THE BARBOUR COLLECTION OF CONNECTICUT TOWN VITAL RECORDS

THE BARBOUR COLLECTION OF CONNECTICUT TOWN VITAL RECORDS

NEW MILFORD 1712–1860

NORFOLK 1758–1850

NORTH STONINGTON 1807–1852

Compiled by
Lorraine Cook White

General Editor
Lorraine Cook White

Copyright © 2000
Genealogical Publishing Co., Inc.
Baltimore, Maryland
All Rights Reserved
Library of Congress Catalogue Card Number 94-76197
International Standard Book Number 0-8063-1643-8
Made in the United States of America

INTRODUCTION

As early as 1640 the Connecticut Court of Election ordered all magistrates to keep a record of the marriages they performed. In 1644 the registration of births and marriages became the official responsibility of town clerks and registrars, with deaths added to their duties in 1650. From 1660 until the close of the Revolutionary War these vital records of birth, marriage, and death were generally well kept, but then for a period of about two generations until the mid-nineteenth century, the faithful recording of vital records declined in some towns.

General Lucius Barnes Barbour was the Connecticut Examiner of Public Records from 1911 to 1934 and in that capacity directed a project in which the vital records kept by the towns up to about 1850 were copied and abstracted. Barbour previously had directed the publication of the Bolton and Vernon vital records for the Connecticut Historical Society. For this new project he hired several individuals who were experienced in copying old records and familiar with the old script.

Barbour presented the completed transcriptions of town vital records to the Connecticut State Library where the information was typed onto printed forms. The form sheets were then cut, producing twelve small slips from each sheet. The slips for most towns were then alphabetized and the information was then typed a second time on large sheets of rag paper, which were subsequently bound into separate volumes for each town. The slips for all towns were then interfiled, forming a statewide alphabetized slip index for most surviving town vital records.

The dates of coverage vary from town to town, and of course the records of some towns are more complete than others. There are many cases in which an entry may appear two or three times, apparently because that entry was entered by one or more persons. Altogether the entire Barbour Collection--one of the great genealogical manuscript collections and one of the last to be published--covers 137 towns and comprises 14,333 typed pages.

TABLE OF CONTENTS

NEW MILFORD	1
NORFOLK	235
NORTH STONINGTON	303

ABBREVIATIONS

ae.------------age
b. ------------born, both
bd.------------buried
B. G.---------Burying Ground
d. ------------died, day, or daughter
decd.---------deceased
f.--------------father
h.--------------hour
J. P.-----------Justice of Peace
m.-------------married or month
res.------------resident
TM ------------Town Meeting Records
s.--------------son
st.--------------stillborn
w. -----------wife
wid.----------widow
wk.-----------week
y. ------------year

THE BARBOUR COLLECTION OF CONNECTICUT TOWN VITAL RECORDS

NEW MILFORD VITAL RECORDS
1712 - 1860

	Vol.	Page
ABBOTT, ABBET, Allen, of Washington, m. Laura **HALL**, of New Milford, Mar. 9, 1823, by Rev. Eleazar Beecher	1	46
Deborah, m. Abram **BROWNSON**, Nov. 28, 1738, by James Benedict, J. P.	LR4	23
ABEL, Ebenezer, of Sharon, m. Julia **KELLOGG**, of New Milford, Sept. 6, 1842, by Rev. Elijah Baldwin	1	373
ADDIS, Emily Ann, of New Milford, m. James **DEWHURST**, of Woodbury, Oct. 12, 1852, by Rev. David P. Sanford	2	79
John W., m. Jane E. **TURRILL**, b. of New Milford, Oct. 24, 1854, by Rev. David Murdock, Jr.	2	105
ADDISON, Elinor, d. James & Lydia, b. Apr. 10, 1741	LR4	4
Mary, d. James & Lydia, b. Sept. 20, 1742	LR4	4
ADKINS, Eliza, m. Miles **BURR**, b. of Patterson, N. Y., June 28, 1821 (Entry crossed out in original)	1	200
Eliza, m. Josiah **BURR**, b. of Patterson, N. Y., June 28, 1821	1	202
AIKIN, AKIN, Isaac, witnessed marriage of Gurdon **SWIFT** & Jane **WANZER**	1	288
William, witnessed marriage of Jehu **HOAG** & Phebe **WANZER**	1	250
ALLEN, Charles E., s. Samuel D. & M. Anna, b. Mar. 27, 1808	1	158
George M., m. Jennette D. **CRANE**, b. of New Milford, Apr. 26, 1849, by Jno Greenwood	2	53
Henry, of Hoosick, N. Y., m. Betsey* S. **TERRILL**, of New Milford, Mar. 15, 1824, by Rev. Andrew Eliot *("Hetty" written above)	1	119
Hetty, m. William N. **MYGATT**, b. of New Milford, Dec. 7, 1840, by Rev. N. Porter	1	353
Mary M., d. Samuel D. & Mehetabel Anna, b. Sept. 20, 1806	1	158
Samuel D., m. M. Anna **FOOT**, b. of New Milford, Apr. 27, 1806, by Elisha Bostwick, J. P.	1	158
Samuel D., d. Feb. 8, 1812	1	158
Sarah E., m. Irwin B. **GAYLORD**, b. of New Milford, Oct. 26, 1848, by John Greenwood	2	44
William, s. Samuel & Susanna, b. Dec. 16, 1780	1	9
ANDREWS, ANDRUS, Cyrus, s. Seth & Sarah, b. Dec. 3, 1769	LR7	2
Henry, of Winchester, Conn., m. Mrs. Susan A. **SAGE**, of New Milford, Dec. 5, 1837, by N. Porter	1	307
Philander, s. Seth & Sarah, b. May 11, 1772	LR7	2
Rebeckah, of Bethelehem, m. Ezra **TERRILL**, of New Milford, Dec. 24, 1747/8, by Rev. Mr. Belemis. Witnesses: Jabez Whitelsee & William Churchel	LR5	10

	Vol.	Page
ANDREWS, ANDRUS, (cont.)		
Robert, s. Seth & Sarah, b. Jan. 25, 1767	LR7	2
Samuel, s. Seth & Sarah, b. Dec. 7, 1764	LR7	2
Seth, m. Sarah **BALDWIN**, Apr. 11, 1764	LR7	2
Thomas, of Brookfield, m. Eunice **PICKET**, of Bridgwater Soc., Jan. 22, 1826, by Rev. Benjamin Benham	1	164
ANGEVINE, John, m. Amy M. **SPERRY**, Feb. 20, 1833, by Josiah L. Dickinson	1	259
ARMSTRONG, Orin Mallery, of Washington, m. Bulah **HINE**, of New Milford, May 22, 1805, by Elisha Bostwick, J. P.	1	121
ARNOLD, ARNOL, Anthony, s. Anthony & Sarah, b. Sept. 14, 1738	LR5	11
David, s. Anthony & Sarah, b. Apr. 27, 1733	LR5	11
Jerome, m. Charlotte **OWEN**, b. of New Milford, Mar. 20, 1836, by E. Huntington	1	296
Mary, m. Capt. Benjamin **BROWNSON**, May 16, 1781	LR13	5
Sarah, d. Anthony & Sarah, b. June 24, 1742. Witnesses: Meriam Pickit & Sarah Ferriss	LR4	12
Sarah, d. Anthony & Sarah, b. June 24, 1742	LR5	11
ARVIN, John, Jr., m. Betsey **BOOTH**, b. of New Milford, Apr. 23, 1828, by Stephen Crane, J. P.	1	205
ASHLEY, Mary, m. William **DUNWELL**, Oct. 14, 1773	LR13	7
ATWEL, Thankful, of Montville, m. John **MOREHOUSE**, of New Milford, Dec. 25, 1808	LR7	2
ATWOOD, ATTWOOD, Alma M., m. Neram **SUMMERS**, b. of Bridgwater, Sept. 21, 1826, by Rev. Fosdick Harrison, of Roxbury	1	153
Hector J., m. Meria **BEACHER**, b. of New Milford, Mar. 1, 1820, by Joel Sanford, J. P.	1	105
Mary, of Woodbury, m. Elijah **WELLER**, of New Milford, Nov. 25, 1773, by Joseph Bebiny	LR12	6
Samuel, of Woodbury, m. Clarinda G.* **JONES**, of New Milford, May 16, 1852, by Rev. J. F. Jones *(Probably "L.")	2	76
AUSTIN, Lydia, m. John **BEECHER**, Nov. 9, 1775	LR13	11
AVERILL, AVEREL, Frederick W., of Bethany, Genesee Co., N. Y., m. Mrs. Louisa **WELTON**, of Bridgewater, Oct. 24, 1839, by Albert B. Camp	1	333
Lucee, m. Christopher **MINOR**, Dec. 1, 1767	LR10	13
Perry, of Washington, m. Sarah **TERRILL**, of New Milford, Dec. 8, 1824, by Rev. C. A. Boradman, of New Preston	1	21
AVERY, John, of Goshen, m. Mary M. **EDWARDS**, of New Milford, Feb. 11, 1829, by Rev. Enoch Huntington	1	230
John, of Cornwall, m. Rebecca **EDWARDS**, of New Milford, Oct. 25, 1835, by E. Huntington	1	295
BABBITT, Philo, m. Lucy M. **GLOVER**, Oct. 14, 1846, by Rev. William Atwill, of Bridgewater	2	27
BADCOCKE, Clarissa, m. Samuel **WHITLOCKE**, Apr. 27, 1817,		

	Vol.	Page
BADCOCKE, (cont.)		
by Elisha Bostwick, J. P.	1	165
BAILEY, Betsey P., m. Benjamin **HANDLIN**, b. of Sharon, June 23, 1839, by Rev. Elijah Baldwin	1	327
Joel W., m. Laura A. **MARSH**, b. of New Milford, Jan. 8, 1833, by Rev. Nathan D. Benedict	1	258
BALDWIN, Abiel, m. Rachel **BUCK**, Dec. 12, 1749, by Samuel Canfield, J. P.	LR6	9
Abiel, d. Sept. 8, 1754	LR6	9
Abiel, s. Israel & Hannah, b. July 12, 1763	LR6	13
Abiel, m. Annis **STONE**, Sept. 10, 1787	1	28
Abiel, of Washington, m. Maria **INGERSOLL**, of New Milford, Jan. 8, 1823, by Rev. Benjamin Benham	1	54
Abigal, d. Abiel & Ratchel, b. Dec. 5, 1752	LR6	9
Abigail, d. Abiel & Rachel, d. Jan. 1, 1754	LR6	9
Abigail, d. Sam[ue]ll & Grace, b. Dec. 30, 1754	LR7	1
Albert, m. Harriet **BALDWIN**, b. of New Milford, Oct. 20, 1835, by E. Huntington	1	294
Amasa, s. Jared, Jr. & Rachel, b. Feb. 8, 178[ ]	1	3
Amos, s. Samuel & Grace, b. Aug. 4, 1740; d. Aug. 5, 1741	LR4	28
Amos, s. Samuel & Grace, b. Feb. 21, 1743/4	LR4	28
Amos, s. Simeon & Rebeckah, b. Dec. 31, 1764	LR7	1
Amos, m. Jared & Damaras, b. Oct. 26, 1769* *(First written "Amos") *(Possibly "1767")	LR7	15
Amos, m. Sally **HICKS**, Feb. 24, 1789	1	58
Andrew J., m. Delia **MERWIN**, b. of New Milford, Oct. 10, [1854], by Rev. David Murdock, Jr.	2	107
Ann, d. Jared & Damaras, b. Mar. 23, 1756	LR7	15
Anna, m. Riverous **STILSON**, Aug. 6, 1767	LR11	4
Anna, m. Gilbert **BUCKINGHAM**, May 1, 1825, by Rev. Andrew Eliot	1	156
Anne, d. Capt. Theophilus & Jerusha, b. Nov. 24, 1744	LR5	2
Annis, d. Israel, Jr. & Elizabeth, b. Apr. 22, 1772	LR7	3
Asa, s. Simeon & Rebeckah, b. Apr. 21, 1769	LR7	1
Asa, m. Betsey **LEWIS**, July 8, 1798	1	73
Assell*, s. Capt. Theophilus & Jerusha, b. June 27, 1739 *(Asahel)	LR2	349
Aurilla, d. Abiel & Annis, b. July 25, 1788	1	28
Betty, d. Ebenezer & Mary, b. Jan. 9, 1727/8	LR2	344
Betty, m. Thomas **BROWNSON**, Jr., Oct. 24, 1751, by Rev. Nathaniel Taylor	LR6	15
Caroline, of New Milford, m. Michael **MEAD**, of Kent, Sept. 4, 1842, by E. Huntington	1	381
Charles, s. Ebenezer & Abiah, b. Apr. 2, 1777	LR13	2
Charles, Jr., m. Mary Jane **HYDE**, b. of Westville, Jan. 3, 1850, at the house of David Hummiston, in Bridgewater, by Rev. W. O. Jarvis	2	59
Cloe, d. Samuel & Grace, b. Apr. 6, 1760	LR7	1

	Vol.	Page
BALDWIN, (cont.)		
Content, d. Israel & Hannah, b. Feb. 8, 1766	LR6	13
Daniel, s. Israel, Jr. & Elisabeth, b. Apr. 18, 1763	LR7	3
Daniel, s. Israel & Elisabeth, b. Nov. 8, 1769	LR7	3
David, s. Capt. Theophilus & Jerusha, b. Dec. 5, 1741	LR2	350
David M., m. Laura M. **FAIRCHILD**, b. of New Milford, Apr. 13, 1829, by Rev. Andrew Eliott	1	230
Davis, s. Isaac & Hannah, b. Aug. 8, 1777	LR7	35
Deborah, of New Milford, m. Herman **BENEDICT**, of Sherman, Nov. 11, 1824, by Rev. Andrew Eliot	1	79
Delia M., m. Sheldon **BUCKINGHAM**, Aug. 30, 1841, by Rev. Merit S. Platt	1	359
Ebenezer, of New Milford, m. Mary **DABON**, of Newtown, Dec. 31, 1735. Witnesses: Paul Welsh & Daniel Hine	LR4	17
Ebenezer, Jr., d. May 27, 1739	LR4	25
Ebenezer, s. Simeon & Mercy, b. Feb. 1, 1755	LR6	8
Ebenezer, m. Abiah **CHAPMAN**, Apr. 18, 1776	LR13	2
Ebenezer, d. Oct. 16, 1776	LR2	364
Ebenezer, m. Eliza **HOIT**, Nov. 28, 1833, by Heman Rood	1	269
Edmond, s. Israel, Jr. & Elisabeth, b. July 7, 1765	LR7	3
Edmond, s. Israel, d. Sept. 28, 1766	LR7	3
Edmond, s. Israel, Jr. & Elizabeth, b. July 6, 1774	LR7	3
Eli, s. Simeon & Rebeccah, b. May 12, 1777	LR7	1
Elijah, s. Abiel & Annis, b. Oct. 5, 1792	1	28
Elizabeth, d. Theophilus & Jerusha, b. Sept. 16, 1725	LR2	349
Elisabeth, m. Samuel **COMSTOCK**, Feb. 7, 1750/1, by Rev. Nathaniell Taylor	LR6	11
Elizabeth, d. Isaac & Hannah, b. Jan. 25, 1782	LR7	35
Ellany, m. Isaac **CLARK**, b. of New Milford, Feb. 3, 1839, by Rev. Alonso F. Selleck	1	323
Elmore, m. Adaline **BENSON**, b. of New Milford, Feb. 15, 1831, by H. Rood	1	242
Elvira, of New Milford, m. Oliver **PARSONS**, of Cornwall, May 28, 1843, by Daniel Baldwin	1	388
Esther, d. Samuel & Grace, b. Aug. 30, 1746	LR4	28
Eunis, d. Sam[ue]ll & Grace, b. Apr. 3, 1750	LR4	28
Gabril, s. Jared & Damaras, b. Jan. 29, 1766	LR7	15
Gamaliel, m. Rebeckah **STEBBINS**, alias **HERRO**, b. of New Milford, Feb. 11, 1741/2, by Samuel Canfield, J. P.	LR4	6
George, m. Abigail J. **NEARING**, b. of New Milford, Apr. 1, 1835, by H. Rood	1	286
Hannah, d. Ebenezer & Mary, b. Nov. 30, 1730	LR2	344
Hannah, d. Ebenezer, d. Mar. 13, 1741/2	LR4	17
Hannah, d. Israel & Hannah, b. June 1, 1752	LR6	13
Hannah, d. Simeon & Mercy, b. Mar. 6, 1763; d. Mar. 12, 1763	LR6	8
Hannah, d. Isaac & Hannah, b. Aug. 10, 1769	LR7	35
Hannah, of New Milford, m. Almon **BEECHER**, of		

	Vol.	Page
BALDWIN, (cont.)		
Hinesburgh, Vt., Mar. 31, 1829, by Rev. Eleazar Beecher	1	214
Harmon, s. Abiel & Annis, b. Mar. 13, 1791	1	28
Harriet, m. Albert BALDWIN, b. of New Milford, Oct. 20, 1835, by E. Huntington	1	294
Harriet, m. Almon HALLOCK, b. of New Milford, Jan. 1, 1844, by John Greenwood	1	390
Harriet E., m. Frederic G. BENNITT, b. of New Milford, Oct. 7, 1845, by Rev. Johnson Howard	1	403
Herman S., of New Milford, m. Elizabeth LANE, of Kent, July 15, 1827, by William Jewett	1	216
Hezekiah, s. Theophilus & Jerusha, b. Sept. 26, 1732	LR2	349
Hezekiah, Lieut., m. Abigail PEAT, Apr. 5, 1759	LR7	38
Hezekiah, s. Hezekiah & Abigail, b. Mar. 25, 1762	LR7	38
Hulda, d. Jared & Damaras, b. Mar. 20, 1758	LR7	15
Hulda*, d. Jared & Damaras, b. May [ ] *(Following this are the words "Asenith, d. to Jared BALDWIN & Damaras, Aug. 30, 1759" crossed out)	LR7	15
Isaac, s. Theophilus & Jerusha, b. Mar. 17, 1735	LR2	349
Isaac, m. Hannah DAVIS, Jan. 2, 1765	LR7	35
Isaac, s. Isaac & Hannah, b. June 10, 1771; d. Feb. 27, 1781	LR7	35
Isaac, s. Thaddeus & Sarah, b. Jan. 5, 1775	LR13	3
Isaac, d. Dec. 16, 1811, in the 77th y. of his age	LR7	35
Israel, s. Lieut. Theophilus & Jerusha, b. Mar. 19, 1736/7	LR2	349
Isural, m. Hannah GUNN, Oct. 9, 1751, by Rev. Nathaniell Taylor	LR6	13
Israel, m. Elisabeth WARNER, Feb. 25, 1761	LR7	3
Israel, Jr., s. Israel & Hannah, b. Mar. 25, 1761	LR6	13
Israel, Jr., d. Mar. 16, 1778	LR7	3
Jacob Hicks, s. Amos & Sally, b. Oct. 13, 1792	1	58
Jane, m. Isaac CLARK, Dec. 6, 1781	1	6
Jane, m. Elihu HOWLAND, b. of New Milford, Sept. 14, 1842, by Rev. Daniel Baldwin	1	375
Jared, s. Jared, Jr. & Rachel, b. Mar. 30, 178[ ]; d. Feb. 25, 1785	1	3
Jared, Jr., m. Rachel BARNS, May 17, 178[ ]	1	3
Jean, d. Israel & Hannah, b. Aug. 31*, 1754 *(First written "30")	LR6	13
Jerusha, d. Theophilus & Jerusha, b. Aug. 22, 1723	LR2	349
Jerusha, m. Jonah DATON, Nov. 20, 1745, by Samuell Canfield, J. P.	LR5	13
Jerusha, d. Hezekiah & Abigail, b. Sept. 9, 1760	LR7	38
Jerusha, d. Thaddeus & Sarah, b. July 26, 1770	LR13	3
Joel, s. Abiel & Ratchel, b. Sept. 27, 1750	LR6	5
Joel, s. Thaddeus & Sarah, b. Oct. 29, 1772	LR13	3
John, s. Israel & Hannah, b. Nov. 20, 1756	LR6	13
John, s. Jared & Damaras, b. Nov. 19, 1768	LR7	15
John Murray, s. Amos & Sally, b. Mar. 3, 1795	1	58

	Vol.	Page
BALDWIN, (cont.)		
Jonah, s. Simeon & Mary, b. Oct. 26, 1753	LR6	8
Lemuel, s. Thaddeus & Sarah, b. May 24, 1766	LR13	3
Lois, d. Sam[ue]ll & Grace, b. Jan. 23, 1758	LR7	1
Lois, d. Simeon & Mercy, b. July 11, 1758	LR6	8
Lois, d. Isaac & Hannah, b. Mar. 11, 1784	LR7	35
Lorette, m. Moses G. **HALLOCK,** b. of New Milford, Sept. 6, 1832, by Rev. Nathaniel Benedict	1	251
Luce, d. Jared & Damaras, b. May 3, 1772	LR7	15
Lucy M., m. John **NEARING,** of New Lisbon, N. Y., Dec. 13, 1821, by Rev. Andrew Eliott	1	9
Martha, d. Theophilus & Jerusha, b. Mar. 26, 1730	LR2	349
Martha, m. Enos **CAMP,** Jr., Dec. 25, 1740, in Milford, by Rev. Samuel Whittelsey, of Milford	LR4	3
Martha*, d. of Theophilus, m. Abel **GUNN,** July 18, 1771, by Rev. Nathaniell Taylor *(Written "Martha **TRYALL**" in mss. copy)	LR11	17
Martha, Mrs., m. Capt. Nathan **BOTSFORD,** Sept. 18, 1771	LR4	4
Martha, d. Isaac & Hannah, b. Aug. 6, 1775	LR7	35
Martha, d. Thaddeus & Sarah, b. June 26, 1780	LR13	3
Matty, of New Milford, m. Elder John **HIGBY,** of Granville, Mass., Apr. 22, 1838, by Rev. Elijah Baldwin	1	317
Mary, w. Ebenezer, d. July 13, 1735	LR2	364
Mary, m. Jonathan **NOBLE,** b. of New Milford, Oct. 15, 1744, by Nathaniel Bostwick, J. P.	LR5	14
Mary, d. Gamaliel & Rebeckah, b. Jan. 1, 1744/5	LR4	6
Mary, d. Simeon & Mercy, b. Aug. 12, 1756	LR6	8
Mary, w. Ebenezer, d. Aug. 20, 1778	LR2	364
Matthew, Dea., m. Lois **PORTER,** b. of New Milford, Dec. 6, 1832, by Eldad C. Jackson, J. P.	1	256
Mercy, d. Israel & Hannah, b. Mar. 6, 1759	LR6	13
Mercy, w. Simeon, d. June 15, 1763	LR6	8
Mercy, d. Simeon & Rebekah, b. Sept. 22, 1767	LR7	1
Minerva, d. Amos & Sally, b. Dec. 5, 1789	1	58
Nathan, s. Samuel & Grace, b. July 14*, 1748 *(Date uncertain)	LR4	28
Nathaniel, s. Ebenezer & Abiah, b. Feb. 3, 1779	LR13	2
Noble, s. Isaac & Hannah, b. Dec. 25, 1779	LR7	35
Orange, s. Israel & Elizabeth, b. Nov. 15, 1776	LR7	3
Pamelia, d. Israel & Elisabeth, b. Oct. 4, 1761; d. July 6, 1762	LR7	3
Pamela, d. Isaac & Hannah, b. Nov. 11, 1765	LR7	35
Pamela, d. Isaac & Hannah, d. Oct. 2, 1766	LR7	35
Pamelea, d. Isriel & Elizabeth, b. July 2, 1767	LR7	3
Patience, twin with Prudence, d. Isaac & Hannah, b. July 3, 1773	LR7	35
Paulina, of New Milford, m. William **WAY,** of New Haven, Mar. 19, 1850, by Seth W. Scofield	2	60
Phebe, d. Ebenezer & Mary, b. June 21, 1738	LR4	17

	Vol.	Page
BALDWIN, (cont.)		
Phebe, m. Joseph **LINES**, Sept. 11, 1758	LR7	35
Phebe Daton, d. Mary, w. of Ebenezer **BALDWIN**, [b. Apr. 23, 1737]*, d. Apr. 28, 1737 *(Supplied from Orcutt's Hist.)	LR4	17
Polly, m. John **BROWNSON**, b. of New Milford, Oct. 12, 1801, by Elisha Bostwick, J. P.	1	42
Prudence, twin with Patience, d. Isaac & Hannah, b. July 3, 1773	LR7	35
Prue, d. Jared & Damaras, b. Nov. 6, 1761	LR7	15
Rachel, m. Robert **HAWKINS**, b. of New Milford, Jan. 3, 1758	LR7	19
Rebeccah, d. Simeon & Rebeccah, b. Mar. 27, 1779	LR7	1
Rebecca, of New Milford, m. Beach **HUNGERFORD**, of Sherman, Oct. 5, 1805, by Elisha Bostwick, J. P.	1	125
Ruben, s. Ebenezer & Mary, b. Apr. 24, 1737; d. May 9, 1737	LR4	17
Rube, d. Thaddeus & Sarah, b. May 30, 1768	LR13	3
Samuel, s. Samuel, m. Grace **BUCK**, d. Enoch, Oct. 31, 1739, by Rev. Daniel Bordman. Witnesses: Job Terrill & Enos Camp	LR4	28
Samuel, d. Dec. 18, 1740	LR4	1
Samuel, s. Gamaliel & Rebeckah, b. Mar. 21, 1742/3	LR4	6
Samuel, m. Mabel **MOREHOUSE**, b. of New Milford, Feb. 14, 1827, by Rev. Andrew Eliot	1	212
Samuel, m. Louisa **CHITTENDEN**, b. of New Milford, Sept. 4, 1836, by Alpheus Fuller, J. P.	1	298
Sarah, d. Samuel & Grace, b. Sept. 23, 1742	LR4	28
Sarah, d. Jared & Damaras, b. Dec. 4, 1759	LR7	15
Sarah, d. Simeon & Mercy, b. Sept. 29, 1760	LR6	8
Sarah, m. Seth **ANDRUS**, Apr. 11, 1764	LR7	2
Sarah, d. Thaddeus & Sarah, b. Mar. 30, 1771	LR13	3
Simeon, s. Ebenezer & Mary, b. July 14, 1724	LR2	344
Simeon, m. Marcy **BROWNSON**, Dec. 20, 1752*, by Rev. Nathanel Taylor *(First Written "1753")	LR6	8
Simeon, m. Rebekah **BUCK**, b. of New Milford, Jan. 4, 1764, by Paul Welch, J. P.	LR7	1
Solomon, s. Thaddeus & Sarah, b. Aug. 21, 1783	LR13	3
Stanley S., of New York **CITY**, m. Harriet **STEVENS**, May 10, 1830, by Heman Rood	1	237
Susan, m. Hiram **BUCKINGHAM**, b. of New Milford, June 10, 1846, by Rev. H. Read	2	16
Susanna, d. Ebenezer & Mary, b. Feb. 6, 1721/2	LR2	344
Thadeus, m. Sarah [ ], July 15*, 1762 *("July 15" written after erasure)	LR13	3
Thadeus Elmer, s. Thaddeus & Sarah, b. Apr. 9, 1764	LR13	3
Thankful, m. Ebenezer **BUCK**, Feb. 29, 1743/4, by Rev. Daniel Bordman	LR5	7
Theophilus, m. Jerusha **BEECHER**, June 5, 1722	LR2	349

	Vol.	Page
BALDWIN, (cont.)		
Theophilus, s. Theophilus & Jerusha, b. Jan. 16, 1728	LR2	349
Theophilus, Capt., d. May 1, 1745	LR5	2
Theophilus, m. Rosanna McEUEN, Feb. 13, 1821, by Rev. Benjamin Benham	1	52
Tibbals, s. Jared & Damaras, b. Nov. 17, 1763	LR7	15
Truman, s. Abiel & Annis, b. Aug. 20, 1789	1	28
Zubah, d. Samuel & Garse*, b. Dec. 26, 1753 *(Grace)	LR4	28
BANKER, Betsey A., [d. Philo & Julia M.], b. Nov. 11, 1854	2	117
Lucinda S., [d. Philo & Julia M.], b. Apr. 10, 1859	2	117
Nancy M., [d. Philo & Julia M.], b. Sept. 25, 1852	2	117
Philo, m. Julia M. FRENCH, Jan. 1, 1850; d. May 6, 1865, ae 36 y.	2	117
BANKS, Nancy O., of Patterson, N. Y., m. Akin INGERSOLL, of Sherman, Dec. 25, 1825, at the house of Elihu Marsh, 2nd, by Homer Boardman, J. P.	1	82
BARLOW, Ambrose, m. Laura SUMMERS, Feb. 1, 1852, by Rev. William McAlister	2	87
Anna, of New Milford, m. Ephraim BENEDICT, of Danbury, May 24, 1827, by Stephen Crane, J. P.	1	215
Bradley B., m. Laura A. BARNS, b. of New Milford, Jan. 1, 1834, by H. Rood	1	270
Harriet, m. Jabesh MOREHOUSE, Jan. 16, [18(?)], by Benjamin Benham	1	240
Harriet N., of Bridgewater, m. Ezra WILDMAN, of Brookfield, Feb. 23, 1841, by Albert B. Camp	1	352
Henry M., m. Sarah SEARS, Nov. 20, 1846, by Rev. Eleazer Beecher	2	20
Mary Ann, of Bridgwater, m. Joseph ELWOOD, of Brookfield, Oct. 2, 1828, by Rev. Fosdick Harrison, of Roxbury	1	226
BARNES, BARNS, Albert, m. Catherine GAYLORD, b. of New Milford, [Feb. 24, 1836], by Maltby Gelston	1	292
Amanda, d. Amos & Anna, b. Jan. 14, 1781	1	59
Amanda, d. Amos & Anna, d. Dec. 24, 1794	1	59
Amos, m. Anna BYINGTON, July 2, 1777, by Rev. Joseph Bellamy, in Bethleham	1	59
Amos, d. June 14, 1788	1	59
Amos Clinton, s. Amos & Anna, b. Sept. 26, 1783	1	59
Betsey, d. Amos & Anna, b. Mar. 11, 1778	1	59
Elisabeth, m. Isaac BUCK, Feb. 10, 1758	LR7	5
Henry, of Sherman, m. Laura ROOT, of Kent, Apr. 24, 1826, by Alpheus Fuller, J. P.	1	189
Laura A., m. Bradley B. BARLOW, b. of New Milford, Jan. 1, 1834, by H. Rood	1	270
Loretta, of New Milford, m. Capt. Levi STARR, of Danbury, Sept. 6, 1827, by Maltby Gleston	1	207
Rachel, m. Jared BALDWIN, Jr., May 17, 178[ ]	1	3

	Vol.	Page
BARNES, BARNS, (cont.)		
Samuel H., m. Sarah **STERLING**, b. of New Milford, June 3, 1834, by H. Rood	1	273
Sarah A., m. Joseph N. **McMAHON**, b. of New Milford, Nov. 27, 1839, by Noah Porter	1	333
BARNUM, Alonzo, of Bridgeport, m. Flora **RANDALL**, of Bridgewater, Jan. 25, 1846, by Rev. J. Kilbourn	2	9
Eli, of Bethel, m. Julia **BARNUM**, of New Milford, Feb. 15, 1846, by E. Huntington	2	11
Julia, of New Milford, m. Eli **BARNUM**, of Bethel, Feb. 15, 1846, by E. Huntington	2	11
Sarah, m. John **HITCHCOCK**, May 27, 1736, by Rev. Daniel Bordman	LR4	17
Sarah, m. John **STURDEVANT**, Jr., Mar. 28, 1782	LR13	1
Sarah, m. Noble **BUCKINGHAM**, Apr. 4, 1802	LR12	19
BARTLETT, BARTLET, Mindwel, m. Oliver **THAIR**, Sept. 12, 1738, by Roger Brownson, J. P.	LR4	28
Thankful, m. Jonathan **WELLER**, Dec. 20, 1733, by John Bostwick, J. P.	LR4	12
BARTRAM, Abba Jane, of New Milford, m. Demon **HOYT**, of Sherman, Oct. 11, 1845, by Rev. Samuel Weeks	2	13
Albert, m. Mary C. **BRONSON**, Aug. 3, 1828, by Rev. E. Huntington	1	221
Caroline, m. Daniel **MOREHOUSE**, June 2, 1842, by Eldad C. Jackson, J. P.	1	370
David, of Sherman, m. Sarah **DUNNING**, of Brookfield, Mar.14, 1847, by E. Huntington	2	34
John L., of Sherman, m. Lydia **JEWEL**, of New Milford, Oct. 25, 1837, by Rev. Alonso F. Selleck	1	307
Julia Ann, of New Milford, m. Dennis **COSIER**, of Brookfield, Jan. 12, 1840, by Nathan Rice	1	355
Laura, d. Phebe, b. Oct. 19, 1794	1	127
Lavinia, of New Milford, m. Thomas **BEARDSLEY**, of Kingsbury, Eng., Nov. 10, 1851, by Rev. David P. Sanford	2	73
Lucy M., of New Milford, m. Silas **ROE**, of Sherman, Mar. 12, 1843, by Z. Davenport	1	386
Marcus, s. Noah & Lucy Maria*, b. Sept. 13, 1820 *(First written "Huldah his wife")	1	317
Marcus, of Washington, m. Sally **PEET**, of New Milford, Aug. 18, 1840, by Rev. Eleazer Beecher	1	346
Phebe, had d. Laura, b. Oct. 19, 1794	1	127
Phebe, m. Elizur **THAYER**, May 5, 1798	1	127
BASS, Anna Meria, d. Josiah & Freelove, b. Sept. 20, 1802	1	6
Caroline, d. Josiah & Freelove, b. Apr. 13, 1805	1	6
Daniel, s. Josiah & Freelove, b. May 30, 1799	1	6
Gideon Noble, s. Josiah & Freelove, b. Nov. 7, 1797	1	6
Joseph Canfield, s. Josiah & Freelove, b. June 1, 1790	1	6

	Vol.	Page

BASS, (cont.)
   Josiah, m. Freelove **CANFIELD**, Mar. 27, 1780 — 1 — 6
   Sarah, d. Josiah & Freelove, b. Dec. 27, 1788 — 1 — 6
[BASSETT], BASSET, Sarah, m. Benjamin **ROGERS**, Oct. 5,
   1834, by E. Huntington — 1 — 426
BATES, Caswel, of New York City, m. Emily E. **BEACH**, of
   Bridgewater, Aug. 27, 1834, by Fosdic Harrison — 1 — 280
   Isaac, of Wallingford, m. Emeline **LEACH**, of New Milford,
     May 9, 1836, by E. Hungtington — 1 — 296
   Sibbel, m. Robert **BROWN**, Aug. 11, 1799, by Elisha
     Bostwick, J. P. — 1 — 66
[BATTELL], BATTEL, Abigal, d. James & Annah, b. July 10,
   1750 — LR6 — 14
BEACH, Abigail Emily, of Bridgewater, m. Elijah S.* **DUNNING**,
   of Brookfield, Oct. 20, 1840, by Rev. Albert B. Camp
   *(Possibly "T") — 1 — 348
   Anna, of Bridgewater, m. Lyman **SHED**, Oct. 11, 1829, by
     Rev. Fosdic Harrison, of Roxbury — 1 — 235
   Anaa Matilda, d. Caleb & Clare, b. Oct. 20, 1793 — 1 — 56
   Benjamin B., m. Mary **STURDEVANT**, b. of New Milford,
     Nov. 2, 1834, by E. Huntington — 1 — 283
   Burroughs, of Brookfield, m. Harriet **WELLER**, of
     Bridgewater, May 14, 1826, by Rev. Fosdic Harrison, of
     Roxbury — 1 — 152
   Caleb, m. Clare **TREAT**, Aug. 16, 1787 — 1 — 56
   Emily, of Oxford, m. Cyrus **BOTCHFORD**, of Derby, Sept.
     15, 1833, by Rev. Nathan D. Benedict — 1 — 265
   Emily E., of Bridgewater, m. Caswel **BATES**, of New York
     City, Aug. 27, 1834, by Fosdic Harrison — 1 — 280
   Isaac, of Bridgewater, m. Emily A. **WHEELER**, Oct. 25, 1829,
     by Rev. Fosdic Harrison, of Roxbury — 1 — 235
   John, m. Fanny Amandy **HAMBLIN**, June 3, 1845, by Gad S.
     Gilbert — 1 — 401
   Julia A., m. William **GILLITT**, Jr., b. of Bridgewater, Feb.
     26, 1822, by Rev. Andrew Eliot — 1 — 34
   Laura, d. Caleb & Clare, b. Aug. 25, 1791 — 1 — 56
   Laura Antonett, m. Othniel **FRENCH**, b. of New Milford,
     Dec. 28, 1828, by Rev. E. Huntington — 1 — 227
   Letitia, m. Maltby **REYNOLDS**, Apr. 24, 1822, by Rev.
     Andrew Eliot — 1 — 31
   Lucy Ann, of New Milford, m. William **REYNOLDS**, of New
     York, Jan. 13, 1822, by Rev. Fosdic Harrison, of
     Roxbury — 1 — 17
   Minty M., of Bridgewater, m. Hiram **HIGLEY**, Sept. 26,
     1830, by Rev. Fosdic Harrison, of Roxbury — 1 — 227
   Ruth, m. Andrew **SUMMERS**, Nov. 15, 1770 — 1 — 39
   Sally J., m. Ephraim **FRENCH**, b. of Bridgewater, Jan. 15,
     1828, by Rev. Fosdic Harrison, of Roxbury — 1 — 124

	Vol.	Page

BEACH, (cont.)
Thalia, d. Caleb & Clare, b. June 1, 1788	1	56
BEARD, David, m. Mary **COMSTOCK,** Mar. 30, 1790	1	46
Homer, s. David & Polly, b. Nov. 2, 1791	1	46
Homer, m. Phebe **MOREHOUSE,** June 10, 1841, by Daniel Baldwin	1	361
Minerva, m. Samuel Beebe **STERLING,** b. of New Milford, Nov. 6, 1828, by Rev. Andrew Eliot	1	225
BEARDSLEY, BEARSLIE, BARDSLEE, Amos, m. Minerva **JENNINGS,** Aug. 17, 1820, by Rev. Andrew Eliot	1	108
Anson, of Monroe, m. Caroline **PHIPPENEY,** of New Milford, May 4, 1830, by E. Huntington	1	133
Byah, of Stratford, m. Abraham **DATON,** of New Milford, Apr. 14, 1743, by Nathaniel Bostwick, J. P.	LR5	5
Eletiaette, m. Charles **TITUS,** Feb. 12, 1828, by Rev. Eleazar Beecher	1	218
Elisha, s. John & Joanna, b. June 23, 1774	LR12	1
Eliza A., m. John M. **HINE,** b. of New Milford, Aug. 14, 1850, by Rev. William McAlister	2	63
Eunice, d. Silas & Catharine, b. Sept. 25, 1790	1	47
Henry, m. Apphia **MEAD,** b. of New Milford, Sept. 22, 1805, by Elisha Bostwick, J. P.	1	123
James B., of Kent, m. Laura M. **PLATT,** of New Milford, Mar. 15, 1836, by Aaron D. Lane	1	293
John, m. Caroline E. **NEARING,** May 24, 1830, by Rev. Eleazer Beecher	1	235
Lucy, m. Stephen **CHITTENTEND,** b. of New Milford, Sept. 26, 1765	LR10	13
Maijary*, m. Daniel **PICKIT,** Sept. 16, 1741, in Streatfield, *("Margaret" in Orcutt's Hist.)	LR4	1
Mary N., m. Edward Francis **PLATT,** b. of New Milford, Dec. 22, 1852, by Rev. James L. Scott, of New Preston	2	85
Polly Ann, m. Edward M. **NOBLE,** b. of New Milford, Oct. 9, 1848, by John Greenwood	2	43
Rebeckah, m. Abel **CANFIELD,** July 11, 1773, by Samuell Canfield, J. P.	LR12	3
Sally, m. Northrop **KELLOGG,** b. of New Milford, June 4, 1834, by Fosdic Harrison	1	280
Silas, m. Catharine **TREADWELL,** May 14, 1789	1	47
Thomas, of Kingsbury, Eng., m. Lavinia **BARTRAM,** of New Milford, Nov. 10, 1851, by Rev. David P. Sanford	2	73
Tryphena, m. David **PLATS,** Mar. 19, 1778	LR13	7
William, s. Silas & Catharine, b. Nov. 22, 1792	1	47

BEARSE, [see under **BEERS**]

BEEBE, Ezenezer, s. Samuel & Hannah, b. Jan.* 8, 1715/16
*("Feb." crossed out)	LR2	355
Hannah, d. Sam[ue]ll, d. Sept. 14, 1714	LR2	358
Jeames, s. Samuell & Hannah, b. Aug. 7, 1704	LR2	355

BEEBE, (cont.)

	Vol.	Page
John, s. Samuell & Hannah, b. Mar. 1, 1705/6* *(Year crossed out and rewritten)	LR2	355
Julia Ann, m. Nelson **HALLOCK**, b. of New Milford, Apr. 16, 1827, by Rev. Benjamin Benham	1	213
Mary, d. Samuel & Hannah, b. Sept. 25, 1699	LR2	355
Mary, m. Enoch **BUCK**, b. of New Milford, May 2, 1717	LR1	351
Nathan, d. July 12, 1773	LR12	1
Rebeckah, of Litchfield, m. Abel **HINE**, of New Milford, July 7, 1763	LR7	36
Samuel, s. Samuell & Hannah, b. Nov. 13, 1701	LR2	355
Sarah, d. Samuell & Hannah, b. Feb. 22, 1712/13	LR2	355
BEECHER, BEACHER, Abagal, d. Elieazer & Frances, b. Nov. 22, 1734	LR2	340
Abagal, d. Elieazer & Frances, d. Oct. [ ], 1737	LR2	340
Abigail, m. Gerardus W. **CAMP**, Oct. 15, 1823, by Rev. Andrew Eliot	1	89
Almon, of Hinesburgh, Vt., m. Hannah **BALDWIN**, of New Milford, Mar. 31, 1829, by Rev. Eleazer Beecher	1	214
Amarillis, of New Milford, m. Moss **LEAVENWORTH**, of Roxbury, Dec. 25, 1827, by Rev. Andrew Eliot	1	216
Annis, d. Elezer, Jr. & Ellice, b. Nov. 25, 1766	LR7	5
Austin, s. John & Lydia, b. Mar. 7, 1782	LR13	11
Elezer, twin with John, s. Elezer & Allice, b. [ ]	LR7	5
Elleazer, m. Francis **OVIAT**, b. of Milford, Oct. 30, 1729	LR2	340
Elleazer, s. Elleazer & Francis, b. Sept. 17, 1732	LR2	340
Elieazer, Jr., m. Allice **BRITTOL**, b. of New Milford, Dec. 24, 1760, by Rev. Nathaniell Taylor	LR7	5
Francis, d. Elleazer & Francis, b. July 5, 1730	LR2	340
Frances, m. Nehemiah **FISHER**, Jan. 18, 1757, by Solomon Palmer	LR7	19
Harvey, s. John & Lydia, b. Mar. 29, 1787	LR13	11
Jerusha, m. Theophilus **BALDWIN**, June 5, 1722	LR2	349
Jerusha, m. James **MORGIN**, b. of New Milford, Feb. 16, 1766* *(1768?)	LR10	14
John, m. Lydia **AUSTIN**, Nov. 9, 1775	LR13	11
John, s. John & Lydia, b. Aug. 31, 1776	LR13	11
John, twin with Elezer, s. Elezer & Allice, b. [ ]	LR7	5
Lucy, d. John & Lydia, b. Dec. 8, 1789	LR13	11
Lydia, d. Elisazer & Frances, b. Nov. 18, 1741	LR4	26
Lydia, m. Daniel **HINE**, Mar. 18, 1769, by Paul Welch	1	18
Lydia, d. John & Lydia, b. Jan. 15, 1778	LR13	11
Lyman, s. Elizer, Jr. & Allice, b. June 4, 1762	LR7	5
Lyman, s. Elizer & Allice, d. Dec. 7, 1766	LR7	5
Lyman, s. John & Lydia, b. Nov. 24, 1779	LR13	11
[Lym]an, of Hinesburgh, m. Elizabeth **STONE**, of New Milford, Feb. 5, 1803, by Elisha Bostwick, J. P.	1	101
Lyman, of Hinesburgh, m. Elizabeth **STONE**, of New Milford,		

	Vol.	Page
BEECHER, BEACHER, (cont.)		
Feb. 5, 1803, by Elisha Bostwick, J. P.	1	103
Maria, m. Hector J. **ATTWOOD**, b. of New Milford, Mar. 1, 1820, by Joel Sanford, J. P.	1	105
Mary Ann, m. Benjamin J. **STONE**, b. of New Milford, Oct. 10, 1838, by N. Porter	1	321
Nathaniel, s. Elieazer & Francis, b. Mar. 19, 1738/9	LR4	26
Phebe, of Milford, m. Benjamin **FERRIS**, of New Milford, Nov. 6, 1728	LR4	3
Phebe, d. Eliezer & Frances, b. Mar. 22, 1736/7	LR2	340
Pheebe, m. John **MOREHOUSE**, b. of New Milford, Dec. 27, 1763	LR7	2
Polly, d. John & Lydia, b. Nov. 3, 1785	LR13	11
Rebecah, d. John & Lydia, b. Aug. 26, 1783	LR13	11
Thaila (?), d. Elezer, Jr. & Allice, b. June 2, 1769	LR7	5
Thalia, m. Daniel **GARLICK**, Nov. 5, 1788	1	19
Urania, d. Elezer, Jr. & Allice, b. May 4, 1764	LR7	5
Urania, m. Salmon **BUCK**, Mar. 5, 1794	1	64
BEEMAN, Rufus, of New Milford, m. Mabel **BENNITT**, of Brookfield, Aug. 18, 1841, by Rev. Z. Davenport	1	359
BEERS, BEARSE, BEARSS, Abel, s. Abijah & Sarah, b. June 5, 1782	1	4
Abijah & Sarah, had 1st s. [ ], b. Dec. 21, 1780; d. 3rd day after	1	4
Anna, wid. James, m. Ephraim **BUCK**, Feb. 27, 1800	LR7	16
Anne, d. Abijah & Sarah, b. Apr. 29, 1784	1	4
Bradley, of New Fairfield, m. Cornelia **BROWNSON**, of New Milford, Nov. 9, 1845, by E. Huntington	2	5
Caroline, m. William **ROWE**, July 11, 1824, by Rev. Eleazar Beecher	1	44
Eli Hervey, s. Josiah & Freelove, b. Feb. 14, 1793	1	6
Eliza, m. Charles B. **MALLORY**, b. o Bridgewater, Mar. 14, 1841, by Albert B. Camp	1	352
Frederick F., m. Mary **COLE**, July 5, 1847, by Rev. Eleazar Beecher	2	30
Joseph, m. Rebecca **SMITH**, b. of New Milford, May 30, 1827, by Nathaniel Perry, J. P.	1	214
[L]aurania, d. Josiah & Freelove, b. Mar. 16, 1784	1	6
Mary A., witnessed marriage of David **SANDS** & Paulina **LEACH**	1	277
Mary S., of Bridgewater, m. Frederick **JACKSON**, of Bethlem, Mar. 2, 1842, by Rev. Albert B. Camp. of Bridgewater	1	369
Patience, d. Josiah & Rebeccah, b. Sept. 3, 1762; m. Joel **SMITH**, s. Jesse & Elizabeth, July 11, 1782	1	34
Paulina, d. Josiah & Freelove, b. July 16, 1782	1	6
Phalina Frances, of Roxbury, m. Charles Lockwood **WARNER**, Nov. 23, 1848, at the house of Wooster		

	Vol.	Page
BEERS, BEARSE, BEARSS, (cont.)		
by George L. Foote	2	47
Rebeckah, d. Josiah & Freelove, b. Sept. 30, 1785	1	6
Sylvia, m. Lewis **FROST**, May 7, 1837, by E. Huntington	1	311
BELL, Huldah, m. Thomas **McCOMBS**, b. of New Milford, Nov. 25, 1841, by Rev. Z. Davenport	1	364
Mary, m. Isaac O. **PETTIT**, b. of New Milford, Oct. 8, 1838, by N. Porter	1	322
Sarah, m. Richard **MORRIS**, b. of Poughkeepsie, N. Y., Oct. 30, 1836, by Rev. F. Donnelly	1	299
BEMIS, Betsey, Mrs., m. William **MALLORY**, Aug. 9, 1846, by Rev. Eleazer Beecher	2	17
BENEDICT, BENEDICK, BENNEDICK, Abel, s. Pitman & Mercy, b. Jan. 24, 1752	LR10	1
Amos N., Rev., of New Marlborough, Mass., m. Emily M. **HOWLAND**, of New Milford, Oct. 27, 1847, by Rev. Johnson Howard	2	33
Benajah, s. Pitman & Mercy, b. Dec. 26, 1758	LR10	1
Cloe, d. Pitman & Mercy, b. Oct. 10, 1762	LR10	1
Elijah, s. Gideon & Dorath, b. Sept. 20, 1738	LR4	23
Elizabeth, d. Lieut. Beeiamin, of Ridgfield, m. William **DRINKWATER**, Dec. 18, 1728, by Rev. Thomas Hawley	LR4	1
Elisabeth, d. John & Elisabeth, d. Jan. 11, 1763	LR7	28
Elisabeth, w. John, d. Jan. 11, 1763	LR7	28
Ephraim, of Danbury, m. Anna **BARLOW**, b. of New Milford, May 24, 1827, by Stephen Crane, J. P.	1	215
Ezra, s. Joseph & Mary, d. Aug. 15, 1758, in Camp, at Lake George	LR7	28
Harmon, m. Philamelia **POTTER**, Feb. 20, 1853, by Rev. David P. Sanford	2	82
Herman, of Sherman, m. Deborah **BALDWIN**, of New Milford, Nov. 11, 1824, by Rev. Andrew Eliot	1	79
Ichabod, s. Pitman & Mercy, b. Jan. 15, 1756	LR10	1
Jane O., m. Henry W. **MALLETT**, b. of New Milford, Oct. 11, 1846, by John Greenwood	2	20
Jehannah, d. Pitman & Mercy, b. Feb. 25, 1754	LR10	1
John, of New Milford, m. Elisabeth **SMITH**, of Darby, Nov. 19, 1760	LR7	24
John, m. Elisabeth **SMITH**, Nov. 19, 1760	LR7	28
Jonathan, m. Margaret **PINNOCK**, Oct. 1, 1778	1	53
Joseph, d. July 4, 1761	LR6	3
Pheebe, d. Pitman & Mercy, b. Apr. 24, 1760	LR10	1
Pitman, m. Mercy **BOSTWICK**, Dec. 6, 1749	LR10	1
Pitman, & w. Mercy, had d. [ ], b. Jan. 26, 1764; d. Jan. 21 [sic], 1764	LR10	1
Priscilla, m. David **JACKSON**, Apr. 4, 1775, by Rev. Mr. Wetmore	LR12	18

	Vol.	Page
BENEDICT, BENEDICK, BENNEDICK, (cont.)		
Sophira, d. Pitman & Mercy, b. Mar. 21, 1750	LR10	1
Tirza, of Danbury, m. Thomas **BRADSHAW**, of New Milford, Mar. 15, 1801	1	144
William, of Kent, m. Amanda **HALLOCK**, of New Milford, Oct. 9, 1822, by Rev. Andrew Eliot	1	56
BENHAM, Caroline, of New Milford, m. Joseph **HAWLEY**, of Bridgeport, May 7, 1826, by Rev. Benjamin Benham	1	203
Lousia Warner, d. Rev. Benjamin, m. Reuben **BURROUGHS**, of Darien, Ga., Aug. 25, 1822, by Rev. Benjamin Benham	1	33
Lovisa, m. Oliver **WARNER**, Jr., Sept. 2, 1809, by Rev. Benjamin Benham	1	165
BENNITT, BENNET, BENNETT, BENNIT, Abagail, d. Benjamin & Byoh, b. Mar. 26, 1742	LR4	27
Abyah, d. Benjamin & Abiah, b. Oct. 25, 1745 (Abiah)	LR4	27
Abijah, m. Abigail **STONE**, Jan. 23, 1777	LR13	13
Ann, d. Caleb & Abigal, b. Mar. 31, 1749* *("1748" 14 erased out)	LR6	1
Ann, m. Solomon **PHINE**, June 28, 1774, by Samuell Bostwick, J. P.	LR12	12
Benjamin, m. Biah **NOBLE**, b. of New Milford, Dec. 4, 1740, by Roger Brownson, J. P.	LR4	27
Caleb, m. Abigail **FOWLER**, b. of New Milford, June 13, 1746, by Rev. Elisha Kent	LR5	14
Canfield, s. Edward & Rhoda, b. Aug. 12, 1784	LR11	8
Canfield P., m. Emily **BOOTH**, Sept. 1, 1844, by E. Huntington	2	10
Edward, m. Rhoda **CANFIELD**, b. of New Milford, Jan. 19, 1769, by Samuell Bostwick, J. P.	LR11	8
Elijah, s. Edward & Rhoda, b. May 26, 1776	LR11	8
Elijah Salmon, s. Stanley G. & Clarrissa, b. Nov. 6, 1840	1	339
Elisabeth, m. Jeremiah B. **BRONSON**, Oct. 20, 1841, by E. Huntington	1	367
Esther, m. Philander **BUCK**, b. of New Milford, Aug. 18, 1799, by Elisha Bostwick, J. P.	1	53
Eunice, d. Edward & Rhoda, b. Jan. 3, 1783	LR11	8
Eunice, d. Thomas & Mary, m. Daniel **BOOTH**, s. Jonathan & Hester, [ ]	1	409
Eunice, d. Thomas & Mary (**BOOTH**), m. Daniel **BOOTH**, s. Jonathan & Hester, [ ], 1725	2	112
Franklin, m. Almira **HINE**, b. of New Milford, Nov. 24, 1853, by Rev. David Murdock, Jr.	2	100
Frederic G., m. Harriet E. **BALDWIN**, b. of New Milford, Oct. 7, 1845, by Rev. Johnson Howard	1	403
Harriet A., m. James E. **WELLS**, b. of New Milford, Jan. 13, 1848, by John Greenwood	2	37
Isaac, s. Caleb & Abigall, b. Apr. 15, 1747	LR6	1

BENNITT, BENNET, BENNETT, BENNIT, (cont.)

	Vol.	Page
Isaac, m. Catharine **DATON**, May 4, 1769	LR10	17
John G., of Brookfield, m. Sophronia **COUCH**, of New Milford, Mar. 18, 1849, by Rev. William Long, of New Preston	2	51
Joseph, s. Edward & Rhoda, b. Oct. 3, 1778	LR11	8
Joseph, m. Polly **CLARK**, b. of New Milford, June 26, 1820, by Rev. Andrew Eliot	1	179
Joseph, m. Eliza **MOREHOUSE**, b. of New Milford, May 4, 1828, by Joel Sanford, J. P.	1	179
Loranai, d. Edward & Rhoda, b. Oct. 29, 1769	LR11	8
Mabel, of Brookfield, m. Rufus **BEEMAN**, of New Milford, Aug. 18, 1841, by Rev. Z. Davenport	1	359
Martha, d. Benjamin & Byah, b. Oct. 26, 1743	LR4	27
Mary, w. Thomas, was d. Ephraim **BOOTH** & his w. Mary (**OSBORN**, of New Haven) & granddaughter of Richard **BOOTH**, of Stratford, formerly of England	2	112
Mary, m. Mark W. **HUNT**, Nov. 14, 1839, by Rev. Eleaser Beecher	1	331
Mary A., of New Milford, m. James F. **YALE**, of Lebanon, Penn., Dec. 6, 1848, by John Greenwood	2	46
Noble, s. Edward & Rhoda, b. Aug. 24, 1786; d. Dec. 3, 1793	LR11	8
Noble S., m. Sarah Maria **MOREHOUSE**, Sept. 15, 1841, by E. Huntington	1	366
Phebe, of New Milford, m. John A. **SHARRA**, of Lancaster, Pa., July 25, [1847], by James Kilbourn	2	31
Polley, d. Edward & Rhoda, b. June 6, 1771	LR11	8
Polly, w. Joseph, d. [ ]	1	179
Polly Ann, of New Milford, m. Benjamin **STEBBINS**, of Brookfield, [Mar. 6, 1836], by Rev. Henry Eames	1	292
Rachel C., of New Milford, m. Elijah B. **FENTON**, of Plymouth, Mar. 6, 1836, by Rev. Henry Eames	1	292
Samuel, s. Abijah & Abigail, b. Nov. 6, 1777	LR13	13
Stanley G., m. Clarrissa **MOREHOUSE**, Jan. 1, 1840, by E. Huntington	1	339
Susan, m. Asahel **SHERWOOD**, Aug. 4, 1846, by Rev. Samuel Weeks	2	39
Truman, s. Edward & Rhoda, b. Apr. 12, 1773	LR11	8
Urania, m. Joseph **PECK**, Dec. 20, 1790	1	29

BENSON

	Vol.	Page
Adaline, m. Elmore **BALDWIN**, b. of New Milford, Feb. 15, 1831, by H. Rood	1	242
Ambrous, s. Benjamin, b. Dec. 14, 1766	LR11	13
Beniamin, s. Benjamin, b. May 11, 1758	LR11	13
Bryent, s. Benjamin, b. Jan. 24, 1769	LR11	13
Caroline, of New Milford, m. John **NASH**, of Newtown, Oct. 19, 1831, by Rev. John Lovejoy	1	194
Elizabeth, d. Benjamin, b. Feb. 19, 1756	LR11	13
John, s. Benjamin, b. Nov. 11, 1759	LR11	13

	Vol.	Page

BENSON, (cont.)
    John, m. Zilla **CANFIELD**, b. of New Milford, Nov. 14, 1830,
      by Joel Sanford, J. P. — 1 — 233
    Lydia, d. Benjamin, b. Jan. 8, 1761 — LR11 — 13
    Rebekah, d. Benjamin, b. July 14, 1764 — LR11 — 13
[**BENTON**], **BINTON**, Meriam, m. Ephraim **BUCK**, Feb. 2, 1763 — LR7 — 17
BERRY, John C., of Kent, m. Ann **MARSH**, of New Milford, Dec.
    15, 1830, by Heman Rood — 1 — 120
    John C., of Kent, m. Ann **MARSH**, of New Milford, Dec. 15,
      1830, by Heman Rood — 1 — 206
BERTRAM], [see under **BUTRAM**]
BETTS, Betsey, d. Nathan & Polly, b. July 13, 1799 — 1 — 77
    Elvira, d. Nathan & Polly, b. Aug. 27, 1797 — 1 — 77
    Judith, m. Jonathan **BROWN**, b. of New Milford, Sept. 6,
      1797 — 1 — 99
    Laurenia, d. Nathan & Polly, b. Aug. 26, 1795 — 1 — 77
    Molly, d. William & Molly, b. Aug. 14, 1760 — 1 — 38
    Molly, m. Isaac M. **RUGGLES**, Nov. 6, 1783 — 1 — 38
    Nathan, m. Polly **TREAT**, Nov. 20, 1794 — — 77
BIDWELL, Stephen, of Litchfield, m. Catharine **LAMSON**, of
    New Milford, Feb. 8, 1841, by E. Huntington — 1 — 365
BIRCH, **BURCH**, Ebenezer, m. Huldah A. **MALLETT**, b. of New
    Milford, Sept. 20, 1835, by Rev. G. L. Brownell, of
    Woodbury — 1 — 289
    Mary A., made affidavit Dec. 28, 1858, Newtown, before
    Theophilus Nichols, J. P. that she was present at the
    wedding of Abraham Seabeary **BOOTH**, s. James &
    Lucinda **SANFORD**, d. Jonathan, Sunday eve before 1st
    Monday in May 1806/7, at Jonathan Sanfords, Newtown,
    by Rev. Daniel Burhans — 2 — 113
[**BIRCHARD**], **BURCHARD**, Sarah, m. Uri **JACKSON**, Apr. 10,
    1770, by Rev. Nathaniell Taylor — LR10 — 13
BISHOP, Betsey Jane, m. Henry **CRANE**, b. of New Milford, Oct.
    14, 1833, by H. Rood — 1 — 266
    Garry, of Washington, m. Emeline **NORTHROP**, of
      New Milford, May 13, 1833, by E. Huntington — 1 — 261
    Jonathan Austin, s. David & Sarah, b. May 25, 1764 — LR7 — 7
    Lydia, d. David & Sarah, b. May 6, 1766 — LR7 — 7
    Susan, of New Milford, m. Bryan **HICKIX**, of Washington,
      Nov. 23, 1826, by Rev. Andrew Eliot — 1 — 204
BLACKMAN, Edwin B., of Danbury, m. Jennette **RUGGLES**, of
    Bridgewater, Jan. 2, 1848, by Rev. James Kilbourn — 2 — 38
    Frederick, m. Betsey **MARSH**, b. of New Milford, Oct. 8,
      1834, by E. Hungtington — 1 — 282
    Isaac, of Newtown, m. Henrietta L. **HOYT**, of New Milford,
      Dec. 25, 1834, by E. Huntington — 1 — 284
    Joseph A., of Newtown, m. Betsey **LOCKWOOD**, of New
      Milford, Sept. 7, 1833, by H. Rood — 1 — 263

	Vol.	Page

BLACKMAN, (cont.)

Judson, of Woodbury, m. Susan **MASTERS**, of New Milford, Apr. 6, 1826, by Rev. Andrew Eliot	1	42
Sally, of Newtown, m. Chauncey **NOBLE**, of New Milford, Dec. 3, 1839, by Nathaniel Perry, J. P.	1	331
Sheldon, m. Julia C. **NOBLE**, b. of New Milford, June 3, 1845, by J. Greenwood	1	400
Theodore, m. Eveline **WYGANT**, b. of New Milford, Nov. 12, 1851, by Rev. David P. Sanford	2	74

BLACKNEY, Eliza A., m. Samuel Addison **LOCKWOOD**, Nov.

25, 1828, by Rev. E. Huntington	1	226
Emily Maria, m. Justus **MILES**, Feb. 7, 1821, by Rev. Benjamin Benham	1	63
Paulina, wid., m. Samuel **WILDMAN**, of Danbury, Apr. 6, 1830, by E. Huntington	1	133
William A., m. Ann **WATSON**, b. of New Milford, Oct. 18, 1821, by Benjamin Benham	1	106
William A., of New Milford, m. Clara **LEACH**, June 22, 1840, by Rev. Daniel Baldwin	1	344

BLAKELYE, [see under **BLAKESLEE**]

[BLAKESLEE], BLAKELYE, BLAKELEY, Ezra, s. Jonathan &

Ruth, b. Feb. 11, 1760	LR7	29
Mehetabel, m. Seelye **RICHMOND**, Aug. 12, 1789	1	27
Ruth, of Woodbury, m. Edward **COLLINS**, of New Milford, June 15, 1763	LR7	2
Sarah, d. Jonathan & Ruth, b. Jan. 13, 1762	LR7	29

BOARDMAN, BORDMAN, Caroline Maria, d. [Elijah & Mary

Ann], b. June 29, 1802	1	102
Caroline Maria, d. [Elijah & Mary Ann], b. June 29, 1802	2	121
Caroline Maria, of New Milford, m. Rev. John Frederick **SCHROEDER**, of New York City, May 22, 1825, by Rev. Benjamin Benham	1	183
Charles Adolphus, s. Homer & Amaryllys, b. Nov. 19, 1788	1	92
Cornelia Elizabeth, d. [Elijah & Mary Ann], b. Aug. 4, 1808	1	102
Cornelia Elizabeth, d. [Elijah & Mary Ann], b. Aug. 4, 1808	2	121
Daniel, of New Milford, m. Hannah **WHEELER**, of Milford, Feb. 20, 1716/17	LR2	357
Daniell, of New Milford, m. Jerusha **CEILIE**, of Stratfield, Nov. 1, 1720	LR2	356
Daniel, s. Sherman & Sarah, b. Mar. 4, 1757	LR7	32
Daniel Homer, s. Homer & Amarillis, b. May 21, 1803	1	92
David, s. Sherman & Sarah, b. Oct. 3, 1758; d. Nov. 11, 1766	LR7	32
David Sherman, s. Sherman & Sarah, b. Dec. 8, 1768	LR7	32
David Sherman, m. Charlotte **TAYLOR**, b. of New Milford, May 18, 1806, by Elisha Bostwick, J. P.	1	130
Elijah, of New Milford, m. Mary Ann **WHITING**, of Great Barrington, Mass., Sept. 25, 17[ ], by Rev. Gideon Bostwick, of Great Barrington	2	121

	Vol.	Page
BOARDMAN, BORDMAN, (cont.)		
Elijah, s. Sherman & Sarah, b. May 7, 1760	LR7	32
Elijah of New Milford, m. Mary Ann **WHITING**, of Great Barrington, Mass., Sept. 25, 1792, at Great Barrington, by Rev. Gideon Bostwick	2	121
Elijah & w. Mary Ann, had sons William Whiting, Henry Mason, George Sherman, bp. May 9, 1802, by Rev. Stanley Griswold	1	102
Elijah, Hon., d. Aug. 18, 1823, at Boardman, Ohio, ae 63 y. 5 m. 18 d., bd. Sept. 5, following, at New Milford	2	30-1
Elijah, Hon., d. Aug. 18, 1823, ae 63 y. 5 m. 18 d., at Boardman, Ohio; bd. Sept. 5, following, at New Milford	2	121
Easter, d. Sherman & Sarah, b. Jan. 29, 1762	LR7	32
Esther Orinda, d. Homer & Amaryllis, b. Jan. 9, 1792	1	92
Frederick, m. Harriet **CANFIELD**, b. of New Milford, Sept. 17, 1845, by John Greenwood	1	402
Frederick A., of Boardman, Ohio, m. Mary **WILLIAMS**, of New Milford, Mar. 20, 1848, by Rev. E. Huntington	2	41
George Sherman, [s. Elijah & Mary Ann], b. Oct. 17, 1799	1	102
George Sherman, [s. Elijah & Mary Ann], b. Oct. 17, 1799; bp. May 9, 1802, by Rev. Stanley Griswold; d. Jan. 18, 1825	2	121
George Sherman, s. [Elijah & Mary Ann], d. Jan. 18, 1825	1	102
Hannah, d. Daniell & Hannah, b. Jan. 12, 1717/18	LR2	357
Harriot Maria, d. Homer & Amarillis, b. Jan. 1, 1795	1	92
Henry Mason, [s. Elijah & Mary Ann], b. Jan. 4, 1797	1	102
Henry Mason, [s. Elijah & Mary Ann], b. Jan. 4, 1797; bp. May 9, 1802, by Rev. Stanley Griswold; d. Dec. 17, 1846	2	121
Homer, s. Sherman & Sarah, b. Oct. 10, 1764	LR7	32
Homer, m. Amarillis **WARNER**, Nov. 14, 1787	1	92
Jerusha, d. Daniel & Jerusha, b. May 4, 1731	LR2	356
Laura A., of New Milford, m. Rev. Aaron D. **LANE**, of Waterloo, N. Y., Oct. 20, 1828, by Rev. C. A. Boardman	1	210
Laura Amarillis, d. Homer & Amerillis, b. Mar. 27, 1806	1	92
Marcy, d. Daniell & Jerusha, b. Feb. 9, 1725/6	LR2	356
Mary Anna, d. [Elijah & Mary Ann], b. Nov. 19, 1805; d. Apr. 7, 1822	1	102
Mary Anna, d. [Elijah & Mary Ann], b. Nov. 19, 1805; d. Apr. 7, 1822	2	121
Mary Anna, wid., b. Oct. 19, 1767; d. June 24, 1848	2	121
Mercy, m. Gilead **SPERY**, b. of New Milford, Jan. 30, 1745/6, by Samuel Canfield, J. P.	LR5	13
Oliver Warner, s. Homer & Amarillis, b. Sept. 14, 1799	1	92
Oliver Warner, s. Homer & Amarillis, d. Oct. 30, 1815	1	92
Orinda, d. Sherman & Sarah, b. July 22, 1767	LR7	32
Penelope, d. Daniel & Jerusha, b. Dec. 26, 1721	LR2	356
Penolope, m. Riverious **CARRINGTON**, July 7, 1742, by Rev. Daniel Bordman	LR4	3

	Vol.	Page
BOARDMAN, BORDMAN, (cont.)		
Sarah, d. Homer & Amarillis, b. Jan. 5, 1798; d. Jan. 13, 1798, ae 8 d.	1	92
Sarah, wid. Sherman, d. Oct. 17, 1818, ae 88 y. 29 d.	LR7	32
Sherman, s. Daniel & Jerusha, b. Aug. 2, 1728	LR2	356
Sherman, m. Sarah **BOSTWICK**, Dec. 3, 1755	LR7	32
Sherman, had negro Tamar, d. Betty, b. Apr. 19, 1786	1	424
Sherman, had negro **OLIVE**, d. Noami, b. May 3, 1792, Jack or Carlton Jackson, s. Naomi, b. Oct. 17, 1796	1	423
Sherman, d. July 19, 1814, ae 86 y. wanting 25 d.	LR7	32
Tamar, d. Daniel & Jerusha, b. Mar. 26, 1723	LR2	356
Tamer, m. Rev. Nathaniel **TAYLARD**, Feb. 23, 1748/9, by Samuell Canfield, J. P.	LR6	6
William Whiting, s. [Elijah & Mary Ann], b. Oct. 10, [ ]	1	102
William Whiting, s. [Elijah & Mary Ann], b. Oct. 10, 1794; bp. May 9, 1802, by Rev. Stanley Griswold	2	121
BOBIT, BOBBIT, Annis, d. Eleanah & Obediance, b. Mar. 28, 1747* *(1748* crossed out)	LR6	8
Daniel, s. Eleanah & Obediance, b. Apr. 28, 1749	LR6	8
David, s. Elkenah & Obedience, b. Aug. 6, 1739	LR4	27
Elkenah, m. Obedience **PRINDLE**, b. of New Milford, Jan. 20, 1736/7	LR4	27
Eleanah*, m. Bediance **PRINDEL**, Dec. 5, 1737, by Rev. Daniel Boardman *(Elkanah. Date is probably an error)	LR6	8
Eleanah, s. Eleanah & Obediance, b. Dec. 5, 1738	LR6	8
Elkenah, s. Eleanah & Obediance, b. Dec. 5, 1737	LR4	27
Loess, d. Eleanah & Obediance, b. Mar. 30, 1743	LR6	8
Lorrin, s. Eleannah & Obediance, b. May 1, 1745	LR6	8
Mary, d. Eleanah & Obediance, b. Apr. 15, 1741	LR6	8
BOLAND, BOLELAND, Frederick, of Sharon, m. Jaimthier **RANDALL**, of New Milford, Feb. 2, 1830, by Joseph S. Covill	1	238
William H., m. Nancy L. **TREAT**, b. of New Milford, May 10, 1853, by David Murdock, Jr.	2	88
[BOLLES], BOLLS, Samuel, a witness at wedding of Elnathan **BOTSFORD** and Dorothy **PRINDLE**, Quakers	LR4	14
Samuel, a witness at wedding of John **FERRIS** and Abigal **TRYON**, Quakers	LR4	22
BOLT, Dabora, of Norwalk, m. David **CAMP**, of New Milford, Apr. 29, 1741, by Rev. Moses Dikinson, of Norwalk	LR4	16
BONESTEEL, Virgil D., of Poughkeepsie, N. Y., m. Sarah Eliza **TODD**, of New Milford, Sept. 30, 1840, by Noah Porter	1	349
BOOTH, Abel, s. Jonathan & Hester, b. July 15, 1707	1	409
Abel, s. Jonathan & Hester, b. July 15, 1707	2	112
Abel, s. Jonathan & Hester, d. Apr. 13, 1774, ae 67 y. 8 m. 29 d.	2	113
Abraham, s. Daniel & Eunice, b. [ ]	1	409

	Vol.	Page
BOOTH, (cont.)		
Abraham, s. Daniel & Eunice, b. [Feb.]*, 1735		
*(Crossed out)	2	112
Abraham, s. Daniel & Eunice, m. Anna **WALKER**, Dec. 3, 1759	2	112
Abraham & w. Anna, had twins, b. Mar. 12, 1764; d. a few days after birth	2	112
Abraham, d. Aug. 20, 1815	2	112
Abraham S., d. Apr. 16, 1822, ae 35 y. 4 m. 10 d.	2	113
Abraham Seabeary, s. James, b. Dec. 21, 1785	2	113
Abraham Seabeary, s. James, m. Lucinda **SANFORD**, d. Jonathan, sunday eve before 1st Monday in May, 1806/7, at Jonathan Sanfords, at Newtown, by Rev. Daniel Burhans. Witness: Mary A. Birch	2	113
Adaline, m. Solomon E. **BOSTWICK**, b. of New Milford, Feb. 26, 1834, by H. Rood	1	272
Alonzo, s. James, b. [ ]	2	113
Alvira, m. Morgan **HALLOCK**, Oct. 21, 1852, by Rev. William McAlister	2	87
Ann, d. Jonathan & Hester, b. Apr. 15, 1710	1	409
Anna, d. John & Dorothy, b. [ ]; m. Ambross **THOMPSON**, June 22, 1707	2	111
Anna, d. Daniel & Eunice, b. [ ]	1	409
Anna, d. Daniel & Eunice, b. [ ]	2	112
Anna, d. Richard, b. Feb. 14, 1643	2	111
Anna, d. Jonathan & Hester, b. Apr. 15, 1710	2	112
Anna, d. Abraham & Anna, b. Oct. 8, 1761	2	112
Anna, d. Abraham S. & Lucinda, b. Mar. 27, 1807	2	113
Bethiah, d. Richard, b. Aug. 18, 1658	2	111
Betsey, m. John **ARVIN**, Jr., b. of New Milford, Apr. 23, 1828, by Stephen Crane, J. P.	1	205
Carlos B., s. Abraham S. & Lucinda, b. Mar. 25, 1815	2	113
Charles, s. David & Hetty, b. July 27, 1824	1	112
Charles M., witnessed marriage of Ebenezer **WANZER**, Jr. & Lucy **LEACH**	1	181
Charles M., s. Abraham S. & L:ucinda, b. Dec. 12, 1810	2	113
Charles M., m. Hellen M. **BROWNSON**, May 16, 1847, by E. Huntington	2	35
Charott, d. David & Hetty, b. Dec. 26, 1826	1	112
Clarinda, [d. Lewis & Jerusha], b. Nov. 5, 1798	1	407
Daniel, s. Jonathan & Hester, m. Eunice **BENNITT**, d. Thomas & Mary, [ ]	1	409
Daniel, s. Daniel & Eunice, m. Hulday **THOMPSON**, [ ]	1	409
Daniel, s. Jonathan & Hester, b. Jan. 12, 1704	1	409
Daniel, s. Jonathan & Hester, b. Jan. 12, 1704	2	112
Daniel, s. Jonathan & Hester, m. Eunice **BENNITT**, d. Thomas & Mary (**BOOTH**), [ ], 1725	2	112
Daniel, s. Daniel & Eunice, b. Oct. 1, 1730	1	409

	Vol.	Page

BOOTH, (cont.)

	Vol.	Page
Daniel, s. Daniel & Eunice, b. Oct. 1, 1730	2	112
Daniel, s. Daniel & Hulday, b. Dec. 11, 1776	1	409
Daniel, Sr., d. Apr. 8, 1777	1	409
Daniel, s. Jonathan & Hester, d. Apr. 8, 1777	2	113
David, [s. Lewis & Jerusha], b. Oct. 23, 1794; d. Nov. 3, 1857	1	407
David, s. Daniel & Eunice, d. Apr. 1, 1814, ae 83 y. 6 m.	2	114
David, m. Hetty **CLARK**, b. of New Milford, Feb. 2, 1820	1	112
Ebenezer, s. Richard, b. Nov. 19, 1651	2	111
Edgar L., of Ohio, m. Lucy L. **BOOTH**, of Penn., Mar. 26, 1837, by Rev. F. Donnelly, at Bridgewater	1	304
Eli, [s. Lewis & Jerusha], b. Nov. 23, 1788	1	407
Eli, see also Ely		
Elizabeth, d. Richard, b. Sept. 10, 1641	2	111
Ely, s. Abraham S. & Lucinda, b. Sept. 13, 1821	2	113
Ely, see also Eli		
Emily, m. Canfield P. **BENNITT**, Sept. 1, 1844, by E. Huntington	2	10
Emma, of New Milford, m. James **HEPBURN**, of Milford, Jan. 24, 1827, by Rev. Benjamin Benham	1	93
Ephriam, s. Richard, b. Aug. 1, 1648	2	111
Ephraim, s. John & Dorothy, b. [ ]; m. Rachel **NICHOLS**, [ ], 1709	2	111
Ester, w. Jonathan, Sr., d. Apr. 2, 1731/ ae 49 y.	2	113
Ester, d. Daniel & Eunice, b. [ ]	1	409
Eunice, d. Daniel & Eunice, b. [ ]	1	409
Eunice, d. Daniel & Eunice, b. Feb. [ ], 1738; m. James **GLOVER**, [ ]; d. Feb. 13, 1795, ae 57 y.	2	112
Eunice, w. Daniel, d. May 14, 1786, in the 83rd y. of her age	2	114
Eunice, w. [Daniel, Sr.], d. May 15, 1786, in the 83rd y. of her age	1	409
Ezra, s. Daniel & Eunice, b. Mar. [ ], 1745; d. July 18, 1812, in the 68th y. of his age	2	112
Ezra, s. Daniel & Eunice, b. [ ]	1	409
Harlow, s. James, b. [ ]	2	113
Henry A., s. Abraham S. & Lucinda, b. July 13, 1817	2	113
Henry W., m. Mary E. **MYGATT**, b. of New Milford, Oct. 6, 1846, by John Greenwood	2	19
Hester, d. Daniel & Eunice, b. [ ]; m. James **HURD**, [ ]; moved to Arlington, Vt.	2	112
Horace M., m. Harriet **COLE**, Mar. 20, 1843, by E. Huntington	1	393
Hulda Matilda, d. Daniel & Huldah, b. Dec. 1, 1783	1	409
James, s. James, b. [ ]	2	113
James, s. Abraham & Anna, m. [ ]	2	113
James, s. Abraham & Anna, b. Aug. 17, 1766	2	112
James, s. Abraham, d. Jan. 16, 1816	2	113
Jerusha, w. [Lewis], b. Sept. 26, 1764; d. Apr. 10, 1852	1	407

	Vol.	Page
BOOTH, (cont.)		
Jerusha, [d. Lewis & Jerusha], b. Dec. 7, 1790; d. [ ], at the age of 2 1/2 y. old	1	407
Jerusha, [d. Lewis & Jerusha], b. Oct. 12, 1796	1	407
Jerusha, m. Eli **ROBURDS**, b. of New Milford, June 21, 1820, by Rev. Fosdic Harrison, of Roxbury	1	178
Johanna, d. Richard, b. Mar. 21, 1661	2	111
John, s. Richard, b. Nov. 5, 1653	2	111
John, s. Richard, of Stratford, m. Dorothy **HAWLEY**, d. Thomas & Dorothy, of Roxbury, Mass., June 14, 1678	2	111
John, s. John & Dorothy, b. [ ]; m. Elizabeth **MALLOREY**, of New Haven, Jan. 9, 1717	2	111
Jonathan, s. John & Dorothy, b. [ ], 1682	2	111
Jonathan, s. John & Dorothy, m. Hester **GALPIN**, Aug. 11, 1703, by Mr. Purdy, J. P., at Rye	2	111
Jonathan, s. Jonathan & Hester, b. June 10, 1715	1	409
Jonathan, s. Jonathan & Hester, b. June 10, 1715	2	112
Jonathan, s. John, Sr. & Dorothy, d. Feb. 8, 1755, ae 73 y.	2	113
Jonathan, s. Jonathan & Hester, d. May 27, 1770, ae 74 y. 11 m. 4 d.	2	114
Joseph, s. Richard, b. Mar. 8, 1656	2	111
Joseph, s. Daniel & Hulday, b. Sept. 17, 1779	1	409
Josiah, [s. Lewis & Jerusha], b. Jan. 11, 1785; d. [ ] at the age of 6 y.	1	407
Josiah C., [s. Lewis & Jerusha], b. [ ]; d. Mar. 28, 1830	1	407
Judson, [s. Lewis & Jerusha], b. Mar. 11, 1801; d. June 23, 1851	1	407
Julia M., of New Milford, m. Andrew **COMSTOCK**, of New York, Aug. 20, 1827, by Rev. Andrew Eliot	1	117
Lavinia, [d. Lewis & Jerusha], b. Feb. 19, 1803	1	407
Lavinna, m. Smith **RANDAL**, Jan. 10, 1821, by Rev. Fosdic Harrison, of Roxbury	1	29
Lavina, m. Elijah **PECK**, Feb. [ ], 1823	1	408
Legrand, s. James, b. [ ]	2	113
Lewis, b. Sept. 2, 1764	1	407
Lewis, m. Jerusha [ ], Aug. 30, 1784	1	407
Lewis, s. David & Hetty, b. June 7, 1821	1	112
Lewis, d. Apr. 29, 1850	1	407
Lewis E., s. Abraham S. & Lucinda, b. Nov. 2, 1813	2	113
Lucy L., of Penn., m. Edgar L. **BOOTH**, of Ohio, Mar. 26, 1837, at Bridgewater, by Rev. F. Donnelly	1	304
Mabel, d. Jonathan & Hester, b. Dec. 13, 1722, in Newtown	1	409
Mabel, d. Jonathan & Hester, b. Dec. 13, 1722	2	112
Mabel, d. Jonathan, d. July 11, 1816	2	114
Mary, d. John & Dorothy, b. [ ]; m. Benjamin **BROOKS**, [ ], 1713	2	111
Mead, [s. Lewis & Jerusha], b. Jan. 24, 1787	1	407
Naoma, d. Daniel & Eunice, b. [ ], 1741; m. Zebulon		

BOOTH, (cont.)

	Vol.	Page
NORTON, [ ]; moved to Bloomfield, Western New York	2	112
Naome, d. Daniel & Huldah, b. Mar. 10, 1786	1	409
Naome, d. Daniel & Eunice, b. [ ]	1	409
Nicholas, s. Daniel & Huldah, b. Mar. 12, 1788	1	409
Parthena, d. Daniel & Hulday, b. Aug. 25, 1773	1	409
Phebe, d. Daniel & Hulday, b. July 22, 1781	1	409
Phebe, w. Jonathan, Jr., d. Jan. 17, 1803, ae 81 y.	2	114
Phebe, ae 76 y. of Newtown, made affidavit July 9, 1858, before David B. Beers, J. P., that she was present at the m. of her brother Thompson **BOOTH** & Eunice **BRISCO**, Feb. [ ], 1798, by Rev. Philo Perry , of Newtown	1	406
Polly, d. Josiah & Sarah, b. Dec. 9, 1783; m. Lambert Lewis **TREADWELL**, s. David (s. Benjamin, s. Edward), Sept. 23, 1800, at the house of Josiah Booth, by Rev. James Johnson; d. Jan. 20, 1850; bd. in Fairport, Munroe Co., N. Y., in Hiram Hayes' family lot	2	93
Polly, m. Lambert Lewis **TREADWLL**, s. David (s. of Benjamin, s. of Edward), Sept. 23, 1800	2	93
Rebecca, w. Abel, d. July 28, 1778, in the 68th y. of her age	2	114
Sabra, d. Daniel & Huldah, b. May 10, 1790	1	409
Sally, [d. Lewis & Jerusha], b. Dec. 7, 1790; d. July 5, 1843	1	407
Sarah, d. Daniel & Eunice, b. Oct. [ ], 1733; m. Ebenezer **PECK**, [ ]; d. Feb. 22, 1783	2	112
Sarah, d. Daniel & Eunice, b. [ ], 1733	1	409
Sarah, d. John & Dorothy, b. [ ]; m. Richard **CHAPMAN**, [ ]	2	111
Sarah B., d. David & Hetty, b. Feb. 28, 1829	1	112
Sarah Elizabeth, of New Milford, m. Forbes **DUNDERDALE**, of New York, June 4, 1845, by J. Greenwood	1	400
Thomas, s. John & Dorothy, b. Mar. 13, 1679	2	111
Thompson, s. Daniel [& Hulday], b. Feb. 23, 1775	1	409
Thompson, m. Eunice **BRISCO**, Feb. [ ], 1798, by Rev. Philo Perry, of Newtown. Witness: Phebe **BOOTH**, sister of Thompson **BOOTH**	1	406
Walker, s. Abraham & Anna, b. July 5, 1762; d, June 7, 1763	2	112
Walker, s. Abraham & [Anna], b. Feb. 5, 1769	2	112
William E., s. Abraham S. & Lucinda, b. Mar. 17, 1809	2	113
BORIE, Charles, of Philadelphia, m. Mary **WELLER**, of New Milford, May 20, 1851, by Rev. David Murdock	2	69
BOSTWICK, BOSTICK, BOSWICK, Abel, s. Joseph & Rebecka, b. Jan. 15, 1734	LR2	339
Abel, m. Sarah **HITCHCOCK**, b. of New Milford, Jan. 28, 1756	LR7	11
Abel, d. Sept. 8, 1797, in the 64th y. of his age	LR7	11
Abigal, m. Japhoth **COLLINS**, Ma[ ] 28, 1734	LR4	13

	Vol.	Page
BOSTWICK, BOSTICK, BOSWICK, (cont.)		
Abagal, d. Nathaniel & Esther, b. July 20, 1737	LR4	10
Abigail, d. Capt. Nathaniel, d. Aug. 9, 1758	LR7	5
Abraham, s. Joseph & Ann, of New Milford, m. Hannah COLLING, d. Daniel & Ruth, of Milford, Sept. 13, 1732, by Samuell Gunn, J. P.	LR4	9
Adoniram, twin with Alvin, s. Mathew & Rebeckah, b. Feb. 8, 1771	LR8	2
Adonirum, twin with Alvin, s. Matthew & Rebeckah, b. Feb. 8, 1771	LR8	3
Agur Bushnell, s. Edmond & Aurelia, b. Feb. 15, 1808	1	166
Alanson, s. Israel & Elizabeth, b. Feb. 17, 1774	LR10	2
Albert, s. Ebenezer & Rebeckah, b. Mar. 14, 1718/19	LR2	362
Almeria, d. Matthew & Rebeckah, b. Mar. 24, 1784	LR8	3
Almon, s. Reuben & Mabel, b. July 4, 1773	LR7	33
Almon, s. Reuben & Mabel, b. Jan. 4, 1777, in the 4th y. of his age	LR7	33
Almon, s. Benjamin Ruggles & Rachel, b. Apr. 19, 1788	1	3
Alvin, twin with Adoniram, s. Mathew & Rebeckah, b. Feb. 8, 1771	LR8	2
Alvin, twin with Adomirum, s. Matthew & Rebeckah, b. Feb. 8, 1771	LR8	3
Amelia, d. Jonathan & Rebeckah, b. Feb. 24, 1766	LR7	12
Aminta Meriah, d. Edmond & Aurilia, b. Sept. 8, 1805	1	166
Amos, m. Sarah **GRANT**, b. of New Milford, Dec. 2, 1766, by Samuell Canfield, J. P.	LR10	1
Andrew, s. Joseph & Mary, b. Feb. 14, 1771	LR8	2
Andrew, s. Ebenezer & Rebeckah, b. Nov. 3, 1778	LR13	12
Ann, d. Abraham & Hannah, b. July 7, 1733	LR4	9
Ann, m. Benjamin **ROBURDS**, b. of New Milford, Nov. 15, 1756, by Bushnell Bostwick, J. P.	LR7	14
Ann, s. Sam[ue]ll, d. Sept. 21, 1783, in the 59th y. of her age	LR5	3
Anna, wid. Lemuel, d. [ ], in Hinesburgh; removed there with her s. Isaac	LR4	9
Anna, m. John D. **WEED**, Oct. 25, 1807, by Elisha Bostwick, J. P.	1	150
Anne, d. Abel & Sarah, b. Oct. 24, 1762	LR7	11
Anne, d. Ichabod & Anne, b. Feb. 13, 1790	1	96
Anne Fisk, d. Samuel & Pollypheme, b. Jan. 6, 1787	1	7
Annis, m. William **CLARK**, b. of New Milford, June [ ], 1775	LR12	11
Arthur, m. Eunice **WARRINER**, July 1, 1752	LR7	16
Asel, s. Abraham & Hannah, b. Mar. 14, 1738/9	LR4	9
Ashlel, [s. Edmond & Mercy], b. Aug. 12, 1766; d. June 20, 1767	LR11	1
Ashbel, s. Elizur & Mercy, b. Jan. 4, 1780	LR13	12
Ashbel, m. Clarra Minerva **BRISTOL**, Aug. 28, 1803	1	122
Barbara, d. Ichabod & Anne, b. June 11, 1786	1	96

	Vol.	Page
BOSTWICK, BOSTICK, BOSWICK, (cont.)		
Bennajah, s. John & Marcy, b. Feb. 8, 1717/18	LR2	361
Benajah, m. Hannah **FISK**, b. of New Milford, Oct. 22, 1741	LR4	25
Benajah, s. Maj. John & Marcy, d. Oct. 23, 1776, in the 59th y. of his age	LR10	5
Benjamin, of New Milford, m. Zerviah **JOHNSON**, of Woodbery, May 2, 1711	LR2	353
Benjamin, s. Benjamin & Zerviah, b. May 2, 1724	LR2	353
Benjamin, d. May 15, 1739	LR4	2
Benjamin, m. Rachel [ ], Jan. 11, 1742/3, by Rev. Jonathan Ingerson	LR5	1
Benjamin, s. Benjamin & Rachel, b. Feb. 13, 1744/5	LR5	1
Benjamin, 2nd, d. Nov. 25, 1748	LR4	2
Benjamin, twin with Joseph, s. Joseph & Mary, b. Feb. 24, 1764; d. Apr. 16, 1764	LR8	2
Benjamin, m. Hester **BOSTWICK**, Apr. 15, 1767, by Samuel Bostwick, J. P.	LR10	12
Benjamin, of New Milford, m. Olive **JUDSON**, of Woodbury, Feb. 8, 1769	LR10	8
Benjamin E., m. Emiline E. **NORTHROP**, b. of New Milford, Sept. [ ], 1831, by H. Rood	1	245
Benjamin Ruggles, s. Reuben & Mabel, b. Sept. 5, 1762	LR7	33
Benjamin Ruggles, m. Rachel **STONE**, Nov. 30, 178[ ]	1	3
Betsy Ann, d. Elisha & Betty, b. July 11, 1792	1	5
Betsey Ann, of New Milford, m. William Morgan **BURRALL**, of Canaan, Nov. 14, 1813, by David S. Boardman; d. Dec. 18, 1851	1	186
Beety, d. Benjamin & Zerviah, b. Mar. 23, 1714/15	LR2	353
Betty, m. Jonathan **BUCK**, Jan. 9, 1732/3, by Rev. D. Bordman	LR4	15
Betty, [w. Elisha], d. July 13, 1834	1	5
Billy, s. Jonathan & Rebeckah, b. Jan. 21, 1774	LR7	12
Bushnell, s. John & Marcy, b. Nov. 16, 1712	LR2	361
Bushnell, of New Milford, m. Merian **SKEELS**, of Woodbury, Jan. 25, 1736/7, by Roger Brownson, J. P.	LR4	19
Bushnell, Col., d. Jan. 31, 1793, in the 81st y. of his age	LR4	19
Bushnel, m. Laura **SANFORD**, b. of New Milford, Feb. 11, 1822, by Rev. Benjamin Benham	1	17
Caleb Noble, s. Israel & Elizabeth, b. Apr. 28, 1772	LR10	2
Charlotte, d. Matthew & Rebecah, b. Oct. 23, 1777	LR8	3
Chloe, m. Henry **THOMAS**, Nov. 6, 1783	LR13	17
Clarra, d. Nathan & Elizabeth, b. Mar. 21, 1770	LR7	23
Cyrus, s. Jonathan & Rebeckah, b. Mar. 28, 1769	LR7	12
Cyrus, m. Tabby **SANFORD**, Jan. 4, 1796	1	66
Daniel, m. Hanah **HITCHCOCK**, b. of New Milford, Dec. 14, 1736, by John Bostwick, J. P.	LR4	19
Daniel, s. Daniel & Hannah, b. Aug. 22, 1737	LR4	19
Daniel, Jr., m. Tamar **BOSTWICK**, b. of New Milford, May		

	Vol.	Page
BOSTWICK, BOSTICK, BOSWICK, (cont.)		
31, 1769, by Samuell Bostwick, J. P.	LR10	7
David, s. John & Marcy, b. Jan. 8, 1720/1	LR2	361
David, twin with Jonathan, s. Bushnell & Meriam, b. Mar. 27, 1738; d. Apr. 10, 1738	LR4	19
David, s. Benajah & Hannah, b. Aug. 3, 1742	LR4	2
David, s. Joseph, Jr. & Bette, b. Apr. 24, 1752	LR7	1
David, s. Jonathan & Rebeckah, b. Mar. 24, 1761	LR7	12
David, m. Hannah HULL, b. of New Milford, Apr. 5, 1770	LR10	7
David, Jr., m. Polly YEATS, Oct. 24, 1780	LR13	17
David, Jr., [ ] Taymar BOSTWICK, [ ] (This entry crossed out)	LR10	12
David E., m. Sophrona M. A. SOMERS, Mar. 16, 1834, by E. Huntington	1	275
DeLauzuny, s. Edmond & Aurelia, b. Sept. 14, 1810	1	166
Doctor, [s. Edmond & Mercy], b. Oct. 6, 1764	LR11	1
Duiadamia*, d. Nathan & Elizabeth, b. Sept. 3, 1771 *("Urania" crossed out)	LR7	23
Ebenezer, m. Rebeckah BUNNELL, b. of New Milford, Apr. 11, 1717	LR2	362
Ebenezer, s. Edmond & Mercy, b. June 22, 1755	LR11	1
Ebenezer, Jr., m. Rebecah NORTHROP, June 10, 1777	LR13	12
Ebenezar, s. Ebenezer, Jr. & Rebecah, b. Oct. 11, 1781	LR13	12
Eden, s. Robert & Sarah, d. Feb. 23, 1760	LR10	2
Edmond, m. Mercy RUGGLES, Sept. 3, 1754	LR11	1
Edmond, [s. Edmond & Mercy], b. Feb. 5, 1763	LR11	1
Edmon, s. Elizur & Mercy, b. July 5, 1782	LR13	12
Edmond, of New Milford, m. Aurelia HAWLEY, of Huntington, June 4, 1804	1	166
Edward, s. John, 3rd & Jemima, b. Dec. 9, 1735	LR4	2
Edward, m. Ann STEVENS, Apr. 10, 1757	LR7	25
Edwin, s. Ashbel & Clarra M., b. July 24, 1804	1	122
Electa, d. Reuben & Mabel, b. Dec. 1, 1764	LR7	33
Elijah, s. Nathaniel & Esther, b. June 8, 1740	LR4	10
Elisha, s. Sam[ue]ll & Ann, b. Dec. 17*, [ ] *(Date "11" doubtful)	LR4	13
Elisha, s. Samuel & Ann, b. Dec. 17, 1748	LR5	3
Elisha, m. Betty FERRISS, May 14, 1786	1	5
Elisha, d. Dec. 11, 1834	1	5
Elisha & Samuel, had Orman s. Dora (d. Patience an emancipated servant), b. Dec. 16, 1800 taking the name of Orman WILSON; m. Cloe JACKLIN, May 18, 1828, by Stephen Crane, J. P.; Frederick, s. Orman & Cloe, b. May 7, 1829	1	420
Elisha & Samuell, had negro Javan WILSON, m. Dora, d. Patience (an emancipated servant), b. of New Milford, Jan. 20, 1802	1	420
Elizabeth, d. Robert & Sarah, d. Jan. 30, 1760	LR10	2

	Vol.	Page
BOSTWICK, BOSTICK, BOSWICK, (cont.)		
Elizabeth, d. Israel & Elizabeth, b. Nov. 25, 1767	LR10	2
Elizabeth, d. Israel & Elizabeth, b. Nov. 25, 1767	LR11	2
Elizabeth, d. Nathan & Elizabeth, b. May 13, 1781	LR7	23
Elizabeth, d. Solomon E. & Adaline, b. Feb. 9, 1837	1	272
Elizur, s. Edom & Mercy, b. Jan. 13, 1757	LR11	1
Elizur, s. Jonathan & Rebeckah, b. Mar. 5, 1771	LR7	12
Elizur, m. Mercy **BOSTWICK**, Dec. 30, 1778	LR13	12
Erastus, s. Jonathan & Rebeckah, b. Aug. 31, 1767	LR7	12
Esther, [w. Capt. Nathaniel], d. Dec. 13, 1747	LR4	10
Easter, d. Arthur & Eunice, b. Dec. 3, 1754	LR7	16
Esther, d. Abel & Sarah, b. May 6, 1765	LR7	11
Esther, m. Nathan **CAMP**, Jr., Dec. 10, 1772, by Rev. Nathaniel Taylor	LR10	2
Easter, m. Nathan **CAMP**, Dec. 10, 1772, by Rev. Nathaniel Taylor	LR11	15
Eunes, d. Lemuel & Annah, b. Jan. 23, 1733/4	LR4	9
Eunice, d. Nathaniel & Ester, b. Aug. 21, 1744	LR4	10
Eunice, m. Jonathan **CLARK**, Jan. 18, 1753	LR7	24
Eunice, m. Ezra **NOBLE**, b. of New Milford, June 24, 1772, by Rev. Nathaniel Taylor	1	116
Eunice, m. Enos **CAMP**, Jr., Apr. 13, 1779	LR7	6
Ezbon, see under Jzbon		
Ezra, s. Reuben & Mabel, b. Oct. 26, 1770	LR7	33
Ezra*, s. Reuben & Mabel, d. Jan. 18, 1777, in the 7th y. of his age *("Azer" crossed out, corrected to "Ezra")	LR7	33
Frederick Elisha, s. Jared & Ann, b. Feb. 3, 1833	1	187
George, s. Jared & Ann, b. [ ]	1	115
George H., m. Elizbeth **PARKS**, Mar. 9, 1843, by E. Huntington	1	393
George Henry, s. Jared & Ann, b. Dec. 5, 1817	1	187
George Henry, s. [Jared & Ann], d. Mar. 2, 1844	1	187
Gershom, [s. Edmond & Mercy], b. July 7, 1761	LR11	1
Gedeon*, s. Nathaniel & Esther, b. Sept. 21, 1742 *(Gideon)	LR4	10
Gilbert, s. John & Jemimah, b. May 26, 1744	LR4	2
Gilbert, s. Nathan & Elizabeth, b. Nov. 22, 1782	LR7	23
Hannah, d. Benjamin & Zerviah, b. Oct. 22, 1711	LR2	353
Hannah, m. Thomas **WELLER**, b. of New Milford, Nov. 5, 1729	LR2	346
Hannah, w. Abraham, d. Dec. 18, 1742	LR4	9
Hannah, m. Lazarus **RUGGLES**, Sept. 3, 1754	LR7	17
Hannah, d. Joel & Sarah, b. July 13, 1769* *(Corrected from "1768")	LR10	5
Hannah, wid. Daniel, d. July 31, 1792	LR4	19
Hannah Lorrain, d. Samuel & Pollypheme, b. May 25, 1789; d. Mar. 31, 179[ ]	1	7
Hannah Lorrain, d. Samuell & Pollypheme, b. Feb. 9, 179[ ]	1	7
Harriet Susanna, d. Ashbel & Clara M., b. June 9, 1815	1	122

BOSTWICK, BOSTICK, BOSWICK, (cont.)

	Vol.	Page
Hecter, s. Nathaniel & Esther, b. June 28, 1729	LR2	342
Heman, [s. Edmond & Mercy], b. Apr. 15, 1777	LR11	1
Henry E., s. Solomon E. & Adaline, b. May 6, 1835	1	272
Hester, d. Daniel & Hannah, b. Sept. 17, 1749	LR6	2
Hester, m. Benjamin **BOSTWICK**, Apr. 15, 1767, by Samuel Bostwick, J. P.	LR10	12
Horatio Nelson, s. Ashbel & Clara M., b. June 15, 1806	1	122
Hulda, d. Edward & Ann, b. Aug. 25, 1758	LR7	25
Huldah, d. Matthew & Rebeckah, b. Feb. 19, 1774	LR8	3
Hulda, of Sharon, m. Joel **BUCK**, July 2, 1778	LR13	4
Ichabod, s. Joseph & Rebecaha, b. Sept. 1, 1737; d. Aug. 16, 1755	LR2	339
Ichabod, s. Capt. Nathaniel & Esther, b. Dec. 13, 1747	LR4	10
Ichabod, s. Abel & Sarah, b. Sept. 1, 1756	LR7	11
Ichabod, m. Lucy **WARNER**, Feb. 27, 1771	LR11	11
Ichabod, d. Sept. 15, 1776" in the Provential Army with out Kingsbridge"	LR11	11
Ichabod, m. Anne **WHEATON**, Oct. 8, 1780	1	96
Isaac, s. Lemuel & Anna, b. Sept. 6, 1732 (?) *(blot)	LR4	9
Isaac, m. Prudence **WARNER**, Nov. 27, 1754, by Rev. Nathaniel Taylor	LR6	7
Israel, s. Bushnel & Meriam, b. Aug. 9, 1740	LR4	19
Israel, s. Bushnell & Meriam, d. Jan. 16, 1745/6	LR4	19
Israel, twin with Marcy, s. Bushnell & Meriam, b. Aug. 7, 1749	LR4	19
Isarall, [twin with Mearcy], s. Bushanell & Meriam, b. Aug. 7, 1749	LR6	4
Israel, m. Elizabeth **MALLERY**, July 12, 1767, by Samuell Canfield, J. P.	LR10	2
Israel, m. Elizabeth **MALLERY**, July 12, 1767, by Samuell Canfield, J. P.	LR11	2
Jared, s. Samuel & Ann, b. Aug. 9*, 1751 *("6th" crossed out)	LR5	3
Jared, s. Sam[ue]ll & Ann, d. Aug. 30, 1778, at Norwich	LR5	3
Jared, s. Israel & Elizabeth, b. Oct. 15, 1778	LR10	2
Jared, s. Elisha & Betty, b. May 24, 1787	1	5
Jared, m. Ann **COPLEY**, b. of New Milford, June 25, 1814, by David S. Boardman, J. P.	1	115
Jared, m. Ann **COPLEY**, b. of New Milford, June 25, 1814, by David S. Boardman, J. P.	1	187
Jehannah, d. Zadock & Darcos, b. Mar. 22, 1780	LR13	11
Jemima, d. Benjamin & Zerviah, b. Aug. 29, 1720	LR2	353
Jemima, w. Dea. John, d. Oct.* 11, 1795, in the 89th y. of her age *(month corrected)	LR4	2
Jerusha, d. Benjamin & Zerviah, b. July 15, 1717	LR2	353
Jerusha, m. Joseph **CANFIELD**, Jan. 15, 1736/7, by John Bostwick, J. P.	LR4	21

	Vol.	Page
BOSTWICK, BOSTICK, BOSWICK, (cont.)		
Jesse, s. John & Jemima, b. Apr. 15, 1733	LR4	2
Joel, m. Sarah **KENEY**, June 21, 1768, by Rev. Noah Wadhams	LR10	5
Joel, s. Benajah & Hannah, d. Apr. 11, 1777	LR10	5
John, s. Jared & Ann, b. [ ]	1	115
John, Jr., of New Milford, m. Marcy **BUSHNELL**, of Danbury, Jan. 30, 1711/12	LR2	360
John, s. John & Marcy, b. Mar. 24, 1714/15	LR2	361
John, m. Jemima **CANFEILD**, b. of New Milford, Jan. 18, 1732/3, by Samuell Brownson, J. P.	LR4	2
John, Dea., d. June 12, 1741	LR4	1
John, s. John & Jemima, b. Sept. 1, 1741	LR4	2
John, s. Nathan & Elizabeth, b. Apr. 6, 1785	LR7	23
John, Dea., d. Dec. 17, 1806, in the 93rd y. of his age	LR4	2
John R., m. Minerva **CLARK**, b. of Bridgewater, Aug. 13, 1826, by Rev. Fosdick Harrison, of Roxbury	1	135
John Robert, s. Jared & Ann, b. Jan. 9, 1820	1	187
John Robert, of New Milford, m. Ann Louisa **PORTER**, of Bridgeport, Dec. 25, 1844, by Rev. Gurdon S. Coit, of Bridgeport	1	404
John Roberts, m. Ann Louisa **PORTER**, Dec. 25, 1844	1	404
Jonathan, twin with David, s. Bushnell & Meriam, b. Mar. 27, 1738	LR4	19
Jonathan, m. Rebeckah **BROWNSON**, Jan. 4, 1761	LR7	12
Jonathan, Jr., s. Jonathan & Rebecckah, b. July 7, 1762	LR7	12
Jonathan, Jr., m. Abigail **TROWBRIDGE**, b. of New Milford, Sept. 22, 1791	1	23
Jonathan, d. Mar. 16, 1812, ae 74 y. wanting 22 d.	LR7	12
Joseph, of New Milford, m. Rebekah **WHEELER**, of Stratfield, July 23, 1724, by [ ]	LR2	339
Joseph, s. Joseph & Rebekah, b. Aug. 19, 1728	LR2	339
Joseph, s. Abraham & Hannah, b. Nov. 14*, 1735 *("Dec. 4" crossed out)	LR4	9
Joseph, Jr., m. Bette [**HURD**(?)], Feb. 7, 1750/1, by Rev. Jeadiah Mills, of Ripton	LR7	1
Joseph, Capt., d. Sept. 27, 1756	LR2	339
Joseph, s. Abel & Sarah, b. Nov. 29, 1757	LR7	11
Joseph, m. Mary **ROBURDS**, Dec. 21, 1760	LR8	2
Joseph, twin with Benjamin, s. Joseph & Mary, b. Feb. 24, 1764	LR8	2
Joseph, s. Abel & Sarah, d. Mar. 15, 1778, in the 21st y. of his age	LR7	11
Joseph Abel, s. Ichabod & Anne, b. Nov. 23, 1781	1	96
Joseph Morton, s. Joseph & Mary, b. Feb. 3, 1773	LR8	2
Joshua, s. Abraham & Hannah, b. Feb. 22, 1749	LR4	9
Jzbon, [s. Edmond & Mercy], b. Mar. 19, 1768	LR11	1
Laury, d. Ebenezer & Rebecah, b. Feb. 27, 1784	LR13	12

BOSTWICK, BOSTICK, BOSWICK, (cont.)

	Vol.	Page
Laura A., m. Samuel C. **WILDMAN**, Sept. 1, 1835, by Edward C. Bull	1	314
Lemuel, of New Milford, m. Anna **JACKSON**, of Stratfeild, Nov. 5, 1729	LR4	9
Lemuel*, m. Ann **FISK**, Mar. 28, 1748, by Samuel Canfield, J. P. *(Perhaps "Samuel")	LR5	3
Lemuel, s. Isaac & Prudence, d. Sept. 12, 1757* *("1767" blotted out)	LR6	7
Lemuel, Jr., s. Isaac & Prudence, b. Dec. 27, 1758	LR6	7
Lemuel, Jr., m. Polly **FRAIL**, June 27, 1784, by Daniel Everitt	1	1
Lemuel, d. Apr. 8, 1791, in the 87th y. of his age	LR4	9
Lodemia, d. Benjamin Ruggles & Rachel, b. Oct. 10, 178[ ]	1	3
Lowis, d. Nathaniel & Esther, b. Mar. 16, 1732/3	LR4	10
Lois, d. Capt. Nathaniel, d. Oct. 24, 1757	LR7	5
Lois, d. Arthur & Eunice, b. Aug. 20, 1758	LR7	16
Loies, d. Reuben & Mabel, b. Nov. 23, 1766	LR7	33
Lois, d. Israel & Elizabeth, b. Dec. 13, 1769	LR10	2
Lois, d. Reuben & Mabel, d. Jan. 18, 1777, in the 11th y. of her age	LR7	33
Lois, d. Reuben & Mabel, b. Nov. 15, 1777	LR7	33
Lois Anna, d. Ichabod & Lucy, b. Jan. 9, 1772	LR11	11
Lucy, [d. Edmond & Mercy], b. Mar. 5, 1772	LR11	1
Lucy, m. Nathanael **DURKE**, Jr., Feb. 22, 1778, by Rev. Nathaniell Taylor	LR13	8
Lucy, d. Salmon & Anne, b. Aug. 14, 1791	1	22
Lucy, m. Sheldon G. **WOODIN**, b. of New Milford, Feb. 24, 1833, by Rev. Henry S. Atwater	1	258
Lydia, m. Orange **MERWIN**, b. of New Milford, Apr. 16, 1807, by Elisha Bostwick, J. P.	1	140
Lydia Sarah, d. Ichabod & Anne, b. Aug. 3, 1783	1	96
Lyman, s. Nathan & Elizabeth, b. Oct. 8, 1768	LR7	23
Mabell, d. Bushnell [& Meriam], b. Aug. 4, 1744	LR4	19
Mable, d. Reuben & Mabel, b. Nov. 30, 1775	LR7	33
Mabel, d. Reuben & Mabel, d. Jan. 14, 1777, in the 2nd y. of her age	LR7	33
Mabel, w. Capt. Reuben, m. June 15, 1804, at Canton, N. Y., in the 69th y. of her age	LR7	33
Marcy, d. Joseph & Rebekah, b. June 12, 1731	LR2	339
Marcy, twin with Israel, d. Bushnell & Meriam, b. Aug. 7, 1749 (This entry written over an erasure)	LR4	19
Marcy, d. Salmon & Anne, b. July 14, 1789	1	22
Mary, d. Benjamin & Zerviah, b. May 19, 1713	LR2	353
Mary, d. Benjamin, d. Oct. 10, 1713	LR2	358
Mary, d. John, Sr. & Abigail, b. Feb. 8, 1714/15	LR2	361
Mary, m. Zarubbael **CANFIELD**, July 26, 1733	LR4	11
Mary A., of New Milford, m. William H. **KELLEY**, of Goshen, Nov. 12, 1850, by Rev. Harley Goodwin, of		

BOSTWICK, BOSTICK, BOSWICK, (cont.)

	Vol.	Page
S. Canaan	2	67
Mary Ann, d. Jared & Ann, b. Nov. 18, 1829	1	187
Mary Ann, Mrs., of New Milford, m. Thomas **IVES**, of Roxbury, Oct. 17, 1852, by D. Williams. Int. Pub.	2	77
Mary M., of Bridgwater, m. Tyrus **WHEATON**, of Brookfield, Dec. 13, 1827, by Abner Brundige	1	219
Matthew, s. John, 3rd & Jemima, b. Aug. 26, 1737	LR4	2
Matthew, m. Rebeckah **BOSTWICK**, Nov. 6, 1766, by Samuell Bostwick, J. P.	LR8	2
Matthew, m. Rebecah **BOSTWICK**, Nov. 6, 1766, by Samuel Bostwick, J. P.	LR8	3
Medad, [s. Edmon & Mercy], b. Jan. 14, 1760	LR11	1
Mercy, Mrs., m. Ens. William **GAYLARD**, Oct. 14*, 1742, by Rev. Daniel Bordman *(Crossed out date)	LR4	2
Mearcy, [twin with Isarall], d. Bushanell & Meriam, b. Aug. 7, 1749	LR6	4
Mercy, m. Pitman **BENEDICK**, Dec. 6, 1749	LR10	1
Mercy, [d. Edmond & Mercy], b. Mar. 11, 1770; d. Sept. 26, 1777	LR11	1
Mercy, m. Elizur **BOSTWICK**, Dec. 30, 1778	LR13	12
Mercy, see Mercy **LOCKWOOD**	LR4	1
Meriam, w. Col. Bushnell, d. Apr. 10, 1783	LR4	19
Nancy, d. Edmond & Aurelia, b. Dec. 22, 1813	1	166
Nathan, s. John & Jemima, b. Nov. 16, 1746	LR3	2
Nathan, m. Elizabeth **COGSWELL**, Jan. 7, 1768, by Rev. Noah Wadhams	LR7	23
Nathan, s. Nathan & Elizabeth, b. Aug. 28, 1778	LR7	23
Nathaniel, m. Esther **HITCHCOCK**, Oct. 7, 1727	LR2	342
Nathaniel, s. Arthur & Eunice, b. Feb. 7, 1757	LR7	16
Noble, s. Joseph & Mary, b. July 18, 1769	LR8	2
Noble, s. Joel & Sarah, b. Apr. 28, 1771	LR10	5
Oliver, s. Ichabod & Lucy, b. Feb. 17, 1776; d. Feb. 18, 1776	LR11	11
Oringe, s. Mathew & Rebeckah, b. Apr. 27, 1769	LR8	2
Orange, s. Matthew & Rebeckah, b. Apr. 27, 1769	LR8	3
Parnell, d. Joseph & Rebekah, b. Mar. 16, 1725/6	LR2	339
Pearnal, m. Ebenezer **PEEKIT***, May 28, 1748, by Nathaniell Bostwick, J. P. *(PICKETT)	LR6	1
Parnel, d. Matthew & Rebeckah, b. Feb. 28, 1776	LR8	3
Paul Yeats, s. David, Jr. & Polly, b. Mar. 22, 1781	LR13	17
Paulina, d. Jonathan & Rebeckah, b. May 24, 1764	LR7	12
Polly, d. Amos & Sarah, b. Oct. 18, 1767	LR10	1
Polley, d. Joel & Sarah, b. Mar. 12, 1771 (?)* *("1773" in Orcutt's Hist.)	LR10	5
Prudence, d. Isaac & Prudence, b. Nov. 30, 1764	LR6	7
Prudence, m. Benoni Stebbins **SANFORD**, [ ]	1	14
Rachel, d. Benjamin & Rachel, b. Dec. 9, 1743	LR5	1
Rachel, m. James **BRADSHAW**, Sept. 19, 1750, by Rev.		

	Vol.	Page
BOSTWICK, BOSTICK, BOSWICK, (cont.)		
Nathaniell Taylor	LR6	11
Rachel, d. Robert & Sarah, d. Feb. 21, 1760	LR10	2
Rachel, m. Isaac **DeFOREST**, Jan. 11, 1763	LR7	34
Rachel, d. Benjamin & Hester, b. Mar. 15, 1769	LR10	12
Rachel, d. Benjamin & Olive, b. May 9, 1770	LR10	8
Rachel, d. Benjamin & Olive, b. May 9, 1770; m. John **STILSON**, s. John & Hannah, Apr. 30, 1794, by Rev. Stanley Griswold	1	243
Rebecha, d. Joseph & Rebecha, b. Sept. 1, 1741	LR2	339
Rebeckah, m. Matthew **BOSTWICK**, Nov. 6, 1766, by Samuell Bostwick, J. P.	LR8	2
Rebeckah, m. Matthew **BOSTWICK**, Nov. 6, 1766, by Samuell Bostwick, J. P.	LR8	3
Rebecah, w. Jonathan, d. June 3, 1806, in the 75th y. of her age	LR7	12
Ruben, s. Nathaniel & Esther, b. Sept. 2, 1734	LR4	10
Reuben, s. Isaac & Prudence, b. May 21, 1757	LR6	7
Reuben, m. Mabel **RUGGLES**, May 27, 1761	LR7	33
Reuben, s. Reuben & Mabel, b. Apr. 24, 1769	LR7	33
Reuben, s. Reuben & Mabel, d. Jan. 20, 1777, in the 8th y. of his age	LR7	33
Robert, of New Milford, m. Rachel **HOLMES**, of Bedford, Jan. 9, 1720/1	LR2	344
Robert, s. Robert & Sarah, d. Nov. 11, 1759	LR10	2
Robert, [s. Edmond & Mercy], b. Mar. 15, 1774	LR11	1
Salley, d. Ichabod & Lucy, b. Oct. 12, 1773	LR11	11
Salley, d. Lemuel, Jr. & Polly, b. Mar. 21, 1786	1	1
Salmon, [s. Edmon & Mercy], b. May 7, 1758	LR11	1
Salmon, s. Joel & Hulda, b. Aug. 2, 1781	LR13	4
Salmon, m. Anne **WARNER**, b. of New Milford, June 22, 1788	1	22
Samuel, s. John & Marcy, b. Aug. 30, 1723	LR2	361
Sam[ue]ll, s. Sam[ue]ll & Ann, b. Jan. 19, 1755	LR5	3
Samuel, s. Isaac & Prudence, b. Aug. 27, 1755	LR6	7
Samuel, Jr., m. Pollypheme **RUGGLES**, May 14, 178[ ]	1	7
Samuell, had negro Doria, d. Patience, b. Feb. 17, 1781, George, b. July 24, 1784, Shubal, b. July 22, 1785, Ira, b. July 2, 1789, Rhoda, b. Oct. 26, 1791, Abel, b. Sept. 1, 1794, Charles, b. Feb. 16, 1797, Julia, b. Oct. 10, 1800	1	424
Samuel, d. Sept. 23, 1789, ae 66 y. 12 d.	LR5	3
Samuel, d. Apr. 3, 1799, in the 45th y. of his age	1	7
Samuel, see Lemuel **BOSTWICK**	LR5	3
Samuel Randolph, s. Elisha & Betty, b. Aug. 16, 1799; d. Dec. 30, 1802, ae 3 y. 4 m. 14 d.	1	5
Saria, d. Nathaniel & Esther, b. Aug. 28, 1730	LR2	342
Sarah, m. Sherman **BORDMAN**, Dec. 3, 1755	LR7	32
Sarah, d. Robert & Sarah, b. June 18, 1760	LR10	2

BOSTWICK, BOSTICK, BOSWICK, (cont.)

	Vol.	Page
Sarah, d. Robert & Sarah, d. Dec. 5, 1784	LR10	2
Seymor, s. Nathan & Elizabeth, b. Apr. 10, 1774	LR7	23
Shadrah, s. Bushnel & Meriam, b. Sept. 25, 1742	LR4	19
Shelburn, s. Matthew & Rebecah, b. Nov. 8, 1781	LR8	3
Solomon, s. Benjamin & Rachel, b. Jan. 13, 1746/7	LR5	1
Solomon, s. Isaac & Prudence, b. Aug. 8, 1762	LR6	7
Solomon, s. Benj[ami]n & Olive, b. June 12, 1774	LR10	8
Solomon E., m. Adaline **BOOTH**, b. of New Milford, Feb. 26, 1834, by H. Rood	1	272
Stanley, s. Jared & Ann, b . July 10, 1815	1	115
Stanley Griswold, s. [Jared & Ann], b. July 10, 1815	1	187
Sylvia, of New Milford, m. John D. **CHAMPLAIN**, of Stonnington, Sept. 12, 1831, by H. Rood	1	236
Tamor, d. Nathaniel [& Ester], b. May 31, 1746	LR4	10
Tamar, m. Daniel **BOSTWICK**, Jr., b. of New Milford, May 31, 1769, by Samuell Bostwick, J. P.	LR10	7
Taymar, [ ] David **BOSTWICK**, Jr. [ ] (This entry crossed out)	LR10	12
Walker B., s. Solomon E. & Adaline, b. Aug. 26, 1840	1	272
William, s. Benjamin & Hester, b. Aug. 21, 1767	LR10	12
William, m. Lucy Maria **SANFORD**, b. of New Milford, Jan. 5, 1842, by N. Porter, Jr.	1	371
William T., of Sherman, m. Amy **HILL**, of New Milford, Dec. 26, 1822, by Rev. Benjamin Benham	1	67
Zachariah, s. Joseph & Mary, b. Nov. 18, 1761	LR8	2
Zadock, s. Nathaniel & Esther, b. Feb. 18, 1735/6	LR4	10

[BOSWORTH], [see under **BOZWORTH**]
BOTCHFORD, [see under **BOTSFORD**]
BOTSFORD, BOTCHFORD, BOSFORD, Abel, s. Jonathan &

Elisabeth, b. Sept. 6, 1747	LR4	24
Abel, m. Mary **HARTWELL**, Aug. 7, 1769, by Bushnel Bostwick, J. P.	LR11	6
Ann, d. Nathan & Sarah, b. Oct. 10, 1744	LR4	4
Ann, m. Benjamin **BUCKINGHAM**, b. of New Milford, June 30, 1762	LR7	38
Anna, d. David & Rebeckah, b. July 2, 1767	LR11	9
Annis, m. Daniel H. **FERRISS**, Jan. 29, 1795	1	37
Benjamin, s. David & Rebeckah, b. Sept. 9, 1765	LR11	9
Cyrus, of Derby, m. Emily **BEACH**, of Oxford, Sept. 15, 1833, by Rev. Nathan D. Benedict	1	265
David, s. Jonathan & Elisabeth, b. Oct. 4, 1744	LR4	24
David, m. Rebekah **PHIPENEY**, b. of New Milford, Oct. 18, 1764, by [Samuel] Boswick, J. P.	LR11	9
David, of Newtown, m. Phebe **HATCH**, of New Milford, May 19, 1824, by Rev. Benjamin Benham	1	104
Doratha, a witness at wedding of Elnathan **BOTSFORD**, & Dorothy **PRINDLE**, Quakers	LR4	14

NEW MILFORD VITAL RECORDS 35

	Vol.	Page
BOTSFORD, BOTCHFORD, BOSFORD, (cont.)		
Elizabeth, d. Jonathan & Elizabeth, b. Sept. 22, 1740	LR4	24
Elizabeth, m. Thomas **OVIATT**, Jr., Jan. 26, 1769	LR13	14
Elizabeth A., m. George **WELTON**, Oct. 25, 1789	1	81
Ella A., of Sherman, m. Isaac L. **SANFORD**, of New Milford, this day, [Sept. 20, 1886), by Sandanett Wheeler, J. P. Witnesses: Juliet Wheeler, of Doyer, Priscilla Hall, of Dover	2	123
Elnathan, s. Samuel & Hannah, of Milford, m. Dorothy **PRINDLE**, d. Samuel & Dorathy, of New Milford, Mar. 18, 1733/4, at the house of Samuel Prindle, Quaker ceremony before 17 witnesses. Intentions declared at Josiah Quinby's house at Momorneck, Chester Co., N. Y.	LR4	14
Elnathan, hus. of Dorothy **PRINDLE**, d. Apr. 13, 1734	LR4	14
Elnathan, s. Jonathan & Elisabeth, b. Nov. 10, 1738	LR4	24
Elnathan, a witness at wedding of Elnathan **BOTSFORD**, & Dorothy **PRINDLE**, Quakers	LR4	14
Hannah, d. Jonathan & Elisabeth, b. Apr. 19, 1750/1	LR4	24
Hannah, m. Abel **BUCKINGHAM**, Dec. 28, 1773, by Rev. Nathaniell Taylor	LR12	19
Hester, d. Nathan & Sarah, b. Jan. 20, 1754	LR4	4
Jonathan, s. Samuel & Hannah, of Milford, m. Elisabeth **CAMP**, d. Samuel & Lydia, of New Milford, Feb. 5, 1735/6, by Rev. Daniel Bordman	LR4	24
Jonathan, s. Jonathan & Elizabeth, b. Sept. 1, 1742 (?)	LR4	24
Martha, d. Jonathan & Elisabeth, b. Mar. 27, 1737; d. Aug. 25, 1740	LR4	24
Martha, w. Capt. Nathan, d. Apr. 8, 1791	LR11	4
Nathan, s. David & Rebeckah, b. June 2, 1769	LR4	9
Nathan, Capt., m. Mrs. Martha **BALDWIN**, Sept. 18, 1771	LR4	4
Nathan, Capt., d. Feb. 14, 1792	LR4	4
Samuel, s. Jonathan & Elisabth, b. Mar. 11, 1753	LR4	24
Sarah, d. Nathan & Sarah, b. June 18, 1740	LR4	4
Sarah, m. Enos **CAMP**, Jr., b. of New Milford, July 5, 1764, by Rev. Nathaniel Taylor	LR7	6
Sarah, w. Capt. Nathan, d. July 26, 1770	LR4	4
BOWDITCH, David, of Dover, N. Y., m. Sally **McGARRY**, Sept. 11, 1834, by H. Rood	1	278
BOWERS, Heman, m. Polly **BUEL**, Nov. 3, 1833, by H. Rood	1	267
Olive, of New Milford, m. Solomon S. **PECK**, of Moreson, Mass., May 13, 1821, by David S. Boardman, J. P.	1	47
Sally, m. Arza **DOWNS**, b. of New Milford, Dec. 13, 1820, by Rev. Fosdic Harrison, of Roxbury	1	106
BOWLIN, Oliver, of Kent, m. Hannah **WARREN**, of New Milford, (colored), Sept. 24, 1850, by Rev. David Murdock	2	64
BOWNE, Samuel, a witness at wedding of Elnathan **BOTSFORD**, & Dorothy **PRINDLE**, Quakers	LR4	14
BOYCE, James F., of Washington, N. Y., m. Loisa		

	Vol.	Page
BOYCE, (cont.)		
MOREHOUSE, of New Milford, June 29, 1854, by Rev. James L. Scott	2	99
BOZWORTH, Daniel, s. Stephen & Abigal, b. Nov. 13, 1750	LR6	7
James, s. Stephen & Abigal, b. Dec. 25, 1747	LR6	7
Nathaniel, s. Stephen & Abigal, b. Feb. 7, 1749	LR6	7
William, m. Sarah FARRAND, b. of New Milford, Aug. 6, 1745, by Roger Brownson, J. P.	LR5	10
BRADLEY, Jennette E., m. Joseph M. PLATT, b. of New Milford, Jan. 24, 1849, by John Greenwood	2	47
Terrissa, m. John MARSH, b. of New Milford, July 28, 1816, by Elisha Bostwick, J. P.	1	141
BRADSHAW, Anna, d. William & Mindwell, b. Dec. 16, 1773	LR10	16
Asahel, s. James & Lydiah, b. Feb. 15, 1761	LR6	11
Betsay, d. John, Jr. & Abigail, b. Jan. 19, 1779	LR12	6
Betsey, m. Lacy CAMP, Apr. 1, 1827, by Abner Brundage	1	213
Daniel, s. William & Mindwell, b. Mar. 3, 1772; d. Apr. 22, 1774	LR10	16
David, s. James & Rachel, b. Dec. 29, 1751; d. Jan*. 13, 1752 *("Dec." crossed out)	LR6	11
David, s. James & Lydia, b. Feb. 5, 1759	LR6	11
Ellenor, m. James MACKENNIE, Feb. 10, 1741/2, by Roger Brownson, J. P.	LR4	2
Ellenor, m. James MACKKENNEY, Feb. 10, 1742	LR6	14
Homer, of Rootstown, O., m. Jane OLMSTED, of New Milford, Oct. 23, 1825, by Rev. Andrew Eliot	1	35
James, m. Rachel BOSTWICK, Sept. 19, 1750, by Rev. Nathaniell Taylor	LR6	11
James, m. Lydiah MOSS, Feb. 13, 1753, by Rev. Nathaniell Taylor	LR6	11
James, s. James & Lidea, b. Apr. 2, 1763	LR6	2
John, of New Milford, m. Sarah VIDDITS, of Danbury, June 4, 1740, by Rev. Ebenezer White, of Danbury. Witnesses: Stephen Vidito & Mary Vidito	LR5	2
John, s. John & Sarah, b. May 4, 1748* *(Written first "1758")	LR5	2
John, Jr., m. Abigail KEELER, Nov. 16, 1775	LR12	6
Lois, d. James & Lydia, b. Sept. 10, 1757	LR6	11
Lucy, of New Milford, m. David P. CAMP, of Brookfield, Apr. 27, 1823, by Abner Brundage	1	109
Mary, d. John & Sarah, b. Feb.* 26, 1743/4 *("Apr." crossed out and "Feb." written above)	LR5	2
Rachel, w. James, d. Jan. 18, 1752	LR6	11
Rachel, d. John & Sarah, b. Jan. 4, 1758	LR5	2
Salmon, s. John, Jr. & Abigail, b. Nov. 4, 1776	LR12	6
Salmon Thomas, s. Thomas & Tirza, b. Dec. 17, 1801	1	144
Sarah, d. John & Sarah, b. July 6, 1745	LR5	2
Sarah, Jr., m. James TERRIL, Jr., b. of New Milford, June		

	Vol.	Page

BRADSHAW, (cont.)
   15, 1768 — LR10, 13
   Sarah, d. William & Mindwell, b. Sept. 4, 1770; d. Apr. 20, 1774 — LR10, 16
   Sarah, m. Abraham **OLMSTED**, Dec. 30, 1823, by Rev. Andrew Eliot — 1, 177
   Thomas, d. Mar. 10, 1753 — LR5, 1
   Thomas, s. James & Lydiah, b. Nov. 25, 1754 — LR6, 11
   Thomas, of New Milford, m. Thirza **BENEDICT**, of Danbury, Mar. 15, 1801 — 1, 144
   William, d. Aug. 7, 1734 — LR4, 1
   William, s. John & Sarah, b. Oct. 9, 1742 — LR5, 2
   William, of New Milford, m. Mindwell **WILDMAN**, of Danbury, June 14, 1769 — LR10, 16
   William, s. John, Jr. & Abigail, b. Aug. 2, 1784 — LR12, 6

BRAIGE, Elizabeth, of New Milford, m. Richard **PORTER**, of Warren, Nov. 22, 1843, by Daniel B. Wilson, J. P. — 1, 389

BRASCHING, John William, journeyman carpenter, s. John **CHRISTIAN**, of Eichberg, m. Maria Dorothea **HENSEL**, d. John **GOBBLOT**, of Augustwalde, Sept. 4, 1853, by Rev. Graefe. Recorded in Marbledale, Litchfield Co., Conn., July 14, 1866, at request of Mrs. Maria Brasching — 2, 115

BRIGGS, Eurania, m. Aaron **GAYLARD**, Feb. 16, 1764 — LR10, 18
   Hermon, m. Lorain **NICHOLS**, Dec. 6, 1821, by Rev. Andrew Eliot — 1, 9
   Iranai, m. Aaron **GAYLARD**, Jr., b. of New Milford, Feb. 16, 1764 — LR7, 9
   James, of Sherman, m. Phebe Ophelia **FERRISS**, of New Milford, Feb. 8, 1808, by Elisha Bostwick, J. P. — 1, 126
   Phebe, of New Fairfield, m. Daniel Hervey **GAYLARD**, of New Milford, Sept. 25, 1799 — 1, 82
   Sally, of New Milford, m. Martin **LEE**, of Sherman (lately from New York State), Mar. 10, 1825, by Daniel Gaylord, J. P. — 1, 110

BRISCO, Eunice, m. Thompson **BOOTH**, Feb. [ ], 1798, by Rev. Philo Perry, of Newtown. Witness: Phebe Booth, sister of Thompson Booth — 1, 406

BRISTOL, BRITTOL. BRISTOLL, Abel, of Washington, m. Luna **PEETS**, of New Milford, Dec. 4, 1837, by N. Porter — 1, 313
   Allice, m. Elieazer **BEECHER**, Jr., b. of New Milford, Dec. 24, 1760, by Rev. Nathaniell Taylor — LR7, 5
   Ann, d. Daniel & Susanna, b. Jan. 8, 1783 — 1, 60
   Clarry, d. Daniel & Susanna, b. Nov. 15, 1784 — 1, 60
   Clarra Minerva, m. Ashbel **BOSTWICK**, Aug. 28, 1803 — 1, 122
   Daniel, m. Susanna **WOOSTER**, July 18, 1775 — 1, 60
   Daniel & w. Susanna, had d. [ ], b. Jan. 22, 1776; d. same day — 1, 60

	Vol.	Page
BRISTOL, BRITTOL, BRISTOLL, (cont.)		
Isaac, twin with Peter, s. Daniel & Susanna, b. Apr. 7, 1794	1	60
Isaac B., m. Annis **ROBERTS**, b. of New Milford, Jan. 7, 1846, by J. Greenwood	2	8
Jabez, s. Daniel & Susanna, b. Apr. 29, 1781	1	60
Lucy, d. Daniel & Susanna, b. Aug. 22, 1779	1	60
Peter, twin with Isaac, s. Daniel & Susanna, b. Apr. 5, 1794	1	60
Susanna, w. Daniel, d. May 7, 1794	1	60
William H., of Derby, m. Harriot A. **PICKETT**, of New Milford, June 5, 1854, by J. W. Hoffman	2	108
BRISTOR, John, Jr., m. Sarah **NEARING**, Jan. 12, 1764	LR7	38
BRITON, Edwin, of Salisbury, m. Mary Jane **SEELY**, of New Milford, Oct. 6, 1833, by Rev. R. B. Canfield	1	264
BROCK, Elisabeth, d. Ezekiel & Elisabeth, b. Oct. 2, 1751	LR7	2
Elizabeth, m. James **DAILY**, Oct. 31, 1771, by Samuell Bostwick, J. P.	LR13	6
BRONSON, BROWNSON, Abel, s. Josiah & Prudence, b. Jan. 14, 1757	LR4	23
Abigal, w. Jacob, d. Apr. 25, 1734	LR4	1
Abigail, d. Jacob & Rebeck[ah], b. Sept. 12, 1738	LR4	1
Abigail, d. Peter & Abigail, b. June 8, 1753	LR5	1
Abigail, of Cornwall, m. Asa **WHITNEY**, of New Preston, Dec. 17, 1772, by Rev. Hezekiah Goold	LR10	17
Abigail, m. Samuel **FERRISS**, Jan. 26, 1774, by Rev. Nathaniell Taylor	LR12	8
Abraham, s. Josiah & Prudance, b. Nov. 3, 1749	LR6	5
Abraham, s. Josiah & Prudance, b. Nov. 3, 1749	LR4	23
Abram, s. Roger, b. Dec. 22, 1707	LR2	359
Abram, m. Deborah **ABBOTT**, Nov. 28, 1738, by James Benedict, J. P.	LR4	23
Abram, d. Jan. 28, 1743/4* *("Feb. 28th" crossed out)	LR4	23
Affa, m. James Charles **DOVEY**, June 20, 1843, by E. Huntington	1	394
Alfred, s. Thomas & Betty*, b. May 22, 1767 *("Elizabeth" crossed out)	LR6	15
Almira, m. Samuel **CALDWELL**, b. of New Milford, Nov. 28, 1821, by Rev. Benjamin Benham	1	118
Ann, d. Josiah & Prudence, b. Apr. 10, 1742	LR4	23
Annah, d. Samuell & Elisabeth, b. Jan. 9, 1752	LR6	5
Armida, m. Elliott **HOYT**, Apr. 5, 1846, by E. Huntington	2	22
Asa, s. Thomas & Betty, b. Oct. 31, 1754	LR6	15
Asa, m. Sarah **WOOD**, Sept. 9, 1777	LR13	10
Asahel, s. Mathew & Mary, b. Dec. 28, 1793	1	48
Austin, s. Noah & Elizabeth, b. Jan. 30, 1768	LR8	2
Benjamin, s. Roger & Ruth, b. Nov. 1, 1735	LR4	6
Benjamin, Capt., m. Mary **ARNOLD**, May 16, 1781	LR13	5
Benjamin, Capt., d. May 9, 1803	LR13	5
Benjamin, s. Samuel & Barbara, b. Sept. 27, 1808	1	138

	Vol.	Page
BRONSON, BROWNSON, (cont.)		
Benjamin, m. Minerva **CLARK**, b. of New Milford, Nov. 17, 1828, by Rev. Andrew Eliot	1	226
Betty, w. Thomas, d. Sept. 12, 1799	LR6	15
Charlotte, of Bridgewater, m. George T. **PACHING**, of Danbury, Jan. 1, 1846, by Rev. J. Kilborn	2	7
Clotilda, d. Peter & Abigail, b. Jan. 26, 1758; d. Feb. 7, 1776	LR5	1
Cornelia, of New Milford, m. Bradley **BEERS**, of New Fairfield, Nov. 9, 1845, by E. Huntington	2	5
Daniel, s. Mathew & Mary, b. Jan. 23, 1796	1	48
Daniel, m. Almira **LAMSON**, b. of New Milford, Jan. 21, 1823, by Rev. Benjamin Benham	1	64
Darehas*, d. Noah & Elizabeth, b. May 7, 1775; d. June 23, 1775 *("Dorcas" in Orcutt's Hist.)	LR8	2
David, s. Josiah & Prudence, b. Oct. 29, 1739	LR4	23
David, s. Matthew & Mary, b. Sept. 16, 1799	1	48
Dabora, w. Abram, d. Nov. 3, 1739	LR4	23
Deborah, d. Josiah & Prudence, b. Feb. 1, 1743/4	LR4	23
Deborah, d. Noah & Elizabeth, b. June 24, 1766	LR8	2
Dorcas, d. Rogger & Dorcas, b. Sept. 9, 1720	LR2	364
Darocus, d. Peter & Abageil, b. Feb. 15, 1746/7	LR5	1
Darcos, w. Roger, d. Oct. 16, 1755	LR6	5
Darcos, m. David **WILKERSON**, Feb. 18, 1764	LR7	1
Dorcas*, d. Noah & Elizabeth, b. May 7, 1775; d. June 23, 1775 *("Darehas" in Brush copy)	LR8	2
Elisabeth, d. Samuell & Elisabeth, b. Aug. 28, 1756	LR6	5
Eunis, d. Thomas & Sarah, b. Feb. 21*, 1738/9 *(First Written "16")	LR4	11
Eunice, m. Moses **JOHNSON**, May 18, 1761	LR7	36
Eunice, m. Herman D. **SUMMERS**, Oct. 28, 1827, by Stephen Crane, J. P.	1	131
Fidelia, of New Milford, m. Rev. Daniel **DYE**, of Brockfield, Madison Co., N. Y., Mar. 2, 1846, by Rev. Johnson Howard	2	12
Gershom, s. Roger, b. Oct. 4, 1713; d. 18th of same month	LR2	359
Hannah, of Waterbury, m. Nathan **GAYLARD**, of New Milford, Sept. 23, 1731	LR4	7
Hannah, of Waterbury, m. Nathan **GAYLARD**, of New Milford, Sept. 23, 1731	LR2	345
Hannah, d. Roger, Jr. & Ruth, b. Oct. 21, 1743	LR4	6
Hannah, m. Jonathan **REED**, b. of New Milford, Sept. 2, 1845, by E. Huntington	2	3
Hellen M., m. Charles M. **BOOTH**, May 16, 1847, by E. Huntington	2	35
Henry, m. Elizabeth **SEELEY**, Nov. 14, 1843, by John Greenwood	1	388
Hermon, s. Asa & Sarah, b. Feb. 8, 1780	LR13	10
Hine, s. John & Mabel, b. Aug. 16, 1767	LR10	1

	Vol.	
BRONSON, BROWNSON, (cont.)		
Isaac, s. Thomas & Betty, b. July 27, 1758	LR6	15
Jacob, s. Samuell & Lydia, b. Sept. 24, 1711	LR2	359
Jacob, of New Milford, m. Abigail **JONES**, or **GRIFFIN**, a transient person, Nov. 13, 1732, by Rev. Daniel Bordmond	LR4	1
Jacob, of New Milford, m. Mrs. Rebeckah **SMITH**, of Milford, May 29, 1735, by Sam[ue]ll Eels	LR4	1
Jacob, s. Jacob & Rebeckah*, b. Dec. [ ], 1740 *(Abagel)	LR4	1
Jeremiah, m. Elizabeth **GREEN**, Mar. 12, 1826, by Rev. Eleazar Beecher	1	200
Jeremiah B., m. Elisabeth **BENNITT**, Oct. 20, 1841, by E. Huntington	1	367
Jerusha, of Waterbury, m. Paul **WELCH**, of New Milford, July 9, 1728	LR2	343
Jerusha, d. Thomas & Sarah, b. Aug. 13, 1729	LR2	346
Jerusha, m. John **WILKINSON***, b. of New Milford, Jan. 14, 1744/5, by Roger Brownson, J. P. *("Jr." crossed out)	LR5	12
John, s. Thomas & Sary, b. July 3, 1736	LR4	11
John, m. Mabel **HINE**, Aug. 29, 1765	LR10	1
John, m. Rachel **STEVENS**, Jan. 5, 1769	LR10	1
John, s. Asa & Sarah, b. Nov. 29, 1781	LR13	10
John, m. Polly **BALDWIN**, b. of New Milford, Oct. 12, 1801, by Elisha Bostwick, J. P.	1	42
John H., m. Maria A. **FOARD**, b. of New Milford, May 1, 1836, by Albert B. Camp	1	294
Joseph, s. Samuel & Barbara, b. Aug. 10, 1812	1	138
Josiah, s. Rogger, b. Feb. 14, 1714/15	LR2	360
Josiah, s. Rogger, b. Feb. 14, 1714/15	LR2	362
Josiah, s. Roger & Darocus, of New Milford, m. Prudence **HULBUT**, d. Joseph, of Woodbury, Jan. 31, 1738/9, by Joseph Minard, J. P.	LR4	23
Laura, m. William R. **WARNER**, Dec. 23, 1823, by Rev. Andrew Eliot	1	147
Lamuel Abott, s. Noah & Elizabeth, b. Sept. 23, 1773	LR8	2
Lewis, s. Matthew & Mary, b. June 11, 1814	1	48
Leucey, d. Thomas & Betty, b. Oct. 13, 1752, by Samuell Canfield	LR6	15
Lucy, m. Lemuel **THAYER**, Mar. 6, 1771	1	28
Lydia, d. Samuell & Lydia, b. Feb. 23, 1701/2	LR2	359
Mabel, w. John, d. Aug. 28, 1767	LR10	1
Marcy, d. Thomas & Sarah, b. Aug. 20, 1727	LR2	346
Marcy, m. Simeon **BALDWIN**, Dec. 20, 1752*, by Rev. Nathanel Taylor *(First written "1753")	LR6	8
Margett, d. Samuell & Lydia, b. Oct. 3, 1715	LR2	359
Marget, m. Thomas **OVIAT**, b. of New Milford, Jan. 18, 1732/3, by Rev. Daniel Bordman	LR4	2
Martha, of Waterbury, m. Jonathan **HILL**, of New Milford,		

	Vol.	Page
BRONSON, BROWNSON, (cont.)		
Dec. 31, 1746, by Roger Brownson, J. P.	LR5	4
Martha, m. Carlostian COLE, b. of New Milford, Nov. 20, 1831, by E. Huntington	1	248
Mary, d. Rogger, b. Feb. 20, 1704	LR2	359
Mary, m. Jonathan HITCHCOCK, b. of New Milford, Oct. 10, 1726	LR2	341
Mary, d. Roger & Ruth, b. Dec. 12, 1733	LR4	6
Mary, d. Isaac, of Waterbury, m. Daniel HINE, of New Milford, Nov. 23, 1737	LR4	21
Mary, of New Milford, m. Lorenzo HULL, of Litchfield, Mar. 24, 1839, by E. Huntington	1	335
Mary, w. Mathew, d. [ ]	1	48
Mary C., m. Albert BARTRAM, Aug. 3, 1828, by Rev. E. Huntington	1	221
Mary Caroline, d. Mathew & Mary, b. Sept. 25, 1806	1	48
Matthew, s. Roger & Ruth, b. June 29, 1741	LR4	6
Matthew, m. Mary RICHMOND, d. Ephraim, Dec. 27, 1792, by Rev. Stanley Griswold	1	48
Matthew, d. Jan. 16, 1816, in the 75th y. of his age	1	48
Nathaniel, s. Roger & Ruth, b. Oct. 3, 1738	LR4	6
Nathaniel, s. Roger, Jr. [& Ruth], d. Nov. 20, 1747	LR4	6
Nathaniel, s. Noah & Elizabeth, b. Nov. 20, 1777	LR8	2
Nathaniel, m. Hannah MERWIN, b. of New Milford, Feb. 13, 1806, by Elisha Bostwick, J. P.	1	129
Nathaniel, m. Betsey WILLIAMS, Apr. 10, 1836, by E. Huntington	1	297
Noah, s. Roger & Dorcas, b. Oct. 2, 1722; d. Dec. 10, 1738* *(Possibly "1733")	LR2	364
Noah, s. Abram & Dabora, b. Oct. 18, 1739	LR4	23
Noah, m. Elisabeth OVIATT, Mar. 16, 1763, by Bushnell Bostwick, J. P.	LR7	18
Noah, m. Elisabeth OVIATT, Mar. 16, 1763	LR8	2
Noah, s. Noah & Elisabeth, b. Oct. 24, 1771	LR8	2
Noah W., m. Susan M. EVATTS, b. of New Milford, Nov. 2, 1834, by H. Rood	1	279
Orra, d. Asa & Sarah, b. Oct. 11, 1778	LR13	10
Orzamus, s. Noah & Elizabeth, b. Mar. 19, 1764	LR8	2
Orzamus, s. Noah & Elizabeth, d. Oct. 1, 1780, in the Continent Army	LR8	2
Orzamus, s. Noah & Elizabeth, b. Aug. 5, 1781	LR8	2
Orsamus, m. Lucy THAYER, Oct. 6, 1803, by Elisha Bostwick, J. P.	1	108
Peter, s. Rogger & Doracus, b. Oct. 22, 1717	LR2	360
Peter, m. Abagal RICE(?), Nov. 11, 1742, by Rev. Nathaniel Bostwick	LR5	1
Peter, d. Feb. 22, 1776	LR5	1
Prudence, d. Josiah & Prudence, b. July 28, 1746	LR4	23

	Vol.	Page
BRONSON, BROWNSON, (cont.)		
Rebeckah, d. Samuell & Lydia, b. Feb. 14, 1707/8	LR2	359
Rebeckah, m. Samuel **HITCHCOCK**, Oct. 10, 1726	LR2	342
Rebeckah, d. Thomas & Sarah, b. Aug. 2, 1731	LR2	346
Rebeckah, m. Jonathan **BOSTWICK**, Jan. 4, 1761	LR7	12
Reuben, s. Thomas, Jr. & Betty, b. June 10, 1761	LR6	15
Roane, m. James **TERRY**, b. of New Milford, Oct. 29, 1826, by Rev. C. A. Boardman	1	207
Rogger, s. Roger, b. Dec. 10, 1702	LR2	359
Roger, Jr., m. Ruth **CASTLE**, d. Henry, Jan. 11, 1732/3, by Rev. Anthony Stoddard, of Woodbury	LR4	6
Roger, d. Feb. 16, 1758	LR6	5
Roger, d. Dec. 11, 1789, ae 87 y. wanting 10 d.	LR4	6
Rosanah, d. Peter & Abagil, b. Nov. 6, 1743	LR5	1
Rosannah, m. James **PHIPPENEY**, Sept. 16, 1772	LR12	20
Ruth, d. Rogger, b. Dec. 25, 1710	LR2	359
Ruth, d. Roger & Darocus, m. Benjamin **HOUGH**, s. Jonathan & Abagal, Aug. 22, 1738	LR4	21
Ruth, w. Roger, d. Mar. 4, 1788, in the 83rd y. of her age	LR4	6
Ruth Meria, d. Mathew & Mary, b. Jan. 5, 1803	1	48
Samuel, s. Samuel & Lydia, b. July 16, 1721	LR2	359
Samuel, d. Oct. 27, 1733	LR4	1
Samuell, s. Samuell & Elisabeth, b. July 14, 1755	LR6	5
Samuel, s. Capt. Benjamin & Mary, b. Apr. 30, 1784	LR13	5
Samuel, of New Milford, m. Barbara **HARTWELL**, of Washington, Jan. 29, 1807, by Elisha Bostwick, J. P.	1	138
Sary, d. Thomas & Sary, b. Nov. 10, 1733	LR4	11
Sarah, w. Asa, d. Dec. 24, 1781	LR13	10
Sarah, d. Capt. Benjamin & Mary, b. Oct. 21, 1782	LR13	5
Sarah, m. David **MERWIN**, s. Stephen, b. of New Milford, Feb. 23, 1804	1	7
Sheldon Myars, of Kent, m. Alma **GOODSELL**, of New Milford, Mar. 10, 1829, by Rev. Harry Finch, of Washington	1	192
Tamer, d. Samuell & Elisabeth, b. Nov. 2, 1749	LR6	5
Thomas, s. Samuell & Lydia, b. Feb. 6, 1703/4	LR2	359
Thomas, m. Sarah **HITCHCOCK**, b. of New Milford, Nov. 5, 1725	LR2	346
Thomas, s. Thomas & Sarah, b. Dec. 25, 1725	LR2	346
Thomas, Jr., m. Betty **BALDWIN**, Oct. 24, 1751, by Rev. Nathaniel Taylor	LR6	15
Thomas, d. Apr. 18, 1802	LR6	15
Timothy, s. Jacob & Rebeckah, b. Feb. 28, 1736/7	LR4	1
BROOKLIN, Mariah, m. William E. **JACKSON** (colored), Apr. 15, 1821, by Reuben Warner, J. P. Int. Pub. by Rev. Mr. Eliot	1	38
BROOKS, Benjamin, m. Mary **BOOTH**, d. John & Dorothy, [ ], 1713	2	111

	Vol.	Page

BROOKS, (cont.)
Benjamin S., of New York, m. Catharine N. **LYON**, of
    Fairfield, Oct. 13, 1847, by John Greenwood   2   32
BROTHERTON, Almerin, of Sherman, m. Mary **MARSH**, of New
    Milford, Oct. 7, 1833, by Rev. Nathan D. Benedict   1   265
Mary, m. Frederick D. **NORTHROP**, b. of New Milford, Nov.
    15, 1848, by Rev. J. B. Stodard   2   44
BROWN, Abigail J., of Monroe, m. David G. **ODELL**, of New
    Milford, Sept. 22, 1844, by William H. Bangs   1   398
Amos H., m. Caroline F. **SHELDON**, Sept. 14, 1851, by
    William Roberts, J. P.   2   70
Anson, m. Almeda **WOODEN**, b. of New Milford, Nov. 30,
    1826, by Rev. C. A. Boardman   1   207
Arabella, m. Jay Stilson **HINE**, b. of New Milford, Mar. 27,
    1832, by Rev. Hervey S. Atwater   1   249
Hiram, s. Jonathan & Judith, b. Jan. 24, 1800   1   99
Jonathan, m. Judith **BETTS**, b. of New Milford, Sept. 6, 1797   1   99
Joseph, m. Sally **MOREHOUSE**, b. of New Milford, Mar. 31,
    1830, by J. S. Covill   1   238
Lucella, of New Milford, m. Edwin **KELLOGG**, of New
    Fairfield, Sept. 31, 1834, by E. Huntington   1   282
Nathaniel, Jr., m. Susan **CARY**, May 20, 1821, by Rev.
    George B. Andrews   1   123
Nathaniel, of Washington, m. Elizabeth A. **SUMMERS**, of
    New Milford, Nov. 16, 1826, by Rev. Andrew Eliot   1   204
Rebecca, m. Solomon Baldwin **HILL**, b. of New Milford, Oct.
    17, 1832, by Rev. Henry S. Atwater   1   253
Robert, m. Sibbel **BATES**, Aug. 11, 1799, by Elisha Bostwick,
    J. P.   1   66
Salmon, of Washington, m. Harriet **WATROUS**, of New
    Milford, Aug. 24, 1825, by Rev. Benjamin Benham   1   125
Zera Anson, s. Jonathan & Judith, b. Apr. 12, 1806   1   99
BROWNSON, [see under **BRONSON**]
BROWNWELL, Elisha, s. Isaac & Ann, b. Feb. 10, 1770   LR10   11
Isaac, m. Ann **NEARING**, Apr. 7, 1769   LR10   11
BRUSH, Sarah, m. Joseph **CANFIELD**, Jr., Dec. 5, 1770   LR12   5
BUCK, Aaron, s. Jonathan & Mary, b. Jan. 20, 1719/20   LR2   361
Abel, s. Joseph & Ann, b. Sept. 23, 1736   LR2   347
Abel, s. Abel & Thankfull, b. Sept. 20, 1755   LR7   13
Abigaill, d. Enoch & Mary, b. Aug. 3, 1721   LR2   351
Abigal, m. James **TERRIL**, b. of New Milford, June 22, 1741,
    by Rev. Daniel Bordman   LR4   2
Abishur, s. Ezekiel & Lydia, b. Nov. 10, 1725, at Litchfield   LR2   354
Abisha, m. Easter **CLINTON**, Sept. 20, 1750   LR7   30
Abishur, s. Abisher & Easther, b. May 6, 1755   LR7   3
Abishur, s. Abishur & Easter, b. May 6, 1755   LR7   30
Abishur, Sr., d. Mar. 23, 1760   LR7   30
Alma, twin with Elizabeth, d. Samuel Beebe & Hannah,

	Vol.	Page

BUCK, (cont.)
b. Dec. 18, 1787	LR12	12
Ann, d. Abel & Thankfull, b. Oct. 9*, 1758 *(Possibly "1" or "7")	LR7	13
Annah, d. Jonathan & Betty, b. Jan. 13, 1745/6	LR4	18
Asaph*, s. James & Elisabeth, b. Apr. 21, 1762 *(blot)	LR6	12
Asaph, of New Milford, m. Phebe **WAINRIGHT**, of Stratford, Sept. 7, 1788	1	15
Asell, s. William & Daborah, b. July 12, 1745	LR5	10
Bariah, s. Ezekiel & Lydia, b. Oct. 25, 1738	LR2	354
Benjamin, s. Daniel & Ann, b. Nov. 21, 1762	LR7	18
Benton, s. Ephraim & Meriam, b. Sept. 23, 1765	LR7	17
Betsey, d. Joel & Huldah, b. Aug. 14, 1779	LR13	4
Betty, d. Jonathan & Betty, b. Jan. 26, 1739/40	LR4	18
Comfort, d. Jonathan & Mary, b. Apr. 19, 1717	LR2	361
Daniel, s. Enoch & Mary, b. Feb. 28, 1736/7	LR4	28
Daniel, of New Milford, m. Ann **DENTON**, of Nine Partners, Dec. 9, 1756, at Sharon, by John Williams, J. P.	LR7	18
Daniel Daton, s. Sam[ue]ll & Mehetibel, b. Aug. 31, 1769	LR7	15
David, s. Joseph & Ann, b. Aug. 2, 1741	LR2	347
David Seelye, m. Susan **MARSH**, May 29, 1807	1	94
Dabaro*, d. Enoch & Mary, b. Oct. 30, 1734 *(Deborah)	LR4	7
Ebenezer, s. Enoch & Mary, b. Jan. 8, 1717/18	LR2	351
Ebenezer, m. Thankful **BALDWIN**, Feb. 29, 1743/4, by Rev. Daniel Boardman	LR5	7
[E]lecta, d. Samuell B. & Hannah, b. July 6, 1792	LR12	12
Elijah, s. Lameul & Bithiah, b. Aug. 31, 1770* *("1770" rewritten)	LR7	10
Elijah Sherman, s. Asaph & Phebe, b. June 14, 1791	1	15
Elizabeth, d. James & Elisabeth, b. Feb. 14, 1760	LR6	12
Elisabeth, d. Isaac & Elisabeth, b. Nov. 28, 1760	LR7	5
Elizabeth, twin with Alma, d. Samuel Beebe & Hannah, b. Dec. 18, 1787	LR12	12
Elizabeth, w. James, d. Jan. 9, 1793	LR6	12
Elizabeth, m. William **CAMP**, b. of New Milford, June 3, 1829, by Rev. C. A. Boardman, of New Preston	1	233
Elvira, m. John T. **WHEELER**, b. of New Milford, Oct. 11, 1829, by Rev. Enoch Huntington	1	233
Enoch, m. Mary **BEEBE**, b. of New Milford, May 2, 1717	LR2	351
Enoch, s. Ebenezer & Thankful, b. Dec. 5, 1747	LR5	7
Ephraim, s. Ezekiell & Lydia, b. Sept. 25, 1729	LR2	354
Ephraim, m. Sarah **CAMP**, June 23, 1757	LR7	17
Ephraim, m. Meriam **BINTON**, Feb. 2, 1763	LR7	17
Ephraim & Meriam, had twin s. & d. [ ], b. Feb. 27, 1772; s. [ ], d. same day; d. [ ], d. Apr. 11, following	LR7	17
Ephraim, s. Ephraim & Miriam, b. Nov. 14, 1773	LR7	17
Ephraim, m. Sarah **STEVENS**, Nov. 28, 1776	LR7	16
Ephraim, s. Ephraim & Meriam, d. Jan. 17, 1779	LR7	16

	Vol.	Page
BUCK, (cont.)		
Ephraim, m. Anna **BEERS,** wid. James, Feb. 27, 1800	LR7	16
Ephraim, d. Oct. 20, 1802, in the 76th y. of his age	LR7	16
Easter, d. Abishur & Easter, b. Mar. 29, 1757	LR7	30
Eunice, w. Moses, d. Nov. 19, 1732	LR2	345
Eunice, d. Isaac & Elisabeth, b. Nov. 11, 1758	LR7	5
Experience, d. Ezekiel & Lydia, b. June 28, 1727	LR2	354
Ezekiel, d. May 10, 1745	LR2	354
Ezekiel, d. May 18, 1745	LR5	3
Ezekiel, s. Ephraim & Meriam, b. Mar. 5, 1764	LR7	17
Falley, d. Samuel & Mehetibel, b. Oct. 25, 1767	LR7	15
George, s. Lemuel & Bethina, b. Nov. 17, 1766	LR7	10
Goold*, s. Lamuel & Bithiah, b. Mar. 14, 1765 *(Or "Gools")	LR7	10
Grace, d. Enoch & Mary, b. Jan. 22, 1718/19	LR2	351
Grace, d. Enoch, m. Samuel **BALDWIN,** s. Samuel, Oct. 31, 1739, by Rev. Daniel Bordman. Witnesses: Job Terrill & Enos Camp	LR4	28
Hannall, d. Enoch & Mary, b. June 9, 1720	LR2	351
Hannah, m. Matthew **HAULEY,** Dec. 3, 1740, by Rev. Daniel Bordman	LR4	20
Hannah, d. Ebenezer & Thankful, b. Nov. 26, 1744	LR5	7
Hannah, d. James & Elizabeth, b. May 15*, 1768 *(May "10" or "16")	LR6	6
Hannah, d. James, m. Jared **TERRILL,** s. Caleb & Hannah, Feb. 22, 1789	1	16
Hariet, d. Asaph & Phebe, b. Dec. 20, 1800	1	15
Ichabod, s. Daniel & Ann, b. Nov. 25, 1757	LR7	18
Isaac, s. Joseph & Ann, b. Mar. 19, 1729/30	LR2	347
Isaac, m. Elisabeth **BARNES,** Feb. 10, 1758	LR7	5
Isaac, s. Isaac & Elisabeth, b. May 23, 1763	LR7	5
Israel, s. John & Elisabeth, b. May 7, 1762	LR7	25
Jacob, s. Enoch & Mary, b. Feb. 29, 1731/2	LR2	351
Jeams, s. Enoch & Mary, b. Mar. 24, 1725	LR2	351
James, m. Elizabeth **SHERMAN,** Feb. 14, 1748/9*, by Rev. Nathaniell Taylor *("Aug. 31, 1750 "crossed out)	LR6	12
James, d. Jan. 28, 1793	LR6	12
James Bebee, s. Samuell Bebee & Hannah, b. June 13, 1789* *(Perhaps intended for "1784")	LR12	12
Jehiel, m. Cynthia **TOWNER,** Nov. 19, 178[ ]	1	5
Jerusha, d. Enoch & Mary, b. Aug. 25, 1739	LR4	28
Jerusha, d. James & Elisabeth, b. Mar. 1, 1758	LR6	12
Joel, s. John & Elisabeth, b. June 4, 1758	LR7	25
Joel, m. Hulda **BOSTWICK,** of Sharon, July 2, 1778	LR13	4
John, s. Ezekiel & Lydia, b. July 25*, 1731 *("26" intended)	LR2	354
John, m. Elisabeth **JUDD,** Feb. 16, 1757	LR7	25
John, s. John & Elizabeth, b. Sept. 6, 1773	LR7	25
Jonathan, a witness at wedding of Elnathan **BOTSFORD** & Dorothy **PRINDLE,** Quakers	LR4	14

BUCK, (cont.)

	Vol.	Page
Jonathan, m. Betty **BOSTWICK**, Jan. 9, 1732/3, by Rev. D. Bordman	LR4	15
Jonathan, s. Jonathan & Bettie, b. Sept. 6, 1748	LR4	18
Joseph, m. Ann **GOULD**, b. of New Milford, June 5, 1729	LR2	347
Joseph, s. Abishur & Easter, b. Feb. 1, 1754	LR7	30
Joseph, s. Lamuel & Bithiah, b. Oct. 11, 1760	LR7	10
Josiah, s. James & Elisabeth, b. Jan. 25, 1756	LR6	12
Josiah Judson, s. Asaph & Phebe, b. Mar. 3, 1794	1	15
Lemuel, s. Joseph & Ann, b. Sept. 6, 1732	LR2	347
Lamuel, m. Bithiah **MacEUEN**, Aug. 27, 1755	LR7	10
Lamuel, s. Lamuel & Bithiah, b. Apr. 8, 1758	LR7	10
Lowes, d. Jonathan & Bety, b. June 5, 1736* *(Erasure)	LR4	18
Lucinda, d. John & Elizabeth, b. July 21, 1767	LR7	25
Luse, d. Joseph & Ann, b. Feb. 18, 1747/8	LR6	2
Lucy, d. Sam[ue]ll Bebee & Hannah, b. Mar. 18, 1781	LR12	12
Lucy, m. Ephraim **STERLING**, Jr., b. of New Milford, Jan. 19, 1804, by Elisha Bostwick, J. P.	1	109
Lydia, d. Ezekiel & Lydia, b. Apr. 27, 1733	LR2	354
Lydia, wid. Ezekiel, d. Jan. 3, 1768	LR2	354
Lydia, m. Dea. Ebenezar **HOTCHKISS**, Nov. 30, 1789	LR5	9
Maria, see under Meriah		
Mary, d. William & Daborah, b. Nov. 2, 1746; d. Dec. 14, following	LR5	10
Mehitebel, d. James & Eliabeth, b. Oct. 6, 1753	LR6	12
Meriah, d. Asaph & Phebe, b. Aug. 12, 1797 *(Maria?)	1	15
Meriam, d. Ephraim & Sarah, b. Dec. 10, 1758	LR7	17
Miriam, w. Ephraim, d. July 14, 1776	LR7	16
Molley, d. Sam[ue]ll & Phebe, b. June 5, 1758	LR7	15
Moses, m. Eunice **MILES**, b. of New Milford, Sept. 29, 1730	LR2	345
Nathan, twin with Zadock, s. Lamuel & Bithina, b. May 26, 1773	LR7	10
Phebie, d. Jonathan & Betty, b. Mar. 18, 1733/4	LR4	15
Pheebe, d. Sam[ue]ll & Pheebe, b. Dec. 14, 1759	LR7	15
Phebe, w. Samuel, d. Nov. 26, 1761	LR7	15
Philander, m. Esther **BENNETT**, b. of New Milford, Aug. 18, 1799, by Elisha Bostwick, J. P.	1	53
Polly, d. Ephraim & Meriam, b. Feb. 6, 1776	LR7	17
Polly, d. Ephraim & Merriam, d. Jan. 21, 1779	LR7	16
Rachell, m. Jonathan **PEIRCE**, b. of New Milford, Sept. 11, 1729	LR4	7
Rachel, d. Enoch & Mary, b. Apr.* 1, 1730 *("May" crossed out)	LR2	351
Rachel, m. Abiel **BALDWIN**, Dec. 12, 1749, by Samuel Canfield, J. P.	LR6	9
Rachel, d. Daniel & Ann, b. Feb. 12, 1760	LR7	18
Rachel, d. Ephraim & Meriam, b. Feb. 25, 1767	LR7	17
Rebeckah, d. Ezekiel & Lydia, b. June 7, 1741	LR2	354

	Vol.	Page
BUCK, (cont.)		
Rebeckah, m. Simeon **BALDWIN**, b. of New Milford, Jan. 4, 1764, by Paul Welch, J. P.	LR7	1
Robert, s. Lemuel & Bithiah, b. Oct. 18, 1762	LR7	10
Ruth, m. Nathan **TERRILL**, b. of New Milford, June 7, 1721	LR2	352
Ruth, d. James & Elizabeth, b. Dec. 28, 1749/50	LR6	12
Sabra, d. Asaph & Phebe, b. July 23, 1789	1	15
Salmon, s. James & Elizabeth, b. May 9, 1766	LR6	12
Salmon, m. Urania **BEACHER**, Mar. 5, 1794	1	64
Samuel, s. Moses & Eunice, b. June 26, 1731	LR2	345
Sam[ue]ll, m. Phebe **DATON**, b. of New Milford, May 12, 1756, by Solomon Palmer	LR7	15
Samuel, m. Mehetibel **Mc[C]OY**, July 1, 1762	LR7	15
Samuel Bebee, s. James & Elisabeth, b. Sept. 21, 1751	LR6	12
Samuell Beebe, m. Hannah **FAIRCHILD**, Aug. 31, 1775	LR12	12
Sarai, d. Ezekiel & Lydia, b. Oct. 5, 1735	LR2	354
Sarah, d. John & Elizabeth, b. Mar. 3, 1761	LR7	25
Sarah, d. Ephraim & Sarah, b. May 22, 1762	LR7	17
Sarah, w. Ephraim, d. July 7, 1762	LR7	17
Sarah, 3rd w. Ephraim, d. Mar. 26, 1799	LR7	16
Sarah, see Sarah **CHASE**	LR7	16
Seymour, s. Salmon & Urania, b. June 27, 1801	1	64
Seymour, m. Rebecca **MERWIN**, b. of New Milford, Feb. 22, 1837, by Noah Porter	1	303
Sibbel, d. Abisha & Easter, b. Oct. 9, 1760	LR7	30
Thayley, d. Samuell Beebe & Hannah, b. Oct. 4, 1776; d. Apr. 22, 1777 (Thalia)	LR12	12
Thaley, d. Sam[ue]l B. & Hannah, b. Jan. 17, 1778	LR12	12
Thalia, m. Benjamin **STONE**, Jr., b. of New Milford, Apr. 23, 1803, by Elisha Bostwick, J. P.	1	105
Thankfull, d. Jonathan & Mary, b. Apr. 30, 1723	LR2	361
Theodore, s. Salmon & Urania, b. Jan. 5, 1795	LR1	64
Theodore, m. Celistea **WALLER**, Dec. 13, 1820, by Rev. Andrew Eliot	1	175
Timothy, s. Jonathan & Mary, b. Oct. 27, 1725	LR2	362
Timmothy, s. Jonathan & Mary, b. Oct. 27, 1725	LR2	363
Tryphena, d. Sam[ue]ll Bebee & Hannah, b. Apr. 16, 1779	LR12	12
William, s. Enoch & Mary, b. Mar. 23, 1723	LR2	351
William, s. Isaac & Elisabeth, b. Aug. 17, 1765	LR7	5
William Sherman, s. James & Elisabeth, b. Feb. 7, 1764	LR6	12
Zadock, s. Jonathan & Betty, b. Feb. 23, 1752	LR4	18
Zadock, twin with Nathan, s. Lemuel & Bithina, b. May 26, 1773	LR7	10
Zerviah, d. Jonathan & Betty, b. Sept. 25, 1742	LR4	18
BUCKINGHAM, Abel, m. Hannah **BOSFORD**, of New Milford, Dec. 28, 1773, by Rev. Nathaniell Taylor	LR12	19
Abel, s. Abel & Hannah, b. July 18, 1776	LR12	19
Abel, Jr., m. Abiah **CLARK**, b. of New Milford, Mar. 9,		

	Vol.	Page
BUCKINGHAM, (cont.)		
1802, by Daniell Everitt	1	98
Abel, Jr., m. Nancy **GAYLORD**, Feb. 18, 1809	1	98
Abel, Jr., d. May 21, 1825, in the 49th y. of his age	1	98
Abiah, w. Abel, Jr., d. Oct. 30, 1807	1	98
Benjamin, m. Ann **BOTCHFORD**, b. of New Milford, June 30, 1762	LR7	38
Benjamin, s. Abel, Jr. & Nancy, b. Jan. 16, 1824	1	98
Biram Botsford, s. Joseph & Sally, b. Sept. 22, 1802	1	94
Caroline, d. Abel, Jr. & Abiah, b. Mar. 2, 1806; d. Apr. 4, 1807	1	98
Caroline, m. Isaac **NICHOLS**, Jr., b. of New Milford, Oct. 26, 1823, by Rev. Benjamin Benham	1	173
Charles Gaylord, s. Abel, Jr. & Nancy, b. Oct. 10, 1815	1	98
Dannis, m. Anna **RICHMOND**, b. of New Milford, May 8, 1853, by Rev. A. B. Pulling	2	86
Emily, d. Abel, Jr. & Nancy, b. Feb. 1, 1821	1	98
Emily, m. Miles J. **BURR**, b. of New Milford, Nov. 27, 1845, by Rev. Joseph L. Morse	2	1
Enoch, m. Anna **SLOCUM**, Dec. 31, 1848, by Thomas A. Welton	2	45
Ephraim, s. Abel & Hannah, b. Aug. 15, 1782	LR12	19
Erastus, m. Mary **EVITTS**, b. of New Milford, Mar. 22, 1829, by Joel Sanford, J. P.	1	231
George, m. Sarah **MORGAN**, b. of New Milford, Mar. 17, 1839, by Alonso F. Selleck	1	324
George Hartwell, s. Abel, Jr. & Nancy, b. Aug. 30, 1813	1	98
Gilbert, s. Abel & Hannah, b. July 25, 1785	LR12	19
Gilbert, m. Anna **BALDWIN**, May 1, 1825, by Rev. Andrew Eliot	1	156
Hannah, w. Abel, d. Sept. 22, 1801	LR12	19
Hannah Marilia, d. Joseph & Sally, b. Mar. 18, 1805	1	94
Harry, m. Thalia **HINE**, b. of New Milford, Mar. 11, 1840, by Noah Porter	1	343
Herman, m. Anne **WELLS**, Aug. 27, 1826, by Rev. Eleazer Beecher	1	187
Hester, m. Samuel **COMSTOCK**, Jr., Dec. 28, 1795	1	65
Hiram, m. Susan **BALDWIN**, b. of New Milford, June 10, 1846, by Rev. H. Read	2	16
Ira, of Brookfield, m. Sally S. **TREAT**, of New Milford, Jan. 4, 1824, by Rev. Bardsley Northrop	1	160
Joseph, s. Abel & Hannah, b. May 5, 1778	LR12	19
Joseph, m. Sally **LOCKWOOD**, Aug. 9, 1801	1	94
Joseph, s. Joseph & Sally, b. Mar. 15, 1807	1	94
Laurens Edward, m. Julia Ann **TAYLOR**, b. of New Preston, June 13, 1832, by Henry S. Atwater	1	249
Martha A., of New Milford, m. P. **CLARK**, of Williston, Vt., Aug. 18, 1844, by J. Greenwood	1	396

	Vol.	Page
BUCKINGHAM, (cont.)		
Minerva, of New Milford, m. Marcus B. **MERWIN**, of New Haven, Jan. 4, 1846, by J. Greenwood	2	8
Nathan, s. Abel, Jr. & Nancy, b. Aug. 28, 1810; d. Sept. 25, 1810	1	98
Nathaniel, s. Abel & Hannah, b. Mar. 3, 1775	LR12	19
Noble, m. Sarah **BARNUM**, Apr. 4, 1802	LR12	19
Orzo, s. Joseph & Sally, b. June 28, 1809	1	94
Phoebe, m. George **SEELEY**, b. of New Milford, Jan. 18, 1835, by E. Huntington	1	284
Ruth Maria, d. Abel, Jr. & Nancy, b. Nov. 13, 1811	1	98
Samuel, s. Abel & Hannah, b. July 4, 1780	LR12	19
Sarah Ann, m. George H. **LAWRENCE**, b. of New Milford, Jan. 26, 1836, by Rev. Elijah Baldwin	1	291
Sheldon, s. Abel, Jr. & Abiah, b. Nov. 22, 1803	1	98
Sheldon, m. Delia M. **BALDWIN**, Aug. 30, 1841, by Rev. Merit S. Platt	1	359
Stanley, s. Abel, Jr. & Nancy, b. Mar. 27, 1818	1	98
BUEL, BUELL, Emila Melissa, m. Isaac **HINE**, b. of New Milford, Feb. 15, 1829, by Rev. Andrew Eliot	1	229
Herman, m. Ann **HOYT**, b. of New Milford, Mar. 31, 1824, by Rev. Andrew Eliot	1	120
John, m. Julia **LOCKWOOD**, Dec. 22, 1823, by Rev. Andrew Eliot	1	146
Marietta, m. Nathan **SMITH**, Oct. 19, 1823, at the house of David Buel, by Seth Higby	1	58
Miranda, m. Henry **SMITH**, b. of New Milford, Jan. 25, 1843, by Rev. Albert B. Camp	1	378
Polly, m. Heman **BOWERS**, Nov. 3, 1833, by H. Rood	1	267
Rebeckah, Mrs. of Kent, m. Capt. John **HITCHCOCK**, May 21, 1760	LR4	17
BULKLEY, Amos R., m. Maria E. **GREGORY**, b. of New Milford, Oct. 21, 1840, by N. Porter	1	350
John R., m. Mary A. **MILES**, Aug. 26, 1827, by Rev. Eleazar Beecher	1	155
Lavinia A., of New Milford, m. William **NEARING**, of New Lisbon, N. Y., Oct. 6, 1840, by Noah Porter	1	349
Nathan, m. Mary Ann **SHERWOOD**, b. of New Milford, Feb. 11, 1839, by Lewis B. Sherwood, J. P.	1	326
Sarah, m. Timothy **COLE**, Jan. 11, 1779	LR13	16
BULL, Emily, m. David C. **SANFORD**, Nov. 28, 1837, by Edward C. Bull	1	315
Epaphras W., of Danbury, m. Polly **WELLS**, of New Milford, Jan. 5, 1804, by Elisha Bostwick, J. P.	1	109
Eunice, of Kent, m. Charles **NORTHROP**, of New Milford, Oct. 28, 1847, by E. Huntington	2	36
BUNCE*, Charlotte E., of New Milford, m. Rodman N. **STONE**, of New York, Jan. 21, 1824, by Rev. Andrew Eliot		

	Vol.	Page

BUNCE*, (cont.)
   *(Name doubtful) — 1 — 87
BUNNELL, BUNNEL, BUNEL, Benjamin, s. Benjamin & Hannah,
   b. Apr. 28, 1704 — LR2 — 363
   Benjamin, of New Milford, m. Patience **MILES**, of Milford,
     Aug. 27, 1717 — LR2 — 363
   Benjamin, Sergt., d. Aug. 20, 1749 — LR6 — 3
   Gershom, s. Benjamin & Hannah, b. May 1, 1708 — LR2 — 363
   Hannah, d. Benjamin & Hannah, b. Apr. 11, 1702 — LR2 — 363
   Hannah, w. Benjamin, d. Nov. 16*, 1716 *(Possibly "15") — LR2 — 358
   Isaac, s. Benjamin & Hannah, b. Aug. 29, 1713 — LR2 — 363
   Keziah, d. Benjamin & Patience, b. Oct. 17, 17[ ] — LR2 — 363
   Caziah, m. Nathan **HAWLYE**, Nov. 8, 1733, by John
     Bostwick, J. P. — LR4 — 10
   Rebeckah, d. Benjamin & Hannah, b. Mar. 8, 1700/1 — LR2 — 363
   Rebeckah, m. Ebenezer **BOSTICK**, b. of New Milford, Apr.
     11, 1717 — LR2 — 362
   Solomon, s. Benjamin & Hannah, b. Oct. 27, 1706 — LR2 — 363
BURCH, [see under **BIRCH**]
BURCHARD, [see under **BIRCHARD**]
BURDEN, BURDIN, Ann, d. Reneldo* & Mary, b. July 4, 1736
   *(Given as "Beneldo" in Orcutt's Hist.) — LR5 — 2
   Ann, m. John **PHILLIPS**, Nov.* 17, 1757 *(First written
     "Dec.") — LR7 — 21
   Elizabeth, d. Reneldo* & Martha, d. Aug. 11, 1737 *(Given
     as "Beneldo" in Orcutt's Hist.) — LR4 — 16
BURNHAM, Rhoda, d. Woolcott & Hannah, b. Jan. 3, 1785 — LR13 — 17
   Woolcott, m. Hannah Shove **STURDEVANT**, Jan. 22, 1784,
     by Nathaniell Taylor — LR13 — 17
BURR, John, s. Miles & Eliza, b. June 15, 1822, in Patterson, N. Y.
   (Entry crossed out in original) — 1 — 200
   John, s. Josiah & Eliza, b. Nov. 28, 1823 — 1 — 202
   Jonathan S., of New York City, m. Mary **STEVENS**, of New
     Milford, May 10, 1830, by Heman Rood — 1 — 237
   Josiah, m. Eliza **ADKINS**, b. of Patterson, N. Y., June 28,
     1821 — 1 — 202
   Maria, d. Josiah & Eliza, b. Sept. 28, 1825 — 1 — 202
   Mariah, d. Miles & Eliza, [ ] (Entry crossed out in
     original) — 1 — 200
   Miles, m. Eliza **ADKINS**, b. of Patterson, N. Y., June 28,
     1821 — 1 — 200
   Miles, s. Josiah & Eliza, b. June 15, 1822, in Patterson, N. Y. — 1 — 202
   Miles J., m. Emily **BUCKINGHAM**, b. of New Milford, Nov.
     27, 1845, by Rev. Joseph L. Morse — 2 — 1
   Sally, of New Milford, Bridgewater Soc., m. Johnson
     WHEELER, Jr., of Southbury, Nov. 29, 1820, by Rev.
     Fosdic Harrison, of Roxbury — 1 — 36
   Sarah M. m. Harrison B. **MERWIN**, b. of New Milford, Jan.

	Vol.	Page
BURR, (cont.)		
24, 1841, by Nathan Rice	1	356
BURRALL, [see also **BURWELL**], Betsey Ann, d. Dec. 18, 1851	1	5
Betsey Ann, [w. William **MORGAN**], d. Dec. 18, 1851	1	186
William Morgan, of Canaan, m. Betsey Ann **BOSTWICK**, of New Milford, Nov. 14, 1813, by David S. Boardman	1	186
BURRITT, BURRIT, Adonirim, s. Daniel & Sarah, b. July 16, 1758	LR7	12
Andrew, m. Eunice **WELLER**, b. of New Milford, Jan. 27, 1763, by Rev. Thomas Davis	LR7	[ ]
Daniel, m. Sarah **COLLINS**, Feb. 8, 1756	LR7	12
Edmond, s. Daniel & Sarah, b. Dec. 7, 1761	LR7	12
Easther, d. Daniel & Sarah, b. May 8, 1765	LR7	12
Hannah Eunice, d. Andrew & Eunice, b. Apr. 5, 1771	LR7	[ ]
Lois, d. Daniel & Sarah, b. Oct. 16, 1796	LR7	12
Molle, d. Andrew & Eunice, b. Nov. 1, 1764	LR7	[ ]
Phebee, d. Daniel & Sarah, b. Oct. 6, 1763	LR7	12
Phebe, m. Thomas **SMITH**, Apr. 8, 1787	1	24
Sarah, m. William **LAMSON**, Jr., Mar. 22, 1768	LR10	15
Stephen, s. Daniel & Sarah, b. Nov. 22, 1759	LR7	12
Truman, s. Andrew & Eunice, b. July 20, 1767	LR7	[ ]
Truman, of Hinesburgh, m. Polly **CLARKE**, of New Milford, Feb. 15, 1805, by Elisha Bostwick, J. P.	1	120
Urania, d. Daniel & Sarah, b. Feb. 13, 1767	LR7	12
BURROUGHS, Reuben, of Darien, Ga., m. Louisa Warner **BENHAM**, d. Rev. Benjamin, Aug. 25, 1822, by Rev. Benjamin Benham	1	33
BURTON, Sarah, m. Lamuel **CANFIELD**, Feb. 10, 1774, by Rev. Nathaniell Taylor	LR12	18
BURWELL, [see also **BURRALL**], Henry, s. Stephen & Sabilliah, b. June 16, 1769	LR11	7
Sarah, d. Ephraim & Sarah, decd., m. Job **TERRILL**, s. Daniel & Mary, decd., May 2, 1735, by Samuel Gunn, J. P.	LR4	16
Sibilluh, w. Stephen, d. Dec. 27, 1769	LR11	7
BUSHNELL, Marcy, of Danbury, m. John **BOSTICK**, Jr., of New Milford, Jan. 30, 1711/12	LR2	360
BUTRAM, Delia, of New Milford, m. Allen **GILBERT**, of Kent, Feb. 2, 1837, by N. Porter. Int. Pub.	1	302
BUTTS, Seneca, of Clinton, N. Y., m. Jane E. **STILSON**, of New Milford, May 28, 1845, by J. Greenwood	1	400
BYINGTON, Anna, m. Amos **BARNS**, July 2, 1777, by Rev. Joseph Bellamy, in Bethleham	1	59
CABLE, Addie S., of New Milford, m. David **HOLBROOK**, of Bridgeport, Oct. 29, 1854, by Rev. William H. Russell	2	104
Elazar, of Stratford, m. Menirva **WAY**, of New Milford, Mar. 13, 1828, by Rev. E. Huntington	1	218
Julius, of New Preston, m. Jane **MARSH**, of New Milford,		

	Vol.	Page
CABLE, (cont.)		
Feb. 21, 1837, by Noah Porter	1	303
Julius, of New Preston, m. Adeline E. **MARSH**, of New Milford, Nov. 19, 1845, by J. Greenwood	1	405
Margaret, of New Milford, m. Harry **HUNGERFORD**, of Sherman, May 15, 1821, by David S. Boardman, J. P.	1	48
Sherman, of Stratford, m. Pamela **FENN**, of New Milford, Jan. 2, 1826, by Rev. Fosdic Harrison, of Roxbury	1	197
Susan, m. Hervey **SANFORD**, b. of New Milford, Aug. 31, 1827, by Daniel Gaylord, J. P.	1	219
CALDWELL, Samuel, m. Almira **BROWNSON**, b. of New Milford, Nov. 28, 1821, by Rev. Benjamin Benham	1	118
CALHOUN, Harmon, of Washington, m. Philema **HOPKINS**, of New Milford, Sept. 7, 1840, by Noah Porter	1	348
CAMP, Aba, m. Nathaniel **NORTHROP**, June 7, 1809, by Elisha Bostwick, J. P.	1	161
Abbey, d. Daniel & Lorainia, b. Dec. 9, 1789	LR11	3
Abel, m. Abigail **GOOLD**, Dec. 20, 175[2]*, by Rev. Nathaniell Taylor *(Supplied from Orcutt's Hist.)	LR6	9
Abel, s. Abel & Abigail, b. Mar. 17, 1756	LR6	9
Abel & Lucy, colored, had Polly, b. Jan. 17, 1798; William, b. Oct. 17, 1799; Oliver, b. May 16, 1801; Maria, b. May 17, 1803	1	423
Abigail, d. Abel & Abigail, b. Aug. 2, 1769; d. Jan. 18, 1770* *("1770" crossed out)	LR6	10
Abigail, d. Enos, Jr. & Lois, b. Oct. 30, 1771	LR7	6
Abigail, d. Abel & Abigail, b. Apr. 27*, 1776; d. June 2, 1776 *(Marked over "26th")	LR6	10
Abigail, d. Enos, Jr. & Lois, b. Jan. 23, 1786	LR7	6
Albert, s. Job & Anna, b. Dec. 28, 1774	LR12	15
Ann, d. Enos & Martha, b. Mar. 25, 1774	LR4	3
Anne, d. Nathan & Esther, b. May 28, 1775	LR10	2
Anne, d. Nathan & Easter, b. May 28, 1775	LR11	15
Annis, d. Abel & Abigail, b. June 22, 1762	LR6	9
Annis, d. Abel & Abigail, d. Jan. 31, 1766	LR6	9
Annis, d. Abel & Abigail, b. May 18, 1773	LR6	10
Anson, s. Nathan & Esther, b. Oct. 17, 1784	LR11	15
Asa W., Jr., m. Susan C. **SMITH**, b. of New Milford, May 18, 1853, by Rev. A. B. Pulling	2	86
Augustus B., of Kent, m. Mary A. **PEET**, of New Milford, Nov. 15, 1853, by Rev. George Tomlinson	2	91
Bille, s. Nathan & Easter, b. Sept. 1, 1777	LR11	15
Bille, s. Job & Anna, b. Apr. 7, 1783	LR12	15
Clark, s. Job & Anne, b. Mar. 12, 1785	LR12	15
Daniel, s. Enos & Martha, b. June 18, 1753* *(Possibly "8"?)	LR4	3
Daniel, m. Loraina **CHITTENDEN**, Aug. 13, 1782	LR11	3
Daniel B., of Kent, m. Laura M. **HILL**, of New Milford, Jan. 14, 1852, by Rev. James L. Scott, of New Preston	2	75

NEW MILFORD VITAL RECORDS 53

	Vol.	Page
CAMP, (cont.)		
David, m. Sarah **TERRILL**, of Woodburie, June 26, 1735, by Rev. Daniel Bordman	LR4	16
David, of New Milford, m. Dabora **BOLT**, of Norwalk, Apr. 29, 1741, by Rev. Moses Dikinson, of Norwalk	LR4	16
Dauied, s. Dauied & Deborah, b. July 17, 1752	LR4	16
David, Jr., m. Sibbel **SMITH**, Jan. 20, 1774, by Bushnel Bostwick, J. P.	LR12	10
David, d. Mar. 18, 1782, in the 82nd y. of his age	LR4	16
David P., of Brookfield, m. Lucy **BRADSHAW**, of New Milford, Apr. 27, 1823, by Abner **BRUNDAGE**	1	109
Diania, colored, d. Abel & Lucy, b. July 16, 1796	1	423
Elijah, s. Job & Anna, b. Nov. 26, 1788	LR12	15
Elijah J., m. Adeline **NORTHROP**, Oct. 19, 1820, by Rev. C. A. Boardman	1	177
Elish[a], s. Enos & Martha, b. Aug. 3, 1751	LR4	3
Elisabeth, d. Samuel & Lydia, of New Milford, m. Jonathan **BOTSFORD**, s. Samuel & Hannah, of Milford, Feb. 5, 1735/6, by Rev. Daniel Bordman	LR4	24
Elizabeth, d. David & Daborah, b. May 6, 1747	LR4	16
Enos, Jr., m. Martha **BALDWIN**, Dec. 25, 1740, in Milford, by Rev. Samuel Whittelsey, of Milford	LR4	3
Enos, s. Enos & Martha, b. Apr. 23, 1742	LR4	3
Enos, Jr., m. Sarah **BOTSFORD**, b. of New Milford, July 5, 1764, by Rev. Nathaniell Taylor	LR7	6
Enos, Jr., m. Lois **WHEELER**, of Darby, May 5, 1767, by Rev. David Brownson	LR7	6
Enos, Jr., m. Eunice **BOSTWICK**, Apr. 13, 1779	LR7	6
Enos, s. Enos, Jr. & Eunice, b. Jan. 17, 1780	LR7	6
Enos, Sr., d. July 1, 1791	LR4	3
Enos, Jr., of New Milford, m. Laura **WHITTLESEY**, of Washington, Apr. 17, 1804	1	172
Enos Ralph, s. Enos, Jr. & Laura, b. Nov. 28, 1812	1	172
Esther, m. Jared **SPERREY**, [ ]	1	1
Eunis, d. Isaral & Ann, b. Nov. 7, 1748	LR4	19
Eunice, m. Asa **WARNER**, b. of New Milford, Dec. 29, 1768, by Nathaniell Taylor	LR10	17
Eunice, w. Enos, d. Mar. 31, 1813	LR7	6
Eunice, m. Riverius C. **MARSH**, Oct. 3, 1825, by Rev. Andrew Eliot	1	189
Eunice Emeline, d. Enos, Jr. & Laura, b. Oct. 2, 1808	1	172
Garry, s. Job & Anna, b. Sept. 12, 1790	LR12	15
George*, s. Abel & Abigail, b. Jan. 20, 1767 *(Name erased)	LR6	10
Gerardus W., m. Abigail **BEECHER**, Oct. 15, 1823, by Rev. Andrew Eliot	LR1	89
Gideon, s. Enos, Jr. & Lois, b. Oct. 19, 1774; d. Aug. 30, 1777	LR7	6
Gideon, s. Enos, Jr. & Lois, b. Oct. 19, 1778	LR7	6
Goold, s. Abel & Abigail, b. July 22, 1760	LR6	9

	Vol.	Page
CAMP, (cont.)		
Henry, of New Milford, m. Julia Emily **FROST**, of Bridgewater, Dec. 25, 1848, by Rev. A. Ogden, of Bridgewater	2	52
Hepsibah, d. David & Daborah, b. Sept. 8, 1744	LR4	16
Hermon, s. Nathan & Esther, b. Oct. 6, 1787	LR11	15
Huldah, w. Riverious, d. Feb. 17, 1782	LR13	5
Isaac, s. Job & Anna, b. Jan. 21, 1782	LR12	15
Isarall, m. Ann **HINE**, b. of New Milford, Jan. 13, 1747/8, by Samuell Camfield, J. P.	LR4	19
Israel, s. Job & Anna, b. Feb. 5, 1779; d. July 4, 1788	LR12	15
Israel, s. Riverious & Huldah, b. Feb. 8, 1782	LR13	5
Jared, s. Abel & Abigail, b. Sept. 20, 1779	LR6	10
Jared, s. Abel & Abigail, d. Jan. 4, 1785	LR6	10
Jesse, s. David & Daborah, b. Jan. 4*, 1757 *(Possibly "9th")	LR7	20
Job, m. Anna **OVIATT**, Feb. 22, 1773	LR12	15
Job, m. Anna **OVIAT**, Feb. 22, 1773	LR10	18
Joel, s. Abell & Abigail, b. Sept. 21, 1753	LR6	9
Lacy, m. Betsey **BRADSHAW**, Apr. 1, 1827, by Abner Brundage	1	213
Laury, d. Daniel & Lorania, b. Aug. 13, 1784	LR11	3
Laura, m. Abner **NORTHROP**, b. of New Milford, Jan. 12, 1808, by Elisha Bostwick, J. P.	1	154
Lois, w. Enos, Jr., d. Oct. 29, 1778	LR7	6
Major, s. Abel & Abigail, b. Jan. 26, 1771	LR6	10
Maria, [d. Abel & Lucy, negroes], b. May 17, 1803	1	422
Martha, m. Henry **JACKSON**, July 9, 1776, by Rev. Mr. Brooks	LR13	2
Martha, d. Nathan & Esther, b. Sept. 22, 1779	LR11	15
Martha, see Justus **MILES**	LR4	2
Mary, d. David & Deborah, b. June 14, 1758* *("Fig. 8" uncertain)	LR4	16
Mary A., m. Francis P. **CRESLY**, b. of New Milford, Dec. 19, 1849, by Rev. William Henry Rees	2	58
Moses, s. David & Deborah, b. Sept. 3, 1754	LR7	20
Nathan, s. Enos & Martha, b. Jan. [ ], 1745/6	LR4	3
Nathan, m. Sarah **SMITH**, Nov. 11, 1767	LR10	14
Nathan, Jr., m. Esther **BOSTWICK**, Dec. 10, 1772, by Rev. Nathaniel Taylor	LR10	2
Nathan, m. Easter **BOSTWICK**, Dec. 10, 1772, by Rev. Nathaniel Taylor	LR11	15
Nathan, s. Nathan & Esther, b. Feb. 18, 1782	LR11	15
Nathan, d. Oct. 26, 1792	LR11	15
Oliver, [s. Abel & Lucy, negroes], b. May 16, 1801	1	422
Polly, d. Job & Anna, b. Dec. 12, 1776	LR12	15
Polly, [d. Abel & Lucy, negroes], b. Jan. 17, 1798	1	422
Rebeckah, d. Riverious & Huldah, b. May 28, 1776	LR13	5
Rebeca Ann, d. Enos, Jr. & Laura, b. Feb. 26, 1811	1	172

	Vol.	Page
CAMP, (cont.)		
Riverious, m. Huldah **CLARK**, Oct. 10, 1775	LR13	5
Salla, d. David, Jr. & Sibbel, b. Apr. 3, 1775	LR12	10
Samuel, s. David & Dabora, b. Oct. 23, 1742	LR4	16
Samuel, s. Enos, Jr. & Lois, b. Mar. 16, 1768	LR7	6
Samuel, s. David, Jr. & Sibbel, b. Mar. 28, 1777	LR12	10
Samuel Orlando, s. Enos, Jr. & Laura, b. May 6, 1806	1	172
Sarah, d. David & Sarah, b. Mar. 28, 1737	LR4	16
Sarah, w. David, d. Mar. 31, 1737	LR4	16
Sarah, m. Ephraim **BUCK**, June 23, 1757	LR7	17
Sarah, w. Enos, Jr., d. Mar. 20, 1765	LR7	6
Sarah Botsford, d. Enos, Jr. & Sarah, b. Feb. 27, 1765	LR7	6
Sheldon, m. Lucy **GAYLORD**, b. of New Milford, Oct. 14, 1838, by N. Porter	1	322
William, s. Abel & Abigail, b. Apr. (?), 9, 1764	LR6	9
William, [s. Abel & Lucy, negroes], b. Oct. 17, 1799	1	422
William, m. Elizabeth **BUCK**, b. of New Milford, June 3, 1829, by Rev. C. A. Boardman, of New Preston	1	233
CAMPBELL, Archebell, m. Sary **POOL**, Dec. 26, 1734, by John Bostwick, J. P.	LR4	12
CANFIELD, CANFEILD, Abel, m. Rebeckah **BARDSLEE**, July 11, 1773, by Samuell Canfield, J. P.	LR12	3
Abel, Jr., m. Phebe **PRIME**, b. of New Milford, Apr. 11, 1804, by Elisha Bostwick, J. P.	1	112
Abigail, d. Sam[ue]ll & Abigaild, b. Aug. 10, 1728	LR2	337
Abigail, d. Jeremiah & Mary, b. Mar. 21, 1762	LR7	26
Abigail, wid. Samuel, d. Sept. 14, 1764	LR2	337
Alanson N., m. Mercy **LINES**, b. of New Milford, Mar. 29, 1837, by N. Porter	1	304
Alanson W., m. Betsey A. **RUSSEL**, b. of New Milford, Apr. 3, 1833, by Rev. H . Rood	1	260
Amasa, s. John & Phebe, b. Jan. 16, 1785	LR13	10
Ann, d. Samuel & Abagail, b. Mar. 31, 1735	LR2	337
Ann, d. Zorobabel & Mary, b. Sept. 1, 1737	LR4	11
Ann, d. Zorobabel & Mary, d. Jan. 23, 1770	LR4	11
Ann, d. Lemuel & Sarah, b. July 26, 1776	LR12	18
Ann E., of New Milford, m. Edward G. **HOWAL** (?), of Bridgeport, Nov. 29, 1849, by Rev. James L. Scott, of New Preston. Int. Pub.	2	57
Anna Jennett, m. Henry **SANFORD**, b. of Bridgeater, Dec. 4, 1828, by Rev. Fosdic Harrison, of Roxbury	1	230
Anne, d. Israel & Mary, b. Oct. 3, 1771	LR7	22
Anne, d. Isaac & Hannah, b. Mar. 28, 1779	LR12	9
Anne, m. Homer **GAYLORD**, b. of New Milford, May 5, 1807, by Elisha Bostwick, J. P.	1	141
Asher, s. Samuel & Elizabeth, b. Dec. 12, 1768	LR7	10
Augustine, m. Betsey **CANFIELD**, b. of New Milford, Oct. 21, 1807, by Elisha Bostwick, J. P.	1	149

	Vol.	Page
CANFIELD, CANFEILD, (cont.)		
Austus*, s. Lemuel & Sarah, b. Jan. 15, 1784 *("Augustine" in Orcutt's Hist.)	LR12	18
Avis, d. Philo & Mary P., b. July 8, 1786	1	190
Avis, d. Philo, m. Joel **NORTHROP**, s. Solomon, b. of New Milford, Sept. 24, 1803, by Elisha Bostwick, J. P.	1	107
Azariah, Jr., m. Mary **HYNIES**, May 7, 1763, by Bushnel Bostwick, J. P.	LR8	1
Benajah, s. Azariah & Mary, b. Oct. 21, 1771	LR8	1
Betsey, d. John & Phebe, b. Mar. 15, 1789	LR13	10
Betsey, m. William **HALLOCK**, Jr., May 12, 1804, by Elisha Bostwick, J. P.	1	113
Betsey, m. Augustine **CANFIELD**, b. of New Milford, Oct. 21, 1807, by Elisha Bostwick, J. P.	1	149
Betty, d. Zarubbabel & Mary, b. Oct. 1, 1735;d. Aug. 25, 1736	LR4	11
Betty, d. Jeremiah & Mary, b. Mar. 10, 1769	LR7	26
Burton, s. Lemuel & Sarah, b. Feb. 28, 1778	LR12	18
Caroline, m. Andrew B. **MYGATT**, b. of New Milford, June 7, 1843, by [ ]	1	387
Catharine, d. Israel & Mary, b. Mar. 29, 1764	LR7	22
Catherine, m. Joel W. **NORTHROP**, b. of New Milford, Aug. 28, 1831, by E. Huntington	1	249
Charles Augustus, s. Lemuel & Sarah, b. Sept. 24, 1781; d. May 2, 1782	LR12	18
Clarissa, m. Benjamin **DeFOREST**, Dec. 13, 1788	1	8
Cornelia A., m. Cyrus **MOREHOUSE**, b. of New Milford, Nov. 20, 1832, by Rev. H. Rood	1	255
Daniel, s. Zerubaber & Mary, b. Nov. 27, 1749	LR6	6
Daniel, s. Zorobabel & Mary, b. Nov. 28, 1749	LR4	11
Daniel, [s. Zorobabel & Mary], d. Aug. 18, 1770	LR4	11
Daniel, s. Lemuel & Sarah, b. Oct. 29, 1774	LR12	18
David, Jr., m. Sarah **GRAY**, Aug. 4, 1772, by Rev. Nathaniell Taylor	LR11	12
Diana L., of New Milford, m. John **HATCH**, of New Preston, Dec. 12, 1839, by E. Huntington	1	339
Elce, w. Jeremiah, d. Jan. 4, 1739/40	LR4	11
Elijah S., m. Betsey **COLE**, b. of New Milford, Mar. 26, 1837, by N. Porter	1	304
Elizabeth, wid. Col. Samuel, d. Aug. 4, 1801, in the 69th y. of her age	LR7	10
Elvira, [twin with Evelina], d. Philo & Mary P., b. Jan. 31, 1796	1	190
Emily A., of New Milford, m. Robert **IRWIN**, of Redhook, N. Y., May 7, 1838, by N. Porter	1	316
Enos, s. Zorubabel & Mary, b. Feb. 8, 1741/2	LR4	11
Eronn*, s. Zorubabel & Mary, d. Dec. 10, 1761 *(Possibly "Enos")	LR4	11
Easter, d. Isaac & Hannah, b. Sept. 20, 1772; d. Jan. 20, 1791	LR12	9

NEW MILFORD VITAL RECORDS 57

	Vol.	Page
CANFIELD, CANFEILD, (cont.)		
Esther, d. David & Sarah, b. June 21, 1773	LR11	12
Eunice, d. Joseph & Jerusha, b. June 18, 1745	LR4	21
Evelina, [twin with Elvira], d. Philo & Mary P., b. Jan. 31, 1796	1	190
Freelove, d. Azariah & Marcy, b. Dec. 29, 1726	LR2	337
Freelove, m. Ebenezer **LACEY**, Dec. 15, 1748	LR7	39
Freelove, m. Josiah **BASS**, Mar. 27, 1780	1	6
Hannah, d. Samuel & Abigail, b. Dec. 5, 1730	LR2	337
Hannah, d. Samuel & Abigal, d. May 17, 1737	LR2	337
Hannah, d. Zerubbale & Mary, b. July 2, 1746	LR4	11
Hannah, m. Thomas **DOWNS**, Jan. 7*, 1782, by Bushnel Bostwick, J. P. *("17" written and erased)	LR13	11
Harriet, m. Frederick **BOARDMAN**, b. of New Milford, Sept. 17, 1845, by John Greenwood	1	402
Heath, s. Sam[ue]ll & Abigail, b. Jan. 7, 1742/3	LR2	337
Heth, s. Samuel & Abigail, b. Jan. 7, 1742/3	LR5	1
Heth, Jr., m. Jerusha **ODLE**, b. of New Milford, Sept. 30, 1807, by Elisha Bostwick, J. P.	1	147
Heth, Jr., d. Jan. 3, 1832	1	147
Herman, s. Samuel & Elizabeth, b. May 19, 1771	LR7	10
Hulda, d. Samuell & Elizabeth, b. Apr. 19, 1766	LR7	10
Ira, m. Harriet **PEET**, b. of New Milford, July 25, 1824, by Homer Boardman, J. P.	1	188
Isaac, s. Joseph & Jerusha, b. Nov. 1, 1740	LR4	21
Isaac, m. Hannah **LAMSON**, Dec. 18, 1771, by Rev. Nathaniell Taylor	LR12	9
Isaac, d. Nov. 4, 1779	LR12	9
Israel, s. Azariah & Marcy, b. Mar. 13, 1733	LR2	337
Israel, m. Mary **SACKET**, Apr. 6, 1758	LR7	22
Israel, s. Israel & Mary, b. Feb. 2, 1761	LR7	22
Ithamer, s. Capt. Samuel & Elizabeth, b. Feb. 19, 1764	LR7	10
Jemima, m. John **BOSTWICK**, b. of New Milford, Jan. 18, 1832/3, by Samuell Brownson, J. P.	LR4	2
Jeremiah, s. Samuel & Abagal, b. Aug. 20, 1737	LR2	337
Jeremiah, d. Mar. 19*, 1739/40 *(Possibly "18th")	LR4	11
Jeremiah, m. Mary **EVERTUN**, Mar. 7, 1759	LR7	26
Jeremiah, s. Jeremiah & Mary, b. Feb. 10, 1774	LR7	26
Jeremiah, [Sr.], d. Mar. 21, 1791	LR7	26
Jerusha, d. Azariah & Mary, b. Oct. 12, 1763	LR8	1
Jerusha, d. Joseph & Sarah, b. May 12, 1774	LR12	5
Jerusha, wid. Capt. Joseph, d. Oct. 22, 1803, ae 88 y.	LR4	21
Joel, s. Joseph, Jr. & Sarah, b. Dec. 23, 1771	LR12	5
John, s. Jeremiah & Mary, b. Feb. 18, 1760	LR7	26
John, m. Phebe **TREAT**, Mar. 6, 1781	LR13	10
John Everton, s. John & Phebe, b. Mar. 10, 1782	LR13	10
Joseph, m. Jerusha **BOSTWICK**, Jan. 15, 1736/7, by John Bostwick, J. P.	LR4	21

	Vol.	Page
CANFIELD, CANFEILD, (cont.)		
Joseph, s. Joseph & Jerusha, b. Jan. 27, 1737/8	LR4	21
Joseph, Jr., m. Sarah **BRUSH**, Dec. 5, 1770	LR12	5
Joseph, Capt., d. [ ], 1776	LR4	21
Judson, s. Samuell & Elizabeth, b. Jan. 23, 1759	LR7	10
Judson, m. Caroline **TERRILL**, Oct. 24, 1824, by Rev. Andrew Eliot	1	171
Lemuel, s. Zerubbabel & Mary, b. Jan. 31, 1743/4	LR4	11
Lamuel, m. Sarah **BURTON**, Feb. 10, 1774, by Rev. Nathaniell Taylor	LR12	18
Lemuel, s. Lemuel & Sarah, b. Mar. 26, 1787	LR12	18
Lorane*, d. Samuel & Elizabeth, b. Aug. 25, 1773 *("Hulda" crossed out)	LR7	10
Lorain, m. Stephen **CHITTENDEN**, Jr., May 3, 1797	1	118
Lucinda, d. Nath[a]n & Lois, b. Aug. 7, 1768	LR7	[ ]
Margrate, d. Azariah & Mary, b. Mar. 31, 1765	LR8	1
Mary, d. Samuel & Abigail, b. Dec. 10, 1732	LR2	337
Mary, m. Benajah **STONE**, Jr., b. of New Milford, Nov. 19, 1755, by Rev. Nathaniell Taylor	LR7	5
Mary, d. Israel & Mary, b. Jan. 11, 1759	LR7	22
Mary, d. Azariah & Mary, b. May 11, 1778	LR8	1
Mary, d. John & Phebe, b. Mar. 9, 1787	LR13	10
Mary, d. Philo & Mary P., b. Nov. 4, 1791	1	190
Mary I., of New Milford, m. Andrew **KIDD**, of Cornwall, Jan. 1, 1851, by Rev. David Murdock, Jr.	2	66
Moses, m. Hannah **LAKE**, b. of New Milford, Sept. 24, 1832, by Homer Boardman, J. P.	1	252
Nathan, s. Zerubbal & Mary, b. July 28, 1739	LR4	11
Nathan, m. Lois **HARD**, Nov. 14, 1765, by Thomas Davies, Miss.	LR10	12
Nathaniel, s. Azariah & Mary, b. June 28, 1773	LR8	1
Oliver, s. Azariah & Marcy, b. Dec. 5, 1729	LR2	337
Orlando, s. Lemuel & Sarah, b. Apr. 4, 1794	LR12	18
Orrilla, of New Milford, m. Philo **IUCKET**, of Sharon, Dec. 28, 1828, by William Jewett	1	227
Phebe, d. David, Jr. & Sarah, b. Dec. 27, 1775	LR11	12
Philo, s. Samuel & Betty, b. June 13, 1762	LR7	10
Philo, s. Samuel & Elizabeth, b. June 13, 1762; m. Mary Parsons **CLARK**, Jan. 1, 1783	1	190
Philo, d. Mar. 11, 1827	1	190
Polley, d. Jeremiah & Mary, b. July 11, 1765	LR7	26
Polly, m. Elijah **HOYT**, Nov. 28, 1833, by Stephen Crane, J. P.	1	270
Rachael, d. Azariah & Mary, b. Mar. 26, 1776	LR8	1
Ransom Clark, s. Philo & Mary P., b. Sept. 7, 1783	1	190
Rebeccah, d. Samuel & Elizabeth, b. Aug. [ ], 1777	LR7	10
Roda, d. Joseph & Jerusha, b. Mar. 17, 1747/8	LR4	21
Rhoda, m. Edward **BENNIT**, b. of New Milford, Jan. 19,		

	Vol.	Page
CANFIELD, CANFEILD, (cont.)		
1769, by Samuell Bostwick, J. P.	LR11	8
Rhoda, of New Milford, m. Martin **GOLDSMITH,** of Plymouth, Jan. 2, 1825*, by Rev. Andrew Eliot *("5" uncertain)	1	20
Sackett, s. Israel & Mary, b. May 19, 1774	LR7	22
Sally, d. Philo & Mary P., b. Jan. 25, 1789	1	190
Sally, of New Milford, m. James Winans **SMITH,** of Northeast, Town Dutches Co., N. Y., Apr. 20, 1803	1	174
Samuel, m. Abigail **PECK,** June 1, 1725	LR2	337
Samuel, s. Samuel & Abigaill, b. Apr. 5, 1726	LR2	337
Sam[ue]ll, d. Dec. 14, 1754	LR2	337
Samuel, of New Milford, m. Elisabeth **JUDSON,** of Woodbury, June 5, 1755, by John Graham, V. D. M.	LR7	10
Samuel, s. Samuel & Elisabeth, b. Jan. 30, 1756	LR7	10
Samuel, Col. had negro Kate, d. Pegg, b. Sept. 11, 1781; negro Belden Whitney & Sheldon Whitney, s. Kate, b. Sept. 28, 1797	1	421
Samuell, Col., d. Aug. 17, 1799, in the 74th y. of his age	LR7	10
Samuel, s. Jeremiah, [ ]	1	188
Sary, d. Zarubbal & Mary, b. Mar. 10, 1733/4	LR4	11
Sarah, d. Isaac & Hannah, b. Aug. 11, 1777	LR12	9
Sarah, m. Renssalaer **GIDDINGS,** b. of New Milford, Jan. 31, 1833, by E. Huntington	1	259
Susanah, d. Azariah & Mary, b. May 19, 1768	LR8	1
Salvanus, s. Israel & Mary, b. Aug. 11, 1765	LR7	22
Tamar, d. Abel & Rebeka, b. Feb. 16, 1774	LR12	3
Urania, d. Israel & Mary, b. May 29, 1768	LR7	22
William N., m. Martha A. **PLATT,** Apr. 8, 1835, by H. Rood	1	287
Zarubbael, m. Mary **BOSTWICK,** July 26, 1733	LR4	11
Zorobabel, d. Aug. 18, 1770	LR4	11
Zilla, m. John **BENSON,** b. of New Milford, Nov. 14, 1830, by Joel Sanford, J. P.	1	233
CARPENTER, Abigail, m. Mason **GANSON,** b. of New Milford, Jan. 1, 1840, by Noah Porter	1	341
Amanda, m. Daniel **JACKLIN,** Oct. 31, 1822, by Rev. Andrew Eliot	1	169
Barney, s. John & Elizabeth, b. Oct. 16, 1784	1	61
Benjamin, s. John & Elizabeth, b. Nov. 21, 1782	1	61
Benson, s. John & Elizabeth, b. Dec. 19, 1775	1	61
Daniel, m. Mary E. **TODD,** Jan. 31, 1841, by B. B. Parsons	1	351
Doctor Barney, s. John & Elizabeth, b. Oct. 23, 1785	1	61
Edna, witnessed marriage of Enoch **CARPENTER,** & Sophia **LANE**	1	184
Elizabeth, d. John & Elizabeth, b. July 16, 1788	1	61
Enoch, of Purchase Monthly meeting Harrison, West Chester Co., N. Y., s. James, decd. & Freelove, m. Sophia **LANE,** d. Gilbert & Susanna, of Monthly Meeting		

	Vol.	Page
CARPENTER, (cont.)		
of Oblong, Sherman, Fairfield Co., Conn., 6th month 19th day, 1822, before 37 witnesses. Int. Pub. at Oblong, N. Y.	1	184
Henry, m. Polly Ann **TREADWELL**, (colored), b. of New Milford, Nov. 24, 1849, in Brooklyn, by Rev. Eli N. Hall. Witnesses: Forbes Dusiderdale, Elizabeth Dusiderdale, Betsey Booth & Mary Robinson	2	56
Hervey, s. John & Elizabeth, b. July 8, 1791	1	61
Jane, m. John **SACKETT**, Oct. 8, 1830, by Birdsey Beardsley, J. P.	1	231
Job, m. witnessed marriage of Enoch **CARPENTER** & Sophia **LANE**	1	184
John, s. John & Elizabeth, b. May 20, 1774	1	61
Joshua, s. John & Elizabeth, b. Feb. 24, 1780	1	61
Rebeccah, d. John & Elizabeth, b. May 25, 1794	1	61
Stanley, m. Abigail **WILDER**, b. of New Milford, (colored), Nov. 25, 1830, by Rev. Heman Rood	1	425
William, s. John & Elizabeth, b. Aug. 31, 1777	1	61
CARRINGTON, CARINGTON, Anna, d. Salmon & Rebecah, b. Aug. 11, 1781; d. Dec. 29, 1781	LR12	2
Annah Willmut, d. Riverious & Penelope, b. May 21, 1745	LR4	3
Daniel, s. Riverious & Penelope, b. Apr. 23, 1743	LR4	3
Daniel, s. Salmon & Rebeckah, b. July 27, 1774	LR12	2
Daniel, s. Salmon & Rebecah, d. Sept. 1, 1777	LR12	2
Daniel Noble, s. Dr. John & Susannah, b. Mar. 8, 1759	LR7	20
Eunice, m. Reuben **WARNER**, Jr., b. of New Milford, Jan. 1, 1781	1	21
John, m. Susannah **NOBLE**, June 16, 1756	LR7	20
John, s. John & Susannah, b. Apr. 14, 1757; d. Nov. 18, 1757	LR7	20
Penelope, d. Salmon & Rebeccah, b. Dec. 13*, 1776; d. Nov. 15, 1777, at Westfield *(Possibly "3")	LR12	2
Polephema, d. John & Susannah, b. Nov. 14, 1760	LR7	20
Polypheme, m. Stephen **COUCH**, Dec. 16, 1781, by Rev. Nathaniell Taylor	LR13	3
Rebeccah, d. Salmon & Rebeccah, b. Mar. 28, 1779; d. May 12, 1780	LR12	2
Rhoda, d. Salmon & Rebecah, b. Oct. 31, 1783	LR12	2
Riverious, m. Penelope **BORDMAN**, July 7, 1742, by Rev. Daniel Bordman	LR4	3
Salmon, s. Riverious & Pennellope, b. Dec. 18, 1747	LR4	3
Salmon, of New Milford, m. Rebecka **SACKETT**, of Westfield, Nov. 6, 1771	LR12	2
Sarah, d. Salmon & Rebeckah*, b. Aug. 13, 1772 *("Sarah" crossed out)	LR12	2
CARTER, Russel, of Warren, m. Rebeccah **STONE**, of New Milford, Jan. 29, 1823, by Rev. Andrew Eliot	1	182
CARY, Susan, m. Nathaniel **BROWN**, Jr., May 20, 1821, by Rev.		

		Vol.	Page
CARY, (cont.)			
	George B. Andrews	1	123
CASTLE, Adeline E., m. David **STERLING**, b. of New Milford, June 13, 1854, by Rev. W. H. Russell		2	103
	Betsey, m. Marvin **WELCH**, Sept. 27, 1806, by Elisha Bostwick, J. P.	1	133
	Emerson W., m. Mrs. Ruth M. **KEELER**, b. of New Milford, Mar. 27, 1842, by Rev. Albert B. Camp, of Bridgewater	1	370
	Easter, of Woodbury, m. Jeptha **HAWLEY**, of New Milford, Dec. 26, 1762	LR7	23
	George, m. Nancey **DAILY**, Feb. 28, 1844, by Rev. James Kilbourn	1	391
	Ruth, d. Henry, m. Roger **BROWNSON**, Jr., Jan. 11, 1732/3, by Rev. Anthony Stoddard, of Woodbury	LR4	6
CASWELL, Ann, d. Josiah & Abigail, b. Apr. 13, 1752		LR7	14
	Daniel, s. Josiah & Abigail, b. Sept. 14, 1754	LR7	14
	Eli, s. Josiah & Abigail, b. Sept. 24, 1757	LR7	8
	Josiah, m. Abigail **KINNE**, Aug. 13, 1751	LR7	14
	Julias, s. Josiah & Abigail, b. Sept. 19, 1759	LR7	8
	Mary, d. Josiah & Abigail, b. Dec. 18, 1755	LR7	14
CATEN, Phelix, m. Mary **LEWIS**, Sept. 11, 1843, by Rev. Eleazer Beecher		1	390
CEILIE, [see under **SEELEY**]			
CHAMBERLAIN, Polly, m. Samuel R. **GARLICK**, Sept. 13, 1821, by Rev. Andrew Eliot		1	49
	William A., m. Laura A. **WYANT**, Mar. 28, 1843, by N. M. Urmston	1	385
CHAMBERS, Abigail, m. Abel **HOLLISTER**, Jan. 28, 1766		1	41
	Amarillis, of Newtown, m. Jonathan **RICHMOND**, of New Milford, Aug. 14, 1779, by Rev. John Beach	1	25
CHAMPLAIN, John D., of Stonnington, m. Sylvia **BOSTWICK**, of New Milford, Sept. 12, 1831, by H. Rood		1	236
CHANDLER, Eunice, d. Simeon & Eunice, b. June 22, 1762		LR7	27
	Ozias*, s. Simeon & Eunice, b. Mar. 12, 1768 *("Green" crossed out)	LR7	27
	Ruba, d. Simeon & Eunice, b. Apr. 13*, 1766 *("13" crossed out and rewritten)	LR7	27
CHAPMAN, [see also **CHIPMAN**], Abiah, m. Ebenezar **BALDWIN**, Apr. 18, 1776		LR13	2
	Alpheus, m. Anna **CLARK**, Apr. 2, 1826, by Rev. Eleazar Beecher	1	201
	Ann, of Parish of Unity, in Stratford, m. Ephraim **HAULEY**, Jr., of New Milford, June 12, 1739, by Rev. Richardson Miner, of Unity	LR4	26
	Mary, m. Stephen **CRANE**, Jan. 22, 1762, by Rev. Elisha Kent	LR10	3
	Richard, m. Sarah **BOOTH**, d. John & Dorothy, [ ]	2	111
	Sarah, m. Samuel **PRINDLE**, Sr., b. of New Milford, Mar. 31, 1747, by Samuell Canfield, J. P.	LR5	2

CHAPMAN, (cont.)

	Vol.	Page
Sarah, m. Samuel **WALLER**, Nov. 23, 1773	LR12	8
Shubel, m. Annice **WELLER**, b. of New Milford, Dec. 29, 1768, by Samuel Canfield, J. P.	LR11	4

CHASE, Perry, of New Fairfield, m. Susan **HOYT**, of New

Milford, Nov. 27, 1844, by William H. Bangs	1	398
Sarah, d. Ephraim **BUCK**, d. Mar. 30, 1844	LR7	16

CHIPMAN, [see also **CHAPMAN**], Hiram S., m. Harriet **STUART**, b. of Bridgewater, Nov. 29, 1846, by James Kilborn — 2 — 21

CHITTENDEN, CHITTENTEND, Catharine, m. Ebenezer

GAYLARD, Apr. 3, 1771	LR11	10
Charles Augustus, s. Stephen, Jr. & Lorain, b. Jan. 29, 1799	1	118
Frederick, s. Stephen, Jr. & Lorain, b. Jan. 17, 1804	1	118
Loraina, m. Daniel **CAMP**, Aug. 13, 1782	LR11	3
Louisa, m. Samuel **BALDWIN**, b. of New Milford, Sept. 4, 1836, by Alpheus Fuller, J. P.	1	298
Miles, s. Stephen & Lucy, b. Mar. 28, 1767	LR10	13
Stephen, m. Lucy **BARDSLEY**, b. of New Milford, Sept. 26, 1765	LR10	13
Stephen, Jr., m. Lorain **CANFIELD**, May 3, 1797	1	118

CHURCH, Lucy, of Sharon, m. William **HALLOCK**, of New Milford, Nov. 29, 1781 — 1 — 8

CHURCHILL, Fanny, of Roxbury, m. Jethro **MOREHOUSE**, of New Milford, Feb. 9, 1834, by E. Huntington — 1 — 274

CLAGET, Lewis, m. Sarah A. **FRANK**, b. of New Milford, Nov. 16, 1845, by J. Greenwood — 1 — 405

CLARK, CLARKE, Abiah, d. Edmond & Charity, b. Feb. 16, 1783 — 1 — 31

Abiah, m. Abel **BUCKINGHAM**, Jr., b. of New Milford, Mar. 9, 1802, by Daniell Everitt	1	98
Amos, s. Thomas & Elizabeth, b. Sept. 1, 1772	LR13	13
Amos, s. Edmond & Charity, b. Mar. 24, 1780	1	31
Amos, s. Edmond & Hannah, b. Oct. 10, 1810	1	71
Andrew, of Trumbull, m. Sarah Jane **HILL**, of New Milford, June 17, 1849, by Rev. William Henry Rees	2	55
Anna, d. Jonathan & Eunice, b. Apr. 24, 1759; d. Feb. 7, 1761	LR7	24
Anna, d. Jonathan & Eunice, b. Oct. 3, 1764* *("4" uncertain)	LR7	24
Anna, d. Richard & Grace, b. Sept. 8, 1781	1	49
Anna, d. Isaac & Jane, b. Nov. 10, 1782	1	6
Anna, m. Alpheus **CHAPMAN**, Apr. 2, 1826, by Rev. Eleazar Beecher	1	201
Anne, d. Edmond & Hannah, b. Aug. 8, 1798	1	71
Anson, s. Joseph, Jr. & Patty, b. Aug. 27, 1796	1	70
Artimesia, d. Joseph, Jr. & Patty, b. Apr. 24, 1800	1	70
Asahel, s. Thomas & Elizabeth, b. June 3, 1770	LR13	13
Aurelia, d. Edmond & Hannah, b. Feb. 25, 1807	1	71
Aurilla, of New Milford, m. Lewis **HUBBELL**, of Washington, Nov. 27, 1834, by Stephen S. Nelson	1	281

	Vol.	Page
CLARK, CLARKE, (cont.)		
Beebe, s. Edmond & Hannah, b. May 10, 1797	1	71
Caroline, d. Joseph & Patty, b. Jan. 1, 1807	1	70
Cornelia, d. Joseph & Patty, b. Jan. 4, 1809	1	70
Daniel, s. Thomas & Elizabeth, b. Jan. 18, 1765	LR13	13
David, s. Richard & Grace, b. May 25, 1779	1	49
Ebenezer H., m. Melissa P. **WHITE**, b. of New Milford, Sept. 21, 1851, by Rev. William Biddle, of Brookfield	2	72
Edmond, m. Charity **STILSON**, July 11, 1770	1	31
Edmond, s. Edmond & Charity, b. Dec. 23, 1776	1	31
Edmond, m. Hannah **LOVEL**, Dec. 13, 1796	1	71
Evaline, m. Stephen **MASTERS**, b. of New Milford, Oct. 5, 1832, by Rev. Heman Rood	1	252
George, s. Jonathan & Eunice, b. Sept. 7, 1761	LR7	24
George, of New Milford, m. Emma E. **SMITH**, of Roxbury, Feb. 20, 1853, by Rev. A. B. Pulling	2	82
Hannah, d. Isaac & Jane, b. Nov. 13, 1788; d. Jan. 17, 1789	1	6
Hannah, m. George **PECK**, Jan. 13, 1824, by Rev. Andrew Eliot	1	86
Hannah, w. Edmond, d. Mar. 1, 1841, ae 71 y.	1	71
Harriet, d. Edmond & Hannah, b. Feb. 3, 1804	1	71
Harriet M., of Bridgewater, m. Herbert **SMITH**, of Oxferd, May 13, 1846, by Rev. James Kilborn	2	15
Hekiah, s. Jonathan & Eunice, b. June 22, 1757	LR7	24
Hetty, m. David **BOOTH**, b. of New Milford, Feb. 2, 1820	1	112
Homer, s. Joseph, Jr. & Patty, b. Feb. 27, 1803	1	70
Huldah, d. Jonathan & Eunice, b. Sept. 15, 1754	LR7	24
Huldah, m. Riverious **CAMP**, Oct. 10, 1775	LR13	5
Isaac, m. Jane **BALDWIN**, Dec. 6, 1781	1	6
Isaac, s. Edmond & Hannah, b. July 5, 1800	1	71
Isaac, of New Milford, m. Ellany **BALDWIN**, of New Milford, Feb. 3, 1839, by Rev. Alonso F. Selleck	1	323
James, s. Thomas & Elizabeth, b. Jan. 23, 1768	LR13	13
Jane, d. Isaac & Jane, b. Jan. 21, 1786	1	6
Jane, m. Joseph **WELLS**, b. of New Milford, Feb. 20, 1803, by Daniel Everitt	1	100
Jane, m. Joseph **WELLS**, b. of New Milford, Feb. 20, 1803, by Daniel Everitt	1	101
Jonas L., m. Elisa **HALLOCK**, d. Joseph, b. of New Milford, June 28, 1838, by Rev. Elijah Baldwin	1	318
Jonathan, m. Eunice **BOSTWICK**, Jan. 18, 1753	LR7	24
Joseph, s. Edmond & Charity, b. May 9, 1774	1	31
Joseph, s. Thomas & Elizabeth, b. Dec. 26, 1774	LR13	13
Joseph, Jr., m. Patty **MILLARD**, Apr. 16, 1795	1	70
Joseph, of Washington, m. Lucy **FARNAM**, of New Milford, Sept. 3, 1821, by Stephen Mason	1	10
Lydia, d. Joseph & Patty, b. Feb. 21, 1811	1	70
Mabel, m. Jonathan **FORD**, Jr., b. of New Milford, Oct. 5,		

	Vol.	Page
CLARK, CLARKE, (cont.)		
1806, by Elisha Bostwick, J. P.	1	134
Marcia, d. Isaac & Jane, b. July 5, 1790	1	6
Marcus, m. Polly **NORTHROP**, Sept. 13, 1835, by Edward C. Bull	1	315
Mary, d. Edmond & Charity, b. Nov. 17, 1771	1	31
Mary Jane, of New Milford, m. Henry W. **GRIFFIN**, of Dover, Dutches Co., N. Y., Oct. 30, 1848, by Rev. Stephen J. Stebbins	2	48
Mary M., of New Milford, m. Abijah M. **MINOR**, of Woodbury, Oct. 9, 1822, by Rev. Fosdic Harrison, of Roxbury	1	57
Mary Parsons, b. Mar. 10, 1765; m. Philo **CANFIELD**, s. Samuel & Elizabeth, Jan. 1, 1783	1	190
Milissa, d. Joseph & Patty, b. May 3, 1798	1	70
Minerva, m. John R. **BOSTWICK**, b. of Bridgwater, Aug. 13, 1826, by Rev. Fosdic Harrison, of Roxbury	1	135
Minerva, m. Benjamin **BROWNSON**, b. of New Milford, Nov. 17, 1828, by Rev. Andrew Eliot	1	226
Molley, d. Thomas & Elizabeth, b. Apr. 19, 1777	LR13	13
P., of Williston, Vt., m. Martha A. **BUCKINGHAM**, of New Milford, Aug. 18, 1844, by J. Greenwood	1	396
Parsons, s. William & Annis, b. Nov. 17, 1783	LR12	11
Polly, d. Richard & Grace, b. Aug. 5, 1783	1	49
Polly, of New Milford, m. Truman **BURRITT**, of Hinesburgh, Feb. 15, 1805, by Elisha Bostwick, J. P.	1	120
Polly, m. Joseph **BENNETT**, b. of New Milford, June 26, 1820, by Rev. Andrew Eliot	1	179
Richard, m. Grace **PLATT**, May 25, 1775	1	49
Ruth, m. Amasa **MOSS**, b. of New Milford, Nov. 3, 1768	LR10	16
Sally, d. William & Annis, b. Feb. 16, 1778	LR12	11
Samuel, m. Lois **GALUSHA**, Nov. 7, 1809, by Elisha Bostwick, J. P.	1	163
Samuel Horatio, m. Elizabeth **HUNT**, b. of New Milford, Dec. 28, 1853, by Rev. N. S. Wheaton	2	105
Samuel R., m. Hetty **EVITTS**, b. of New Milford, Mar. 7, 1830, by Joel Sanford, J. P.	1	168
Sarah, d. Thomas & Elizabeth, b. Aug. 18, 1763	LR13	13
Seeley, of New Milford, m. Mary **SHELDON**, of Kent, Sept. 18, 1833, by Joel Sanford, J. P.	1	264
Susannah, m. Benjamin **STONE***, Dec. 19, 1830, by Rev. Eleazar Beecher *(Possibly "**STOWE***)	1	94
Thomas, m. Elizabeth **PRIME**, Feb. 15, 1763	LR13	13
Walker, s. William & Annis, b. Oct. 12, 1775	LR12	11
William, m. Annis **BOSTWICK**, b. of New Milford, June [ ], 1775	LR12	11
William, s. William & Annis, b. Aug. 18, 1780	LR12	11
William, m. Harriet **SPERRY**, b. of Bridgwater Soc., Jan.		

	Vol.	Page
CLARK, CLARKE, (cont)		
1, 1826, by Rev. Fosdic Harrison, of Roxbury	1	196
CLINTON, Easter, m. Abisha **BUCK,** Sept. 20, 1750	LR7	30
COADY, Mary, b. June 11, 1759; m. Jonathan **HILL,** May 25, 1782	1	151
COAN, George, witnessed marriage of David **SANDS** & Paulina **LEACH**	1	277
COGER, Caroline E., of Huntington, m. Harmon M. **CRITTENDEN,** of New Milford, Apr. 9, 1854, at Northville, by Rev. James F. Jones	2	96
COGSHALL, John, m. Eunice **JUDD,** b. of New Milford, Dec. 19, 1834, by E. Huntington	1	284
COGSWELL, COGGSWELL, COGSWEL, Almira, of Roxbury, m. Marcus D. **RUGGLES,** of New Milford, Sept. 6, 1837, by A. B. Camp	1	309
Anna, d. William & Anna, b. Dec. 7, 1774	LR11	16
Dolley, d. William & Anna, b. May 22, 1767	LR11	16
Edward, Jr., m. Jane **OWEN,** Apr. 17, 1758	LR7	3
Elizabeth, m. Nathan **BOSTWICK,** Jan. 7, 1768, by Rev. Noah Wadhams	LR7	23
Emerson, of Washington, m. Deborah **SQUIER,** of New Milford, Feb. 5, 1804, by Elisha Bostwick, J. P.	1	110
Eunice, m. Caleb **TURRIL,** Jr., b. of New Milford, Jan. 27, 1768, by Samuell Bostwick, J. P.	LR10	11
Hannah, d. Edward & Jane, b. Sept. 22, 1762	LR7	3
Hannah, d. William & Anna, b. Mar. 15, 1765	LR11	16
Joel, s. Samuel & Lydia, b. Aug. 19, 1747	1	9
Lydia, d. Edward & Jane, b. Nov. 18, 1760	LR7	3
Molly, d. Edward & Jane, b. Sept. 4, 1764	LR7	3
Nathaniel, s. William & Anna, b. Jan. 18, 1776	LR11	16
Patience, m. Gideon **MORGAN,** June 16, 1772, by Rev. Jeremiah Day	LR11	1
Roger, s. William & Anna, b. July 24, 1763	LR11	16
Stephen, s. William & Anna, b. Sept. 1, 1771	LR11	16
William, m. Ann **WHITTLESEY,** Nov. 4, 1762, by Rev. Noah Wadhams	LR11	16
William, s. William & Anna, b. July 23, 1769	LR11	16
William Riley, of Cornwall, m. Mary Ann **PHILLIPS,** of New Milford, Jan. 21, 1849, by John Greenwood	2	46
COLE, Andrew, s. Nathaniel & Abigail, b. Aug. 8, 1775	LR10	8
Ansalon*, s. Nathaniel & Abigail, b. Sept. 28, 1773 *("Ansel" crossed out. Probably "Anselm")	LR10	8
Betsey, m. Elijah S. **CANFIELD,** b. of New Milford, Mar. 26, 1837, by N. Porter	1	304
Carlostian, m. Martha **BRONSON,** b. of New Milford, Nov. 20, 1831, by E. Huntington	1	248
David, of New Milford, m. Mary **FOX,** of Hartland, May 2, 1790, by Rev. Nathaniell Taylor	1	35

	Vol.	Page
COLE, (cont.)		
Edmond, s. John & Abigail, b. Oct. 24, 1786	1	35
Eliza, m. Philo R. **WELLER**, b. of New Milford, Mar. 9, 1834, by Rev. Nathan D. Benedict	1	271
Hannah, d. Timothy & Sarah, b. Aug. 30, 1779	LR13	16
Hannah, m. James **WRIGHT**, Dec. 17, 1801, by Elisha Bostwick, J. P.	1	54
Harriet, m. Horace M. **BOOTH**, Mar. 20, 1843, by E. Huntington	1	393
Ichabod, s. Jesse & Eunice, b. Sept. 8, 1786	1	4
Ichabod, m. Lucy **HOYT**, July 30, 1808, by Elisha Bostwick, J. P.	1	157
Ira D., s. John & Abigail, b. Oct. 6, 1790	1	35
Ithamar, m. Betsey **FORD**, Jan. 23, 1821, by Rev. Andrew Eliot	1	32
Jesse, m. Eunice **WILKINSON**, Feb. 8, 1783	1	4
John, m. Abigail **WOOD**, Oct. 20, 1785	1	35
John, m. Laura **GLOVER**, May 6, 1846, by E. Huntington	2	22
Lysander, m. Sally **WILDMAN**, Jan. 8, 1839, by E. Huntington	1	334
Martin, s. John & Abigail, b. Dec. 14, 1791	1	35
Mary, m. Frederick F. **BEERS**, July 5, 1847, by Rev. Eleazer Beecher	2	30
Nathaniel, m. Abigail **OVIATT**, July 21, 1771	LR10	8
Parmelia, of New Milford, m. Isaac **POLOMON**, of Watertown, Dec. 31, 1853, by J. F. Jones	2	92
Paulina, d. Jesse & Eunice, b. Oct. 8, 1784	1	4
Paulina, of New Milford, m. Hiram **MANVILLE**, of Woodbury, Feb. 11, 1849, by Rev. J. Kelbourn	2	50
Rachel, d. David & Mary, b. Jan. 2, 1792	1	35
Sarah, d. Nathaniel & Abigail, b. Jan. 13, 1772	LR10	8
Timothy, m. Sarah **BULKLEY**, Jan. 11, 1779	LR13	16
COLLINS, COLLING, Abigail, d. Edward & Ruth, b. Aug. 24, 1765	LR7	2
Amos, m. Prudence **NOBLE**, May 10, 1741, by John Bostwick, J. P.	LR7	7
Amos, s. Amos & Prudence, b. Nov. 1, 1745* *(Or "1755" first written)	LR7	7
Amos, d. May 30, 1778	LR7	7
Amos, s. Amos & Prudence, d. July 11, 1792	LR7	7
Daniel, s. Nathan & Phebe, b. June 24, 1739	LR4	2
Daniel, m. Hannah **HOTCHKISS**, Mar. 11, 1767, by Bushnell Bostwick, J. P.	LR7	24
Daniel, s. Daniel & Hannah, b. Oct. 28, 1771	LR7	24
David, s. Daniel & Hannah, b. Mar. 2, 1777	LR7	24
Edmond, s. Daniel & Hannah, b. Nov. 8, 1779	LR7	24
Edward, s. Japheth & Abigail, b. July 25, 1736	LR4	13

	Vol.	Page
COLLINS, COLLING, (cont.)		
Edward, of New Milford, m. Ruth BLAKELEE, of Woodbury, June 15, 1763	LR7	2
Enos, s. Edward & Ruth, b. Mar. 15, 1764	LR7	2
Hannah, d. Daniel & Ruth, of Milford, m. Abraham BOSTWICK, s. Joseph & Ann, of New Milford, Sept. 13, 1732, by Samuell Gunn, J. P.	LR4	9
Hannah, d. Amos & Prudence, b. Mar. 11, 1733* *(Year doubtful, third figure may be "5" or "4")	LR7	7
Hannah, d. Daniel & Hannah, b. June 30, 1775	LR7	24
Hannah, d. Daniel & Hannah, d. Aug. 16, 1777	LR7	24
Japheth, s. Edward & Ruth, b. July 26, 1767	LR7	2
Japhoth, m. Abigal BOSTWICK, Ma[ ] 28, 1734	LR4	13
Nathan, m. Ann STEVENS, b. of New Milford, Apr. 8, 1759	LR4	2
Nathan, s. Daniel & Hannah, b. Apr. 6, 1770	LR7	24
Pheebie, d. Nathan & Phebe, b. Aug. 6, 1730	LR4	2
Phebe, w. Nathan, d. Nov. 16, 1758	LR4	2
Phebe, d. Daniel & Hannah, b. Oct. 19, 1773	LR7	24
Phipe, m. John GRISWOOLD, Nov. 29, 1750, by Rev. Nathaniel Taylard	LR7	1
Prudence, w. Amos, d. Jan. 23, 1804*, 83 y.	LR7	7
Ruth, d. Japheth & Abigal, b. Feb. 28, 1738/9	LR4	13
Sarah, d. Nathan & Phebe, b. May 1, 1733	LR4	2
Sarah, m. Daniel BURRIT, Feb. 8, 1756	LR7	12
Stephen, s. Amos & Prudence, b. Nov. 1, 1754	LR7	7
COMSTOCK, COMSTACKE, Abigaile, of Kent, m. David FERRISS, of New Milford, Feb. 26, 1755, by Rev. Cyrus Marsh, of Kent	LR7	4
Achillies, s. Samuel & Elisabeth, b. Nov. 26, 1757	LR6	11
Andrew, of New York, m. Julia M. BOOTH, of New Milford, Aug. 20, 1827, by Rev. Andrew Eliot	1	117
Anne, d. Samuel & Hester, b. Nov. 7, 1796	1	65
Anne, d. Samuel & Hester, m. Perry SMITH, [ ]	1	65
Anson, s. John & Deborah, b. June 13, 1764	LR5	6
Chloe, d. Samuel & Elisabeth, b. Oct. 5, 1751	LR6	11
Cyrus, s. Samuel & Elizabeth, b. Dec. 3, 1765	LR6	1
Daniel, s. Samuel & Elisabeth, b. Mar. 2, 1756; d. June 3, 1759	LR6	11
Deborah, d. John & Deborah, b. Mar. 16, 1750	LR5	6
Deborah, d. John & Deborah, d. Apr. 24, 1753	LR5	6
Deborah, d. John & Deborah, b. Nov. 5, 1755	LR5	6
Deborah, m. Reuben STONE, Sept. 21, 1773	1	79
Deborah, w. John, d. Feb. 5, 1787	LR5	6
Elisabeth, d. Samuel & Elisabeth, b. Mar. 7, 1762	LR6	11
Fanny, m. David MERWIN, Jr., July 15, 1771	1	33
Frances, d. John & Deborah, b. July 14, 1752	LR5	6
John, s. Samuel & Elizabeth, b. Jan. 1, 1741 (?)	LR6	1
John, m. Deborah WELCH, Dec. 14, 1743, by Rev. Daniel		

	Vol.	Page
COMSTOCK, COMSTACKE, (cont.)		
Bordman	LR5	6
John, d. Aug. 24, 1798	LR5	6
Lucinda*, d. John & Deborah, b. Aug. 6, 1758 *(Word crossed out)	LR5	6
Martha, d. Samuel & Elisabeth, b. June 24*, 1760 *(Perhaps "29?")	LR6	11
Mary, d. John & Deborah, b. Nov. 7, 1768* *("1768" crossed out)	LR5	6
Mary, m. David **BEARD**, Mar. 30, 1790	1	46
Samuel, m. Elisabeth **BALDWIN**, Feb. 7, 1750/1, by Rev. Nathaniell Taylor	LR6	11
Sam[ue]ll, s. John & Deborah, b. Feb. 16, 1762	LR5	6
Samuel, Jr., m. Hester **BUCKINGHAM**, Dec. 28, 1795	1	65
Sarah, d. John & Deborah, b. D[ ]*, Nov. 12, 1747 *(Crossed out)	LR4	7
Sarah, d. John & Deborah, b. Nov. 12, 1747	LR5	6
Sarah, m. Daniel **PICKET**, Jr., Nov. 5, 1767, by Richard Clark, Miss.	LR10	12
Sarah, m. Daniel **PICKET**, Jr., Nov. 5, 1767	LR10	16
Theophilus, s. Samuell & Elisabeth, b. Oct. 5, 1753	LR6	11
CONGDON, Daniel S., m. Sarah A. **WANZER**, 9th month 25th day, 1845, by William Wanzer, Clerk	1	403
CONKWRIGHT, Alexander E., s. Jabez & Electa, b. Sept. 21, 1844* *(Year not clear)	1	341
Jabez, m. Electa **HALLOCK**, b. of New Milford, Mar. 23, 1840, by Rev. Elijah Baldwin	1	341
CONNER, Patrick, m. Mary **McCONE**, Feb. 3, 1852, by Rev. Michael O'Farrel	2	75
CONNOVER, Benjamin, m. Julia **JENNINGS**, b. of Bridgewater, Feb. 23, 1842, by Rev. Albert B. Camp, of Bridgewater	1	369
COPLEY, Almon, s. Daniel & Mary, b. July 16, 1802	1	83
Almen, [s. Daniel, Jr. & Mary], d. Mar. 24, 1844, in Montgomery, N. Y.	1	83
Ann, m. Jared **BOSTWICK**, b. of New Milford, June 25, 1814, by David S. Boardman, J. P.	1	115
Ann, m. Jared **BOSTWICK**, b. of New Milford, June 25, 1814, by David S. Boardman, J. P.	1	187
Calvin O., of Montgomery, m. Electa **MARSH**, of New Milford, Oct. 14, 1835, by E. Huntington	1	294
Calvin Orvill, s. Daniel, Jr. & Mary, b. Apr. 1, 1807	1	83
Calvin Orvill, [s. Daniel, Jr. & Mary], d. Sept. 27, 1841, in Fishkill, N. Y.	1	83
Daniel, s. Daniel, b. Nov. 13, 1777; m. Mary **PEET**, May 31, 1798	1	83
Daniel Harvey, s. Daniel, Jr. & Mary, b. Mar. 26, 1809	1	83
Joel, s. Daniel, Jr. & Mary, b. Feb. 11, 1800	1	83
Joel, [s. Daniel, Jr. & Mary], d. Feb. 14, 1814	1	83

NEW MILFORD VITAL RECORDS

	Vol.	Page
COPLEY, (cont.)		
Lucinda Bostwick, d. Daniel, Jr. & Mary, b. Apr. 23, 1805	1	83
Mary, w. Daniel, Jr., d. Oct. 20, 1841, in Montgomery, N. Y.	1	83
Sarah Ann, d. Daniel, Jr. & Mary, b. Apr. 21, 1811	1	83
CORNING, Edson B., of Brooksfield, m. Polly Ann WARNER, of New Milford, Dec. 29, 1836, at Bridgwater, by Rev. F. Donnelly	1	302
CORNWELL, Joshua, a witness at wedding of Elnathan BOTSFORD, & Dorothy PRINDLE, Quakers	LR4	14
Richard, at witness at wedding of Elnathan BOTSFORD, & Dorothy PRINDLE, Quakers	LR4	14
Richard, at witness at wedding of John FERRIS & Abigal TRYON, Quakers	LR4	22
COSIER, Dennis, of Brookfield, m. Julia Ann BARTRAM, of New Milford, Jan. 12, 1840, by Nathan Rice	1	355
COUCH, Charlotte K., of New Milford, m. Cyrus A. CROMMER, of Roxbury, Feb. 7, 1853, by Rev. A. B. Pulling	2	81
Daniel, s. Stephen & Pollypheme, b. Sept. 5, 1782	LR13	3
Harriet, of New Milford, m. Glover HUNGERFORD, of Sherman, [Sept.] 10, [1840], by B. B. Parsons	1	347
Harriet, m. Perry WALKER, b. of New Milford, June 9, 1850, by Rev. W. O. Jarvis, of Bridgewater	2	61
Harry, m. Almira HALLOCK, May 14, 1848, by Rev. Eleazer Beecher	2	41
Marcus Betts, s. Samuel & Hannah, b. May 26, 1790	1	15
Mary, m. Curtis KINNEY, Mar. 12, 1837, by E. Huntington	1	312
Pollypheme, d. Stephen & Pollypheme, b. July 11, 1787	LR13	3
Sally, d. Stephen & Pollypheme, b. Jan. 21, 1785	LR13	3
Samuel, m. Hannah FERRISS, Mar. 19, 1789	1	15
Sophronia, of New Milford, m. John G. BENNITT, of Brookfield, Mar. 18, 1849, by Rev. William Long, of New Preston	2	51
Stephen, m. Polypheme CARRINGTON, Dec. 16, 1781, by Rev. Nathaniell Taylor	LR13	3
Sylvia, wid. of New Milford, m. Harlow H. NORTON, of Washington, May 30, 1831, by Rev. Henry S. Atwater	1	112
COY, [see also COYES], Ann M., m. Reuben P.* WHITNEY (colored), b. of New Milford, Apr. 9, 1854, by Rev. A. B. Pulling *("P" uncertain)	2	97
COYES, [see also COY], Samuel, of Cornwall, m. Susan WELDON, of New Milford, Sept. 28, 1834, by E. Huntington	1	426
[CRAMMER], [see under CROMMER]		
CRANE, Abigail, d. Stephen & Mary, b. Nov. 24, 1765	LR10	3
Ann, m. Joseph SANFORD, b. of New Milford, Bridgewater Soc., Feb. 10, 1822, by Rev. Fosdic Harrison, of Roxbury	1	26
Caroline, of New Milford, m. Hiram SNYDER, of Bridgeport, Jan. 2, 1844, by John Greenwood	1	391

	Vol.	Page
CRANE, (cont.)		
Ezra, s. Stephen & Mary, b. Dec. 22, 1763	LR10	3
Henry, m. Betsey Jane **BISHOP**, b. of New Milford, Oct. 14, 1833, by H. Rood	1	266
Isaac Chapman, s. Stephen & Mary, b. Nov. 17, 1767	LR10	3
Jennette D., m. George M. **ALLEN**, b. of New Milford, Apr. 26, 1849, by Jno Greenwood	2	53
Joseph, s. Stephen & Mary, b. Aug. 24, 1775	LR10	3
Mary, d. Stephen & Mary, b. June 8, 1773	LR10	3
Noah, s. Stephen & Mary, b. May 6, 1771	LR10	3
Noah, s. Stephen, b. May 6, 1771	LR11	3
Stephen, m. Mary **CHAPMAN**, Jan. 22, 1762, by Rev. Elisha Kent	LR10	3
Stephen, s. Stephen & Mary, b. Jan. 6, 1769	LR10	3
CRANK, Phila, of Kent, m. Aaron **POTTER**, of New Milford, Oct. 16, 1827, by Daniel Gaylord, J. P.	1	220
CRESLY, Francis P., m. Mary A. **CAMP**, b. of New Milford, Dec. 19, 1849, by Rev. William Henry Rees	2	58
CRITTENDEN, Harmon M., of New Milford, m. Caroline E. **COGER**, of Huntington, Apr. 9, 1854, at Northville, by Rev. James F. Jones	2	96
CROCKER, Ziba, of Vermont, m. Abigh **SWEETLOVE**, of New Milford, June 8, 1818, by Joel Sanford, J. P.	1	105
CROMMER, Cyrus A., of Roxbury, m. Charlotte K. **COUCH**, of New Milford, Feb. 7, 1853, by Rev. A. B. Pulling	2	81
CROSBY, CROSSBY, Eliza E., m. Daniel D. **MARSH**, Jan. 6, 1842, by E. Huntington	1	379
George N., of Phelps, N. Y., m. Betsey **NORTHROP**, of New Milford, Nov. 8, 1837, by N. Porter	1	306
Gilbert N., of New Milford, m. Mothe* **MARSH**, of New Milford, Mar. 16, 1844, by William H. Bangs *(Possibly "Mattie")	1	397
James, m. Harriet **MOREHOUSE**, b. of New Milford, July 5, 1846, by Rev. Joseph L. Morse	2	17
CROSSMAN, Calvin, m. Anah **GUNN**, b. of New Milford, Oct. 9, 1831, by E. Huntington	1	246
[CUMMINGS], CUMMINS, Annis, d. John & Phebe, b. Apr. 27, 1775	LR12	14
Bilie, s. John & Phebe, b. Sept. 26, 1776	LR12	14
Elias, s. John & Phebe, b. Mar. 8, 1778	LR12	14
Elizabeth, m. Amos **TOLES**, Apr. 1, 1765, by Paul Welch, J. P.	LR7	5
John, m. Phebe **STILSON**, Nov. 3, 1774, by John Beach, Miss.	LR12	14
Polly, d. John & Phebe, b. Jan. 5, 1781	LR12	14
Sally, d. John & Phebe, b. July 28, 1782	LR12	14
CURRIE, Julia, b. Dec. 14, 1810	1	423
Julia, m. Cato **NICHOLS**, Sept. 16, 1828, by Rev. Andrew		

	Vol.	Page
CURRIE, (cont.)		
Eliot	1	423
CURTIS, CURTISS, CARTISS, Abel, s. Elnathan & Roase, b. Feb. 17, 1740/1	LR4	20
Abigal, w. Isarall, d. Feb. 28, 1747	LR6	1
Betsey, m. Homer **GIFFORD**, Dec. 25, 1820, at the house of William Camp, by Eleazar Beecher, Elder	1	21
Elizabeth, d. Elnathan & Rose, b. Mar. 23, 1737/8	LR4	20
Elnathan, of New Milford, m. Rose **WELLER**, of Woodbury, Mar. 10, 1736/7, by John Bostwick, J. P.	LR4	20
Elnathan, s. Elnathan & Roose, b. Oct. 16, 1754	LR4	20
Isaac, s. Elnathan & Rose, b. June 4, 1749	LR4	20
Isaral, d. Apr. 21, 1748	LR6	1
Judson, of New Haven, m. Elizabeth L. **MARSH**, of New Milford, last evening, [Sept. 5, 1824], by Maltby Gelston	1	91
Lois, d. Elnathan & Rose, b. June 7, 1747	LR4	20
Lorania, m. Joseph C. **GOLDSMITH**, Aug. 15, 1853, by Rev. A. B. Pulling	2	89
Lusie, d. Elnathan & Rose, b. June 6, 1739; d. Dec. 30, 1756	LR4	20
Marcy, of Farmington, d. Thomas, m. John **WARNER**, of New Milford, July 3, 1727, by Rev. William Burnham	LR2	338
Mary, d. Capt. Thomas, of Kensington in Farmington, m. Thomas **NOBLE**, of New Milford, June 29, 1737, witnesses: John Noble & John Warner	LR4	24
Mary, d. Elnathan & Rose, b. Apr. 9, 1743	LR4	20
Rhoda, d. Elnathan & Roos, b. Dec. 29, 1751	LR4	20
Samuel, s. Elnathan & Roase, b. Apr. 12, 1745; d. Apr. 30, 1747	LR4	20
CUSHMAN, Shubael R., m. Betsey **MILES**, Aug. 29, 1807, by Elisha Bostwick, J. P.	1	145
DAILY, DALY, James, m. Elizabeth **BROCK**, Oct. 31, 1771, by Samuell Bostwick, J. P.	LR13	6
James, s. James & Elizabeth, b. Nov. 18, 1775	LR13	6
Mehitebel, d. James & Elizabeth, b. July 11, 1773	LR13	6
Nancey,, m. George **CASTLE**, Feb. 28, 1844, by Rev. James Kilbourn	1	391
Orson, of Sherman, m. Sarah A. **OSBORN**, of New Milford, Feb. 14, 1849, by Rev. William Henry Rees	2	54
DANSLO, Mary, m. Amos **DATON**, June 2, 1752, by Rev. Timothy Collins	LR6	16
DARLING, DERLING, Harriet, m. Samuel **GORHAM**, b. of New Milford, Oct. 25, 1835, by E. Huntington	1	295
Sarah, of Redding, m. Henry **WILLIAMS**, of Sharon, Dec. 9, 1839, by E. Huntington	1	338
Senica, of Buhmanville, N. Y., m. Bular **FRANKLIN**, of New Milford, Feb. 5, 1854, by Rev. A. B. Pulling	2	94
DART, Abijah, s. George & Eunice, b. May 22, 1786	LR12	7
Elijah, s. George & Eunice, b. Feb. 1, 1788	LR12	7

	Vol.	Page
DART, (cont.)		
George, m. Eunice **PROUT**, July 17, 1783, by Rev. Nathaniell Taylor	LR12	7
George, s. George & Eunice, b. Dec. 2, 1784	LR12	7
[DAVENPORT], DEAVENPORT, David, s. John & Elisabeth, b. Mar. 13, 1758	LR7	21
William, s. John & Elisabeth, b. Dec. 27, 1756	LR7	21
DAVIS, DAVIES, Benedick, m. Hannah **MERWIN**, twin d. David & Mary, [ ]	LR5	10
Hannah, m. Isaac **BALDWIN**, Jan. 2, 1765	LR7	35
Hannah, w. Benedick, d. Mar. 1, 1809	LR5	10
Laura, Mrs., m. Isaac **WHITLOCK**, Nov. 1, 1827, by Rev. Eleazar Beecher	1	130
Royal, m. Orinda A. **SMITH**, Nov. 25, 1827, by Stephen Crane, J. P.	1	204
Thomas, Rev. of New Milford, m. Mrs. Mary **HARVY**, of Sharon, Apr. 1, 1762	LR7	32
William, s. Thomas & Mary, b. Mar. 21, 1763	LR7	32
DAY, Jeremiah, Rev., m. Abigail **OSBORN**, Oct. 7, 1772	LR13	17
Jeremiah, s. Jeremiah & Abigail, b. Aug. 3, 1773	LR13	17
Mills, s. Jeremiah & Abigail, b. Sept. 30, 1783	LR13	17
Noble, s. Jeremiah & Abigail, b. May 20, 1779	LR13	17
Sarah, d. Jeremiah & Abigail, b. Dec. 9, 1781; d. Dec. 31, 1782	LR13	17
Thomas, s. Jeremiah & Abigail, b. July 6, 1777	LR13	17
DAYTON, DABON, DATON, Abraham, of New Milford, m. Byah **BEARSLIE**, of Stratford, Apr. 14, 1743, by Nathaniel Bostwick, J. P.	LR5	5
Abraham, s. Abraham & Byah, b. Sept. 14, 1745	LR5	5
Amos, m. Mary **DANSLO**, June 2, 1752, by Rev. Timothy Collins	LR6	16
Annis, d. Abraham & Abiah, b. Nov. 17, 1751	LR6	4
Calab, m. Sarah **TAYLOR**, Apr. 19, 1759	LR7	26
Catharine, d. Josiah & Hannah, b. Mar. 19, 1748	LR6	15
Catharine, m. Isaac **BENNIT**, May 4, 1769	LR10	17
Daniel, s. Josiah & Catharine, d. Oct. 5, 1760, in Camp at Ovoagoe	LR6	15
Daniel, s. Caleb & Sarah, b. Feb. 14, 1769	LR7	26
Daniel, s. Eli & Hannah, b. Mar. 2, 1788	1	42
Eli, s. Josiah & Hannah, b. Aug. 9, 1750	LR6	15
Elizabeth, d. Abraham & Abiah, b. July 14, 1747	LR5	5
Elisabeth, [d. Abraham & Abiah], d. Oct. 20, 1757	LR5	5
Elisabeth, d. Abraham & Abiah, b. Aug. 21, 1759	LR5	5
Eunice, d. Abraham & Biah, b. Dec. 21, 1743	LR5	5
Eunice, m. Uriah **TUCKER**, Feb. 2, 1762	LR10	4
Friend, s. Abraham & Abiah, b. Mar. 25, 1765	LR5	5
Hannah, w. Josiah, d. May 25, 1758	LR6	15
Isaac, s. Josiah & Hannah, b. Mar. 3, 1746	LR6	15

	Vol.	Page
DAYTON, DABON, DATON, (cont.)		
Isaac, s. Eli & Hannah, b. Sept. 18, 1791	1	42
Jonah, m. Jerusha **BALDWIN**, Nov. 20, 1745, by Samuell Canfield, J. P.	LR5	13
Jonah, s. Abraham & Abiah, b. July 20, 1757	LR5	5
Josiah, Sergt., d. May 18, 1758	LR6	15
Josiah, s. Caleb & Sarah, b. June 28, 1761	LR7	26
Iuleas*, s. Jonah & Jerusha, b. July 11, 1753 *(Julius)	LR5	13
Lucinda, d. Eli & Hannah, b. Jan. 10, 1785	1	42
Mary, of Newtown, m. Ebenezer **BALDWIN**, of New Milford, Dec. 31, 1735. Witnesses: Paul Welsh & Daniel Hine	LR4	17
Mary, d. Josiah & Catharine, d. May 30, 1758	LR6	15
Nathan, s. Abraham & Abiah, b. Aug. 1, 1749	LF6	4
Phebe, d. Mary, w. of Ebenezer **BALDWIN**, d. Apr. 28, 1737	LR4	17
Phebe, m. Sam[ue]ll **BUCK**, b. of New Milford, May 12, 1756, by Solomon Palmer	LR7	15
Reuben Bardslee, s. Abraham & Abiah, b. May 13, 1754; d. Oct. 11, 1757	LR6	4
Reuben Bardsley, s. Abraham & Abiah, b. Feb. 4, 1762	LR5	5
Rhodah, d. Amos & Mary, b. June 18, 1753	LR6	16
Salmon, s. Amos & Maray, b. Aug. 20, 1755	LR6	16
Sarah, d. Josiah & Hannah, b. Dec. * 28, 1752 *("Feb." crossed out and "2" crossed out)	LR6	15
Thomas, s. Caleb & Sarah, b. Jan. 11, 1767	LR7	26
William, m. Mary Ann **WATSON**, Mar. 16, 1842, by E. Huntington	1	380
DEAN, Lidia Mary Anne, of Stratford, m. Isaac **HITCHCOCK**, of New Milford, Dec. 16, 1764	LR7	6
DeFOREST, DeFORIST, Anne, d. Isaac & Rachel, b. Jan. 17, 1774	LR7	34
Benjamin, s. Isaac & Rachel, b. June 27, 1764	LR7	34
Benjamin, m. Clarissa **CANFIELD**, Dec. 13, 1788	1	8
Benjamin & Clarissa, had s. [ ], b. Nov. 20, 1789; d. 4th day after	1	8
Elizabeth, m. Caleb **MALERY**, b. of New Milford, Dec. 5, 1734, by John Bostwick, J. P.	LR4	15
Elisabeth, d. Isaac & Rachel, b. July 1, 1767	LR7	34
Elizabeth, had s. John **ROBURDS**, b. Jan. 7, 1789	1	9
Isaac, m. Elizabeth **NOBLE**, b. of New Milford, Aug. 17, 1732	LR4	3
Isaac, m. Rachel **BOSTWICK**, Jan. 11, 1763	LR7	34
Isaac, s. Benjamin & Clarissa, b. Sept. 19, 1791	1	8
John P., m. Mary Jennette **MORRISS**, of Bridgewater, Feb. 10, 1847, by Rev. William Atwill, of Bridgewater	2	28
DEMMON, Olive, m. John **MAIN**, Nov. 9, 1820, at the house of Walker Platt, by Eleazar Beacher	1	179
DENTON, Ann, of Nine Partners, m. Daniel **BUCK**, of New Milford, Dec. 9, 1756, at Sharon, by John Williams, J P.	LR7	18

	Vol.	Page
DERLING, [see under **DARLING**]		
DERRY, James, m. Martha E. **MOORE**, b. of New Milford, Mar. 9, 1834, by H. Rood	1	272
DEWHURST, James, of Woodbury, m. Emily Ann **ADDIS**, of New Milford, Oct. 12, 1852, by Rev. David P. Sanford	2	79
DIBBLE, DIBBEL, Freelove, of Danbury, m. Zadock **NOBLE**, of New Milford, Oct. 27, 1747, by Rev. Ebenezer White	LR6	16
Orson, of Bethel, m. Julia A. **FRENCH**, of Bridgwater, Dec. 27, 1827, by Rev. Fosdic Harrison, of Roxbury	1	45
Sarah, m. Joseph **WALLAR**, Jr., Nov. 9, 1757	LR7	7
------, wid., m. John **MERWIN**, [ ]	LR10	5
DICKERSON, Molly, m. Josiah **LOCKWOOD**, Sept. [ ], 1784	1	78
DODGE, Moses, of Charlton, Mass., m. Elisabeth **EGGLESTON**, of New Milford, June 30, 1839, by Noah Porter	1	328
DORLAND, Lydia C., witnessed marriage of David **SANDS** & Paulina **LEACH**	1	277
Reuben, witnessed marriage of David **SANDS** & Paulina **LEACH**	1	277
Samuel P., witnessed marriage of David **SANDS** & Paulina **LEACH**	1	277
[DOUGLAS], DUGLAS, Domini, m. Mary **WARNER**, May 5, 1761	LR7	29
Joseph, s. Dominey & Sarah, b. Oct. 9, 1763	LR7	29
Sarah, d. Dominy & Sarah, b. Oct. 7, 1761	LR7	29
DOVEY, James Charles, m. Affa **BRONSON**, June 20, 1843, by E. Huntington	1	394
DOWNES, DOWNS, Anne, d. Jonathan & Sarah, b. May 17, 1767	LR7	5
Arza, s. Isaac & Prudence, b. May 16, 1798	1	86
Arza, m. Sally **BOWERS**, b. of New Milford, Dec. 13, 1820, by Rev. Fosdic Harrison, of Roxbury	1	106
Benjamin P., of South Britain, m. Phebe **PAINE**, of New Milford, Jan. 25, 1843, by E. Huntington	1	383
Edward F., s. Elisha & Eunice, b. Dec. 24, 1806	1	106
Elijah, s. Jonathan & Sarah, b. Dec. 16, 1758	LR7	5
Elijah, m. Ruth **TAYLOR**, Oct. 13, 1785	LR12	4
Elijah Welch, s. Elijah & Ruth, b. Sept. 2, 1786	LR12	4
Elijah Welch, [s. Elijah & Ruth], d. Sept. 14, 1807	LR12	4
Elisha, s. Jonathan & Sarah, b. Sept. 16, 1760	LR7	5
Elisha, of New Milford, m. Eunice **FRISBIE**, of Washington, May 13, 1802, by [ ]	1	106
Elisha, d. Feb. 1, 1812	1	106
Elisha Saymour, s. Elijah & Ruth, b. Dec. 13, 1791	LR12	4
Eunice, of New Milford, m. John M. **WINANS**, of Pine Plains, Dutchess Co., N. Y., Jan. 31, 1813	1	107
Hannah, d. Thomas & Hannah, b. May 26, 1784	LR13	11
Hannah, m. Benjamin **ROBURDS**, b. of New Milford, Oct. 12, 1812, by [ ]	1	173
Hannah, w. Thomas, d. Jan. 1, 1814, ae 64 y.	LR13	11

	Vol.	Page
DOWNES, DOWNS, (cont.)		
Irene, m. Nathan **GAYLORD**, Oct. 15, 1807, by Elisha Bostwick, J. P.	1	148
Isaac, s. Jonathan & Sarah, b. Apr. 12, 1763	LR7	5
Isaac, of New Milford, m. Prudence Polly **SPERRY**, of Huntington, Jan. 4, 1796	1	86
Jonah, s. Jonathan & Sarah, b. Sept. 16, 1760	LR7	5
Jonathan, s. Jonathan & Sarah, b. Apr. 11, 1745	LR7	5
Jonathan, d. July 4, 1801	LR7	5
Jonathan E., s. Elisha & Eunice, b. Dec. 12, 1804	1	106
Jonathan Fitch, s. Elijah & Ruth, b. Jan. 1, 1788	LR12	4
Levi Taylor, s. Elijah & Ruth, b. Jan. 10, 1790	LR12	4
Mabel, m. Thomas **REYNOLDS**, b. of New Milford, Apr. 17, 1823, by Stephens Crane, J. P.	1	314
Mabel, of New Milford, m. Miles **MONSON**, of Bethleham, June 7, 1849, by Ezra Noble, J. P.	2	53
Maretta, d. Isaac & Prudence, b. June 22, 1802; d. Feb. 15, 1812	1	86
Mary, d. Jonathan & Sarah, b. Feb. 15, 1756	LR7	5
Samuel, s. Jonathan & Sarah, b. Oct. 19, 1750	LR7	5
Sarah, d. Jonathan & Sarah, b. Mar. 17, 1747	LR7	5
Sarah, w. Jonathan, d. Apr. 12, 1802	LR7	5
Thomas, s. Jonathan & Sarah, b. Mar. 20*, 1753 *("20" crossed out)	LR7	5
Thomas, m. Hannah **CANFIELD**, Jan. 7*, 1782, by Bushnel Bostwick, J. P. *("17" written and erased)	LR13	11
Thomas*, d. Jan. 31, 1812, ae 55 y. *("Lyman, s. John **BEECHER**" erased)	LR13	11
William, s. Isaac & Prudence, b. July 25, 1800	1	86
William, m. Phebe Ann **PATTERSON**, b. of New Milford, July 9, 1834, by Fosdic Harrison	1	280
DRAKE, Ezra, m. Elizabeth **FERRISS**, May 5, 1801, by Elisha Bostwick, J. P.	1	80
Lutilda, [d. Prince & Susanna], b. July 11, 1808	1	422
Nancey, [d. Prince & Susanna], b. Feb. 19, 1812	1	422
Orinda, [d. Prince & Susanna], b. Mar. 14, 1815	1	422
Prince & Susanna (colored), had Lutilda, b. July 11, 1808; Nancey, b. Feb. 19, 1812; Orinda, b. Mar. 14, 1815; Rhiley, s. Susanna before her marriage, b. Oct. 9, 1804, in Brookfield	1	422
DRINKWATER, Abagal, d. William & Elizabeth, b. Mar. 15, 1736/7	LR4	1
Ann, d. William & Elizabeth, b. June 11, 1746	LR4	1
Ann, d. William, decd. & Susannah, b. May 17*, 1758 *(Possibly "19th")	LR7	3
Clarilla, d. Sam[ue]ll & Olive, b. Aug. 5, 1770	LR11	5
David Northrup, s. Sarah, b. June 17, 1764* *(Corrected from "1765")	LR7	7

	Vol.	Page

DRINKWATER, (cont.)

	Vol.	Page
Ebenezer, s. William & Suzannah, b. Dec. 25, 1751	LR4	26
Ebenezer, s. William & Susanah, b. Dec. 25, 1751	LR6	7
Elizabeth, d. William & Elizabeth, b. Apr. 2, 1733	LR4	1
Elisabeth, w. William, d. July 30, 1749, in the 45th y. of her age	LR4	1
Hanah, d. William & Elizabeth, b. Aug. 11, 1734	LR4	1
Jerusha, d. William & Elizabeth, b. June 16, 1740	LR4	1
Jerusha, m. Gamaliel **HURLBUT**, Feb. 19, 1758* *("8" rewritten over "9")	LR7	29
Joannah, d. William & Suzannah, b. July 26, 1753	LR4	26
Johannah, d. William & Suzannah, b. July 26, 1753	LR6	7
John, s. William & Elizabeth, b. July 7, 1731	LR4	1
John, s. William, d. Sept. 8, 1755, at the camp at Lake George, under Capt. Benjamin Hinman	LR7	3
Mary, d. William & Elizabeth, b. Feb. 5, 1735/6	LR4	1
Mercy, d. William & Elizabeth, b. Mar. 25, 1748	LR4	1
Prudence, d. John & Welthe, b. Apr. 2, 1747	LR5	14
Samuel, s. William & Elizabeth, b. June 27, 174[ ]* *(Last figure doubtful)	LR4	1
Samuel, b. Mar. 27, 1744, O. S., according to affidavit made Mar. 28, 1765, before Paul Welch, J. P., by Justus Miles & Martha Camp, w. of Enos	LR4	2
Samuel, m. Olive **GRAY**, July 27, 1769	LR11	5
Sarah, d. William & Elizabeth, b. Feb. 18*, 1738* *("18" uncertain) *("1738" repeated in pencil)	LR4	1
Sarah, had s. David **NORTHRUP**, b. June 17, 1764* *(Corrected from "1765")	LR7	7
Sarah, m. Stephen **FERRISS**, Aug. 27, 1771	LR12	3
Thomas, s. William & Elizabeth, b. Nov. 3, 1729	LR4	1
Thomas, s. William, d. Nov. 3, 1755, at the camp at Fort Edward, under Capt. Samuel Demmik	LR7	3
Thomas, s. William & Susannah, b. Jan. 13, 1756	LR6	7
Warren, s. John & Welthe, b. Sept. 3, 1745	LR5	14
Welthe, d. John & Welthe, b. Dec. 16, 1743	LR5	14
Welhy, m. Abraham* **SMITH**, Sept. 25, 1767, by Samuell Bostwick, J. P. *("Abel" crossed out)	LR11	3
William, m. Elizabeth **BENEDICT**, d. Lieut. Beeiamin, of Ridgfield, Dec. 18, 1728, by Rev. Thomas Hawley	LR4	1
William, s. William & Elizabeth, b. May 3, 1742	LR4	1
William, m. Susanah **WASHBURN**, Mar. 14, 1751, by Samuel Canfield, J. P.	LR6	7
DUNBAR, Caroline, d. [Charles], b. Feb. [ ], 1839	1	420
Charles, d. June 11, 1847	1	420
Hannah Maria, w. Charles, d. July 22, 1845	1	420
William, s. [Charles], b. Feb. [ ], 1841	1	420
DUNCOMBE, Charles & Elisabeth, had s. [ ], b. July 28, 1745; d. Aug. 10, following	LR5	12

	Vol.	Page
DUNDERDALE, Forbes, of New York, m. Sarah Elizabeth **BOOTH**, of New Milford, June 4, 1845, by J. Greenwood	1	400
DUNN, Ann, m. John **RILEY**, May 23, 1847, by E. Huntington	2	35
DUNNING, Amasa, m. Polly **SQUIER**, b. of New Milford, Dec. 18, 1806, by Elisha Bostwick, J. P.	1	137
Cyrus, of New Milford, m. Sally **WHEELER**, of Southbury, [ ]	1	200
Elijah S., of Brookfield, m. Liberta R. **STONE**, of Bridgwater, June 17, 1828, by Rev. Andrew Eliot	1	220
Elijah S.*, of Brookfield, m. Abigail Emily **BEACH**, of Bridgewater, Oct. 20, 1840, by Rev. Albert B. Camp *(Possibly "T")	1	348
Eunice E., d. Cyrus & Sally, b. Aug. 29, 1825	1	200
Mary R., d. Cyrus & Sally, b. Nov. 4, 1819	1	200
Oliver w., s. Cyrus & Sally, b. Sept. 27, 1821	1	200
Phebe, m. Noah **TITUS**, Apr. 18, 1781	1	10
Sarah, of Brookfield, m. David **BARTRAM**, of Sherman, Mar. 14, 1847, by E. Huntington	2	34
Sarah M., d. Cyrus & Sally, b. Feb. 20, 1823	1	200
DUNWELL, Daniel, s. William & Mary, b. Sept. 21, 1774	LR13	7
George, s. William & Mary, b. July 27, 1783	LR13	7
Hannah, d. William & Mary, b. Sept. 20, 1777	LR13	7
Polly, d. William & Mary, b. Apr. 20, 1780	LR13	7
William, m. Mary **ASHLEY**, Oct. 14, 1773	LR13	7
DURAN, Abagail, of Derby, m. Eli **ROBURDS**, of New Milford, May 31, 1763	LR8	1
DURKE, Nathanael, Jr., m. Lucy **BOSTWICK**, Feb. 22, 1778, by Rev. Nathaniell Taylor	LR13	8
DYE, Daniel, Rev. of Brockfield, Madison Co., N. Y., m. Fidelia **BRONSON**, of New Milford, Mar. 2, 1846, by Rev. Johnson Howard	2	12
EASTMAN, Amherst, s. Benjamin & Mary, b. Aug. 14, 1768	LR7	6
Benjamin, m. Mary **HITCHCOCK**, June 16, 1756, by Solomon Palmer	LR7	6
Benjamin, s. Benjamin & Mary, b. Oct. 3, 1759	LR7	6
David, s. Benjamin & Mary, b. Sept. 14, 1770	LR7	6
Deiclainice*, d. Benjamin & Mary, b. May 31, 1765; d. July 30, 1765 *(Possibly "Deidamia")	LR7	6
Mehetibel, d. Benjamin & Mary, b. June 9, 1766	LR7	6
Nadab, s. Benjamin & Mary, b. Apr. 23, 1757; d. Sept. 24, 1757	LR7	6
Nadab, s. Benjamin & Mary, b. July 11, 1761	LR7	6
Rachel, d. Benjamin & Mary, b. June 18, 1763	LR7	6
EDDY, Abel A., m. Lavinia **LOCKWOOD**, Oct. 20, 1841, by E. Huntington	1	368
Philomela N., of New Haven, m. Joshua L. **RIDER**, of New Milford, Jan. 16, 1839, by Rev. Edwin C. Griswold	1	363

	Vol.	Page
EDMONDS, Esther J., m. Wilkes **EDWARDS**, b. of New Milford, Apr. 23, 1834, by E. Huntington	1	275
Mary C., m. Robert E. **HULL**, b. of New Milford, May 8, 1854, by Rev. H. G. Noble	2	98
Ruth E., m. Silas **RICHMOND**, b. of New Milford, Dec. 18, 1831, by Heman Rood	1	85
EDWARDS, Abel, of Sherman, m. Ruth **LYON**, of New Milford, Nov. 27, 1833, by E. Huntington	1	274
Anne, d. Edward & Margaret, b. May 28, 1783	LR11	14
Apphia, m. Orange **WARNER**, 3rd, b. of New Milford, Dec. 19, 1822, by Rev. Benjamin Benham	1	145
Dyadamia, d. Edward & Margrate, b. Jan. 11, 1777	LR11	14
Edward, m. Margrate **OVIATT**, Oct. 10, last past [1771], by Nathaniell Taylor	LR11	11
Edward, m. Margrate **OVIATT**, Oct. 10, 1771, by Nathaniell Taylor	LR11	14
Edward, d. Oct. 29, 1823	LR11	14
John Calvin, s. Edward & Margaret, b. Apr. 5, 1778	LR11	14
John Wilks, s. Edward & Marget, b. Sept. 12, 1775	LR11	14
Margaret, w. Edward, d. June 5, 1824, ae 82 y. wanting 24 d.	LR11	14
Martin Luther, s. Edward & Margaret, b. May 18, 1781	LR11	14
Mary M., of New Milford, m. John **AVERY**, of Goshen, Feb. 11, 1829, by Rev. Enoch Huntington	1	230
Ophelia, d. Edward & Margrate, b. June 13, 1774	LR11	14
Rebecca, of New Milford, m. John **AVERY**, of Cornwall, Oct. 25, 1835, by E. Huntington	1	295
Sylvia, d. Edward & Margaret, b. Sept. 1, 1779	LR11	14
Urania, d. Edward & Marget, b. Aug. 19, 1772	LR11	14
Urania, m. David **SMITH**, Jan. 27, 1794	1	77
Wilkes, m. Esther J. **EDMONDS**, b. of New Milford, Apr. 23, 1834, by E. Huntington	1	275
EGGLESTON, Artemas W., m. Mary E. **WHEELER**, b. of New Milford, Mar. 13, 1854, by Rev. A. B. Pulling	2	96
Charles L., m. Catharine **RICHMOND**, b. of New Milford, Sept. 5, 1854, by J. W. Hoffman	2	110
Elisabeth, of New Milford, m. Moses **DODGE**, of Charlton, Mass., June 30, 1839, by Noah Porter	1	328
Fanny, of New Milford, m. Edwin **WILCOX**, of Chester, Mass., June 14, 1840, by Rev. E. Huntington	2	38
Hannah, m. Charles **FORD**, Oct. 26, 1834, by E. Huntington	1	282
ELDERKIN, Minerva, m. William **NARIGON**, b. of New Milford, Dec. 17, 1826, by Rev. Benjamin Benham	1	209
Sarah, m. Jair **MOREHOUSE**, 2nd, Mar. 28, 1830, by Rev. Eleazer Beecher	1	236
ELLIOTT, ELIOT, Andrew, Rev. of New Milford, m. Sophia **WASSON**, of Fairfield, Sept. 19, 1820	1	192
Andrew, Rev., d. May 9, 1829, ae 48 y. 9 m.	1	192
George, m. Charlotte **SKIDMORE**, b. of Bridgewater, Nov.		

	Vol.	Page
ELLIOTT, ELIOT, (cont.)		
20, 1849, at the house of John Skidmore, by W. C. Jarvis	2	57
Henry, of Bridgeport, m. Anna C. **GAYLORD**, of New Milford, Oct. 15, 1850, by Rev. David Murdock	2	64
Martha, of the oblong or Woster Sheer, m. Joseph **OVIAT**, s. Thomas & Lydia, of New Milford, May 12, 1740, by Roger Brownson, J. P.	LR4	28
Sophia, w. Rev. Andrew, d. Nov. 17, 1822	1	192
Sophia Wasson, d. Rev. Andrew & Sophia, b. Nov. 13, 1822	1	192
ELLISON, Gahelisne, witnessed marriage of Jehu **HOAG** & Phebe **WANZER**	1	250
ELWOOD, Joseph, of Brookfield, m. Mary Ann **BARLOW**, of Bridgwater, Oct. 2, 1828, by Rev. Fosdick Harrison, of Roxbury	1	226
ERWIN, Epenetus, m. Julia M. **PECK**, b. of Bridgewater, Nov. 29, 1854, by Rev. Fosdic Harrison	2	104
Maria, m. Augustine **EVITTS**, b. of New Milford, Jan. 29, 1850, by William Henry Rees	2	58
Silas, m. Caroline **WEEKS**, b. of New Milford, Dec. 16, 1832, by E. Huntington	1	256
EVANS, James N., of Sherman, m. Fanny M. **KELLOGG**, of New Milford, Nov. 23, 1841, by N. M. Urmston	1	362
EVERITT, EVERIT, Catharine, m. Thomas A. **FOLLETT**, b. of Franklin, N. Y., July 13, 1841, by E. Huntington	1	366
Daniel, m. Urania **TAYLOR**, Jan. 1, 1778, by Rev. Nathaniel Taylor	LR13	10
Daniel, d. Jan. 20, 1805, in the 57th y. of his age	LR13	10
Daniel Taylor, s. Daniel & Urainah, b. Mar. 20, 1784	LR13	10
Hannah, m. Benjamin **HALLOCK**, Jr., Jan. 12, 1805, by Elisha Bostwick, J. P.	1	103
Harmon, s. Daniel & Urania, b. Sept. 23, 1778	LR13	10
Harmon, s. Daniell & Uraniah, d. Mar. 3, 1812, in the 34th y. of his age	LR13	10
Nathaniell Shelton, s. Daniell & Urania, b. Dec. 7, 1796; d. Nov. 27, 1799, ae 3 y. wanting 10 d.	LR13	10
Tamar Urania, d. Daniel & Urania, b. July 1, 1786	LR13	10
Tamar Urania, d. [Daniel & Urania], d. Mar. 14, 1812, in the 26th y. of her age	LR13	10
Uraniah, wid. Daniel, d. May 28, 1823, in the 72nd y. of her age	LR13	10
William, s. Daniel & Urania, b. Nov. 11, 1780	LR13	10
EVERTUN, Mary, m. Jeremiah **CANFIELD**, Mar. 7, 1759	LR7	26
EVITTS, EVATTS, Augustine, m. Maria **ERWIN**, b. of New Milford, Jan. 29, 1850, by William Henry Rees	2	58
Hetty, m. Samuel R. **CLARK**, b. of New Milford, Mar. 7, 1830, by Joel Sanford, J. P.	1	168
Laura, m. Charles **THOMPSON**, b. of New Milford, Oct. 28, 1839, by N. Porter	1	330

	Vol.	Page
EVITTS, EVATTS, (cont.)		
Mary, m. Erastus **BUCKINGHAM**, b. of New Milford, Mar. 22, 1829, by Joel Sanford, J. P.	1	231
Sally, of New Milford, m. Stephen **TURRILL**, of Roxbury, June 4, 1854, by Joshua R. **BROWN**, of New Haven	2	102
Susan M., m. Noah W. **BROWNSON**, b. of New Milford, Nov. 2, 1834, by H. Rood	1	279
[FABRIQUE], FABRAGUE, FABRAGE, Ann, d. David & Deborah, b. Aug. 27, 1766; d. Dec. 24, 1766	LR8	3
Anna, d. David & Deborah, b. Dec. 14, 1767	LR8	3
David, of New Milford, m. Deborah **WOOSTER**, of Derby, May 13, 1766	LR8	3
Deborah, d. David & Deborah, b. June 6, 1769	LR8	3
John, s. David & Deborah, b. Sept. 9, 1770	LR8	3
FAIRCHILD, Amos Leach, s. Eleazar, Jr. & Deborah, b. Nov. 6, 1788	1	55
Anne, d. Eleazar & Deborah, b. Nov. 6, 1792	1	55
Benajah, m. Hannah **NOBLE**, Jan. 29, 1806, by Elisha Bostwick, J. P.	1	128
Clary, d. Eleazar & Deborah, b. Sept. 2, 1797	1	55
Daniel, s. Eleazar, Jr. & Deborah, b. Sept. 26, 1790	1	55
Daniel Munson, m. Phebe **GAYLORD**, Oct. 19, 1802, by Elisha Bostwick, J. P.	1	100
Eleazar, Jr., m. Deborah **LEACH**, Jan. 18, 1786	1	55
Eleazar Curtiss, s. Eleazar, Jr. & Deborah, b. Feb. 16, 1787	1	55
Hannah, m. Samuel Beebe **BUCK**, Aug. 31, 1775	LR12	12
Laura M., m. David M. **BALDWIN**, b. of New Milford, Apr. 13, 1829, by Rev. Andrew Eliott	1	230
Lewis, of Roxbury, m. Harriet **ODELL**, of New Milford, Jan. 22, 1833, by E. Huntington	1	257
Paulina, m. Drake H. **PHILLIPS**, b. of New Milford, Sept. 24, 1838, by N. Porter	1	321
Ruth Amy, d. Eleazar, Jr. & Deborah, b. July 28, 1795	1	55
Samuel, m. Polly M. **TITUS**, Sept. 26, 1824, by Rev. Benjamin Benham	1	171
William H., m. Abigail **MARSH**, Nov. 21, 1825, by Rev. Andrew Eliot	1	157
FARNAM, Lucy, of New Milford, m. Joseph **CLARK**, of Washington, Sept. 3, 1821, by Stephen Mason	1	10
FARRAND, Asah*, s. Joseph & Marcy, b. June 5, 1757 *("John" crossed out)	LR7	11
Benjamin, twin with Joseph, s. Joseph, Jr. & Mary, b. Jan. 7, 1759	LR7	11
Daniel, a witness at wedding of John **FERRIS**, & Abigal **TRYON**, Quakers	LR4	22
John, s. Joseph, Jr. & Mary*, b. Feb. 25, 1756 *("h" crossed out)	LR7	11
Joseph, twin with Benjamin, s. Joseph, Jr. & Mary, b. Jan. 7,		

	Vol.	Page
FARRAND, (cont.)		
Sarah, m. William **BOZWORTH**, b. of New Milford, Aug. 6, 1745, by Roger Brownson, J. P.	LR5	10
FARVOUR, Gerardus, m. Eliza **WILDMAN**, June 26, 1832, by Nathan Gaylord, J. P.	1	252
FED, Phebie, a transient person, m. Daniel **PRINDLE**, of New Milford, Oct. 4, 1737, by John Bostwick, J. P.	LR4	8
FELLOWS, Thomas S., of Northfield, N. H., m. Flora E. WATERBURY, of Bridgewater, Aug. 8, 1850, at the New England House, by Rev. Gilbert B. Hayden	2	62
FENN, Dorcas, m. Peter **PHIPPENCY**, b. of New Milford, Sept. 29, 1808, by Elisha Bostwick, J. P.	1	159
Pamela, of New Milford, m. Sherman **CABLE**, of Stratford, Jan. 2, 1826, by Rev. Fosdic Harrison, of Roxbury	1	197
FENTON, Elijah B., of Plymouth, m. Rachel C. **BENNET**, of New Milford, Mar. 6, 1836, by Rev. Henry Eames	1	292
Fanny, m. John **NEWTON**, Nov. 7, 1801, by Elisha Bostwick, J. P.	1	89
Washington, m. Sally **MEAD**, b. of New Milford, Aug. 15, 1799, by Elisha Bostwick, J. P.	1	74
FERGUSON, John, m. Polly **FULLER**, Jan. 5, 1806	1	156
William Henry, s. John & Polly, b. Feb. 5, 1807	1	156
[**FERRILL**], **FERRIL**, Phebe, d. Calab, Jr. & Eunice, b. Sept. 8, 1768	LR10	11
FERRISS, FEARISS, FARRISS, FERISS, Aaron Gaylard, s. Zachariah & Phebe, b. May 15, 1770	LR7	4
Abigal, a witness at wedding of John **FERRIS**, & Abigal **TRYON**, Quakers	LR4	22
Abigail, w. David, d. Sept. 11, 1797, in the 67th y. of her age	LR7	4
Allson, s. David & Abigail, b. Aug. 10, 1763 (Alanson)	LR7	4
Alanson, m. Esther **WASHBURN**, Nov. 16, 1783	1	40
Albert, [s. George & Amy (**STONE**), b. Nov. 9, 1844	2	125
Amasa, s. David & Abigail, b. Nov. 5, 1760	LR7	4
Amasa, m. Molly **MILES**, Dec. 16, 1781	1	43
Amasa, Capt., d. Apr. 26, 1811, in the 51st y. of his age	1	43
Angus, s. Zachariah & Phebe, b. Oct. 19, 1772	LR7	4
Angus, m. Apphia **HILLISTER**, b. of New Milford, July 21, 1822, by Rev. Benjamin Benham	1	51
Annis, w. Daniel H., d. Feb. 19, 1852	1	37
Arabella, m. Walter **MARSH**, b. of New Milford, Sept. 15, 1852, by Rev. David P. Sanford	2	84
Benjamin, a witness at wedding of Elnathan **BOTSFORD** & Dorothy **PRINDLE**, Quakers	LR4	14
Benjamin, a witness at wedding of John **FERRIS** & Abigal **TRYON**, Quakers	LR4	22
Benjamin, s. Zechariah & Sarah, b. Nov. 10, 1708	LR2	360
Benjamin, of New Milford, m. Phebe **BEECHER**, of Milford, Nov. 6, 1728	LR4	3

	Vol.	Page
FERRISS, FEARISS, FARRISS, FERISS, (cont.)		
Betty, d. David & Abigail, b. May 25, 1768	LR7	4
Betty, m. Elisha **BOSTWICK**, May 14, 1786	1	5
Caroline, of New Milford, m. Henry **STEWARD**, of Sherman, Apr. 17, 1826, by Rev. Benjamin Benham	1	202
Charlania, of New Milford, m. Israel **NOBLES**, of Kent, Nov. 23, 1834, by E. Huntington	1	283
Charlena, [d. George & Amy (**STONE**)], b. June 9, 1848	2	125
Charles M., m. Mary A. **MARSH**, of New Milford, June 12, 1839, by E. Huntington	1	336
Constantine W., m. Rachel A. **NORTHROP**, Feb. 24, 1839, by E. Huntington	1	336
Constantine Wright, s. Joseph, Jr. & Anna, b. Nov. 22, 1808	1	90
Curtis, [s. George & Amy (**STONE**)], b. Jan. 20, 1835	2	125
Daniel H., m. Annis **BOTSFORD**, Jan. 29, 1795	1	37
Daniel H., d. Apr. 2, 1843	1	37
Daniel Hutton, s. David & Abigail, b. Mar. 1, 1771	LR7	4
Daniel Picket, s. Amasa & Molly, b. Mar. 17, 1792	1	43
Daniel Pickett, m. Elizabeth **FURLONG**, Apr. 23, 1821, at New York	2	49
Daniel Pickett, Jr., [s. Daniel Pickett & Elizabeth], b. Feb. 17, 1827	2	49
Daniel Pickett, s. Amasa & Molly, d. Sept. 17, 1831, in New York	1	43
Daniel Pickett, d. Sept. 17, 1831, at New York	2	49
David, Jr., m. Amaryllis **STILSON**, Jan. 11, 17[ ], by Rev. Nathaniel Taylor	1	3
David, s. Zachariah & Sarah, b. May 10, 1707	LR2	360
David, s. Joseph & Hannah, b. Sept. 18, 1726	LR2	340
David, of New Milford, m. Abigaile **COMSTOCK**, of Kent, Feb. 26, 1755, by Rev. Cyrus Marsh, of Kent.	LR7	4
David, s. David & Abigail, b. Feb. 8, 1766	LR7	4
David, s. Daniel H. & Annis, b. Sept. 2, 1798; d. Jan. 2, 1799	1	37
David, d. July 20, 1800, in the 74th y. of his age	LR7	4
David, s. Daniell H. & Annis, b. June 30, 1802	1	37
Deborah, d. Zechariah & Sarah, b. June 17, 1700	LR2	360
Deborah, m. John **WELCH**, b. of New Milford, Aug. 27, 1719	LR2	349
Daborah, twin with Rachel, d. John & Abigal, b. 12th m. 7th d. 1738/9. Witnesses: Lydiah Brownson, midwife, Sarah Ferriss, Hannah Gaylard, Hanah Weller & Daborah Seelye	LR4	22
Edeth, of New Milford, m. Levi **LEACH**, of Sherman, Mar. 9, 1826, by Rev. Andrew Eliot	1	193
Elizabeth, d. Stephen & Sarah, b. Apr. 29, 1775	LR12	3
Elizabeth, m. Ezra **DRAKE**, May 5, 1801, Elisha Bostwich, J. P.	1	80
Elizabeth, see Elizabeth **FROST**	2	49
Easter, d. Gilbert & Merriam, b. Sept. 8, 1780	LR12	9

	Vol.	Page
FERRISS, FEARISS, FARRISS, FERISS, (cont.)		
Esther Ann, [d. Daniel Pickett & Elizabeth], b. Nov. 12, 1825; d. [ ], 1827, at New York	2	49
Eugene, s. Daniell H. & Annis, b. June 18, 1806	1	37
Eugene, m. Laura **HOYT**, b. of New Milford, Oct. 26, 1829, by Rev. E. Huntington	1	234
Fitch, of Canaan, m. Mary Ann **NOBLE**, of New Milford, Aug. 22, 1838, by Noah Porter	1	318
Gariway, s. Steephen & Sarah, b. Mar. 18, 1779	LR12	3
George Alexander, s. Joseph, Jr. & Anna, b. Mar. 19, 1807	1	90
Gerardus, 2nd, m. Harriet **HOYT**, May 3, 1843, by E. Huntington	1	394
Gilburt, s. Joseph & Hannah, b. July 16, 1747	LR4	26
Gilbert, m. Meriam **NICHOLS**, Apr. 15, 1778	LR12	9
Gilbert, m. Meriam **NICHOLS**, Apr. 28, 1778	LR13	9
Gilbert, s. Gilbert & Meriam, b. May 6, 1779	LR12	9
Gilbert, d. May 9, 1782	LR12	9
Hannah, d. Zechariah & Sarah, b. Aug. 6, 1712	LR2	360
Hannah, m. Nathan **TALLCOT**, b. of New Milford, Dec. 24, 1730	LR4	8
Hannah, d. Zachariah & Phebe, b. June 19, 1768	LR7	4
Hannah, d. Zachariah & Pheebe, b. June 19, 1768	LR7	4
Hannah, m. Samuel **COUCH**, Mar. 19, 1789	1	15
Hannah, m. William **WANZER**, Sept. 27, 1832, by E. Huntington	1	253
Hannah Meria, d. Joseph, Jr. & Anna, b. Jan. 14, 1811	1	90
Henry, s. Daniell H. & Rhuma, b. Oct. 27, 1793	1	37
Henry, s. Daniell H. & Rumah, d. Oct. 1, 1794	1	37
Henry Bilson, s. Alanson & Esther, b. Feb. 8, 1784; d. Mar. 9, 1784	1	40
Henry Bilson, 2nd, s. Alanson & Esther, b. Jan. 16, 1785	1	40
James Fitch, s. David & Abil, b. June 1, 1774; d. Aug. 26, 1775	LR7	4
Jane E., of New Milford, m. William **PAINE**, of Cato, N. Y., May 29, 1853, by Rev. D. P. Sanford	2	83
Joann Caroline, d. Joseph, Jr. & Anna, b. Apr. 4, 1805	1	90
John, a witness at wedding of John **FERRIS** & Abigal **TRYON**, Quakers	LR4	22
John, s. Zechariah & Sarah, b. Feb. 6, 1713/14	LR2	360
John, of New Milford, s. Zachariah & Sarah, m. Abigal **TRYON**, of New Fairfield, Mar. 15, 1738. Quaker ceremony before 27 witnesses at Joseph Ferris. Intentions declared at Momorneck	LR4	22
John, s. Steephen & Sarah, b. Feb. 24, 1777	LR12	2
John, s. Daniell Hutton & Rhumah, b. Dec. 18, 1790	1	37
John, [s. George & Amy (**STONE**)], b. Apr. 21, 1837	2	125
John Furlong, [s. Daniel Pickett & Elizabeth], b. Aug. 11, 1829	2	49
Joseph, a witness at wedding of John **FERRIS** & Abigal		

FERRISS, FEARISS, FARRISS, FERISS, (cont.)

	Vol.	Page
TRYON, Quakers	LR4	22
Joseph, s. Zechariah & Sarah, b. Sept. 27, 1703	LR2	360
Joseph, of Newington, m. Hannah **WELCH**, of Milford, Nov. 11, 1725	LR2	340
Joseph, s. Joseph & Hannah, b. Jan. 15, 1731/2	LR2	340
Joseph, Jr., m. Johannah **GAYLOR**, Jan. 19, 1758	LR7	37
Joseph, s. Joseph, Jr. & Johannah, b. Jan. 26, 1778	LR7	37
Joseph, Jr., m. Anna **McMAHON**, Dec. 11, 1796	1	90
Joseph, d. Feb. 14, 1814, ae 82 y.	LR7	37
Jude, s. Joseph & Hanah, b. May 14, 1735	LR2	340
Jude, s. Joseph, d. Sept. 28, 1757	LR7	5
Jude, s. David & Abigail, b. Feb. 12, 1758	LR7	4
Jude, s. David & Abigal, d. Sept. 9, 1775	LR7	4
Jude Fitch, s. Amasa & Molly, b. Jan. 9, 1786	1	43
Julia, d. Daniel H. & Annis, b. Mar. 18, 1796	1	37
Julia Ann, d. Joseph, Jr. & Anna, b. July 6, 1801	1	90
Julia Ann, [d. Joseph, Jr. & Anna], d. [ ]	1	90
Laura, of New Milford, m. Levi **LEACH**, of Sherman, Jan. 22, 1833, by E. Huntington	1	257
Lydia Ann, m. Charles **GREGORY**, Jan. 10, 1847, by E. Huntington	2	33
Maria, of New Milford, m. Elijah **JUDD**, of Kent, Oct. 18, 1826, by Rev. Eleazar Beecher	1	201
Mariett, d. Daniell H. & Annis, b. Jan. 17, 1800	1	37
Mariett, m. Edwin Gavin **KNAPP**, b. of New Milford, Nov. 29, 1815, by Rev. Andrew Eliot	1	174
Mary A., of New Milford, m. John **OSBORN**, of Sherman, Sept. 1, 1842, by E. Huntington	1	380
Mary Ann, m. John W. **HAVILAND**, b. of New Milford, Aug. 29, 1831, by H. Rood	1	228
Mary Jane, [d. Daniel Pickett & Elizabeth], b. Mar. 23, 1822; lost at New York in 1833	2	49
Mercy, d. Stephen & Sarah, b. Sept. 29, 1773	LR12	3
Miranda, m. Ellis **SWEETLOVE**, Oct. 27, 1824, at the house of John Ferriss, by Rev. Eleazar Beecher	1	170
Molly Picket, d. Amasa & Molly, b. Feb. 27, 1789	1	43
Molly Picket, see Molly Picket **REID**	1	43
Nathan, s. John & Abigal, b. 6th m. 7th d., 1740. Witness: Lydia Brownson, midwife, Sarah Ferriss, Doratha Frion, Hannah, Brigs, Mary Weller, Hannah Talcott & Dabora Seelye	LR4	22
Nathan Langrish, s. Zachariah & Phebe, b. Feb. 15, 1775	LR7	4
Oringe, s. David & Abigal, b. Dec. 14, 1755	LR7	4
Orange, s. David & Abigale, d. Sept. 13, 1775, in Army at Crown Point	LR7	4
Orange Miles, s. Amasa & Molly, b. Mar. 21, 1783	1	43
Orange Miles, [s. Amasa & Molly], d. Feb. 9, 1834, ae 52 y.,		

	Vol.	Page
FERRISS, FEARISS, FARRISS, FERISS, (cont.)		
at New York	1	43
Phebe, wid. Zechariah, d. May 14, 1811	LR7	4
Phebe, m. George W[illia]m **MARSH**, b. of New Milford, Nov. 29, 1827, by Rev. Andrew Eliot	1	217
Phebe Joan, of New Milford, m. Abraham **HOAG**, of New York, May 8, 1831, by E. Huntington	1	246
Phebe Ophelia, d. Zechariah & Phebe, b. Nov. 16, 1784	LR7	4
Phebe Ophelia, of New Milford, m. James **BRIGGS**, of Sherman, Feb. 8, 1808, by Elisha Bostwick, J. P.	1	126
Rachel, twin with Daborah, d. John & Abigal, b. 12th m. 7th d. 1738/9. Witnesses: Lydiah Brownson, midwife, Sarah Ferriss, Hannah Gaylard, Hanah Weller & Deborah	LR4	22
Seelye	LR4	3
Reed, s. Benjamin & Phebe, b. Oct. 17, 1730	1	37
Rhuma, w. Daniell H., d. Nov. 3, 1793	2	49
Robert Palmer, [s. Daniel Pickett & Elizabeth], b. Jan. 1, 1823		
Rozannah, d. John & Abigil, b. 11th m. 7th d. 1741/2. Witnesses: Lydia Brownson, midwife, Doratha Tryon, Hannah Sherwood, Mary Weller, Phebe Gaylard &	LR4	22
Debora Seelye	LR7	4
Rufus, s. Zachariah & Phebe, b. Mar. 21, 1780	LR4	26
Samuel, s. Joseph & Hannah, b. Sept. 11, 1743		
Samuel, m. Abigail **BROWNSON**, Jan. 26, 1774, by Rev.	LR12	8
Nathaniell Taylor	LR12	8
Samuel, d. Oct. 14, 1775	1	43
Samuel Frederick, s. Amasa & Molly, b. Mar. 9, 1795		
Sarah, d. Zechariah & Sarah, b. Nov*. 10, 1710 *("May"	LR2	360
crossed out)	LR2	340
Sarah, d. Joseph & Hannah, b. Sept. 11, 1728		
Sarah, d. Zachariah & Sarah, m. Stephen **NOBLE**, Jr., s. Capt. Stephen & Abigail, July 18, 1733	LR4	24
Sarah, a witness at wedding of John **FERRIS** & Abigal	LR4	22
TRYON, Quakers	LR12	3
Stephen, m. Sarah **DRINKWATER**, Aug. 27, 1771	LR12	3
Stephen, s. Stephen & Sarah, b. May 1, 1772		
Stephen C., m. Martha **PAINE**, b. of New Milford, Nov. 3,	2	79
1852, by Rev. David P. Sanford	LR4	3
Susanna, d. Benjamin & Phebe, b. Nov. 7, 1732	LR7	4
Thirza, d. Zechariah & Phebe, b. Jan. 2, 1787		
Thirza, m. Squier **JOHNSON**, b. of New Milford, Aug. 9,	1	143
1807, by Elisha Bostwick, J. P.	1	37
Urania, d. Daniell H. & Rhumah, b. Feb. 17, 1792		
Urania, m. Wanzer **MARSH**, b. of New Milford, Nov. 11,	1	66
1822, by Rev. Andrew Eliot	LR2	360
Zechariah, s. Zechariah & Sarah, b. Sept. 30, 1717	LR2	340
Zachariah, s. Joseph & Hannah, b. Mar. 25, 1739	LR4	26
Zachariah, s. Joseph & Hannah, b. Mar. 25, 1739		

	Vol.	Page
FERRISS, FEARISS, FARRISS, FERISS, (cont.)		
1766, by Rev. Nathaniell Taylor	LR7	4
Zachariah, s. Zachariah & Phebe, b. July 11, 1778	LR7	4
Zechariah, Jr., m. Hannah **MARSH**, Sept. 15, 1802, by Elisha Bostwick, J. P.	1	97
Zechariah, d. Feb. 19, 1804	LR7	4
Zachariah, a witness at wedding of John **FERRIS** & Abigal **TRYON**, Quakers	LR4	22
Zebulon, s. Benjamin & Phebe, b. May 20, 1729	LR4	3
Zina, s. Zachariah & Phebe, b. Oct. 6, 1782	LR7	4
Zina, s. Zechariah & Phebe, d. Jan. 20, 1794	LR7	4
[ ]h, a witness at wedding of Elnathan **BOTSFORD** & Dorothy **PRINDLE**, Quakers	LR4	14
[ ]h, a witness at wedding of Elnathan **BOTSFORD** & Dorothy **PRINDLE**, Quakers	LR4	14
[FINNEY], [See under **PHINE**]		
FISH*, [see also **FISK**], Ichabor Ebenezer, s. Ebenezer & Sarah, b. Oct. 19, 1747 *(Possibly "FISK")	LR5	15
FISHER, Chloe, m. Abner G. **LEWIS**, Feb. 5, 1720/1, by Rev. Andrew Eliot	1	62
Luce, d. Nehemiah & Frances, b. Feb. 20, 1759	LR7	19
Nehemiah, m. Frances **BEACHER**, Jan. 18, 1757, by Solomon Palmer	LR7	19
Nehemiah Beacher, s. Nehemiah & Frances, b. Apr. 1, 1761	LR7	19
Sarah, d. Nehemiah & Frances, b. Mar. 15, 1758	LR7	19
FISK, Ann, m. Lemuel* **BOSTWICK**, Mar. 28, 1748, by Samuel Canfield, J. P. *(Perhaps "Samuel")	LR5	3
Ebenezer, d. Oct. 4, 1747	LR4	3
Hannah, m. Benajah **BOSTWICK**, b. of New Milford, Oct. 22, 1741	LR4	25
FLAGG, Elizabeth, of East Hartford, m. Stanley **GRISWOLD** (Rev.), of New Milford, Aug. 5, 1789	1	51
FLOWERS, Horatio N., of Roxbury, m. Eliza **PATTERSON**, of New Milford, Nov. 7, 1833, by Rev. Fosdic Harrison, of Roxbury	1	268
FOGHERTY, Huldah A., of New Milford, m. Hiram R. **GILBERT**, of Southbury, Aug. 4, 1839, by Albert B. Camp	1	329
FOLLETT, Thomas A., of Franklin, N. Y., m. Catharine **EVERITT**, of Franklin, N. Y., July 13, 1841, by E. Huntington	1	356
FOOT, FOOTS, Deborah, of Woodbury, m. Paul **TERRIL**, of New Milford, Sept. 11, 1758	LR7	15
M. Anna, m. Samuel D. **ALLEN**, b. of New Milford, Apr. 27, 1806, by Elisha Bostwick, J. P.	1	158
FORCE, Edward B., of Pyramus, N. J., m. Jennet **ROBERTS**, of New Milford, Oct. 17, 1843, by J. Greenwood	1	389
FORD, FOARD, Aaron N., s. Charles & Hannah, b. Jan. 18, 1836	1	282

	Vol.	Page
FORD, FOARD, (cont.)		
Anna, m. John **WILKINSON**, b. of New Milford, Nov. 1, 1807, by Elisha Bostwick, J. P.	1	152
Betsey, m. Ithamar **COLE**, Jan. 23, 1821, by Rev. Andrew Eliot	1	32
Charles, m. Hannah **EGGLESTON**, Oct. 26, 1834, by E. Huntington	1	282
Clark, m. Anne **FULLER**, b. of New Milford, Nov. 29, 1832, by Rev. H. Rood	1	255
Emily, of New Milford, m. Allen S. **LANE**, of Kent, Aug. 8, 1830, by Rev. H. Rood	1	193
Fanny E., m. Isaac E. **WARNER**, b. of New Milford, Apr. 2, 1854, by Rev. A. B. Pulling	2	97
Harriet, m. Asher **MALLET**, Dec. 18, 1822, by Rev. Andrew Eliot	1	175
Jane, of New Milford, m. George **HITCHCOCK**, of Woodbury, Apr. 22, 1835, by H. Rood	1	287
Jonathan, Jr., m. Mabel **CLARK**, b. of New Milford, Oct. 5, 1806, by Elisha Bostwick, J. P.	1	134
Loiza, m. Ithamar **MALLETT**, b. of New Milford, Apr. 28, 1827, by Rev. Josiah L. Dickerson	1	129
Maria A., m. John H. **BRONSON**, b. of New Milford, May 1, 1836, by Albert B. Camp	1	294
FORWARD, Lydia, of Danbury, m. David **NOBLE**, of New Milford, June 15, 1720	LR2	348
FOSTER, David A., of Brookfield, m. Marietta **NOBLE**, of New Milford, Dec. 24, 1820, by Rev. Benjamin Benham	1	22
FOWLER, Abigail, m. Caleb **BENNITT**, b. of New Milford, June 13, 1746, by Rev. Elisha Kent	LR5	14
Philo, s. Benjamin & Rachel, b. Jan. 13, 177[ ]	LR10	17
Rachel, mother of Philo made statement, Apr. 21, 1791, that her s. Philo was 21 y. of age Jan. 13, last, by which account the time of his birth was on Jan. 13, 1770	LR10	17
FOX, Mary, of Hartland, m. David **COLE**, of New Milford, May 2, 1790, by Rev. Nathaniel Taylor	1	35
FRAIL, Polly, m. Lemuel **BOSTWICK**, Jr., June 27, 1784, by Daniel Everitt	1	1
FRANK, Sarah A., m. Lewis **CLAGET**, b. of New Milford, Nov. 16, 1845, by J. Greenwood	1	405
FRANKLIN, Bular, of New Milford, m. Senica **DERLING**, of Buhmanville, N. Y., Feb. 5, 1854, by Rev. A. B. Pulling	2	94
Charles, m. Sally Minerva **PHILLYIS**, b. of New Milford, (colored), Oct. 26, 1829, by Eldad C. Jackson, J. P.	1	426
FREEMAN, Hopeful, of Litchfield, m. Cyrus **THATCHER**, of New Milford, June 17, 1811, at Litchfield South Farms, by James Morriss	1	419
Levi, of Goshen, m. Almira **ROBERTS**, of Canaan, Dec. 18, 1852, by Rev. David Murdock, Jr.	2	80

	Vol.	Page

FREEMAN, (cont.)
Robert, of Hartford, m. Mary E. **HINE**, of New Milford,
Sept. 11, 1854, by Rev. David Murdock, Jr. — 2 — 106
Thaddeus, of Reading, m. Sophia **PHILLIPS**, of New Milford,
Oct. 3, 1821, by Rev. Andrew Eliott — 1 — 49
FRENCH, Benjamin, of New Haven, m. Lucinda **HALL**, of New
Milford, July 2, 1832, by Rev. Nathan D. Benedict — 1 — 246
Chester, m. Lucy A. **SUDLOW**, Nov. 23, 1835, by E.
Huntington — 1 — 296
Elizebeth Ann, m. Alonzo **WARNER**, Nov. 16, 1831, by E.
Huntington — 1 — 248
Ephraim, m. Sally J. **BEACH**, b. of Bridgwater, Jan. 15, 1828,
by Rev. Fosdic Harrison, of Roxbury — 1 — 124
Julia A., of Bridgwater, m. Orson **DIBBLE**, of Bethel, Dec.
27, 1827, by Rev. Fosdic Harriosn, of Roxbury — 1 — 45
Julia M., m. Philo **BANKER**, Jan. 1, 1850 (see Julia M.
HARTWELL) — 2 — 117
Laura A., Mrs., m. Elanson D. **YOUNG**, Feb. 14, 1836, by
Albert B. Camp — 1 — 292
Lucinda, m. Charles **LOVEMAN**, b. of New Milford, Oct. 3,
1842, by Rev. Daniel Baldwin — 1 — 375
Nancy, of New Milford, m. Homer **LAKE**, of Brookfield,
May 27, 1830, by J. S. Covill — 1 — 238
Othniel, m. Laura Antonett **BEACH**, b. of New Milford, Dec.
28, 1828, by Rev. E. Huntington — 1 — 227
FRISBIE, Eunice, of Washington, m. Elisha **DOWNS**, of New
Milford, May 13, 1802 — 1 — 106
Huldah, m. Edmund **RICHMOND**, Dec. 1, 1785 — 1 — 36
FROST, Elizabeth, 1st w. Daniel Pickett **FERRISS**, d. June 8,
1847, at East Port, Me. — 2 — 49
Julia Emily, of Bridgewater, m. Henry **CAMP**, of New
Milford, Dec. 25, 1848, by Rev. A. Ogden, of
Bridgewater — 2 — 52
Lewis, m. Sylvia **BEERS**, May 7, 1837, by E. Huntington — 1 — 311
FULLER, Anne, m. Clark **FORD**, b. of New Milford, Nov. 29,
1832, by Rev. H. Rood — 1 — 255
Baton, s. Ichabod & Jemimah, of Balmans Patten, b.
Oct. 2, 1749 — LR5 — 13
Henry C., of Ludlow, Mass., m. Julia E. **PARK**, of New
Milford, Nov. 24, 1853, by Rev. David Murdock, Jr. — 2 — 100
Jonathan, E., m. Julia A. **GILLET**, b. of New Milford, Sept.
6, 1832, by E. Huntington — 1 — 254
Lucy, m. Joseph **LUDLOW**, b. of New Milford, Oct. 12,
1815, by Elisha Bostwick, J. P. — 1 — 10
Polly, m. John **FERGUSON**, Jan. 5, 1806 — 1 — 156
Thirza, m. George **SUDLOW**, b. of New Milford, July 4, 1809 — 1 — 164
----, Mrs. of Bridgeport, m. John **LEACH**, of Trumbull,
Mar. 10, 1844, by Rev. James Kilborn, of Bridgeport — 1 — 392

	Vol.	Page
FURLONG, Elizabeth, m. Daniel Pickett **FERRISS**, Apr. 23, 1821, at New York	2	49
GALARD, [see under **GAYLORD**]		
GALBRITIA, Nathaniel T., b. Apr. 8, 1782, in Williamstown, m. Esther **MOREHOUSE**, Nov. 15, 1806, by Elisha Bostwick, J. P.	1	136
GALPIN, Hester, m. Jonathan **BOOTH**, s. John & Dorothy, Aug. 11, 1703, by Mr. Purdy, J. P., at Rye	2	111
Nathaniel J., of Washington, m. Sally **ODLE**, Nov. 24, 1825, by Rev. Andrew Eliot	1	176
GALUSHA, Lois, m. Samuel **CLARK**, Nov. 7, 1809, by Elisha Bostwick, J. P.	1	163
GANSON, Manson, m. Abigail **CARPENTER**, b. of New Milford, Jan. 1, 1840, by Noah Porter	1	341
Nathan, m. Rachel **JACKSON**, Dec. 22, 1825, by Rev. Andrew Eliot	1	29
GARDERNER, Eliza O., of Beekman, Dutchess Co., N. Y., m. David D. **HOAG**, of South Dover, Sept. 11, 1844, at the house of Mrs. Jane Gardener, Green Haven, by Rev. Thomas Sparkes	2	115
GARLICK, Abel, s. Henry & Mary, b. June 20, 1749	LR5	3
Anna, m. Reuben **HITCHCOCK**, Nov. 7, 1807, by Elisha Bostwick, J. P.	1	153
Daniel, s. Heath & Sarah, b. Oct. 19, 1766	1	50
Daniel, m. Thalia **BEECHER**, Nov. 5, 1788	1	19
Ebenezer, s. Daniel & Thalia, b. June 4, 1790	1	19
Elizabeth, d. Heath & Sarah, b. Nov. 11, 1764	1	50
Emlen, d. Henry & Elizabeth, b. Mar. 3, 1721/2	LR4	6
Eunice, twin with Sarah, d. Heath & Sarah, b. Oct. 3, 1772	1	50
Heath, s. Henry & Elizabeth, b. Oct. 21, 1733	LR4	6
Heath, of New Milford, m. Sarah **SEELYE**, of Kent, Feb. 8, 1764	1	50
Henry, s. Henry & Elizabeth, b. Apr. 5, 1727	LR4	6
Henry, m. Mary **WILLIAMS**, Jan. 18, 1741	LR5	3
Leman, m. Mary **HITCHCOCK**, b. of New Milford, Sept. 5, 1799, by Elisha Bostwick, J. P.	1	19
Read, s. Henry & Elizabeth, b. Dec. 24, 1730	LR4	6
Read, m. Mary **STONE**, b. of New Milford, Dec. 7, 1752	LR6	4
Reuben, s. Henry & Mary, b. Mar. 29, 1743	LR4	6
Reuben, s. Henry & Mary, b. Mar. 29, 1743	LR5	3
Samuel R., m. Polly **CHAMBERLAIN**, Sept. 13, 1821, by Rev. Andrew Eliot	1	49
Sarah, d. Henry & Elizabeth, b. Dec. 22, 1718, at Milford	LR4	6
Sarah, d. Henry & Elizabeth, m. William* **PRIME**, s. James & Ann, Oct. 31, 1739, by John Beach *("James" crossed out, "William" written underneath)	LR4	21
Sarah, d. Henry & Elizabeth, m. William **PRIME**, s. James & Annah, Oct. 31, 1739, by John Beach, of Newtown	LR4	27

GARLICK, (cont.)

	Vol.	Page
Sarah, twin with Eunice, d. Heath & Sarah, b. Oct. 3, 1772	1	50
Seth, s. Henry & Mary, b. Nov. 26, 1752	LR5	3
William, s. Henry & Elizabeth, b. Jan. 2, 1724/5	LR4	6

GAYLORD, GAYLARD, GALARD, Aaron, of New Milford, m. Phebe **SMITH**, of Ridgfeild, Sept. 22, 1732, by Rev.

	Vol.	Page
Thomas Hauley	LR4	1
Aaron, s. Aaron & Phebe, b. Dec. 21, 1735	LR4	1
Aaron, Jr., m. Iranai **BRIGGS**, b. of New Milford, Feb. 16, 1764, by [ ]	LR7	9
Aaron, m. Eurania **BRIGGS**, Feb. 16, 1764	LR10	18
Aaron, s. Aaron & Urania, b. Oct. 6, 1773	LR7	9
Ahner Mosely, s. Nathan & Hannah, d. Mar. 18, 1768	LR4	7
Albert, s. Daniel H. & Phebe, b. July 11, 1800	1	82
Albert A., of New Milford, m. Julia M. **SANFORD**, of Bridgwater, May 23, 1827, by Rev. Andrew Eliot	1	215
Anna C., of New Milford, m. Henry **ELLIOTT**, of Bridgeport, Oct. 15, 1850, by Rev. David Murdock	2	64
Benjamin, s. William & Jahanan, b. Aug. 28, 1715	LR2	345
Benjamin, s. William, d. Feb. 11, 1717/18	LR2	358
Benjamin, s. William & Johanna b. Sept. 12, 1721	LR2	345
Benjamin, s. William & Johanah, b. Sept. 12, 1721	LR2	361
Benjamin, m. Trial **MOREHOUS**, Oct. 2, 1745, by Timothy Hutch, J. P.	LR6	12
Benjamin, m. Ruth **SHERMAN**, Sept. 28, 1756	LR6	12
Benjamin, s. Nathan & Ruth, b. Apr. 4, 1779; d. [ ]	LR12	13
Benj[ami]n, Dea., d. Apr. 6, 1792	LR6	12
Betsey, d. Peter & Sarah, b. Aug. 1, 1781	1	17
Betsey, m. Orra **WARNER**, b. of New Milford, Mar. 26, 1834, by H. Rood	1	273
Caroline J., m. Charles S. **GAYLORD**, b. of New Milford, Oct. 4, 1848, by John Greenwood	2	43
Catharine, m. Albert **BARNS**, b. of New Milford, [Feb. 24, 1836], by Maltby Gelston	1	292
Charles S., of New Milford, m. Caroline J. **GAYLORD**, of New Milford, Oct. 4, 1848, by John Greenwood	2	43
Cornelia, of New Milford, m. Hugh **GELSTON**, of Sherman, May 21, 1828, by Rev. Andrew Eliot	1	211
Daniel, s. Benjamin & Tryal, b. May 19, 1755	LR6	12
Daniel, s. Peter & Sarah, b. May 14, 1779	1	17
Daniel Harvey, s. Ebenezer & Catharine, b. May 1, 1776	LR11	10
Daniel Hervey, of New Milford, m. Phebe **BRIGGS**, of New Fairfield, Sept. 25, 1799	1	82
David, s. William & Eunice, b. Jan. 5, 1770	LR7	9
David, of New Milford, m. Armida **GIDDINGS**, of New Fairfield, Oct. 21, 1798	1	83
Dinena*, d. Ebenezer & Catharine, b. Feb. 13, 1772 *("Demice")	LR11	10

	Vol.	Page
GAYLORD, GAYLARD, GALARD, (cont.)		
Ebenezer, s. Aaron & Phebe, b. July 12, 1746	LR4	1
Ebenezer, m. Catharine CHITTENDEN, Apr. 3, 1771	LR11	10
Ebenezer & w. Catharine, had d. [ ], d. Dec. 3, 1779; d. Dec. 7, 1779	LR11	10
Ebenezer, d. [ ]	LR11	10
Elijah, s. Peter & Sarah, b. Mar. 18, 1786	1	17
Eliza, d. David & Armida, b. July 4, 1800	1	83
Eliza, d. David, m. William ROBURDS, Oct. 25, 1820, by Rev. Andrew Eliot	1	178
Easter, d. Nathan & Ruth, b. Apr. 16, 1777	LR12	13
Esther, m. Daniel LATHROP, June 17, 1821, at the house of Hervey Benson, by Elder Eleazar Beecher	1	56
Hannah, w. Nathan, d. Aug. 14, 1757	LR4	7
Hannah, a witness at wedding of Elnathan BOTSFORD, & Dorothy PRINDLE, Quakers	LR4	14
Homer, s. Nathan & Ruth, b. Apr. 3, 1784	LR12	13
Homer, m. Anne CANFIELD, b. of New Milford, May 5, 1807, by Elisha Bostwick, J. P.	1	141
Irwin B., m. Sarah E. ALLEN, b. of New Milford, Oct. 26, 1848, by John Greenwood	2	44
Jahanah*, d. William & Jahanah, b. Aug. 16, 1717 *("Johanah" written over, "Ruth" crossed out)	LR2	345
Johannah, d. William & Johanna, b. Aug. 16, 1717	LR2	361
Joannah, d. Aaron & Phebe, b. Oct. 10, 1737	LR4	1
Joannah, w. William, d. May 24, 1741	LR4	1
Johannah, m. Joseph FERRISS, Jr., Jan. 19, 1758	LR7	37
Joanna, d. Aaron & Urania, b. Mar. 31, 1769	LR7	9
Joseph, s. Nathan & Ruth, b. Nov. 19, 1781	LR12	13
Julia, of New Milford, m. Phinehas HUNT, of Sherman, Oct. 15, 1822, by Rev. Andrew Eliot	1	57
Lucy, m. Sheldon CAMP, b. of New Milford, Oct. 14, 1838, by N. Porter	1	322
Mary, d. William & Jahannah, b. Nov. 22, 1725	LR2	345
Miner, s. William & Eunice, b. Mar. 6, 1774	LR7	9
Nancy, d. Nathan & Ruth, b. Apr. 21, 1786	LR12	13
Nancy, m. Abel BUCKINGHAM, Jr., Feb. 18, 1809	1	98
Nathan, of New Milford, m. Hannah BROWNSON, of Waterbury, Sept. 23, 1731	LR2	345
Nathan, of New Milford, m. Hannah BROWNSON, of Waterbury, Sept. 23, 1731	LR4	7
Nathan, s. Benjemen & Trial, b. Dec. [ ]*, 1748 *(Probably "7")	LR6	12
Nathan, Dea., of New Milford, m. Mrs. Hannah MOSELEY, of Westfield, Mar. [ ], 1758* *("1768" crossed out)	LR4	7
Nathan, s. Isaac & Hannah, b. Apr. 27, 1767	LR7	35
Nathan, m. Ruth HARTWELL, June 30, 1774, by Rev. Nathaniel Taylor	LR12	13

GAYLORD, GAYLARD, GALARD, (cont.)

	Vol.	Page
Nathan, s. Ebenezar & Catharine, b. Nov. 10, 1783	LR11	10
Nathan, d. July 29, 1806	LR12	13
Nathan, m. Irene **DOWNS**, Oct. 15, 1807, by Elisha Bostwick, J. P.	1	148
Nathan, a. witness at wedding of Elnathan **BOTSFORD** & Dorothy **PRINDLE**, Quakers	LR4	14
Nathan, a witness at wedding of John **FERRIS** & Abigail **TRYON**, Quakers	LR4	22
Orra A., m. Marcus E. **MERWIN**, b. of New Milford, Jan. 10, 1844, by John Greenwood	1	390
Paulina, d. William & Eunice, b. Dec. 1, 1775	LR7	9
Peter, s. [William] & [Johanna], b. Feb. 18, 172[ ]	LR2	361
Peter, s. William & Johanah, b. Feb. 18, 1723/4	LR2	345
Peter, s. William, d. June 28, 1724	LR2	343
Peter, s. Benjemen & Trial, b. July 21, 1751	LR6	12
Peter, s. Dea. Benjamin, m. Sarah **HARTWELL**, d. Joseph Feb. 20, 1778	1	17
Peter, s. Peter & Sarah, b. June 1, 1784	1	17
Peter, d. Sept. 28, 1793	1	17
Phebe, d. Aaron & Phebe, b. Jan. 9, 1742/3	LR4	1
Phebe, m. Zachariah **FERRISS**, b. of New Milford, Mar. 13, 1766, by Rev. Nathaniell Taylor	LR7	4
Phebe, d. Ebenezer & Catharine, b. Apr. 24, 1774	LR11	10
Phebe, m. Daniel Munson **FAIRCHILD**, Oct. 19, 1802, by Elisha Bostwick, J. P.	1	100
Ruth, d. William, d. Aug. 31, 1714	LR2	358
Ruth, d. William & Johanah, b. Mar. 28, 1719	LR2	345
Ruth*, d. William & Johannah, b. Mar. 28, 1719 *("Ruth" crossed out)	LR2	361
Ruth, d. Benjamin & Trial, b. July 27, 1746	LR6	12
Ruth, d. Nathan & Ruth, b. [ ]	LR12	13
Ruth, w. Nathan, d. [ ]	LR12	13
Salome, d. Peter & Sarah, b. Oct. 26, 1791	1	17
Sary, d. Aaron & Phebe, b. Sept. 13, 1733	LR4	1
Sarah*, m. Lamuel **WARNER**, Feb. 15, 1758 *("Phebee" crossed out)	LR7	36
Sarah, d. William & Eunice, b. Aug. 12, 1766	LR7	9
Susan, m. Henry **MERWIN**, b. of New Milford, Oct. 2, 1828, by Rev. Andrew Eliot	1	222
Truman, s. Aaron & Urania, b. Oct. 13, 1766	LR7	9
Truman, s. Aaron & Eurania, b. [ ]	LR10	18
Tryal, w. Benjamin, d. July 17, 1755	LR6	12
William, s. Benjamin & Jahanna, b. Aug. 28, 1715	LR2	361
William, s. Aaron & Phebe, b. Mar. 10, 1739/40* *("1740 crossed out)	LR4	1
William, Ens., m. Mrs. Mercy **BOSTWICK**, Oct. 14*, 1742, by Rev. Daniel Bordman *(Date crossed out)	LR4	2

	Vol.	Page
GAYLORD, GAYLARD, GALARD, (cont.)		
William, d. Oct. 25, 1753	LR6	6
William, m. Eunice **HITCHCOCK**, b. of New Milford, Mar. 20, 1766, by Samuell Bostwick, J. P.	LR7	6
William, m. Eunice **HITCHCOCK**, Mar. 20, 1766	LR7	9
William, s. William & Eunice, b. Dec. 9, 1777	LR7	9
William, m. Martha **JACKSON**, b. of New Milford, Feb. 25, 1836, by Abner Brundage	1	293
GAYSON, Lois, m. Robert **SMITH**, b. of New Milford, Nov. 19, 1845, by Daniel B. Wilson, J. P.	1	405
GELSTON, Hugh, of Sherman, m. Cornelia **GAYLORD**, of New Milford, May 21, 1828, by Rev. Andrew Eliot	1	211
Maltby, Rev. of Clyde, N. Y., m. Marcia H. **MERWIN**, of New Milford, Oct. 20, 1834, by H. Rood	1	279
GIBBS, Elisabeth, m. Justice **SEELEY**, Mar. 10, 1746/7, by Rev. Timothy Collins	LR6	3
GIDDINGS, Armida, of New Fairfield, m. David **GAYLORD**, of New Milford, Oct. 21, 1798	1	83
Daniel E., of Sherman, m. Lavinia **MARSH**, of New Milford, Jan. 20, 1835, by H. Rood	1	286
John P., m. Martha W. **MERWIN**, b. of New Milford, Feb. 27, 1849, by Jno Greenwood	2	51
Renssalaer, m. Sarah **CANFIELD**, b. of New Milford, Jan. 31, 1833, by E. Huntington	1	259
Samuel, of Sherman, m. Armida **SANFORD**, of New Milford, Oct. 16, 1831, by Rev. C. A. Boardman, of New Haven	1	229
GIFFORD, Eunice, m. Henry **GUNN**, Dec. 2, 1839, by E. Huntington	1	338
Hiram S., m. Mrs. Maricha **RICHMOND**, b. of New Milford, May 3, 1846, by Rev. Joseph L. Morse	2	14
Homer, m. Betsey **CURTISS**, Dec. 25, 1820, at the house of William Camp, by Eleazer Beecher, Elder	1	21
GILBERT, Abigail, of Sherman, m. Elijah **LEONARD**, of Kent, Nov. 10, 1822, by Daniel Gaylord, J. P.	1	52
Allen, of Kent, m. Delia **BUTRAM**, of New Milford, Feb. 2, 1837, by N. Porter. Int. Pub.	1	302
Burton, of Warren, m. Marcia **STONE**, of New Milford, July 9, 1837, by Rev. Joseph Whittlesey	1	305
Clarissa, of New Milford, m. Daniel **MALLORY**, of Bridgeport, Feb. 13, 1825, by Rev. Andrew Eliot	1	137
Hiram R., of Southbury, m. Huldah A. **FOGHERTY**, of New Milford, Aug. 4, 1839, by Albert B. Camp	1	329
Larania, m. Nirom **HALEY**, Dec. 31, 1823, by Rev. Benjamin Benham	1	166
GILLET, GILLIT, GILLITT, Abigail, d. Abraham & Abigail, b. July 19, 1732	LR2	344
Abraham, m. Abigail **PRINDLE**, b. of New Milford, Jan. 28, 1729/30	LR2	344

	Vol.	Page
GILLET, GILLIT, GILLITT, (cont.)		
Abraham, a witness at wedding of Elnathan **BOTSFORD** & Dorothy **PRINDLE**, Quakers	LR4	14
Hannah, d. Abraham & Abigail, b. July 24, 1730	LR2	344
Hannah, m. Nathaniel **TAYLOR**, Mar. 5, 1760	LR7	25
Jonathan, s. Abram & Abigal, b. Dec. 16, 1734	LR4	14
Julia A., m. Jonathan E. **FULLER**, b. of New Milford, Sept. 6, 1832, by E. Huntington	1	254
William, Jr., m. Julia A. **BEACH**, b. of Bridgewater, Feb. 26, 1822, by Rev. Andrew Eliot	1	34
GLASFORD, Betsy, d. Hugh & Thankfull, b. Feb. 19, 1778	LR13	11
Polly, d. Hugh & Thankfull, b. July 2, 1770	LR13	11
GLOVER, Charles, m. Charlotte **NORTHROP**, b. of Newtown, Sept. 3, 1837, by A. B. Camp	1	308
Emily, m. George M. **SHERMAN**, Feb. 1, 1843, by E. Huntington	1	384
Esmily, m. George B. **SHERMAN**, Feb. 1, 1843, by E. Huntington	1	392
Eunice, w. James, d. Feb. 13, 1795, ae 57 y.	2	112
James, m. Eunice **BOOTH**, d. Daniel & Eunice, [ ]	2	112
Laura, m. John **COLE**, May 6, 1846, by E. Huntington	2	22
Lucy M., m. Philo **BABBITT**, Oct. 14, 1846, by Rev. William Atwill, of Bridgewater	2	27
GOLD, Rachel, d. Job & Sarah, b. Mar. 12, 1734/5	LR4	12
GOLDSMITH, Joseph C., m. Lorania **CURTIS**, Aug. 15, 1853, by Rev. A. B. Pulling	2	89
Martin, of Plymouth, m. Rhoda **CANFIELD**, of New Milford, Jan. 2, 1825*, by Rev. Andrew Eliot *("5" uncertain)	1	20
Sarah, of New Milford, m. Edward B. **THOMPSON**, of New Haven, Dec. 17, 1845, by Rev. William Atwill, of Bridgewater	2	6
GOODSELL, GOODWILL, Alma, of New Milford, m. Sheldon Myars **BRONSON**, of Kent, Mar. 10, 1829, by Rev. Harry Finch, of Washington	1	192
Eliza, of New Milford, m. Eli **SOMMERS**, of Dover, N. Y., Jan. 21, 1837, by Rev. William W. Andrews, of Kent	1	303
Surges, m. Maria Ann **KNAPP**, b. of New Milford, Apr. 2, 1840, by Nathan Rice	1	355
GORDON, Charles W., m. Harriet C. **WINTERS**, d. Curtis, July 29, 1849, by Rev. James L. Scott, of New Preston. Int. Pub.	2	56
GORHAM, GORAM, Eliza Jane, d. Samuel & Betsey, b. Jan. 28, 1841	1	342
Eunis Maria, d. Samuel & Betsey L., b. Aug. 23, 1844	1	342
George Burr, s. Samuel & Betsey L., b. Mar. 21, 1845	1	342
Hellen Sasan, d. Samuel & Betsey L., b. Apr. 6, 1847	1	342
Isaac E., m. Oliver Ann **IVES**, Sept. 27, 1840, by Rev. Albert B. Camp, of Bridgewater	1	347

NEW MILFORD VITAL RECORS 95

	Vol.	Page
GORHAM, GORAM, (cont.)		
Laura Ann, d. Samuel & Betsey L., b. June 28, 1842	1	342
Mary Ellen, d. Samuel & Betsey L., b. Nov. 25, 1849	1	342
Phinehas, m. wid. Patty **SPERRY**, b. of New Milford, Jan. 10, 1819, by Joel Sanford, J. P.	1	117
Samuel, m. Harriet **DARLING**, b. of New Milford, Oct. 25, 1835, by E. Huntington	1	295
Samuel, m. Betsey L. **KEITH**, b. of New Milford, Mar. 5, 1840, by Noah Porter	1	342
Sarah, of New Milford, m. Isaac **SANFORD**, of Newtown, Oct. 30, 1825, by Rev. Newton Tuttle	1	188
GOULD, GOOLD, COOLD, Abigail, d. William & Mary, b. July 23, 1718	LR2	355
Abigal, d. Job & Sary, b. Aug. 3, 1733	LR4	12
Abigail, m. Abel **CAMP**, Dec. 20, 175[2]*, by Rev. Nathaniell Taylor (Supplied from Orcutt's Hist.)	LR6	9
Ann, m. Joseph **BUCK**, b. of New Milford, June 5, 1729	LR2	347
Annis, d. Job & Sarah, b. July 31, 1748; d. Feb. 28, 1753	LR4	12
Charlotte, m. Charles **THATCHER**, b. of New Milford, Mar. 19, 1844, by John Greenwood	1	392
Charlotte, m. Charles **THATCHER**, b. of New Milford, Mar. 19, 1844, by John Greenwood	1	395
David, s. Job & Sarah, b. Nov.* 16, 1745 *("Feb." crossed out)	LR4	12
Job, m. Sarah **PRINDLE**, b. of New Milford, June 17, 1730	LR2	355
Job, s. Job & Sarah, b. Dec. 28, 1736* *(Possibly "8")	LR4	12
Job, of New Milford, m. Martha **HURLBUT**, of Sharon, Mar. 24, 1767, by Rev. Cotton Mather Smith, of Sharon	LR9	[ ]
Job, a witness at wedding of Elnathan **BOTSFORD** & Dorothy **PRINDLE**, Quaker	LR4	14
Joel, s. Job & Sarah, b. Mar. 5, 1731/2; d. Mar. 22, 1751	LR2	355
Lyman, s. Job & Martha, b. Dec. 23, 1769	LR9	[ ]
Mary, d. William & Mary, b. Aug. 1, 1724; d. Aug. 25, 1724	LR2	355
Rachel, m. Zachariah **SANFORD**, May 28, 1761	LR8	1
Samuell, s. William & Mary, d. Jan. 20, 1718/19	LR2	358
Samuell, s. William & Mary, b. June 14, 1720	LR2	355
Samuell, s. William & Mary, d. June 26, 1720	LR2	358
Sarah, d. Job & Sarah, b. Sept. 14, 1743	LR4	12
Sarah, a witness at wedding of Elnathan **BOTSFORD** & Dorothy **PRINDLE**, Quakers	LR4	14
William, Sr., d. Feb 15, 1729/30	LR2	353
William, s. Job & Sarah, b. May 14, 1740	LR4	12
GRAHAM, Amy, m. George R. **McEWEN**, Sept. 13, 1847, by E. Huntington	2	36
Ann E., m. Samuel Marcus **MARSH**, Nov. 23, 1846, by E. Huntington	2	24
GRANGER, Eunice, m. Thomas **GREEN**, Nov. 23, 1795	1	75
Laura, m. Ezra **LACEY**, Jan. 5, 1806, by Elisha Bostwick, J. P.	1	126

	Vol.	Page
GRANT, Anne, m. Amos **NORTHRUP**, Jr., Dec. 7, 1768, by Paul Welch, J. P.	LR10	4
Rachel, Mrs. of Litchfield, m. Paul **WELCH**, of New Milford, Dec. 29, 1756	LR4	2
Rachel, m. David **NORTHRUP**, July 3, 1769, by Paul Welch, J. P.	LR12	15
Sarah, m. Amos **BOSTWICK**, b. of New Milford, Dec. 2, 1766, by Samuell Canfield, J. P.	LR10	1
Thomas, s. Capt. Thomas, of Litchfield, decd. & Rachel Welch, formerly w. Capt. Thomas, d. Jan. 8, 1759	LR4	2
GRATIS, Dan, of New Milford, m. Genne **GRATIS**, of Stratford, Nov. 24, 1758	LR7	1
Genne, of Stratford, m. Dan **GRATIS**, of New Milford, Nov. 24, 1758	LR7	1
GRAVES, Samuel Brown, m. Betsey **WELCH**, Feb. 7, 1805, by Elisha Bostwick, J. P.	1	120
GRAY, Caroline D., of New Milford, m. Benajah H. **PEET**, of Danbury, Nov. 16, 1845, by Samuel Weeks	2	14
Olive, m. Samuel **DRINKWATER**, July 27, 1769	LR11	5
Sarah, m. David **CANFIELD**, Jr., Aug. 4, 1772, by Rev. Nathaniell Taylor	LR11	12
GREEN, GREENE, Amarillis, d. Thomas & Eunice, b. July 3, 1802	1	75
Aurillia, d. Thomas & Eunice, b. June 10, 1804	1	75
Aurilla, of New Milford, m. William **HUNT**, of Woodbury, Sept. 30, 1823, by Rev. Benjamin Benham	1	172
David, m. Margery **SACKETTE**, July 12, 1759	LR7	27
David, s. David & Margary, b. Aug. 24, 1761	LR7	27
Elijah, m. Polly **SMITH**, Apr. 18, 1832, by Rev. Eleazar Beecher	1	100
Elizabeth, m. Jeremiah **BROWNSON**, Mar. 12, 1826, by Rev. Eleazar Beecher	1	200
Gideon, s. David & Margery, b. Aug. 10, 1763	LR7	27
Isaac, witnessed marriage of David **SANDS** & Paulina **LEACH**	1	277
Jarius, s. David & Margery, b. Jan. 20, 1766	LR7	27
Martha, d. David & Margery, b. Dec. 6, 1773	LR7	27
Mary, d. David & Margery, b. Feb. 11, 1768	LR7	27
Mary E., of New Milford, m. Edmund V. **HAWES**, of Sherman, Sept. 8, 1846, by J. Greenwood	2	18
Phebe, witnessed marriage of David **SANDS** & Paulina **LEACH**	1	277
Polly, d. Thomas & Eunice, b. Sept. 9, 1796	1	75
Polly, witnessed marriage of Ebenezer **WANZER**, Jr. & Lucy **LEACH**	1	181
Polly, witnessed marriage of Jehu **HOAG** & Phebe **WANZER**	1	250
Polly, witnessed marriage of Gurdon **SWIFT**, & Jane **WANZER**	1	288

	Vol.	Page
GREEN, GREENE, (cont.)		
Rebecah, d. Thomas & Eunice, b. Jan. 9, 1799	1	75
Tabatha Broughton, d. David & Margary, b. Jan. 20, 1771	LR7	27
Thomas, m. Eunice **GRANGER**, Nov. 23, 1795	1	75
Thomas, d. May [ ], 1823	1	75
GREGORY, Anne, m. Ezra D. **NOBLE**, June 22, 1805, by Elisha Bostwick, J. P.	1	116
Charles, m. Lydia Ann **FERRISS**, Jan. 10, 1847, by E. Huntington	2	33
Edgar, m. Catharine E. **TIBBETTS**, b. of New Milford, Mar. 9, 1840, by Noah Porter	1	342
Elizabeth, m. Nathan **HITCHCOCK**, Jr., b. of New Milford, Jan. 8, 1801, by Elisha Bostwick, J. P.	1	85
Elvira, m. Riverious **STILSON**, b. of New Milford, Jan. 22, 1826, by Rev. Andrew Eliot	1	197
Lucinda S., of Norwalk, m. Eli C. **NORTHROP**, of Brookfield, Dec. 3, 1823, by Rev. Benjamin Benham	1	149
Maria E., m. Amos R. **BULKLEY**, b. of New Milford, Oct. 21, 1840, by N. Porter	1	350
William, m. Irene **WYANT**, Feb. 21, 1841, by Rev. Maltby Gelston	1	364
William, m. Irene **WYANT**, Feb. 21, 1842, by Maltby Gleston	1	376
GRIFFIN, GRIFFEN, Abigail, see Abigail **JONES**	LR4	1
Henry W., of Dover, Dutches Co., N. Y., m. Mary Jane **CLARK**, of New Milford, Oct. 30, 1848, by Rev. Stephen J. Stebbins	2	48
Joseph, of Summers, N. Y., m. Elizabeth **WANZER**, of New Fairfield, 9th m. 25th d., 1834, by Abraham Wanzer	1	278
Joseph, witnessed marriage of Gurdon **SWIFT** and Jane **WANZER**	1	288
GRIFFITH, Hepzibah, of Reading, m. Stephen **TERRILL**, of New Milford, Feb. 7, 1781, by Rev. Nathaniell Bartlet	1	16
GRINDEL, Samuel, a witness at wedding of Elnathan **BOTSFORD** & Dorothy **PRINDLE**, Quakers	LR4	14
GRISWOLD, GRISWOULD, GRISWOOLD, Adonijah, s. John & Phebe, b. June 11, 1759	LR7	1
Anne, d. David & Siverance, b. Feb. 22, 1715* *(Possibly "1716")	LR2	350
Asahel, s. Jeremiah & Hannah, b. Jan. 23, 1743/4	LR6	3
Asaph, s. John & Phebe, b. Oct. 17, 1766	LR7	1
Cornelia, d. Rev. Stanley & Elizabeth, b. May 6, 1801	1	51
David, s. John & Phebe, b. July 29, 1761	LR7	1
Doctor, s. John & Phebe, b. Nov. 30, 1770	LR7	1
Elijah, s. David & Siverance, b. May 20, 1719	LR2	350
Gideon, s. David & Siverance, b. Oct. 2, 1717	LR2	350
Henry William, s. Rev. Stanley & Elizabeth, b. Oct. 5, 1795	1	51
James Fitzherbert, s. Rev. Stanley & Elizabeth, b. Aug. 18, 1790	1	51

	Vol.	Page
GRISWOLD, GRISWOULD, GRISWOOLD, (cont.)		
John, d. Dec. 24, 1719	LR2	358
John, s. John, decd. & Mabel, b. Mar. 1, 1720	LR2	353
John, m. Phipe COLLINS, Nov. 29, 1750, by Rev. Nathaniel Taylard	LR7	1
John, s. John & Phebe, b. Sept. 16, 1751	LR7	1
Mabell, d. John & Mabell, b. Mar. 12, 1717/18	LR2	353
Mabell, d. Jeremiah & Hannah, b. Mar. 5, 1746	LR6	3
Mary, d. David & Siverance, b. Feb. 15, 1720/1	LR2	350
Mary, d. David, d. Jan. 20*, 1721/2 *(Possibly "21")	LR2	343
Nathan, s. John [& Phebe], b. Mar. 5, 1756	LR7	1
Seth, s. Jeremiah & Hannah, b. May 30, 1740	LR6	3
Stanley, Rev. of New Milford, m. Elizabeth **FLAGG**, of East Hartford, Aug. 5, 1789	1	51
GUNN, Abell, s. Nathan & Hannah, b. Sept. 20, 1747	LR4	25
Abel, m. Martha **TYRALL**, July 18, 1771, by Rev. Nathaniell Taylor	LR11	17
Abner, s. Nathan & Abigail, b. July 5, 1783	LF13	5
Ann, d. Nathan & Hannah, b. Apr. 6, 1742	LR4	25
Anah, m. Calvin **CROSSMAN**, b. of New Milford, Oct. 9, 1831, by E. Huntington	1	246
Anne, m. Jacob **KENEY**, Jr., b. of New Milford, Jan. 3, 1764	LR7	3
Hannah, m. Isural **BALDWIN**, Oct. 9, 1751, by Rev. Nathaniell Taylor	LR6	13
Harriet, m. Cyrus **REYNOLDS**, Oct. 2, 1839, by E. Huntington	1	337
Henry, m. Eunice **GIFFORD**, Dec. 2, 1839, by E. Huntington	1	338
Jane, d. Nathan & Hannah, b. Jan. 4, 1749/50	LR4	25
John Nathan, s. Nathan & Abigail, b. Dec. 28, 1779	LR13	5
Nathan, m. Hannah **WELSH**, May 10, 1741, by Rev. Daniel Bordman	LR4	25
Nathan, s. Abel & Martha, b. Sept. 23, 1772	LR11	17
Nathan, m. Abigail **NORTHROP**, May 30, 1776, by [ ]	LR13	5
Rueben, s. Nathan & Hannah, b. Dec. 17, 1745	LR4	25
Ruth, d. Nathan & Hannah, b. Dec. 20, 1743	LR4	25
Susanna, wid. Abner, m. Nathaniel **TAYLOR**, Dec. 7, 1812	1	30
HAIGHT, HATE, [see also **HOYT**], Catharine E., of New Milford, m. D. **MERAMBLE**, of Naugatuck, Oct. 8, 1854, by Rev. David Murdock, Jr.	2	107
James H., m. Lydia **WANZER**, 5th month (May) 19th day, 1846, by William Wanzer, Clerk	2	16
HALEY, [see under **HAWLEY**]		
HALL, [see also **HULL**], David, of New Milford, m. Mehitebel **TICKNER**, of Sharon, Aug. 2, 1764	LR7	7
Laura, of New Milford, m. Allen **ABBET**, of Washington, Mar. 9, 1823, by Rev. Eleazar Beecher	1	46
Lois, m. Ebenezer **TERRIL**, Feb. 26, 1766, by Rev. Noah Wadhams, of New Preston	LR8	3

	Vol.	Page
HALL, (cont.)		
Lucinda, of New Milford, m. Benjamin **FRENCH**, of New Haven, July 2, 1832, by Rev. Nathan D. Benedict	1	246
Olive, m. Isaac **NORTHROP**, Apr. 11, 1825, by Rev. Benjamin Benham	1	190
Olive, m. Michael **WATERS**, Dec. 13, 1846, by E. Huntingon	2	25
HALLETT, Richard, a witness at wedding of Elnathan **BOTSFORD** & Dorothy **PRINDLE**, Quakers	LR4	14
Richard, a witness at wedding of John **FERRIS** & Abigal **TRYON**, Quakers	LR4	22
HALLOCK HALLOK, Adolphus, m. Laura **MORGAN**, Feb. 23, 1823, by Rev. Andrew Eliot	1	81
Albert B., of Litchfield, m. Cynthia **MAIN**, of New Milford, Oct. 26, 1853, by Rev. A. B. Pulling	2	90
Almira, m. Harry **COUCH**, May 14, 1848, by Rev. Eleazer Beecher	2	41
Almon, m. Harriet **BALDWIN**, b. of New Milford, Jan. 1, 1844, by John Greenwood	1	390
Amanda, d. William & Lucy, b. Nov. 8, 1798	1	8
Amanda, of New Milford, m. William **BENEDICK**, of Kent, Oct. 9, 1822, by Rev. Andrew Eliot	1	56
Amos, of Washington, Conn., m. Mary A. **SULLIVAN**, of New Milford, Jan. 31, 1849, by Rev. John Howard	2	48
Barbara, m. Almon **LANE**, b. of New Milford, Dec. 12, 1838, by Rev. Elijah Baldwin	1	320
Benjamin, m. Pheebe **PRINDLE**, Aug. 7, 1755	LR7	33
Benjamin, s. Benjamin & Phebe, b. Feb. 1, 1760	LR7	33
Benjamin, s. William & Lucy, b. Aug. 17, 1784	1	8
Benjamin, Jr., m. Hannah **EVERITT**, Jan. 12, 1805, by Elisha Bostwick, J. P.	1	103
Daniel, s. Benjamin & Phebee, b. Mar. 21, 1758	LR7	33
Electa, m. Jabez **CONKWRIGHT**, b. of New Milford, Mar. 23, 1840, by Rev. Elijah Baldwin	1	341
Elisa, d. Joseph, m. Jonas L. **CLARK**, b. of New Milford, June 28, 1838, by Rev. Elijah Baldwin	1	318
Elmer, of Kent, m. Betsey Ann **VIDETS**, of New Milford, June 2, 1830, by Rev. Fosdic Harrison, of Roxbury	1	226
Fanny, m. Martin **WRIGHT**, Mar. 14, 1824, by Daniel Gaylord	1	162
Homer, m. Caroline **HENDRIX**, Dec. 24, 1840, by Rev. Eleazer Beecher	1	351
Jane, m. David T. **WHITEHEAD**, Nov. 27, 1833, by Rev. Nathan D. Benedict	1	269
Jehiel, s. William & Lucy, b. Dec. 2, 1785	1	8
Laury A., m. Russel **STONE**, b. of New Milford, Apr. 8, 1835, by Daniel Baldwin	1	285
Lucy, d. William & Lucy, b. Nov. 14, 1787	1	8
Mirza Maria, of New Milford, m. Curtis Erastus **LAMSON**, of		

	Vol.	Page

HALLOCK, HALLOK, (cont.)
of New Preston, May 1, 1833, by Rev. Henry S. Atwater	1	261
Morgan, m. Alvira **BOOTH**, Oct. 21, 1852, by Rev. William McAlister	2	87
Moses G., m. Lorette **BALDWIN**, b. of New Milford, Sept. 6, 1832, by Rev. Nathaniel Benedict	1	251
Nelson, m. Julia Ann **BEEBE**, b. of New Milford, Apr. 16, 1827, by Rev. Benjamin Benham	1	213
Phebe, d. William & Lucy, b. Apr. 8, 1801	1	8
Phebe, of New Milford, m. Hervey **TERRILL**, of Kent, Feb. 20, 1825, by Daniel Gaylord, J. P.	1	121
Phebe, of New Milford, m. Hervey **TERRILL**, of Kent, Feb. 13, 1825, by Daniel Gaylord, J. P.	1	140
Polly, d. William & Lucy, b. Sept. 7, 1792	1	8
Rebecca A., of New Milford, m. Burtis **JUDD**, of Roxbury, Dec. 31, 1838, by Rev. Alonso F. Sellick	1	320
Russel, s. William & Lucy, b. Aug. 23, 1789	1	8
Ryle, s. William & Lucy, b. Oct. 13, 1794; d. Mar. 15, 1794* *(As written)	1	8
Sally Ann, m. William A. **SULIVAN**, Dec. 27, 1846, by E. Huntington	2	26
Sarah, d. William & Lucy, b. Dec. 8, 1802	1	8
William, s. Benj[ami]n & Phebe, b. Feb. 21, 1756	LR7	33
William, of New Milford, m. Lucy **CHURCH**, of Sharon, Nov. 29, 1781	1	8
William, s. William & Lucy, b. Jan. 8, 1783	1	8
William, Jr., m. Betsey **CANFIELD**, May 12, 1804, by Elisha Bostwick, J. P.	1	113

HAMBLIN, HAMLIN, [see also **HANDLIN & HAMILTON**],
Abagail, d. Ruth **SEELYE**, single woman, b. May 25, 1739	LR4	1
Abigail, m. Arthrew **KNOWLS**, Jan. 15, 1761	LR10	3
Fanny Amandy, m. John **BEACH**, June 3, 1845, by Gad S. Gilbert	1	401
Garry B., m. Frances A. **PALMER**, b. of New Milford, Jan. 2, 1854, by Rev. A. B. Pulling	2	92
Hannah, of Sharon, m. Samuel **PRINDLE**, of New Milford, June 8, 1768, by Rev. Nathaniell Taylor	LR11	16
Hannah Bostwick, d. Sarah, b. Oct. 22, 1768	LR10	2
Hopestil, m. Ephraim **PLATT**, June 30, 1773, by Rev. Nathaniell Taylor	LR12	16
Joel, s. Nathaniel, d. Sept. 21, 1755*, at Albany, a soldier under Capt. Benjamin Hinman *("Oct. 4, 1755" written and crossed out)	LR7	3
Lovice, had s. John Henry **WARNER**, b. Oct. 12, 1785	1	5
Luman B., m. Mary Ann **WELLER**, Nov. 7, 1821, by Rev. Fosdic Harrison, of Roxbury	1	100
Mary Ann, m. William **SPERRY**, May 26, 1822, by Rev. Benjamin Benham	1	33

	Vol.	Page
HAMBLIN, HAMLIN, (cont.)		
Sarah, had d. Hannah **BOSTWICK**, b. Oct. 22, 1768	LR10	2
HAMILTON, HAMLETON, [see also **HAMBLIN** & **HANDLIN**],		
Catharine, of New Milford, m. Charles F. **POTTER**, of Shelby, Orleans Co., N. Y., Apr. 17, 1844, by John Greenwood	1	395
Judith, m. Ezra **TERRILL**, Aug. 31, 1752, by Increas Mosley, J. P.	LR5	10
Sumner, of Banger, Me., m. Caroline **NOBLE**, of New Milford, June 23, 1841, by Noah Porter, Jr.	1	358
HANDLIN, [see also **HAMBLIN** & **HAMILTON**], Benjamin, m. Betsey P. **BAILEY**, b. of Sharon, June 23, 1839, by Rev. Elijah Baldwin	1	327
H[A]NFORD, Lydia A., m. Marquis D. **RANDAL**, b. of Bridgwater, Nov. 16, 1826, by Rev. Fosdic Harrison	1	211
HARD, [see also **HURD**], Abraham, s. Abraham & Charrity, b. July 7, 1766	LR10	3
Ann, m. Andrew **HAWLEY**, Jan. 2, 1757	LR7	20
Betty, d. Abraham & Charity, b. Apr. 29, 1762	LR10	3
Lisander, s. Abraham & Charity, b. Mar. 25, 1769	LR10	3
Lois, m. Nathan **CANFIELD**, Nov. 14, 1765, by Thomas Davies, Miss.	LR10	12
HARRISS, David, Corp., d. Sept. 4, 1760	LR7	2
HARTWELL, Barbara, of Washington, m. Samuel **BROWNSON**, of New Milford, Jan. 29, 1807, by Elisha Bostwick, J. P.	1	138
Elisabeth, of Staten, m. Roger **SHERMAN**, of New Milford, Nov. 17, 1749, by Rev. Samuell Dunbar, of Staten	LR6	7
Elisabeth, d. Joseph & Rebeckah, b. Apr. 24, 1763	LR7	31
Isaac, s. Joseph & Rebeckah, b. June 14, 1768	LR7	31
Joseph, m. Rebeckah **SHERMAN**, Apr. [ ], 1752	LR7	31
Joseph, s. Joseph & Rebekah, b. Mar. 7, 1766	LR7	31
Julia M., made affidavit Apr. 23, 1870, before Gould C. Whittlesey, Notary Public, that her maiden name was Julia M. **FRENCH**, m. Philo **BANKER**, Jan. 1, 1850, children: Nancy M. **BANKER**, b. Sept. 25, 1852, Betsey A. **BANKER**, b. Nov. 11, 1854, Lucinda S. **BANKER**, b. Apr. 10, 1859; hus. carriage, maker, d. May 6, 1865, ae 36	2	117
Mary, d. Joseph & Rebeckah, b. Sept. 30, 1752	LR7	31
Mary, m. Abel **BOTSFORD**, Aug. 7, 1769, by Bushnel Bostwick, J. P.	LR11	6
Rebeckah, d. Joseph & Rebeckah, b. Aug. 1, 1770	LR7	31
Ruth, d. Joseph & Rebeckah, b. Mar. 6, 1755	LR7	31
Ruth, m. Nathan **GAYLARD**, June 30, 1774, by Rev. Nathaniel Taylor	LR12	13
Samuel, s. Joseph & Rebeckah, b. Apr. 13, 1760	LR7	31
Sarah, d. Joseph & Rebeckah, b. June 14, 1757	LR7	31
Sarah, d. Joseph, m. Peter **GAYLARD**, s. Dea. Benjamin,		

	Vol.	Page
HARTWELL, (cont.)		
Feb. 20, 1778	1	17
HARVEY, [see under **HERVEY**]		
HATCH, Abigail S., of New Milford, m. John W. **JONES**, of Canaan, Sept. 26, 1837, by Rev. Alonzo F. Sellick	1	309
Henry W., m. Sarah M. **STEPHENS**, b. of New Milford, Aug. 10, 1835, by C. Shumway	1	271
John, of New Preston, m. Diana L. **CANFIELD**, of New Milford, Dec. 12, 1839, by E. Huntington	1	339
Phebe, of New Milford, m. David **BOTSFORD**, of Newtown, May 19, 1824, by Rev. Benjamin Benham	1	104
HAVILAND, HEVLEND, Alexander Y., witnessed marriage of Jehu **HOAG** & Phebe **WANZER**	1	250
Alexander Y., witnessed marriage of David **SANDS** & Paulina **LEACH**	1	277
Alexander Y., witnessed marriage of Gurdon **SWIFT** & Jane **WANZER**	1	288
Betsey, witnessed marriage of Jehu **HOAG** & Phebe **WANZER**	1	250
Betsey P., of New Milford, m. Robert **POST**, of Westbury, N. Y., 2nd month 22nd day, 1849, by William Wanzer, Clerk	2	52
Betsey P., witnessed marriage of Gurdon **SWIFT**, & Jane **WANZER**	1	288
Ebenezar N., witnessed marriage of Jehu **HOAG** & Phebe **WANZER**	1	250
Elizabeth, of New Milford, m. Ira **LEACH**, of Sherman, Nov. 12, 1829, by Rev. E. Huntington	1	232
Elizabeth, witnessed marriage of Enoch **CARPENTER** & Sophia **LANE**	1	184
Elizabeth, witnessed marriage of Jacob **WANZER** & Phebe **LEACH**	1	208
Isaac, Jr., witnessed marriage of Jehu **HOAG** & Phebe **WANZER**	1	250
Isaac, Jr., witnessed marriage of Gurdon **SWIFT**, & Jane **WANZER**	1	288
Isaac E., witnessed marriage of Enoch **CARPENTER** & Sophia **LANE**	1	184
Jane, of New Milford, m. Simeon **HINMAN**, of Oxford, May 29, 1831, by Eldad C. Jackson, J. P.	1	245
Jane, witnessed marriage of Ebenezer **WANZER**, Jr. & Lucy **LEACH**	1	181
Jane, witnessed marriage of Enoch **CARPENTER**, & Sophia **LANE**	1	184
John W., m. Mary Ann **FERRISS**, b. of New Milford, Aug. 29, 1831, by H. Rood	1	228
John W., witnessed marriage of Enoch **CARPENTER** & Sophia **LANE**	1	184

	Vol.	Page
HAVILAND, HEVLEND, (cont.)		
John W., witnessed marriage of Gurdon **SWIFT** & Jane **WANZER**	1	288
Joseph, witnessed marriage of Jehu **HOAG** & Phebe **WANZER**	1	250
Lewis, witnessed marriage of Jehu **HOAG** & Phebe **WANZER**	1	250
Lewis, witnessed marriage of Gurdon **SWIFT** & Jane **WANZER**	1	288
Loren, m. Susan Maria **ROBERTS**, b. of New Milford, Jan. 5, 1843, by Rev. Albert B. Camp, of Bridgewater	1	377
Mary Ann, witnessed marriage of Jehu **HOAG** & Phebe **WANZER**	1	250
Mary Ann, witnessed marriage of Gurdon **SWIFT** & Jane **WANZER**	1	288
Mercy, witnessed marriage of David **SANDS** & Paulina **LEACH**	1	277
Mercy, witnessed marriage of Gurdon **SWIFT** & Jane **WANZER**	1	288
Phebe, witnessed marriage of Ebenezer **WANZER**, Jr. & Lucy **LEACH**	1	181
Phebe, witnessed marriage of Enoch **CARPENTER** & Sophia **LANE**	1	184
Phebe, witnessed marriage of Jehu **HOAG** & Phebe **WANZER**	1	250
Sarah, witnessed marriage of David **SANDS** & Paulina **LEACH**	1	277
Sarah W., witnessed marriage of Gurdon **SWIFT** & Jane **WANZER**	1	288
Sarah W., witnessed marriage of Jehu **HOAG** & Phebe **WANZER**	1	250
HAWES, Edmund V., of Sherman, m. Mary E. **GREEN**, of New Milford, Sept. 8, 1846, by J. Greenwood	2	18
HAWKINS, HAUKINS, Abiel, s. Robert & Rachel, b. May 27, 1760	LR7	19
Damares, d. Zadock & Lydiah, d. Jan. 22, 1758	LR7	37
Damaras, d. Zadok & Lydia, b. July 29, 1766	LR7	37
Lydia, d. Zadok & Lydia, b. Dec. 26, 1762	LR7	37
Lydia, m. Reuben **MOGER**, Nov. 29, 1768	LR13	16
Peter, s. Zadock & Lydia, b. Jan. 24, 1761	LR7	37
Rebeckah, w. Robert, d. Aug. 25, 1756* *(1757?)	LR7	19
Reuben, s. Zadock & Lydia, b. Feb. 5, 1765	LR7	37
Robert, m. Rachel **BALDWIN**, b. of New Milford, Jan. 3. 1758	LR7	19
William Willmot, s. Zadok & Lydia, b. Nov. 16, 1757	LR7	37
Zadok, s. Zadok & Lydia, b. Oct. 6, 1759	LR7	37
HAWLEY, HAULEY, HALEY, HAWLYE, Abagal, w. Matthew, d. Oct. 30, 1738	LR4	20

104   BARBOUR COLLECTION

	Vol.	Page
HAWLEY, HAULEY, HALEY, HAWLYE, (cont.)		
Abagail, d. Matthew & Hannah, b. Feb. 3, 1743/4	LR4	20
Abijah, s. Jehiel & Sarah, b. Jan. 30, 1737/8	LR5	15
Abijah, s. Nathan & Keziah, b. Dec. 6, 1751	LR6	3
Abner, s. Nathan & Sarah, b. Mar. 22, 1766	LR7	19
Adoniram, s. Andrew & Ann, b. Aug. 28, 1763	LR7	20
Alonzo, m. Roccelania KINGSLEY, Jan. 24, 1827, by E. B. Kellogg	1	181
Amos, s. Ephraim & Ann, b. Oct. 26, 1739	LR4	26
Andrew, s. Jehiel & Sarah, b. June 22, 1732	LR5	15
Andrew, m. Ann HARD, Jan. 2, 1757	LR7	20
Ann, twin with Ephraim, d. Ephraim & Ann, b. Sept. 25, 1748	LR4	26
Annah, d. Jehiel & Sarah, b. Nov. 26, 1736	LR5	15
Anna, m. Phineas HURD, Jan. 2, 1757	LR10	2
Asahel, s. Mathew & Hannah, b. Oct. 28, 1748	LR4	5
Aurelia, of Huntington, m. Edmond BOSTWICK, of New Milford, June 4, 1804	1	166
Benjamin, twin with Nathan, s. Nathan & Keziah, b. July 31, 1743	LR4	10
Curtis, s. Jehiel & Sarah, b. Apr. 24, 1747	LR5	15
Daniel, s. Matthew & Hannah, b. Sept. 4, 1741	LR4	20
Dorothy, d. Thomas & Dorothy, of Roxbury, Mass., m. John BOOTH, s. Richard, of Stratford, June 14, 1678	2	111
Eli, s. Andrew & Ann, b. Nov. 20, 1757	LR7	20
Elijah, of Trumbull, m. Harriet HONYE, of Bridgwater, Nov. 16, 1826, by Rev. Fosdic Harrison, of Roxbury	1	211
Ephraim, Jr., of New Milford, m. Ann CHAPMAN, of Parish of Unity, in Stratford, June 12, 1739, by Rev. Richardson Miner, of Unity	LR4	26
Ephraim, twin with Ann, s. Epraim & Ann, b. Sept. 25, 1748	LR4	26
Eunis, d. Nathan & Keziah, b. Jan. 12, 1739/40	LR4	10
Hezekiah, of New Milford, m. Sarah PHELPS, of Harwinton, Feb. 7, 1750/1, by Rev. Andrew Bartholomew, of Harrington	LR7	1
Ira, s. Nathan & Kaziah, b. Aug. 10, 1745	LR4	10
Ira, of New Milford, m. Abigail HITCHCOCK, of Kent, Nov. 27, 1765, by Cyrus Marsh, J. P.	LR7	38
Jubez*, s. Nathan & Keziah, b. Aug. 29, 1749 *(Jabez)	LR6	3
Jehial, s. Ephraim, b. Feb. 14, 1712/13	LR5	15
Jehiel, m. Sarah [ ], Mar. 30, 1731	LR5	15
Jehiel, s. Jehiel & Sarah, b. Sept. 16, 1744	LR5	15
Jehiel, s. Andrew & Anna, b. May 31, 1765	LR7	20
Jephtha, s. Jehiel & Sarah, b. Sept. 22, 1740	LR5	15
Jeptha, of New Milford, m. Easter CASTLE, of Woodbury, Dec. 26, 1762	LR7	23
Joseph, s. David & Ruth, b. July 13, 1750	LR6	10
Joseph, of Bridgeport, m. Caroline BENHAM, of New Milford, May 7, 1826, by Rev. Benjamin Benham	1	203

	Vol.	Page
HAWLEY, HAULEY, HALEY, HAWLYE, (cont.)		
Joseph Chrysostoni, s. Hezekiah & Sarah, b. Oct. 10, 1757	LR7	1
Keiziah, d. Nathan & Keiziah, b. Dec. 19, 1736	LR4	10
Martha, m. William NICHOLS, May 20, 1775	1	32
Martin, s. Jeptha & Easter, b. Feb. 20, 1764	LR7	23
Mary, d. Jehiel & Sarah, b. Mar. 24, 1739	LR5	15
Mary, d. Hezekiah & Sarah, b. Oct. 22, 1751; d. Nov. 27, 1751	LR7	1
Matthew, s. Ephraim, m. Abagal NOBLE, d. Capt. Stephen, Dec. 21, 1737	LR4	20
Matthew, m. Hannah BUCK, Dec. 3, 1740, by Rev. Daniel Bordman	LR4	20
Nathan, m. Caziah BUNEL, Nov. 8, 1733, by John Bostwick, J. P.	LR4	10
Nathan, twin with Benjamin, s. Nathan & Keziah, b. July 31, 1743	LR4	10
Nathan, Jr., m. Sarah KENT, May 1, 1765	LR7	19
Nirom, m. Larania GILBERT, Dec. 31, 1823, by Rev. Benjamin Benham	1	166
Patience, d. Nathan & Kaziah, b. July 26, 1741	LR4	10
Patience, m. James MURRY, b. of New Milford, Nov. 5, 1755	LR7	3
Peter, s. Ephraim, Jr. & Ann, b. Feb. 14, 1740/1	LR4	26
Phebie, d. Jehiel & Sarah, b. July 1, 1734* *("Nov. 2"crossed out)	LR5	15
Phebe, m. John TREAT, Nov. 23, 1749	LR7	8
Phebe, d. David & Ruth, b. May 12, 1752	LR6	10
Philo, s. Andrew & Ann, b. July 3, 1759	LR7	20
Ruth, d. Jehiel & Sarah, b. Aug. 19, 1742	LR5	15
Samuel, s. Hezekiah & Sarah, b. Oct. 18, 1752	LR7	1
Sarah, w. Jehiel, b. Aug. 14, 1713	LR5	15
Sarah, d. Hezekiah & Sarah, b. May 28, 1754	LR7	1
Sarah, of Newtown, m. Stephen MOREHOUSE, Jr., of New Milford, Apr. 8, 1759	LR7	34
Stephen, s. Hezekiah & Sarah, b. Jan. 30, 1756	LR7	1
Zadock, s. Andrew & Ann, b. June 15, 1761	LR7	20
HAWNHURSTE, Sarah C., witnessed marriage of Gurdon SWIFT & Jane WANZER	1	288
HAYES, Isaac, of Unadilla Otsego Co., N. Y., m. Minerva McMAHON, of New Milford, Sept. 26, 1831, by H. Rood	1	169
Samuel, m. Patty WARNER, b. of New Milford, Jan. 31, 1847, by Rev. Samuel Weeks	2	40
HEACOCK, Philo N., m. Olive STILSON, Sept. 2, 1822, by Rev. Andrew Eliot	1	76
Philo N., d. Apr. 20, 1825, ae 41 y.	1	76
HEINZE, Charles, journeyman turner, s. Joseph, decd., master turner, m. wid. Anna Maria Theresa ZEIDLER, b. a. Kuschmann, Oct. 17, 1858, (Evangelical Pastorate)	2	118
HENDRIX, HENDRYX, Caroline, m. Homer HALLOCK, Dec.		

	Vol.	Page
HENDRIX, HENDRYX, (cont.)		
24, 1840, by Rev. Eleazer Beecher	1	351
Eleazar, m. Martha **STONE**, Oct. 2, 1782	LR13	8
Julia, m. George N. **MALLORY**, Apr. 1, 1829, by Rev. Eleazar Beecher	1	215
Laura, m. John **PAYNE**, b. of New Milford, Jan. 7, 1841, by Nathan Rice	1	356
Sarah, m. James **LAKE**, Jr., Jan. 23, 1760	LR7	37
Sarah, d. Eleazar & Martha, b. Sept. 14, 1783	LR13	8
HENSEL, Maria Dorothea, d. John **GOBBLOT**, of Augustwalde, b. Oct. 17, 1835; m. John William **BRASCHING**, journeyman carpenter, s. John **CHRISTIAN**, of Eichberg, Sept. 4, 1853, by Rev. Graefe. Recorded in Marbledale, Litchfield Co., Conn., July 14, 1866, at request of Mrs. Maria Brasching	2	115
HEPBURN, James, of Milford, m. Emma **BOOTH**, of New Milford, Jan. 24, 1827, by Rev. Benjamin Benham	1	93
Joseph, m. Harriet **RANDAL**, b. of New Milford, Bridgewater Soc., Jan. 16, 1822, by Rev. Fosdic Harrison, of Roxbury	1	18
HERROW, HERRO, Elisabeth, m. James **MOGER**, May 23, 1744, by Nathaniel Bostwick, J. P.	LR5	11
Rebeckah, see Rebeckah **STEBBINS**	LR4	6
HERVEY, HARVEY, HARVY, Ann, d. Joel & Sarah, b. Sept. 4, 1740	LR4	25
Joel, of New Milford, m. Sarah **THACHER**, of Lebanon, Dec. 13, 1737	LR4	25
Mary, d. Joel & Sarah, b. Jan. 26, 1738/9	LR4	25
Mary, Mrs. of Sharon, m. Rev. Thomas **DAVIES**, of New Milford, Apr. 1, 1762	LR7	32
Patience, d. Joel & Sarah, b. May 2, 1742	LR4	25
HICKIX, [see also **HITCHCOCK**], Bryan, of Washington, m. Susan **BISHOP**, of New Milford, Nov. 23, 1826, by Rev. Andrew Eliot	1	204
HICKS, Sally, m. Amos **BALDWIN**, Feb. 24, 1789	1	58
HIDDEN, Hiram, of Neward, N. J., m. Elisebeth M. **ROOD**, of New Milford, Oct. 10, 1841, by Rev. Z. Davenport	1	361
HIGBY, John, Elder, of Granville, Mass., m. Matty **BALDWIN**, of New Milford, Apr. 22, 1838, by Rev. Elijah Baldwin	1	317
HIGGINS, Anne, m. Nathan **PEET**, Jr., b. of New Milford, Apr. 7, 1804, by Elisha Bostwick, J. P.	1	111
Betsey, m. David **WILLIAMS**, b. of New Milford, Dec. 17, 1826, by Grove S. Brownell	1	210
HIGLEY, Hiram, m. Minty M. **BEACH**, of Bridgwater, Sept. 25, 1830, by Rev. Fosdic Harrison, of Roxbury	1	227
HILL, Albert S., m. Elizabeth T. **WELLS**, b. of New Milford, Nov. 16, 1845, by E. Huntington	2	5
Amy, d. [Ebenezar & Philothete], b. Jan. 30, 1803	1	232
Amy, of New Milford, m. William T. **BOSTWICK**, of		

	Vol.	Page
HILL, (cont.)		
Sherman, Dec. 26, 1822, by Rev. Benjamin Benham	1	67
Amy Maria, d. Solomon & Amy, b. July 5, 1809	1	67
Anna, d. Jonathan & Mary, b. Feb. 12, 1789	1	151
Catharine, m. Daniel **SULLIVAN**, Aug. 17, 1823, by Rev. Benjamin Benham	1	97
Ebenezar, s. Silas & Sarah, b. Dec. 15, 1778, in the New Milford; m. Philothete **LESSEY**, d. John F. & Anna, of New Fairfield, Nov. 27, 1800	1	232
Eliza Ann, 2nd d. [Ebenezar & Philothete], b. June 8, 1806	1	232
Eliza Ann, m. Henry S. **WARNER**, b. of New Milford, Jan. 7, 1829, by Rev. John Lovejoy	1	227
Elizabeth, of Fairfield, m. John **McEUEN**, of New Milford, Apr. 30, 1754	LR7	13
Elizabeth, m. John **McEUNE**, Apr. 29, [ ]	LR11	1
Ephraim, m. Charlotte **PRINCE**, Apr. 7, 1803, by Elisha Bostwick J. P.	1	104
Garner, see under Gomer **HILL**		
George J., s. Ephraim & Charlotte, b. Aug. 21, 1805	1	104
Gomer*, s. Solomon & Amey, b. Aug. 13, 1796; d. May 11, 1819 *("Garner, b. Aug. 3" in Orcutt's Hist.)	1	67
Jane Charlotte, d. Ephraim & Charlotte, b. Aug. 18, 1807	1	104
Jonathan, of New Milford, m. Martha **BROWNSON**, of Waterbury, Dec. 31, 1746, by Roger Brownson	LR5	4
Jonathan, b. Apr. 8, 1755; m. Mary **COADY**, May 25, 1782	1	151
Jonathan, m. Mary **COADY**, May 25, 1782	1	151
Joysee*, d. Solomon & Amey, b. June 25, 1791 *(Joyce)	1	67
Julia Maria, m. Marshall **MARSH**, Nov. 20, 1844, by E. Huntington	2	2
Laura, m. George **McMAHON**, Nov. 12, 1839, by E. Huntington	1	337
Laura Caroline, [d. Silas & Polly], b. June 1, 1822	1	290
Laura M., of New Milford, m. Daniel B. **CAMP**, of Kent, Jan. 14, 1852, by Rev. James L. Scott, of New Preston	2	75
Love Mariah, d. Jonathan & Mary, b. Mar. 5, 1792	1	151
Lucius M., m. Mary W. **SHERWOOD**, b. of New Milford, Feb. 14, 1849, by Rev. William Henry Rees	2	54
Maria, 3rd d. [Ebenezar & Philothete], b. Dec. 22, 1809	1	232
Maria, m. Ormond **MARSH**, Apr. 5, 1832, by E. Huntington	1	255
Meria T., m. Orrin B. **MARSH**, b. of New Milford, Oct. 14, 1829, by Rev. John Lovejoy *(Maria)	1	234
Marshall Gomer, [s. Silas & Polly], b. Mar. 11, 1820	1	290
Martial*, m. Serena **PLATT**, Dec. 21, 1842, by E. Huntington *(Marshall)	1	382
Mary Eliza, d. Jonathan & Mary, b. Aug. 29, 1799	1	151
Merieha*, d. Jonathan & Mary, b. June 9, 1796 *("Mericha" in Orcutt's Hist.)	1	151
Merwin, m. Cornelia **MARSH**, b. of New Milford, Sept. 18,		

BARBOUR COLLECTION

	Vol.	Page
HILL, (cont.)		
1845, by E. Huntington	2	4
Merwin Platt, [s. Silas & Polly], b. Nov. 28, 1817	1	290
Noah Ingersoll, s. Solomon & Amey, b. Dec. 16, 1785	1	67
Rachel, d. Jonathan & Mary, b. May 19, 1794	1	151
Sally, d. Solomon & Amey, b. Dec. 8, 1787	1	67
Samuel, s. Jonathan & Mary, b. Mar. 22, 1783	1	151
Sarah, d. Silas & Sarah, b. Nov. 16, 1761	LR7	22
Sarah, d. Jonathan & Mary, b. June 30, 1785	1	151
Sarah, w. Silas, d. Apr. 3, 1792	LR7	22
Sarah Ann, 4th d. [Ebenezar & Philothete], b. Mar. 12, 1813	1	232
Sarah Jane, of New Milford, m. Andrew **CLARK**, of Trumbull, June 17, 1849, by Rev. William Henry Rees	2	55
Silas, s. Solomon & Amey, b. Apr. 16, 1789	1	67
Silas, d. Oct. 1, 1798	LR7	22
Silas, m. Polly **PLATT**, Feb. 28, 1813	1	290
Silas Bryon, [s. Silas & Polly], b. Aug. 21, 1834	1	290
Solomon, m. Amy **STONE**, Jan. 16, 1783	1	67
Solomon, s. Solomon & Amey, b. Feb. 8, 1784	1	67
Solomon, Jr., m. Hannah **TUTTLE**, July 26, 1807, by Elisha Bostwick, J. P.	1	142
Solomon Baldwin, m. Rebecca **BROWN**, b. of New Milford, Oct. 17, 1832, by Rev. Henry S. Atwater	1	253
Susan, [d. Silas & Polly], b. Dec. 1, 1814	1	290
William Prince, s. Ephraim & Charlotte, b. Feb. 28, 1804	1	104
HINE, [see also **HYNIES**], Abell, s. Jeams & Margaret, b. Mar. 4, 1730/1* *("Aug. 16, 1731" crossed out)	LR2	348
Abel, of New Milford, m. Rebekah **BEEBE**, of Litchfield, July 7, 1763	LR7	36
Abel, s. Noble & Patience, b. Jan. 30, 1779	LR11	10
Abel, d. May 9, 1820, in the 89th y of his age	LR7	36
Alfred, s. Abel & Rebekah, b. June 25, 1765	LR7	36
Almira, m. Franklin **BENNITT**, b. of New Milford, Nov. 24, 1853, by Rev. David Murdock, Jr.	2	100
Anan, s. Stephen & Naomi, b. Feb. 4, 1789	1	87
Ann, d. Jeams & Margaret, b. Mar. 14, 1728/9	LR2	348
Ann, m. Isarall **CAMP**, b. of New Milford, Jan. 13, 1747/8, by Samuell Camfield, J. P.	LR4	19
Beebe, s. Abel & Rebeckah, b. Jan. 27, 1770	LR7	36
Betsey N., m. Henry N. **MERWIN**, b. of New Milford, Nov. 27, 1845, by J. Greenwood	2	7
B[e]ulah, of New Milford, m. Orin Mallery **ARMSTRONG**, of Washington, May 22, 1805, by Elisha Bostwick, J. P.	1	121
B[e]ula Moulton, d. Noble & Patience, b. June 11, 1783	LR11	10
Bildad, s. Noble & Patience, b. Mar. 18, 1774	LR11	10
Charles B., m. Mary **LOCKWOOD**, b. of New Milford, Jan. 15, 1834, by E. Huntington	1	274
Charlotte, of New Milford, m. Oliver C. **STANLEY**, of		

	Vol.	Page
HINE, (cont.)		
Berlin, Conn., Oct. 13, 1847, by John Greenwood	2	31
Clark, s. Stephen & Naomi, b. Nov. 23, 1783	1	87
Clark, m. Mary E. **WELLS**, Jan. 1, 1846, by E. Huntington	2	11
Daniel, of New Milford, m. Mary **BROWNSON**, d. Isaac, of Waterbury, Nov. 23, 1737	LR4	21
Daniel, claims on Dec. 30, 1737, was 30 y. of age	LR4	21
Daniel, s. Daniel & Mary, b. Feb. 18, 1748/9	LR4	21
Daniel, m. Lydia **BEACHER**, Mar. 18, 1769, by Paul Welch	1	18
Daniel, s. Daniel & Lydia, b. Dec. 18, 1780	1	18
Fanny, d. Noble & Patience, b. Oct. 15, 1790	LR11	10
Fanny, of New Milford, m. Constantine **McMAHON**, of Washington, Nov. 28, 1822, by Rev. Andrew Eliot	1	38
Homer, s. Noble & Patience, b. July 25, 1776	LR11	10
Isaac, s. Stephen & Naomi, b. June 23, 1791	LR1	87
Isaac, m. Emila Melissa **BUEL**, b. of New Milford, Feb. 15, 1829, by Rev. Andrew Eliot	1	229
Jeams, m. Margaret **NOBLE**, Dec. 23, 1726 (b. of New Milford)	LR2	348
Jay Stilson, m. Arabella **BROWN**, b. of New Milford, Mar. 27, 1832, by Rev. Hervey S. Atwater	1	249
John M., m. Eliza A. **BEARDSLEY**, b. of New Milford, Aug. 14, 1850, by Rev. William McAlister	2	63
L. Julia, of New Milford, m. Henry **WALTER**, of New York City, Mar. 14, 1843, by John Greenwood	1	384
Laura, m. John Buckley **MARSH**, b. of New Milford, Oct. 19, 1823, by Rev. Andrew Eliot	1	185
Laura M., m. Charles W. **JACKSON**, b. of New Milford, Aug. 27, 1851, by Rev. David Murdock, Jr.	2	71
Lucy, d. Daniel & Lydia, b. Apr. 10, 1778	1	18
Lydia, d. Daniel & Lydia, b. Jan. 3, 1775	1	18
Lyman, s. Stephen & Naomi, b. Jan. 28, 1793	1	87
Maben*, d. James & Margret, b. Dec. 7, 1740 *("Mabel" in Orcutt's Hist.)	LR4	13
Mabel, m. John **BROWNSON**, Aug. 29, 1765	LR10	1
Mabel, d. Noble & Patience, b. Nov. 11, 1769	LR11	10
Mary, d. Daniel & Mary, b. July 9*, 1742 *(Possibly "7th")	LR4	21
Mary, d. Daniel & Lydia, b. Dec. 19, 1769	1	18
Mary, m. Henry S. **MYGATT**, b. of New Milford, Sept. 17, 1839, by N. Porter	1	330
Mary E., of New Milford, m. Robert **FREEMAN**, of Hartford, Sept. 11, 1854, by Rev. David Murdock, Jr.	2	106
Mahittabel, d. Daniel & Mary, b. Aug. 6, 1739	LR4	21
Naomi, w. Stephen, d. Oct. 5, 1818	1	87
Noble, s. Jeams & Margaret, b. Sept. 26, 1727	LR2	348
Noble, s. Jeams & Margaret, d. Mar. 29, 1730/1	LR2	348
Noble, s. James & Margrit, b. Aug. 12, 1744	LR4	13
Noble, m. Patience **HUBBEL**, Feb. 2, 1768	LR11	10

110   BARBOUR COLLECTION

	Vol.	Page
HINE, (cont.)		
Noble, Capt., d. Oct. 15, 1796	LR11	10
Patience, [w. Noble], d. Mar. 5, 1829	LR11	10
Polly, d. Noble & Patience, b. Sept. 19, 1785	LR11	10
Rachel, d. James & Margrit, b. [ ] 12, 1733/4	LR4	13
Sarah, d. Daniel & Mary, b. July 14, 1745	LR4	21
Sarah, d. Daniel & Lydia, b. Apr. 26, 1772	1	18
Sophia, d. Noble & Patience, b. Dec. 2, 1787	LR11	10
Stephen, b. Jan. 13, 1754	1	87
Stephen, of New Milford, m. Naomi **PECK**, of Woodbridge, June 19, 1782	1	87
Stephen, m. Anna **STILSON**, [ ]	1	87
Thalia, d. Abel & Rebeckah, b. Oct. 29, 1766	LR7	36
Thalia, d. Noble & Patience, b. Aug. 12, 1781	LR11	10
Thalia, m. Harry **BUCKINGHAM**, b. of New Milford, Mar. 11, 1840, by Noah Porter	1	343
Urania, d. Noble & Patience, b. Feb. 11, 1772	LR11	10
Urania, of New Milford, m. Capt. Deliverance **PAINTER**, of Roxbury, Jan. 13, 1802, by Elisha Bostwick, J. P.	1	69
William, s. Stephen & Naomi, b. Nov. 4, 1785	1	87
William, m. Phebe Abigail **MERWIN**, b. of New Milford, Dec. 9, 1804, by Elisha Bostwick, J. P.	1	114
HINKLEY, Amos, of Kent, m. Viola V. **LATHROP**, of New Milford, July 9, 1854, by J. W. Hoffman	2	109
HINMAN, Phebe, witnessed marriage of Ebenezer **WANZER**, Jr. & Lucy **LEACH**	1	181
Robinson S., witnessed marriage of Ebenezer **WANZER**. Jr. & Lucy **LEACH**	1	181
Simeon, of Oxford, m. Jane **HAVILAND**, of New Milford, May 29, 1831, by Eldad C. Jackson, J. P.	1	245
Weller, of New Milford, m. Ruth **STONE**, of Bridgwater, Jan. 23, 1827, by Rev. Andrew Eliot	1	115
HITCHCOCK, HICHCOCK, [see also **HICKIX**], Aaron, s. Jonathan & Meriam, b. Nov. 25, 1743	LR4	10
Aaron, m. Elisabeth **TROBRIDGE**, Mar. 31, 1763	LR7	31
Aaron, s. Aaron & Elizabeth, b. July 8, 1773	LR7	31
Abagail, d. John & Sarah, b. Oct. 29, 1747	LR4	17
Abigail, d. David & Abigail, b. July 5, 1763	LR7	27
Abigail, of Kent, m. Ira **HAWLEY**, of New Milford, Nov. 27, 1765, by Cyrus Marsh, J. P.	LR7	38
Abner, s. Samuel & Dabora, b. Jan. 2, 1742/3	LR4	18
Almera, d. Isaac & Anna, b. Sept. 18, 1765* *(Date crossed out)	LR7	6
Amarillia, d. Ira & Hannah, b. Dec. 29, 1788	1	24
Annis, d. David & Abigail, b. July 15, 1769	LR7	27
Asael, s. John & Sarah, b. Sept. 16, 1740	LR4	17
Barzillia Dean, s. Isaac & Anna, b. Oct. 29, 1769	LR7	6
Betty, d. Aaron & Elisabeth, b. Mar. 21, 1764	LR7	31

	Vol.	Page
HITCHCOCK, HICHCOCK, (cont.)		
Betty, d. Aaron & Elizabeth, b. Nov. 27, 1765	LR7	31
Betty, d. Daniel & Comfort, b. Nov. 24, 1775	LR12	7
Caleb, s. Samuel & Dabora, b. Mar. 8, 1734/5	LR2	342
Caleb, s. Samuel & Daborah, d. Aug. 29, 1736	LR4	18
Caleb, s. Samuel & Debora, b. Feb. 26, 1736/7	LR4	18
Comfort, w. Daniel, d. Nov. 2, 1776	LR12	7
Comfort, d. Daniel & Deborah, b. Sept. 24, 1779	LR12	7
Dan, s. Samuell & Deborah, b. Aug. 24, 1751; d. Apr. 9, 1753	LR4	18
Daniel, s. Jonathan & Meriam, b. May 22, 1739	LR4	10
Daniel, s. Jonathan & Meriam, d. Sept. 16, 1751	LR4	10
Daniel, s. Jonathan & Meriam, b. Dec. 31, 1751	LR4	10
Daniel, m. Comford **PORTER**, Nov. 3, 1773, by Rev. Nathaniell Taylor	LR12	7
Daniel, s. Deborah **KETCHAM**, Mar. 12, 1777, by Bushnel Bostwick	LR12	7
David, s. Jonathan & Miriam, b. Nov. 3, 1731	LR2	341
David, m. Abigail **TROBRIGE**, Sept. 11, 1759	LR7	27
David, s. David & Abigail, b. Sept. 1, 1771	LR7	27
Deborah, d. Sam[ue]ll & Sarah, b. Oct. 4, 1710	LR2	354
Deborah, d. Sam[ue]ll & Deborah, b. Feb. 4, 1732/3	LR2	342
Debora, d. Samuel, decd. & Sarah, m. Beniamin **SEELYE**, s. John & Martha, b. Apr. 11, 1735	LR4	16
Ebenezer, s. Samuel & Daborah, b. Jan. 10*, 1746/7; d. Sept. 3, 1747 *(Possibly "16th")	LR4	18
Ebenezer, s. Samuell & Debarah, b. Agu. 6, 1748	LR4	18
Ebenezer, s. Nathan & Rebeckah, b. Feb. 9, 1777	LR11	7
Ebenezar, s. Ira & Hannah, b. Nov. 23, 1786	1	24
Elisabeth, d. Samuel & Daborah, b. June 18, 1755	LR4	18
Elizabeth, d. Nathan & Rebecah, b. June 6, 1793	LR11	7
Elizabeth M., of New Milford, m. John H. **NETTLETON**, of Watertown, June 13, 1837, by N. Porter, Jr.	1	305
Esther, d. Sam[ue]ll & Sarah, b. July 11, 1705	LR2	354
Esther, m. Nathaniel **BOSTWICK**, Oct. 7, 1727	LR2	342
Esther, d. Samuel & Dabora, b. Mar. 5, 1738/9	LR4	18
[E]unice, d. John & Sarah, b. Apr. 12, 1743	LR4	17
Eunice, m. William **GAYLARD**, b. of New Milford, Mar. 20, 1766, by Samuel Bostwick, J. P.	LR7	6
Eunice, m. William **GAYLARD**, Mar. 20, 1766	LR7	9
Ezra, s. Nathan & Rebeckah, b. Mar. 16, 1773	LR11	7
George, of Woodbury, m. Jane **FORD**, of New Milford, Apr. 22, 1835, by H. Rood	1	287
Hannah, d. Sam[ue]ll & Sarah, b. Jan. 1, 1718/19	LR2	354
Hannah, m. Daniel **BOSTWICK**, b. of New Milford, Dec. 14, 1736, by John Bostwick, J. P.	LR4	19
Hanah, d. Jonathan & Meriam, b. June 24, 1737	LR4	10
Hannah, d. Nathan & Rebecah, b. May 23, 1791	LR11	7
Hulda, d. Jonathan & Meriam, b. Dec. 30, 1745/6; d. June 14,		

HITCHCOCK, HICHCOCK, (cont.)

	Vol.	Page
1746	LR4	10
Hulda, d. David & Abigail, b. Oct. 4, 1765	LR7	27
Ira, m. Hannah **HOTCHKISS**, Oct. 27, 1785	1	24
Isaac, s. John & Sarah, b. Feb. 26, 1736/7	LR4	17
Isaac, of New Milford, m. Lidia Mary Anne **DEAN**, of Stratford, Dec. 16, 1764	LR7	6
John, s. Sam[ue]ll & Sarah, b. Sept. 28, 1716	LR2	354
John, m. Sarah **BARNUM**, May 27, 1736, by Rev. Daniel Bordman	LR4	17
John, s. John & Sarah, b. May 17, 1753	LR4	17
John, of New Milford, m. Sybbel **SHERWOOD**, of Woodbury, Dec. 20, 1754*, by [ ] *(First written "1755")	LR4	17
John, of New Milford, m. Sibble **SHERWOOD**, of Woodbury, Dec. 20, 1754, by [ ]	LR7	1
John, Capt., m. Mrs. Rebeckah **BUEL**, of Kent, May 21, 1760, by [ ]	LR4	17
Jonathan, s. Samuell & Sarah, b. Apr. 25, 1701	LR2	354
Jonathan, m. Mary **BROWNSON**, b. of New Milford, Oct. 10, 1726	LR2	341
Jonathan, s. Jonathan & Mary, b. Oct. 16, 1727	LR2	341
Jonathan, m. Miriam **MALLERY**, b. of New Milford, Oct. 16, 1728	LR2	341
Jonathan, Jr., m. Christian **WARNER**, Nov. 16, 1757	LR7	28
Jonathan, s. Jonathan, Jr. & Christian, b. Aug. 25, 1770	LR7	28
Joseph, s. Nathan & Rebeckah, b. Jan. 10, 1781	LR11	7
Julius, s. Daniel & Deborah, b. Dec. 20, 1777	LR12	7
Lowis, d. Jonathan & Meriam, b. July 5, 1741	LR4	10
Lois, m. Solomon **PALMER**, Jr., May 15, 1758	LR7	31
Luke, s. Samuel & Daborah, b. Dec. 27, 1744	LR4	18
Mary, w. Jonathan, d. Oct. 24, 1727	LR2	341
Mary, d. Jonathan & Meriam, b. Aug. 24, 1733	LR4	10
Mary, m. Benjamin **EASTMAN**, June 16, 1756, by Solomon Palmer	LR7	6
Mary, d. Jonathan, Jr. & Christian, b. Nov. 12, 1766	LR7	28
Mary, d. Nathan & Rebeckah, b. Jan. 28, 1783	LR11	7
Mary, m. Leman **GARLICK**, b. of New Milford, Sept. 5, 1799, by Elisha Bostwick, J. P.	1	19
Meriam, d. Nathan & Rebeckah, b. Mar. 23, 1775	LR11	7
Miriam, d. Jonathan & Mirriam, b. July 26, 1729	LR2	341
Nathan, s. Jonathan & Meriam, b. Aug. 11, 1747	LR4	10
Nathan, m. Rebeckah **KEELER**, Aug. 21, 1769, by Rev. Mr. Brooks, of Newberry Parish	LR11	7
Nathan, s. Nathan & Rebeckah, b. Mar. 20, 1779	LR11	7
Nathan, Jr., m. Elizabeth **GREGORY**, b. of New Milford, Jan. 8, 1801, by Elisha Bostwick, J. P.	1	85
Philo, s. Nathan & Rebecah, b. June 8, 1787	LR11	7

	Vol.	Page
HITCHCOCK, HICHCOCK, (cont.)		
Polly, d. Aaron & Elizabeth, b. Jan. 17, 1768	LR7	31
Rebeckah, d. Samuel & Rebekah, b. Nov. 15, 1727	LR2	342
Rebeckah, w. Samuel, d. Dec. 5, 1727	LR2	342
Rebeckah, d. Sam[uel]ll, d. Dec. 24, 1727	LR2	342
Rebeckah, d. Nathan & Rebeckah, b. Sept. 27, 1771	LR11	7
Reuben, s. Nathan & Rebecah, b. Sept. 9, 1785	LR11	7
Reuben, m. Anna **GARLICK**, Nov. 7, 1807, by Elisha Bostwick, J. P.	1	153
Ruth, d. Samuel & Dabora, b. Feb. 2, 1740/1	LR4	18
Sally, d. Ira & Hannah, b. Apr. 22, 1791	1	24
Samuel, s. Samuel & Sarah, b. Sept. 17, 1699	LR2	354
Samuel, m. Rebeckah **BROWNSON**, Oct. 10, 1726	LR2	342
Samuel, Sr., d. Dec. 9, 1727	LR2	342
Samuel, Sr., d. Dec. 9, 1727	LR2	354
Sam[ue]ll, m. Deborah **MALLERY**, b. of New Milford, Apr. 23, 1730	LR2	342
Samuel, s. Samuel & Deborah, b. Feb. 28, 1730/1	LR2	342
Sarah, d. Sam[ue]ll & Sarah, b. Feb. 5, 1702/3	LR2	354
Sarah, m. Thomas **BROWNSON**, b. of New Milford, Nov. 5, 1725	LR2	346
Sarai, d. Jonathan & Meriam, b. July 30*, 1735 *("12" crossed out)	LR4	10
Sarah, w. John, d. May 10, 1754	LR4	17
Sarah, m. Abel **BOSWICK**, b. of New Milford, Jan. 28, 1756	LR7	11
Sarah, d. Capt. John & Rebecka, b. Feb. 22, 1761	LR4	17
Sarah, wid. Samuel, d. Apr. 13, 1761, ae 83 y.	LR2	342
Sarah, d. Aaron & Elizabeth, b. Nov. 15, 1770	LR7	31
Spencer, s. Nathan & Rebeckah, b. Oct. 2, 1795	LR11	7
Stephen, s. Nathan & Rebecah, b. June 21, 1789	LR11	7
Sybel, w. John, d. July 12, 1759	LR4	17
William, s. David & Abigail, b. Oct. 1, 1760	LR7	27
Zina, s. John & Sybbel, b. Nov. 6, 1755	LR4	17
HOAG, Abraham, of New York, m. Phebe Joan **FERRISS**, of New Milford, May 8, 1831, by E. Huntington	1	246
David D., of South Dover, m. Eliza O. **GARDERNER**, of Beekman, Dutchess Co., N. Y., Sept. 11, 1844, at the house of Mrs. Jane Gardener, Green Haven, by Rev. Thomas Sparkes	2	115
Henry P., witnessed marriage of Jehu **HOAG**, & Phebe **WANZER**	1	250
Jehu, of Washington, Cty. of Dutchess, N. Y., s. Phillip & Phebe, m. Phebe **WANZER**, d. Moses and Sarah, of New Fairfild, 5th month 22nd day, 1832, before 38 witnesses. Int. Pub. at Oblong & New Milford	1	250
John, witnessed marriage of Gurdon **SWIFT** & Jane **WANZER**	1	288
Phebe W., witnessed marriage of Gurdon **SWIFT** & Jane		

BARBOUR COLLECTION

	Vol.	Page
HOAG, (cont.)		
WANZER	1	288
HODGE, Albert L., m. Jane WELLS, Oct. 25, 1846, by E. Huntington	2	23
Thomas K., m. Mary Ann RITTON, Apr. 6, 1846, by Henry Elliott, J. P.	2	12
HOLBROOK, David, of Bridgeport, m. Addie S. CABLE, of New Milford, Oct. 29, 1854, by Rev. William H. Russell	2	104
HOLCOMB, William, of Brookfield, m. Lydia OLMSTED, of New Milford, Sept. 24, 1826, by Rev. Benjamin Benham	1	206
HOLLISTER, Abel, m. Abigail CHAMBERS, Jan. 28, 1766	1	41
Abel, s. Abel & Abigail, b. Nov. 4, 1771	1	41
Abel, d. Jan. [ ], 1821	1	41
Amarillis, d. Abel & Abigail, b. Apr. 16, 1767	1	41
Anna, d. Abel & Abigail, b. Jan. 17, 1776	1	41
Anson, s. Abel & Abigail, b. Mar. 4, 1785	1	41
Apphia, m. Angus FERRISS, b. of New Milford, July 21, 1822, by Rev. Benjamin Benham	1	51
James Harvey, s. Abel & Abigail, b. Sept. 8, 1782	1	41
Jesse Chambers, s. Abel & Abigail, b. Nov. 17, 1780	1	41
Lucy, d. Abel & Abigail, b. Oct. 9, 1769	1	41
Lyman, s. Abel & Abigail, b. May 8, 1787	1	41
Marcy, d. Abel & Abigail, b. Mar. 1, 1774	1	41
Polly, d. Abel & Abigail, b. Apr. 24, 1778	1	41
Will Russel, s. Abel & Abigail, b. Nov. 17, 1789	1	41
HOLMES, Rachel, of Bedford, m. Robert BOSTWICK, of New Milford, Jan. 9, 1720/1	LR2	344
HONYE, Harriet, of Bridgwater, m. Elijah HAWLEY, of Trumbull, Nov. 16, 1826, by Rev. Fosdic Harrison, of Roxbury	1	211
HOPHUAS, [see also HOPKINS], George, of New Fairfield, m. Rebecca McGRAW, of New Milford, Feb. 6, 1843, by E. Huntington	1	394
HOPKINS, [see also HOPHUAS], Philema, of New Milford, m. Harmon CALHOUN, of Washington, Sept. 7, 1840, by Noah Porter	1	348
HORFORD, Neri, m. Caroline WRIGHT, Jan. 19, 1823, by Elder Eleazar Beacher	1	80
HOTCHKISS, HOTCHKINS, Ann, 2nd w. Dea. Ebenezar, d. Aug. 29, 1789	LR5	9
Asael, s. Ebenezer & Hannah, b. Aug. 16, 1744	LR5	8
Asahel, m. Philene WASHBORN, b. of New Milford, Nov. 26, 1766	LR7	32
Asahel, s. Asahel & Phileney, b. Oct. 14, 1772; d. Feb. 28, 1788	LR7	32
Charles, s. Solomon & Lois, b. Nov. 11, 1782	LR7	3
Daniel, s. Solomon & Lois, b. Aug. 10, 1779	LR7	3
Ebenezer, m. Hannah TERRILL, Jan. 10, 1741/2, by Roger Brownson, J. P.	LR5	8

	Vol.	Page
HOTCHKISS, HOTCHKINS, (cont.)		
Ebenezer, s. Solomon & Lois, b. Feb. 28, 1763	LR7	3
Ebenezar, Dea., m. Ann **ROBURDS**, Apr. 30, 1783	LR5	9
Ebenezar, Dea., m. Lydia **BUCK**, Nov. 30, 1789	LR5	9
Ebenezar, Dea., d. Jan. 12, 1796	LR5	9
Hannah, d. Ebenezer & Hannah, b. Apr. 9, 1746	LR5	8
Hannah, m. Daniel **COLLINS**, Mar. 11, 1767, by Bushnell Bostwick, J. P.	LR7	24
Hannah, d. Solomon & Lois, b. Aug. 20, 1767	LR7	3
Hannah, 1st w. Dea. Ebenezer, d. Dec. 29, 1782	LR5	8
Hannah, m. Ira **HITCHCOCK**, Oct. 27, 1785	1	24
Hulda, d. Sollomon & Lois, b. June 24, 1776	LR7	3
Lois, d. Solomon & Lois, b. Jan. 16, 1773; d. July 21, 1789	LR7	3
Lois, w. Solomon, d. Sept. 11, 1800, in the 58th y. of her age	LR7	3
Mary, of New Milford*, m. Silas **LAMSON**, of New Milford, Jan. 22, 1771 *(Guilford crossed out)	LR11	14
Mercy, d. Solomon & Lois, b. Aug. 14, 1765	LR7	3
Noble, s. Asahel & Philene, b. Apr. 16, 1782	LR7	32
Olive, d.* [Asahel & Philene], b. Mar. 9, 1768 *("Benjamin **HALLOCK**, & P" crossed out)	LR11	2
Olive, d. Asahel & Philene, b. Mar. 9, 1768	LR7	32
Philene, d. Asahel & Philene, b. Apr. 21, 1770	LR7	32
Philo, s. Asahel & Philene, b. Feb. 28, 1778	LR7	32
Solomon, s. Ebenezer & Hannah, b. Sept. 18, 1742	LR5	8
Solomon, m. Lois **WOOSTER**, b. of New Milford, July 21, 1762	LR7	3
Solomon, s. Solomon & Lois, b. July 18, 1770	LR7	3
William, s. Asahel & Philene, b. Sept. 10, 1775	LR7	32
HOUGH, [see also **HUFF**], Benjamin, s. Jonathan & Abagal, m. Ruth **BROWNSON**, d. Roger & Darocus, Aug. 22, 1738	LR4	21
Noah, s. Benjamin & Ruth, b. Feb. 5, 1738/9;d. Feb. 9, 1738/9	LR4	21
HOWAL (?), Edward G., of Bridgeport, m. Ann E. **CANFIELD**, of New Milford, Nov. 29, 1849, by Rev. James L. Scott, of New Preston. Int. Pub.	2	57
HOWARD, Abigal, m. Nathaniell **SELYE**, May 9, 1745, by John Yeomans, J. P.	LR6	9
Martha, m. John **MURRY**, May 30, 1751	LR7	28
[**HOWE**], HOW, HOWES, Elizabeth, m. Samuel **JACKSON**, s. Daniel, Aug. 9, 1734? by Roger Brownson, J. P.	LR4	14
Elisabeth, Mrs., d. Oct. 1, 1755	LR7	2
Jasper Moody, of South East, m. Betsey Ann **MARSH**, of New Milford, Mar. 21, 1830, by Rev. E. Huntington	1	133
HOWLAND, Elihu, m. Jane **BALDWIN**, b. of New Milford, Sept. 14, 1842, by Rev. Daniel Baldwin	1	375
Emily M., of New Milford, m. Amos N. **BENEDICT**, Rev., of New Marlborough, Mass., Oct. 27, 1847, by Rev. Johnson Howard	2	33
John T., m. Mary **OSBORN**, b. of New Milford, May 1, 1850,		

116   BARBOUR COLLECTION

	Vol.	Page
HOWLAND, (cont.)		
by Rev. A. N. Benedict	2	60
HOYT, HOIT, [see also **HAIGHT**], Ann, m. Herman **BUEL,** b. of New Milford, Mar. 31, 1824, by Rev. Andrew Eliot	1	120
Charles, m. Nancy **IVES,** Oct. 22, 1828, by Joel Sanford, J. P.	1	225
Demon, of Sherman, m. Abba Jane **BARTRAM,** of New Milford, Oct. 11, 1845, by Rev. Samuel Weeks	2	13
Elijah, m. Polly **CANFIELD,** Nov. 28, 1833, by Stephen Crane, J. P.	1	270
Eliza, m. Ebenezer **BALDWIN,** Nov. 28, 1833, by Heman Rood	1	269
Elliott, m. Armida **BROWNSON,** Apr. 5, 1846, by E. Huntington	2	22
Elsie E., m. George **NORTHROP,** b. of New Milford, Feb. 17, 1852, by Rev. David Murdock, Jr.	2	80
George, of Sherman, m. Emeline **MEAD,** of New Milford, Dec. 12, 1830, by Abner Brundage	1	239
Harriet, m. Gerardus **FERRISS,** 2nd, May 3, 1843, by E. Huntington	1	394
Henrietta L., of New Milford, m. Isaac **BLACKMAN,** of Newtown, Dec. 25, 1834, by E. Huntington	1	284
Laura, m. Eugene **FERRISS,** b. of New Milford, Oct. 26, 1829, by Rev. E. Huntington	1	234
Lucy, m. Ichabod **COLE,** July 30, 1808, by Elisha Bostwick, J. P.	1	157
Sarah, of New Milford, m. Charles **SMITH,** of Fairfield, Aug. 15, 1834, by E. Huntington	1	281
Susan, of New Milford, m. Perry **CHASE,** of New Fairfield, Nov. 27, 1844, by William H. Bangs	1	398
HUBBARD, Eunice, m. Philip **JACKLIN,** Dec. 9, 1832, by Eleazer Beecher	1	416
HUBBELL, HUBBEL, Clement, s. Peter & Hepzibah, b. Sept. 21, 1742; d. Aug. 12, 1747	LR7	38
Clement, s. Peter & Hepzibah, b. June 3, 1752	LR7	38
Hepzibah, d. Peter & Hepzibah, b. Jan. 23, 1749	LR7	38
John, s. Peter & Hepzibah, b. June 10, 1746	LR7	38
Lewis, of Washington, m. Aurilla **CLARK,** of New Milford, Nov. 27, 1834, by Stephen S. Nelson	1	281
Patience, d. Peter & Hepzibah, b. Apr. 11, 1757	LR7	38
Patience, m. Noble **HINE,** Feb. 2, 1768	LR11	10
Peter, s. Peter & Hepzibah, b. May 1, 1760	LR7	38
Sarah, d. Peter & Hepzibah, b. July 27, 1738	LR7	38
Shadrach, s. Peter & Hepzibah, b. July 22, 1740	LR7	38
Susan, m. George B. **WALLER,** May 11, 1841, by B. B. Parsons	1	357
Urania, m. Abraham **McDONELL,** May 11, 1841, by B. B. Parsons	1	358
HUFF*, [see also **HOUGH**], Mary, d. Ruth **HUFF,** b. June 24,		

	Vol.	Page
HUFF, (cont.)		
1748; d. Jan. 30, 1824 *("HUFF" crossed out)	LR5	10
Ruth, had d. Mary **HUFF***, b. June 24, 1748; d. Jan. 30, 1824 *("HUFF" crossed out)	LR5	10
Ruth, m. Ezra **TERRILL**, Apr. 10, 1752, by Samuell Canfield, J. P.	LR5	10
HULL, [see also **HALL**], Abigail Terril, [twin with Mary Basset], d. Samuell & Abigail, b. Mar. 1, 1772	LR11	13
David, s. John & Eunice, b. Aug. 29, 1767	1	4
Deborah, d. John & Eunice, b. Feb. 4, 1777	1	4
Eliza, of New Milford, m. George G. **WILDMAN**, of Danbury, May 16, 1837, by Rev. Francis Donnelly	1	305
Eunice, d. John & Eunice, b. Aug. 17, 1771	1	4
Eunice, m. Curtiss **WARNER**, Nov. 4, 1792	1	73
Eunice, wid. John, d. Mar. 16, 183[ ], ae 93 y. wanting 1 day	1	4
Gideon, s. John & Eunice, b. July 1, 1769; d. Jan. 14, 1770	1	4
Hannah, d. John & Eunice, b. June 26, 1763	1	4
Hannah, m. David **BOSTWICK**, b. of New Milford, Apr. 5, 1770	LR10	7
John*, s. John & Abagail, b. May 28, 1738 *(Possibly "John **HALL**")	LR4	26
John, m. Eunice **JACKSON**, Apr. 20, 1762	1	4
John, d. Dec. 28, 1808	1	4
Julia Ann, m. Mrkenzia **ROOT**, Nov. 20, 1836, by Rev. Francis Donnelly	1	301
Lorenzo, of Litchfield, m. Mary **BRONSON**, of New Milford, Mar. 24, 1839, by E. Huntington	1	335
Mary Basset, [twin with Abigail Terril], d. Samuell & Abigail, b. Mar. 1, 1772	LR11	13
Reumah, d. John & Eunice, b. July 4, 1765	1	4
Robert E., m. Mary E. **EDMONDS**, b. of New Milford, May 8, 1854, by Rev. H. G. Noble	2	98
Urania, d. John & Eunice, b. Sept. 7, 1773	1	4
Urania, d. John & Eunice, d. Feb. 10, 18[ ]	1	4
HUMESON, Mary Ann, m. Chancy **WILMOT**, Sept. 17, 1828, by Stephen Crane, J. P.	1	222
HUNGERFORD, Akin, m. Patty **LANE**, Feb. 24, 1824, by Daniel Gaylord, J. P.	1	59
Beach, of Sherman, m. Rebecca **BALDWIN**, of New Milford, Oct. 5, 1805, by Elisha Bostwick, J. P.	1	125
Glover, of Sherman, m. Harriet **COUCH**, of New Milford, [Sept.] 10, [1840], by B. B. Parsons	1	347
Harry, of Sherman, m. Margaret **CABLE**, of New Milford, May 15, 1821, by David S. Boardman, J. P.	1	48
Josiah, m. Mary **MILES**, Jan. 5, 1807, by Elisha Bostwick, J. P.	1	128
Julia Ann, of New Milford, m. John A. **ROOD**, of Brookfield, Nov. 21, 1820, by Rev. Andrew Eliott	1	182

	Vol.	Page

HUNGERFORD, (cont.)
Thomas, of Sherman, m. Rachel M. **SMITH**, of Bridgewater, Nov. 19, 1838, by Albert B. Camp — 1, 319

HUNT, Elizabeth, m. Josiah G.* **MINOR**, b. of New Milford, Sept. 11, 1851, at Northville, by Rev. J. F. Jones, of Northville *(Probably "L") — 2, 73

Elizabeth, m. Samuel Horatio **CLARK**, b. of New Milford, Dec. 28, 1853, by Rev. N. S. Wheaton — 2, 105

Gideon L., m. Sophia **NORTHROP**, Feb. 10, 1836, by E. Huntington — 1, 298

Horace, m. Mary Ann **WAY**, Nov. 2, 1835, by E. Huntington — 1, 295

John, m. Laura **WAY**, Dec. 19, 1839, by Rev. Daniel Baldwin — 1, 340

Julia Samantha, m. Maron **WOODIN**, b. of New Milford, Nov. 1, [1831], at the house of Edward Hunt, by Henry S. Atwater — 1, 245

Mark W., m. Mary **BENNITT**, Nov. 14, 1839, by Rev. Eleaser Beecher — 1, 331

Mary Ann, m. Noble **READ**, b. of New Milford, Dec. 10, 1837, by Rev. Alonzo F. Selleck — 1, 307

Phinehas, of Sherman, m. Julia **GAYLORD**, of New Milford, Oct. 15, 1822, by Rev. Andrew Eliot — 1, 57

William, of Woodbury, m. Aurilla **GREEN**, of New Milford, Sept. 30, 1823, by Rev. Benjamin Benham — 1, 172

HUNTINGTON, Mary G., of Middletown, m. William E. **HURLBUT**, June 3, 1833, by E. Huntington — 1, 262

HURD, [see also **HARD**], Abigal, w. Dr. George, d. Oct. 22, 1776 — LR11, 12

Abijah, s. William & Rebekah, b. Sept. 13, 1757 — LR7, 4

Anna, d. William & Rebeckah, b. Oct. 7, 1761 — LR7, 4

Carles DeLancy, s. Dr. George & Abigail, b. May 8, 1775 — LR11, 12

Cintha, twin with Silvia, d. Dr. George & Abigail, b. Dec. 3, 1773; d. Dec. 20, 1773 — LR11, 12

Clarinda, d. Phineas & Anna, b. June 13, 1765 — LR10, 2

Cooleye, s. William & Rebeckah, b. July 1, 1757 — LR7, 4

Easter, d. Phineas & Anna, b. July 20, 1757; d. Jan. 7, 1760 — LR10, 2

George, Dr., m. Abigail **PALMER**, Nov. 5, 1767, by Solomon Palmer, Miss. — LR11, 12

George Albert Hall, s. George & Abigail, b. June 24, 1771 — LR11, 12

Hester, d. Phineas & Anna, b. Feb. 23, 1767 — LR10, 2

Hinman, s. William & Rebeckah, b. May 1, 1764 — LR7, 4

James, m. Hester **BOOTH**, d. Daniel & Eunice, [ ]; moved to Arlington, Vt. — 2, 112

Jehiel, s. Phineas & Anna, b. Nov. 8*, 1760 *(Possibly 18th") — LR10, 2

Jonathan, s. William & Rebekah, b. Dec. 10, 1755 — LR7, 4

Lois, d. William & Rebeckah, b. Jan. 27, 1767 — LR7, 4

Lyman, s. Phineas & Anna, b. Nov. 3, 1762 — LR10, 2

Ophelia, d. George & Abigail, b. Apr. 19, 1769 — LR11, 12

Ophelia, d. Dr. George & Abigail, d. Dec. 30, 1773 — LR11, 12

	Vol.	Page
HURD, (cont.)		
Phineas, m. Anna **HAWLEY,** Jan. 2, 1757	LR10	2
Silvia, twin with Cintha, d. Dr. George & Abigail, b. Dec. 3, 1773	LR11	12
Sylvia, d. Dr. George & Abigail, d. Dec. 30, 1773	LR11	12
Tyrus, s. Phineas & Anna, b. July 1, 1759	LR10	2
William, m. Rebekah **WELLER,** b. of New Milford, Nov. 1, 1753, by Rev. Nathaniell Taylor	LR7	4
HURLBUT, HURLBUTT, HULBUT, Fanny, m. Marvin S. **TODD,** Dec. 3, 1837, by Abner Brundage	1	308
Gamaliel, m. Jerusha **DRINKWATER,** Feb. 19, 1758* *("8" rewritten over "9")	LR7	29
Hannah, d. Gamaliel & Jerusha, b. Oct. 6, 1779	LR7	29
Henry, of Roxbury, m. Fanny **PATTERSON,** of New Milford, Mar. 19, 1834, by Rev. Fosdic Harrison, of Roxbury	1	275
Job, s. Gamaliel & Jerusha, b. Apr. 14, 1764	LR7	29
John, s. Gamaliel & Jerusha, b. Mar. 6, 1760	LR7	29
Martha, of Sharon, m. Job **GOOLD,** of New Milford, Mar. 24, 1767, by Rev. Cotton Mather Smith, of Sharon	LR9	[ ]
Prudence, d. Joseph, of Woodbury, m. Josiah **BROWNSON,** s. Roger & Darocus, of New Milford, Jan. 31, 1738/9, by Joseph Minard, J. P.	LR4	23
William E., m. Mary G. **HUNTINGTON,** of Middletown, June 3, 1833, by E. Huntington	1	262
HYDE, Mary Jane, m. Charles **BALDWIN,** Jr., b. of Westville, Jan. 3, 1850, at the house of David Hummiston, in Bridgewater, by Rev. W. O. Jarvis	2	59
HYNIES, [see also **HINE**], Mary, m. Azariah **CANFIELD,** Jr., May 7, 1763, by Bushnel Bostwick, J. P.	LR8	1
INGERSOLL, INGERSOL, Akin, of Sherman, m. Nancy O. **BANKS,** of Patterson, N. Y., Dec. 25, 1825, at the house of Elihu Marsh, 2nd, by Homer Boardman, J. P.	1	82
Elizabeth, of Sheffield, m. Noah **WADHAMS,** of New Milford, Nov. 8, 1758, by Rev. Samuel Hopkins, of Great Barrington	LR7	7
Maria, of New Milford, m. Abiel **BALDWIN,** of Washington, Jan. 8, 1823, by Rev. Benjamin Benham	1	54
IRWIN, Robert, of Redhook, N. Y., m. Emily A. **CANFIELD,** of New Milford, May 7, 1838, by N. Porter	1	316
ISBELL, ISBEL, Jared S., of Woodbury, m. Polly Ann **MALLETT,** of New Milford, Dec. 25, 1834, by Rev. Fosdic Harrison, of Roxbury	1	287
Martin, of Naugatuck, m. Susan **MALLET,** of New Milford, Apr. 22, 1839, by E. Huntington	1	335
IUCKET, Philo, of Sharon, m. Orrilla **CANDFIELD,** of New Milford, Dec. 28, 1828, by William Jewett	1	227
IVES, Abigail, m. Daniel B. **SMITH,** Jan. 4, 1824, by Rev. Benjamin Benham	1	160

	Vol.	Page
IVES, (cont.)		
Betsey Ann, of Bridgewater, m. Stephen **LAMSON**, of New Milford, Aug. 28, 1842, by Rev. Albert B. Camp, of Bridgewater	1	373
James, m. Sarah Elvira **IVES**, b. of New Milford, Nov. 24, 1841, by Rev. Z. Davenport	1	363
Julia Jennet, of New Milford, m. Hiram **LOBDELL**, of Brookfield, [ ], 1840, by Nathan Rice	1	357
Nancy, m. Charles **HOYT**, Oct. 22, 1828, by Joel Sanford, J. P.	1	225
Oliver* Ann, m. Isaac E. **GORHAM**, Sept. 27, 1840, by Rev. Albert B. Camp *("Olive or "Olivia"?)	1	347
Sarah A., of Bridgwater, m. Edwin **SMITH**, of Hadley, Mass., Mar. 14, 1847, by James Kilborn	2	28
Sarah Elvira, m. James **IVES**, b. of New Milford, Nov. 24, 1841, by Rev. Z. Davenport	1	363
Thomas, of Roxbury, m. Mrs. Mary Ann **BOSTWICK**, of New Milford, Oct. 17, 1852, by D. Williams. Int. Pub.	2	77
JACKLIN, C[h]loe, m. Orman **WILSON**, May 18, 1828, by Stephen Crane, J. P.	1	420
Daniel, m. Amanda **CARPENTER**, Oct. 31, 1822, by Rev. Andrew Eliot	1	169
Huldah, m. Hervey **PHILLIPS**, July 18, 1807, by Elisha Bostwick, J. P.	1	417
Philip, m. Eunice **HUBBARD**, Dec. 9, 1832, by Eleazer Beecher	1	416
Phillip H., m. Charlotte S. **PHILLIPS**, b. of New Milford, June 9, 1850, by Rev. Amos N. Benedict	2	61
JACKSON, Andrew Eliot, s. Eldad C. & Cynthia, b. Nov. 19, 1830	1	40
Anna, of Stratfeild, m. Lemuel **BOSTWICK**, of New Milford, Nov. 5, 1729	LR4	9
Avice, d. David & Priscilla, b. May 12, 1777	LR12	18
Azar, s. Uri & Sarah, b. Feb. 26, 1771	LR10	13
Charles W., m. Laura M. **HINE**, b. of New Milford, Aug. 27, 1851, by Rev. David Murdock, Jr.	2	71
Daniel, s. Uri & Sarah, b. Mar. 6, 1776	LR10	13
David, m. Priscilla **BENEDICT**, Apr. 4, 1775, by Rev. Mr. Wetmore	LR12	18
David, s. David & Priscillia, b. Apr. 23, 1790	LR12	18
Eldad, s. Henry & Martha, b. May 1, 1777; d. 13th of same month	LR13	2
Eldad, s. Henry & Martha, b. Mar. 29, 1788	LR13	2
Eldad C., m. Cynthia **STARR**, May 28, 1808	1	40
Elias, s. Uri & Sarah, b. Dec. 15, 1781* *(Possibly "1787")	LR10	13
Elijah, s. Uri & Sarah, b. Oct. 27, 1772	LR10	13
Elizabeth, d. Uri & Sarah, b. May 25* 1774 *("21" or "25")	LR10	13
Eunice, m. John **HULL**, Apr. 20, 1762	1	4
Frederick, of Bethlem, m. Mary S. **BEERS**, of Bridgewater,		

NEW MILFORD VITAL RECORDS

	Vol.	Page
JACKSON, (cont.)		
Mar. 2, 1842, by Rev. Albert B. Camp, of Bridgewater	1	369
Frederick William, s. Eldad C. & Cynthia, b. June 7, 1822	1	40
Hannah, d. David & Priscilla, b. Apr. 22, 1785; d. same day	LR12	18
Hannah, d. David & Priscillia, b. Feb. 27, 1787	LR12	18
Harriet, of New Milford, m. Oliver **RYDER**, of Elyria, O., Apr. 24, 1839, by Noah Porter	1	327
Harriot Rachel, d. Eldad C. & Cynthia, b. Jan. 7, 1813	1	40
Henry, m. Martha **CAMP**, July 9, 1776, by Rev. Mr. Brooks	LR13	2
Henry, s. Henry & Martha, b. Mar. 13, 1786	LR13	2
Henry, [Sr.], d. Nov. 24, 1790	LR13	2
Henry, s. Eldad C. & Cynthia, b. Aug. 1, 1816	1	40
Hervey, s. Henry & Martha, b. Mar. 29, 1780; d. Jan. 29, 1782	LR13	2
Huldah, m. Peter **McFARLAND**, b. of Brookfield, Sept. 13, 1846, by Rev. Samuel Weeks	2	39
Isaac, s. David & Priscillia, b. June 25, 1792	LR12	18
Jane, sister of Polly Ann, b. Oct. 10, 1829 (colored)	1	421
Joanna, d. David & Prissillia, b. Dec. 19, 1781	LR12	18
John, m. Fanny **THOMAS**, Nov. 4, 1830, by Rev. Eleazer Beecher	1	239
Levi, s. David & Priscillia, b. Mar. 7, 1779	LR12	18
Lyman, s. Uri & Sarah, b. Mar. 9, 1780; d. Feb. 2, 1781	LR10	13
Martha, d. Henry & Martha, b. Mar. 9, 1784	LR13	2
Martha, m. William **GAYLORD**, b. of New Milford, Feb. 25, 1836, by Abner Brundage	1	293
Martha Maria, d. Eldad C. & Cynthia, b. Nov. 6, 1820	1	40
Oliver Parsons, s. Eldad C. & Cynthia, b. Feb. 27, 1809	1	40
Oliver Parsons, [s. Eldad C. & Cynthia], d. Sept. 8, 1830	1	40
Priscilla, d. David & Priscilla, b. Nov. 24, 1783; d. Mar. 2, 1784	LR12	18
Rachel, m. Nathan **GANSON**, Dec. 22, 1825, by Rev. Andrew Eliot	1	29
Rebeccah, d. David & Prisilla, b. Nov. 3, 1775	LR12	18
Sally, of New Milford, m. Benedict W. **NICHOLS**, of Bridgeport, May 29, 1842, by N. Porter, Jr.	1	372
Samuel, s. Daniel, m. Elizabeth **HOW**, Aug. 9, 1734 (?), by Roger Brownson, J. P.	LR4	14
Uri, m. Sarah **BURCHARD**, Apr. 10, 1770, by Rev. Nathaniell Taylor	LR10	13
Uri, s. Uri & Sarah, b. Apr. 18, 1778	LR10	13
William, m. Eliza **PHILLIPS**, of New Milford, Sept. 4, 1841, by N. Porter, Jr.	1	371
William E., m. Mariah **BROOKLIN**, (colored), Apr. 15, 1821, by Reuben Warner, J. P. Int. Pub. by Rev. Mr. Eliot	1	38
JAGGAR, Samuel B., of Orid, N. Y., m. Pamela **TERRILL**, of New Milford, Jan. 16, 1822, by Rev. C. A. Boardman	1	13
JENNINGS, Ann, of New Milford, m. David **WALKER**, of Washington, Jan. 12, 1831, by E. Huntington	1	246

	Vol.	Page
JENNINGS, (cont.)		
Ann, of New Milford, m. David **WALKER**, of Washington, Jan. 12, 1831, by E. Huntington	1	247
Elmor*, m. Polly Ann **OLMSTED**, b. of New Milford, Sept. 14, 1828, by Rev. E. Huntington *(Rewritten and not clear)	1	223
Harriet, m. Henry A. **SOULE**, b. of New Milford, Nov. 11, 1849, by Rev. William Henry Rees	2	59
Hiram, m. Florilla **ROOT**, b. of New Milford, Dec. 4, 1839, by Benjamin B. Parsons	1	332
Julia, m. Benjamin **CONNOVER**, b. of Bridgewater, Feb. 23, 1842, by Rev. Albert B. Camp, of Bridgewater	1	369
Maria, m. Frederick A. **MONSON**, Sept. 27, 1843, by E. Huntington	1	395
Minerva, m. Amos **BEARDSLEY**, Aug. 17, 1820, by Rev. Andrew Eliot	1	108
Polly, of New Milford, m. Asa H. **WAY**, of Goshen, Sept. 21, 1828, by Rev. E. Huntington	1	223
[JESSUP], JESUP, Jonathan, m. Abigail **MINOR**, b. of Bridgewater, Jan. 24, 1821, by Rev. Fosdic Harrison, of Roxbury	1	61
Laura A., m. Eli H. **WELTON**, b. of New Milford, Sept. 11, 1850, by Rev. D. Williams	2	68
JEWEL, Lydia, of New Milford, m. John L. **BARTRAM**, of Sherman, Oct. 25, 1837, by Rev. Alonso F. Selleck	1	307
JOHNSON, Cyrus, s. Moses & Eunice, b. Aug. 12, 1776	LR7	36
Daniel, s. Moses & Eunice, b. Oct. 2, 1763	LR7	36
Elijah, s. Moses & Eunice, b. Mar. 26, 1774	LR7	36
Gideon, s. Moses & Eunice, b. July 14, 1769	LR7	36
Isaac, s. Peter & Deborah, b. Mar. 12, 1768	LR10	6
Jeremiah, s. Peter & Deborah, b. Mar. 24, 1772	LR10	6
Joseph, of Monroe, m. Huldah **WHEELER**, of New Milford, May 17, 1825, by Newton Tuttle. Witnesses: Charles Smith, David Warner, Belden Warner & Rev. Nathan Tuttle	1	98
Laura, d. James & Sarah (colored), b. Aug. 1, 1813	1	421
Miles, s. Peter & Deborah, b. Sept. 6, 1770	LR10	6
Minerva, d. James & Sally (colored), b. May 10, 1819	1	421
Moses, m. Eunice **BROWNSON**, May 18, 1761	LR7	36
Moses, s. Moses & Eunice, b. Dec. 6, 1778	LR7	36
Peter, m. Deborah **MERRILDS**, Jan. 1, 1767	LR10	6
Phebe, d. Peter & Deborah, b. Jan. 13, 1774	LR10	6
Salmon, s. Moses & Eunice, b. Apr. 26, 1767	LR7	36
Solomon, of Newtown, m. Polly **PALMER**, of New Milford, Oct. 5, 1823, by Joel Sanford, J. P.	1	183
Squier, m. Thirza **FERRISS**, b. of New Milford, Aug. 9, 1807, by Elisha Bostwick, J. P.	1	143
Urania, d. Moses & Eunice, b. Aug. 2, 1771	LR7	36

	Vol.	Page
JOHNSON, (cont.)		
Zerviah, of Woodbery, m. Benjamin **BOSTWICK**, of New Milford, May 2, 1711	LR2	353
JONES, Abigail, or Griffin, a transient person, m. Jacob **BROWNSON**, of New Milford, Nov. 13, 1732, by Rev. Daniel Bordmond	LR4	1
Clarinda G*. of New Milford, m. Samuel **ATWOOD**, of Woodbury, May 16, 1852, by Rev. J. F. Jones *(Probably "L")	2	76
Electa, m. Charles **READ**, July 6, 1840, by Eleazer Beecher	1	345
George D., of New Milford, m. Mary J. **PAGE**, of Sherman, Mar. 19, 1843, by E. Huntington	1	393
Hannah, m. Samuel **PRINCE**, Jr., Feb. 2, 1780	LR13	16
John W., of Canaan, m. Abigail S. **HATCH**, of New Milford, Sept. 26, 1837, by Rev. Alonzo F. Sellick	1	309
Rebecca, m. Henry R. **PIEREY**, b. of New Milford, Nov. 7, 1847, by Rev. E. P. Ackerman	2	40
Ruth, d. Joseph & Hannah, b. Dec. 9, 1758	LR7	24
JORLOMON, Charlotte, formerly of New York, m. Merwin **LAMSON**, of Bridgewater, Dec. 25, 1841, by Rev. Albert B. Camp	1	365
JOYCE, Abigail, m. Ira **NORTHROP**, b. of New Milford, Dec. 24, 1820, by Homer Boardman, J. P.	1	20
JUDD, Burtis, of Roxbury, m. Rebecca A. **HALLOCK**, of New Milford, Dec. 31, 1838, by Rev. Alonso F. Sellick	1	320
Elijah, of Kent, m. Maria **FERRISS**, of New Milford, Oct. 18, 1826, by Rev. Eleazar Beecher	1	201
Elisabeth, m. John **BUCK**, Feb. 16, 1757	LR7	25
Eunice, m. John **COGSHALL**, b. of New Milford, Dec. 19, 1834, by E. Huntington	1	284
Joel W., of New Milford, m. Annis E. **SMITH**, of Bridgewater Dec. 22, 1842, by Rev. Albert B. Camp, of Bridgewater	1	376
JUDSON, Elisabeth, of Woodbury, m. Samuel **CANFIELD**, of New Milford, June 5, 1755, by John Graham, V. D. M.	LR7	10
Harris, Dr., m. Emily A. **WARNER**, b. of Bridgwater, Apr. 13, 1830, by Rev. Fosdick Harrison, of Roxbury	1	231
Mary E., m. Edwin G. **SANFORD**, b. of New Milford, May 29, 1854, by Rev. H. G. Noble	2	99
Olive, of Woodbury, m. Benjamin **BOSTWICK**, of New Milford, Feb. 8, 1769	LR10	8
Oliver W.*, of Roxbury, m. Flora M. **RUGGLES**, of New Milford, July 3, 1851, by D. Williams *(Possibly "N")	2	71
Reuben W., m. Esther Ann **SMITH**, b. of New Milford, Feb. 15, 1854, by Rev. David Murdock, Jr.	2	101
Samuel W., of Woodbury, m. Almira **TERRILL**, of New Milford, Mar. 31, 1835, by H. Rood	1	286
KAHAM, Amy, m. Truman **YOUNG**, Feb. 4, 1824, by Rev. Andrew Eliott	1	65

	Vol.	Page
KEELER, Abigail, m. John **BRADSHAW**, Jr., Nov. 16, 1775	LR12	6
Cornelia, m. George **WHITTELSEY**, Feb. 28, 1822, by Rev. Andrew Eliot	1	39
Eli, m. Clarinda **OVIATT**, Aug. 18, 1807, by Elisha Bostwick, J. P.	1	144
Eliza, m. Isaac **MALLET**, Apr. 18, 1822, by Rev. Benjamin Benham	1	23
Hiram, m. Sarah **PECK**, b. of Bridgwater Soc., Dec. 12, 1826, by Rev. Andrew Eliot	1	210
Ira, of Brookfield, m. Mary J. **SANFORD**, of New Milford, June 27, 1850, by Rev. H. D. Noble, of Brookfield	2	62
Rebeckah, m. Nathan **HITCHCOCK**, Aug. 21, 1769, by Rev. Mr. Brooks, of Newberry Parish	LR11	7
Ruth M., Mrs. m. Emerson W. **CASTLE**, b. of New Milford, Mar. 27, 1842, by Rev. Albert B. Camp, of Bridgewater	1	370
[**KEENEY**], KENEY, KENNEY, KINNE, [see also **KINNEY**], Abigail, m. Josiah **CASWELL**, Aug. 13, 1751	LR7	14
Abigail, d. Jacob, Jr. & Anna, b. Feb. 18, 1769	LR7	3
Anson, s. Jacob, Jr., & Ann, b. Apr. 7, 1771	LR7	3
Elias, m. Lois **STONE**, Jan. 25, 1759	LR7	9
Jacob, Jr., m. Anne **GUNN**, b. of New Milford, Jan. 3, 1764	LR7	3
Joseph, s. Jacob, Jr. & Anne, b. June 5, 1766	LR7	3
Leucinda, d. Jacob, Jr. & Anna, b. Mar. 11, 1776	LR7	3
Sarah, m. Joel **BOSTWICK**, June 21, 1768, by Rev. Noah Wadhams	LR10	5
Silvina, d. Jacob, Jr. & Anne, b. Aug. 10, 1764	LR7	3
[ ]*anson, s. Jacob, Jr. & Ann, b. Apr. 7, 1771 *(Letter crossed out)	LR7	3
KEITH, Betsey L., m. Samuel **GORHAM**, b. of New Milford, Mar. 5, 1840, by Noah Porter	1	342
KELLEY, Mary A. B., d. William H. & Mary A., b. May 28, 1852	2	67
William H.,of Goshen, m. Mary A. **BOSTWICK**, of New Milford, Nov. 12, 1850, by Rev. Harley Goodwin, of S. Canaan	2	67
KELLOGG, Edwin, of New Fairfield, m. Lucella **BROWN**, of New Milford, Sept. 31, 1834, by E. Huntington	1	282
Fanny M., of New Milford, m. James N. **EVANS**, of Sherman, Nov. 23, 1841, by N. M. Urmston	1	362
Julia, of New Milford, m. Ebenezer **ABEL**, of Sharon, Sept. 6, 1842, by Rev. Elijah Baldwin	1	373
Northrop, m. Sally **BEARDSLEE**, b. of New Milford, June 4, 1834, by Fosdic Harrison	1	280
KENT, Eri, s. Seth & Lois, b. Nov. 1, 1760	LR7	16
Sarah, m. Nathan **HAWLEY**, Jr., May 1, 1765	LR7	19
KETCHAM, Deborah, m. Daniel **HITCHCOCK**, Mar. 12, 1777, by Bushnel Bostwick	LR12	7
KIDD, Andrew, of Cornwall, m. Mary I. **CANFIELD**, of New Milford, Jan. 1, 1851, by Rev. David Murdock, Jr.	2	66

	Vol.	Page
KILSON, Delia, of Kent, m. Reuben ROGERS, of New Milford, May 24, 1846, by J. Greenwood	2	15
KING, Edward W., of Painsville, O., m. Eliza LOCKWOOD, of New Milford, Oct. 26, 1837, by E. Huntington	1	310
KINGSLEY, Alonzo C., of New Milford, m. Marilla PARSONS, of Sharon, May 18, 1847, by Rev. George Tomlinson	2	29
Roccelania, m. Alonzo HAWLEY, Jan. 24, 1827, by E. B. Kellogg	1	181
KINNEY, [see also KEENEY], Curtis, m. Mary COUCH, Mar. 12, 1837, by E. Huntington	1	312
Narusia, of New Milford, m. Joseph SPERRY, of Woodbridge, Mar. 13, 1842, by E. Huntington	1	379
KIRBY, Jestus, see under Jestus RUBY		
Mary, of Milford, m. Benoni STEBBINS, of New Milford, Dec. 10, 1717	LR2	352
KNAPP, KNAP, Arche Warner, s. Joshua & Lodema, b. Sept. 10, 1786	1	20
Edwin Gavin, s. Joshua & Lodema, b. Aug. 24, 1795	1	20
Edwin Gavin, m. Mariett FERRISS, b. of New Milford, Nov. 29, 1815, by Rev. Andrew Eliot	1	174
Edwin Joshua, s. Edwin G. & Mariett, b. Dec. 22, 1817, at Cairo, N. Y.	1	174
Geliad*, s. Moses & Sarah, b. May 25, 1751 *("nu" crossed out)	LR6	15
Joshua, Jr., of Danbury, m. Lodema WARNER, of New Milford, Oct. 26, 1785	1	20
Levi Philetus, s. Joshua & Lodema, b. Mar. 4, 1789	1	20
Levi S., m. Eliza ROBURDS, Dec. 9, 1823, by Rev. Andrew Eliot	1	103
Lucy, of Danbury, m. Benjamin PAYNE, of New Milford, Apr. 13, 1791	1	117
Maria Ann, m. Surges GOODSILL, b. of New Milford, Apr. 2, 1840, by Nathan Rice	1 1	355
Moses, m. Sarah WARNER, May 29, 1751, by Rev. Nathaniel Taylor	LR6	15
Rebecca, of New Milford, m. Austin MOREHOUSE, of Kent, Jan. 25, 1831, by H. Rood	1	240
Samuel, m. Phebe McMAHON, Feb. 14, 1796, by Rev. Nathaniel Taylor	1	62
Terrissa, witnessed marriage of Enoch CARPENTER & Sophia LANE	1	184
Uraina Cordelia, d. Edwin G. & Mariett, b. Apr. 18, 1820	1	174
William A., m. Lucy LINES, Feb. 10, 1836, by E. Huntington	1	297
William Albert, m. Eliza SANFORD, b. of New Milford, Oct. 27, 1847, by John Greenwood	2	32
KNOWLES, KNOLES, KNOWLS, Amelia, m. Preserve SMITH, Jan. 1, 1824, by Rev. Andrew Eliot	1	163
Arthur, s. William & Innocent, b. Dec. 29, 1743* *("4"		

	Vol.	Page
KNOWLES, KNOLES, KNOWLS, (cont.)		
blotted and uncertain)	LR7	6
Arthrew, m. Abigail HAMBLIN, Jan. 15, 1761	LR10	3
Betsey, m. Samuel C. NICHOLS, b. of New Milford, Nov. 24, 1824, by Rev. Benjamin Benham	1	161
Elisabeth, d. William & Innocent, b. Feb. 20, 1741	LR7	6
Elizar, s. Arthrew & Abigail, b. Jan. 21, 1763	LR10	3
Gideon Benedict, s. Arthrew & Abigail, b. Aug. 1, 1766	LR10	3
Nelson, of New Milford, m. Eunice A. WARNER, of New Milford, Apr. 2, 1829, by Rev. John Lovejoy	1	144
Selvine, d. Arthrew & Abigail, b. Jan. 7, 1765	LR10	3
William, s. Arthrew & Abigail, b. Jan. 2, 1762	LR10	3
KNOWLTON, Asa, m. Ruth WOOSTER, [ ]	1	54
Polly, d. Asa & Ruth, b. June 20, 1793	1	54
KUSCHMANN, Anna Maria Theresa, see under Anna Maria Theresa* ZEILDER	2	118
LACEY, LACY, Annah, [d. Ebenezer & Freelove], b.June 23, 1758	LR7	39
Betsey Ann, m. Harvey PLATT, b. of New Milford, May 13, 1827, by Nathaniel Perry, J. P.	1	214
Daniel, s. Ebenezer & Freelove, b. Sept. 17, 1766; d. Oct. 17, 1766	LR7	39
David, [s. Ebenezer & Freelove], b. Aug. 4, 1752	LR7	39
Ebenezer, m. Freelove CANFIELD, Dec. 15, 1748	LR7	39
Edwin A., of Brookfield, m. Flora M. SANFORD, of New Milford, Nov. 17, 1828, by Rev. E. Huntington	1	226
Ezra, m. Laura GRANGER, Jan. 5, 1806, by Elisha Bostwick, J. P.	1	126
George C., m. Harriet MORE, b. of New Milford, Oct. 30, 1838, by N. Porter	1	323
Isaac, [s. Ebenezer & Freelove], b. Apr. 2, 1754	LR7	39
Jedidiah, [s. Ebenezer & Freelove], b. Oct. 14, 1762	LR7	39
Lucana, d. Ebenezer & Freelove, b. Nov. 1, 1767	LR7	39
Mercy, [d. Ebenezer & Freelove], b. July 28, 1760	LR7	39
Ollive, d. Ebenezer & Frelove, b. Oct. 1, 1749	LR7	39
Penelope, [d. Ebenezer & Freelove], b. Aug. 25, 1756	LR7	39
Rhodah, d. Ebenezer & Freelove, b. Sept. 4, 1764	LR7	39
Susan E., m. Israel POTTER, Jan. 6, 1828, by Rev. E. Huntington	1	217
Thomas B., m. Rachel Ann NOBLE, b. of New Milford, Sept. 11, 1838, by N. Porter	1	319
LAKE, Charity, d. Jeams & Mary, b. May 6, 1729	LR4	5
Charles, m. Hannah MORE, b. of New Milford, Mar. 17, 1841, by N. Porter	1	353
Daniel, s. Jeams & Mary, b. Nov. 12, 1730	LR4	5
David, s. James, Jr. & Sarah, b. June 6, 1761	LR7	37
David, s. James, Jr. & Sarah, d. Sept. 14, 1763	LR7	37
David, s. James & Sarah, b. July 14, 1765	LR7	37
Hannah, m. Moses CANFIELD, b. of New Milford, Sept. 24,		

NEW MILFORD VITAL RECORDS

	Vol.	Page
LAKE, (cont.)		
1832, by Homer Boardman, J. P.	1	252
Homer, of Brookfield, m. Nancy **FRENCH**, of New Milford, May 27, 1830, by J. S. Covill	1	238
Isaac, s. James, Jr. & Sarah, b. June 27, 1763	LR7	37
Jeams, s. Jeams & Mary, b. Aug. 16, 1728	LR4	5
James, Jr., m. Sarah **HENDRYX**, Jan. 23, 1760	LR7	37
Rogers, s. Jeams & Mary, b. Sept. 12, 1732	LR4	5
Samuel, s. Jeams & Mary, b. Feb. 10, 1725	LR4	5
LAMSON, Almira, m. Daniel **BROWNSON**, b. of New Milford, Jan. 21, 1823, by Rev. Benjamin Benham	1	64
Amos. s. William & Sarah, b. June 8, 1769	LR10	15
Andrew, s. Will[ia]m & Sarah, b. Feb. 20, 1774	LR10	15
Catharine, of New Milford, m. Stephen **BIDWELL**, of Litchfield, Feb. 8, 1841, by E. Huntington	1	365
Curtis Erastus, of New Preston, m. Mirza Maria **HALLOCK**, of New Milford, May 1, 1833, by Rev. Henry S. Atwater	1	261
Hannah, d. William & Hannah, b. Oct. 24, 1749	LR6	13
Hannah, m. Isaac **CANFIELD**, Dec. 18, 1771, by Rev. Nathaniell Taylor	LR12	9
John, s. William & Hannah, b. Oct. 27, 1747	LR6	13
John, s. Silas & Mary, b. June 1, 1774	LR11	14
Joseph, s. William & Hannah, b. June 11, 1746	LR6	13
Joseph, s. Silas & Mary, b. Aug. 14, 1779	LR11	14
Laura, m. George N. **SANFORD**, b. of New Milford, Jan. 19, 1831, E. Huntington	1	247
Merwin, of Bridgewater, m. Charlotte **JORLOMON**, formerly of New York, Dec. 25, 1841, by Rev. Albert B. Camp	1	365
Molly, d. William & Hannah, b. July 19, 1757	LR6	13
Nathan, s. Silas & Mary, b. May 12, 1772	LR11	14
Nehemiah, s. Silas & Mary, b. July 5, 1777; d. Apr. 15, 1778	LR11	14
Rowzel*, s. William, Jr. & Sarah, b. Apr. 28, 1771 *("Ros" crossed out)	LR10	15
Silas, of New Milford, m. Mary **HOTCHKISS**, of New Milford*, Jan. 22, 1771 *("Guilford" crossed out)	LR11	14
Stephen, of New Milford, m. Betsey Ann **IVES**, of Bridgewater, Aug. 28, 1842, by Rev. Albert B. Camp, of Bridgewater	1	373
William, Jr., m. Sarah **BURRITT**, Mar. 22, 1768	LR10	15
William, m. Chloe **LEWIS**, Jan. 29, 1843, by Rev. Eleazer Beecher	1	378
LANE, LAIN, Aaron D., Rev. of Waterloo, N. Y., m. Laura A. **BOARDMAN**, of New Milford, Oct. 20, 1828, by Rev. C. A. Boardman	1	210
Abbey, witnessed marriage of Enoch **CARPENTER** & Sophia **LANE**	1	184
Abbey, witnessed marriage of Jocob **WANZER** & Phebe **LEACH**	1	208

	Vol.	Page
LANE, LAIN, (cont.)		
Allen S., of Kent, m. Emily **FORD**, of New Milford, Aug. 8, 1830, by Rev. H. Rood	1	193
Almon, m. Barbara **HALLOCK**, b. of New Milford, Dec. 12, 1838, by Rev. Elijah Baldwin	1	320
Alonzo B., witnessed marriage of Enoch **CARPENTER** & Sophia **LANE**	1	18
Anne, of New Milford, m. Abraham **LEE**, of Fishkill, N. Y., Dec. 26, 1824, by Daniel Gaylord	1	111
Catharine C., witnessed marriage of Enoch **CARPENTER** & Sophia **LANE**	1	184
Elizabeth, of Kent, m. Herman S. **BALDWIN**, of New Milford, July 15, 1827, by William Jewett	1	216
Gilbert, witnessed marriage of Enoch **CARPENTER** & Sophia **LANE**	1	184
Harman, of Washington, m. Esther M. **RIGBY**, of New Milford, Oct. 30, 1853, by Rev. A. B. Pulling	2	90
Lucena, witnessed marriage of Enoch **CARPENTER** & Sophia **LANE**	1	184
Mary, witnessed marriage of Enoch **CARPENTER** & Sophia **LANE**	1	184
Park, witnessed marriage of Ebenezer **WANZER**, Jr. & Lucy **LEACH**	1	181
Park H., witnessed marriage of Enoch **CARPENTER** & Sophia **LANE**	1	184
Patty, m. Akin **HUNGERFORD**, Feb. 24, 1824, by Daniel Gaylord, J. P.	1	59
Samuel, witnessed marriage of Enoch **CARPENTER** & Sophia **LANE**	1	184
Sophia, d. Gilbert & Susanna, of Monthly Meeting of Oblong, Sherman, Conn., m. Enoch **CARPENTER**, of Purchase Monthly Meeting, Harrison, West Chester Co., N. Y., s. James, decd. & Freelove, 6th month 19th day, 1822, before 37 witnesses. Int. Pub. at Oblong, N. Y.	1	184
Sophia, witnessed marriage of Ebenezer **WANZER**, Jr. & Lucy **LEACH**	1	181
Susanna, witnessed marriage of Enoch **CARPENTER** & Sophia **LANE**	1	184
Susanna, witnessed marriage of Jacob **WANZER** & Phebe **LEACH**	1	208
William, witnessed marriage Enoch **CARPENTER** & Sophia **LANE**	1	184
LAPHAM, Betsey A., m. Alfred T. **MURPHY**, b. of New Milford, June 18, 1854, by J. W. Hoffman	2	109
LATHROP, Ann, m. Clark **MOREHOUSE**, Oct. 24, 1842, by E. Huntington	1	381
Daniel, m. Esther **GAYLORD**, June 17, 1821, at the house of Hervey Benson, by Eleazar Beecher, Elder	1	56

NEW MILFORD VITAL RECORDS 129

	Vol.	Page
LATHROP, (cont.)		
Daniel, m. Livia Ann **RUNNELS**, b. of New Milford, Mar. 31, 1839, by Alonso F. Sellick	1	325
Jerome, m. Laura **MOREHOUSE**, b. of New Milford, May 8, 1848, by J. Kilbourn	2	42
Viola V., of New Milford, m. Amos **HINKLEY**, of Kent, July 9, 1854, by J. W. Hoffman	2	109
LAW, Sidney A., m. Lucy Ann **TONG**, b. of New Milford, Apr. 28, 1851, by Rev. G. B. Haden	2	67
LAWRENCE, George H., m. Sarah Ann **BUCKINGHAM**, b. of New Milford, Jan. 26, 1836, by Rev. Elijah Baldwin	1	291
LAWTON, Charles W., of West Killingly, m. Charloote L. **SEELEY**, of Sherman, May 28, 1844, by John Greenwood	1	396
LEACH, LEACK, Catharine, witnessed marriage of David **SANDS** & Paulina **LEACH**	1	277
Charlotte, witness marriage of Ebenezer **WANZER**, Jr. & Lucy **LEACH**	1	181
Charlotta, witnessed marriage of Jacob **WANZER** & Phebe **LEACH**	1	208
Charlotte, witnessed marriage of Jehu **HOAG** & Phebe **WANZER**	1	250
Charlotte, witnessed marriage of David **SANDS** & Paulina **LEACH**	1	277
Clara, m. William A. **BLACKNEY**, June 22, 1840, by Rev. Daniel Baldwin	1	344
Deborah, m. Eleazar **FAIRCHILD**, Jr., Jan. 18, 1786	1	55
Elizabeth, witnessed marriage of Jacob **WANZER**, & Phebe **LEACH**	1	208
Emeline, of New Milford, m. Isaac **BATES**, of Wallingford, May 9, 1836, by E. Huntington	1	296
Ephraim, witnessed marriage of David **SANDS** & Paulina **LEACH**	1	277
Flora, witnessed marriage of Ebenezer **WANZER**, Jr. & Lucy **LEACH**	1	181
Flora, witnessed marriage of Enoch **CARPENTER** & Sophia **LANE**	1	184
Ira, of Sherman, m. Elizabeth **HAVILAND**, of New Milford, Nov. 12, 1829, by Rev. E. Huntington	1	232
Ira, witnessed marriage of David **SANDS** & Paulina **LEACH**	1	277
Jane, witnessed marriage of Jacob **WANZER** & Phebe **LEACH**	1	208
Jane C., witnessed marriage of Jehu **HOAG** & Phebe **WANZER**	1	250
Jane C., witnessed marriage of David **SANDS** & Paulina **LEACH**	1	277
Jane C., witnessed marriage of Gurdon **SWIFT** & Jane **WANZER**	1	288

	Vol.	Page

LEACH, LEACK, (cont.)

	Vol.	Page
John, of Trumbull, m. Mrs. **FULLAR**, of Bridgeport, Mar. 10, 1844, by Rev. James Kilborn, of Bridgeport	1	392
Levi, of Sherman, m. Edeth **FERRISS**, of New Milford, Mar. 9, 1826, by Rev. Andrew Eliot	1	193
Levi, of Sherman, m. Laura **FERRISS**, of New Milford, Jan. 22, 1833, by E. Huntington	1	257
Levi, witnessed marriage of Enoch **CARPENTER** & Sophia **LANE**	1	184
Luce, d. Amos & Deborah, b. Aug. 14, 1769	LR11	9
Lucy, d. William & Charlotte, of Sherman, m. Ebenezer **WANZER**, Jr., of New Fairfield, s. Ebenezar & Betsey, 10th m. 26th d., 1820, before 31 witnesses. Int. Pub. at Oblong, N. Y.	1	180
Mary, witness marrige of Ebenzer **WANZER**, Jr. & Lucy **LEACH**	1	181
Meriam, m. Samuel **MARSH**, Nov. 15, 1771	1	44
Merritt, witnessed marriage of Gurdon **SWIFT** & Jane **WANZER**	1	288
Merritt H., witnessed marriage of Jehu **HOAG** & Phebe **WANZER**	1	250
Merritt H., witnessed marriage of David **SANDS** & Paulina **LEACH**	1	277
Moses W., witness marriage of Ebenezer **WANZER**, Jr. & Lucy **LEACH**	1	181
Moses W., witnessed marriage of Enoch **CARPENTER** & Sophia **LANE**	1	184
Moses W., witnessed marriage of Jacob **WANZER** & Phebe **LEACH**	1	208
Naomi, d. Amos & Deborah, b. July 17, 1766	LR8	1
Paulina, witnessed marriage of Jehu **HOAG** & Phebe **WANZER**	1	250
Paulina, d. William & Charlotte, of Sherman, Conn., m. David **SANDS**, of New Windsor, Co. of Orange, N. Y., s. Nathaniel & Rebecca, 6th m. 18th d., 1834, before 46 witnesses. Int. Pub. at Oblong, N. Y.	1	276-7
Phebe, d. William & Charlotte, of Sherman, m. Jacob **WANZER**, of New Fairfield, s. John & Grace, 10th m. 26th d., 1826, before 26 witnesses. Int. Pub. at Oblong, N. Y.	1	208
Phebe, witnessed marriage of Ebenezer **WANZER**, Jr. & Lucy **LEACH**	1	181
Phebe, witnessed marriage of Jacob **WANZER** & Phebe **LEACH**	1	208
Phebe P., witnessed marriage of Enoch **CARPENTER** & Sophia **LANE**	1	184
Susan, witnessed marriage of Ebenezer **WANZER**, Jr. & Lucy **LEACH**	1	181

	Vol.	Page
LEACH, LEACK, (cont.)		
Susan, witnessed marriage of Enoch **CARPENTER** & Sophia **LANE**	1	184
William, witness marraige of Ebenezer **WANZER,** Jr. & Lucy **LEACH**	1	181
William, witnessed marriage of Enoch **CARPENTER** & Sophia **LANE**	1	184
William, witnessed marriage of Jacob **WANZER** & Phebe **LEACH**	1	208
William, Jr., witnessed marriage of Jehu **HOAG** & Phebe **WANZER**	1	250
W[illia]m, witnessed marriage of Jehu **HOAG** & Phebe **WANZER**	1	250
William, witnessed marriage of David **SANDS** & Paulina **LEACH**	1	277
William, Jr., witnessed marriage of David **SANDS** & Paulina **LEACH**	1	277
William, witnessed marriage of Gurdon **SWIFT** & Jane **WANZER**	1	288
Zubah, d. Amos & Deborah, b. Aug. 7, 1767	LR11	9
LEAVENWORTH, Moss, of Roxbury, m. Amarillis **BEECHER,** of New Milford, Dec. 25, 1827, by Rev. Andrew Eliot	1	216
LEE, Abraham, of Fishkill, N. Y., m. Anne **LANE,** of New Milford, Dec. 26, 1824, by Daniel Gaylord	1	111
Martin, of Sherman (lately from New York State), m. Sally **BRIGGS,** of New Milford, Mar. 10, 1825, by Daniel Gaylord, J. P.	1	110
Sally, of New Milford, m. Samuel **PAGE,** of Sherman, Dec. 25, 1822, by Daniel Gaylord, J. P.	1	55
Susan A., m. John R. **WAY,** b. of New Milford, Mar. 8, 1853, by Rev. A. B. Pulling	2	85
LEONARD, LENARD, Ebenezer, m. Miriam **STEVENS,** Jan. 5, 1758	LR6	2
Elijah, of Kent, m. Abigail **GILBERT,** of Sherman, Nov. 10, 1822, by Daniel Gaylord, J. P.	1	52
LESSEY, Philothete, d. John F. & Anna, b. June 16, 1781, in new Fairfield, m. Ebenezer **HILL,** s. Silas & Sarah, of New Milford, Nov. 27, 1800	1	232
LEWIS, Abner G., m. Chloe **FISHER,** Feb. 5, 1721*, by Rev. Andrew Eliot *(Written "1720/1")	1	62
Betsey, m. Asa **BALDWIN,** July 8, 1798	1	73
Caroline, m. Orlando **MORGAN,** Apr. 2, 1854, by Rev. Eleazer Beecher	2	98
Charles, m. Catherine **THATCHERRE,** b. of New Milford, Dec. 26, 1850, by Rev. David Murdock, Jr.	2	66
Chloe, m. William **LAMSON,** Jan. 29, 1843, by Rev. Eleazer Beecher	1	378
Deborah, d. Thomas & Mary, b. Nov. 17, 1770	LR10	2

	Vol.	Page
LEWIS, (cont.)		
Ebenezer, s. Thomas & Mary, b. Apr. 14, 1774	LR10	2
James, s. Thomas & Mary, b. Nov. 5, 1782	LR10	2
Jeremiah, s. Thomas & Mary, b. Feb. 11, 1776	LR10	2
John, s. Thomas & Mary, b. June 24, 1779	LR10	2
John H., of New Milford, m. Lucy J. **PATCHEN**, of Danbury, Dec. 13, 1846, by J. Kilborn	2	21
Mary, m. Phelix **CATEN**, Sept. 11, 1843, by Rev. Eleazer Beecher	1	390
Sarah, d. Thomas & Mary, b. Mar. 1, 1769	LR10	2
Thomas, m. Mary **TERRIL**, May 1, 1768	LR10	2
LINES, Clarissa, d. Joseph & Phebe, b. Mar. 12, 1759	LR7	35
Daniel, s. Joseph & Phebe, b. Jan. 3, 1766	LR7	35
Erwin, m. Maria **ROSWELL**, Oct. 3, 1852, at Southville, by Rev. Richard D. Kirby	2	78
Joseph, m. Phebe **BALDWIN**, Sept. 11, 1758	LR7	35
Joseph, d. July 29, 1792	LR7	35
Lucy, m. William A. **KNAPP**, Feb. 10, 1836, by E. Huntington	1	297
Mercy, m. Alanson N. **CANFIELD**, b. of New Milford, Mar. 29, 1837, by N. Porter	1	304
Philo, s. Joseph & Phebe, b. Jan. 11, 1769	LR7	35
Reuben, s. Joseph & Phebe, b. Jan. 21, 1761	LR7	35
William A., m. Betsey A. **SULLIVAN**, b. of New Milford, June 1, 1843, by J. Greenwood	1	387
LIVINGSTON, Lois, Mrs., of Roxbury, m. Sherman **PECK**, of Bridgewater, Apr. 10, 1836, by Albert B. Camp	1	293
LOBDELL, Hiram, of Brookfield, m. Julia Jennet **IVES**, of New Milford, [ ], 1840, by Nathan Rice	1	357
LOCKWOOD, Abigail, m. William **WILLIAMS**, b. of. New Milford, Apr. 8, 1838, by N. Porter	1	316
Anna, d. Josiah & Molly, b. July 9, 1791	1	78
Asher, [s. Nehemiah & Dinah], b. Nov. 29, 1790	1	422
Belden, [s. Nehemiah & Dinah], b. Mar. 19, 1787	1	422
Betsey, of New Milford, m. Joseph A. **BLACKMAN**, of Newtown, Sept. 7, 1833, by H. Rood	1	263
Charles, s. Josiah & Molly, b. Nov. 27, 1802	1	78
Diana, [d. Nehemiah & Dinah], b. May 11, 1794	1	422
Edmond, [s. Nehemiah & Dinah], b. Mar. 15, 1785	1	422
Eliza, of New Milford, m. Edward W. **KING**, of Painsville, O., Oct. 26, 1837, by E. Huntington	1	310
Emily, m. Josiah L. **MINER***, Jan. 15, 1840, by Albert B. Camp *("MINER doubtful)	1	340
Henry G., m. Cornelia A. **MEAD**, b. of Bridgewater, Nov. 30, 1843, by John Greenwood	1	388
Josiah, m. Molly **DICKERSON**, Sept. [ ], 1784	1	78
Josiah, m. Abigail **WILKINSON**, Apr. 21, 1808, by Elisha Bostwick, J. P.	1	78

	Vol.	Page
LOCKWOOD, (cont.)		
Josiah, d. [ ], 1828		
Julia, m. John **BUEL**, Dec. 22, 1823, by Rev. Andrew Eliot	1	78
Julia, m. Asa **PICKETT**, Jan. 12, 1843, by E. Huntington	1	146
Lavinia, m. Abel A. **EDEY**, Oct. 20, 1841, by E. Huntington	1	383
Lyman, of Newtown, m. Ruth **SMITH**, of Bridgewater, Soc., Feb. 24, 1822, by Rev. Fosdic Harrison, of Roxbury	1	368
Marcus, s. Josiah & Molly, b. Dec. 29, 1786	1	30
Marcus, m. Mercy **RICHMOND**, b. of New Milford, June 16, 1811, by [ ]	1	78
Mary, m. Charles B. **HINE**, b. of New Milford, Jan. 15, 1834, by E. Huntington	1	169
Mercy, formerly w. of Maj. John **BOSTWICK**, d. Sept. 5, 1767	LR4	274
Molly, w. Josiah, d. Nov. 14, 1807, in the 43rd y. of her age	1	1
Nehemiah, free negro, m. Dinah [ ], Oct. 20, 1783	1	78
Nehemiah & Dinah, had Edmond, b. Mar. 15, 1785, Belden, b. Mar. 19, 1787, Asher, b. Nov. 29, 1790, Orra, b. Nov. 15, 1792, Dina, b. May 11, 1794, Rachel, b. Sept. 2, 1798 (colored)	1	422
Orra, [d. Nehemiah & Dinah], b. Nov. 15, 1792	1	422
Rachel, [d. Nehemiah & Dinah], b. Sept. 2, 1798	1	422
Sally, m. Joseph **BUCKINGHAM**, Aug. 9, 1801	1	422
Samuel Addison, m. Eliza A. **BLACKNEY**, Nov. 25, 1828, by Rev. E. Huntington	1	94
Stanley, s. Josiah & Molly, b. Nov. 4, 1793	1	226
Sukey, d. Josiah & Molly, b. Mar. 7, 1785; d. Jan. 17, 1786	1	78
LOVEL, Hannah, m. Edmond **CLARK**, Dec. 13, 1796	1	78
LOVEMAN, Charles, m. Lucinda **FRENCH**, b. of New Milford, Oct. 3, 1842, by Rev. Daniel Baldwin	1	71
LOVERIDGE, LOVERIDG, Emeline, m. David J. **STONE**, b. of New Milford, Sept. 13, 1831, by E. Huntington	1	375
Orissa, of New Milford, m. Orrin **YOUNG**, of Roxbury, Jan. 15, 1829, by Rev. Andrew Eliot	1	247
LUDLOW, Joseph, m. Lucy **FULLER**, b. of New Milford, Oct. 12, 1815, by Elisha Bostwick, J. P.	1	227
LUMM, Andrew, s. Samuel & Hannah, b. Feb. 25, 1742/3	LR5	10
Jonathan, s. Samuel & Hannah, b. Apr. 20, 1738	LR5	5
LYNDS, Annita, d. Joseph & Phebe, b. June 9, 1763	LR7	5
LYON, LION, Barbary, d. Ephraim & Marcy, b. May 19, 1798	1	35
Catharine N., of Fairfield, m. Benjamin S. **BROOKS**, of New York, Oct. 13, 1847, by John Greenwood	2	143
Ephraim, b. Oct. 15, 1768, in Fairfield, m. Marcy **TERRILL** Mar. 20, 1793	1	32
Henry, s. Ephraim & Marcey, b. Dec. 9, 1794	1	143
Noble, s. Ephraim & Marcey, b. Oct. 20, 1796	1	143
Noble, m. Sally **STONE**, Jan. 30, 1821, by Rev. Benjamin Benham	1	143

	Vol.	Page

LYON, LION, (cont.)
Noble, of New Milford, m. Hannah **PAGE**, of Sherman, Aug.
   31, 1845, by Rev. Johnson Howard — 1, 401
Ruth, of New Milford, m. Abel **EDWARDS**, of Sherman,
   Nov. 27, 1833, by E. Huntington — 1, 274

McCOMBS, Thomas, m. Huldah **BELL**, b. of New Milford, Nov.
   25, 1841, by Rev. Z. Davenport — 1, 364

McCONE, Mary, m. Patrick **CONNER**, Feb. 3, 1852, by Rev.
   Michael O'Farrell — 2, 75

Mc[C]OY, Mehetibel, m. Samuel **BUCK**, July 1, 1762 — LR7, 15

McDONELL, Abraham, m. Urania **HUBBELL**, May 11, 1841, by
   B. B. Parsons — 1, 358

McDURFE, John, m. Abigail S. **SCOT**, June 28, 1840, by Rev.
   Eleazer Beecher — 1, 345

McEWEN, MacEUEN, McEUEN, McEUNE, Anna Charlana, of
   New Milford, m. Jonas Fowler **MERWIN**, of Orange,
   Dec. 28, 1823, by Rev. Benjamin Benham — 1, 150
Bithiah, m. Lamuel **BUCK**, Aug. 27, 1755 — LR7, 10
Elizabeth, [d. John & Elizabeth], b. Feb. 18, 1768 — LR11, 1
George, s. John & Elizabeth, b. Mar. 13, 1755 — LR7, 13
George, s. John & Elizabeth, b. Mar. 13, 1755 — LR11, 1
George R., m. Amy **GRAHAM**, Sept. 13, 1847, by E.
   Huntington — 2, 36
James, s. John & Elizabeth, b. Apr. 25, 1757 — LR7, 13
James, s. John & Elizabeth, b. Apr. 25, 1757 — LR11, 1
John, of New Milford, m. Elizabeth **HILL**, of Fairfield,
   Apr. 30, 1754 — LR7, 13
John, m. Elizabeth **HILL**, Apr. 29, [ ] — LR11, 1
John, [s. John & Elizabeth], b. Jan. 9, 1762 — LR11, 1
Robert, [s. John & Elizabeth], b. Apr. 24, 1764 — LR11, 1
Rosanna, m. Theophilus **BALDWIN**, Feb. 13, 1821, by Rev.
   Benjamin Benham — 1, 52
William, s. John & Elizabeth, b. Sept. 18, 1759 — LR11, 1

McFARLAND, Peter, m. Huldah **JACKSON**, b. of Brookfield,
   Sept. 13, 1846, by Rev. Samuel Weeks — 2, 39

McGARRY, Sally, m. David **BOWDITCH**, of Dover, N. Y., Sept.
   11, 1834, by H. Rood — 1, 278

McGRAW, Louise, m. George S. **WELTON**, b. of Bridgwater, Feb.
   19, 1826, by Rev. Fosdic Harrison, of Roxbury — 1, 199
Rebecca, of New Milford, m. George **HOPHUAS***, of New
   Fairfield, Feb. 6, 1843, by E. Huntington *(Probably
   "HOPKINS") — 1, 394

**McKINNEY, MACKENEY, MACKENNIE, MACKENNEY,
MACKENIE, MACKKINE**, Amos, s. James & Elenor, b. June 4,
   1749 — LR6, 14
James, m. Ellenor **BRADSHAW**, Feb. 10, 1741/2, by Roger
   Brownson, J. P. — LR4, 2
James, m. Ellenor **BRADSHAW**, Feb. 10, 1742 — LR6, 14

	Vol.	Page

McKINNEY, MACKENEY, MACKENNIE, MACKENNEY, MACKENIE, MACKKINE, (cont.)

	Vol.	Page
James F., m. Sarah SHERWOOD, b. of New Milford, Jan. 15, 1845, by William H. Bangs	1	399
John, s. James & Ellenor, b. May 3, 1743	LR4	2
John, s. James & Elenor, b. May 3, 1743	LR6	14
Mary, d. James & Elenor, b. June 16, 1754	LR6	14
McMAHON, Anna, m. Joseph FERRISS, Jr., Dec. 11, 1796	1	90
Constantine, of Washington, m. Fanny HINE, of New Milford, Nov. 28, 1822, by Rev. Andrew Eliot	1	38
Cornelius, s. John & Sophia, b. Apr. 30, 1822	1	43
George, m. Laura HILL, Nov. 12, 1839, by E. Huntington	1	337
Henry C., m. Mary [ ], b. of New Milford, Aug. 29, 1831, by H. Rood	1	244
John, m. Sophia WELLS, Jan. 10, 1821, by Rev. Andrew Eliot	1	43
Joseph N., m. Sarah A. BARNES, b. of New Milford, Nov. 27, 1839, by Noah Porter	1	333
Minerva, of New Milford, m. Isaac HAYES, of Unadilla Otsego Co., N. Y., Sept. 26, 1831, by H. Rood	1	169
Phebe, m. Samuel KNAPP, Feb. 14, 1796, by Rev. Nathaniel Taylor	1	62
Thalia Maria, of New Milford, m. Alexis PAINTOR, of Westfield, Mass., Apr. 24, 1826, by Rev. Andrew Eliot	1	203
MAIN, Cynthia, of New Milford, m. Albert B. HALLOCK, of Litchfield, Oct. 26, 1853, by Rev. A. B. Pulling	2	90
John, m. Olive DEMMON, Nov. 9, 1820, at the house of Walker Platt, by Eleazar Beacher	1	179
MALLET, MALLETT, Asher, s. Matthew & Anna, b. Aug. 4, 1796	1	72
Asher, m. Harriet FORD, Dec. 18, 1822, by Rev. Andrew Eliot	1	175
Charlotte, of New Milford, m. John RUTHERFORD, of Savannah, July 28, 1853, by David Murdock, Jr.	2	88
Henry W., m. Jane O. BENEDICT, b. of New Milford, Oct. 11, 1846, by John Greenwood	2	20
Huldah A., m. Ebenezer BURCH, b. of New Milford, Sept. 20, 1835, by Rev. G. L. Brownell, of Woodbury	1	289
Isaac, m. Eliza KEELER, Apr. 18, 1822, by Rev. Benjamin Benham	1	23
Ithamar, m. Loiza FORD, b. of New Milford, Apr. 28, 1827, by Rev. Josiah L. Dickerson	1	129
Matthew, m. Anna MOREHOUSE, July 5, 1795	1	72
Polly Ann, of New Milford, m. Jared S. ISBEL, of Woodbury, Dec. 25, 1834, by Rev. Fosdic Harrison, of Roxbury	1	287
Sally, m. Eli PEET, b. of New Milford, Oct. 4, 1833, by H. Rood	1	266
Susan, of New Milford, m. Martin ISBELL, of Naugatuck, Apr. 22, 1839, by E. Huntington	1	335

MALLORY, MALERY, MALLERY, MALLOREY, Caleb, [s.

	Vol.	Page
Caleb & Miriam], b. Aug. 3, 1712	LR2	364
Caleb, d. Aug. 20, 1716	LR2	358
Caleb, m. Elizabeth DeFORIST, b. of New Milford, Dec. 5, 1734, by John Bostwick, J. P.	LR4	15
Caleb, s. Caleb & Elisabeth, b. Oct. 23, 1749	LR6	1
Charles B., m. Eliza BEERS, b. of Bridgewater, Mar. 14, 1841, by Albert B. Camp	1	352
Daniel, of Bridgeport, m. Clarissa GILBERT, of New Milford, Feb. 13, 1825, by Rev. Andrew Eliot	1	137
Deborah, [d. Caleb & Miriam], b. May 11, 1710	LR2	364
Deborah, m. Sam[ue]ll HITCHCOCK, b. of New Milford, Apr. 23, 1730	LR2	342
Elizabeth, of New Haven, m. John BOOTH, s. John & Dorothy, Jan. 9, 1717	2	111
Elisabeth, d. Caleb & Elisabeth, b. May 7, 1743	LR4	15
Elizabeth, m. Israel BOSTWICK, July 12, 1767, by Samuell Canfield, J. P.	LR10	2
Elizabeth, m. Israel BOSTWICK, July 12, 1767, by Samuell Canfield, J. P.	LR11	2
Eunice, d. Caleb & Elisabeth, b. Sept. 7, 1746	LR4	15
George N., m. Julia HENDRIX, Apr. 1, 1829, by Rev. Eleazar Beecher	1	215
John, [s. Caleb & Miriam], b. Apr. 7, 1715	LR2	364
John, of New Milford, m. Ann WOODRUFF, of the parish of Kensington, Farmington, May 7, 1740, by Rev. William Burnam, of Kensington	LR4	3
Lois, d. Caleb & Elizabeth, b. Dec. 10, 1735	LR4	15
Loois, d. Caleb & Elizabeth, b. Apr. 5, 1738	LR4	15
Lois, m. Solomon NORTHRUP, Apr. 5, 1764*, by Samuell Bostwick, J. P. *("4" not clear)	LR7	1
Martin, m. Sally J. RANDALL, b. of Bridgewater, Sept. 30, 1846, by Rev. J. Kilborn	2	19
Miriam, [d. Caleb & Miriam], b. May 23, 1708	LR2	364
Miriam, m. Thomas PICKET, b. of New Milford, Dec. 13, 1716	LR2	357
Miriam, m. Jonathan HITCHCOCK, b. of New Milford, Oct. 16, 1728	LR2	341
Nancy, m. Edwin PEARCE, b. of South Britain, Nov. 29, 1836, by A. B. Camp	1	301
Sarah, d. John & Ann, b. Dec. 29, 1742	LR4	3
Simmons, s. John & Ann, b. July 29, 1741	LR4	3
William, m. Mrs. Betsey BEMIS, Aug. 9, 1846, by Rev. Eleazer Beecher	2	17

MANVILLE, Hiram, of Woodbury, m. Paulina COLE, of New

Milford, Feb. 11, 1849, by Rev. J. Kelbourn	2	50

MARSH, Abigail, w. Joseph, d. Jan. 28, 1793

	1	45
Abigail, d. Joseph & Deborah, b. Aug. 18, 1799	1	45

	Vol.	Page
MARSH, (cont.)		
Abigail, m. William H. **FAIRCHILD**, Nov. 21, 1825, by Rev. Andrew Eliot	1	157
Abigail, m. Herman **SHERWOOD**, Dec. 29, 1825, by Rev. Andrew Eliot	1	194
Abraham, s. John & Rachel, b. July 9, 1780	LR12	5
Adeline E., of New Milford, m. Julius **CABLE**, of New Preston, Nov. 19, 1845, by J. Greenwood	1	405
Albert Francis, s. Elihu, 2nd & Elizabeth, b. June 25, 1805	1	167
Allen, s. Joseph & Deborah, b. June 8, 1797	1	45
Allen, of New Milford, m. Abigail Ellen **TERRILL**, of New Fairfield, Mar. 9, 1820, in New Fairfield	1	72
Amos Horrace, s. Samuell & Meriam, b. Mar. 23, 1785	1	44
Amos Horrace, m. Ann **SHERWOOD**, b. of New Milford, Feb. 15, 1819	1	186
Amy Lorain, d. William & Rachel, b. Jan. 26, 1808	1	162
Anan, m. Lucy A. **PEET**, b. of New Milford, [Nov. 20, 1839], by B. B. Parsons	1	332
Ann, of New Milford, m. John C. **BERRY**, of Kent, Dec. 15, 1830, by Heman Rood	1	120
Ann, of New Milford, m. John C. **BERRY**, of Kent, Dec. 15, 1830, by Heman Rood	1	206
Ann Jennet, d. John & Terrissa, b. Oct. 31, 1823	1	141
Anthony, s. John & Abigail, b. Aug. 12, 1778	LR12	13
Betsey, m. Frederick **BLACKMAN**, b. of New Milford, Oct. 8, 1834, by E. Huntington	1	282
Betsey Ann, d. Bradley & Sally, b. Sept. 11, 1813	1	115
Betsey Ann, of New Milford, m. Jasper Moody **HOWES**, of South East, Mar. 21, 1830, by Rev. E. Huntington	1	133
Betsey Avis, d. Elihu, 2nd & Elizabeth, b. Mar. 14, 1814	1	167
Bradley, s. Samuel & Meriam, b. Apr. 23, 1780	1	44
Bradley, m. Sally **WELLS**, b. of New Milford, Jan. 10, 1805, by Elisha Bostwick, J. P.	1	115
Caroline Elizabeth, d. John & Terrissa, b. Mar. 31, 1829	1	141
Clark, m. Mary Esther **STONE**, Sept. 4, 1851, at the house of Chauncey Stone, by Rev. James L. Scott	2	70
Cordelia, d. William & Rachel, b. Jan. 12, 1806	1	162
Cornelia, m. Merwin **HILL**, b. of New Milford, Sept. 18, 1845, by E. Huntington	2	4
Cornelia Abigail, d. Allen & Abigail, b. Aug. 25, 1822	1	72
Daniel, m. Charlotte **WILLIAMS**, June 11, 1833, by E. Huntington	1	263
Daniel D., m. Eliza E. **CROSBY**, Jan. 6, 1842, by E. Huntington	1	379
Ebenezer B., s. Orrin B. & Maria, b. July 12, 1830	1	234
Edwin, s. Allen & Abigail, b. Dec. 18, 1820	1	72
Electa, d. Elihu, 2nd & Elizabeth, b. July 21, 1799	1	167
Electa, of New Milford, m. Calvin O. **COPLEY**, of		

138   BARBOUR COLLECTION

	Vol.	Page
MARSH, (cont.)		
Montgomery, Oct. 14, 1835, by E. Huntington	1	294
Elihu, s. John & Abigail, b. July 18, 1774	LR12	13
Elihu, s. Samuel & Meriam, b. June 9, 1776	1	44
Elihu, 2nd, m. Elizabeth SWORDS, Jan. 13, 1793	1	167
Elihu, d. Dec. 1, 1830, ae 54 y. 5 m. 21 d.	1	167
Elizabeth L., of New Milford, m. Judson CURTIS, of New Haven, last evening, [Sept. 5, 1824], by Maltby Gelston	1	91
Elizabeth Lune, d. Bradley & Sally, b. Feb. 8, 1806	1	115
Ellet, s. William & Rachel, b. Nov. 14, 1802	1	162
Esther, d. John & Rachel, b. Dec. 24, 1771	LR12	5
Esther, m. Isaac C. WELLS, b. of New Milford, May 7, 1826, by Rev. C. A. Boardman	1	206
Eunice, d. Elihu & Elizabeth, b. Jan. 30, 1793 *(Entry crossed out in original)	1	167
Eunice, d. Elihu & Elizabeth, b. July 30, 1793	1	167
George, s. Samuel & Meriam, b. May 12, 1789	1	44
George Martin, m. Betsey SHERWOOD, Mar. 14, 1811, by [ ]	1	138
George W[illiam], m. Phebe FERRIS, b. of New Milford, Nov. 29, 1827, by Rev. Andrew Eliot	1	217
Hannah, d. Joseph & Abigail, b. Sept. 10, 1784	1	45
Hannah, m. Zechariah FERRISS, Jr., Sept. 15, 1802, by Elisha Bostwick, J. P.	1	97
Hannah, w. Riverius C., d. [ ]	1	189
Henry, m. Nancy STONE, b. of New Milford, Dec. 23, 1847, by E. Huntington	2	37
Henry Leach, s. John & Terrissa, b. Sept. 6, 1818	1	141
Holman, s. Joseph & Deborah, b. Apr. 28, 1802	1	45
Horace, s. Elihu, 2nd & Elizabeth, b. Sept. 2, 1795 (Entry crossed out in original)	1	167
Horace, s. Elihu & Elizabeth, b. Sept. 2, 1795	1	167
Horace, m. Fanny SHERMAN, b. of New Milford, Jan. 4, 1821, by Rev. Benjamin Benham	1	22
Hulda, d. Allen & Abigail, b. Mar. 15, 1831	1	72
James, s. Wanzer & Urania, b. Mar. 18, 1825; d. Oct. 24, 1860	1	66
Jane, of New Milford, m. Julius CABLE, of New Preston, Feb. 21, 1837, by Noah Porter	1	303
John, m. Rachel PRINDLE, Feb. 11, 1771	LR12	5
John, Jr., m. Abigail WANZER, Mar. 2, 1772	LR12	13
John, s. Samuell & Meriam, b. July 19, 1795	1	44
John, m. Terrissa BRADLEY, b. of New Milford, July 28, 1816, by Elisha Bostwick, J. P.	1	141
John Buckley, m. Laura HINE, b. of New Milford, Oct. 19, 1823, by Rev. Andrwew Eliot	1	185
John Read, s. John & Abigail, b. Feb. 11, 1776	LR12	13
Joseph, s. Sameul & Meriam, b. Mar. 16, 1778	1	44
Joseph, m. Abigail WALDO, Nov. 29, 1781	1	45

NEW MILFORD VITAL RECORDS 139

	Vol.	Page
MARSH, (cont.)		
Joseph, m. Deborah **WALDO**, Nov. 19, 1793	1	45
Joseph Jackson, s. Allen & Abigail, b. Aug. 17, 1824	1	72
Laura A., m. Joel W. **BAILEY**, b. of New Milford, Jan. 8, 1833, by Rev. Nathan D. Benedict	1	258
Lavinia, of New Milford, m. Daniel E. **GIDDINGS**, of Sherman, Jan. 20, 1835, by H. Rood	1	286
Lois, d. John & Rachel, b. Oct. 23, 1773	LR12	5
Lucy, d. John & Rachel, b. Mar. 13, 1778	LR12	5
Marshall, m. Julia Maria **HILL**, Nov. 20, 1844, by E. Huntington	2	2
Mary, d. John & Abigail, b. Jan. 16, 1773	LR12	13
Mary, of New Milford, m. Almerin **BROTHERTON**, of Sherman, Oct. 7, 1833, by Rev. Nathan D. Benedict	1	265
Mary A., m. Charles M. **FERRISS**, June 12, 1839, by E. Huntington	1	336
Meriam, [w. Samuel], d. [ ], "previous to her husband"	1	44
Mira Ann, of New Milford, m. Thomas A. **WELTON**, of Oxford, Oct. 12, 1837, by E. Huntington	1	310
Mothe*, of New Milford, m. Gilbert N. **CROSSBY**, of New Milford, Mar. 16, 1844, by William H. Bangs *(Possibly Mattie")	1	397
Oliver T., s. Allen & Abigail, b. Jan. 25, 1839	1	72
Orabilla, d. Joseph & Abigail, b. Feb. 2, 1789	1	45
Orman Bradley, s. Elihu, 2nd & Elizabeth, b. July 7, 1803	1	167
Ormond, m. Maria **HILL**, Apr. 5, 1832, by E. Huntington	1	255
Orrin B., m. Meria T. **HILL**, b. of New Milford, Oct. 14, 1829, by Rev. John Lovejoy	1	234
Orrin Bradley, s. Bradley & Sally, b. Jan. 9, 1808	1	115
Phillip Wells, s. Bradley & Sally, b. Dec. 22, 1815	1	115
Philo Judson, s. John & Terrissa, b. Oct. 27, 1821	1	141
Phineas, s. John & Rachel, b. Jan. 30, 1776	LR12	5
Rachel, w. William, d. Jan. 28, 1810	1	162
Riverius C., m. Eunice **CAMP**, Oct. 3, 1825, by Rev. Andrew Eliot	1	189
Riverius Chauncey, m. Hannah **MILES**, b. of New Milford, May 27, 1824, by Rev. Benjamin Benham	1	189
Royal, s. John & Terrissa, b. July 11, 1827	1	141
Sally, w. Bradley, d. Dec. 8, 1827	1	115
Samuel, m. Meriam **LEACH**, Nov. 15, 1771	1	44
Samuel, d. May 14, 1822, in the 71st y. of his age	1	44
Samuel David, s. Samuel & Meriam, b. Oct. 22, 1792	1	44
Samuel Marcus, s. Amos H. & Ann, b. Nov. 26, 1819	1	186
Samuel Marcus, m. Ann E. **GRAHAM**, Nov. 23, 1846, by E. Huntington	2	24
Samuel Waldo, s. Joseph & Abigail, b. Apr. 18, 1791	1	45
Sophia Abba, d. Bradley & Sally, b. Jan. 18, 1820	1	115
Surizah, d. Joseph & Abigail, b. Apr. 3, 1787	1	45

MARSH, (cont.)

	Vol.	Page
Susan, m. David Seelye **BUCK**, May 29, 1807	1	94
Susan, of New Milford, m. Sylvester **STEWART**, of Sherman, Apr. 6, 1840, by Rev. Elijah Baldwin	1	344
Susan E., m. David G. **ODELL**, b. of New Milford, Oct. 9, 1844, by William H. Bangs (Entry crossed out in original)	1	397
Susan E., of New Milford, m. Orange **PEPPER**, of New Fairfield, Oct. 9, 1844, by William H. Bangs	1	398
Susan Emily, d. John & Terrissa, b. Jan. 30, 1820	1	141
Susan Maria, d. John & Terrissa, b. Mar. 11, 1817	1	141
Susanna, d. Samuel & Meriam, b. Nov. 17, 1786	1	44
Villeroy, s. John & Terrissa, b. July 26, 1825	1	141
Walter, s. Amos H. & Ann, b. June 27, 1821	1	186
Walter, m. Arabella **FERRISS**, b. of New Milford, Sept. 15, 1852, by Rev. David P. Sanford	2	84
Wanzer, m. Urania **FERRISS**, b. of New Milford, Nov. 11, 1822, by Rev. Andrew Eliot	1	66
Warner, s. Elihu, 2nd & Elizabeth, b. Dec. 3, 1797	1	167
Warner, s. Elihu & Elizabeth, b. Dec. [ ] (Entry crossed out in original)	1	167
Wealthy, d. William & Rachel, b. Oct. 18, 1804	1	162
William, s. Joseph & Abigail, b. Jan. 25, 1783	1	45
William, m. Rachel **NICHOLS**, Feb. 18, 1802	1	162
MASTERS, Stephen, m. Evaline **CLARK**, b. New Milford, Oct. 5, 1832, by Rev. Heman Rood	1	252
Susan, of New Milford, m. Judson **BLACKMAN**, of Woodbury, Apr. 6, 1826, by Rev. Andrew Eliot	1	42
MAXFIELD, Jerusha, m. Nathan **PEET**, b. of New Milford, Sept. 10, 1854, by Rev. w. H. Russell	2	102
William J., m. Jerusha **MOREHOUSE**, Dec. 3, 1826, by Rev. Eleazar Beecher	1	209
MEAD, Abigail L., m. Jeremiah G. **RANDALL**, Jan. 1, 1839, by E. Huntington	1	334
Apphia, m. Henry **BEARDSLEY**, b. of New Milford, Sept. 22, 1805, by Elisha Bostwick, J. P.	1	123
Cornelia A., m. Henry G. **LOCKWOOD**, b. of Bridgewater, Nov. 30, 1843, by John Greenwood	1	388
Emeline, of New Milford, m. George **HOYT**, of Sherman, Dec. 12, 1830, by Abner Brundage	1	239
Michael, of Kent, m. Caroline **BALDWIN**, of New Milford, Sept. 4, 1842, by E. Huntington	1	381
Peter, m. Phebe **SMITH**, b. of New Milford, Dec. 9, 1824, by Rev. Fosdick Harrison, of Roxbury	1	159
Sally, m. Washington **FENTON**, b. of New Milford, Aug. 15, 1799, by Elisha Bostwick, J. P.	1	74
MERAMBLE, D., of Naugatuck, m. Catharine E. **HAIGHT**, of New Milford, Oct. 8, 1854, by Rev. David Murdock, Jr.	2	107

	Vol.	Page
MERRILDS, Deborah, m. Peter **JOHNSON**, Jan. 1, 1767	LR10	6
MERWIN, MURWIN, Abbey M., m. David D. **NOBLE**, b. of New Milford, Apr. 10, 1839, by Noah Porter	1	326
Abel, s. David & Mary, b. Sept. 18, 1750	LR5	6
Abel, m. Rebeckah **NOBLE**, b. of New Milford, June 15, 1774, by Bushnel Bostwick, J. P.	LR12	17
Abel, d. Mar. 30, 1823	LR12	17
Abigail, d. David & Mary, b. Mar. 22, 1764	LR5	10
Abigail, d. Abel & Rebeckah, b. Mar. 13, 1777	LR12	17
Anna, d. Stephen & Martha, b. Nov. 17, 1782	LR13	1
Betsey, d. John & Ruth, b. Oct. 12, 1783	LR10	5
Caroline T., of New Milford, m. David C. **SANFORD**, of Litchfield, Sept. 1, 1822, by Rev. Benjamin Benham	1	74
Charlotte, m. Ezra **MURRAY**, Nov. 9, 1834, by E. Huntington	1	283
Clarinda, d. John & Mercy, b. Feb. 17, 1769	LR10	5
Cornelia Mary Ann, d. David, 3rd & Sarah, b. Apr. 20, 1807	1	7
Daniel, s. John & Ruth, b. Mar. 28, 1788	LR10	5
David, m. Mary **NOBLE**, b. of New Milford, Dec. 23, 1742*, by Nathaniell Bostwick, J. P. *(Corrected. Perhaps "1743")	LR5	6
David, s. David & Mary, b. Mar. 7, 1742/3	LR5	6
David, s. David & Mary, d. May 7, 1754	LR5	6
David, s. David & Mary, b. July 3, 1757	LR5	10
David, Jr., m. Fanny **COMSTOCK**, July 15, 1771	1	33
David, s. Stephen & Martha, b. Nov. 11, 1777	LR13	1
David, d. Apr. 19, 1792	LR5	10
David, s. Stephen, m. Sarah **BROWNSON**, b. of New Milford, Feb. 23, 1804	1	7
David, d. [ ]	1	33
Delia, m. Andrew J. **BALDWIN**, b. of New Milford, Oct. 10, [1854], by Rev. David Murdock, Jr.	2	107
Elias C., of New Haven, m. Mary Jane **PICKETT**, of Bridgewater, Mar. 22, 1847, by James Kilborn	2	29
Elizabeth Mary, d. Stephen & Martha, b. Apr. 10, 1790	LR13	1
Hannah, twin with Jonathan, d. David & Mary, b. Nov. 14, 1760; m. Benedick **DAVIS**, [ ]; d. Mar. 1, 1809	LR5	10
Hannah, d. John & Ruth, b. Mar. 12, 1781	LR10	5
Hannah, m. Nathaniel **BROWNSON**, b. of New Milford, Feb. 13, 1806, by Elisha Bostwick, J. P.	1	129
Harriet O., m. Charles S. **TROWBRIDGE**, Dec. 5, 1854, by Rev. David Murdock	2	106
Harrison B., m. Sarah M. **BURR**, b. of New Milford, Jan. 24, 1841, by Nathan Rice	1	356
Harrison Brownson, s. David & Sarah, b. July 20, 1813	1	7
Henry, m. Susan **GAYLORD**, b. of New Milford, Oct. 2, 1828, by Rev. Andrew Eliot	1	222
Henry N., m. Betsey N. **HINE**, b. of New Milford, Nov. 27, 1845, by J. Greenwood	2	7

MERWIN, MURWIN, (cont.)

	Vol.	Page
Homer, s. John & Ruth, b. Jan. 15, 1792; d. June 3, 1816	LR10	5
Horace, m. Florinda PEET, b. of New Milford, Dec. 4, 1837, by N. Porter	1	313
Huldah, m. Eli SMITH, June 17, 1782, by Rev. David Brownson	LR13	16
Ichabod, s. John & Mary, b. July [ ], 1776; d. Mar. [ ], 1778	LR10	5
John, s. David & Mary, b. Aug. 24, 1744	LR5	6
John, m. Mercy WARNER, Nov. 6, 1766	LR10	5
John, m. Ruth WELCH, Dec. 31, 1777	LR10	5
John, d. May 22, 1826, ae 81 y. 8 m. 29 d.	LR10	5
John, m. wid. [ ] DIBBLE, [ ]	LR10	5
John Warner, s. John & Mercy, b. Sept. 16, 1774	LR10	5
Jonas Fowler, of Orange, m. Anna Charlana McEUEN, of New Milford, Dec. 28, 1823, by Rev. Benjamin Benham	1	150
Jonathan, twin with Hannah, s. David & Mary, b. Nov. 14, 1760	LR5	10
Jonathan, s. John & Ruth, b. Nov. 8, 1778; d. Apr. 12, 1782	LR10	5
Levi, m. Lois RUGGLES, Feb. 24, 1774	LR13	9
Lois, d. John & Ruth, b. July 25, 1785	LR10	5
Lois, m. Joshua STONE, b. of New Milford, Oct. 1, 1805, by Elisha Bostwick, J. P.	1	124
Lorain, of New Milford, m. Abel STUART, of Sherman, Mar. 5, 1807, by Elisha Bostwick, J. P.	1	139
Marcia H., of New Milford, m. Rev. Maltby GELSTON, of Clyde, N. Y., Oct. 20, 1834, by H. Rood	1	279
Marcus B., of New Haven, m. Minerva BUCKINGHAM, of New Milford, Jan. 4, 1846, by J. Greenwood	2	8
Marcus E., m. Orra A. GAYLORD, b. of New Milford, Jan. 10, 1844, by John Greenwood	1	390
Maria, m. William J. STONE, b. of New Milford, Sept. 1, 1836, by Noah Porter, Jr.	1	299
Martha, d. Stephen & Martha, b. Feb. 2, 1785	LR13	1
Martha, w. Stephen, d. Apr. 16, 1812	LR13	1
Martha W., m. John P. GIDDINGS, b. of New Milford, Feb. 27, 1849, by Jno Greenwood	2	51
Mary, d. David & Mary, b. Apr. 21, 1748	LR5	6
Mary, d. Miles & Mary, b. Dec. 18, 1753, in Milford; m. Jeremiah PLATT, s. Jeremiah & Hannah, Mar. 17, 1770	1	14
Mary, d. David & Mary, d. May 13, 1754	LR5	6
Mary, d. David & Mary, b. Apr. 5, 1755	LR5	6
Mary, d. John & Mercy, b. Dec. 12, 1772; d. Oct. [ ], 1776	LR10	5
Mary, w. David, d. [ ]	LR5	10
Mary G., m. Daniel B. WILSON, b. of New Milford, Jan. 21, 1845, by John Greenwood	1	397
Mercy, d. John & Mercy, b. Aug. 9, 1767	LR10	5
Mercy, w. John, d. Nov. 7, 1776	LR10	5
Miles, s. Stephen & Martha, b. Oct. 14, 1787	LR13	1

	Vol.	Page
MERWIN, MURWIN, (cont.)		
Noble, s. Abel & Rebekah, b. Mar. 31, 1775	LR12	17
Onor, d. John & Mercy, b. June 16, 1771; m. Truman **STONE**, [ ]; d. Aug. 8, 1799	LR10	5
Orange, s. David & Fanney, b. Apr. 7, 1776	1	33
Orange, m. Lydia **BOSTWICK**, b. of New Milford, Apr. 16, 1807, by Elisha Bostwick, J. P.	1	140
Phebe Abigail, m. William **HINE**, b. of New Milford, Dec. 9, 1804, by Elisha Bostwick, J. P.	1	114
Rebecca, m. Seymour **BUCK**, b. of New MIlford, Feb. 22, 1837, by Noah Porter	1	303
Ruth, w. John, d. Mar. 14, 1816	LR10	5
Samuel Tibbals, s. Stephen & Martha, b. Dec. 23, 1792	LR13	1
Sarah, d. David & Fanney, b. Apr. 15, 1773	1	33
Sarah, d. Levi & Lois, b. Apr. 30, 1782	LR13	9
Sarah, w. David, d. June 14, 1831, in the 49th y. of her age	1	7
Sarah, m. Oliver **SMITH**, b. of Bridgewater, Nov. 24, 1841, by Rev. Albert B. Camp	1	362
Stephen, s. Miles & Mary, b. Sept. 4, 1751	LR13	1
Stephen, m. Marthar **SMITH**, June 7, 1775, by Bushnel Bostwick, J. P.	LR13	1
Stephen, s. Stephen & Martha, b. May 4, 1780	LR13	1
Susan Almira, of New Milford, m. Samuel **SAGE**, of Colebrook, Jan. 29, 1834, by H. Rood	1	271
Tryphena, m. Marshall S. **PLATT**, Mar. 20, 1825, by Rev. C. A. Boardman	1	194
MESSER, Hannah, m. James **WILDMAN**, Apr. 4, 1833, by Rev. Luther Mead	1	260
MILES, Aville*, d. Samuel & Molly, b. Aug. 29, 1768 *("Arilla" in Orcutt's Hist.)	LR7	4
Betsey, m. Shubael R. **CUSHMAN**, Aug. 29, 1807, by Elisha Bostwick, J. P.	1	145
Elijah, s. Justis & Hannah, b. Jan. 16, 1753	LR5	4
Elijah, m. Harriet **PECK**, Jan. 15, 1826, by Rev. Eleazar Beacher	1	199
Eunice, m. Moses **BUCK**, b. of New Milford, Sept. 29, 1730	LR2	345
Eunice, d. Joseph & Dabora, b. Aug. 23, 1739	LR4	25
Hannah, d. Justus & Hannah, b. Dec. 13, 1758	LR5	4
Hannah, m. Riverius Chauncey **MARSH**, b. of New Milford, May 27, 1824, by Rev. Benjamin Benham, d. [ ]	1	189
Joseph, m. Daboroh **WELSH**, wid. John, b. of New Milford, Sept. 25, 1732, by Rev. Daniel Bordman	LR4	25
Joseph, s. Joseph & Dabora, b. July 4, 1737	LR4	25
Justus, s. Justus & Hannah, b. Aug. 3, 1740	LR5	4
Justus, & Martha Camp, w. Enos, made affidavit Mar. 28, 1765, before Paul Welch, J. P., that Samuel **DRINKWATER**, b. Mar. 27, 1744 O. S.	LR4	2
Justus, m. Emily Maria **BLACKNEY**, Feb. 7, 1821, by Rev.		

MILES, (cont.)

	Vol.	Page
Benjamin Benham	1	63
Mary, d. Joseph & Dabora, b. Oct. 14, 1733* *(Last "3" uncertain)	LR4	25
Mary, m. Josiah HUNGERFORD, Jan. 5, 1807, by Elisha Bostwick, J. P.	1	128
Mary A., m. John R. BUCKLEY, Aug. 26, 1827, by Rev. Eleazar Beecher	1	155
Mercy, d. Joseph & Daborah, b. Jan. 5, 1735/6* *("175/6" crossed out)	LR4	25
Molly, d. Samuel & Molly, b. Aug. 11, 1765	LR7	4
Molly, w. Samuel, d. June 27, 1775	LR7	4
Molly, m. Amasa FERRISS, Dec. 16, 1781	1	43
Patience, of Milford, m. Benjamin BUNNELL, of New Milford, Aug. 27, 1717	LR2	363
Patience, m. Ebenezer WASHBORN, June 29, 1721	LR4	20
Patiance, d. Jabe & Daboroh, b. May 6, 1745	LR4	25
Samuel, s. Justus & Hannah, b. Oct. 21, 1743	LR5	4
Samuel, m. Molly PICKET, b. of New Milford, Oct. 17, 1764, by [ ]	LR7	4
Sarah, d. Joseph & Dabora, b. July 23, 1742	LR4	25
Stephen, s. Justus & Hannah, b. Feb. 19, 1746/7	LR5	4
MILLARD, Patty, d. Joshua & Lydia, b. May 15, 1776, in Williamstown; m. Joseph CLARK, Jr., [Apr. 16, 1795]	1	70
Patty, m. Joseph CLARK, Jr., Apr. 16, 1795	1	70
MILLIGAN, George, m. Catharine TAYLOR, Nov. 13, 1788	1	37
John, s. George & Catharine, b. Jan. 17, 1792	1	37
Mary, d. George & Catharine, b. Mar. 17, 1796	1	37
William, s. George & Catharine, b. Feb. 6, 1790	1	37
MINOR, Abigail, d. Truman & Sarah, b. May 10, 1801	1	63
Abigail, m. Jonathan JESUP, b. of Bridgwater, Jan. 24, 1821, by Rev. Fosdic Harrison, of Roxbury	1	61
Abijah M., of Woodbury, m. Mary M. CLARK, of New Milford, Oct. 9, 1822, by Rev. Fosdic Harrison, of Roxbury	1	57
Anna, d. Christopher & Lucee, b. Feb. 26, 1769; d. Mar. 22, 1771* *(Date crossed out)	LR10	13
Christopher, m. Lucee AVEREL, Dec. 1, 1767	LR10	13
Daniel, s. Truman & Sarah, b. Oct. 17, 1794	1	63
George C., m. Esther RIGBY, b. of New Milford, May 20, 1849, by Mr. Butterfield	2	63
Gilbert S., of Cornwall, m. Julia A. PICKETT, of New Milford, Apr. 27, 1847, by E. Huntington	2	34
John, s. Truman & Sarah, b. Oct. 18, 1797	1	63
Josiah G.*, m. Elizabeth HUNT, b. of New Milford, Sept. 11, 1851, at Northville, by Rev. J. F. Jones, of Northville *(Probably "L")	2	73
Josiah L.*, m. Emily LOCKWOOD, Jan. 15, 1840, by Albert	1	340

NEW MILFORD VITAL RECORDS 145

	Vol.	Page
MINOR, (cont.)		
B. Camp *("MINER" doubtful)	1	340
Nathan, s. Christopher & Luece, b. Mar. 29, 1771	LR10	13
Sally, m. Hiram **RUGGLES**, b. of Bridgwater, May 8, 1823, by Rev. Fosdic Harrison, of Roxbury	1	75
Sarah, m. Truman **MINOR**, July 5, 1792, in Woodbury, by Rev. Noah Benedick	1	63
Truman, m. Sarah **MINOR**, July 5, 1792, in Woodbury, by Rev. Noah Benedick	1	63
MOGER, Hannah, d. James & Elisabeth, b. Feb. [ ], 1747/8	LR5	11
Isaac, s. James & Elisabeth, b. Mar. 3, 1744/5	LR5	11
James, m. Elisabeth **HERROW**, May 23, 1744, by Nathaniel Bostwick, J. P.	LR5	11
Jesse, m. Anna **WOOSTER**, Feb. 25, 1773, by Bushnel Boswick, J. P.	LR11	13
Rebecah Bowers, d. Reuben & Lydia, b. Apr. 1, 1780	LR13	16
Reuben, m. Lydia **HAWKINS**, Nov. 29, 1768	LR13	16
Silvester Wooster, s. Jesse & Anna, b. Feb. 3, 1774	LR11	13
Truman, s. Jesse & Anna, b. Oct. 18, 1775	LR11	13
MONROE, Henry, m. Phebe **MOSELEY**, Sept. 16, 1828, by Rev. Andrew Eliot	1	423
MOONEY, Susan, witnessed marriage of Jacob **WANZER** & Phebe **LEACH**	1	208
MOORE, MORE, [see also **MOOSE**], Ellen, m. Joseph E. **TREAT**, b. of New Milford, Mar. 6, 1844, by John Greenwood	1	391
Hannah, m. Charles **LAKE**, b. of New Milford, Mar. 17, 1841, by N. Porter	1	353
Harriet, m. George G. **LACY**, b. of New Milford, Oct. 30, 1838, by N. Porter	1	323
Martha E., m. James **DERRY**, b. of New Milford, Mar. 9, 1834, by H. Rood	1	272
Phebe R., m. S. J. **STILSON**, Feb. 1, 1837, by N. Porter. Int. Pub.	1	302
MOOSE, [see also **MOORE**], Sarah, d. John & Lydiah, b. July 5, 1751	LR6	3
MOREHOUSE, MOREHOUS, MORHOUSE, Abigail, d. Jair & Elizabeth, b. Nov. 30, 1817	1	176
Adonijah, s. John & Deborah, b. Mar. 11, 1771	LR12	2
Amanda Jane, d. Minor & Betsey Ann, b. May 6, 1832	1	148
Ammon, s. Lemuel & Mehetabel, b. June 24, 1797; d. Sept. 23, 1797	1	93
Ammon, m. Elisa A. **MORGAN**, b. of New Milford, June 5, 1853, by Rev. A. B. Pulling	2	82
Ammon, m. Eliza A. **MORGAN**, b. of New Milford, June 5, 1853, by Rev. A. B. Pulling	2	83
Ammon Brush, s. Lemuel & Mehetabel, b. July 24, 1798	1	93
Anna, d. John & Pheebe, b. Dec. 2, 1764	LR7	2

MOREHOUSE, MOREHOUS, MORHOUSE, (cont.)

	Vol.	Page
Anna, m. Matthew **MALLETT**, July 5, 1795	1	72
Anna, d. Daniel & Elizabeth, b. Nov. 28, 1799	1	95
Annar, d. John, Jr. & Sarah, b. Aug. 11, 1803	1	84
Anna, w. Stephen, d. Mar. 31, 1805, in the 61st y. of her age	LR7	34
Anna, d. Jair & Elizabeth, b. Mar. 16, 1816	1	176
Asher, s. Jair & Elizabeth, b. Mar. 5, 1822	1	176
Augustine, s. Stephen & Anna, b. Sept. 20, 1785	LR7	34
Austin, of Kent, m. Rebecca **KNAPP**, of New Milford, Jan. 25, 1831, by H. Rood	1	240
Benjamin, s. Stephen, Jr. & Sarah, b. Apr. 21, 1760	LR7	34
Caroline, d. Jair & Elizabeth, b. Aug. 30, 1806	1	176
Catharine, d. Lemuel & Mehetabel, b. Oct. 15, 1794	1	93
Catharine, d. John, Jr. & Sarah, b. Oct. 18, 1811	1	84
Clark, m. Ann **LATHROP**, Oct. 24, 1842, by E. Huntington	1	381
Clarrissa,m. Stanley G. **BENNITT**,Jan. 1,1840,by E. Huntington	1	339
Clarry, d. Jair & Elizabeth, b. Mar. 4, 1808	1	176
Cyrus, s. John, Jr. & Sarah, b. Nov. 11, 1808	1	84
Cyrus, m. Cornelia A. **CANFIELD**, b. of New Milford, Nov. 20, 1832, by Rev. H. Rood	1	255
Daniel, s. John & Phebe, b. Apr. 27, 1768	LR7	2
Daniel, m. Elizabeth **TUCKER**, Apr. 11, 1797	1	95
Daniel, s. Jair & Elizabeth, b. Apr. 15, 1813	1	176
Daniel, m. Caroline **BARTRAM**, June 2, 1842, by Eldad C. Jackson, J. P.	1	370
Edward Fitch, s. Minor & Betsey Ann, b. Apr. 22, 1828	1	148
Edward H., m. Bessie A. **SHERWOOD**, b. of New Milford, June 5, 1854, by J. W. Hoffman	2	108
Eliza, m. Joseph **BENNETT**, b. of New Milford, May 4, 1828, by Joel Sanford, J. P.	1	179
Eliza, Mrs., of New Milford, m. Curtis **PEET**, of Warren, Conn., Oct. 2, 1853, by J. F. Jones	2	89
Elizabeth, d. Jair & Elizabeth, b. Feb. 28, 1811	1	176
Elizabeth, of New Milford, m. Joel **SMITH**, of Kent, July 6, 1824, by Rev. C. A. Boardman, of New Preston	1	69
Ellen, m. Emmon H. **NEARING**, b. of New Milford, Mar. 25, 1839, by Noah Porter	1	325
Esther, b. Oct. 28, 1788; m. Nathaniel T. **GALBRITIA**, Nov. 15, 1806, by Elisha Bostwick, J. P.	1	136
Goold, s. John & Deborah, b. Dec. 3, 1774; d. Sept. 19, 1775	LR12	2
Hannah, d. Stephen & Sarah, b. May 9, 1772	LR7	34
Harriet, m. James **CROSBY**, b. of New Milford, July 5, 1846, by Rev. Joseph L. Morse	2	17
Helen, d. [Jabesh & Harriet], b. Mar. 31, 1840	1	240
Henry, s. [Jabesh & Harriet], b. Oct. 1, 1826	1	240
Isaac, s. John, Jr. & Sarah, b. Apr. 19, 1794	1	84
Jabez, s. John & Phebe, b. June 12, 1775	LR7	2

	Vol.	Page
MOREHOUSE, MOREHOUS, MORHOUSE, (cont.)		
Jabez, s. John, Jr. & Sarah, b. Sept. 22, 1797	1	84
Jabesh, m. Harriet BARLOW, Jan. 16, [ ], by Benjamin	1	240
Benham	LR7	2
Jair, s. John & Phebe, b. Mar. 14, 1781	1	176
Jair, m. Elizabeth MORGAN, July 2, 1802, by Daniel Everitt	1	176
Jair, s. Jair & Elizabeth, b. June 27, 1809		
Jair, 2nd, m. Sarah ELDERKIN, Mar. 28, 1830, by Rev.	1	236
Eleazer Beecher	1	176
Jerusha, d. Jair & Elizabeth, b. Aug. 7, 1803		
Jerusha, m. William J. MAXFIELD, Dec. 3, 1826, by Rev.	1	209
Eleazer Beecher	1	176
Jethro, s. Jair & Elizabeth, b. Sept. 19, 1814		
Jethro, of New Milford, m. Fanny CHURCHILL, of Roxbury,	1	274
Feb. 9, 1834, by E. Huntington	1	95
Joel, s. Daniel & Elizabeth, b. Oct. 9, 1797	1	176
Joel, s. Jair & Elizabeth, b. July 23, 1819		
John, m. Pheebe BEECHER, b. of New Milford, Dec. 27,1763	LR7	2
John, s. John & Phebee, b. Jan. 21, 1770	LR7	2
John, Jr., m. Sarah STRAIGHT, b. of New Milford, Jan. 22, 1793	1	84
John, of New Milford, m. Thankful ATWELL, of Montville, Dec. 25, 1808	LR7	2
John, 4th, m. Sally SMITH, b. of New Milford, Feb. 7, 1822, by Rev. Benjamin Benham	1	27
Julia, m. Merwin WALLER, b. of New Milford, Dec. 31, 1850, by Rev. James L. Scott	2	65
Laura, m. Jerome LATHROP, b. of New Milford, May 8, 1848, by J. Kilbourn	2	42
Lemuel, m. Mehetabel TREADWELL, Sept. 1, 1791	1	93
Loisa, of New Milford, m. James F. BOYCE, of Washington, N. Y., June 29, 1854, by Rev. James L. Scott	2	99
Lucy*, d. [Jabesh & Harriet], b. Dec. 20, 1827 *(Written "Suesa")	1	240
Lyman Banks, s. Lemuel & Mehetabel, b. Jan. 8, 1801	1	93
Mabel, m. Samuel BALDWIN, b. of New Milford, Feb. 14, 1827, by Rev. Andrew Eliot	1	212
Minor, s. Lemuel & Mehetabel, b. Aug. 11, 1792	1	93
Minor, s. Daniel & Elizabeth, b. Apr. 19, 1801	1	95
Minor, m. Betsey Ann PORTER, b. of New Milford, Dec. 1, 1823, by Rev. Benjamin Benham	1	148
Mortimer Bruce, s. Minor & Betsey Ann, b. Sept. 28, 1824	1	148
Olive, d. Stephen & Sarah, b. Dec. 6, 1768	LR7	34
Phebe, d. John & Phebe, b. Dec. 13, 1776	LR7	2
Phebe, d. Jair & Elizabeth, b. Feb. 2, 1805	1	176
Phebe, w. John, d. Feb. 20, 1807, in the 70th y. of her age	LR7	2
Phebe, m. Homer BEARD, June 10, 1841, by Daniel Baldwin	1	361
Ralph, s. [Jabesh & Harriet], b. Aug. 16, 1825	1	240

	Vol.	Page
MOREHOUSE, MOREHOUS, MORHOUSE, (cont.)		
Rebeckah, d. John & Debora, b. Apr. 4, 1773	LR12	2
Rhode, d. Stephen & Sarah, b. Oct. 31, 1766	LR7	34
Ruth, d. Stephen & Sarah, b. Mar. 27, 1774	LR7	34
Sally, m. Joseph **BROWN**, b. of New Milford, Mar. 31, 1830, by J. S. Covill	1	238
Sarah, d. Stephen & Sarah, b. Apr. 21, 1764	LR7	34
Sarah, w. Stephen, d. Mar. 28, 1776, in the 42nd y. of her age	LR7	34
Sarah Maria, m. Noble S. **BENNITT**, Sept. 15, 1841, by E. Huntington	1	366
Seymour, of Washington, m. Harriet **NORTHROP**, of New Milford, Sept. 7, 1828, by Rev. Harry Finch, of Washington	1	192
Stephen, Jr., of New Milford, m. Sarah **HAWLEY**, of Newtown, Apr. 8, 1759	LR7	34
Stephen, Jr., s. Stephen & Sarah, b. Mar. 8, 1762	LR7	34
Stephen, of New Milford, m. Anna **STILES**, of Lanesborough, Oct. 3, 1779, by Rev. Gideon Bostwick	LR7	34
Stiles, s. Stephen & Anna, b. Apr. 15, 1783	LR7	34
Suesa*, d. [Jabesh & Harriet], b. Dec. 20, 1827 *("Lucy" in Orcott's Hist.)	1	240
Sylvia, d. John, Jr. & Sarah, b. June 25, 1800	1	84
Tamar, m. Daniel **SHERMAN**, Jan. 1, 1826, by Rev. Andrew Eliot	1	195
Trial, m. Benjamin **GAYLARD**, Oct. 2, 1745, by Timothy Hatch, J. P.	LR6	12
MOREY, Aueintee M., m. Isaac **REYNOLDS**, b. of New Milford, Sept. 21, 1851, by D. Williams	2	72
David P., of West Stockbridge, Mass., m. Aminta M. **STONE**, of Bridgewater, Feb. 14, 1841, by Rev. Albert B. Camp	1	354
MORGAN, MORGIN, Abigail, d. James & Jerusha, b. June 1, 1785	LR10	14
Anna, d. James & Jerusha, b. Apr. 24, 1787	LR10	14
Anne, of New Milford, m. Epaphroditus **STRONG**, of Warren, Mar. 20, 1804, by Elisha Bostwick, J. P.	1	110
Daniel, s. James & Jerusha, b. July 17, 1769	LR10	14
Daniel, s. James & Jerusha, d. Nov. 19, 1794	LR10	14
Elijah, s. James & Jerusha, b. Apr. 8, 1793	LR10	14
Elisa A., m. Ammon **MOREHOUSE**, b. of New Milford, June 5, 1853, by Rev. A. B. Pulling	2	82
Eliza A., m. Ammon **MOREHOUSE**, b. of New Milford, June 5, 1853, by Rev. A. B. Pulling	2	83
Elizabeth, d. James & Jerusha, b. June 30, 1781	LR10	14
Elizabeth, m. Jair **MOREHOUSE**, July 2, 1802, by Daniel Everitt	1	176
Esther, d. James & Jerusha, b. Jan. 21, 1773	LR10	14
Esther, d. James & Jerusha, d. July 31, 1793	LR10	14
Gideon, m. Patience **COGSWELL**, June 16, 1772, by Rev.		

	Vol.	Page
MORGAN, MORGIN, (cont.)		
Jeremiah Day	LR11	1
James, m. Jerusha **BEECHER**, b. of New Milford, Feb. 16, 1766* (Perhaps "1768")	LR10	14
James, s. James & Jerusha, b. June 5, 1777	LR10	14
James, d. [ ]	LR10	14
Jerusha, d. James & Jerusha, b. Aug. 24, 1775	LR10	14
Jerusha, [w. James], d. Apr. 17, 1826	LR10	14
Laura, m. Adolphus **HALLOCK**, Feb. 23, 1823, by Rev. Andrew Eliot	1	81
Laury, d. James & Jerusha, b. Feb. 22, 1790	LR10	14
Laury, d. James & Jerusha, d. Oct. 5, 1793	LR10	14
Lyman, s. James & Jerusha, b. June 13, 1768; d. June 2, 1780	LR10	14
Lyman, s. James & Jerusha, b. Apr. 12, 1783	LR10	14
Orlando, m. Caroline **LEWIS**, Apr. 2, 1854, by Rev. Eleazer Beecher	2	98
Samuel, s. James & Jerusha, b. Apr. 5, 1779	LR10	14
Sarah, m. George **BUCKINGHAM**, b. of New Milford, Mar. 17, 1839, by Alonso F. Selleck	1	324
Tamar, d. James & Jerusha, b. Feb. 14, 1771	LR10	14
MORRIS, MORRISS, Caroline, m. Peter **WOOSTER**, b. of New Milford, Oct. 14, 1845, by Rev. William Atwill, of Bridgewater	2	6
Emily E., m. Charles G. **SANFORD**, June 6, 1837, by E. Huntington	1	311
Levi, m. Polly M. **SMITH**, Sept. 24, 1807, by Elisha Bostwick, J. P.	1	146
Mary Jennette, of Bridgewater, m. John P. **DeFOREST**, Feb. 10, 1847, by Rev. William Atwill, of Bridgewater	2	28
Richard, m. Sarah **BELL**, b. of Poughkeepsie, N. Y., Oct. 30, 1836, by Rev. F. Donnelly	1	299
Sarah, m. Joseph **WALLAR**, of New Preston, Aug. 5, 1756	LR8	1
MORRISON, William E. L., s. Abraham J. & Emeline C., b. Sept. 12, 1843	2	116
MOSELEY, Hannah, Mrs. of Westfield, m. Dea. Nathan **GAYLARD**, of New Milford, Mar. [ ], 1758* *("1768" crossed out)	LR4	7
Phebe, m. Henry **MONROE**, Sept. 16, 1828, by Rev. Andrew Eliot	1	423
MOSS, Amasa, m. Ruth **CLARK**, b. of New Milford, Nov. 3, 1768	LR10	16
Isaac, s. Isaac & Anna, b. Jan. 2, 1755	LR6	16
Lydiah, m. James **BRADSHAW**, Feb. 13, 1753, by Rev. Nathaniell Taylor	LR6	11
Lydia, d. Amasa & Ruth, b. May 8, 1769	LR10	16
Mary, d. Isaac & Anna, b. Aug. 27, 1760	LR6	16
Mehittabel, d. Isaac & Anna, b. Mar. 12, 1753	LR6	16
MOTT, Abel, m. Rachel **PIERCE**, May 11, 1756	LR7	23
Isaac, s. Abel & Rachel, b. Sept. 12, 1760	LR7	23

	Vol.	Page
MOTT, (cont.)		
Lucy, d. Abel & Rachel, b. Mar. 8, 1757	LR7	23
Lyman, s. Abel & Rachel, b. Sept. 18, 1758	LR7	23
Rhoda, d. Abel & Rachael, b. Jan. 20, 1763	LR7	23
MUDG, Abigail, see Abigail **SKINNER**	LR4	14
MUNSON, MONSON, Frederick A., m. Maria **JENNINGS**, Sept. 27, 1843, by E. Huntington	1	395
Mabel, m. Nathaniel **SMITH**, b. of New Milford, Jan. 19, 1854, by Rev. A. B. Pulling	2	94
Miles, of Bethlehem, m. Mabel **DOWNES**, of New Milford, June 7, 1849, by Ezra Noble, J. P.	2	53
MUNCY, [see also **MURRY**], Mary Ann, b. Mar. 28, 1798	1	289
MURPHY, Alfred T., m. Betsey A. **LAPHAM**, b. of New Milford, June 18, 1854, by J. W. Hoffman	2	109
David H., of Roxbury, m. Mahala **RICHMOND**, of New Milford, July 23, 1848, by E. Huntington	2	42
Orrin, of Brookfield, m. Julia Ann **STEWART**, of Bridgwater, Nov. 27, 1836, by A. B. Camp	1	301
MURRY, MURRAY, [see also **MUNCY**], Benjamin, s. John & Martha, b. Oct. 8, 1755	LR7	28
Elisabeth, m. John Henry **NEARING**, May 5, 1743, by Roger Brownson, J. P.	LR5	3
Eunice, d. John & Martha, b. Jan. 28, 1752	LR7	28
Ezra, m. Charlotte **MERWIN**, Nov. 9, 1834, by E. Huntington	1	283
George, s. John & Martha, b. Aug. 9, 1757	LR7	28
George A., witnessed marriage of Jacob **WANZER** & Phebe **LEACH**	1	208
James, m. Patience **HAULEY**, b. of New Milford, Nov. 5, 1755, by [ ]	LR7	3
Jasper, s. John & Martha, b. Aug. 3, 1753	LR7	28
John, of New Milford, m. Martha **HOWARD**, May 30, 1751	LR7	28
John, Sergt., d. Sept. 7, 1760, in Camp	LR7	28
Mary Ann, m. Asa **REED**, Apr. 20, 1784	1	1
Saul, s. John & Martha, b. Jan. 20, 1759	LR7	28
MYGATT, MYGAT, Abigail S., m. John G. **NOBLE**, b. of New Milford, Feb. 4, 1821, by Rev. Andrew Eliot	1	60
Andrew B., m. Caroline **CANFIELD**, b. of New Milford, June 7, 1843, by [ ]	1	387
Augustine, s. Benjamin Starr & Tryphene, b. Apr. 6, 1776	LR12	20
Benjamin Starr, m. Tryphena **WARNER**, Apr. 5, 1775	LR12	20
Benstar*, s. Joseph & Elizabeth, b. Oct. 15, 1774; d. Nov. 16, 1776 *("Benjamin Starr" in Orcutt's Hist.)	LR13	4
Eli, Jr., of New York City, m. Sophia **NORTHROP**, of New Milford, Oct. 24, 1837, by N. Porter	1	306
Ezra, s. Joseph & Elizabeth, b. Oct. 21, 1771	LR13	4
Henry S., m. Mary **HINE**, b. of New Milford, Sept. 17, 1839, by N. Porter	1	330
Joseph, m. Elizabeth **RICHMON**, May 15, 1771	LR13	4

MYGATT, MYGAT, (cont.)

	Vol.	Page
Martha D., of New Milford, m. Henry R. TREADWELL, of New York, May 16, 1843, by John Greenwood	1	386
Mary E., m. Henry W. BOOTH, b. of New Milford, Oct. 6, 1846, by John Greenwood	2	19
Noadia, witnessed marriage of Enoch CARPENTER & Sophia LANE	1	184
Rebecca, d. Benjamin Starr & Tryphene, b. Dec. 22, 1777; d. Mar. 15, 1778	LR12	20
Rebecca, d. Benjamin Starr & Tryphena, b. May 7, 1787	LR12	20
Sarah, d. Benjamin Starr & Tryphene, b. May 16, 1779	LR12	20
William N., m. Hetty ALLEN, b. of New Milford, Dec. 7, 1840, by Rev. N. Porter	1	353

NARIGON, William, m. Minerva ELDERKIN, b. of New Milford, Dec. 17, 1826, by Rev. Benjamin Benham — 1, 209

NASH, John, of Newtown, m. Caroline BENSON, of New Milford, Oct. 19, 1831, by Rev. John Lovejoy — 1, 194

NEARING,

	Vol.	Page
Abigail J., m. George BALDWIN, b. of New Milford, Apr. 1, 1835, by H. Rood	1	286
Ann, d. John & Elizabeth, b. May 12, 1746	LR5	3
Ann, d. John Henry & Elisabeth, b. May 12, 1746	LR7	33
Ann, m. Isaac BROWNWELL, Apr. 7, 1769	LR10	11
Caroline E., m. John BEARDSLEY, May 24, 1830, by Rev. Eleazer Beecher	1	235
Elisabeth, d. John & Elisabeth, b. Oct. 2, 1760	LR7	33
Emmon H., m. Ellen MOREHOUSE, b. of New Milford, Mar. 25, 1839, by Noah Porter	1	325
Hannah, [d. John & Elizabeth], b. Apr. 6, 1753	LR5	3
Hannah, d. John & Elisabeth, b. Apr. 6, 1753	LR7	33
Henry, [s. John & Elizabeth], b. Jan. 29, 1758	LR5	3
John, [s. John & Elizabeth], b. Apr. 12, 1748	LR5	3
John, s. John Henry & Elisabeth, b. Apr. 12, 1748	LR7	33
John, of New Lisbon, N. Y., m. Lucy M. BALDWIN, Dec. 13, 1821, by Rev. Andrew Eliott	1	9
John Henry, m. Elisabeth MURRY, May 5, 1743, by Roger Brownson, J. P.	LR5	3
Joseph, s. John Henry & Elisabeth, b. June 3, 1762	LR5	3
Maray, [d. John & Elizabeth], b. Apr. 14, 1751	LR5	3
Mary, d. John & Elisabeth, b. Apr. 14, 1751	LR7	33
Ruby, [d. John & Elizabeth], b. Mar. 3, 1756	LR5	3
Ruby, [d. John & Elizabeth], b. Jan. 29, 1758	LR7	33
Sarah, d. John & Betty, b. May 15*, 1744 *(Possibly "13th")	LR5	3
Sarah, d. Jno Henry & Elisabeth, b. May 25, 1744	LR7	33
Sarah, m. John BRISTER, Jr., Jan. 12, 1764	LR7	38
William, of New Lisbon, N. Y., m. Lavinia A. BULKLEY, of New Milford, Oct. 6, 1840, by Noah Porter	1	349

NETTLETON, John H., of Watertown, m. Elizabeth M. HITCHCOCK, of New Milford, June 13, 1837, by N.

	Vol.	Page
NETTLETON, (cont.)		
Porter, Jr.	1	305
NEWCOMB, William F., m. Esther **WELLS**, Feb. 27, 1831, by Rev. Eleazar Beecher	1	114
NEWTON, Edward E.*, of New Preston, m. Caroline **NORTHROP**, of New Milford, July 7, 1830, by H. Rood *("Ezekiel N." written over)	1	239
John, m. Fanny **FENTON**, Nov. 7, 1801, by Elisha Bostwick, J. P.	1	89
NICHOLS, Abiah, d. Isaac & Sarah, b. Apr. 20, 1790	LR13	14
Andrew B., s. [Cato & Julia], b. Jan. 15, 1840	1	423
Asa, s. Isaac & Sarah, b. Nov. 4, 1786	LR13	14
Benedict W., of Bridgeport, m. Sally **JACKSON**, of New Milford, May 29, 1842, by N. Porter, Jr.	1	372
Cato, b. Feb. 19, 1804	1	423
Cato, m. Julia **CURRIE**, Sept. 16, 1828, by Rev. Andrew Eliot	1	423
Cato, d. July 31, 1847, ae 43 y. 6 m.	1	423
Chloe, of New Milford, m. Hiram **TURRELL**, of Roxbury, Sept. 29, 1834, by E. Huntington	1	281
Ezra L., s. [Cato & Julia], b. Oct. 10, 1844	1	423
Hanford, s. Isaac & Sarah, b. Oct. 3, 1788	LR13	14
Henry S., s. [Cato & Julia], b. Nov. 6, 1841	1	423
Isaac, m. Sarah **STEVENS**, June 15, 1779	LR13	14
Isaac, Jr., m. Caroline **BUCKINGHAM**, b. of New Milford, Oct. 26, 1823, by Rev. Benjamin Benham	1	173
Laura M., d. [Cato & Julia], b. Nov. 19, 1835	1	423
Lorain, m. Hermon **BRIGGS**, Dec. 6, 1821, by Rev. Andrew Eliot	1	9
Mary, d. Isaac & Sarah, b. Nov. 3, 1783	LR13	14
Meriam, m. Gilbert **FERRISS**, Apr. 15, 1778	LR12	9
Meriam, m. Gilbert **FERRISS**, Apr. 28, 1778	LR13	9
Peter, s. Isaac & Sarah, b. Feb. 14, 1782	LR13	14
Rachel, m. Ephraim **BOOTH**, s. John & Dorothy, [ ], 1709	2	111
Rachel, d. Isaac & Sarah, b. Apr. 3, 1780	LR13	14
Rachel, m. William **MARSH**, Feb. 18, 1802	1	162
Samuel C., m. Betsey **KNOWLES**, b. of New Milford, Nov. 24, 1824, by Rev. Benjamin Benham	1	161
Sarah, d. Isaac & Sarah, b. Mar. 8, 1785	LR13	14
Theophilus, of Newtown, m. Lucia **NOBLE**, of New Milford, May 2, 1822, by Rev. Andrew Eliot	1	44
William, m. Martha **HAWLEY**, May 20, 1775	1	32
[NICHOLSON], NICKELSON, Angus, m. Sarah **PLAT[T]**, b. of New Milford, May 11, 1767, by Rev. Nathaniel Taylor	LR10	6
Angus, m. Sarah **PLATT**, May 11, 1767	1	68
Angus, s. Angus & Sarah, b. Oct. 4, 1786	1	68
Angus, d. Mar. 26, 1804	1	68
Anny, d. Angus & Sarah, b. Aug. 17, 1768; d. Nov. 17, 1769	1	68
Anny*, d. Angus & Sarah, b. Aug. 17, 1768; d. Nov. 16, 1769		

	Vol.	Page
[NICHOLSON], NICKELSON, (cont.)		
*(Name rubbed out)	LR10	6
Anny, d. Angus & Sarah, b. Mar. 3, 1773	1	68
Barbara, d. Angus & Sarah, b. Mar. 14, 1771	LR10	6
Barbary, d. Angus & Sarah, b. Mar. 14, 1771	1	68
Donald, s. Angus & Sarah, b. Aug. 16, 1789; d. Sept. 26, 1791	1	68
Mary, d. Angus & Sarah, b. Sept. 1, 1779	1	68
Mary, [d. Angus & Sarah], d. Nov. 24, 1781	1	68
Mary Ann, alias Polly, d. Angus & Sarah, b. Oct. 30, 1784	1	68
Polly, see Mary Ann NICKELSON	1	68
Samuel Malcolm, s. Angus & Sarah, b. Aug. 19, 1781	1	68
Sarah, d. Angus & Sarah, b. June 23, 1777	1	68
Sarah, wid. Angus, d. [ ]	1	68
NOBLE, NOBLES, Abagal, d. Capt. Stephen, m. Matthew HAULEY, s. Ephraim, Dec. 21, 1737	LR4	20
Abigail, d. John, Jr. & Annah, b. May 12, 1746	LR5	15
Abraham, s. John, Jr. & Annah, b. Sept. 23, 1748	LR5	15
Anna, m. Ichabod Betts PALMER, Sept. 23, 1759	LR8	1
Anne, wid. Ezra D., d. Aug. 22, 1815, ae 65	1	116
Asahel, m. Catharn PEAT, Jan. 3, 1750	LR7	39
Asahel, d. Mar. 8, 1796	LR7	39
Asell, s. David & Susanna, b. Oct. 7, 1725	LR2	348
Biah, d. John & Abigaill, b. May 19, 1721	LR2	362
Biah, m. Benjamin BENNITT, b. of New Milford, Dec. 4, 1740, by Roger Brownson, J. P.	LR4	27
Bostwick, s. Elnathan & Jehannah, b. Dec. 30, 1788	1	2
Caroline, of New Milford, m. Sumner HAMILTON, of Bangor, Me., June 23, 1841, by Noah Porter, Jr.	1	358
Chauncey, of New Milford, m. Sally BLACKMAN, of Newtown, Dec. 3, 1839, by Nathaniel Perry, J. P.	1	331
Clolie, d. Thomas & Mary, b. Feb. 11, 1739/40	LR4	24
Curtiss, s. Elnathan & Jehannah, b. Nov. 18, 1774	1	2
Cyrenius, s. Elnathan & Jehannah, b. Sept. 27, 1776	1	2
Daniel, s. David & Lydia, b. July 22, 1721	LR2	348
Daniel, s. Zadock & Freelove, b. Jan. 11, 1762	LR6	16
David, of New Milford, m. Lydia FORWARD, of Danbury, June 15, 1720	LR2	348
David, of New Milford, m. Susanna SHERMAN, of Woodbery, June 1*, 1722, by [ ] *(Possibly "2" intended)	LR2	348
David, s. Zadok & Freelove, b. Dec. 26, 1759	LR6	16
David D., m. Abbey M. MERWIN, b. of New Milford, Apr. 10, 1839, by Noah Porter	1	326
Diamia, d. Zadok & Freelove, b. Mar. 5, 1768	LR6	16
Edward M., m. Polly Ann BEARDSLEY, b. of New Milford, Oct. 9, 1848, by John Greenwood	2	43
Elijah, s. Ezra D. & Eunice, b. Feb. 6, 1776; d. Oct. 17, 1777, ae 1 y. 8 m. 11 d.	1	116

NOBLE, NOBLES, (cont.)

	Vol.	Page
Elisha, s. Asahel & Catharn, b. Oct. 25, 1750	LR7	39
Elizabeth, d. Stephen & Abigall, b. Dec. 13, 1715	LR2	360
Elizabeth, m. Isaac **DeFOREST**, b. of New Milford, Aug. 17, 1732	LR4	3
Elisabeth, d. Gideon & Martha, b. Sept. 15, 1754	LR6	4
Elnathan, m. Jehannah [ ], Feb. 10, 1774	1	2
Elnathan, s. Elnathan & Jehannah, b. July 15, 1779	1	2
Esther, d. Ezra D. & Eunice, b. May 28, 1783; d. Sept. 10, 1784, ae 15 m. 12 d.	1	116
Esther, 2nd, d. Ezra D. & Eunice, b. Feb. 1, 1787	1	116
Eunice, d. David & Susanna, b. Jan. 13, 1727/8	LR2	348
Eunice, d. Gideon & Martha, b. Nov. 12, 1750	LR6	4
Eunice, d. Zadok & Freelove, b. May 17, 1764	LR6	16
Eunice, w. Ezra D., d. Feb. 24, 1804, ae 59 y. 5 m. 22 d.	1	116
Ezra, m. Eunice **BOSTWICK**, b. of New Milford, June 24, 1772, by Rev. Nathaniel Taylor	1	116
Ezra, s. Ezra D. & Eunice, b. July 9, 1779	1	116
Ezra, d. Mar. 26, 1808, ae 59 y. 2 m. 11 d.	1	116
Ezra D., m. Anne **GREGORY**, June 22, 1805, by Elisha Bostwick, J. P.	1	116
Ezra Dibble, s. Zadock & Freelove, b. Jan. 3, 1749	LR6	16
Gideon, s. Stephen & Abigaill, b. Mar. 10, 1725/6	LR2	350
Gideon, m. Martha **PRIME**, Mar. 22, 1747	LR6	4
Grace, d. John, b. Jan. 22, 1718/19	LR2	362
Grace, d. John, d. Feb. 1, 1718/19	LR2	358
Hannah, w. John, d. Mar. 1, 1716	LR2	343
Hannah, d. John & Abgail, b. [ ]; bp. July 5, 1730	LR2	363
Hannah, d. Thomas & Mary, b. Aug. 23, 1738	LR4	24
Hannah, d. Ezra D. & Eunice, b. Jan. 1, 1781	1	116
Hannah, m. Benajah **FAIRCHILD**, Jan. 29, 1806, by Elisha Bostwick, J. P.	1	128
Hephe*, d. Thomas & Mary, b. Mar. 31, 1742 *("Heziba" in Orcutt's Hist.)	LR4	24
Ichabod, s. Zadock & Freelove, b. July 5, 1750	LR6	16
Ichabod, s. Zadock & Freelove, d. July 28, 1753	LR6	16
Ichabod, s. Ezra D. & Eunice, b. Mar. 30, 1773	1	116
Israel, s. Stephen & Sarah, b. Mar. 25, 1735	LR4	24
Israel, of Kent, m. Charlania **FERRIS**, of New Milford, Nov. 23, 1834, by E. Huntington	1	283
Jerusha, d. Stephen & Sarah, b. Feb. 6, 1733/4	LR4	24
John, Sr., d. Aug. 17, 1714	LR2	358
John, his twins [ ], d. Dec. [ ], 1715	LR2	343
John, s. John & Abigaill, b. Sept. 21, 1717	LR2	362
John, Jr., of New Milford, m. Anna **PEETE**, of Stratford, Aug. 23, 1743, in parish of Unity, by Rev. Richardson Miner, of Unity	LR5	15
John, s. John, Jr. & Annah, b. June 31, 1751; d. Oct. 31, 1751	LR5	15

	Vol.	Page
NOBLE, NOBLES, (cont.)		
John G., m. Abigail S. **MYGATT**, b. of New Milford, Feb. 4, 1821, by Rev. Andrew Eliot	1	60
Jonathan, s. Stephen & Abigaill, b. Mar. 14, 1717/18	LR2	360
Jonathan, m. Mary **BALDWIN**, b. of New Milford, Oct. 15, 1744, by Nathaniel Bostwick, J. P.	LR5	14
Jonathan, s. Gideon & Martha, b. Jan. 9, 1748/9* *("4" written over "5")	LR6	4
Jonathan, s. Gideon & Martha, d. *Sept. 9, 1753 *("was b." crossed out)	LR6	4
Julia C., m. Sheldon **BLACKMAN**, b. of New Milford, June 3, 1845, by J. Greenwood	1	400
Lucia, of New Milford, m. Theophilus **NICHOLS**, of Newtown, May 2, 1822, by Rev. Andrew Eliot	1	44
Marah, m. Nathan **NOBLE**, May 2, 1748	LR7	3
Marcia, m. Stephen **SMITH**, b. of New Milford, Dec. 30, 1828, by Rev. Andrew Eliot	1	226
Marcy, d. John & Abigail, b. [ ]; bp. June 29, 1729	LR2	363
Margaret, m. Jeams **HINE**, b. of New Milford, Dec. 23, 1726	LR2	348
Maria A., of New Milford, m. John M. **THOMPSON**, of Bridgeport, Oct. 14, 1840, by Noah Porter	1	350
Marietta, of New Milford, m. David A. **FOSTER**, of Brookfield, Dec. 24, 1820, by Rev. Benjamin Benham	1	22
Martha, d. Gideon & Martha, b. Aug. 16, 1752	LR6	4
Marten, s. Zadock & Freelove, b. Feb. 6, 1752	LR6	16
Marten, s. Zadock & Freelove, d. July 29, 1753	LR6	16
Martin, s. Ezra D. & Eunice, b. June 18, 1774	1	116
Mary, d. Stephen & Abigail, b. June 27, 1723	LR2	360
Mary, m. David **MERWIN**, b. of New Milford, Dec. 23, 1742*, by Nathaniel Bostwick, J. P. *(Corrected. Perhaps "1743")	LR5	6
Mary, d. Thomas & Mary, b. Jan. 8, 1745*/6 *(Possible "6")	LR4	24
Mary Ann, of New Milford, m. Fitch **FERRIS**, of Canaan, Aug. 22, 1838, by Noah Porter	1	318
Mary L., of New Milford, m. Austin B. **TROWBRIDGE**, of Danbury, June 11, 1831, by David S. Boardman, J. P.	1	244
Matilda, d. Morgan & Patience, b. Dec. 5, 1774	LR13	3
Micahel, s. Nathan & Marah, b. Jan. 3, 1754* *("1751") in Orcutt's Hist.)	LR7	3
Morgin, s. Stephen & Sarah, b. Jan. 10, 1738/9	LR4	24
Nathan, s. John & Abigail, b. Feb. 4, 1722; bp. Feb. 4, 1722	LR2	363
Nathan, m. Marah **NOBLE**, May 2, 1748	LR7	3
Nathan & Marah, had twins [ ], b. May 26, 1754	LR7	3
Nathaniel, s. Elnathan & Jehanna, b. May 10, 1792	1	2
Phebie, d. Thomas & Mary, b. May 11, 1744	LR4	24
Phebe, d. Nathan & Marah, b. May 15, 1754* *("1749" in Orcutt's Hist.)	LR7	3
Philo, s. Ezra D. & Eunice, b. Feb. 6, 1778	1	116

NOBLE, NOBLES, (cont.)

	Vol.	Page
Prudence, d. Stephen & Abigail, b. May 3, 1721	LR2	360
Prudence, m. Amos COLLINS, May 10, 1741, by John Bostwick, J. P.	LR7	7
Rachel, d. John & Abigail, b. July 3, 1726	LR2	363
Rachel Ann, m. Thomas B. LACEY, b. of New Milford, Sept. 11, 1838, by N. Porter	1	319
Rebeckah, d. Zadock & Freelove, b. Feb. 24, 1756	LR6	16
Rebeckah, m. Abel MERWIN, b. of New Milford, June 15, 1774, by Bushnel Bostwick, J. P.	LR12	17
Reuben, s. Asahel & Cathern, b. Oct. 5, 1756	LR7	39
Salley, d. Elnathan & Jehannah, b. Apr. 12, 1783	1	2
Sarah, d. John & Abigail, bp. Aug. [ ], 1724	LR2	363
Sarah, d. John & Annah, b. July 23, 1744	LR5	15
Sarah, a witness at wedding of John FERRIS & Abigal TRYON, Quakers	LR4	22
Sherman, s. Asael & Cathern, b. Sept. 14, 1752	LR7	39
Stephen, Jr., s. Capt. Stephen & Abagil, m. Sarah FERRISS, d. Zachariah & Sarah, July 18, 1733	LR4	24
Stephen, Capt., d. Dec. 10, 1755	LR2	358
Susanna, d. David & Susanna, b. July 19, 1730) *("30" crossed out)	LR2	348
Susannah, m. John CARRINGTON, June 16, 1756	LR7	20
Susannah, d. Zadok & Freelove, b. Jan. 25, 1758	LR6	16
Sylvanus, s. Elnathan & Jehannah, b. Apr. 17, 1785	1	2
Thomas, s. John & Hannah, b. Jan. 16, 1711/12 (This transcribed in N. M. "Sept. 24, 1717)	LR2	362
Thomas, of New Milford, s. John & Hannah, m. Mary CURTISS, d. Capt. Thomas, of Kensington, in Farmington, June 29, 1737. Witnesses: John Noble & John Warner	LR4	24
Thomas, s. Thomas & Mary, b. Sept. 28, 1748	LR4	24
Thomas, s. Elnathan & Jehannah, b. July 18, 1781; d. Oct. 14, 1781	1	2
Wakefield, s. Zadok & Freelove, b. Jan. 14, 1766	LR6	16
William, s. John & Abigal, b. Mar. 2, 1719/20	LR2	362
William, s. John, d. May 8, 1720	LR2	358
Zachariah, s. Stephen & Sarah, b. Apr. 10, 1737	LR4	24
Zadock, s. David & Susanah, b. Sept. 17, 1723	LR2	344
Zadock, s. David & Susanna, b. Sept. 17, 1723	LR2	348
Zadock, of New Milford, m. Freelove DIBBEL, of Danbury, Oct. 27, 1747, by Rev. Ebenezer White	LR6	16
Zadok, s. Zadok & Freelove, b. Dec. 20, 1772	LR6	16

NORTHROP, NORTHRUP, Abba, d. Cyrus & Betsey, b. Oct. 14, 1799

	Vol.	Page
	1	91
Abigail, m. Nathan GUNN, May 30, 1776	LR13	5
Abner, m. Laura CAMP, b. of New Milford, Jan. 12, 1808, by Elisha Bostwick, J. P.	1	154

	Vol.	Page
NORTHROP, NORTHRUP, (cont.)		
Adeline, m. Elijah J. **CAMP**, Oct. 19, 1820, by Rev. C. A. Boardman	1	177
Amos, Jr., m. Anne **GRANT**, Dec. 7, 1768, by Paul Welch, J. P.	LR10	4
Amos, s. Amos, Jr. & Anne, b. Oct. 11, 1772	LR10	4
Ann, d. Amos & Ann, b. Apr. 3, 1751	LR5	9
Ann B., m. Joseph **TOMLINSON**, b. of New Milford, Dec. 10, 1843, by John Greenwood	1	389
Anne, wid. of Amos, Jr., b. Sept. 11, 1752, in Litchfield; m. Thomas **WELLS**, Jan. 11, 1780	1	13
Anne, m. Nathanael **TAYLOR**, 3rd, Aug. 31, 1774	1	30
Betsey, m. Isaac **SANFORD**, b. of New Milford, Sept. 11, 1806, by Elisha Bostwick, J. P.	1	132
Betsey, of New Milford, m. George N. **CROSBY**, of Phelps, N. Y., Nov. 8, 1837, by N. Porter	1	306
Bette, d. David & Rachel, b. Apr. 20, 1772	LR12	15
Billey, s. Solomon & Lois, b. Nov. 27, 1767* *(Date crossed out)	LR7	1
Caroline, d. Cyrus & Betsey, b. July 27, 1796	1	91
Caroline, of New Milford, m. Edward E.* **NEWTON**, of New Preston, July 7, 1830, by H. Rood *("Ezekiel N." written over)	1	239
Charles, of New Milford, m. Eunice **BULL**, of Kent, Oct. 28, 1847, by E. Huntington	2	36
Charlotte, m. Charles **GLOVER**, b. of Newtown, Sept. 3, 1837, by A. B. Camp	1	308
Clarry, d. Cyrus & Betsey, b. Nov. 12, 1805	1	91
Cyrus, m. Betsey **WELLS**, July 31, 1795	1	91
Cyrus, s. Joel W. & Catharine, b. May 26, 1838	1	249
David, s. Amos & Ann, b. July 27, 1746	LR5	9
David, m. Rachel **GRANT**, July 3, 1769, by Paul Welch, J. P.	LR12	15
David, m. Mary **PICKETT**, Oct. 25, 1846, by E. Huntington	2	24
David D., m. Laura **WOODRUFF**, b. of New Milford, Apr. 25, 1841, by Rev. Elijah Baldwin	1	354
Eli C., of Brookfield, m. Lucinda S. **GREGORY**, of Norwalk, Dec. 3, 1823, by Rev. Benjamin Benham	1	149
Elvira, of New Milford, m. Levi **TUCKER**, of Washington, June 20, 1830, by H. Rood	1	53
Emeline, of New Milford, m. Garry **BISHOP**, of Washington, May 13, 1833, by E. Huntington	1	261
Emiline E., m. Benjamin E. **BOSTWICK**, b. of New Milford, Sept. [ ], 1831, by H. Rood	1	245
Emily, d. Cyrus & Betsey, b. Oct. 7, 1803	1	91
Frederick D., m. Mary **BROTHERTON**, b. of New Milford, Nov. 15, 1848, by Rev. J. B. Stodard	2	44
Friend Grant, s. David & Rachel, b. Jan. 14, 1770	LR12	15
George, m. Elsie E. **HOYT**, b. of New Milford, Feb. 17, 1852,		

	Vol.	Page
NORTHROP, NORTHRUP, (cont.)		
by Rev. David Murdock, Jr.	2	80
Harriet, of New Milford, m. Seymour **MOREHOUSE**, of Washington, Sept. 7, 1828, by Rev. Harry Finch, of Washington	1	192
Henrietta, m. Walter B. **PECK**, Apr. 13, 1842, by N. Porter, Jr.	1	372
Ira, m. Abigail **JOYCE**, b. of New Milford, Dec. 24, 1820, by Homer Boardman, J. P.	1	20
Isaac, m. Olive **HALL**, Apr. 11, 1825, by Rev. Benjamin Benham	1	190
Joel, s. Amos & Ann, b. July 27, 1753	LR5	9
Joel, s. Solomon, m. Avis **CANFIELD**, d. Philo, b. of New Milford, Sept. 24, 1803, by Elisha Bostwick, J. P.	1	107
Joel W., m. Catherine **CANFIELD**, b. of New Milford, Aug. 28, 1831, by E. Huntington	1	249
Joel Wells, s. Cyrus & Betsey, b. Sept. 3, 1801	1	91
John Wilks, s. David & Rachel, b. Feb. 9, 1774	LR12	15
Lawrence, s. Joel W. & Catharine, b. June 29, 1835	1	249
Lois, d. Amos & Ann, b. Sept. 17, 1748	LR5	9
Lois, m. Eli **SHERMAN**, b. of New Milford, Dec. 25, 1844, by E. Huntington	2	2
Mary, of New Milford, m. Bethuel **TREAT**, of South Britain, Feb. 15, 1849, by Jno Greenwood	2	50
Nathaniel, m. Aba **CAMP**, June 7, 1809, by Elisha Bostwick, J. P.	1	161
Olanor, m. Daniel J. **SUMMERS**, Jan. 1, 1830, by Rev. Josiah P. Dickinson	1	236
Orinda, of New Milford, m. Joel B. **PRATT**, of Kent, Sept. 1, 1844, by E. Huntington	2	10
Orval, of New Milford, m. Ann **WAY**, of Goshen, Nov. 30, 1828, by Rev. E. Huntington	1	227
Polly, d. Solomon & Lois, b. Dec. 14, 1765	LR7	1
Polly, m. Marcus **CLARK**, Sept. 13, 1835, by Edward C. Bull	1	315
Rachel A., m. Constantine W. **FERRISS**, Feb. 24, 1839, by E. Huntington	1	336
Rebecah, m. Ebenezer **BOSTWICK**, Jr., June 10, 1777	LR13	12
Sally, d. Amos, Jr. & Anne, b. June 28, 1776	LR10	4
Sally, d. Cyrus & Betsey, b. Nov. 9, 1807	1	91
Samuel Canfield, s. Joel W. & Catharine, b. May 16, 1833	1	249
Sarah, m. William J. **STARR**, b. of New Milford, Apr. 15, 1830, by Hinman Rood	1	237
Solomon, s. Amos, b. Aug. 3, 1744	LR5	9
Solomon, m. Lois **MALLERY**, Apr. 5, 1764*, by Samuell Bostwick, J. P. *("4" not clear)	LR7	1
Sophia, m. Gideon L. **HUNT**, Feb. 10, 1836, by E. Huntington	1	208
Sophia, of New Milford, m. Eli **MYGATT**, Jr., of New York City, Oct. 24, 1837, by N. Porter	LR10	306

	Vol.	Page
NORTHROP, NORTHRUP, (cont.)		
Thomas Grant, s. Amos, Jr. & Anne, b. Jan 5, 1771	LR10	4
Urania, d. Amos, Jr. & Anne, b. Jan. 28, 1779; d. Apr. 14, 1788	LR10	4
NORTON, NORTEN, Harlow H., of Washington, m. wid. Sylvia **COUCH,** of New Milford, May 30, 1831, by Rev. Henry S. Atwater	1	112
Rowland, s. Rowland & Elidah, b. Feb. 19, 1750/1	LR6	11
ODELL, ODLE, Amanda, m. Elijah **TURRILL,** b. of New Milford, Mar. 15, 1846, by J. Greenwood	2	9
David G., of New Milford, m. Abigail J. **BROWN,** of Monroe, Sept. 22, 1844, by William H. Bangs	1	398
David G., m. Susan E. **MARSH,** b. of New Milford, Oct. 9, 1844, by William H. Bangs (Entry crossed out in original)	1	397
Harriet, of New Milford, m. Lewis **FAIRCHILD,** of Roxbury, Jan. 22, 1833, by E. Huntington	1	257
Jerusha, m. Heth **CANFIELD,** Jr., b. of New Milford, Sept. 30, 1807, by Elisha Bostwick, J. P.	1	147
Sally, m. Nathaniel J. **GALPIN,** of Washington, Nov. 24, 1825, by Rev. Andrew Eliot	1	176
OGDEN, Dayton, of Woodbury, m. Flora **SHERMAN,** of New Milford, Jan. 10, 1833, by E. Huntington	1	257
OLCOTT, Charles, of Woodbury, m. Amanda **STONE,** of New Milford, Feb. 3, 1829, by Rev. Eleazar Beecher	1	229
OLMSTED, Abraham, m. Sarah **BRADSHAW,** Dec. 30, 1823, by Rev. Andrew Eliot	1	177
Adolphus, s. David & Sarah, b. Oct. 12, 1795	1	88
Amarillis, d. David & Sarah, b. Apr. 26, 1789	1	88
Asa, s. David & Sarah, b. Aug. 8, 1780	1	88
Catharine, d. David & Sarah, b. June 30, 1799	1	88
David, m. Sarah **WALLER,** Feb. 7, 1774, by Rev. Jeremiah [ ], at New Preston	LR12	11
David, m. Sarah **WALLER,** Feb. 7, 1774, by [ ]	1	88
Esther, d. David & Sarah, b. June 30, 1783, in Kent	1	88
Jane, of New Milford, m. Homer **BRADSHAW,** of Rootstown, O., Oct. 23, 1825, by Rev. Andrew Eliot	1	35
Lois, d. David & Sarah, b. Oct. 24, 1774	1	88
Lydia, of New Milford, m. William **HOLCOMB,** of Brookfield, Sept. 24, 1826, by Rev. Benjamin Benham	1	206
Mary, d. David & Sarah, b. Dec. 9, 1776, in Kent	1	88
Polly Ann, m. Elmor* **JENNINGS,** b. of New Milford, Sept. 14, 1828, by Rev. E. Huntington *(Rewritten and not clear)	1	223
Sarah, d, Davud & Sarah, b. Oct. 29, 1778, in Kent	1	88
OSBORN, OSBORNE, Abigail, m. Rev. Jeremiah **DAY,** Oct. 7, 1772	LR13	17
Cynthia, m. Daniel **WANZER,** 3rd month 17th day, 1846,		

	Vol.	Page

OSBORN, OSBORNE, (cont.)

	Vol.	Page
by William Wanzer, Clerk	2	13
John, of Sherman, m. Mary A. **FERRISS**, of New Milford, Sept. 1, 1842, by E. Huntington	1	380
Mary, m. John T. **HOWLAND**, b. of New Milford, May 1, 1850, by Rev. A. N. Benedict	2	60
Richard T., witnessed marriage of Jehu **HOAG** & Phebe **WANZER**	1	250
Sarah A., of New Milford, m. Orson **DALY**, of Sherman, Feb. 14, 1849, by Rev. William Henry Rees	2	54
Stephen, d. Mar. 4, 1825, ae 76 y. 4 m.	1	127
Susan P., m. Emmon H. **SHERMAN**, b. of New Milford, Jan. 1, 1852, by Rev. David P. Sanford	2	74
William, witnessed marriage of Gurdon **SWIFT** & Jane **WANZER**	1	288

OVIATT, OVIAT, OUERT, OVIATTE, Abigail, m. Daniell **PRINDLE**, b. of New Milford, Jan. 17, 1732/3, by John Bostwick, J. P. — LR4, 8

Abagal, d. Joseph & Martha, b. Apr. 16, 1741	LR4	28
Abigail, m. Nathaniel **COLE**, July 21, 1771	LR0	8
Amie, d. Benjamin & Francis, b. Mar. 11, 1745/6	LR5	7
Anna, m. Job **CAMP**, Feb. 22, 1773	LR10	18
Anna, m. Job **CAMP**, Feb. 22, 1773	LR12	15
Annas, d. John & Abigail, b. Dec. 4, 1761 *("Annis" blotted out)	LR6	10
Anne, d. Thomas & Margret, b. Jan. 17, 1749/50	LR6	7
Annis, of New Milford, m. John **SEELYE**, of Wilton, Dec. 6, 1821, by Joel Sanford, J. P.	1	183
Benjamin, m. Francis **WARNER**, Apr. 17, 1744, by Joseph Minor, J. P.	LR5	7
Benjamin, m. James* **WARNER**, Apr. 17, [ ], by Joseph Minor, J. P. *(Probably "Frances")	LR5	5
Benjamin, twin with Ebenezer, s. Benjamin & Frances, b. May 3, 1760	LR5	7
Charlotte, of New Milford, m. Marcus D. **SMITH**, of Woodbury, May 29, 1845, by E. Huntington	2	3
Clarinda, m. Eli **KEELER**, Aug. 18, 1807, by Elisha Bostwick, J. P.	1	144
Ebenezer, twin with Benjamin, s. Benjamin & Frances, b. May 3, 1760	LR5	7
Elisabeth, m. Noah **BROWNSON**, Mar. 16, 1763	LR8	2
Elisabeth, m. Noah **BROWNSON**, Mar. 16, 1763, by Bushnell Bostwick, J. P.	LR7	18
Elizabeth, d. Thomas & Elizabeth, b. Aug. 13, 1775	LR13	14
Easter, d. Isaac & Easter, b. Mar. 18, 1776	LR13	1
Faphath*, d. Benjamin & Francis, b. Sept. 29, 1755 *("Japheth" in Orcutt's Hist.)	LR5	7
Faser(?)*, d. Benjamin & Frances, b. Feb. 2, 1747/8		

	Vol.	Page
OVIATT, OVIAT, OUERT, OVIATTE, (cont.)		
*("Frances" in Orcutt's Hist.)	LR5	7
Francis, m. Elleazer **BEECHER**, b. of Milford, Oct. 30, 1729	LR2	340
Hannah, d. Gyles & Elisabeth, b. Nov. 20, 1744	LR5	4
Huldah, d. John & Abigail, b. Apr. 22, 1759	LR6	10
Huldah, m. Edward Howel **PRINCE**, Feb. 4, 1779	LR13	15
Isaac, s. Thomas & Margret, b. Sept. 29, 1734	LR4	2
Israel, s. Thomas & Margrate, b. Dec. 20, 1755	LR4	2
Japheth*, child of Benjamin & Francis, b. Sept. 29, 1755		
*(Written "Faphath")	LR5	7
John, s. John & Abigail, b. Feb. 7, 1767	LR6	10
John, d. May 2*, 1777 *(Possibly "22nd")	LR6	10
Joseph, s. Thomas & Lydia, of New Milford, m. Martha **ELIOT**, of the oblong or Woster Sheer, May 12, 1740, by Roger Brownson, J. P.	LR4	28
Joseph, d. Mar. 2, 1741/2	LR4	1
Joseph, s. Thomas & Margret, b. July 22, 1746	LR4	2
Joseph, s. Thomas, Jr. & Elizabeth, b. July 3, 1777	LR13	14
Lowis, d. Thomas & Margrit, b. Feb. 25, 1752	LR6	7
Lydia, d. Thomas & Margret, b. July 31, 1739	LR4	2
Lydia, w. Thomas, d. July 4, 1742	LR4	1
Lydia, d. Jan. 23, 1760	LR4	2
Lydia, d. Thomas & Elizabeth, b. Nov. 22, 1772	LR13	14
Marget, d. Thomas & Margrit, b. June 29, 1742	LR4	2
Margrate, m. Edward **EDWARDS**, Oct. 10, last past [1771], by Nathaniell Taylor	LR11	11
Margrate, m. Edward **EDWARDS**, Oct. 10, 1771, by Rev. Nathaniell Taylor	LR11	14
Mary, d. Gyels & Elisabeth, b. Feb. 20, 1742/3	LR5	4
Naomi, d. Benjamin & Francis, b. Feb. 1, 1757	LR5	7
Sarah, d. John & Abigail, b. May 4, 1764; d. Apr. 6, 1766	LR6	10
Sarah, m. John **TURNER**, Jan. 21, 1773	1	2
Sibbil, d. Thomas & Margret, b. June 13, 1744	LR4	2
Tamar, d. Benjamin & Tranasis*, b. May 8, 1762 *("Francis")	LR5	7
Tamar, d. John & Abigail, b. Oct. 31, 1774	LR6	10
Thomas, m. Marget **BROWNSON**, b. of New Milford, Jan. 18, 1732/3, by Rev. Daniel Bordman	LR4	2
Thomas, Jr., s. Thomas & Marget, b. Oct. 27, 1736	LR4	2
Thomas, d. Jan. 13, 1740/1	LR4	1
Thomas, Jr., m. Elizabeth **BOTSFORD**, Jan. 26, 1769	LR13	14
Thomas, s. Thomas, Jr. & Elizabeth, b. Nov. 4, 1781	LR13	14
William, m. Urania **RICHMOND**, Dec. 6, 1846, by E. Huntington	2	25
OWEN, Charlotte, m. Jerome **ARNOLD**, b. of New Milford, Mar. 20, 1836, by E. Huntington	1	296
Jane, m. Edward **COGSWILL**, Jr., Apr. 17, 1758	LR7	3
Mary, w. Daniel, d. Sept. 12, 1756	LR7	13
PACHING, George T., of Danbury, m. Charlotte **BRONSON**, of		

162   BARBOUR COLLECTION

	Vol.	Page
PACHING, (cont.)		
Bridgewater, Jan. 1, 1846, by Rev. J. Kilborn	2	7
PAGE, Hannah, of Sherman, m. Noble LION, of New Milford, Aug. 31, 1845, by Rev. Johnson Howard	1	401
James N., witnessed marriage of David SANDS & Paulina LEACH	1	277
Mary J., of Sherman, m. George D. JONES, of New Milford, Mar. 19, 1843, by E. Huntington	1	393
Paulina, witnessed marriage of David SANDS & Paulina LEACH	1	277
Samuel, of Sherman, m. Sally LEE, of New Milford, Dec. 25, 1822, by Daniel Gaylord, J. P.	1	55
PAINE, PAYNE, Abigail Benedict, d. Benjamin & Lucy, b. Apr. 3, 1793	1	117
Benjamin, of New Milford, m. Lucy KNAPP, of Danbury, Apr. 13, 1791	1	117
Benjamin & Lucy, had s. [ ], b. Jan. 19, 1792; d. Feb. 16, 1792	1	117
Benjamin Franklin, s. Benjamin & Lucy, b. Dec. 29, 1800	1	117
Elisabeth Beardsley, d. Benjamin & Lucy, b. Feb. 16, 1803	1	117
Francis D., s. Ephraim, b. Mar. 15, 1797, in Milford. Witnessed: Jabez Beardsley, Jr. & Elijah Stone	1	18
Hiram Mark, s. Benjamin & Lucy, b. Sept. 6, 1797	1	117
John, m. Laura HENDRIX, b. of New Milford, Jan. 7, 1841, by Nathan Rice	1	356
Judd, m. Sally PICKETT, b. of New Milford, May 24, 1828, by Daniel Gaylord, J. P.	1	220
Lucy Knapp, d. Benjamin & Lucy, b. Dec. 14, 1798	1	117
Martha, m. Stephen C. FERRISS, b. of New Milford, Nov. 3, 1852, by Rev. David P. Sanford	2	79
Phebe, of New Milford, m. Benjamin P. DOWNS, of South Britain, Jan. 25, 1843, by E. Huntington	1	383
Sally Hubbell, d. Aaron & Sarah, b. Mar. 4, 1780	1	66
Sally Hubbell, d. Benjamin & Lucy, b. Apr. 19, 1795	1	117
William, of Cato, N. Y., m. Jane E. FERRISS, of New Milford, May 29, 1853, by Rev. D. P. Sanford	2	83
PAINTER, PAINTOR, Alexis, of Westfield, Mass., m. Thalia Maria McMAHON, of New Milford, Apr. 24, 1826, by Rev. Andrew Eliot	1	203
Deliverance, Capt. of Roxbury, m. Urania HINE, of New Milford, Jan. 13, 1802, by Elisha Bostwick, J. P.	1	69
PALMER, Abigail, d. Solomon & Lois, b. May 19, 1765	LR7	31
Abigail, m. Dr. George HURD, Nov. 5, 1767, by Solomon Palmer, Miss.	LR11	12
Benjamin Curtiss, s. Solomon & Lois, b. July 2, 1782	LR7	31
Chiliab, s. Solomon & Lois, b. Jan. 10, 1763	LR7	31
Cloe, d. Ichabod & Anna, b. Nov. 1, 1760; d. Jan. 14, 1762	LR8	1
Frances A., m. Garry B. HAMLIN, b. of New Milford, Jan.		

	Vol.	Page
PALMER, (cont.)		
2, 1854, by Rev. A. B. Pulling	2	92
George, d. Dec. 13, 1758* *(Possibly "1746")	LR6	15
Hulda, d. Solomon & Lois, b. Dec. 29, 1760	LR7	31
Ichabod Betts, m. Anna NOBLE, Sept. 23, 1759	LR8	1
Milo, s. Solomon & Lois, b. Apr. 23, 1767	LR7	31
Polly, of New Milford, m. Solomon JOHNSON, of Newtown, Oct. 5, 1823, by Joel Sanford, J. P.	1	183
Rufus, s. Ichabod Betts & Anna, b. Apr. 30, 1762	LR8	1
Sarah, d. Solomon & Lois, b. Aug. 16*, 1778 *(Or "6th" possibly)	LR7	31
Solomon, Jr., m. Lois HITCHOCK, May 15, 1758	LR7	31
Solomon, s. Sollomon & Lois, b. June 10, 1775	LR7	31
Tamar, d. Salmon & Lois, b. July 5, 1771	LR7	31
PARKS, PARK, Elizabeth, m. George H. BOSTWICK, Mar. 9, 1843, by E. Huntington	1	393
Julia E., of New Milford, m. Henry C. FULLER, of Ludlow, Mass., Nov. 24, 1853, by Rev. David Murdock, Jr.	2	100
PARSONS, Eliza, of New Milford, m. Jehiel B. THOMPSON, of Warren, Sept. 11, 1836, by N. Porter, Jr.	1	299
Marilla, of Sharon, m. Alonzo C. KINGSLEY, of New Milford, May 18, 1847, by Rev. George Tomlinson	2	29
Oliver, of Cornwall, m. Elvira BALDWIN, of New Milford, May 28, 1843, by Daniel Baldwin	1	388
PARTRIDGE, Benjamin, s. Perez & Naomi, b. Nov. 30, 1769	LR11	17
Grover, s. Parez, b. June 5, 1777	LR11	17
Naomi, w. Parez, d. June 11, 1777	LR11	17
Sarah, d. Parez & Naomi, b. Apr. 10, 1773	LR11	17
PATCHEN, Lucy J., of Danbury, m. John H. LEWIS, of New Milford, Dec. 13, 1846, by J. Kilborn	2	21
PATTERSON, Eliza, of New Milford, m. Horatio N. FLOWERS, of Roxbury, Nov. 7, 1833, by Rev. Fosdic Harrison, of Roxbury	1	268
Fanny, of New Milford, m. Henry HURLBUT, of Roxbury, Mar. 19, 1834, by Rev. Fosdic Harrison, of Roxbury	1	275
Phebe Ann, m. William DOWNS, b. of New Milford, July 9, 1834, by Fosdic Harrison	1	280
PAYNE, [see under PAINE]		
PEABODY, Frederick, of Bridgeport, m. Lydia RICHMOND, of New Milford, Dec. 6, 1842, by E. Huntington	1	382
PEARCE, [see under PIERCE]		
PEAT, [see under PEET]		
PECK, Abigail, m. Samuel CANFELD, June 1, 1725	LR2	337
Adaline Minor, [d. Elijah & Lavina], b. Sept. 5, 1837	1	408
Clarinda Booth, [d. Elijah & Lavina], b. Oct. 4, 1843	1	408
Clark Skinner, [s. Elijah & Lavina], b. Nov. 13, 1825	1	408
Cornelius W., m. Mary E. YOUNG, b. of New Milford, Oct. 4, 1853, by Rev. Rufus King	2	95

PECK, (cont.)

	Vol.	Page
Cornelius Wooster, [s. Elijah & Lavina], b. Sept. 3, 1824	1	408
Daniel, s. Peter & Sarah, b. Jan. 22, 1775	LR12	10
Dwight Woodruff, [s. Elijah & Lavina], b. Mar. 17, 1828	1	408
Ebenezer, m. Sarah BOOTH, d. Daniel & Eunice, [ ]	2	112
Edmund, s. Peter & Sarah, b. Nov. 21, 1778	LR12	10
Elijah, m. Lavina BOOTH, Feb. [ ], 1823	1	408
Elijah, m. Lavinna RANDALL, Feb. 9, 1824, by Rev. Fosdic Harrison, of Roxbury	1	84
Ellen Amanda, [d. Elijah & Lavina], b. Aug. 25, 1849; d. June 29, 1850, ae 10 m. 4 d.	1	408
George, m. Hannah CLARK, Jan. 13, 1824, by Rev. Andrew Eliot	1	86
Harriet, m. Elijah MILES, Jan. 15, 1826, by Rev. Eleazar Beacher	1	199
Jane Morris, [d. Elijah & Lavina], b. Sept. 13, 1829	1	408
John B., m. Hester YOUNG, b. of New Milford, Feb. 12, 1854, by Rev. David Murdock, Jr.	2	101
Joseph, of New Milford, m. Priscilla STARR, of Danbury, Nov. 1, 1787, by Rev. Joseph Peck	1	29
Joseph, m. Urania BENNETT, Dec. 20, 1790	1	29
Julia M., m. Epenetus ERWIN, b. of Bridgewater, Nov. 29, 1854, by Rev. Fosdic Harrison	2	104
Loiza, m. Alonzo TAYLOR, b. of Newtown, Sept. 5, 1830, by Rev. Eleazer Beecher	1	201
Loiza Emeline, [d. Elijah & Lavina], b. Mar. 8, 1835	1	408
Naomi, of Woodbridge, b. May 8, 1758	1	87
Naomi, of Woodbridge, m. Stephen HINE, of New Milford, June 19, 1782	1	87
Peter, m. Sarah TERRIL, Dec. 7, 1768	LR12	10
Preston, of Ansonia, m. Charlotte PICKETT, of New Milford, Nov. 26, 1850, at the house of Sheldon Pickett, by Rev. Gilbert B. Hayden	2	65
Priscilla, d. Joseph & Priscilla, b. Oct. 8, 1788	1	29
Priscilla, w. Joseph, d. Nov. 20, 1788	1	29
Reuben, s. Peter & Sarah, b. Feb. 8, 1772	LR12	10
Sarah, w. Ebenezer, d. Feb. 22, 1783	2	112
Sarah, m. Hiram KEELER, b. of Bridgwater Soc., Dec. 12, 1826, by Rev. Andrew Eliot	1	210
Sherman, of Bridgewater, m. Mrs. Lois LIVINGSTON, of Roxbury, Apr. 10, 1836, by Albert B. Camp	1	293
Sidney S., of Bethel, m. Mary Jane WILDMAN, of New Milford, Nov. 27, 1850, by Rev. D. Williams	2	69
Solomon S., of Moreson, Mass., m. Olive BOWERS, of New Milford, May 13, 1821, by David S. Boardman, J. P.	1	47
Walter B., m. Henrietta NORTHROP, Apr. 13, 1842, by N. Porter, Jr.	1	372
Welthy Mareah, [d. Elijah & Lavina], b. May 12, 1832	1	408

	Vol.	Page
PEET, PEAT, PEATT, PEETE, Abigail, d. John & Rebeckah, b. Aug. 20, 1752	LR4	16
Abigail, m. Lieut. Hezekiah **BALDWIN**, Apr. 5, 1759	LR7	38
Abraham, m. Hannah **ROBURDS**, Mar. 16, 1775, by Rev. Nathaniell Taylor	LR12	19
Amarillis, m. Samuel **SMITH**, b. of New Milford, Sept. 5, 1821, by Rev. Benjamin Benham	1	7
Annah, of Stratford, m. John **NOBLE**, Jr., of New Milford, Aug. 23, 1743, in parish of Unity, by Rev. Richardson Miner, of Unity	LR5	15
Ashbel, m. Phebe **WINTERS**, Mar. 9, 1823, at the house of Edmond Clark, by Rev. Eleazar Beecher	1	99
Benajah H., of Danbury, m. Caroline D. **GRAY**, of New Milford, Nov. 16, 1845, by Samuel Weeks	2	14
Catharn, m. Asahel **NOBLE**, Jan. 3, 1750	LR7	39
Curtis, of Warren, Conn., m. Mrs. Eliza **MOREHOUSE**, of New Milford, Oct. 2, 1853, by J. F. Jones	2	89
Daniel, s. John & Rebeckah, b. Dec. 30, 1749	LR4	16
Eli, m. Sally **MALLET**, b. of New Milford, Oct. 4, 1833, by H. Rood	1	266
Elijah, s. John & Rebecka, b. Feb. 17, 1760	LR4	16
Elnathan, d. Jan. 19, 1823	1	19
Ethiel, of Warren, m. Sarah **PEET**, of New Milford, July 6, 1820, by Rev. Benjamin Benham	1	48
Florinda, m. Horace **MERWIN**, b. of New Milford, Dec. 4, 1837, by N. Porter	1	313
Hannah, w. Abraham, d. Apr. 14, 1776	LR12	19
Hannah Robard, d. Abraham & Hannah, b. Apr. 6, 1776	LR12	19
Harriet, m. Ira **CANFIELD**, b. of New Milford, July 25, 1824, by Homer Boardman, J. P.	1	188
Laura Maria, [d. Riley & Sarah], b. July 24, 1815	1	329
Lehman Turrill, [s. Riley & Sarah], b. July 9, 1837	1	329
Lucy A., m. Anan **MARSH**, b. of New Milford, [Nov. 20, 1839], by B. B. Parsons	1	332
Lucy Amarillus, [d. Riley & Sarah], b. July 8, 1820	1	329
Luna, of New Milford, m. Abel **BRISTOL**, of Washington, Dec. 4, 1837, by N. Porter	1	313
Martha, of Unity, m. Joseph **WELLER**, of New Milford, Dec. 8, 1741, in Unity, by Rev. Richardson Miner, of Unity. Witnesses: Daniel Bostwick & Annah Peet	LR4	5
Mary, d. Thadeus, b. Dec. 25, 1781; m. Daniel **COPLEY**, s. Daniel, May 31, 1798	1	83
Mary, m. Alonso **STEWART**, b. of New Milford, Feb. 17, 1839, by Rev. Alonso F. Selleck	1	324
Mary A., of New Milford, m. Augustus B. **CAMP**, of Kent, Nov. 15, 1853, by Rev. George Tomlinson	2	91
Mary Augusta, [d. Riley & Sarah], b. June 6, 1834	1	329
Mahitabel, d. John & Rebeckah, b. Nov. 14, 1757	LR4	16

	Vol.	Page

PEET, PEAT, PEATT, PEETE, (cont.)

Nathan, Jr., m. Anne **HIGGINS**, b. of New Milford, Apr. 7, 1804, by Elisha Bostwick, J. P.	1	111
Nathan, m. Jerusha **MAXFIELD**, b. of New Milford, Sept. 10, 1854, by Rev. W. H. Russell	2	102
Rachel, of New Milford, m. John **STRAIGHT**, of Kent, Nov. 9, 1852, by Albert N. Baldwin, J. P.	2	78
Rachel Ann, [d. Riley & Sarah], b. Apr. 25, 1829	1	329
Rebekah, d. John & Rebeckah, b. May 7, 1755	LR4	16
Roccelania, [d. Riley & Sarah], b. Jan. 26, 1824	1	329
Sally, of New Milford, m. Marcus **BARTRAM**, of Washington, Aug. 18, 1840, by Rev. Eleazer Beecher	1	346
Samuel Riley, [s. Riley & Sarah], b. Jan. 10, 1827	1	329
Sarah, of New Milford, m. Ethiel **PEET**, of Warren, July 6, 1820, by Rev. Benjamin Benham	1	48
Sarah Florinda, [d. Riley & Sarah], b. June 3, 1818	1	329
Susan, of New Milford, m. John A. **WILLIAMS**, of Greenfield, Mar. 8, 1831, by H. Rood	1	113

PEPPER, Orange, of New Fairfield, m. Susan E. **MARSH**, of New Milford, Oct. 9, 1844, by William H. Bangs — 1 — 398

PERCEY, Thadeus, of Woodbury, m. Emeline **STONE**, of New Milford, Oct. 29, 1828, by Rev. Andrew Eliot — 1 — 224

PERRY, [see also **PIEREY**], Elijah, m. Lois **WILKINSON**, b. of New Milford, Feb. 14, [ ] — 1 — 69

PETTIT, Isaac O. m. Mary **BELL**, b. of New Milford, Oct. 8, 1838, by N. Porter — 1 — 322

PHELPS, Dorothy, m. Nathan **TERRILL**, Feb. 26, 1778, by Ephraim Hubbell, in New Fairfield — LR12 — 8

Polley, d. W[illia]m & Ann, b. Aug. 25, 1770	LR10	15
Reuman, d. William & Ann, b. May 31, 1766	LR10	15
Sarah, of Harwinton, m. Hezekiah **HAULEY**, of New Milford, Feb. 7, 1750/1, by Rev. Andrew Bartholomew, of Harrington	LR7	1
William, m. Ann **RUGGLES**, Nov. 6, 1765, by Samuell Bostwick, J. P.	LR7	5
William, m. Ann **RUGGLES**, Nov. 6, 1765	LR10	15
William Routhbon*, s. William & Ann, b. Mar. 29, 1769 *(Rathburn)	LR10	15

PHILLIPS, Buler M., of New Milford, m. John **ROGERS**, of Fairfield, May 27, 1832, by Ezra Noble, J. P. — 1 — 188

Charlotte S., m. Phillip H. **JACKLIN**, b. of New Milford, June 9, 1850, by Rev. Amos N. Benedict	2	61
Drake H., m. Paulina **FAIRCHILD**, b. of New Milford, Sept. 24, 1838, by N. Porter	1	321
Elisha, s. John & Ann, b. Jan. 23, 1759	LR7	21
Eliza, m. William **JACKSON**, b. of New Milford, Sept. 4, 1841, by N. Porter, Jr.	1	371
Elizabeth, d. Benjamin & Mary, b. Aug. 29, 1764	LR7	4

NEW MILFORD VITAL RECORDS 167

	Vol.	Page
PHILLIPS, (cont.)		
Hervey, m. Huldah **JACKLIN**, July 18, 1807, by Elisha Bostwick, J. P.	1	417
Hulda, d. Benjamin & Mary, b. Aug. 4, 1756	LR7	4
Jaruel, s. Benjamin & Mary, b. Aug. 31, 1758	LR7	4
John, s. Elisha & Innocent, b. May 28, 1737	LR7	6
John, m. Ann **BURDEN**, Nov.* 17, 1757 *("Dec."crossed out)	LR7	21
John, of New Milford, m. Margaret **RAYMOND**, of Dover, N. Y., Nov. 18, 1824, by Rev. Andrew Eliot	1	71
Mary, d. Benjamin & Mary, b. July 14, 1762	LR7	4
Mary Ann, of New Milford, m. William Riley **COGSWELL**, of Cornwall, Jan. 21, 1849, by John Greenwood	2	46
Onla, d. Benjamin & Mary, b. Jan. 15, 1766	LR7	4
Reuben, s. Benjamin & Mary, b. May 8, 1755	LR7	4
Shubel, s. Benjamin & Mary, b. Dec. 10, 1760	LR7	4
Sophia, of New Milford, m. Thaddeus **FREEMAN**, of Reading, Oct. 3, 1821, by Rev. Andrew Eliot	1	49
PHILLYIS, Minerva, m. Charles **FRANKLIN**, b. of New Milford, (colored), Oct. 26, 1829, by Eldad C. Jackson, J. P.	1	426
PHINE, Solomon, m. Ann **BENNIT**, June 28, 1774, by Samuell Bostwick, J. P.	LR12	12
PHIPPENY, PHIPPENEY, PHIPNEY, PHIPPENCY, PHIPENEY, PHIPPENNE, Abigail, d. James & Rosannah, b. Jan. 29, 1775	LR12	20
Caroline, of New Milford, m. Anson **BEARDSLEY**, of Monroe, May 4, 1830, by E. Huntington	1	133
Clotilda, d. James & Rosannah, b. Aug. 6, 1782	LR12	20
Esther, d. James & Rosannah, b. Mar. 27, 1777	LR12	20
James, m. Rosannah **BROWNSON**, Sept. 16, 1772	LR12	20
James Madison, m. Harriet **RUGGLES**, b. of Bridgewater, Jan. 6, 1836, by Albert B. Camp	1	291
Joel, s. James & Rosannah, b. Aug. 7, 1773	LR12	20
Peter, s. James & Rosannah, b. Jan. 31, 1779	LR12	20
Peter, m. Dorcas **FENN**, b. of New Milford, Sept. 29, 1808, by Elisha Bostwick, J. P.	1	159
Rebekah, m. David **BOTSFORD**, b. of New Milford, Oct. 18, 1764, by [Samuel] Boswick, J. P.	LR11	9
Sararah, of Stratford, m. Samuel **PRINDLE**, of New Milford, Jan. 6, 1740/1, by Rev. Richardson Miner, of Unity	LR4	14
PICKETT, PEEKIT, PICKET, PICKIT, Abigail, m. Daniel H. **WARNER**, b. of New Milford, Jan. 14, 1829, by Rev. Andrew Eliot	1	228
Abijah, s. Ebenezer & Parnil, b. Oct. 13, 1754	LR6	1
Albert, m. Mary R. **ROBURDS**, b. of New Milford, Jan. 6, 1825, by Rev. Andrew Eliot	1	191
Anson Daniel, s. Daniel & Sarah, b. Sept. 19, 1768	LR10	16
Asa, m. Julia **LOCKWOOD**, Jan. 12, 1843, by E. Huntington	1	383
Benjamin, s. Thomas & Miriam, b. Oct. 2, 1724	LR2	357

PICKETT, PEEKIT, PICKET, PICKIT, (cont.)

	Vol.	Page
Charlotte, of New Milford, m. Preston **PECK**, of Ansonia, Nov. 26, 1850, at the house of Sheldon Pickett, by Rev. Gilbert B. Hayden	2	65
Daniell, s. Thomas & Miriam, b. Aug. 23, 1719	LR2	357
Daniel, m. Maijary* **BEARSLIE**, Sept. 16, 1741, in Streatfield *("Margaret" in Orcutt's Hist.)	LR4	1
Daniel, s. Daniel & Majary, b. Apr. 17, 1742	LR4	1
Daniel, Jr., m. Sarah **COMSTOCK**, Nov. 5, 1767, by Richard Clark, Miss.	LR10	12
Daniel, Jr., m. Sarah **COMSTOCK**, Nov. 5, 1767	LR10	16
Daniel, Jr., d. Jan. 22, 1769	LR10	16
Daniel, d. Dec. 14, 1794	LR4	1
Ebenezer, s. Thomas & Miriam, b. Dec. 20, 1717	LR2	357
Ebenezer, m. Pearnal **BOSTWICK**, May 28, 1748, by Nathaniell Bostwick, J. P.	LR6	1
Ebenezer, Jr., m. Zeruiah **TERRIL**, June 9, 1767, by Samuell Boswick, J. P.	LR11	8
Eldad, s. Ebenezer & Pearnal, b. Aug. 14, 1748	LR6	1
Eunice, of Bridgwater Soc., m. Thomas **ANDREWS**, of Brookfield, Jan. 22, 1826, by Rev. Benjamin Benham	1	164
Hannah, d. Thomas & Miriam, b. Mar. 26, 1728	LR2	357
Harriot A., of New Milford, m. William H. **BRISTOL**, of Derby, June 5, 1854, by J. W. Hoffman	2	108
Huldah, d. Ebenezer & Parnel, b. July 24, 1750	LR6	1
Hulda, d. Ebenezer & Parnil, d. Apr. 29, 1770	LR6	1
Julia A., of New Milford, m. Gilbert S. **MINOR**, of Cornwall, Apr. 27, 1847, by E. Huntington	2	34
Margery, wid. Daniel, d. Sept. 21, 1795	LR4	1
Mary, m. David **NORTHROP**, Oct. 25, 1846, by E. Huntington	2	24
Mary Jane, of Bridgewater, m. Elias C. **MERWIN**, of New Haven, Mar. 22, 1847, by James Kilborn	2	29
Matilda, d. Ebenezer & Parnil, b. Apr. 30, 1767	LR6	1
Medad, s. Ebenezer & Pearnall, b. Nov. 20, 1752	LR6	1
Meriam, d. Ebenezer & Parnal, b. July 10, 1756	LR6	1
Meriam, wid. Dr. Thomas, d. June 23, 1776	LR2	357
Molly, d. Daniel & Margary, b. Mar. 9, 1745	LR4	1
Molly, m. Samuel **MILES**, b. of New Milford, Oct. 17, 1764	LR7	4
Parnil, d. Ebenezer & Parnil, b. Oct. 14, 1758	LR6	1
Philene, d. Ebenezer & Parnil, b. Jan. 19, 1761	LR6	1
Philo, s. Ebenezer & Zeruiah, b. Aug. 2, 1769	LR11	8
Sally, m. Judd **PAINE**, b. of New Milford, May 24, 1828, by Daniel Gaylord, J. P.	1	220
Sarah, d. Ebenezer & Zeruiah, b. Jan. 10, 1768	LR11	8
Thomas, m. Miram **MALLERY**, b. of New Milford, Dec. 13, 1716	LR2	357
Thomas, s. Eben & Parnil, b. May 21, 1763	LR6	1

	Vol.	Page
PICKETT, PEEKIT, PICKET, PICKIT, (cont.)		
Thomas, Dr., d. June 17, 1774, in the 86th y. of his age	LR2	357
PIERCE, PEARCE, PEIRCE, Azael, s. Jonathan & Sarah, b. Dec. 14, 1772	LR7	8
Edwin, m. Nancy **MALLORY**, b. of South Britain, Nov. 29, 1836, by A. B. Camp	1	301
Jonathan, m. Rachell **BUCK**, b. of New Milford, Sept. 11, 1729	LR4	7
Jonathan, s. Jonathan & Rachel, b. Aug. 5, 1738	LR4	7
Jonathan, Jr., of New Milford, m. Sarah **RICHMAN**, of Litchfield, Oct. 4, 1764	LR7	7
Jonathan, f. Jonathan, Jr., d. Oct. 25, 1765	LR7	7
Jonathan, a witness at wedding of Elnathan **BOTSFORD** & Dorothy **PRINDLE**, Quakers	LR4	14
Lydia, d. Jonathan & Rachel, b. Mar. 26, 1744	LR4	7
Lydia, m. John **WILKINSON**, Jr., Feb. 22, 1780	1	4
Orange, s. Jonathan & Sarah, b. Apr. 30, 1771	LR7	8
Rachel, d. Jonathan & Rachel, b. Aug. 21, 1734	LR4	7
Rachel, m. Abel **MOTT**, May 11, 1756	LR7	23
Rachel, d. Jonathan & Sarah, b. Dec. 17, 1767	LR7	8
Silas, s. Jonathan, Jr. & Sarah, b. July 18, 1765	LR7	7
Truelove, d. Jonathan & Rachel, b. Nov. 26, 1730	LR4	7
PIEREY, [see also **PERRY**], Henry R., m. Rebecca **JONES**, b. of New Milford, Nov. 7, 1847, by Rev. E. P. Ackerman	2	40
PINNOCK, Margaret, m. Jonathan **BENEDICK**, Oct. 1, 1778	1	53
PLATT, PLAT, PLATS, Betsey, d. Ephraim & Hopestill, b. Dec. 13, 1776; d. June 21, 1778, ae 18 m. 8 d.	LR12	16
Betsey, d. Ephraim & Hopestill, b. July 22, 1781	LR12	16
Charles, s. Ephraim & Hopestill, b. June 28, 1788	LR12	16
Daniel, s. Ephraim & Hopestill, b. Aug. 17, 1790	LR12	16
David, m. Tryphena **BARDSLEE**, Mar. 19, 1778	LR13	7
Edward Francis, m. Mary N. **BEARDSLEY**, b. of New Milford, Dec. 22, 1852, by Rev. James L. Scott, of New Preston	2	85
Ephraim, m. Hopestil **HAMBLIN**, June 30, 1773, by Rev. Nathaniell Taylor	LR12	16
Ephraim, d. Sept. 26, 1798, in the 50th y. of his age	LR12	16
Grace, m. Richard **CLARK**, May 25, 1775	1	49
Hannah, d. Jeremiah & Mary, b. May 1, 1777	1	14
Harvey, m. Betsey Ann **LACEY**, b. of New Milford, May 13, 1827, by Nathaniel Perry, J. P.	1	214
Henry James, s. Ephraim & Hopestill, b. Mar. 23, 1786	LR12	16
Hiram, m. Harriot **SUMMERS**, b. of New Milford, Nov. 30, 1815, by Elisha Bostwick, J. P.	1	164
Jacob Begardus, s. Ephraim & Hopestill, b. Aug. 14, 1774	LR12	16
Jeremiah, s. Jeremiah & Hannah, b. of Milford, b. Dec. 12, 1747, in Milford; m. Mary **MERWIN**, d. Miles & Mary, Mar. 17, 1770	1	14

PLATT, PLAT, PLATS, (cont.)

	Vol.	Page
Jeremiah, s. Jeremiah & Mary, b. Oct. 20, 1772	1	14
Jerusha, d. Samuel & Anne, b. May 23, 1754	LR7	2
Joseph M., m. Jennette E. BRADLEY, b. of New Milford, Jan., 24, 1849, by John Greenwood	2	47
Laura, m. Nathan TERRILL, May 20, 1807, by Elisha Bostwick, J. P.	1	142
Laura M., of New Milford, m. James B. BEARDSLEY, of Kent, Mar. 15, 1836, by Aaron D. Lane	1	293
Marshall S., m. Tryphena MERWIN, Mar. 20, 1825, by Rev. C. A. Boardman	1	194
Martha A., m. William N. CANFIELD, Apr. 8, 1835, by H. Rood	1	287
Merrit S., m. Orinda [ ]* TAYLOR, Sept. 18, 1832, by Rev. R. B. Canfield, of New Preston *("Gaylord" written over)	1	251
Newton, s. Jeremiah & Mary, b. Oct. 18, 1779	1	14
Polly, m. Silas HILL, Feb. 28, 1813	1	290
Samuel, m. Anne WELCH, Aug. 17, 1749, by Rev. Nathaniell Taylor	LR7	2
Sarah, d. Sam[ue]ll & Anne, b. Oct. 19, 1750	LR7	2
Sarah, m. Angus NICKELSON, b. of New Milford, May 11, 1767, by Rev. Nathaniel Taylor	LR10	6
Sarah, m. Angus NICKELSON, May 11, 1767	1	68
Serena, m. Martial HILL, Dec. 21, 1842, by E. Huntington	1	382
Slosson, of Butternuts, N. Y., m. Minerva SHERWOOD, of New Milford, June 18, 1822, by Rev. Andrew Eliot	1	36
William, [twin with [ ]], s. Ephraim & Hopestill, b. Mar. 19, 1784	LR12	16
Zalmon, s. Ephraim & Hopestill, b. Apr. 10, 1779	LR12	16
Zalmon, s. Ephraim & Hopestill, d. Dec. 12, 1802, in the 24th y. of his age	LR12	16
-----, [twin with William], s. Ephraim & Hopestill, b. Mar. 19, 1784; d. Mar. 21, 1784	LR12	16
PLUM, Sarah, of Milford, m. Samuel SMITH, Jr., of New Milford, May 21, 1772, by Rev. Mr. Waller	LR12	1
POLOMON, Isaac, of Watertown, m. Parmelia COLE, of New Milford, Dec. 31, 1853, by J. F. Jones	2	92
POMROY, John, m. Irene WELCH, b. of New Milford, May 3, 1800, by Elisha Bostwick, J. P.	1	23
POOL, Sary, m. Archebell CAMPBELL, Dec. 26, 1734, by John Bostwick, J. P.	LR4	12
PORTER, Ann Louisa, of Bridgeport, m. John Robert BOSTWICK, of New Milford, Dec. 25, 1844, by Rev. Gurdon S. Coit, of Bridgeport	1	404
Ann Louisa, m. John Roberts BOSTWICK, Dec. 25, 1844	1	404
Betsey Ann, m. Minor MOREHOUSE, b. of New Milford, Dec. 1, 1823, by Rev. Benjamin Benham	1	148

NEW MILFORD VITAL RECORDS

	Vol.	Page
PORTER, (cont.)		
Comford, m. Daniel **HITCHCOCK,** Nov. 3, 1773, by Rev. Nathaniel Taylor	LR12	7
Lois, m. Dea. Matthew **BALDWIN,** b. of New Milford, Dec. 6, 1832, by Eldad C. Jackson, J. P.	1	256
Richard, of Warren, m. Elizabeth **BRAIGE,** of New Milford, Nov. 22, 1843, by Daniel B. Wilson, J. P.	1	389
POST, Robert, of Westbury, N. Y., m. Betsey P. **HAVILAND,** of New Milford, 2nd m. 22nd d., 1849, by William Wanzer, Clerk	2	52
POTTER, Aaron, of New Milford, m. Phila **CRANK,** of Kent, Oct. 16, 1827, by Daniel Gaylord, J. P.	1	220
Charles F., of Shelby Orleans Co., N. Y., m. Catharine **HAMILTON,** of New Milford, Apr. 17, 1844, by John Greenwood	1	395
Israel, m. Phebe Meria **THAYER,** Mar. 14, 1819, by Elisha Bostwick, J. P.	1	168
Israel, m. Susan E. **LACY,** Jan. 6, 1828, by Rev. E. Huntington	1	217
Philamelia, m. Harmon **BENEDICT,** Feb. 20, 1853, by Rev. David P. Sanford	2	82
POWERS, Emeline, d. William C. & Polly, b. Apr. 24, 1805, at Middletown	1	168
Lucy Ann, d. William C. & Polly, b. May 4, 1812	1	168
William, s. William C. & Polly, b. Mar. 2, 1808; d. Nov. 8, 1808	1	168
William C., m. Polly **WOOD,** b. of Middletown, Nov. 21, 1803	1	168
William C., d. [ ]	1	168
William Martin, s. William C. & Polly, b. Jan. 20, 1810	1	168
PRATT, Joel B., of Kent, m. Orinda **NORTHROP,** of New Milford, Sept. 1, 1844, by E. Huntington	2	10
PRIME, Amos, s. William & Sarah, b. Oct. 30, 1744	LR4	21
Ann, d. Jeams & Ann, b. June 11, 1723	LR2	351
Asa, s. William & Sarah, b. July 15, 1753	LR4	21
Asa, m. Phebe **RESSIGUE,** June 25, 1777	LR13	9
Asa, s. Asa & Phebe, b. Nov. 16, 1791	LR13	9
Elisabeth, d. William & Sarah, b. Jan. 6, 1742/3	LR4	21
Elizabeth, m. Thomas **CLARK,** Feb. 15, 1763	LR13	13
Jeames, s. Jeames & Anna, b. Mar. 15, 1720/1	LR2	351
James, s. William & Sarah, b. Aug. 25, 1740	LR4	21
Jane, d. Asa & Phebe, b. Nov. 11, 1782	LR13	9
Martha, d. Jeames & Anna, b. July 19, 1719	LR2	351
Martha, m. John **PRINDLE,** b. of New Milford, Feb. 5, 1729/30	LR4	4
Martha, m. Gideon **NOBLE,** Mar. 22, 1747	LR6	4
Mahetable, d. Dea. James & Annah, b. Apr. 23, 1735	LR4	19
Phebe, d. Asa & Phebe, b. May 4, 1781	LR13	9

172   BARBOUR COLLECTION

	Vol.	Page
PRIME, (cont.)		
Phebe, m. Abel **CANFIELD**, Jr., b. of New Milford, Apr. 11, 1804, by Elisha Bostwick, J. P.	1	112
Sarah, d. William & Sarah, b. Dec. 3, 1748/9	LR4	21
Sarah, m. Nathan **WHEELER**, Sept. 4, 1758	LR4	1
Sarah, m. Josiah **SMITH**, Jr., b. of New Milford, Sept. 10, 1767, by Bushnel Bostwick, J. P.	LR10	12
Sarah, m. Josiah **SMITH**, Sept. 10, 1767, by Bushnel Bostwick, J. P.	LR12	14
William*, s. James & Ann, m. Sarah **GARLICK**, d. Henry & Elizabeth, Oct. 31, 1739, by John Beach *("James" crossed out, "William" written underneath)	LR4	21
William, s. James & Annah, m. Sarah **GARLICK**, d. Henry & Elizabeth, Oct. 31, 1739, by John Beach, of Newtown	LR4	27
William, s. Asa & Phebe, b. June 7, 1778	LR13	9
PRINCE, Charlotte, d. Edward Howel & Huldah, b. Dec. 10, 1781	LR13	15
Charlotte, m. Ephraim **HILL**, Apr. 7, 1803, by Elisha Bostwick, J. P.	1	104
Czar, s. Edward Howel & Huldah, b. Aug. 5, 1792	LR13	15
Edward Howel, m. Huldah **OVIATT**, Feb. 4, 1779	LR13	15
Electa, see under Lecta		
Huldah, d. Edward Howel & Huldah, b. May 23, 1790	LR13	15
Jervis, s. Edward Howel & Huldah, b. Dec. 8, 1794	LR13	15
Lecta, d. Edward Howel & Huldah, b. Oct. 23, 1787	LR13	15
Lecta, d. Edward Howel & Huldah, d. Feb. 7, 1793	LR13	15
Lucy, d. Edward Howel & Huldah, b. Aug. 20, 1779	LR13	15
Noble, s. Edward Howel & Huldah, b. Sept. 15, 1784	LR13	15
Samuel, Jr., m. Hannah **JONES**, Feb. 2, 1780	LR13	16
Sarah, m. Isaack **TERRIL**, b. of New Milford, Jan. 25, 1774, by Rev. Nathaniel Taylor	LR12	17
PRINDLE, PRINDEL, Aaron, s. Daniel & Abiael, b. Nov. 7, 1733	LR4	8
Abigail, d. Sam[ue]ll & Dorothy, b. Dec. 30, 1711	LR2	347
Abigail, m. Abraham **GILLIT**, b. of New Milford, Jan. 28, 1729/30	LR2	344
Abigail, d. Samuell, Jr. & Abagail, b. July 20, 1745, in Sharon	LR4	14
Abigail, m. Orange **WARNER**, Dec. 5, 1765, by Samuell Bostwick, J. P.	LR11	6
Abigail, Jr., m. Orange **WARNER**, Dec. 5, [ ], by Samuel Bostwick, J. P.	LR7	7
Abigal, a witness at wedding of Elnathan **BOTSFORD** & Dorothy **PRINDLE**, Quakers	LR4	14
Bediance, m. Eleanah **BOBIT**, Dec. 5, 1737, by Rev. Daniel Boardman	LR6	8
Daniell, s. Sam[ue]ll & Dorothy, b. June 2, 1709	LR2	347
Daniell, m. Abigail **OVIAT**, b. of New Milford, Jan. 17, 1732/3, by John Bostwick, J. P.	LR4	8
Daniel, of New Milford, m. Phebe **FED**, a transient person, Oct. 4, 1737, by John Bostwick, J. P.	LR4	8

	Vol.	Page
PRINDLE, PRINDEL, (cont.)		
Daniel, a witness at wedding of Elnathan **BOTSFORD** & Dorothy **PRINDLE**, Quakers	LR4	14
Daniel, a witness at wedding of John **FERRIS** & Abigal **TRYON**, Quakers	LR4	22
David, s. Daniel & Phebie, b. Jan. 19, 1742/3	LR4	7
Dorothy, a witness at wedding of Elnathan **BOTSFORD** & Dorothy **PRINDLE**, Quakers	LR4	14
Dorathy, twin with Sarah, d. Sam[ue]ll & Dorythy, b. Jan. 19, 1706/7	LR2	347
Dorathy, d. Samuel & Dorathy, of New Milford, m. Elnathan **BOTSFORD**, s. Samuel & Hannah, of Milford, Mar. 18, 1733/4, at the house of Samuel Prindle. Quaker ceremony before 17 witnesses. Intentions declared at Josiah Quinby's house at Momorneck, Chester Co., N. Y.	LR4	14
Elizabeth, d. Daniel & Phebe, b. June 16, 1747	LR4	8
Elesibath, a witness at wedding of Elnathan **BOTSFORD** & Dorothy **PRINDLE**, Quakers	LR4	14
Gedion, m. Lettice **TOWNER**, Apr. 11, 1753, by Ephraim Hubbel, J. P.	LR7	2
Gedeon, see Gomaras **PRINDLE**	LR4	4
Gomaras*, s. John & Martha, b. Apr. 30, 1732 *("Gomaras" changed to Gedeon, Feb. [ ], 1739/40)	LR4	4
Hannah, d. Daniel & Phebie, b. Feb. 26, 1740/1	LR4	7
John, m. Martha **PRIME**, b. of New Milford, Feb. 5, 1729/30	LR4	4
John, s. Gedion & Lettice, b. Apr. 27, 1756	LR7	2
John, a witness at wedding of John **FERRIS** & Abigal **TRYON**, Quakers	LR4	22
Joseph, s. John & Martha, b. Dec. 16, 1730	LR4	4
Landar*, s. Samuel & Hannah, b. Mar. 7, 1769 *("Leander" in Orcutt's Hist.)	LR11	16
Mark, s. John & Martha, b. Mar. 9, 1733/4	LR4	4
Martha, d. Gedion & Lettice, b. Apr. 17, 1754	LR7	2
Martha, a witness at wedding of John **FERRIS** & Abigal **TRYON**, Quakers	LR4	22
Mary, d. Sam[ue]ll & Dorothy, b. Nov. 14, 1713	LR2	347
Obedience, d. Sam[ue]ll & Dorothy, b. May 13, 1716	LR2	347
Obedience, m. Elkenah **BOBBIT**, b. of New Milford, Jan. 20, 1736/7	LR4	27
Phebie, d. Daniel & Phebie, b. Dec. 31, 1738	LR4	8
Pheebe, m. Benjamin **HALLOK**, Aug. 7, 1755	LR7	33
Racher, d. Daniel & Phebie, b. Dec. 30, 1744	LR4	7
Rachel, m. John **MARSH**, Feb. 11, 1771	LR12	5
Samuel, of New Milford, m. Sararah **PHIPPENNE**, of Stratford, Jan. 6, 1740/1, by Rev. Richardson Miner, of Unity	LR4	14
Samuel, of New Milford, m. Abigail **SKINNER**, wid., of Sharon, formerly Abigail **MUDG**, Sept. 12, 1744, by		

BARBOUR COLLECTION

	Vol.	Page
PRINDLE, PRINDEL, (cont.)		
Rev. Peter Prat, of Sharon	LR4	14
Samuel, s. Samuel & Abagail, b. Mar. 19, 1747	LR4	14
Samuel, Sr., m. Sarah **CHAPMAN**, b. of New Milford, Mar. 31, 1747, by Samuell Canfield, J. P.	LR5	2
Samuel, d. Sept. 29, 1750	LR6	3
Samuel, of New Milford, m. Hannah **HAMBLIN**, of Sharon, June 8, 1768, by Rev. Nathaniell Taylor	LR11	16
Samuel, s. Samuel & Hannah, b. May 15, 1771	LR11	16
Samuel, a witness at wedding of John **FERRIS** & Abigal **TRYON**, Quakers	LR4	22
Sarah, twin with Dorathy, d. Sam[ue]ll & Dorythy, b. Jan. 19, 1706/7	LR2	347
Sarah, m. Job **GOULD**, b. of New Milford, June 17, 1730	LR2	355
Sarah, w. Samuel, Jr., d. Jan. 27, 1743/4	LR4	14
Sarah, d. Samuel, Jr. [& Sarah], b. Jan. 27, 1743/4	LR4	14
----, a witness at wedding of Elnathan **BOTSFORD** & Dorothy **PRINDLE**, Quakers	LR4	14
PROUT, Eunice, m. George **DART**, July 17, 1783, by Rev. Nathaniell Taylor	LR12	7
Meriah, d. Sherman & Assenath, b. Feb. 10, 1799; d. May 2, 1799	1	119
Meriah, 2nd, d. Sherman & Assenath, b. Jan. 25, 1801	1	119
Sherman, of New Milford, m. Assenath **SHOFIELD**, of Kent, Nov. 28, 1796, by Rev. Joel Bordwell	1	119
RANDALL, RANDAL, Cordelia, m. Charles M. **WYANT**, b. of New Milford, Dec. 18, 1853, by Rev. A. B. Pulling	2	91
Flora, of Bridgewater, m. Alonzo **BARNUM**, of Bridgeport, Jan. 25, 1846, by Rev. J. Kilbourn	2	9
Hannah, m. Almon **TREAT**, b. of Bridgwater, Dec. 13, 1821, by Rev. Fosdic Harrison, of Roxbury	1	25
Harriet, m. Joseph **HEPBURN**, b. of New Milford, Bridgewater Soc., Jan. 16, 1822, by Rev. Fosdick Harrison, of Roxbury	1	18
Jaimthier, of New Milford, m. Frederick **BOLELAND**, of Sharon, Feb. 2, 1830, by Joseph S. Covill	1	238
Jeremiah G., m. Abigail L. **MEAD**, Jan. 1, 1839, by E. Huntington	1	334
Lavinna, m. Elijah **PECK**, Feb. 9, 1824, by Rev. Fosdic Harrison, of Roxbury	1	84
Marquis D., m. Lydia A. **H[A]NFORD** (?), b. of Bridgwater, Nov. 16, 1826, by Rev. Fosdic Harrison	1	211
Mary Ann J., m. Sherman **TERRY**, Oct. 28, 1828, by Rev. E. Huntington	1	224
Sally, m. John H. **TREAT**, Nov. 25, 1794	1	76
Sally J., m. Martin **MALLORY**, b. of Bridgewater, Sept. 30, 1846, by Rev. J. Kilborn	2	19
Smith, m. Lavinna **BOOTH**, Jan. 10, 1821, by Rev. Fosdic		

NEW MILFORD VITAL RECORDS 175

	Vol.	Page
RANDALL, RANDAL, (cont.)		
Harrison, of Roxbury	1	29
RAYMOND, Margaret, of Dover, N. Y., m. John **PHILLIPS,** of New Milford, Nov. 18, 1824, by Rev. Andrew Eliot	1	71
REED, READ, REID, Ann, [d. Asa & Mary], b. Jan. 6, 178[ ]	1	1
Asa, m. Mary Ann **MURRAY,** Apr. 20, 1784	1	1
Charles, m. Electa **JONES,** July 6, 1840, by Eleazer Beecher	1	345
Esther, d. Asa & Mary, b. [ ]	1	1
Jonathan, m. Hannah **BROWNSON,** b. of New Milford, Sept. 2, 1845, by E. Huntington	2	3
Joseph Jonathan, s. Asa & Mary Ann, b. Oct. 13, 178*		
*(Edge of leaf gone)	1	1
Molly Picket, w. Samuel Chester & d. Capt. Amasa & Molly **FERRISS,** d. Feb. 20, 1812, at New York	1	43
Noble, m. Mary Ann **HUNT,** b. of New Milford, Dec. 10, 1837, by Rev. Alonzo F. Selleck	1	307
Polly, m. Jeremiah **SMITH,** Mar. 6, 1802, by Elisha Bostwick, J. P.	1	95
RESSIGUE, Phebe, m. Asa **PRIME,** June 25, 1777	LR13	9
REYNOLDS, RENNELS, [see also **RUNNELS**], Cyrus, m. Harriet **GUNN,** Oct. 2, 1839, by E. Huntington	1	337
Isaac , m. Aueintee M. **MOREY,** b. of New Milford, Sept. 21, 1851, by D. Williams	2	72
Joseph, a witness at wedding of John **FERRIS** & Abigal **TRYON,** Quakers	LR4	22
Maltby, m. Letitia **BEACH,** Apr. 24, 1822, by Rev. Andrew Eliot	1	31
Thomas, m. Mabel **DOWNS,** b. of New Milford, Apr. 17, 1823, by Stephen Crane, J. P.	1	314
William, of New York, m. Lucy Ann **BEACH,** of New Milford, Bridgewater Soc., Jan. 13, 1822, by Rev. Fosdick Harrison, of Roxbury	1	17
RICE (?), Abagal, m. Peter **BROWNSON,** Nov. 11, 1742, by Rev. Nathaniel Bostwick	LR5	1
RICH RIECH, Abigail, d. Jonathan & Abigail, b. Apr. 27, 1750	LR7	1
Bersheba, d. Jonathan & Abigail, b. Feb. 13, 1752	LR7	1
David, s. Jonathan & Abigail, b. Mar. 29, 1756	LR7	1
Elizabeth, d. Jonathan & Abigail, b. June 29, 1760	LR7	1
James, s. Jonathan & Abigail, b. Aug. 20, 1764	LR7	1
Jonathan, s. Jonathan & Abigail, b. Feb. 20, 1754	LR7	1
Levi, s. Jonathan & Abigail, b. Aug. 18, 1766	LR7	1
Mehitibel, d. Jonathan & Abigail, b. May 30, 1762	LR7	1
Samuel, s. Jonathan & Abigail, b. May 24, 1758	LR7	1
Zeruiah, d. Jonathan & Abigail, b. Aug. 28, 1768	LR7	1
RICHMOND, RICHMAN, Anna, m. Dennis **BUCKINGHAM,** b. of New Milford, May 8, 1853, by Rev. A. B. Pulling	2	86
Annis, d. Ephraim & Martha, b. Nov. 5, 1762	1	26
Annis, d. Jonathan & Amarillis, b. Apr. 25, 1786	1	25

BARBOUR COLLECTION

	Vol.	Page
RICHMOND, RICHMAN, (cont.)		
Assal, [s. Ephraim], b. June 6, 1833	2	68
Aszel, s. Ephraim & Martha, b. July 6, 1767	1	26
Aszel, s. Ephraim & Martha, d. Nov. 18, 1772	1	26
Auville, d. Jonathan & Amarillis, b. Dec. 28, 1783, in Woodbury	1	25
Avis, d. Ephraim & Martha, b. Sept. 21, 1775	1	26
Catharine, m. Charles L. **EGGLESTON**, b. of New Milford, Sept. 5, 1854, by J. W. Hoffman	2	110
David, s. Edmond & Huldah, b. Aug. 1, 1799	1	36
Edmund, s. Ephraim & Martha, b. May 3, 1765	1	26
Edmund, m. Huldah **FRISBIE**, Dec. 1, 1785	1	36
Edmund, s. Edmund & Huldah, b. Nov. 19, 1791	1	36
Eliza, of New Milford, m. Nelson **WHITE**, of Sherman, Apr. 10, 1842, by Rev. Daniel Baldwin	1	374
Elizabeth, m. Joseph **MYGATT**, May 15, 1771	LR13	4
Ephraim, m. Martha **SEELYE**, Dec. 2, 1754	1	26
Ephraim, s. Ephraim & Martha, b. Jan. 28, 1783	1	26
Ephraim, d. Oct. 22, 1800	1	26
Guy, s. Edmond & Huldah, b. Feb. 26, 1797	1	36
John, 2nd, [s. Ephraim], b. Jan. 12, 1842	2	68
Jonathan, s. Ephraim & Martha, b. Jan. 20, 1756	1	26
Jonathan, of New Milford, m. Amarillis **CHAMBERS**, of Newtown, Aug. 14, 1779, by Rev. John Beach	1	25
Lorrey, d. Jonathan & Amarillis, b. Nov. 16, 1790	1	25
Lydia, m. Henry S. **WELLER**, b. of New Milford, Dec. 17, 1837, by Rev. Alonzo F. Selleck	1	307
Lydia, of New Milford, m. Frederick **PEABODY**, of Bridgeport, Dec. 6, 1842, by E. Huntington	1	382
Mahala, of New Milford, m. David H. **MURPHY**, of Roxbury, July 23, 1848, by E. Huntington	2	42
Maricha, Mrs., m. Hiram S. **GIFFORD**, b. of New Milford, May 3, 1846, by Rev. Joseph L. Morse	2	14
Martha, d. Ephraim & Martha, b. July 5, 1777	1	26
Mary, d. Ephriam & Martha, b. Apr. 7, 1773	1	26
Mary, d. Ephraim, m. Matthew **BROWNSON**, Dec. 27, 1792, by Rev. Stanley Griswold	1	48
Mercy, m. Marcus **LOCKWOOD**, b. of New Milford, June 16, 1811	1	169
Nathaniel, s. Edmund & Huldah, b. Aug. 19, 1789	1	36
Philetus, [s. Ephraim], b. Mar. 31, 1829	2	68
Polline, d. Jonathan & Amarillis, b. June 13, 1788	1	25
Rhoda, d. Ephraim & Martha, b. Feb. 27, 1758	1	26
Roswel, s. Edmund & Huldah, b. July 14, 1787	1	36
Sarah, of Litchfield, m. Jonathan **PIERCE**, Jr., of New Milford, Oct. 4, 1764	LR7	7
Sarah Anne, d. Jonathan & Amarillis, b. Apr. 14, 1782	1	25
Seelye, s. Ephraim & Martha, b. Mar. 8, 1770	1	26

	Vol.	Page
RICHMOND, RICHMAN, (cont.)		
Seelye, m. Mehetabel **BLAKELEY**, Aug. 12, 1789	1	27
Seelye & Mehetabel, had d. [ ], b. Nov. 5, 1791;		
d. next day Nov. 6, 1791	1	27
Seth, s. Edmund & Huldah, b. Dec. 23, 1794	1	36
Silas, f. Ephraim, d. Feb. 21, 1784	1	26
Silas, m. Ruth E. **EDMONDS**, b. of New Milford, Dec. 18, 1831, by Heman Rood	1	85
Thomas Chambers, s. Jonathan & Amarillis, b. Mar. 30, 1780, in Woodbury	1	25
Truman, s. Ephraim & Martha, b. Aug. 14, 1760	1	26
Truman, s. Seely & Mehetabel, b. Apr. 27, 1790	1	27
Urania, m. William **OVIATT**, Dec. 6, 1846, by E. Huntington	2	25
RIDER, Helen Maria, d. Joshua L. & Philomela N., b. July 23, 1840	1	363
Joshua L., of New Milford, m. Philomela N. **EDDY**, of New Haven, Jan. 16, 1839, by Rev. Edwin C. Griswold	1	363
RIGBY, Esther, m. George C. **MINOR**, b. of New Milford, May 20, 1849, by Mr. Butterfield	2	63
Esther M., of New Milford, m. Harman **LAIN**, of Washington, Oct. 30, 1853, by Rev. A. B. Pulling	2	90
RILEY, John, m. Ann **DUNN**, May 23, 1847, by E. Huntington	2	35
RITTON, Mary Ann, m. Thomas K. **HODGE**, Apr. 6, 1846, by Henry Elliott, J. P.	2	12
ROBERTS, ROBURDS, Abraham, s. Benjamin & Ann, b. Oct. 7, 1759	LR7	14
Adrian, s. Eli & Abigail, b. Mar. 29, 1767	LR8	1
Almira, of Canaan, m. Levi **FREEMAN**, of Goshen, Dec. 18, 1852, by Rev. David Murdock, Jr.	2	80
Ann, m. Dea. Ebenezar **HOTCHKISS**, Apr. 30, 1783	LR5	9
Annis, d. Benjamin & Hannah, b. Oct. 30, 1821	1	173
Annis, m. Isaac B. **BRISTOL**, b. of New Milford, Jan. 7, 1846, by J. Greenwood	2	8
Benjamin, m. Ann **BOSTWICK**, b. of New Milford, Nov. 15, 1756, by Bushnell Bostwick, J. P.	LR7	14
Benjamin, s. Benjamin & Ann, b. June 21, 1765	LR7	14
Benjamin, m. Hannah **DOWNS**, b. of New Milford, Oct. 12, 1812, by [ ]	1	173
Benjamin & Hannah, had d. [ ], b. Aug. 1, 1813; d. same day	1	173
Duran, s. Eli & Abigail, b. Feb. 17, 1764	LR8	1
Eli, d. Sept. 23, 1754	LR6	14
Eli, of New Milford, m. Abagail **DURAN**, of Derby, May 31, 1763	LR8	1
Eli, s. Benjamin & Ann, b. June 28, 1769	LR7	14
Eli, m. Jerusha **BOOTH**, b. of New Milford, June 21, 1820, by Rev. Fosdick Harrison, of Roxbury	1	178
Eliakim, s. Peter & Mary, b. Dec. 6, 1761	LR6	14
Eliza, m. Levi S. **KNAPP**, Dec. 9, 1823, by Rev. Andrew		

	Vol.	Page
ROBERTS, ROBURDS, (cont.)		
Eliot	1	103
Elisabeth, d. Peter & Mary, b. Sept. 15, 1752	LR6	14
Elisabeth, d. Peter & Mary, d. Aug. 15, 1753	LR6	14
Hannah, m. Abraham **PEAT**, Mar. 16, 1775, by Rev. Nathaniell Taylor	LR12	19
Hannah C., d. Benjamin & Ann, b. Nov. 20, 1757	LR7	14
Hannah Harriet, d. Benjamin & Hannah, b. Mar. 26, 1817	1	173
Harriet H., of New Milford, m. Elmer **WARNER**, of Brookfield, June 12, 1844, by John Greenwood	1	396
Jennet, of New Milford, m. Edward B. **FORCE**, of Pyramus, N. J., Oct. 17, 1843, by J. Greenwood	1	389
John, s. Benjamin & Ann, b. Mar. 30, 1762	LR7	14
John, s. Elizabeth **DeFOREST**, b. Jan. 7, 1789	1	9
Josiah Cornelius, s. Eli & Jerusha, b. Dec. 3, 1823	1	178
Mary, m. Joseph **BOSTWICK**, Dec. 21, 1760	LR8	2
Mary R., m. Albert **PICKET**, b. of New Milford, Jan. 6, 1825, by Rev. Andrew Eliot	1	191
Molly, m. Minor **TREADWELL**, b. of New Milford, Sept. 3, 1805, by Elisha Bostwick, J. P.	1	121
Sam[ue]ll, s. Peter & Mary, b. Sept. 30, 1754	LR6	14
Susan Maria, d. Eli & Jerusha, b. Mar. 13, 1821	1	178
Susan Maria, m. Loren **HEVLEND**, b. of New Milford, Jan. 5, 1843, by Rev. Albert B. Camp, of Bridgewater	1	377
William, m. Eliza **GAYLORD**, d. David, Oct. 25, 1820, by Rev. Andrew Eliot	1	178
RODMON, Joseph, a witness at wedding of John **FERRIS** & Abigal **TRYON**, Quakers	LR4	22
ROE, Silas, of Sherman, m. Lucy M. **BARTRAM**, of New Milford, Mar. 12, 1843, by Z. Davenport	1	386
ROGERS, Benjamin, m. Sarah **BASSET**, Oct. 5, 1834, by E. Huntington	1	426
John, of Fairfield, m. Buler M. **PHILLIPS**, of New Milford, May 27, 1832, by Ezra Noble, J. P.	1	188
Polly Ann, of New Milford, m. Samuel **SCOTT**, of New Haven, Jan. 10, 1833, by Ezra Noble, J. P.	1	416
Reuben, of New Milford, m. Delia **KILSON**, of Kent, May 24, 1846, by J. Greenwood	2	15
ROOD, Elisebeth M., of New Milford, m. Hiram **HIDDEN**, of Neward, N. J., Oct. 10, 1841, by Rev. Z. Davenport	1	361
John A., of Brookfield, m. Julia Ann **HUNGERFORD**, of New Milford, Nov. 21, 1820, by Rev. Andrew Eliott	1	182
ROOT, Ann, of Kent, m. John **WATERS**, of New Milford, Nov. 13, 1842, by Z. Davenport	1	374
Florilla, m. Hiram **JENNINGS**, b. of New Milford, Dec. 4, 1839, by Benjamin B. Parsons	1	332
Laura, of Kent, m. Henry **BARNES**, of Sherman, Apr. 24, 1826, by Alpheus Fuller, J. P.	1	189

	Vol.	Page
ROOT, (cont.)		
Mrkenzia, m. Julia Ann **HULL**, Nov. 20, 1836, by Rev. Francis Donnelly	1	301
ROSWELL, Maria, m. Erwin **LINES**, Oct. 3, 1852, at Southville, by Rev. Richard D. Kirby	2	78
ROWE, Sylvia, d. Capt. Thomas & Christian, b. Sept. 27, 1784	LR12	1
William, m. Caroline **BEARSE**, July 11, 1824, by Rev. Eleazar Beecher	1	44
RUBY*, Jestus, of Stafford, m. Miranda **STUART**, of New Milford, Feb. 15, 1835, by H. Rood *("Ruby" uncertain, possibly "Kerby" or "Seely")	1	285
RUGGLES, Abijah, s. Isaac M. & Molly, b. Jan. 21, 1787	1	38
Adaline, m. Albert **THOMSON**, b. of Bridgewater, Sept. 12, 1841, by Rev. Albert B. Camp, of Bridgewater	1	360
Amasa, s. Timothy & Sibel, b. Sept. 20, 1780	1	3
Ann, m. William **PHELPS**, Nov. 6, 1765, by Samuell Bostwick, J. P.	LR7	5
Ann, m. William **PHELPS**, Nov. 6, 1765	LR10	15
Anna, d. Lazarus & Hannah, b. July 4, 1773	LR7	17
Apphia, d. Lazarus & Hannah, b. June 26, 1755	LR7	17
Ashbel, twin with Timothy, s. Timothy & Sibel, b. Mar. 7, 1783; d. Mar. 30, 1783	1	3
David, s. Lazarus & Hannah, b. Jan. 19*, 1759 *(Possibly "17th")	LR7	17
David, d. [ ], 177*, on Long Island, a prisoner in the British Army *(Last fig. erased or faded)	LR7	17
Eldad, s. Samuel & Huldah, b. Feb. 11, 1785	LR13	15
Eli, s. Samuel & Huldah, b. June 9, 1781	LR13	15
Elihu, s. Timothy & Sibel, b. July 4, 1764	1	3
Esther, d. Elihu & Rachel, b. June 12, 1791, at Brookfield	1	57
Esther, d. Elihu & Rachel, d. May 7, 1796	1	57
Ezra, s. Lazarus & Hannah, b. May 9, 1771	LR7	17
Flora M., of New Milford, m. Oliver W*. **JUDSON**, of Roxbury, July 3, 1851, by D. Williams *(Possibly "N.")	2	71
Hannah, d. Lazarus & Hannah, b. Mar. 26, 1780	LR7	17
Hannah, wid. Capt. Lazarus, d. Nov. 17, 1812, at Pougkeepsie, in the 76th y. of her age	LR7	17
Harriet, m. James Madison **PHIPPENY**, b. of Bridgewater, Jan. 6, 1836, by Albert B. Camp	1	291
Hermon, s. Lazarus & Hannah, b. Mar. 20, 1778	LR7	17
Hervey, s. Timothy & Sibel, b. Dec. 11, 1770	1	3
Hiram, m. Sally **MINOR**, b. of Bridgewater, May 8, 1823, by Rev. Fosdic Harrison, of Roxbury	1	75
Hiram F., m. Mary Ann **RUGGLES**, b. of New Milford, Jan. 26, 1826, by Rev. Andrew Eliot	1	75
Homer, s. Isaac M. & Molly, b. Dec. 30, 1791	1	38
Huldah, d. Samuell & Huldah, b. Dec. 14, 1786	LR13	15
Isaac M., m. Molly **BETTS**, Nov. 6, 1783	1	38

BARBOUR COLLECTION

	Vol.	Page
RUGGLES, (cont.)		
Isaac Matthew, s. Abijah & Hannah, b. Nov. 25, 1754	1	38
Isaac Wakelee, s. Samuel & Huldah, b. July 14, 1783	LR13	15
Jehiel, s. Isaac M. & Molly, b. Jan. 16, 1785	1	38
Jennette, of Bridgewater, m. Edwin B. **BLACKMAN,** of Danbury, Jan. 2, 1848, by Rev. James Kilbourn	2	38
John, s. Timothy & Sibel, b. Sept. 21, 1766	1	3
Joseph, s. Lazarus & Hannah, b. Mar. 2, 1757	LR7	17
Lazarus, m. Hannah **BOSTWICK,** Sept. 3, 1754	LR7	17
Lazarus, s. Lazarus & Hannah, b. June 4, 1769	LR7	17
Lazarus, Capt., d. May 6, [ ]	LR7	17
Lois, m. Oliver **WARNER,** Oct. 16, 1751	LR7	30
Lois, m. Levi **MERWIN,** Feb. 24, 1774	LR13	9
Lucy, d. Timothy & Sibel, b. Dec. 13, 1775	1	3
Mabel, d. Lazarus & Hannah, b. Nov. 8, 1760	LR7	17
Mabel, m. Reuben **BOSTWICK,** May 27, 1761	LR7	33
Marcus D., of New Milford, m. Almira **COGSWELL,** of Roxbury, Sept. 6, 1837, by A. B. Camp	1	309
Martha, d. Timothy & Sibel, b. Dec. 18, 176[ ]; d. Feb. 21, 1768	1	3
Martha, d. Timothy & Sibel, b. Apr. 14, 1773	1	3
Mary Ann, m. Hiram F. **RUGGLES,** b. of New Milford, Jan. 26, 1826, by Rev. Andrew Eliot	1	75
Mercy, m. Edmond **BOSTWICK,** Sept. 3, 1754	LR11	1
Nathaniel, s. Timothy & Sibel, b. Feb. 18, 1769	1	3
Oliver, s. Lazarus & Hannah, b. June 8, 1767	LR7	17
Philo, s. Lazarus & Hannah, b. Feb. 22, 1765	LR7	17
Polly, m. Nathan A. **SUMMERS,** b. of New Milford, Oct. 12, 1825, by Rev. Fosdic Harrison, of Roxbury	1	195
Polypheme, d. Lazarus & Hannah, b. Dec. 4, 1763	LR7	17
Pollypheme, m. Samuel **BOSTWICK,** Jr., May 14, 178[ ]	1	7
Rachel, w. Elihu, d. Oct. 4, 1794, in the 26th y. of her age	1	57
Sally E., m. Almon **SPERRY,** Feb. 6, 1826, by Rev. Fosdic Harrison, of Roxbury	1	198
Samuell, m. Huldah **WAKLEE,** June 1, 1779	LR13	15
Sarah, m. David **SMITH,** b. of New Milford, June 16*, 1746, by Rev. Elisha Kent *(Possibly "18th")	LR7	2
Sherman, s. Isaac M. & Molly, b. Feb. 4, 1789	1	38
Thalia, d. Lazarus & Hannah, b. Dec. 4, 1775	LR7	17
Thirza, d. Samuel & Huldah, b. Feb. 29, 1780	LR13	15
Timothy, m. Sibel **WOODIN,** Apr. 30, 176[ ]	1	3
Timothy, twin with Ashbel, s. Timothy & Sibel, b. Mar. 7, 1783	1	3
Tryphene, m. William **WHITELEY,** Feb. 1, 1779	1	2
William, s. Elihu & Rachel, b. Oct. 10, 1792	1	57
RUNDLE, Lucretia, m. Merwin **SMITH,** b. of New Milford, Dec. 24, 1807, by Elisha Bostwick, J. P.	1	154
RUNNELS, [see also **REYNOLDS**], Livia Ann, m. Daniel		

	Vol.	Page
RUNNELS, (cont.)		
LATHROP, b. of New Milford, Mar. 31, 1839, by Alonso F. Sellick	1	325
RUSSEL[L], Betsey A., m. Alanson W. **CANFIELD**, b. of New Milford, Apr. 3, 1833, by Rev. H. Rood	1	260
RUTHERFORD, John, of Savannah, m. Charlotte **MALLETT**, of New Milford, July 28, 1853, by David Murdock, Jr.	2	88
RYDER, Oliver, of Elyria, O., m. Harriet **JACKSON**, of New Milford, Apr. 24, 1839, by Noah Porter	1	327
SACKETT, SACKETTE, SACKIT, Abigail, m. Joseph **THARE**, May 8, 1776	LR12	19
Cathren, twin with Elisabeth, d. Ritchard & Mary, b. Oct. 14, 1751	LR6	10
Elisabeth, twin with Cathren, d. Ritchard & Mary, b. Oct. 14, 1751	LR6	10
John, m. Jane **CARPENTER**, Oct. 8, 1830, by Birdsey Beardsley, J. P.	1	231
Margery, m. David **GREEN**, July 12, 1759	LR7	27
Mary, m. Israel **CANFIELD**, Apr. 6, 1758	LR7	22
Rebecka, of Westfield, m. Salmon **CARRINGTON**, of New Milford, Nov. 6, 1771	LR13	2
Ritchard, s. Ritchard & Mary, b. July 15, 1749	LR6	10
SAGE, Samuel, of Colebrook, m. Susan Almira **MERWIN**, of New Milford, Jan. 29, 1834, by H. Rood	1	271
Susan A., Mrs. of New Milford, m. Henry **ANDREWS**, of Winchester, Conn., Dec. 5, 1837, by N. Porter	1	307
SANDS, Abraham B., witnessed marriage of David **SANDS** & Paulina **LEACH**	1	277
Catharine, witnessed marriage of David **SANDS** & Paulina **LEACH**	1	277
Catharine E., witnessed marriage of David **SANDS** & Paulina **LEACH**	1	277
David, of New Windsor, Co. Orange, N. Y., s. Nathaniel & Rebecca, m. Paulina **LEACH**, d. William & Charlotte, of Sherman, Conn., 6th m. 18th d., 1834, before 46 witnesses. Int. Pub. at Oblong, N. Y.	1	276-7
Nathaniel, witnessed marriage of David **SANDS** & Paulina **LEACH**	1	277
R. C., witnessed marriage of David **SANDS** & Paulina **LEACH**	1	277
SANFORD, Anne, m. Stephen **STURDEVANT**, Nov. 20, 1791	1	52
Armida, of New Milford, m. Samuel **GIDDINGS**, of Sherman, Oct. 16, 1831, by Rev. C. A. Boardman, of New Haven	1	229
Beach, m. Lucy **SMITH**, b. of New Milford, Nov. 15, 1825, by Rev. Fosdic Harrison, of Roxbury	1	196
Benoni S., d. [Oct. 24*], 1816, [ae 54]* *(Supplied from Orcutt's Hist.)	1	14
Benoni Stebins, s. Zachariah & Rachel, b. Mar. 5, 1762	LR8	1

182   BARBOUR COLLECTION

	Vol.	Page
SANFORD, (cont.)		
Benoni Stebbins, m. Prudence **BOSTWICK,** [ ]	1	14
Betsey Maria, m. Marcus **WAGNN,** May 4, 1836, by E. Huntington	1	297
Charles G., m. Emily E. **MORRIS,** June 6, 1837, by E. Huntington	1	311
Charles Grandison, s. [Joel & Huldah], b. Feb. 25, 1814	1	212
Charles H., m. Susan A. **SMITH,** b. of Bridgewater, Jan. 20, 1847, by James Kilborne	2	26
David, s. Zachariah & Rachel, b. Nov. 14, 1769	LR8	1
David C., of Litchfield, m. Caroline T. **MERWIN,** of New Milford, Sept. 1, 1822, by Rev. Benjamin Benham	1	74
David C., m. Emily **BULL,** Nov. 28, 1837, by Edward C. Bull	1	315
David Curtiss, s. [Joel & Huldah], b. Jan. 23, 1798	1	212
Edwin G., m. Mary E. **JUDSON,** b. of New Milford, May 29, 1854, by Rev. H. G. Noble	2	99
Eliza, m. William Albert **KNAPP,** b. of New Milford, Oct. 27, 1847, by John Greenwood	2	32
Flora M., of New Milford, m. Edwin A. **LACEY,** of Brookfield, Nov. 17, 1828, by Rev. E. Huntington	1	226
Frederick S., m. Mary Adaline **TREAT,** b. of Bridgewater, May 21, 1849, by Rev. J. Kilborn	2	55
George N., m. Laura **LAMPSON,** b. of New Milford, Jan. 19, 1831, by E. Huntington	1	247
George Northrop, s. Isaac & Betsey, b. Sept. 3, 1807	1	132
Goold, s. Benoni S. & Prudence, b. Oct. 31, 1786	1	14
Harriot, d. Joel & Huldah, b. Oct. 31, 1796	1	212
Harry, s. Isaac & Betsey, b. Sept. 23, 1809	1	132
Henry, m. Anna Jennett **CANFIELD,** b. of Bridgwater, Dec. 4, 1828, by Rev. Fosdic Harrison, of Roxbury	1	230
Hervey, m. Susan **CABLE,** b. of New Milford, Aug. 31, 1827, by Daniel Gaylord, J. P.	1	219
Isaac, s. Benoni S. & Prudence, b. Feb. 9, 1785	1	14
Isaac, m. Betsey **NORTHROP,** b. of New Milford, Sept. 11, 1806, by Elisha Bostwick, J. P.	1	132
Isaac, d. June 23, 1824, ae 39 y. 4 m. 14 d.	1	132
Isaac, of Newtown, m. Sarah **GORHAM,** of New Milford, Oct. 30, 1825, by Rev. Newton Tuttle	1	188
Isaac L., of New Milford, m. Ella A. **BOTSFORD,** of Sherman, this day, [Sept. 20, 1886], by Sandanett Wheeler, J. P. Witnesses: Juliet Wheeler, of Dover, Pricilla Hall, of Dover	2	123
Jeremiah, m. Sally **WAKELEE,** Jan. 29, 1809, by Elisha Bostwick, J. P.	1	160
Joseph, m. Ann **CRANE,** b. of New Milford, Bridgewater Soc., Feb. 10, 1822, by Rev. Fosdic Harrison, of Roxbury	1	26
Julia M., of Bridgwater, m. Albert A. **GAYLORD,** of New Milford, May 23, 1827, by Rev. Andrew Eliot	1	215

	Vol.	Page
SANFORD, (cont.)		
Julia Maria, d. [Joel & Huldah], b. May 9, 1803	1	212
Laura, m. Bushnel **BOSTWICK**, b. of New Milford, Feb. 11, 1822, by Rev. Benjamin Benham	1	17
Lorenzo D., m. Susan **WOOSTER**, b. of Bridgewater, Nov. 8, 1848, by J. Kilbourn	2	45
Luca, d. Samuel & Sarah, b. Apr. 27, 1772	LR10	11
Lucinda, d. Jonathan, m. Abraham Seabeary **BOOTH**, s. James, May sunday eve before 1st Monday, 1806/7, at Jonathan Sanfords at Newtown, by Rev. Daniel Burhans. Witness: May A. Birch	2	113
Lucy Maria, m. William **BOSTWICK**, b. of New Milford, Jan. 5, 1842, by N. Porter, Jr.	1	371
Mabel, d. Samuel & Sarah, b. Dec. 7, 1774	LR10	11
Mary, d. Zachariah & Rachel, b. Jan. 26, 1765	LR8	1
Mary J., of New Milford, m. Ira **KEELER**, of Brookfield, June 27, 1850, by Rev. H. D. Noble, of Brookfield	2	62
Meriah, d. Isaac & Betsey, b. Feb. 16, 1816	1	132
Polly, d. Samuel & Sarah, b. May 8, 1788; d. Jan. 17, 1792	LR10	11
Samuel, s. Samuel & Sarah, b. Dec. 29, 1779; d. July 5, 1783	LR10	11
Sarah, d. Samuel & Sarah, b. Aug. 27, 1777	LR10	11
Sarah, d. Benoni S. & Prudence, b. Mar. 2, 1788	1	14
Solomon, s. Isaac & Betsey, b. Apr. 7, 1812	1	132
Tabby, m. Cyrus **BOSTWICK**, Jan. 4, 1796	1	66
Thomas, s. Samuell & Sarah, b. Oct. 27, 1769, at Reading	LR10	11
Uriah, s. Samuel & Sarah, b. Dec. 18, 1767, at Reading	LR10	11
Walker, m. Mabel **SQUIRE**, b. of New Milford, June 3, 1806, by Elisha Bostwick, J. P.	1	131
Zachariah, m. Rachel **GOOLD**, May 28, 1761	LR8	1
SCHROEDER, John Frederick, Rev. of New York City, m. Caroline Maria **BOARDMAN**, of New Milford, May 22, 1825, by Rev. Benjamin Benham	1	183
[SCOFIELD], SHOFIELD, Assenath, of Kent, m. Sherman **PROUT**, of New Milford, Nov. 28, 1796, by Rev. Joel Bordwell	1	119
SCOTT, SCOT, Abigail S., m. John **McDURFE**, June 28, 1840, by Rev. Eleazer Beecher	1	345
Elisabeth, of Waterbury, m. Gamaliel **TERRILL**, of New Milford, May 17, 1725	LR2	339
Samuel, of New Haven, m. Polly Ann **ROGERS**, of New Milford, Jan. 10, 1833, by Ezra Noble, J. P.	1	416
SEARS, Sarah, m. Henry M. **BARLOW**, Nov. 20, 1846, by Rev. Eleazer Beecher	2	20
SEELEY, CEILIE, SEALEY, SEELY, SEELYE, SELYE, Abner, s. Joseph & Thankful, b. Feb. 17, 1739/40	LR4	17
Abner, m. Hannah **THAIR**, Mar. 22, 1759	LR7	29
Abner, s. Abner & Hannah, b. May 31, 1768	LR7	29
Beniamin, s. John & Martha, m. Debora **HITCHCOCK**, d.		

	Vol.	Page

SEELEY, CEILIE, SEALEY, SEELY, SEELYE, SELYE, (cont.)

Samuel, decd. & Sarah, Apr. 11, 1735	LR4	16
Benjamin, had negro Cato, s. Tempe, Oct. 1, 1788; d. same day; Maries, b. Dec. 11, 1791, in New Fairfield, Frederick, b. May 22, 1794, William, b. Jan. [ ], 1799, Amanda, b. Feb. 17, 1801, Julia, b. Mar. 31, 1803, John Stanley, b. Nov. 17, 1805	1	425
Benjamin, of Warren, m. Elizabeth **TAYLOR**, of New Milford, June 20, 1821, by Rev. George B. Andrews	1	122
Charlotte, d. Joseph, Jr. & Mercy, b. May 7, 1767	LR7	29
Charloote L., of Sherman, m. Charles W. **LAWTON**, of West Killingly, May 28, 1844, by John Greenwood	1	396
David, s. John & Martha, b. Sept. 4, 1731	LR4	1
Deborah, had d. Polley, b. Jan. 1, 1762* *("1775" rubbed out)	LR10	3
Ebenezer, s. John & Martha, b. Sept. 25, 1729	LR4	1
Elizabeth, m. Henry **BRONSON**, Nov. 14, 1843, by John Greenwood	1	388
George, m. Phoebe **BUCKINGHAM**, b. of New Milford, Jan. 18, 1835, by E. Huntington	1	284
Jehannah, d. Nathaniell & Abigal, b. July 11, 1747	LR6	9
Jerusha, of Stratford, m. Daniell **BORDMAN**, of New Milford, Nov. 1, 1720	LR2	356
Jestus, see under Jestus **RUBY**		
John, d. May 20, 1740	LR4	1
John, of Wilton, m. Annis **OVIATT**, of New Milford, Dec. 6, 1821, by Joel Sanford, J. P.	1	183
Joseph, m. Thankfull **WELLER**, July 28, 1735	LR4	17
Joseph, Jr., of New Milford, m. Mercy **TUPPER**, of Sailsbury, Jan. 24, 1764	LR7	29
Justice, m. Elisabeth **GIBBS**, Mar. 10, 1746/7, by Rev. Timothy Collins	LR6	3
Justus, s. Joseph, Jr. & Mercy, b. Feb. 4, 1766	LR7	29
Justus, of New Milford, m. Sarah **STUART**, of Litchfield, July 17, 1766, by Rev. Champion, of Litchfield	LR9	[ ]
Lusee, d. Nathaniell & Abigal, b. July 1, 1750	LR6	9
Margrit, d. Joseph & Thankful, b. Dec. 17, 1741	LR4	17
Martha, d. Joseph & Thankfull, b. Jan. 8, 1735/6	LR4	18
Martha, d. Joseph & Thankful, b. Apr. 26, 1738	LR4	17
Martha, m. Ephraim **RICHMOND**, Dec. 2, 1754	1	26
Mary, m. Obadiah **WELLER**, b. of New Milford, Nov. 12, 1728	LR4	4
Mary Jane, of New Milford, m. Edwin **BRITON**, of Salisbury, Oct. 6, 1833, by Rev. R. B. Canfield	1	264
Mary Jane, m. David T. **WHITEHEAD**, Apr. 3, 1843, by Eleazer Beecher	1	385
Nathaniell, m. Abigal **HOWARD**, May 9, 1745, by John Yeomans, J. P.	LR6	9
Oliver, s. Abner & Hannah, b. Feb. 28, 1766	LR7	29

	Vol.	Page
SEELEY, CEILIE, SEALEY, SEELY, SEELYE, SELYE, (cont.)		
Orange, s. Justus & Sarah, b. Feb. 5, 1767	LR9	[ ]
Philo, s. Justus & Sarah, b. Apr. 11, 1769	LR9	[ ]
Polley, d. Deborah, b. Jan. 1, 1762* *("1775" rubbed)	LR10	3
Ruth, single woman, had d. Abagail **HAMLIN**, b. May 25, 1739	LR4	1
Sarah, of Kent, m. Heath **GARLICK**, of New Milford, Feb. 8, 1764	1	50
Shelden, s. Abner & Hannah, b. Nov. 22, 1760	LR7	29
Steward, s. Justus & Sarah, b. Jan. 28, 1771	LR9	[ ]
Thankful, d. Abner & Hannah, b. July 6, 1763	LR7	29
Zadock, s. Justice & Elisabeth, b. Feb. 4, 1748/9	LR6	3
SHARRA, John A., of Lancaster, Pa., m. Phebe **BENNITT**, of New Milford, July 25, [1847], by James Kilbourn	2	31
SHED, Lyman, m. Anna **BEACH**, of Bridgwater, Oct. 11, 1829, by Rev. Fosdic Harrison, of Roxbury	1	235
SHELDON, Caroline F., m. Amos H. **BROWN**, Sept. 14, 1851, by William Roberts, J. P.	2	70
Homer, m. Melinda **WHITNEY**, Oct. 8, 1846, by E. Huntington	2	23
Mary, of Kent, m. Seeley **CLARK**, of New Milford, Sept. 18, 1833, by Joel Sanford, J. P.	1	264
SHERMAN, Almira, m. Daniel Allen **TREAT**, b. of New Milford, Nov. 30, 1809, by Elisha Bostwick, J. P.	1	139
Benjamin M., of New Haven, m. Sophia D. **TAYLOR**, of New Milford, June 9, 1833, by E. Huntington	1	262
Chloe, d. Roger & Elisabeth, b. Dec. 26, 1754; d. Nov. 13, 1757	LR6	7
Daniel, m. Tamar **MOREHOUSE**, Jan. 1, 1826, by Rev. Andrew Eliot	1	195
Eli, m. Lois **NORTHROP**, b. of New Milford, Dec. 25, 1844, by E. Huntington	2	2
Elizabeth, m. James **BUCK**, Feb. 14, 1748/9*, by Rev. Nathaniell Taylor *("Aug. 31, 1750" crossed out)	LR6	12
Elisabeth, d. Roger & Elisabeth, b. Sept. 28, 1760	LR6	7
Elisabeth, d. Roger & Elisabeth, b. Sept. 28, 1769	LR6	7
Emily C., m. David C. **WOOSTER**, b. of Bridgewater, Oct. 27, 1846, by Rev. William Atwill, of Bridgewater	2	27
Emmon H., m. Susan P. **OSBORN**, b. of New Milford, Jan. 1, 1852, by Rev. David P. Sanford	2	74
Ezra, s. Justin, d. Aug. 25, 1725	1	132
Fanny, m. Horace **MARSH**, b. of New Milford, Jan. 4, 1821, by Rev. Benjamin Benham	1	22
Flora, of New Milford, m. Dayton **OGDEN**, of Woodbury, Jan. 10, 1833, by E. Huntington	1	257
George B., m Emily **GLOVER**, Feb. 1, 1843, by E. Huntington	1	392
George M., m. Emily **GLOVER**, Feb. 1, 1843, by E.		

SHERMAN, (cont.)

	Vol.	Page
Huntington	1	384
Isaac, s. Roger & Elizabeth, b. June 17, 1753	LR6	7
Isaac, witnessed marriage of Jacob WANZER & Phebe LEACH	1	208
John, s. Roger & Elisabeth, b. July 8, 1750	LR6	7
Lucy E., m. Eli E. WORDEN, b. of New Milford, Mar. 11, 1840, by Noah Porter	1	343
Mary Jane, m. Stephen WELLS, b. of New Milford, Sept. 14, 1846, by Rev. George L. Foote	2	18
Oliver, s. Roger & Elisabeth, b. July 25, 1756	LR6	7
Rebekah, m. Joseph HARTWELL, Apr. [ ], 1752	LR7	31
Roger, of New Milford, m. Elisabeth HARTWELL, of Staten, Nov. 17, 1749, by Rev. Samuell Dunbar, of Staten	LR6	7
Ruth, m. Benjamin GAYLARD, Sept. 28, 1756	LR6	12
Susanna, of Woodbery, m. David NOBLE, of New Milford, June 1*, 1722 *(Possibly "2" intended)	LR2	348
William, m. Ruth TERRILL, b. of New Milford, Apr. 18, 1743, by Roger Brownson, J. P.	LR5	3
William, s. Roger & Elisabeth, b. Nov. 12, 1751	LR6	7
William, d. Apr. 20, 1756	LR5	3

SHERWOOD, Ann, m. Amos Horrace MARSH, b. of New

Milford, Feb. 15, 1819	1	186
Ann N., [d. Asahael & Caroline], b. Sept. 23, 1858	2	116
Asahel, of New Milford, m. Susan BENNITT, Aug. 4, 1846, by Rev. Samuel Weeks	2	39
Asahael M., [s. Asahael & Caroline], b. Sept. 3, 1855	2	116
Bessie A., m. Edward H. MOREHOUSE, b. of New Milford, June 5, 1854, by J. W. Hoffman	2	108
Betsey, m. George Martin MARSH, Mar. 14, 1811	1	138
Caroline, wid. Asahael, made affidavit Dec. 4, 1869, before James H. McMahon, J. P., the births of five children residence, New Milford, father, farmer, 1st w. Susan [ ]	2	116
Daniel, s. Hervey & Cynthia, b. May 11, 1815	1	124
Daniel F., s. Asahael & Caroline, b. Aug. 3, 1851	2	116
Herman, m. Abigail MARSH, Dec. 29, 1825, by Rev. Andrew Eliot	1	194
Hervey, m. Cynthia WHEATON, Dec. 17, 1814	1	124
Mary Ann, m. Nathan BULKLEY, b. of New Milford, Feb. 11, 1839, by Lewis B. Sherwood, J. P.	1	326
Mary W., m. Lucius M. HILL, b. of New Milford, Feb. 14, 1849, by Rev. William Henry Rees	2	54
Minerva, of New Milford, m. Slosson PLATT, of Butternuts, N. Y., June 18, 1822, by Rev. Andrew Eliot	1	36
Myron E., [s. Asahael & Caroline], b. July 7, 1853	2	116
Sarah, m. James F. McKINNEY, b. of New Milford, Jan. 15, 1845, by William H. Bangs	1	399

	Vol.	Page
SHERWOOD, (cont.)		
Susan, 1st w. of Asahael, according to affidavit made Dec. 4, 1869, by Caroline, wid. of Ashael	2	116
Susan M., [d. Asahael & Caroline], b. Mar. 30, 1860	2	116
Sybbel, of Woodbury, m. John **HITCHCOCK**, of New Milford, Dec. 20, 1754* *(First written "1755")	LR4	17
Sibble, of Woodbury, m. John **HITCHCOCK**, of New Milford, Dec. 20, 1754	LR7	1
SHOFIELD, [see under **SCOFIELD**]		
SKEELS, Merian, of Woodbury, m. Bushnell **BOSTWICK**, of New Milford, Jan. 25, 1736/7, by Roger Brownson, J. P.	LR4	19
SKILMORE, Charlotte, m. George **ELLIOTT**, b. of Bridgewater, Nov. 20, 1849, at the house of John Skidmore, by Rev. William Oscar Jarvis	2	57
SKINNER, Abigail, wid. of Sharon, formerly Abigail **MUDG**, m. Samuel **PRINDLE**, of New Milford, Sept. 12, 1744, by Rev. Peter Prat, of Sharon	LR4	14
SLOCUM, Anna, m. Enock **BUCKINGHAM**, Dec. 31, 1848, by Thomas A. Welton	2	45
SMITH, Abigail F., of Kent, m. Joseph B. **STEVENS**, of Prospect, Jan. 8, 1853, by Rev. A. B. Pulling	2	81
Abraham, s. Josiah & Mary, b. Jan. 26, 1731/2	LR5	2
Abraham, m. Mary **SMITH**, Feb. 24*, 1757 *(Possibly "29th")	LR7	2
Abraham*, m. Welhy **DRINKWATER**, Sept. 25, 1767, by Samuell Bostwick, J. P. *("Abel" crossed out0	LR11	3
Abraham, s. Abraham & Mary, b. Dec. 4, 1767	LR7	2
Alonzo B., of Naugatuck, m. Attha M. **WARNER**, of New Milford, Sept. 24, 1854, by Rev. William H. Russell	2	103
Amanda, d. David & Urania, b. Mar. 2, 1799, in Gallway, Saratoga Co., N. Y., d. Mar. 2, 1804	1	77
Amasa, m. Dorcas **WILKINSON**, b. of New Milford, Jan. 15, 1808, by Elisha Bostwick, J. P.	1	155
Andrew, s. John & Anne, b. Nov. 18, 1779	LR11	5
Anne, m. Thomas B. **WAKLEY**, Feb. 22, 1783	1	50
Anne, w. Perry & d. Samuel & Hester **COMSTOCK**, d. [ ]	1	65
Annis, d. Nathaniel & Annis, b. Feb. 28, 1775	LR7	4
Annis, d. Joel & Patience, b. Mar. 23, 1786	1	34
Annis E., of Bridgewater, m. Joel W. **JUDD**, of New Milford, Dec. 22, 1842, by Rev. Albert B. Camp, of Bridgewater	1	376
Beebe, s. Nathaniel & Annis, b. Apr. 17, 1787	LR7	4
Betsey Ann, m. Smith R. **WEEKS**, b. of Bridgewater, Oct. 15, 1845, by J. Kilbourn	1	404
Betty, d. Abraham & Mary, b. Feb. 14, 1770	LR7	2
Charles, m. Hannah **WARNER**, b. of New Milford, Jan. 19, 1826, by Rev. Eli Denniston	1	198
Charles, of Fairfield, m. Sarah **HOYT**, of New Milford, Aug. 15, 1834, by E. Huntington	1	281

SMITH, (cont.)

	Vol.	Page
Clara, m. Stephen **TREAT**, b. of Bridgwater, Oct. 1, 1833, by Rev. Fosdic Harrison, of Roxbury	1	268
Daniel, s. John & Anne, b. Oct. 26, 1768; d. Nov. 13, 1768	LR11	5
Daniel, s. John & Anne, b. Mar. 4, 1770	LR11	5
Daniel B., m. Abigail **IVES**, Jan. 4, 1824, by Rev. Benjamin Benham	1	160
Daniel Barlow, s. Thomas & Phebe, b. June 4, 1794	1	24
David, m. Sarah **RUGGLES**, b. of New Milford, June 16*, 1746, by Rev. Elisha Kent *(Possibly "18th")	LR7	2
David, s. David & Sarah, b. Mar. 30, 1747	LR7	2
David, s. Josiah, Jr. & Sarah, b. Sept. 10, 1768	LR10	12
David, s. Josiah & Sarah, b. Sept. 10, 1768	LR12	14
David, s. Jesse, d. Aug. 13, 1774	LR12	1
David, s. Joel & Patience, b. Apr. 13, 1783	1	34
David, m. Urania **EDWARDS**, Jan. 27, 1794	1	77
Davis, s. Nathaniell & Annis, b. Mar. 6, 1782; d. Mar. 9, 1782	LR7	4
Doctor, s. John & Anne, b. Jan. 27, 1782	LR11	5
Doctor, s. Joel & Patience, b. Dec. 9, 1798* *("Figure "8" uncertain)	1	34
Edwin, of Hadley, Mass., m. Sarah A. **IVES**, of Bridgewater, Mar. 14, 1847, by James Kilborn	2	28
Eli, s. Jesse & Elizabeth, b. June 10, 1754	LR12	13
Eli, m. Huldah **MERWIN**, June 17, 1782, by Rev. David Brownson	LR13	16
Eli Merwin, s. Eli & Huldah, b. Aug. 25, 1784	LR13	16
Elisha, s. John & Anne, b. July 22, 1777	LR11	5
Elisabeth, of Darby, m. John **BENEDICK**, of New Milford, Nov. 19, 1760	LR7	24
Elisabeth, m. John **BENEDICK**, Nov. 19, 1760	LR7	28
Elizabeth, d. Faithful & Elizabeth, b. May 15, 1803, in Pittsfield, N. Y.	1	47
Emma E., of Roxbury, m. George **CLARK**, of New Milford, Feb. 20, 1853, by Rev. A. B. Pulling	2	82
Esther Ann, m. Reuben W. **JUDSON**, b. of New Milford, Feb. 15, 1854, by Rev. David Murdock, Jr.	2	101
Eunice, [d. Abraham & Welthy], b. June 25, 1768	LR11	3
[E]unice, d. Josiah & Sarah, b. Mar. 5, 1772	LR12	14
Faithfull, s. Faithful & Elizabeth, b. Oct. 1, 1800	1	47
George, s. Joel & Patience, b. June 26, 1791	1	34
Hannah, d. Nathaniell & Annis, b. Dec. 19, 1769	LR7	4
Henry, m. Miranda **BUELL**, b. of New Milford, Jan. 25, 1843, by Rev. Albert B. Camp	1	378
Herbert, of Oxferd, m. Harriet M. **CLARK**, of Bridgewater, May 13, 1846, by Rev. James Kilborn	2	15
Hester, d. Nathaniel & Annis, b. Nov. 11, 1767	LR7	4
Huldah, d. Thomas & Phebe, b. May 9, 1792	1	24
Isaac, s. Joel & Patience, b. Apr. 10, 1793; d. Mar. 17, 1795	1	34

NEW MILFORD VITAL RECORDS 189

	Vol.	Page
SMITH, (cont.)		
Isaac, s. Joel & Patience, b. May 12, 1795	1	34
Isaac Canfield, s. James W. & Sally, b. July 11, 1805	1	174
James Mortimer, s. James W. & Sally, b. Aug. 22, 1809	1	174
James Winans, of Northeast Town, Dutches Co., N. Y., m. Sally **CANFIELD**, of New Milford, Apr. 20, 1803	1	174
Jane, d. Jesse & Elizabeth, b. Mar. 30, 1758	LR12	13
Jeremiah, m. Polly **REED**, Mar. 6, 1802, by Elisha Bostwick, J. P.	1	95
Jeremiah, of Milford, m. Berentha **TERRILL**, of New Milford, Apr. 29, 1827, by Rev. Andrew Eliot	1	128
Jesse, d. Dec. 1, 1783, in the 76th y. of his age	LR13	16
Joel, s. Jesse & Elizabeth, b. Dec. 22, 1756	LR12	13
Joel, s. Jesse & Elizabeth, b. Dec. 22, 1756; m. Patience **BEARSS**, d. Josiah & Rebeccah, July 11, 1782	1	34
Joel, s. [Abraham] & Wetthy, b. Mar. 14, 1765	LR11	3
Joel, of Kent, m. Elizabeth **MOREHOUSE**, of New Milford, July 6, 1824, by Rev. C. A. Boardman, of New Preston	1	69
Joel Bearss, s. Joel & Patience, b. Feb. 2, 1788	1	34
John, s. Josiah & Mary, b. Oct. 21, 1745	LR5	2
John, m. Anne **WILKERSON**, Mar. 3, 1768	LR11	5
John, s. Army **WASHBURN**, b. June 23, 1771	1	6
John, s. John & Anna, b. Apr. 5, 1773	LR11	5
John, d. Aug. 5, 1827, ae 82 y. 9 m. 14 d.	LR11	5
John, made affidavit May 26, 1879, before Lyman P. Eastman, J. P., that his s. Wilber F. **SMITH**, s. John & Esther M., b. July 4, 1839, New Milford, Bridgewater Soc.	2	120
Jonah, s. Abraham & Mary, b. Mar. 25, 1764	LR7	2
Joseph, s. David & Sarah, b. June 25, 1754	LR7	2
Josiah, s. Josiah & Mary, b. Feb. 14, 1741/2	LR5	2
Josiah, Jr., m. Sarah **PRIME**, b. of New Milford, Sept. 10, 1767, by Bushnel Bostwick, J. P.	LR10	12
Josiah, m. Sarah **PRIME**, Sept. 10, 1767, by Bushnel Bostwick, J. P.	LR12	14
Josiah, Sr., d. Feb. 21, 1776	LR5	2
Julia Ann, d. David & Urania, b. July 27, 1794	1	77
Laura, d. David & Urania, b. Mar. 16, 1796, in Gallway, Saratoga Co., N. Y.	1	77
Leander, s. James W. & Sally, b. June 26, 1807	1	174
Leonard, Jr., m. Rhoda Abigail **SMITH**, Apr. 17, 1824, by Seth Higley	1	134
Levi, s. Joel & Patience, b. Nov. 12, 1789	1	34
Lucena, m. James **STOCKER**, b. of New Milford, Oct. 24, 1833, by Alpheus Fuller, J. P.	1	267
Lucy, m. Beach **SANFORD**, b. of New Milford, Nov. 15, 1825, by Rev. Fosdic Harrison, of Roxbury	1	196
Mabel, d. John & Anne, b. Jan. 9, 1784	LR11	5
Marcus D., of Woodbury, m. Charlotte **OVIATT**, of New		

190   BARBOUR COLLECTION

	Vol.	Page
SMITH, (cont.)		
Milford, May 29, 1845, by E. Huntington	2	3
Martha, d. Jesse & Elizabeth, b. Mar. 24, 1751	LR12	13
Marthar, m. Stephen **MURWIN**, June 7, 1775, by Bushnel Bostwick, J. P.	LR13	1
Martin, s. Joel & Patience, b. Apr. 6, 1797	1	34
Mary, d. David & Sarah, b. Dec. 16, 1750	LR7	2
Mary, m. Abraham **SMITH**, Feb. 24*, 1757 *(Possibly "29th")	LR7	2
Mary, d. Abraham & Mary, b. Oct. 6, 1761	LR7	2
Mary, w. Josiah, d. Feb. last day, 1775	LR5	2
Mary, d. Samuell & Sarah, b. Apr. 5, 1777	LR12	1
Mary A., m. John **WATSON**, b. of New Milford, Oct. 5, 1845, by E. Huntington	2	4
Merrit, s. Samuel, Jr. & Sarah, b. Apr. 18, 1773	LR12	1
Merwin, s. Eli & Huldah, b. July 14, 1783; d. Oct. 22, 1783	LR13	16
Merwin, m. Lucretia **RUNDLE**, b. of New Milford, Dec. 24, 1807, by Elisha Bostwick, J. P.	1	154
Mindwell, d. Nathaniel & Annis, b. Sept. 5, 1765	LR7	4
Nathan, m. Marietta **BUEL**, Oct. 19, 1823, by Seth Higby, at the house of David Buel	1	58
Nathaniel, s. Josiah & Mary, b. Dec. 1, 1733	LR5	2
Nathaniel, m. Annis **THARE**, b. of New Milford, Sept. 27, 1764	LR7	4
Nathaniel, s. Nathaniell & Annis, b. Aug. 6, 1772; d. May 18, 1775	LR7	4
Nathaniel, s. Nathaniel & Annis, b. Mar. 17, 1780	LR7	4
Nathaniel, m. Mabel **MONSON**, b. of New Milford, Jan. 19, 1854, by Rev. A. B. Pulling	2	94
Olive, d. Thomas & Phebe, b. July 9, 1790	1	24
Oliver, m. Sarah **MERWIN**, b. of Bridgewater, Nov. 24, 1841, by Rev. Albert B. Camp	1	362
Olivia, d. David & Urania, b. Oct. 9, 1801, in Milton, Saratoga Co., N. Y.	1	77
Orilla, m. John **WARNER**, Jr., b. of New Milford, Feb. 10, 1825, by Rev. Andrew Eliot	1	136
Orinda A., m. Royal **DAVIS**, Nov. 25, 1827, by Stephen Crane, J. P.	1	204
Perry, m. Anne **COMSTOCK**, d. Samuel & Hester, [ ]	1	65
Phebe, of Ridgfeild, m. Aaron **GAYLARD**, of New Milford, Sept. 22, 1732, by Rev. Thomas Hauley	LR4	1
Phebe, m. Peter **MEAD**, b. of New Milford, Dec. 9, 1824, by Rev. Fosdick Harrison, of Roxbury	1	159
Polly, d. Thomas & Phebe, b. Oct. 19, 1787	1	24
Polly, m. Elijah **GREEN**, Apr. 18, 1832, by Rev. Eleazar Beecher	1	100
Polly Huldah, d. Eli & Huldah, b. Nov. 20, 1785	LR13	16
Polly M., m. Levi **MORRISS**, Sept. 24, 1807, by Elisha		

	Vol.	Page

SMITH, (cont.)

	Vol.	Page
Bostwick, J. P.	1	146
Preserve, m. Amelia **KNOWLES**, Jan. 1, 1824, by Rev. Andrew Eliot	1	163
Rachel M., of Bridgewater, m. Thomas **HUNGERFORD**, of Sherman, Nov. 19, 1838, by Albert B. Camp	1	319
Rebeckah, Mrs. of Milford, m. Jacob **BROWNSON**, of New Milford, May 29, 1735, by Sam[ue]ll Eels	LR4	1
Rebecca, m. Joseph **BEERS**, b. of New Milford, May 30, 1827, by Nathaniel Perry, J. P.	1	214
Reuben, s. Joel & Patience, b. July 8, 1784	1	34
Rhoda Abigail, m. Leonard **SMITH**, Jr., Apr. 17, 1824, by Seth Higley	1	134
Robert, m. Lois **GAYSON**, b. of New Milford, Nov. 19, 1845, by Daniel B. Wilson, J. P.	1	405
Ruth, d. Eli & Huldah, b. Jan. 20, 1789	LR13	16
Ruth, of Bridgewater Soc., m. Lyman **LOCKWOOD**, of Newtown, Feb. 24, 1822, by Rev. Fosdic Harrison, of Roxbury	1	30
Sally, m. John **MOREHOUSE**, 4th, b. of New Milford, Feb. 7, 1822, by Rev. Benjamin Benham	1	27
Sally Ann, d. James W. & Sally, b. Dec. 21, 1812	1	174
Samuel, m. Sarah **WILKINSON**, July 30, 1744, by Samuel Canfield, J. P.	LR5	7
Samuel, Jr., of New Milford, m. Sarah **PLUM**, of Milford, May 21, 1772, by Rev. Mr. Waller	LR12	1
Samuel, m. Amarillis **PEET**, b. of New Milford, Sept. 5, 1821, by Rev. Benjamin Benham	1	7
Samuel W., m. Harriet **YOUNG**, Dec. 20, 1836, by E. Huntington	1	312
Sarah, d. David & Sarah, b. Dec. 15, 1748	LR7	2
Sarah, m. Nathan **CAMP**, Nov. 11, 1767	LR10	14
Sarah, d. Josiah & Sarah, b. Jan. 30, 1775	LR12	14
Sarah Prime, d. David & Urania, b. Oct. 28, 1803, in Greenfield, Saratoga Co., N. Y.	1	77
Shubal, s. John & Anne, b. Mar. 11, 1775	LR11	5
Stephen, m. Marcia **NOBLE**, b. of New Milford, Dec. 30, 1828, by Rev. Andrew Eliot	1	226
Susan A., m. Charles H. **SANFORD**, b. of Bridgewater, Jan. 20, 1847, by James Kilborne	2	26
Susan C., m. Asa W. **CAMP**, Jr., b. of New Milford, May 18, 1853, by Rev. A. B. Pulling	2	86
Sibbel, m. David **CAMP**, Jr., Jan. 20, 1774, by Bushnel Bostwick, J. P.	LR12	10
Tamar, d. Nathaniel & Annis, b. May 24, 1777	LR7	4
Tamar, m. Isaac **WILKINSON**, Dec. 18, 1791	1	32
Thomas, s. Abraham & Mary, b. Apr. 10, 1760	LR7	2
Thomas, m. Phebe **BURRITT**, Apr. 8, 1787	1	24

	Vol.	Page
SMITH, (cont.)		
Thomas, [s. James W. **SALLY**], [ ]	1	174
Urania Runette, d. David & Urania, b. Sept. 4, 1805	1	77
Wilber F., s. John & Esther M., b. July 4, 1839	2	120
Ziphora, d. Abraham & Mary, b. June 6, 1774	LR7	2
SNYDER, Hiram, of Bridgeport, m. Caroline **CRANE**, of New Milford, Jan. 2, 1844, by John Greenwood	1	391
SOMERS, SOMMERS, [see under **SUMMERS**]		
SOULE, SOLES, Edwin, b. Apr. 8, 1829, Kent, Conn.	1	289
Elisha, b. Sept. 26, 1830	1	289
Henry A., m. Harriet **JENNINGS**, b. of New Milford, Nov. 11, 1849, by Rev. William Henry Rees	2	59
Henry Albert, b. Jan. 3, 1827, Franklin, N. Y.	1	289
John, m. Lucinda **WHITEHEAD**, b. of New Milford, Jan. 19, [ ], by Daniel Gaylord, J. P.	1	185
John Milton, b. Mar. 29, 1804, Dover, N. Y.	1	289
Marsia Elizabeth, b. July 5, 1833, Stanford, N. Y.	1	289
Nathaniel, b. Sept. 28, 1840	1	289
Polly, of New Milford, m. Spencer **WARD**, of Dover, Nov. 27, 1822, by Daniel Gaylord, J. P.	1	51
Sary Jane, b. May 10, 1838, Danbury, Conn.	1	289
Simeon C., b. Nov. 15, 1835, Kent, Conn.	1	289
SPERRY, SPEARY, SPERREY, SPERY, Almon, m. Sally E. **RUGGLES**, Feb. 6, 1826, by Rev. Fosdic Harrison, of Roxbury	1	198
Amy, w. Jared, d. [ ]	1	1
Amy M., m. John **ANGEVINE**, Feb. 20, 1833, by Josiah L. Dickinson	1	259
Dolly M., of New Milford, m. Harvey **WHITTLESEY**, of Farmington, Aug. 31, 1842, by N. Porter	1	377
Esther Henrietta, d. Jared & Esther, b. July 6, [ ]	1	1
Gilead, m. Mercy **BORDMAN**, b. of New Milford, Jan. 30, 1745/6, by Samuel Canfield, J. P.	LR5	13
Harriet, m. William **CLARK**, b. of Bridgwater Soc., Jan. 1, 1826, by Rev. Fosdic Harrison, of Roxbury	1	196
Jared, m. Amy **WHEATON**, Nov. 5, [ ]	1	1
Jared, m. Esther **CAMP**, [ ]	1	1
Joseph, of Woodbridge, m. Narusia **KINNEY**, of New Milford, Mar. 13, 1842, by E. Huntington	1	379
Patty, wid., m. Phinehas **GORAM**, b. of New Milford, Jan. 10, 1819, by Joel Sanford, J. P.	1	117
Prudence Polly, of Huntington, m. Isaac **DOWNS**, of New Milford, Jan. 4, 1796	1	86
William, m. Mary Ann **HAMLIN**, May 26, 1822, by Rev. Benjamin Benham	1	33
Wilmot, s. Jared & Amy, b. July 21, 1[ ]	1	1
SPROUL, Henry R., s. Robert E., ae 28, peddler & Eliza E., ae 18, b. Nov. 25, 1843	2	119

NEW MILFORD VITAL RECORDS

	Vol.	Page
SPROUL, (cont.)		
Robert E., made affidavit Apr. 23, 1879, before Lyman P. Eastman, Judge of Probate for Roxbury Dis. that he, ae 28, peddler, & w. Eliza E., ae 18, had s. Henry R. SPROUL, b. Nov. 25, 1843, in New Milford	2	119
SQUIRE, SQUIER, SQUIRES, Deborah, of New Milford, m. Emerson **COGGSWELL**, of Washington, Feb. 5, 1804, by Elisha Bostwick, J. P.	1	110
Harriet W., of New Milford, m. Miletus **WILSON**, of Sharon, Oct. 9, 1823, by Rev. Benjamin Benham	1	31
Mabel, m. Walker **SANFORD**, b. of New Milford, June 3, 1806, by Elisha Bostwick, J. P.	1	131
Polly, m. Amasa **DUNNING**, b. of New Milford, Dec. 18, 1806, by Elisha Bostwick, J. P.	1	137
Samuel, m. Sarah **SOMERS**, Nov. 11, 1841, by E. Huntington	1	368
STANLEY, Oliver C., of Berlin, Conn., m. Charlotte **HINE**, of New Milford, Oct. 13, 1847, by John Greenwood	2	31
STARR, Abigal, m. Joseph **WALLER**, Sept. 22, 1748	LR7	1
Cynthia, m. Eldad C. **JACKSON**, May 28, 1808	1	40
Levi, Capt. of Danbury, m. Loretta **BARNS**, of New Milford, Sept. 6, 1827, by Maltby Gleston	1	207
Priscilla, of Danbury, m. Joseph **PECK**, of New Milford, Nov. 1, 1787, by Rev. Joseph Peck	1	29
William J., m. Sarah **NORTHROP**, b. of New Milford, Apr. 15, 1830, by Hinman Rood	1	237
STEBBINS, STEBINS, Benjamin, of Brookfield, m. Polly Ann **BENNET**, of New Milford, [Mar. 6, 1836], by Rev. Henry Eames	1	292
Benoni, of New Milford, m. Mary **KIRBY**, of Milford, Dec. 10, 1717	LR2	352
Bononi, d. Nov. 14, 1758	LR7	2
Mary, w. Benoni, d. Feb. 17, 1771	LR7	2
Rebeckah, alias **HERRO**, m. Gamaliel **BALDWIN**, b. of New Milford, Feb. 11, 1741/2, by Samuel Canfield, J. P.	LR4	6
Sanford, adopted s. Benoni & Mary, d. Apr. 1, 1757	LR7	7
STEELE, John B., of Humphreysville, m. Emeline A. **STUART**, of Bridgwater, May 11, 1845, by James Kilbourn	1	236
John B., of Humphreysville, m. Emeline A. **STUART**, of Bridgewater, May 11, 1845, by James Kilbourn	1	399
STEPHENS, [see under **STEVENS**]		
STERLING, David, m. Adeline E. **CASTLE**, b. of New Milford, June 13, 1854, by Rev. W. H. Russell	2	103
Emily, of New Milford, m. Brice B. **WEAVER**, of Dover, N. Y., June 17, 1839, by Noah Porter	1	328
Ephraim, Jr., m. Lucy **BUCK**, b. of New Milford, Jan. 19, 1804, by Elisha Bostwick, J. P.	1	109
Samuel Beebe, m. Minerva **BEARD**, b. of New Milford, Nov. 6, 1828, by Rev. Andrew Eliot	1	225

	Vol.	Page
STERLING, (cont.)		
Sarah, m. Samuel H. **BARNS**, b. of New Milford, June 3, 1834, by H. Rood	1	273
STEVENS, STEPHENS, Ann, m. Edward **BOSTWICK,** Apr. 10, 1757	LR7	25
Ann, m. Nathan **COLLINS**, b. of New Milford, Apr. 8, 1759	LR4	2
Harriet, m. Stanley S. **BALDWIN**, of New York City, May 10, 1830, by Heman Rood	1	237
Joseph B., of Prospect, m. Abigail F. **SMITH**, of Kent, Jan. 8, 1853, by Rev. A. B. Pulling	2	81
Mary, of New Milford, m. Jonathan S. **BURR**, of New York City, May 10, 1830, by Heman Rood	1	237
Miriam, m. Ebenezer **LENARD**, Jan. 5, 1758	LR6	2
Rachel, m. John **BROWNSON**, Jan. 5, 1769	LR10	1
Sarah, m. Ephraim **BUCK**, Nov. 28, 1776	LR7	16
Sarah, m. Isaac **NICHOLS**, June 15, 1779	LR13	14
Sarah M., m. Henry W. **HATCH**, b. of New Milford, Aug. 10, 1835, by C. Shumway	1	271
STEWART, STEWARD, [see also **STUART**], Alonso, m. Mary **PEET**, b. of New Milford, Feb. 17, 1839, by Rev. Alonso F. Selleck	1	324
Eliza, m. William **WATERBURY**, Nov. 6, 1836, by Rev. Francis Donnelly	1	300
Henry, of Sherman, m. Caroline **FERRISS**, of New Milford, Apr. 17, 1826, by Rev. Benjamin Benham	1	202
Julia Ann, of Bridgwater, m. Orrin **MURPHY**, of Brookfield, Nov. 27, 1836, by A. B. Camp	1	301
Sylvester, of Sherman, m. Susan **MARSH**, of New Milford, Apr. 6, 1840, by Rev. Elijah Baldwin	1	344
STILES, Anna, of Lanesborough, m. Stephen **MOREHOUSE**, of New Milford, Oct. 3, 1779, by Rev. Gideon Bostwick	LR7	34
STILSON, Albert H., m. Jane E. **STONE**, b. of New Milford, Oct. 4, 1837, N. Porter		306
Amaryllis, m. David **FERRISS**, Jr., Jan. 11, 17[ ], by Rev. Nathaniel Taylor	1	3
Anna, m. Stephen **HINE**, [ ]	1	87
Anne, d. Riverius & Anna, b. Feb. 9, 1772	LR11	4
Anthey, d. Samuell & Mary, b. Nov. 20, 1759	LR7	2
Aurelia, d. Riverius & Anna, b. May 23, 1783	LR11	4
Bille, s. [John & Hannah], b. Aug. 8, 1773; d. Sept. 12, 1777	1	242
Charity, m. Edmond **CLARK**, July 11, 1770	1	31
Dorcas, d. [John & Hannah], b. Apr. 13, 1780; d. Feb. 15, 1814	1	242
Eben, s. Samuel & Mary, b. Nov. 22, 1761	LR7	2
Enoch, m. Freelove **STILSON**, Oct. last day, 1754	LR7	28
Eunice, d. Samuell & Mary, b. May 23, 1764; d. Nov. 4, 1776	LR7	2
Freelove, m. Enoch **STILSON**, Oct. last day, 1754	LR7	28
Hannah, [w. John], d. Mar. 25, 1795	1	242

	Vol.	Page
STILSON, (cont.)		
Jane E., of New Milford, m. Seneca **BUTTS**, of Clinton, N. Y., May 28, 1845, by J. Greenwood	1	400
John, s. Moses, b. Oct. 16, 1742, at Newtown; m. Hannah **TROWBRIDGE**, Aug. 11, 1763	1	242
John, s. [John & Hannah], b. May 2, 1771	1	242
John, s. John & Hannah, b. May 2, 1771; m. Rachel **BOSTWICK**, d. Benjamin & Olive, Apr. 30, 1794, by Rev. Stanley Griswold	1	243
John, d. Mar. 29, 1821	1	242
John, d. Apr. 1, 1831, ae 60 y. wanting 28 d.	1	243
John J., m. Elvira **TURREL**, Aug. 29, [1832], by E. Huntington	1	254
John Judson, s. [John & Rachel], b. Mar. 5, 1804	1	243
Mary, d. Enoch & Freelove, b. Feb. 7, 1755	LR7	28
Nieanor*, s. Riverius & Anna, b. May 3, 1776 *("Nicanor" in Orcutt's Hist.)	LR11	4
Olive, m. Philo N. **HEACOCK**, Sept. 2, 1822, by Rev. Andrew Eliot	1	76
Olive Hannah, d. [John & Rachel], b. Mar. 9, 1797	1	243
Phebe, m. John **CUMMINS**, Nov. 3, 1774, by John Beach, Miss.	LR12	14
Polly, d. Riverus & Anna, b. Mar. 17, 1770	LR11	4
Riverous, m. Anna **BALDWIN**, Aug. 6, 1767	LR11	4
Riverius & Anna, had s. [ ], b. May 18, [1768]; d. May 19, 1768	LR11	4
Riverius, m. Elvira **GREGORY**, b. of New Milford, Jan. 22, 1826, by Rev. Andrew Eliot	1	197
S. J., m. Phebe R. **MOORE**, Feb. 1, 1837, by N. Porter. Int. Pub.	1	302
Samuel Trowbridge, s. [John & Hannah], b. Aug. 2, 1775; d. Sept. 4, 1777	1	242
Sarah, d. [John & Hannah], b. Mar. 20, 1764; d. May 9, 1769	1	242
Semanthe Eudoxia, d. [John & Rachel], b. Feb. 23, 1799	1	243
Solomon Jay, s. [John & Rachel], b. June 27, 1801	1	243
Tamar, d. Riverius & Anna, b. Aug. 23, 1774; d. Sept. 6, 1777, ae 3 y. 14 d.	LR11	4
Tamar, d. Riverius & Anna, b. Mar. 17, 1778	LR11	4
Thaley, d. [John & Hannah], b. Feb. 11, 1777	1	242
Truman, s. Enoch & Freelove, b. May 4, 1757	LR7	28
Urania, d. Riverius & Anna, b. Sept. 14, 1781	LR11	4
William Bostwick, s. [John & Rachel], b. Mar. 24, 1795; d. May 30, 1819, at Louiseville, Kty.	1	243
STOCKER, Alma, m. Hiram **WALKER**, Oct. 31, 1830, by Alvin Brown, J. P.	1	142
James, m. Lucena **SMITH**, b. of New Milford, Oct. 24, 1833, by Alpheus Fuller, J. P.	1	267
STONE, Abigail, m. Abijah **BENNITT**, Jan. 23, 1777	LR13	13

STONE, (cont.)

	Vol.	Page
Almira, of New Milford, m. John **VARNEY**, of Russia, N. Y., Sept. 15, 1834, by Rev. William W. Andrews, of Kent.	1	279
Alvina, m. James E. **WELLS**, Oct. 7, 1841, by E. Huntington	1	367
Amanda, of New Milford, m. Charles **OLCOTT**, of Woodbury, Feb. 3, 1829, by Rev. Eleazar Beecher	1	229
Amaryllis, m. Johnson **WATSON**, b. of New Milford, Jan. 21, 1822, by Rev. C. A. Boardman	1	13
Aminta M., of Bridgewater, m. David P. **MOREY**, of West Stockbridge, Mass., Feb. 14, 1841, by Rev. Albert B. Camp	1	354
Amy, m. Solomon **HILL**, Jan. 16, 1783	1	67
Annis, m. Abiel **BALDWIN**, Sept. 10, 1787	1	28
Benajah, Jr., m. Mary **CANFIELD**, b. of New Milford, Nov. 19, 1755, by Rev. Nathaniell Taylor	LR7	5
Benajah, m. Barentha **STUART**, b. of New Milford, Nov. 5, 1825, by Alpheus Fuller, J. P.	1	191
Benjamin, Jr., m. Thalia **BUCK**, b. of New Milford, Apr. 23, 1803, by Elisha Bostwick, J. P.	1	105
Benjamin*, m. Susannah **CLARKE**, Dec. 19, 1830, by Rev. Eleazar Beecher *(Possibly "Benjamin **STOWE**")	1	94
Benjamin J., m. Mary Ann **BEECHER**, b. of New Milford, Oct. 10, 1838, by N. Porter	1	321
Daniel, s. Reuben & Deborah, b. Aug. 12, 1782	1	79
David J., m. Emeline **LOVERIDGE**, b. of New Milford, Sept. 13, 1831, by E. Huntington	1	247
Elizabeth, of New Milford, m. [Lym]an **BEECHER**, of Hinesburgh, Feb. 5, 1803, by Elisha Bostwick, J. P.	1	101
Elizabeth, of New Milford, m. Lyman **BEECHER**, of Hinesburgh, Feb. 5, 1803, by Elisha Bostwick, J. P.	1	103
Emeline, of New Milford, m. Thadeus **PERCEY**, of Woodbury, Oct. 29, 1828, by Rev. Andrew Eliot	1	224
Esther Orinda, m. Leonard **THOMPSON**, Feb. 6, 1805, by Elisha Bostwick, J. P.	1	114
Francis, of Warren, m. Sarah Jane **WELLS**, of New Milford, Sept. 23, 1845, by Rev. Johnson Howard, at Dover, N. Y.	1	402
Harriot, d. Reuben & Deborah, b. Sept. 19, 1796	1	79
Harriet E., m. Daniel G. **THORP**, b. of Bridgwater, Oct. 30, 1836, by A. B. Camp	1	300
Ithiel, s. Reuben & Deborah, b. Aug. 16, 1774	1	79
Jane E., m. Albert H. **STILSON**, b. of New Milford, Oct. 4, 1837, by N. Porter	1	306
John, s. Reuben & Deborah, b. Aug. 12, 1776	1	79
Joshua, m. Lois **MERWIN**, b. of New Milford, Oct. 1, 1805, by Elisha Bostwick, J. P.	1	124
Liberta R., of Bridgwater, m. Elijah S. **DUNNING**, of Brookfield, June 17, 1828, by Rev. Andrew Eliot	1	220
Lois, m. Elias **KENNE**, Jan. 25, 1759	LR7	9

	Vol.	Page
STONE, (cont.)		
Lucinda, d. Reuben & Deborah, b. May 26, 1779	1	79
Marcia, of New Milford, m. Burton **GILBERT**, of Warren, July 9, 1837, by Rev. Joseph Whittlesey	1	305
Martha, m. Eleazar **HENDRYX**, Oct. 2, 1782	LR13	8
Mary, m. Read **GARLICK**, b. of New Milford, Dec. 7, 1752	LR6	4
Mary Esther, m. Clark **MARSH**, Sept. 4, 1851, at the house of Chauncey Stone, by Rev. James L. Scott	2	70
Nancy, m. Henry **MARSH**, b. of New Milford, Dec. 23, 1847, by E. Huntington	2	37
Onor, w. Truman, d. Aug. 8, 1799	LR10	5
Rachel, m. Benjamin Ruggles **BOSTWICK**, Nov. 30, 178[ ]	1	3
Rebeccah, of New Milford, m. Russel **CARTER**, of Warren, Jan. 29, 1823, by Rev. Andrew Eliot	1	182
Reuben, m. Deborah **COMSTOCK**, Sept. 21, 1773	1	79
Rodman N., of New York, m. Charlotte E. **BUNCE***, of New Milford, Jan. 21, 1824, by Rev. Andrew Eliot *(Name doubtful)	1	87
Russel, m. Laury A. **HALLOCK**, Apr. 8, 1835, by Daniel Baldwin	1	285
Ruth, of Bridgwater, m. Weller **HINMAN**, of New Milford, Jan. 23, 1827, by Rev. Andrew Eliot	1	115
Sally, m. Noble **LYON**, Jan. 30, 1821, by Rev. Benjamin Benham	1	62
Solomon, s. Reuben & Deborah, b. Aug. 1, 1785	1	79
Saphronia, of New Milford, m. Orlin J. **WHEATON**, of Pompey, N. Y., Nov. 22, 1821, by Rev. C. A. Boardman	1	41
Tainmisin, d. Reuben & Deborah, b. Mar. 20, 1787	1	79
Truman, m. Onor **MERWIN**, d. John & Mercy, [ ]	LR10	5
William J., m. Maria **MERWIN**, b. of New Milford, Sept. 1, 1836, by Noah Porter, Jr.	1	299
STOW, David L., witnessed marriage of Enoch **CARPENTER** & Sophia **LANE**	1	184
STRAIGHT, John, of Kent, m. Rachel **PEET**, of New Milford, Nov. 9, 1852, by Albert N. Baldwin, J. P.	2	78
Sarah, m. John **MOREHOUSE**, Jr., b. of New Milford, Jan. 22, 1793	1	84
STRONG, Epaphroditus, of Warren, m. Anne **MORGAN**, of New Milford, Mar. 20, 1804, by Elisha Bostwick, J. P.	1	110
STUART, [see also **STEWART**], Abel, of Sherman, m. Lorain **MERWIN**, of New Milford, Mar. 5, 1807, by Elisha Bostwick, J. P.	1	139
Barentha, m. Benajah **STONE**, b. of New Milford, Nov. 5, 1825, by Alpheus Fuller, J. P.	1	191
Emeline A., of Bridgwater, m. John B. **STEELE**, of Humphreysville, May 11, 1845, by James Kilbourn	1	236
Emeline A., of Bridgewater, m. John B. **STEELE**, of Humphreysville, May 11, 1845, by James Kilbourn	1	399

	Vol.	Page
STUART, (cont.)		
Harriet, m. Hiram S. **CHIPMAN**, b. of Bridgewater, Nov. 29, 1846, by James Kilborn	2	21
Miranda, of New Milford, m. Jestus **RUBY***, of Stafford, Feb. 15, 1835, by H. Rood *("Ruby" uncertain, possibly "Kerby" or "Seely")	1	285
Sarah, of Litchfield, m. Justus **SEELY**, of New Milford, July 17, 1766, by Rev. Champion, of Litchfield	LR9	[ ]
STURDEVANT, Andrew, s. John, Jr. & Sarah, b. Jan. 17, 1785	LR13	1
Hannah, d. John, Jr. & Sarah, b. May 6, 1792	LR13	1
Hannah Shove, m. Woolcott **BURNHAM**, Jan. 22, 1784, by Nathaniell Taylor	LR13	17
John, Jr., m. Sarah **BARNUM**, Mar. 28, 1782	LR13	1
John Sanford, s. John, Jr. & Sarah, b. June 2, 1798	LR13	1
Lucy, d. John, Jr. & Sarah, b. May 3, 1796	LR13	1
Mary, m. Benjamin B. **BEACH**, b. of New Milford, Nov. 2, 1834, by E. Huntington	1	283
Molly, d. Stephen & Anne, b. Aug. 19, 1792	1	52
Sarah Ann, d. John, Jr. & Sarah, b. Dec. 11, 1789	LR13	1
Stephen, m. Anne **SANFORD**, Nov. 20, 1791	1	52
SUDLOW, George, m. Thirza **FULLER**, b. of New Milford, July 4, 1809	1	164
George, witnessed marriage of Ebenezer **WANZER**, Jr. & Lucy **LEACH**	1	181
Henry Wyllys, s. George & Thirza, b. Feb. 28, 1811	1	164
Lucy A., m. Chester **FRENCH**, Nov. 23, 1835, by E. Huntington	1	296
SULLIVAN, SULIVAN, Betsey A., m. William A. **LINES**, b. of New Milford, June 1, 1843, by J. Greenwood	1	387
Daniel, m. Catharine **HILL**, Aug. 17, 1823, by Rev. Benjamin Benham	1	97
Mary A., of New Milford, m. Amos **HALLOCK**, of Washington, Conn., Jan. 31, 1849, by Rev. John Howard	2	48
William A., m. Sally Ann **HALLOCK**, Dec. 27, 1846, by E. Huntington	2	26
SUMMERS, SOMERS, SOMMERS, SUMERS, Andrew, m. Ruth **BEACH**, Nov. 15, 1770	1	39
Andrew, s. Andrew & Ruth, b. July 13, 1784	1	39
Augustine, s. Andrew & Ruth, b. Mar. 19, 1773; d. Nov. 15, 1775	1	39
Augustine, s. Andrew & Ruth, b. Feb. 12, 1776	1	39
Augustine, s. Andrew & Ruth, d. Mar. 8, 1796	1	39
Beach, s. Andrew & Ruth, b. Aug. 23, 1780	1	39
Daniel J., m. Olanor **NORTHROP**, Jan. 1, 1830, by Rev. Josiah P. Dickinson	1	236
David, m. Sarah **TREAT**, Apr. 30, 1773, by Rev. Nathaniell Taylor	LR12	4
Eli, of Dover, N. Y., m. Eliza **GOODSELL**, of New Milford,		

	Vol.	Page

SUMMERS, SOMERS, SOMMERS, SUMERS, (cont.)
    Jan. 21, 1837, by Rev. William W. Andrews, of Kent

Elijah, s. Andrew & Ruth, b. Apr. 26, 1778	1	303
Elizabeth A., of New Milford, m. Nathaniel **BROWN**, of Washington, Nov. 16, 1826, by Rev. Andrew Eliot	1	39
Hannah, m. Abel **WILKERSON**, b. of New Milford, Dec. 23, 1773, by Samuell Bostwick, J. P.	1	204
Hannah, d. Andrew & Ruth, b. July 2, 1792	LR12	4
Harriot, m. Hiram **PLATT**, b. of New Milford, Nov. 30, 1815, by Elisha Bostwick, J. P.	1	39
Herman D., m. Eunice **BROWNSON**, Oct. 28, 1827, by Stephen Crane, J. P.	1	164
Laura, m. Ambrose **BARLOW**, Feb. 1, 1852, by Rev. William McAlister	1	131
Mary D., m. Luther **TUTTLE**, Dec. 9, 1827, by Stephen Crane, J. P.	2	87
Nathan A., m. Polly **RUGGLES**, b. of New Milford, Oct. 12, 1825, by Rev. Fosdic Harrison, of Roxbury	1	205
Neram, m. Alma M. **ATWOOD**, b. of Bridgwater, Sept. 21, 1826, by Rev. Fosdick Harrison, of Roxbury	1	195
Ruth, d. Andrew & Ruth, b. Feb. 7, 1787	1	153
Sarah, d. Andrew & Ruth, b. July 26, 1789	1	39
Sarah, m. Samuel **SQUIERS**, Nov. 11, 1841, by E. Huntington	1	39
Sophrona M. A., m. David E. **BOSTWICK**, Mar. 16, 1834, by E. Huntington	1	368
Taylor, m. Mariett **WILLIAMS**, Jan. 10, 1833, by Rev. Luther Mead	1	275
SWEETLOVE, Abiah, of New Milford, m. Ziba **CROCKER,** of Vermont, June 8, 1818, by Joel Sanford, J. P.	1	256
Ellis, m. Miranda **FERRISS**, Oct. 27, 1824, at the house of John Ferriss, by Rev. Eleazar Beecher	1	105
SWIFT, Gudon, witnessed marriage of David **SANDS** & Paulina **LEACH**	1	170
Gurdon, of Washington, Dutchess Co., N. Y., s. Beriah & Elizabeth, m. Jane **WANZER**, d. Moses & Sarah, of New Fairfield, 8th m. 27th d., 1835, before 37 witnesses. Int. Pub. at Pawling, N. Y. & New Milford	1	277
Jane, witnessed marriage of Gurdon **SWIFT** & Jane **WANZER**	1	288
Joanna W., witnessed marriage of David **SANDS** & Paulina **LEACH**	1	288
Joanna W., witnessed marriage of Gurdon **SWIFT** & Jane **WANZER**	1	277
Maria Ann, witnessed marriage of David **SANDS** & Paulina **LEACH**	1	288
Nathan, witnessed marriage of Gurdon **SWIFT** & Jane **WANZER**	1	277
	1	288

	Vol.	Page
SWIFT, (cont.)		
Reuben, of Waterloo, N. Y., m. Harriet M. **TAYLOR**, of New Milford, Oct. 19, 1823, by Rev. Andrew Eliot	1	119
Susan, witnessed marriage of David **SANDS** & Paulina **LEACH**	1	277
Susan, witnessed marriage of Gurdon **SWIFT** & Jane **WANZER**	1	288
William, witnessed marriage of Gurdon **SWIFT** & Jane **WANZER**	1	288
William, of Washington, Dutchess Co., N. Y., m. Anna **WANSER**, d. Moses, of New Fairfield, 9th m. 24th d. 1840, by Abraham Wanser, Clerk, at the Friends Meeting House	1	346
William, witnessed marriage of David **SANDS** & Paulina **LEACH**	1	277
SWORDS, Elizabeth, m. Elihu **MARSH**, 2nd, Jan. 13, 1793	1	167
TALCOTT, TALLCOT, Annah, d. Nathan & Hanah, b. July 30, 1734	LR4	8
Gains*, s. Nathan & Hanah, b. Nov. 2, 1736 *(Gaius?)	LR4	8
Hannah H., a witness at wedding of John **FERRIS** & Abigal **TRYON**, Quakers	LR4	22
Nathan, m. Hannah **FARRISS**, b. of New Milford, Dec. 24, 1730	LR4	8
Nathan, d. Aug. 13, 1738	LR4	8
Nathan, a witness at wedding of Elnathan **BOTSFORD** & Dorothy **PRINDLE**, Quakers	LR4	14
Nathan, a witness at wedding of John **FERRIS** & Abigal **TRYON**, Quakers	LR4	22
TAPPING, Helen, witnessed marriage of Jehu **HOAG** & Phebe **WANZER**	1	250
TAYLOR, TAYLARD, Abraham, s. Thomas, d. Sept. 8, 1755, at the camp at Lake George, being one of Capt. Benjamin Hinmans Co.	LR7	3
Abraham, d. Sept. 8, 1755, at the camp at Lake George, being one of Capt. Benjamin Hinmans Co.	LR7	3
Abraham, s. Nathaniel & Hannah, b. May 17, 1764 (Entry crossed out in original)	LR7	25
Alonzo, m. Loiza **PECK**, b. of Newtown, Sept. 5, 1830, by Rev. Eleazer Beecher	1	201
Anna, m. Ichabod **WILKINSON**, Apr. 13, 1775	LR13	6
Anne, w. Nathaniel, d. [ ]	1	30
Augustin, s. Nathaniell & Tamer, b. Nov. 28, 1755	LR6	6
Catharine, d. Nathaniell & Hannah, b. June 30, 1765	LR7	25
Catharine, m. George **MILLIGAN**, Nov. 13, 1788	1	37
Charlotte, d. Nathaniell, 3rd & Anne, b. Mar. 20, 1782	1	30
Charlotte, m. David Sherman **BOARDMAN**, b. of New Milford, May 18, 1806, by Elisha Bostwick, J. P.	1	130
Deidamia, d. Nathaniell & Hannah, b. Nov. 21, 1763	LR7	25

NEW MILFORD VITAL RECORDS 201

	Vol.	Page
TAYLOR, TAYLARD, (cont.)		
Elizabeth, d. Nathaniell & Hannah, b. July 22, 1761* *(Date crossed out and corrected)	LR7	25
Elizabeth, of New Milford, m. Benjamin SEELYE, of Warren, June 20, 1821, by Rev. George B. Andrews	1	122
Eunice, d. Eli & Eunice, b. June 20, 1763	LR7	13
Eunice, d. Nathaniell & Hannah, b. Jan. 10, 1767 (Entry crossed out in original)	LR7	25
Harriet M., of New Milford, m. Reuben SWIFT, of Waterloo, N. Y., Oct. 19, 1823, by Rev. Andrew Eliot	1	119
John, s. Eli & Eunice, b. Aug. 1, 1765	LR7	13
John, s. Nathaniell, 3rd & Anne, b. Sept. 20, 1777	1	30
John Boardman, s. Rev. Nathaniel & Tamer, b. Jan. 17, 1749/50; d. Feb. 4, 1749	LR6	6
Julia Ann, m. Laurens Edward BUCKINGHAM, b. of New Preston, June 13, 1832, by Henry S. Atwater	1	249
Laurea, d. Nathaniell, 3rd & Anne, b. Oct. 11, 1775; d. Sept. 11, 1776	1	30
Luana, [d. Nathaniel & Hannah,] (Entry crossed out in original)	LR7	25
Millison, d. Nathaniell & Hannah, b. Sept. 15, 1762 (Entry crossed out in original)	LR7	25
Nathaniel, Rev., m. Tamer BOARDMAN, of New Milford, Feb. 23, 1748/9, by Samuell Canfield, J. P.	LR6	6
Nathaniell, s. Nathaniell & Tamer, b. Apr. 7, 1753	LR6	6
Nathaniel, m. Hannah GILLIT, Mar. 5, 1760	LR7	25
Nathanael, 3rd, m. Anne NORTHROP, Aug. 31, 1774	1	30
Nathaniell, 3rd, had negro Peter, s. Hagar, b. Nov. 23, 1788; Michael, b. Apr. 27, 1791; Phebe, b. June 27, 1795; Peter, d. Feb. 27, 1830	1	425
Nathaniel, Rev., d. Dec. 9, 1800, in the 79th y. of his age	LR6	6
Nathaniel, m. Susanna GUNN, wid. Abner, Dec. 7, 1812	1	30
Nathaniel, d. Feb. 14, 1818	1	30
Orinda [ ]*, m. Merrit S. PLATT, Sept. 18, 1832, by Rev. R. B. Canfield, of New Preston *("Gaylord" written over)	1	251
Ruth, m. Elijah DOWNS, Oct. 13, 1785	LR12	4
Sarah, m. Calab DATON, Apr. 19, 1759	LR7	26
Sophia D., of New Milford, m. Benjamin M. SHERMAN, of New Haven, June 9, 1833, by E. Huntington	1	262
Tamar, d. Nathaniell & Tamar, b. July 4, 1759	LR6	6
Tamar, w. Rev. Nathaniell, d. June 27, 1795	LR6	6
Thomas, s. Nathaniel & Hannah, b. Mar. 6, 1768 (Entry crossed out in original)	LR7	25
Urania, d. Nathaniell & Tamar, b. July 23, 1751	LR6	6
Urania, m. Daniel EVERIT, Jan. 1, 1778, by Rev. Nathaniel Taylor	LR13	10
William, s. Nathaniell & Tamar, b. Mar. 20, 1764* *(Date erased)	LR6	6

	Vol.	Page
TAYLOR, TAYLARD, (cont.)		
William Nathaniel, s. Nathaniel, 3rd & Anne, b. June 23, 1786	1	30
Ziba, s. Eli & Eunice, b. July 16, 1767	LR7	13
TERRILL, TERRIL, TIRRIL, TURRILL, TURREL, TARRIL,		
Abigail, d. Nathan & Ruth, b. Mar. 24, 1727/8	LR2	352
Abigael, d. Caleb & Abigaile, b. Nov. 15, 1744	LR11	1
Abigal, m. Paul **TURRIL**, Jan. 29, 1744/5, by Samuell Cook, pastor	LR5	13
Abiagal, d. Paull & Abigail, b. Dec. 23, 1747	LR5	13
Abigail, w. Paul, d. July 11, 1757	LR7	15
Abigail, d. James & Abigail, b. June 30, 1762	LR5	8
Abigail, w. Capt. James, d. Jan. 9, 1774	LR5	8
Abigail, d. James, Jr. & Sarah, b. Jan. 25, 1774	LR10	13
Abigail Ellen, of New Fairfield, m. Allen **MARSH**, of New Milford, Mar. 9, 1820, in New Fairfield	1	72
Abijah, m. Naomi **TROWBRIDGE**, Sept. 5, 1808, by Elisha Bostwick, J. P.	1	158
Almira, of New Milford, m. Samuel W. **JUDSON**, of Woodbury, Mar. 31, 1835, by H. Rood	1	286
Amos, s. Gamaliel & Elizabeth, b. May 11, 1732	LR2	339
Amos, s. Ezra & Judith, b. July 1, 1760	LR5	12
Anna, d. Nathan & Dorothy, b. Feb. 1, 1789	LR12	8
Anne, d. James & Abigal, b. Apr. 8, 1754	LR5	8
Aranah, d. Nathan & Dorothy, b. Mar. 13, 1779, in New Fairfield	LR12	8
Asehel, s. Paul & Abigiel, b. Mar. 13, 1757	LR7	15
Asiel, s. Nathan & Ruth, b. Sept. 20, 1739	LR4	28
Beebe, s. James & Abigal, b. Sept. 25, 1750	LR5	8
Bebe, s. James & Abigal, d. Nov. 15, 1751	LR5	8
Beebe, s. Ebenezer & Lois, b. Feb. 16, 1767	LR8	3
Benjamin, s. Gamaliel & Elizabeth, b. Apr. 17, 1728	LR2	339
Benjamin, s. Caleb & Abigail, b. Dec. 15, 1765	LR11	1
Berentha, of New Milford, m. Jeremiah **SMITH**, of Milford, Apr. 29, 1827, by Rev. Andrew Eliot	1	128
Betsey, d. Stephen & Hepzibah, b. Aug. 9, 1786	1	16
Betsey* S., of New Milford, m. Henry **ALLEN**, of Hoosick, N. Y., Mar. 15, 1824, by Rev. Andrew Eliot *("Hetty" written above)	1	119
Britania, d. Leman & Lucy, b. July 25, 1798	1	80
Calab, [s. Caleb & Abigail], b. Nov. 10, 1742	LR11	1
Caleb, Jr., m. Eunice **COGSWELL**, b. of New Milford, Jan. 27, 1768, by Samuell Bostwick, J. P.	LR10	11
Calab, s. Calab, Jr. & Eunice, b. Mar. 2, 1773	LR10	11
Caroline, m. Judson **CANFIELD**, Oct. 24, 1824, by Rev. Andrew Eliot	1	171
Comfort, d. Nathan & Ruth, b. Jan. 17, 1731/2	LR2	352
Curtiss, s. Nathan & Dorothy, b. Feb. 27, 1787	LR12	8
Daniel, s. Nathan & Ruth, b. July 11, 1726	LR2	352

	Vol.	Page
TERRILL, TERRIL, TIRRIL, TURRILL, TURREL, TARRIL, (cont.)		
David, s. Nathan & Ruth, b. Apr. 22, 1723	LR2	352
Doctor, twin with Magore*, s. Caleb & Abigail, b. Nov. 26, 1768 *("Major" in Orcutt's Hist.)	LR11	1
Ebenezer, s. James & Abgaall, b. Apr. 3*, 1742 *("2" crossed out)	LR4	2
Ebenezer, m. Lois HALL, Feb. 26, 1766, by Noah Wadhams, Pastor of the Church in New Preston	LR8	3
Elijah, s. Nathan & Dorothy, b. Apr. 1, 1791	LR12	8
Elijah, m. Amanda ODELL, b. of New Milford, Mar. 15, 1846, by J. Greenwood	2	9
Elizabeth, d. Gamiliel & Elizabeth, b. Jan. 14, 1729/30	LR2	339
Elvira, m. John J. STILSON, Aug. 29, [1832], by E. Huntington	1	254
Enoch, s. Calab & Abiguel, b. Aug. 12, 1740	LR11	1
Eunis*, d. Nathan & Ruth, b. June 4, 1735 *("B" crossed out)	LR2	352
Eunis, d. Paul & Abigail, b. May 27, 1751	LR5	13
Eunice, d. Caleb, Jr. & Eunice, b. Nov. 3, 1770	LR10	11
Ezra, of New Milford, m. Rebeckah ANDREWS, of Bethelehem, Dec. 24, 1747/8, by Rev. Mr. Belemis. Witnesses: Jabez Whitelsee & William Churchel	LR5	10
Ezra, m. Ruth HUFF, Apr. 10, 1752, by Samuell Canfield, J. P.	LR5	10
Ezra, m. Judith HAMLETON, Aug. 31, 1752, by Increas Mosley, J. P.	LR5	10
Ezra, made affidavit Dec. 25, 1752, that Mary, d. Ruth HUFF, was his child and heir to his estate. Witnesses: Samuell Canfield, Samuel Canfield, Jr. & Nathenel Henrey	LR5	11
Fanny, d. Jared & Hannah, b. Oct. 7, 1794	1	16
Freelove, d. Caleb & Abigal, b. Sept. 22, 1751 (This entry crossed out)	LR11	1
Frelove, d. Caleb & Abigal, b. Sept. 22, 1751	LR11	1
Freelove, m. Samuel TURNER, Feb. 6, 1772	LR12	16
Gamaliel, of New Milford, m. Elisabeth SCOTT, of Waterbury, May 17, 1725	LR2	339
Hannah, m. Ebenezer HOTCHKINS, Jan. 10, 1741/2, by Roger Brownson, J. P.	LR5	8
Hervey, of Kent, m. Phebe HALLOCK, of New Milford, Feb. 20, 1825, by Daniel Gaylord, J. P.	1	121
Hervey, of Kent, m. Phebe HALLOCK, of New Milford, Feb. 13, 1825, by Daniel Gaylord, J. P.	1	140
Hiram, s. Nathan & Dorothy, b. July 29, 1800	LR12	8
Hiram, of Roxbury, m. Chloe NICHOLS, of New Milford, Sept. 29, 1834, by E. Huntington	1	281
Isuaak, s. Caleb & Abigaill, b. May 22, 1749	LR11	1
Isaack, m. Sarah PRINCE, b. of New Milford, Jan. 25, 1774, by Rev. Nathaniell Taylor	LR12	17

TERRILL, TERRIL, TIRRIL, TURRILL, TURREL, TARRIL, (cont.)

	Vol.	Page
James, m. Abigal **BUCK**, b. of New Milford, June 22, 1741, by Rev. Daniel Bordman	LR4	2
James, s. James & Abigail, b. Dec. 31, 1744	LR5	8
James, Jr., m. Sarah **BRADSHAW**, Jr., b. of New Milford, June 15, 1768	LR10	13
James, s. Isaac & Sarah, b. Aug. 16, 1781	LR12	17
James, Jr., d. May 2, 1812	LR10	13
James, m. Roane **BRONSON**, b. of New Milford, Oct. 29, 1826, by Rev. C. A. Boardman	1	207
James Beebe, s. James & Sarah, b. June 20, 1785	LR10	13
James Beebe, m. Phebe **TERRILL**, Jan. 24, 1807	1	170
James Horrace, s. James B. & Phebe, b. Nov. 1, 1809	1	170
Jane E., m. John W. **ADDIS**, b. of New Milford, Oct. 24, 1854, by Rev. David Murdock, Jr.	2	105
Jared, s. Caleb & Abigial, b. Oct. 18, 1762	LR11	1
Jared, s. Caleb, m. Hannah **BUCK**, d. James, Feb. 22, 1789	1	16
Jerome Beebe, s. James Beebe & Phebe, b. Dec. 8, 1807	1	170
Job, s. Daniel & Mary, decd., m. Sarah **BURWELL**, d. Ephraim & Sarah, decd., May 2, 1735, by Samuel Gunn, J. P.	LR4	16
Job, s. Job & Sarah, b. Nov. 3, 1736; d. Nov. 13, 1736	LR4	16
Job, s. James & Abigail, b. July 3, 1743	LR5	8
Job, s. Caleb & Abigial, b. Apr. 17, 1758	LR11	1
Job, s. James & Abigail, b. Apr. 27, 1760	LR5	8
Job, m. Kezia **YORK**, Dec. 9, 1781, by Rev. Levi Hart	LR13	8
Joel, s. Caleb & Abigael, b. June 8, 1760	LR11	1
Joel, s. Stephen & Hepzibah, b. May 13, 1784	1	16
Joel, s. Leman & Lucy, b. Nov. 1, 1801	1	80
John, s. James & Abigal, d. Nov. 24, 1751	LR5	8
John, s. Paul & Abigal, b. Apr. 12, 1753	LR5	13
John, s. Calab & Abigial, b. Mar. 16, 1756	LR11	1
Jonathan, s. Nathan & Ruth, b. May 29, 1730	LR2	352
Joseph Prince, s. Isaac & Sarah, b. July 13, 1783	LR12	17
Joshua, s. Gamaliel & Elizabeth, b. Dec. 18, 1725	LR2	339
Leaman, s. James & Sarah, b. July 5, 1776	LR10	13
Leman, of New Milford, m. Lucy **TERRILL**, of Kent, Mar. 5, 1797	1	80
Leman Minor, s. Leman & Lucy, b. Jan. 6, 1808	1	80
Leman Walter, s. James B. & Phebe, b. Dec. 8, 1811	1	170
Lerra, d. Jared & Hannah, b. May 2, 1790	1	16
Louis, d. Nathan & Ruth, b. May 27, 1741	LR4	28
Lucy, d. Stephen & Hepzibah, b. Apr. 13, 1782	1	16
Lucy, d. Nathan & Dorothy, b. Oct. 31, 1793	LR12	8
Lucy, of Kent, m. Leman **TERRILL**, of New Milford, Mar. 5, 1797	1	80
Magore*, twin with Doctor, s. Caleb & Abigial, b. Nov. 26,		

NEW MILFORD VITAL RECORDS

	Vol.	Page
TERRILL, TERRIL, TIRRIL, TURRILL, TURREL, TARRIL, (cont.)		
1768 *("Major" in Orcutt's Hist.)	LR11	1
Marcy, b. Dec. 31, 1771, in New Milford; m. Ephraim LYON, Mar. 20, 1793	1	143
Mary, d. Dea. Job & Sarah, b. July 27, 1740	LR4	16
Mary, d. James & Abagain, b. Nov. 10, 1746; d. Jan. 5, 1746/7	LR5	8
Mary, d. James & Abigail, b. Feb. 28, 1747/8	LR5	8
Mary, d. Caleb & Abigael, b. Dec. 6, 1753	LR11	1
Mary, m. Thomas LEWIS, May 1, 1768	LR10	2
Mercy, d. Gamaliel & Elizabeth, b. Dec. 22, 1733; d. June 23, 1737	LR4	12
Mercy, d. Gamaliel & Elizabeth, b. Apr. 4, 1738	LR4	12
Mercy, d. James, Jr. & Sarah, b. Dec. 31, 1771	LR10	13
Nathan, m. Ruth BUCK, b. of New Milford, June 7, 1721	LR2	352
Nathan, s. Nathan & Ruth, b. Feb. 26, 1736/7	LR2	352
Nathan, s. Paul & Abigail, b. Apr. 12, 1755	LR5	13
Nathan, m. Dorothy PHELPS, Feb. 26, 1778, by Ephraim Hubbell, in New Fairfield	LR12	8
Nathan, m. Laura PLATT, of New Milford, May 20, 1807, by Elisha Bostwick, J. P.	1	142
Pamela, of New Milford, m. Samuel B. JAGGAR, of Orid, N. Y., Jan. 16, 1822, by Rev. C. A. Boardman	1	13
Paul, m. Abigal TERRIL, Jan. 29, 1744/5, by Samuell Cook, pastor	LR5	13
Paul, of New Milford, m. Deborah FOOTS, of Woodbury, Sept. 11, 1758	LR7	15
Phebe, d. James & Abigail, b. June 20, 1756	LR5	8
Phebe, d. Nathan & Dorothy, b. Jan. 5, 1783	LR12	8
Phebe, m. James Beebe TERRILL, Jan. 24, 1807	1	170
Polle, d. Isaac & Sarah, b. Nov. 1, 1778	LR12	17
Polly, d. Nathan & Dorothy, b. Aug. 4, 1784	LR12	8
Rachel, d. James & Abigail, b. May 1, 1758	LR5	8
Rachel, d. James & Sarah, b. Jan. 11, 1779	LR10	13
Rebecah, d. Isaac & Sarah, b. Nov. 18, 1774	LR12	17
Ruth, d. Nathan & Ruth, b. Nov. 22, 1724	LR2	352
Ruth, m. William SHERMAN, b. of New Milford, Apr. 18, 1743, by Roger Brownson, J. P.	LR5	3
Ruth, d. Pual & Abigal, b. Apr. 29, 1746	LR5	13
Sally, d. Nathan & Dorothy, b. Sept. 26, 1795; d. Apr. 1, 1798	LR12	8
Salmon, s. Jared & Hannah, b. Apr. 24, 1792	1	16
Samuel, s. Ezra & Judath, b. Feb. 22, 1758	LR5	11
Sarah, of Woodburie, m. David CAMP, June 26, 1735, by Rev. Daniel Bordman	LR4	16
Sarah, d. Paul & Abigal, b. Dec. 28, 1749/50* *(blotted)	LR5	13
Sarah, m. Peter PECK, Dec. 7, 1768	LR12	10
Sarah, d. James, Jr. & Sarah, b. Aug. 15, 1791	LR10	13
Sarah, of New Milford, m. Perry AVERILL, of Washington,		

	Vol.	Page

TERRILL, TERRIL, TIRRIL, TURRILL, TURREL, TARRIL,
(cont.)

Dec. 8, 1824, by Rev. C. A. Boardman, of New Preston	1	21
Stanley, s. Leman & Lucy, b. Feb. 19, 1800	1	80
Stephen, s. Caleb & Abigal, b. Nov. 7, 1746	LR11	1
Stephen, of New Milford, m. Hepzibah **GRIFFITH**, of Reading, Feb. 7, 1781, by Rev. Nathaniell Bartlet	1	16
Stephen, of Roxbury, m. Sally **EVITTS**, of New Milford, June 4, 1854, by Joshua R. Brown, of New Haven	2	102
Stephen Sanford, s. Stephen & Hepzibah, b. Jan. 23, 1789	1	16
Tamar, d. Nathan & Dorothy, b. July 30, 1781	LR12	8
Urania, d. James, Jr. & Sarah, b. Apr. 2, 1769	LR10	13
William, s. Ezra & Judath, b. Feb. 22, 1754	LR5	11
William, s. James & Sarah, b. Feb. 28, 1781	LR10	13
Zeruiah, d. James & Abigail, b. Apr. 25, 1752	LR5	8
Zeruiah, m. Ebenezer **WARNER***, b. of New Milford, June 9, 1767, by Samuell Bostwick, J. P. *(Probably "Picket")	LR7	[ ]
Zeruiah, m. Ebenezer **PICKET**, Jr., June 9, 1767, by Samuell Bostwick, J. P.	LR11	8

TERRY, Sherman, m. Mary Ann J. **RANDALL**, Oct. 28, 1828, by Rev. E. Huntington   1   224

THATCHER, THATCHERRE, THACHER, Catharine, d. Cyrus

& Hopeful, b. Dec. 20, 1818	1	419
Catherine, m. Charles **LEWIS**, b. of New Milford, Dec. 26, 1850, by Rev. David Murdock, Jr.	2	66
Charles, m. Charlotte **GOULD**, b. of New Milford, Mar. 19, 1844, by John Greenwood	1	392
Charles, m. Charlotte **GOULD**, b. of New Milford, Mar. 19, 1844, by John Greenwood	1	395
Charles Jacob, s. Cyrus & Hopeful, b. Mar. 11, 1812	1	419
Cyrus, of New Milford, m. Hopeful **FREEMAN**, of Litchfield, June 17, 1811, by James Morriss, at Litchfield, South Farms	1	419
Mary, d. Cyrus & Hopeful, b. Aug. 19, 1816	1	419
Partridge, had negro Jacob, ae about 11 y. & Dinah aged about 10 y. formerly belonging to Capt. Jabez **DEAN**, of Norwich, (June [ ], 1749]. They were married by Capt. Nathaniel Bostwick, after having them 3 years	1	418
Partridge, had negroes Sybil, d. Jacob & Dinah, b. Jan. 28, 1753, N. S., Heber, s. Jacob & Dinah, b. July 4, 1755, Peleg, s. Jacob & Dinah, b. Dec. 4, 1757, Terah, s. Jacob & Dinah, b. Jan. 25, 1761; d. Sept. 4, 1762, Rhoda, d. Jacob & Dinah, b. June 18, 1763	1	418

Partridge, had negroes Huldah, d. Jacob & Dinah, b. May 26, 1766, Phebe, d. Jacob & Dinah, b. Apr. 17, 1768, Rachel, d. Jacob & Dinah, b. Apr. 11, 1770, Jacob, s. Jacob & Dinah, b. [ ]; d. [ ], at Boston, had negro Cyrus, s. Jacob & Dinah, b. Apr. 28, 1778, Dinah, w. of Jacob, d.

	Vol.	Page
THATCHER, THATCHERRE, THACHER, (cont.)		
July 14, 1806	1	418
Partridge, had negroes Rachel, d. Jacob & Dinah, d. Feb. 19, 1811; Huldah, d. Jacob & Dinah, d. Nov. 15, 1817, at New York; had negro Jacob, d. May 24, 1823	1	418
Peter, a witness at wedding of John **FERRIS** & Abigal **TRYON**, Quakers	LR4	22
Sarah, of Lebanon, m. Joel **HERVEY**, of New Milford, Dec. 13, 1737	LR4	25
THAYER, THAIR, THARE, THAYR, Abigail, d. Joseph & Abigail, b. June 19, 1776; d. June 30, 1776	LR12	19
Annis, d. Oliver & Mindwel, b. Sept. 19, 1741	LR4	28
Annis, m. Nathaniel **SMITH**, b. of New Milford, Sept. 27, 1764	LR7	4
Annis, d. Lemuel & Lucy, b. Sept. 3, 1771	1	28
Annis, d. Elizur & Phebe, b. Nov. 27, 1799	1	127
Annis, m. Amos **WILKINSON**, June 30, 1806, by Elisha Bostwick, J. P.	1	125
Augustine, s. Lemuel & Lucy, b. Oct. 12, 1775	1	28
Benoni, s. Oliver & Mindwell, b. Feb. 4, 1757	LR7	2
Betsey, d. Lemuel & Lucy, b. Apr. 8, 1789	1	28
Elizur, s. Lemuel & Lucy, b. Feb. 17, 1778	1	28
Elizur, m. Phebe **BARTRAM**, May 5, 1798	1	127
George Washington, s. Elizur & Phebe, b. Nov. 6, 1811	1	127
Hannah, d. Oliver & Mindwel, b. July 28, 1739	LR4	28
Hannah, m. Abner **SEELEY**, Mar. 22, 1759	LR7	29
Hetty, d. Lemuel & Lucy, b. Apr. 15, 1793	1	28
Joseph, m. Abigail **SACKETT**, May 8, 1776	LR12	19
Laura, d. Lemuel & Lucy, b. Mar. 28, 1791	1	28
Lemuel, m. Lucy **BROWNSON**, Mar. 6, 1771	1	28
Lemuel, s. Lemuel & Lucy, b. Mar. 6, 1797	1	28
Leoisa, d. Elizur & Phebe, b. Feb. 24, 1810	1	127
Lucy, d. Lemuel & Lucy, b. May 20, 1782	1	28
Lucy, m. Orsamus **BROWNSON**, Oct. 6, 1803, by Elisha Bostwick, J. P.	1	108
Lucy Ann, d. Elizur & Phebe, b. Nov. 13, 1804	1	127
Mary, d. Oliver & Mindwell, b. Oct. 6, 1760	LR7	2
Mary, d. Elizur & Phebe, b. Feb. 8, 1814	1	127
Oliver, m. Mindwel **BARTLET**, Sept. 12, 1738, by Roger Brownson, J. P.	LR4	28
Oliver Bartram, s. Elizur & Phebe, b. Feb. 2, 1808	1	127
Phebe Meria, d. Elizur & Phebe, b. Feb. 5, 1802	1	127
Phebe Meria, m. Israel **POTTER**, Mar. 14, 1819, by Elisha Bostwick, J. P.	1	168
Sally, d. Lemuel & Lucy, b. Feb. 11, 1787	1	28
Sally, d. Elizur & Phebe, b. Sept. 9, 1805	1	127
William, s. Lemuel & Lucy, b. Oct. 31, 1773	1	28
THOMAS, Fanny, m. John **JACKSON**, Nov. 4, 1830, by Rev.		

	Vol.	Page
THOMAS, (cont.)		
Eleazer Beecher	1	239
George Walden, s. Henry & Chloe, b. Mar. 18, 1784	LR13	17
Henry, m. Chloe **BOSTWICK**, Nov. 6, 1783	LR13	17
THOMPSON, THOMSON, Albert, m. Adaline **RUGGLES**, b. of Bridgewater, Sept. 12, 1841, by Rev. Albert B. Camp, of Bridgewater	1	360
Ambross, m. Anna **BOOTH**, d. John & Dorothy, June 22, 1707	2	111
Charles, m. Laura **EVITTS**, b. of New Milford, Oct. 28, 1839, by N. Porter	1	330
Edward B., of New Haven, m. Sarah **GOLDSMITH**, of New Milford, Dec. 17, 1845, by Rev. William Atwill, of Bridgewater	2	6
Hulday, m. Daniel **BOOTH**, s. Daniel & Eunice, [ ]	1	409
Jehiel B., of Warren, m. Eliza **PARSONS**, of New Milford, Sept. 11, 1836, by N. Porter, Jr.	1	299
John M., of Bridgeport, m. Maria A. **NOBLE**, of New Milford, Oct. 14, 1840, by Noah Porter	1	350
Leonard, m. Esther Orinda **STONE**, Feb. 6, 1805, by Elisha Bostwick, J. P.	1	114
Sally, m. Jehiel **WILLIAMS**, Apr. 20, 1825, by Rev. Andrew Eliot	1	193
THORNE, THORN, Anna M., witnessed marriage of Gurdon **SWIFT** & Jane **WANZER**	1	288
Anne M., witnessed marriage of Jehu **HOAG** & Phebe **WANZER**	1	250
Isaac, witnessed marraige of Jehu **HOAG** & Phebe **WANZER**	1	250
Isaac, witnessed marriage of Gurdon **SWIFT** & Jane **WANZER**	1	288
THORP, Daniel G., m. Harriet E. **STONE**, b. of Bridgwater, Oct. 30, 1836, by A. B. Camp	1	300
TIBBETTS, Catharine E., m. Edgar **GREGORY**, b. of New Milford, Mar. 9, 1840, by Noah Porter	1	342
TICKNER, Mehitebel, of Sharon, m. David **HALL**, of New Milford, Aug. 2, 1764	LR7	7
TITUS, Abigail, d. Noah & Phebe, b. Feb. 8, 1786	1	10
Benjamin, s. Noah & Phebe, b. Feb. 23, 1796	1	10
Charles, s. Noah & Phebe, b. Feb. 2, 1805	1	10
Charles, m. Eletiaette **BEARDSLEY**, Feb. 12, 1828, by Rev. Eleazar Beecher	1	218
Desire, d. Noah & Phebe, b. Nov. 11, 1783	1	10
Jared, s. Noah & Phebe, b. Jan. 14, 1793	1	10
John, m. Noah & Phebe, b. Aug. 13, 1790	1	10
Mary, d. Noah & Phebe, b. Jan. 12, 1788	1	10
Noah, m. Phebe **DUNNING**, Apr. 18, 1781	1	10
Polly M., m. Samuel **FAIRCHILD**, Sept. 26, 1824, by Rev.		

	Vol.	Page
TITUS, (cont.)		
Benjamin Benham	1	171
Samuel, s. Noah & Phebe, b. Apr. 6, 1782	1	10
TODD, Jonah, Dr., m. Jane **WELCH**, Mar. 23, 1756, by Paul Welch, J. P.	LR7	9
Marvin S., m. Fanny **HURLBUT**, Dec. 3, 1837, by Abner Brundage	1	308
Mary E., m. Daniel **CARPENTER**, Jan. 31, 1841, by B. B. Parsons	1	351
Sarah Eliza, of New Milford, m. Virgil D. **BONESTEEL**, of Poughkeepsie, N. Y., Sept. 30, 1840, by Noah Porter	1	349
TOLES, Amos, m. Elizabeth **CUMMINS**, Apr. 1, 1765, by Paul Welch, J. P.	LR7	5
TOMLINSON, Joseph, m. Ann B. **NORTHROP**, b. of New Milford, Dec. 10, 1843, by John Greenwood	1	389
TONG, Lucy Ann, m. Sidney A. **LAW**, b. of New Milford, Apr. 28, 1851, by Rev. G. B. Haden	2	67
TOTMAN, Lyra Ann, m. Elezier **WARNER**, b. of New Milford, Sept. 30, 1828, by Rev. Andrew Eliot	1	221
TOWNER, Cynthia, m. Jehiel **BUCK**, Nov. 19, 178[ ]	1	5
Lettice, m. Gedion **PRINDEL**, Apr. 11, 1753, by Ephraim Hubbel, J. P.	LR7	2
TREADWELL, Caroline Elizabeth, d. Lambert L. & Polly, b. Mar. 25, 1816	2	93
Catharine, m. Silas **BEARDSLEE**, May 14, 1789	1	47
David, s. Lambert L. & Polly, b. Apr. 4, 1801	2	93
Harriett, d. Lambert L. & Polly, b. Aug. 2, 1821	2	93
Henry R., of New York, m. Martha D. **MYGATT**, of New Milford, May 16, 1843, by John Greenwood	1	386
Hoyt Bradley, s. Lambert L. & Polly, b. Feb. 4, 1823	2	93
Lambert Lewis, s. David (s. Benjamin, s. Edward), b. Sept. 23, 1783; m. Polly **BOOTH**, d. Josiah & Sarah, Sept. 23, 1800, at the house of Josiah Booth, by Rev. James Johnson	2	93
Lambert Lewis, s. of David (s. of Benjamin, s. Edward), b. Sept. 23, 1783; m. Polly **BOOTH**, Sept. 23, 1800	2	93
Laura Ann, d. Lambert L. & Polly, b. June 26, 1814	2	93
Mehetabel, m. Lemuel **MOREHOUSE**, Sept. 1, 1791	1	93
Minor, m. Molly **ROBURDS**, b. of New Milford, Sept. 3, 1805, by Elisha Bostwick, J. P.	1	121
Orrin Bronson, s. Lambert L. & Polly, b. Sept. 5, 1812	2	93
Polly, w. Lambert L. & d. Josiah **BOOTH**, d. Jan. 20, 1850; bd. [ ], in Fairport Munroe Co., N. Y., in Hiram Hayes' Family lot	2	93
Polly Ann, colored, d. Sally **JACKSON** (Javan **WILSON'S** d.), had d. Lydia **ROGERS**, b. Nov. 17, 1833	1	420
Polly Ann, m. Henry **CARPENTER** (colored), b. of New Milford, Nov. 24, 1849, in Brooklyn, by Rev. Eli N.		

210   BARBOUR COLLECTION

	Vol.	Page
TREADWELL, (cont.)		
Hall. Witnesses: Forbes Dusiderdale, Elizabeth Dusiderdale, Betsey Booth & Mary Robinson	2	56
Polly Nan, b. Aug. 31, 1815	1	420
Sarah Emeline, d. Lambert L. & Polly, b. Dec. 19, 1808	2	93
TREAT, Abijah, s. John & Phebe, b. Dec. 30, 1761	LR7	8
Abijah*, [child of John & Phebe], d. Mar. 29, [ ] *(First written "Abigall" and crossed out)	LR7	8
Alfred A., of Southbury, m. Phebe **TREAT**, of New Milford, Apr. 1, 1835, by Rev. B. Y. Messenger	1	285
Almon, m. Hannah **RANDAL**, b. of Bridgwater, Dec. 13, 1821, by Rev. Fosdic Harrison, of Roxbury	1	25
Anna, d. John & Phebe, b. June 25, 1766	LR7	8
Anna A., m. Horatio N. **WELTON**, b. of New Milford, Nov. 29, 1820, by Rev. Fosdic Harrison, of Roxbury	1	32
Azel, s. Gideon & Leucrcy, b. Nov. 14, 1775	LR9	[ ]
Azel, s. Gideon & Luercy, d. Mar. 15, 1776	LR9	[ ]
Bethuel, of South Britian, m. Mary **NORTHROP**, of New Milford, Feb. 15, 1849, by Jno Greenwood	2	50
Clare, d. John & Phebe, b. Dec. 19, 1768	LR7	8
Clare, m. Caleb **BEACH**, Aug. 16, 1787	1	56
Daniel A., d. Feb. 1, 1828	1	139
Daniel Allen, s. Gideon & Lucrcey, b. May 8, 1778	LR9	[ ]
Daniel Allen, m. Almira **SHERMAN**, b. of New Milford, Nov. 30, 1809, by Elisha Bostwick, J. P.	1	139
Gideon, m. Lucretia **WASHBORN**, b. of New Milford, Nov. 13, 1770, by Rev. Nathaniell Taylor	LR9	[ ]
Gideon, d. July 11, 1811, in the 64th y. of his age	LR9	[ ]
Gideon Washbon, s. Gideon & Lurecy, b. Feb. 3, 1777	LR9	[ ]
Hannah, d. John & Phebe, b. Nov. 3, 1752; d. Feb. 25, 1754	LR7	8
Hannah, d. John & Phebe, b. Mar. 29, 1757	LR7	8
Harmon, m. Mary E. **WOOSTER**, b. of Bridgewater, May 26, 1852, by D. Williams	2	7
Homer, s. Gideon & Lucretia, b. Aug. 7, 1788	LR9	[ ]
Horace, s. John H. & Sally, b. Sept. 14, 1795	1	76
John, m. Phebe **HAULEY**, Nov. 23, 1749	LR7	8
John, s. John & Phebe, b. Apr. 26, 1771; d. May 6, 1771	LR7	8
John H., m. Sally **RANDLE**, Nov. 25, 1794	1	76
Joseph, s. Gideon & Lucrecy, b. July 25, 1771	LR9	[ ]
Joseph, s. Gideon & Lucey, d. Jan. 20, 1774	LR9	[ ]
Joseph, s. Gideon & Lucy, b. July 3, 1774	LR9	[ ]
Joseph, s. Gideon & Lucerey, d. Mar. 26, 1776	LR9	[ ]
Joseph, s. Gideon & Lucretia, b. Dec. 10, 1783	LR9	[ ]
Joseph, [s. Gideon & Lucretia], d. May 9, 1841, at Windham, Portage Co., O., in the 58th y. of his age	LR9	[ ]
Joseph E., m. Ellen **MOORE**, b. of New Milford, Mar. 6, 1844, by John Greenwood	1	391
Lucretia, d. Gideon & Lucretia, b. Oct. 23, 1779	LR9	[ ]

NEW MILFORD VITAL RECORDS   211

	Vol.	Page
TREAT, (cont.)		
Lucretia, w. Gideon, d. Mar. 3, 1847, ae 96 y. 5 m. 15 d.	LR9	[ ]
Mary Adaline, m. Frederick S. **SANFORD**, b. of Bridgewater, May 21, 1849, by Rev. J. Kilborn	2	55
Minorice, d. Gideon & Lucey, b. Feb. 22, 1773; d. Feb. 4, 1776	LR9	[ ]
Nancy L., m. William H. **BOLAND**, b. of New Milford, May 10, 1853, by David Murdock, Jr.	2	88
Phebe, m. John **CANFIELD**, Mar. 6, 1781	LR13	10
Phebe, of New Milford, m. Alfred A. **TREAT**, of Southbury, Apr. 1, 1835, by Rev. B. Y. Messenger	1	285
Polly, m. Nathan **BETTS**, Nov. 20, 1794	1	77
Sally S., of New Milford, m. Ira **BUCKINGHAM**, of Brookfield, Jan. 4, 1824, by Rev. Bardsley Northrop	1	160
Sarah, d. John & Phebe, b. Oct. 3, 1750	LR7	8
Sarah, m. David **SUMERS**, Apr. 30, 1773, by Rev. Nathaniell Taylor	LR12	4
Stephen, s. Gideon & Lucretia, b. Aug. 9, 1781	LR9	[ ]
Stephen, m. Clara **SMITH**, b. of Bridgewater, Oct. 1, 1833, by Rev. Fosdic Harrison, of Roxbury	1	268
TROWBRIDGE, TROBRIGE, Abigail, m. David **HITCHCOCK**, Sept. 11, 1759	LR7	27
Abigail, m. Jonathan **BOSTWICK**, Jr., b. of New Milford, Sept. 22, 1791	1	23
Austin B., of Danbury, m. Mary L. **NOBLE**, of New Milford, June 11, 1831, by David S. Boardman, J. P.	1	244
Charles S., m. Harriet O. **MERWIN**, Dec. 5, 1854, by Rev. David Murdock	2	106
Elisabeth, m. Aaron **HITCHCOCK**, Mar. 31, 1763	LR7	31
Hannah, b. Feb. 24, 1741, at Stratford; m. John **STILSON**, s. Moses, Aug. 11, 1763	1	242
James, m. Sally **WAKELEE**, Oct. 15, 1806, by Elisha Bostwick, J. P.	1	135
Naomi, m. Abijah **TERRILL**, Sept. 5, 1808, by Elisha Bostwick, J. P.	1	158
TRYALL, Martha*, m. Abel **GUNN**, July 18, 1771, by Rev. Nathaniell Taylor *(Given as "Martha, d. of Theophilus **BALDWIN**" in Orcutt's Hist.)	LR11	17
TRYON, Abigal, of New Fairfield, m. John **FERRIS**, of New Milford, s. Zachariah & Sarah, b. Mar. 15, 1738. Quaker ceremony before 27 witnesses at Joseph Ferris. Intention declared at Momorneck	LR4	22
James, a witness at wedding of John **FERRIS** & Abigal **TRYON**, Quakers	LR4	22
Jane, a witness at wedding of John **FERRIS** & Abigal **TRYON**, Quakers	LR4	22
Oliver, a witness at wedding of John **FERRIS** & Abigal **TRYON**, Quakers	LR4	22

	Vol.	Page
TRYON, (cont.)		
Ziba, a witness at wedding of John **FERRIS** & Abigal **TRYON**, Quakers	LR4	22
TUCKER, Anne, d. Uriah & Eunice, b. June 27, 1778	LR10	4
Chloe, d. Uriah & Eunice, b. Feb. 28, 1764	LR10	4
Eli, s. Uriah & Eunice, b. Aug. 4, 1785	LR10	4
Elizabeth, m. Daniel **MOREHOUSE**, Apr. 11, 1797	1	95
Eunice, d. Uriah & Eunice, b. Apr. 7, 1766	LR10	4
Levi, of Washington, m. Elvira **NORTHROP**, of New Milford, June 20, 1830, by H. Rood	1	53
Lois, d. Uriah & Eunice, b. Nov. 16, 1762	LR10	4
Sarah, d. Uriah & Eunice, b. Oct. 26, 1775	LR10	4
Uriah, m. Eunice **DATON**, Feb. 2, 1762	LR10	4
TUPPER, Mercy, of Sailsbury, m. Joseph **SEELEY**, Jr., of New Milford, Jan. 24, 1764	LR7	29
TURNER, Abigail, d. John & Sarah, b. Nov. 13, 1775	1	2
Ammedilla, d. Sam[ue]ll & Freelove, b. Apr. 7, 1776	LR12	16
Amos, s. John & Sarah, b. Aug. 29, 1773	1	2
Daniel, s. Sam[ue]ll & Freelove, b. Mar. 15*, 1780 *(Possibly "18")	LR12	16
Hannah, d. Samuel & Freelove, b. Aug. 16, 1772	LR12	16
John, m. Sarah **OVIATT**, Jan. 21, 1773	1	2
John, s. John & Sarah, b. Apr. 17, 1774	1	2
Samuel, m. Freelove **TERRIL**, Feb. 6, 1772	LR12	16
Samuel, s. Samuel & Frelove, b. Jan. 16, 1774	LR12	16
TUTTLE, Hannah, m. Solomon **HILL**, Jr., July 26, 1807, by Elisha Bostwick, J. P.	1	152
Luther, m. Mary D. **SUMMERS**, Dec. 9, 1827, by Stephen Crane, J. P.	1	205
VAIL, John, of Danbury, m. Harriet M. **WARNER**, of New Milford, Nov. 25, 1852, by Rev. David P. Sanford	2	84
VARNEY, John, of Russia, N. Y., m. Almira **STONE**, of New Milford, Sept. 15, 1834, by Rev. William W. Andrews, of Kent	1	279
VIDETS, VIDDITS, Betsey Ann, of New Milford, m. Elmer **HALLOCK**, of Kent, June 2, 1830, by Rev. Fosdic Harrison, of Roxbury	1	226
Sarah, of Danbury, m. John **BRADSHAW**, of New Milford, June 4, 1740, by Rev. Ebenezer White, of Danbury. Witnesses: Stephen Vidito & Mary Vidito	LR5	2
VINSON, Absalom, of Sherman, m. Harriot **WALKER**, of New Milford, Feb. 29, 1852, by Rev. J. F. Jones	2	76
WADHAMS, Annis, d. Noah & Elizabeth, b. Nov. 20, 1763	LR7	7
Calvin, s. Noah & Elizebeth, b. Dec. 22, 1765	LR7	7
Noah, of New Milford, m. Elizabeth **INGERSOL**, of Sheffield, Nov. 8, 1758, by Rev. Samuel Hopkins, of Great Barrington	LR7	7
Noah Ingersol, s. Noah & Elizebeth, b. Oct. 14, 1761	LR7	7

	Vol.	Page
WAGNN, Marcus, m. Betsey Maria **SANFORD**, May 4, 1836, by E. Huntington	1	297
WAINRIGHT, Phebe, of Stratford, m. Asaph **BUCK**, of New Milford, Sept. 7, 1788	1	15
WAKELEE, WAKLEY, WAKLEE, Eleazer H., s. Thomas B. & Anne, b. Mar. 6, 1784	1	50
Harry, s. Thomas B. & Anne, b. Apr. 19, 1796	1	50
Huldah, m. Samuell **RUGGLES**, June 1, 1779	LR13	15
John S., s. Thomas B. & Anne, b. Oct. 3, 1786	1	50
Sally, d. Thomas B. & Anne, b. May 5, 1788	1	50
Sally, m. James **TROWBRIDGE**, Oct. 15, 1806, by Elisha Bostwick, J. P.	1	135
Sally, m. Jeremiah **SANFORD**, Jan. 29, 1809, by Elisha Bostwick, J. P.	1	160
Solomon, s. Thomas B. & Anne, b. Mar. 17, 1793	1	50
Thomas, s. Thomas B. & Anne, b. May 10, 1791	1	50
Thomas B., m. Anne **SMITH**, Feb. 22, 1783	1	50
William S., s. Thomas B. & Anne, b. Apr. 17, 1799	1	50
WALDO, Abigail, m. Joseph **MARSH**, Nov. 29, 1781	1	45
Deborah, m. Joseph **MARSH**, Nov. 19, 1793	1	45
WALKER, Anna, m. Abraham **BOOTH**, s. Daniel & Eunice, Dec. 3, 1759	2	112
David, of Washington, m. Ann **JENNINGS**, of New Milford, Jan. 12, 1831, by E. Huntington	1	246
David, of Washington, m. Ann **JENNINGS**, of New Milford, Jan. 12, 1831, by E. Huntington	1	247
Harriot, of New Milford, m. Absalom **VINSON**, of Sherman, Feb. 29, 1852, by Rev. J. F. Jones	2	76
Hiram, m. Alma **STOCKER**, Oct. 31, 1830, by Alvin Brown, J. P.	1	142
Perry, m. Harriet **COUCH**, b. of New Milford, June 9, 1850, by Rev. W. O. Jarvis, of Bridgewater	2	61
WALLER, WALLAR, Abigail, d. Joseph & Hannah, b. Oct. 1, 1727, at Litchfield	LR2	338
Asahel, s. Joseph & Sarah, b. Mar. 6, 1770	LR11	15
Benjamin, s. Joseph & Hannah, b. Dec. 4, 1742	LR4	13
Benjamin, s. Joseph & Hannah, d. Sept. 3, 1745	LR4	13
Celistea, m. Theodore **BUCK**, Dec. 13, 1820, by Rev. Andrew Eliot	1	175
Comfort, d. Joseph & Sarah, b. Mar. 27, 1772	LR11	15
David, s. Joseph & Sarah, b. Sept. 1, 1768	LR11	15
Eunis, d. Joseph & Hanah, b. July 4, 1736	LR4	13
George B., m. Susan **HUBBELL**, May 11, 1841, by B. B. Parsons	1	357
Hannah, d. Joseph & Hannah, b. Apr. 18, 1729	LR2	338
Hannah, w. Joseph, d. Feb. 4, 1746/7	LR4	13
Hannah, d. Joseph, Jr. & Sarah, b. Aug. 10, 1758	LR7	7
John, s. Joseph, Jr. & Sarah, b. Oct. 7, 1759	LR7	7

	Vol.	Page
WALLER, WALLAR, (cont.)		
Joseph, s. Joseph & Hannah, b. Oct. 25, 1731	LR2	338
Joseph, m. Abigal **STARR,** Sept. 22, 1748	LR7	1
Joseph, of New Preston, m. Sarah **MORRISS,** Aug. 5, 1756	LR8	1
Joseph, Jr., m. Sarah **DIBBLE,** Nov. 9, 1757	LR7	7
Lydia, of Woodbury, m. John **WELLER,** of New Milford, Dec. 12, 1723	LR4	5
Merwin, m. Julia **MOREHOUSE,** b. of New Milford, Dec. 31, 1850, by Rev. James L. Scott	2	65
Ollive, d. Joseph & Hannah, b. Oct. 4, 1738; d. Sept. 15, 1739	LR4	13
Ollive, d. Joseph & Hannah, b. Dec. 6, 1740	LR4	13
Rachel, d. Joseph & Hanah, b. Mar. 26, 1734	LR4	13
Samuel, m. Sarah **CHAPMAN,** Nov. 23, 1773	LR12	8
Samuel, s. Samuel & Sarah, b. Nov. 21, 1774	LR12	7
Sarah, d. Joseph & Sarah, b. July 29, 1759	LR8	1
Sarah, m. David **OLMSTED,** Feb. 7, 1774, by Rev. Jeremiah [ ], at New Preston	LR12	11
Sarah, m. David **OLMSTED,** Feb. 7, 1774	1	88
WALTER, Henry, of New York City, m. L. Julia **HINE,** of New Milford, Mar. 14, 1843, by John Greenwood	1	384
WANZER, WANZAR, Abbey Jane, witnessed marriage of David **SANDS** & Paulina **LEACH**	1	277
Abbey Jane, witnessed marriage of Gurdon **SWIFT** & Jane **WANZER**	1	288
Abigail, m. John **MARSH,** Jr., Mar. 2, 1772	LR12	13
Abraham, witnessed marriage of Ebenezer **WANZER,** Jr. & Lucy **LEACH**	1	181
Abraham, witnessed marriage of Jacob **WANZER** & Phebe **LEACH**	1	208
Abraham, witnessed marriage of Jehu **HOAG** & Phebe **WANZER**	1	250
Abraham, witnessed marriage of David **SANDS** & Paulina **LEACH**	1	277
Abraham, witnessed marriage of Gurdon **SWIFT** & Jane **WANZER**	1	288
Anna, d. Moses, of New Fairfield, m. William **SWIFT,** of Washington, Dutchess Co., N. Y., 9th m. 24th d., 1840, at the Friends Meeting House, by Abraham Wanzer, Clerk	1	346
Anna, witnessed marriage of Ebenezer **WANZER,** Jr. & Lucy **LEACH**	1	181
Anna, witnessed marriage of Jacob **WANZER** & Phebe **LEACH**	1	208
Anna, witnessed marriage of David **SANDS** & Paulina **LEACH**	1	277
Anna, witnessed marriage of Gurdon **SWIFT** & Jane **WANZER**	1	288
Anna, witnessed marriage of Jehu **HOAG** & Phebe **WANZER**	1	250

	Vol.	Page
WANZER, WANZAR, (cont.)		
Armittia, witnessed marriage of Jacob **WANZER** & Phebe **LEACH**	1	208
Betsey, witnessed marriage of Ebenezer **WANZER**, Jr. & Lucy **LEACH**	1	181
Betsey, witnessed marriage of Jehu **HOAG** & Phebe **WANZER**	1	250
Betsey, witnessed marriage of Gurdon **SWIFT** & Jane **WANZER**	1	288
Daniel, m. Cynthia **OSBORN**, 3rd m. 17th d., 1846, by William Wanzer, Clerk	2	13
Ebenezar, witnessed marriage of Ebenezer **WANZER**, Jr. & Lucy **LEACH**	1	181
Ebenezer, Jr., witnessed marriage of Enoch **CARPENTER** & Sophia **LANE**	1	184
Ebenezer, Jr., witnessed marriage of David **SANDS** & Paulina **LEACH**	1	277
Ebenezer, Jr., witnessed marriage of Gurdon **SWIFT** & Jane **WANZER**	1	288
Ebenezer, Jr., of New Fairfield, s. Ebenezar & Betsey, m. Lucy **LEACH**, d. William & Charlotte, of Sherman, 10th m. 26th d., 1820, before 31 witnesses. Int. Pub. at Oblong, N. Y.	1	180
Ebenezer L., witnessed marriage of Ebenezer **WANZER**, Jr. & Lucy **LEACH**	1	181
Eliza, witnessed marriage of Enoch **CARPENTER** & Sophia **LANE**	1	184
Eliza, witnessed marriage of Jacob **WANZER** & Phebe **LEACH**	1	208
Elizabeth, of New Fairfield, m. Joseph **GRIFFEN**, of Summers, N. Y., 9th m. 25th d., 1834, by Abraham Wanzer	1	278
Elizabeth, witnessed marriage of Jacob **WANZER** & Phebe **LEACH**	1	208
Elizabeth, witnessed marriage of Jehu **HOAG** & Phebe **WANZER**	1	250
Elizabeth, witnessed marriage of David **SANDS** & Paulina **LEACH**	1	277
Francis D., witnessed marriage of David **SANDS** & Paulina **LEACH**	1	277
Francis D., witnessed marriage of Gurdon **SWIFT** & Jane **WANZER**	1	288
Grace, witnessed marriage of Jacob **WANZER** & Phebe **LEACH**	1	208
Hiram, witnessed marriage of Ebenezer **WANZER**, Jr. & Lucy **LEACH**	1	181
Hiram, witnessed marriage of Enoch **CARPENTER** & Sophia **LANE**	1	184

216   BARBOUR COLLECTION

	Vol.	Page
WANZER, WANZAR, (cont.)		
Hiram, witnessed marriage of Jehu **HOAG** & Phebe **WANZER**	1	250
Ira, witnessed marriage of Ebenezer **WANZER**, Jr. & Lucy **LEACH**	1	181
Ira, witnessed marriage of Jehu **HOAG** & Phebe **WANZER**	1	250
Isaac, witnessed marriage of Ebenezer **WANZER**, Jr. & Lucy **LEACH**	1	181
Isaac, witnessed marriage of Enoch **CARPENTER** & Sophia **LANE**	1	184
Ithamar, witnessed marriage of Enoch **CARPENTER** & Sophia **LANE**	1	184
Jacob, of New Fairfield, s. John & Grace, m. Phebe **LEACH**, d. William & Charlotte, of Sherman, 10th m. 26th d., 1826, before 26 witnesses. Int. Pub. at Oblong, N. Y.	1	208
Jacob, witnessed marriage of Ebenezer **WANZER**, Jr. & Lucy **LEACH**	1	181
Jane, d. Moses & Sarah, of New Fairfield, m. Gurdon **SWIFT**, of Washington, Dutchess Co., N. Y., s. Beriah & Elizabeth, 8th m., 27th d. 1835, before 37 witnesses. Int. Pub. at Pawling, N. Y. & New Milford	1	288
Jane, witnessed marriage of Ebenezer **WANZER**, Jr. & Lucy **LEACH**	1	181
Jane, witnessed marriage of David **SANDS** & Paulina **LEACH**	1	277
John, witnessed marriage of Jacob **WANZER** & Phebe **LEACH**	1	208
Lucy, witnessed marriage of Enoch **CARPENTER** & Sophia **LANE**	1	184
Lucy, witnessed marriage of Jacob **WANZER** & Phebe **LEACH**	1	208
Lucy, witnessed marriage of Jehu **HOAG** & Phebe **WANZER**	1	250
Lucy, witnessed marriage of David **SANDS** & Paulina **LEACH**	1	277
Lucy, witnessed marriage of Gurdon **SWIFT** & Jane **WANZER**	1	288
Lydia, m. James H. **HATE**, 5th m. (May) 19th d., 1846, by William Wanzer, Clerk	2	16
Lydia, witnessed marriage of Gurdon **SWIFT** & Jane **WANZER**	1	288
Martha, witnessed marriage of David **SANDS** & Paulina **LEACH**	1	277
Moses, witnessed marriage of Ebenezer **WANZER**, Jr. & Lucy **LEACH**	1	181
Moses, witnessed marriage of Enoch **CARPENTER** & Sophia **LANE**	1	184
Moses, witnessed marriage of Jehu **HOAG** & Phebe **WANZER**	1	250
Moses, witnessed marriage of David **SANDS** & Paulina		

	Vol.	Page

WANZER, WANZAR, (cont.)

LEACH	1	277
Moses, witnessed marriage of Jacob **WANZER** & Phebe		
LEACH	1	208
Moses, witnessed marriage of Gurdon **SWIFT** & Jane		
WANZER	1	288
Moses, Jr., witnessed marriage of Gurdon **SWIFT** & Jane		
WANZER	1	288
Nicholas, witnessed marriage of Ebenezer **WANZER**, Jr. &		
Lucy **LEACH**	1	181
Nicholas, witnessed marriage of Enoch **CARPENTER** &		
Sophia **LANE**	1	184
Phebe, d. Moses & Sarah, of New Fairfield, m. Jehu **HOAG**, of Washington, Cty. of Dutchess, N. Y., s. Phillip & Phebe, 5th m. 22nd d., 1832, before 38 witnesses. Int. Pub. at Oblong & New Milford	1	250
Phebe, witnessed marriage of Ebenezer **WANZER**, Jr. &		
Lucy **LEACH**	1	181
Phebe, witnessed marriage of Jacob **WANZER** & Phebe		
LEACH	1	208
Phebe, witnessed marriage of Jehu **HOAG** & Phebe		
WANZER	1	250
Phebe, witnessed marriage of David **SANDS** & Paulina		
LEACH	1	277
Phebe, witnessed marriage of Gurdon **SWIFT** & Jane		
WANZER	1	288
Sarah, witnessed marriage of Ebenezer **WANZER**, Jr. &		
Lucy **LEACH**	1	181
Sarah, witnessed marriage of Jacob **WANZER** & Phebe		
LEACH	1	208
Sarah, witnessed marriage of Jehu **HOAG** & Phebe **WANZER**	1	250
Sarah, witnessed marriage of David **SANDS** & Paulina		
LEACH	1	277
Sarah A., m. Daniel S. **CONGDON**, 9th m. 25th d., 1845, by William Wanzer, Clerk	1	403
Sarah S., witnessed marriage of Ebenezer **WANZER**, Jr. &		
Lucy **LEACH**	1	181
William, m. Hannah **FERRISS**, Sept. 27, 1832, by E. Huntington	1	253
Willis H., witnessed marriage of David **SANDS** & Paulina		
LEACH	1	277

WARD, Spencer, of Dover, m. Polly **SOULE**, of New Milford, Nov. 27, 1822, by Daniel Gaylord, J. P. — 1, 51

WARNER, [see also **WARREN**], Abigail, d. Orange & Abigail, b. Nov. 9, 1778 — LR11, 6

Alonzo, m. Elizebeth Ann **FRENCH**, Nov. 16, 1831, by E. Huntington — 1, 248

Amarillis, d. Elizer & Mary, b. Aug. 8, 1764 — LR7, 30

	Vol.	Page
WARNER, (cont.)		
Amarillis, m. Homer **BOARDMAN**, Nov. 14, 1787	1	92
Anne, d. Asa & Eunice, b. Oct. 20, 1769	LR10	17
Anne, m. Salmon **BOSTWICK**, b. of New Milford, June 22, 1788	1	22
Aphia, d. Asa & Eunis, b. May 21, 1774	LR10	17
Asa, s. John & Mercy, b. Oct. 1, 1743	LR4	8
Asa, m. Eunice **CAMP**, b. of New Milford, Dec. 29, 1768, by Nathaniell Taylor	LR10	17
Attha M., of New Milford, m. Alonzo B. **SMITH**, of Naugatuck, Sept. 24, 1854, by Rev. William H. Russell	2	103
Charles, s. Curtiss & Eunice, b. Dec. 27, 1793	1	73
Charles Lockwood, m. Phalina Frances **BEERS**, of Roxbury, Nov. 23, 1848, at the house of Wooster Beers, by George L. Foote	2	47
Cloe, d. Orange & Abigail, b. June 25, 1774	LR11	6
Christian, d. Joseph & Sary, b. Feb. 2, 1734/5	LR4	15
Christian, m. Jonathan **HITCHCOCK**, Jr., Nov. 16, 1757	LR7	28
Curtiss, s. Orange & Abigail, b. July 14, 1766	LR11	6
Curtiss, m. Eunice **HULL**, Nov. 4, 1792	1	73
Cyrus, s. Orange & Abigail, b. Jan. 6, 1773	LR11	6
Daniel H., m. Abigail **PICKET**, b. of New Milford, Jan. 14, 1829, by Rev. Andrew Eliot	1	228
David, s. Orange & Abigail, b. Jan. 7, 1768	LR11	6
Deborah, d. Curtiss & Eunice, b. Sept. 20, 1797	1	73
Ebenezer, m. Zeruiah **TERRIL**, b. of New Milford, June 9, 1767, by Samuell Bostwick, J. P.	LR7	[ ]
Elizabeth, d. Joseph & Sarah, b. July 28, 1739	LR4	15
Elizer, s. John & Mercy, b. Dec. 17, 1737	LR4	8
Elizer, m. Mary **WELCH**, Oct. 26, 1763, by Nathaniell Taylor	LR7	30
Elizer, s. Elizer & Mary, b. Mar. 10, 1770	LR7	30
Elezier, m. Lyra Ann **TOTMAN**, b. of New Milford, Sept. 30, 1828, by Rev. Andrew Eliot	1	221
Elisabeth, m. Israel **BALDWIN**, Feb. 25, 1761	LR7	3
Elmer, of Brookfield, m. Harriet H. **ROBERTS**, of New Milford, June 12, 1844, by John Greenwood	1	396
Emily A., m. Dr. Harris **JUDSON**, b. of Bridgwater, Apr. 13, 1830, by Rev. Fosdick Harrison, of Roxbury	1	231
Eunice A., of New Milford, m. Nelson **KNOWLES**, of New Milford, Apr. 2, 1829, by Rev. John Lovejoy	1	144
Francis, m. Benjamin **OVIAT**, Apr. 17, 1744, by Joseph Minor, J. P.	LR5	7
George, s. Curtiss & Eunice, b. Feb. 27, 1808	1	73
Hannah, m. Charles **SMITH**, b. of New Milford, Jan. 19, 1826, by Rev. Eli Denniston	1	198
Harriet, d. Reuben, Jr. & Eunice, b. June 29, 1788	1	21
Harriet M., of New Milford, m. John **VAIL**, of Danbury, Nov. 25, 1852, by Rev. David P. Sanford	2	84

NEW MILFORD VITAL RECORDS 219

	Vol.	Page
WARNER, (cont.)		
Henry, s. Curtiss & Eunice, b. Oct. 14, 1795	1	73
Henry S., of New Milford, m. Eliza Ann HILL, of New Milford, Jan. 7, 1829, by Rev. John Lovejoy	1	227
Horrace, s. Reuben, Jr. & Eunice, b. Aug. 29, 1790	1	21
Hull, s. Curtiss & Eunice, b. May 20, 1801	1	73
Isaac E., m. Fanny E. FORD, b. of New Milford, Apr. 2, 1854, by Rev. A. B. Pulling	2	97
James*, m. Benjamin OVIAT, Apr. 17, [ ], by Joseph Minor, J. P. *(Probably "Frances")	LR5	5
John, of New Milford, m. Marcy CURTICE, of Farmington, d. Thomas, July 3, 1727, by Rev. William Burnham	LR2	338
John, s. John & Mercy, b. Oct. 27, 1739	LR4	8
John, Capt., d. Dec. 9, 1762	LR2	338
John, m. Hannah WESTOVER, July 6, 1763	LR8	2
John, s. John & Hannah, b. Apr. 10, 1764	LR8	2
John, Jr., m. Orilla SMITH, b. of New Milford, Feb. 10, 1825, by Rev. Andrew Eliot	1	136
John Carrington, s. Reuben, Jr. & Eunice, b. Feb. 18, 1782	1	21
John Henry, s. Lovice HAMBLIN, b. Oct. 12, 1785	1	5
Joseph, s. Joseph & Sarah, b. Sept. 12, 1741	LR4	15
Joseph, d. [ ] 21, 1743	LR4	1
Lauria, d. Curtiss & Eunice, b. Sept. 14, 1799	1	73
Lemuel, s. John & Marcy, b. Sept. 6, 1731	LR2	352
Lamuel, m. Sarah* GAYLARD, Feb. 15, 1758 *("Phebee" crossed out)	LR7	36
Lemuel, d. Feb. 20, 1814	LR7	36
Lodema, d. Lamuel & Sarah, b. July 27, 1765	LR7	36
Lodema, of New Milford, m. Joshua KNAPP, Jr., of Danbury, Oct. 26, 1785	1	20
Lois, w. Oliver, d. Oct. 14, 1781	LR7	30
Loria, d. Reuben, Jr. & Eunice, b. Dec. 25, 1783; d. Feb. 15, 1789	1	21
Lucy, d. Oliver & Lois, b. Sept. 17, 1752	LR7	30
Lucy, m. Ichabod BOSTWICK, Feb. 27, 1771	LR11	11
Mabel, d. Oliver & Lois, b. Sept. 30, 1756	LR7	30
Martin, s. John & Mercy, b. Jan. 11, 1735/6	LR4	8
Mary, d. Joseph, decd. & Sarah, b. Dec. 10, 1743	LR4	1
Mary*, m. Domini DUGLAS, May 5, 1761 *("Mary WARREN" in Orcutt's Hist.)	LR7	29
Mercy, d. John & Marcy, b. Dec. 21, 1747	LR4	8
Mercy, w. Capt. John, d. Oct. 1, 1757* *("176" rubbed out)	LR2	338
Mercy, d. Lamuel & Sarah, b. Sept. 22, 1761	LR7	36
Mercy, m. John MERWIN, Nov. 6, 1766	LR10	5
Olliver, s. John & Marcy, b. Oct. 12, 1729	LR2	352
Oliver, m. Lois RUGGLES, Oct. 16, 1751	LR7	30
Oliver, s. Elizer & Maray, b. July 18, 1774	LR7	30
Oliver, s. Reuben, Jr. & Eunice, b. Mar. 3, 1786	1	21

WARNER, (cont.)

	Vol.	Page
Oliver, s. Elizur & Mary, d. June 4, 1796, at Albany, N. Y., in the 22nd y. of his age	LR7	30
Oliver, Jr., m. Lovisa **BENHAM**, Sept. 2, 1809, by Rev. Benjamin Benham	1	165
Oliver, d. Feb. 21, 1814	LR7	30
Orange, s. John & Marcy, b. Jan. 18, 1745/6	LR4	8
Orange, m. Abigail **PRINDLE**, Dec. 5, 1765, by Samuell Bostwick, J. P.	LR11	6
Orange, s. Orange & Abigail, b. Apr. 13, 1770	LR11	6
Orange, 3rd, m. Apphia **EDWARDS**, b. of New Milford, Dec. 19, 1822, by Rev. Benjamin Benham	1	145
Orange, m. Abigail **PRINDLE**, Jr., Dec. 5, [ ], by Samuell Bostwick, J. P.	LR7	7
Orra, m. Betsey **GAYLORD**, b. of New Milford, Mar. 26, 1834, by H. Rood	1	273
Patty, m. Samuel **HAYES**, b. of New Milford, Jan. 31, 1847, by Rev. Samuel Weeks	2	40
Phebee, d. Lamuel & Sarah*, b. Nov. 14, 1758 *("Phebee" crossed out)	LR7	36
Polly Ann, of New Milford, m. Edson B. **CORNING**, of Brookfield, Dec. 29, 1836, at Bridgewater, by Rev. F. Donnelly	1	302
Prudence, d. John & Mercy, b. Dec. 3, 1733	LR4	8
Prudence, m. Isaac **BOSTWICK**, Nov. 27, 1754, by Rev. Nathaniel Taylor	LR6	7
Prudence, d. Oliver & Lois, b. Aug. 28, 1761	LR7	30
Reuben, s. Oliver & Lois, b. May 23, 1759	LR7	30
Reuben, Jr., m. Eunice **CARRINGTON**, b. of New Milford, Jan. 1, 1781	1	21
Roahde, d. Joseph & Sarah, b. Aug. 25, 1732	LR2	343
Sally Caroline, d. Curtiss & Eunice, b. Feb. 3, 1803	1	73
Sarah, d. Joseph & Sarah, b. Mar. 12, 1736/7	LR4	15
Sarah, m. Moses **KNAP**, May 29, 1751, by Rev. Nathaniel Taylor	LR6	15
Sarah, w. Lemuel, d. Dec. 23, 1819, ae 77 y.	LR7	36
Solomon, s. John & Mercy, b. Oct. 13, 1741	LR4	8
Solomon, s. Capt. John & Mercy, d. Sept. 20, 1760, at Montreal, in the English Camp	LR2	338
Tamar, d. Oliver & Lois, b. July 20, 1764	LR7	30
Thale, d. Asa & Eunice, b. Mar. 24, 1772	LR10	17
Thankfull, d. Joseph & Sarah, b. Aug. 26, 1730	LR2	343
Tryphena, d. Oliver & Lois, b. Dec. 14, 1753	LR7	30
Tryphena, m. Benjamin Starr **MYGATT**, Apr. 5, 1775	LR12	20
William, s. Curtiss & Eunice, b. May 5, 1806	1	73
William R., m. Laura **BROWNSON**, Dec. 23, 1823, by Rev. Andrew Eliot	1	147

WARREN, Hannah, of New Milford, m. Olive **BOWLIN**, of Kent

	Vol.	Page
WARREN, (cont.)		
(colored), Sept. 24, 1850, by Rev. David Murdock Mary*, m. Domini **DUGLAS**, May 5, 1761 *(Written "Mary WARNER" in mss. copy)	2 LR7	64 29
WARRINER, Eunice, m. Arthur **BOSTWICK**, July 1, 1752	LR7	16
WASHBURN, WASHBORN, WASHPORN, Army, had s. John **SMITH**, b. June 23, 1771	1	6
Ebenezer, m. Patience **MILES**, June 29, 1721	LR4	20
Esther, m. Alanson **FERRISS**, Nov. 16, 1783	1	40
Eunis, d. Ebenezer & Patiance, b. Apr. 26, 1729	LR4	20
Hester, d. Gideon & Hester, b. Dec. 16, 1763	LR7	7
Jonathan, s. Ebenezer & Patiance, b. Feb. 20, 1732/3	LR4	20
Joseph, s. Ebenezer & Patiance, b. May 16, 1727	LR4	20
Lucretia, m. Gideon **TREAT**, b. of New Milford, Nov. 13, 1770, by Rev. Nathaniell Taylor	LR9	[ ]
Miles, s. Ebenezer & Patiance, b. Jan. 10, 1730/1	LR4	20
Patience, d. Ebenezer & Patience, b. May 2, 1722	LR4	20
Philene, m. Asahel **HOTCHKISS**, b. of New Milford, Nov. 26, 1766	LR7	32
Rebeckah, d. Ebenezer & Patience, b. Mar. 5, 1736/7	LR4	20
Stephen, s. Ebenezer & Patience, b. Feb. 19, 1734/5	LR4	20
Susanah, d. Ebenezer & Patience, b. May 9, 1725	LR4	20
Susanah, m. William **DRINKWATER**, Mar. 14, 1751, by Samuel Canfield, J. R.	LR6	7
WASSON, Sophia, of Fairfield, m. Rev. Andrew **ELIOT**, of New Milford, Sept. 19, 1820	1	192
WATERBURY, Flora E., of Bridgewater, m. Thomas S. **FELLOWS**, of Northfield, N. H., Aug. 8, 1850, at the New England House by Rev. Gilbert B. Hayden	2	62
William, m. Eliza **STEWART**, Nov. 6, 1836, by Rev. Francis Donnelly	1	300
WATERS, John, of New Milford, m. Ann **ROOT**, of Kent, Nov. 13, 1842, by Z. Davenport	1	374
Michael, m. Olive **HALL**, Dec. 13, 1846, by E. Huntington	2	25
WATROUS, Harriet, of New Milford, m. Salmon **BROWN**, of Washington, Aug. 24, 1825, by Rev. Benjamin Benham	1	125
WATSON, Ann, m. William A. **BLACKNEY**, b. of New Milford, Oct. 18, 1821, by Benjamin Benham	1	106
John, m. Mary A. **SMITH**, b. of New Milford, Oct. 5, 1845, by E. Huntington	2	4
Johnson, m. Amaryllis **STONE**, b. of New Milford, Jan. 21, 1822, by Rev. C. A. Boardman	1	13
Mary Ann, m. William **DAYTON**, Mar. 16, 1842, by E. Huntington	1	380
Nancy, m. Phillip **WELLS**, Mar. 14, 1821, by Rev. Benjamin Benham	1	107
WAY, Ann, of Goshen, m. Orval **NORTHROP**, of New Milford, Nov. 30, 1828, by Rev. E. Huntington	1	227

	Vol.	Page
WAY, (cont.)		
Asa H., of Goshen, m. Polly **JENNINGS**, of New Milford, Sept. 21, 1828, by Rev. E. Huntington	1	223
Elvira, m. David **WHEATON**, b. of New Milford, Feb. 12, 1854, by Rev. A. B. Pulling	2	95
Jerome, of New Milford, m. Polly **WILDMAN**, of Brookfield, Feb. 4, 1829, by Rev. John Lovejoy	1	228
John R., m. Susan A. **LEE**, b. of New Milford, Mar. 8, 1853, by Rev. A. B. Pulling	2	85
Laura, m. John **HUNT**, Dec. 19, 1839, by Rev. Daniel Baldwin	1	340
Mary Ann, m. Horace **HUNT**, Nov. 2, 1835, by E. Huntington	1	295
Menirva, of New Milford, m. Eleazar **CABLE**, of Stratford, Mar. 13, 1828, by Rev. E. Huntington	1	218
William, of New Haven, m. Paulina **BALDWIN**, of New Milford, Mar. 19, 1850, by Seth W. Scofield	2	60
WEAVER, Brice B., of Dover, N. Y., m. Emily **STERLING**, of New Milford, June 17, 1839, by Noah Porter	1	328
WEED, John D., m. Anna **BOSTWICK**, Oct. 25, 1807, by Elisha Bostwick, J. P.	1	150
Marshall Hill, s. John D. & Anna, b. Sept. 16, 1808	1	150
Susan, d. John D. & Anna, b. Oct. 2, 1810	1	150
WEEKS, Caroline, m. Silas **ERWIN**, b. of New Milford, Dec. 16, 1832, by E. Huntington	1	256
Smith R., m. Betsey Ann **SMITH**, b. of Bridgewater, Oct. 15, 1845, by J. Kilbourn	1	404
WELCH, WELSH, Ann, d. Paul & Jerusha, b. Mar. 1, 1730/1	LR2	343
Anne, m. Samuel **PLAT[T]**, Aug. 17, 1749, by Rev. Nathaniell Taylor	LR7	2
Betsey, m. Samuel Brown **GRAVES**, Feb. 7, 1805, by Elisha Bostwick, J. P.	1	120
David, s. John & Deborah, b. Jan. 3, 1724/5	LR2	349
Deborah, d. John & Deborah, b. Aug. 7, 1721	LR2	349
Daboroh, wid, John, m. Joseph **MILES**, b. of New Milford, Sept. 25, 1732, by Rev. Daniel Bordman	LR4	25
Deborah, m. John **COMSTACKE**, Dec. 14, 1743, by Rev. Daniel Bordman	LR5	6
Elizabeth, d. Paul & Jerusha, b. Oct. 23, 1736	LR4	2
Hannah, d. John & Deborah, b. Mar. 30, 1723	LR2	349
Hannah, of Milford, m. Joseph **FERRIS**, of Newington, Nov. 11, 1725	LR2	340
Hannah, m. Nathan **GUNN**, May 10, 1741, by Rev. Daniel Bordman	LR4	25
Irene, m. John **POMROY**, b. of New Milford, May 3, 1800, by Elisha Bostwick, J. P.	1	23
Jane, d. John & Deborah, b. Mar. 3, 1728/9	LR2	349
Jane, m. Dr. Jonah **TODD**, Mar. 23, 1756, by Paul Welch, J. P.	LR7	9

	Vol.	Page
WELCH, WELSH, (cont.)		
Jerusha, d. Paul & Jerusha, b. Aug. 6, 1734	LR4	2
Jerusha, w. Paul, d. Sept. 28, 1755	LR4	2
John, of New Milford, m. Deborah **FERRIS**, of New Milford, Aug. 27, 1719	LR2	349
John, s. John & Deborah, b. Feb. 27, 1719/20	LR2	349
John, Sergt., d. May 25, 1732, ae 38 years " and something more"	LR2	358
John, s. Paul & Jerusha, b. Nov. 8, 1744; d. Jan.* 6, 1744/5 *("Dec. 6, 1744")	LR4	2
Marvin, m. Betsey **CASTLE**, Sept. 27, 1806, by Elisha Bostwick J. P.	1	133
Mary, d. Thomas, of Milford, b. Oct. 19, 1740	LR4	26
Mary, m. Elizer **WARNER**, Oct. 26, 1763, by Nathaniell Taylor	LR7	30
Paul, s. John & Deborah, b. June 17, 1727	LR2	349
Paul, of New Milford, m. Jerusha **BRONSON**, of Waterbury, July 9, 1728	LR2	343
Paul, of New Milford, m. Mrs. Rachel **GRANT**, of Litchfield, Dec. 29, 1756	LR4	2
Paul, s. Paul & Rachel, b. Jan. 9, 1759	LR4	2
Ruth, d. Paul & Jerush[a], b. Dec. 19, 1739	LR4	2
Ruth, m. John **MERWIN**, Dec. 31, 1777	LR10	5
Thomas, s. John & Deborah, b. May 17, 1731	LR2	349
WELDON, Susan, of New Milford, m. Samuel **COYES**, of Cornwall, Sept. 28, 1834, by E. Huntington	1	426
WELLER, WELLAR, WELLOUR, Aaron, see Merrick **WELLER**	LR4	4
Abel, s. Joseph & Martha, b. Jan. 4, 1743; d. Feb. 6, 1743	LR4	5
Abel, s. Thomas & Hannah, b. Mar. 24, 1746/7	LR4	9
Amos, s. Obadiah & Mary, b. Sept. 19, 1731	LR4	4
Annis, d. Benjamin & Sarah, b. Aug. 21, 1749	LR7	35
Annice, m. Shubel **CHAPMAN**, b. of New Milford, Dec. 29, 1768, by Samuel Canfield, J. P.	LR11	4
Azel, s. Joseph & Martha, b. Feb. 4, 1747	LR4	5
Benjamin, s. Obadiah & Mary, b. Aug. 18, 1729	LR4	4
Bruce, m. Mary Jane **WILMOT**, Aug. 3, 1847, by Julius B. Harrison, J. P.	2	30
Cocly*, s. Thomas & Hannah, b. Apr. 9, 1732 *("Cooly" in Orcutt's Hist.)	LR2	346
Conley*, s. Thomas & Hannah, b. Apr. 9, 1732 *("Cooley")	LR4	9
Coole, s. Benjamin & Sarah, b. Oct. 6, 1760	LR7	35
David, s. John & Lydia, b. Dec. 12, 1726	LR4	5
Eliakem, s. John & Lydia, b. Oct. 20, 1737	LR4	5
Elijah, s. Benjamin & Sarah, b. Apr. 9, 1751	LR7	35
Elijah, of New Milford, m. Mary **ATTWOOD**, of Woodbury, Nov. 25, 1773, by Joseph Bebiny	LR12	6
Eunice, d. Thomas & Hannah, b. Aug. 6, 1739	LR4	9

WELLER, WELLAR, WELLOUR, (cont.)

	Vol.	Page
Eunice, m. Andrew BURRITT, b. of New Milford, Jan. 27, 1763, by Rev. Thomas Davis	LR7	[ ]
Fllie*, s. Thomas & Hannah, b. Nov. 1, 1741 *(Fillie)	LR4	9
Hannah, d. Thomas & Hannah, b. Mar. 15, 1743/4* *("Sept. 1743" crossed out)	LR4	9
Harriet, of Bridgwater, m. Burroughs BEACH, of Brookfield, May 14, 1826, by Rev. Fosdic Harrison, of Roxbury	1	152
Henry S., m. Lydia RICHMOND, b. of New Milford, Dec. 17, 1837, by Rev. Alonzo F. Selleck	1	307
Heppe, d. Joseph & Martha, b. Aug. 6, 1749	LR4	5
Huldah, d. Elijah & Mary, b. Dec. 17, 1774	LR12	6
John, s. John & Rebeckah, b. Dec. 27, 1694	LR2	359
John, of New Milford, m. Lydia WALLER, of Woodbury, Dec. 12, 1723	LR4	5
John, s. John & Lydia, b. Mar. 19, 1729/30* *(Letter or number crossed out)	LR4	5
John, Sr., d. Apr. 3, 1734	LR4	12
Jonathan, s. John & Rebeckah, b. July 1, 1705	LR2	359
Jonathan, m. Thankful BARTLETT, Dec. 20, 1733, by John Bostwick, J. P.	LR4	12
Jonathan, d. Mar. 23, 1733/4	LR4	12
Jonathan, s. Thomas & Hannah, b. Sept. 6, 1734	LR4	9
Jonathan, s. John & Lydia, b. Apr. 25, 1735	LR4	18
Jonathan, s. John & Lydeah, b. Apr. 26, 1735* *("174" rubbed out)	LR4	5
Joseph, s. John & Rebeckah, b. Feb. 10, 17*10/11 *("17" crossed out)	LR2	359
Joseph, of New Milford, m. Martha PEET, of Unity, Dec. 8, 1741, in Unity, by Rev. Richardson Miner, of Unity. Witnesses: Daniel Bostwick & Annah Peet	LR4	5
Joseph, s. Joseph & Martha, b. June 1, 1752; d. same day	LR4	5
Lurany, d. Elijah & Mary, b. Dec. 9, 1776	LR12	6
Martha, w. Joseph, d. Sept. 15, 1752	LR4	5
Mary, d. Benjamin & Sarah, b. Oct. 8, 1753	LR7	35
Mary, of New Milford, m. Charles BORIE, of Philadelphia, May 20, 1851, by Rev. David Murdock	2	69
Mary Ann, m. Luman B. HAMLIN, Nov. 7, 1821, by Rev. Fosdic Harrison, of Roxbury	1	100
Merrick*, s. Obadiah & Mary, b. Oct. 10, 1742 *("Merrick" changed to "Aaron", Feb. 8, 1742/3	LR4	4
Nathan, s. John & Lydia, b. Dec. 19, 1732	LR4	5
Obadiah, s. John & Rebeckah, b. Feb. 6, 1697	LR2	359
Obadiah, s. John & Rebeckah, b. Aug. 2, 1699	LR2	359
Obadiah, m. Mary SEELVE, b. of New Milford, Nov. 12, 1728	LR4	4
Phebe, d. Joseph & Martha, b. Jan. 6, 1745	LR4	5
Philo R., m. Eliza COLE, b. of New Milford, Mar. 9, 1834,		

	Vol.	Page
WELLER, WELLAR, WELLOUR, (cont.)		
by Rev. Nathan D. Benedict	1	271
Rebeckah, d. John & Rebeckah, b. Nov. [ ], 1708	LR2	359
Rebeckah, d. Thomas & Hannah, b. Sept. 8, 1730	LR2	346
Rebeckah, d. Thomas & Hannah, b. Sept. 8, 1730	LR4	9
Rebekah, m. William **HURD**, b. of New Milford, Nov. 1, 1753, by Rev. Nathaniell Taylor	LR7	4
Rose, of Woodbury, m. Elnathan **CURTIS**, of New Milford, Mar. 10, 1736/7, by John Bostwick, J. P.	LR4	20
Silas, s. Joseph & Sarah, b. May 19, 1757	LR8	1
Thankfull, m. Joseph **SEELYE**, July 28, 1735	LR4	17
Thomas, s. John & Rebeckah, b. Sept. 4, 1702	LR2	359
Thomas, m. Hannah **BOSTWICK**, b. of New Milford, Nov. 5, 1729	LR2	346
Thomas, a witness at wedding of John **FERRIS** & Abigal **TRYON**, Quakers	LR4	22
WELLS, Anna, d. Joseph & Jane, b. Apr. 24, 1805	1	100
Anna, d. Joseph & Jane, b. Apr. 24, [ ]	1	101
Anne, d. Thomas & Anne, b. Nov. 19, 1780	1	13
Anne, m. Herman **BUCKINGHAM**, Aug. 27, 1826, by Rev. Eleazar Beecher	1	187
Betsey, m. Cyrus **NORTHROP**, July 31, 1795	1	91
Elizabeth T., m. Albert S. **HILL**, b. of New Milford, Nov. 16, 1845, by E. Huntington	2	5
Esther, m. William F. **NEWCOMB**, Feb. 27, 1831, by Rev. Eleazar Beecher	1	114
Isaac C., m. Esther **MARSH**, b. of New Milford, May 7, 1826, by Rev. C. A. Boardman	1	206
Isaac Clark, s. Joseph & Jane, b. Jan. 10, 1804	1	100
Isaac Clark, s. Joseph & Jane, b. Jan. 10, [ ]	1	101
James E., m. Alvina **STONE**, Oct. 7, 1841, by E. Huntington	1	367
James E., m. Harriet A. **BENNITT**, b. of New Milford, Jan. 13, 1848, by John Greenwood	2	37
Jane, m. Albert L. **HODGE**, Oct. 25, 1846, by E. Huntington	2	23
Joseph, m. Jane **CLARK**, b. of New Milford, Feb. 20, 1803, by Daniel Everitt	1	100
Joseph, m. Jane **CLARK**, b. of New Milford, Feb. 20, 1803, by Daniel Everitt	1	101
Lois, d. Thomas & Anne, b. Mar. 3, 1786	1	13
Mary E., m. Clark **HINE**, Jan. 1, 1846, by E. Huntington	2	11
Phillip, m. Nancy **WATSON**, Mar. 14, 1821, by Rev. Benjamin Benham	1	107
Polly, d. Thomas & Anne, b. Mar. 16, 1784	1	13
Polly, of New Milford, m. Epaphras W. **BULL**, of Danbury, Jan. 5, 1804, by Elisha Bostwick, J. P.	1	109
Sally, m. Bradley **MARSH**, b. of New Milford, Jan. 10, 1805, by Elisha Bostwick, J. P.	1	115
Sarah Jane, of New Milford, m. Francis **STONE**, of Warren,		

	Vol.	Page
WELLS, (cont.)		
Sept. 23, 1845, by Rev. Johnson Howard, at Dover, N. Y.	1	402
Sophia, m. John **McMAHON**, Jan. 10, 1821, by Rev. Andrew Eliot	1	43
Stephen, m. Mary Jane **SHERMAN**, b. of New Milford, Sept. 14, 1846, by Rev. George L. Foote	2	18
Thomas, b. Mar. 28, 1752, in Stratford; m. Anne **NORTHROP**, wid. of Amos, Jr., Jan. 11, 1780	1	13
Thomas, s. Thomas & Anne, b. June 2, 1790	1	13
Thomas, d. [ ]	1	13
WELTON, Eli H., m. Laura A. **JESUP**, b. of New Milford, Sept. 11, 1850, by Rev. D. Williams	2	68
George, m. Elizabeth A. **BOTSFORD**, Oct. 25, 1789	1	81
George S., m. Louise **McGRAW**, b. of Bridgwater, Feb. 19, 1826, by Rev. Fosdic Harrison, of Roxbury	1	199
Harriet, d. George & Elizabeth, b. Dec. 4, 1795	1	81
Harriet, of Bridgewater, m. David **YOUNG**, of Roxbury, Sept. 15, 1841, by Rev. Albert B. Camp, of Bridgewater	1	360
Horatio N., m. Anna A. **TREAT**, b. of New Milford, Nov. 29, 1820, by Rev. Fosdic Harrison, of Roxbury	1	32
Horatio Nelson, s. George & Elizabeth, b. Oct. 21, 1798	1	81
Louisa, Mrs. of Bridgewater, m. Frederick W. **AVERILL**, of Bethany, Genesee Co., N. Y., Oct. 24, 1839, by Albert B. Camp	1	333
Minerva, d. George & Elizbeth, b. Aug. 15, 1793	1	81
Thomas A., of Oxford, m. Mira Ann **MARSH**, of New Milford, Oct. 12, 1837, by E. Huntington	1	310
WESTOVER, Hannah, m. John **WARNER**, July 6, 1763	LR8	2
WHEATON, WHEATTON, WHEETEN, WHETEN, WHETTON, Amy, m. Jared **SPEARY**, Nov. 5, [ ]	1	1
Anny, d. Joseph & Lydia, b. Feb. 10, 1757	LR5	9
Anne, m. Ichabod **BOSTWICK**, Oct. 8, 1780	1	96
Benjamin, s. Josiph & Lydeah, b. Nov. 30, 1749	LR4	4
Cynthia, m. Hervey **SHERWOOD**, Dec. 17, 1814	1	124
David, m. Elvira **WAY**, b. of New Milford, Feb. 12, 1854, by Rev. A. B. Pulling	2	95
Esseck, s. Joseph & Lydeah, b. Jan. 5, 1747/8	LR4	4
Joseph, s. Joseph & Lydeah, b. Mar. 1, 1745/6	LR4	4
Joseph, s. Joseph & Lydia, b. Mar. 1, 1745/6	LR5	9
Lydeah, d. Joseph & Lydeah, b. July 13, 1744	LR4	4
Lydia, d. Joseph & Lydia, b. July 13, 1744	LR5	9
Molly, d. Esa & Eunice, b. Apr. 27, 1774	LR10	12
Orange, s. Joseph & Lydia, b. Sept. 19, 1760	LR5	9
Orlin J., of Pompey, N. Y., m. Saphronia **STONE**, of New Milford, Nov. 22, 1821, by Rev. C. A. Boardman	1	41
Salmon, s. Joseph & Lyiay, b. Oct. 29, 1754	LR5	9
Salvester*, s. Joseph & Lydiah, b. July 14, 1752 *("Salvester, s. Joseph "crossed out)	LR4	4

	Vol.	Page
WHEATON, WHEATTON, WHEETEN, WHETEN, WHETTON, (cont.)		
Tyrus, of Brookfield, m. Mary M. **BOSTWICK**, of Bridgwater, Dec. 13, 1827, by Abner Brundige	1	219
WHEELER, WHEELR, WHEALER, Ann, d. Nathan & Mary, b. Sept. 20, 1754	LR4	1
David, s. Nathan & Sarah, b. Nov. 27, 1764	LR5	9
David, witnessed marriage of Enoch **CARPENTER** & Sophia **LANE**	1	184
Elisabeth, d. Nathan & Mary, b. Aug. 7, 1744	LR5	9
Emily A., m. Isaac **BEACH**, of Bridgwater, Oct. 25, 1829, by Rev. Fosdic Harrison, of Roxbury	1	235
Easter, d. Nathan & Mary, b. Nov. 5, 1756	LR4	1
Eunice, d. Nathan & Sarah, b. July 18, 1760	LR4	1
Hannah, of Milford, m. Daniel **BORDMAN**, of New Milford, Feb. 20, 1716/17	LR2	357
Hannah, d. Nathan & Mary, b. Nov. 2, 1746	LR5	9
Huldah, of New Milford, m. Joseph **JOHNSON**, of Monroe, May 17, 1825, by Newton Tuttle. Witnesses: Charles Smith, David Warner, Belden Warner & Rev. Nathan Tuttle	1	98
John T., m. Elvira **BUCK**, b. of New Milford, Oct. 11, 1829, by Rev. Enoch Huntington	1	233
Johnson, Jr., of Southbury, m. Sally **BURR**, of New Milford, Bridgewater Soc., Nov. 29, 1820, by Rev. Fosdic Harrison, of Roxbury	1	36
Lois, of Darby, m. Enos **CAMP**, Jr., May 5, 1767, by Rev. David Brownson	LR7	6
Mary, d. Nathan & Mary, b. Nov. 31, [sic], 1749	LR4	1
Mary, w. Nathan, d. Aug. 10, 1758	LR4	1
Mary E., m. Artemas W. **EGELSTON**, b. of New Milford, Mar. 13, 1854, by Rev. A. B. Pulling	2	96
Nathan, s. Nathan & Mary, b. Apr. 11, 1752	LR4	1
Nathan, m. Sarah **PRIME**, Sept. 4, 1758	LR4	1
Rebekah, of Stratfield, m. Joseph **BOSTWICK**, of New Milford, July 23, 1724	LR2	339
Ruth, d. Nathan & Merry, b. Oct. 21, 1748	LR4	1
Sally, of Southbury, m. Cyrus **DUNNING**, of New Milford, [ ]	1	200
WHITE, Melissa P., m. Ebenezer H. **CLARK**, b. of New Milford, Sept. 21, 1851, by Rev. William Biddle, of Brookfield	2	72
Nelson, of Sherman, m. Eliza **RICHMOND**, of New Milford, Apr. 10, 1842, by Rev. Daniel Baldwin	1	374
WHITEHEAD, David T., m. Jane **HALLOCK**, of New Milford, Nov. 27, 1833, by Rev. Nathan D. Benedict	1	269
David T., m. Mary Jane **SEELEY**, Apr. 3, 1843, by Eleazer Beecher	1	385
Lucinda, m. John **SOULE**, b. of New Milford, Jan. 19, [ ],		

	Vol.	Page

WHITEHEAD, (cont.)
    by Daniel Gaylord, J. P.   1   185
WHITELEY, WHITELY, Abijah Ruggles, s. William & Tryphene,
    b. Jan. 11, 1784   1   2
    Amynta, d. William & Tryphene, b. Mar. 16, 1788; d. July 18,
        1788   1   2
    Hannah, d. William & Tryphene, b. Apr. 16, 1786   1   2
    Hermon, s. William & Tryphene, b. Oct. 8, 1781   1   2
    Homer, s. William & Tryphene, b. May 7, 1789   1   2
    William, m. Tryphene RUGGLES, Feb. 1, 1779   1   2
    William, s. William & Tryphene, b. July 18, 1779   1   2
WHITING, Mary Ann, see Mary Anna BOARDMAN   2   121
    Mary Ann, of Great Barrington, Mass., m. Elijah
        BOARDMAN, of New Milford, Sept. 25, 17[ ], by Rev.
        Gideon Bostwick, of Great Barrington   1   102
    Mary Ann, of Great Barrington, Mass., m. Elijah
        BOARDMAN, of New Milford, Sept. 25, 1792, at Great
        Barrington, by Rev. Gideon Bostwick   2   121
WHITLOCK, WHITLOCKE, Isaac, m. Mrs. Laura DAVIS, Nov.
    1, 1827, by Rev. Eleazar Beecher   1   130
    Samuel, m. Clarissa BADCOCKE, Apr. 27, 1817, by Elisha
        Bostwick, J. P.   1   165
WHITNEY, Asa, of New Preston, m. Abigail BROWNSON, of
    Cornwall, Dec. 17, 1772, by Rev. Hezekiah Goold   LR10   17
    Melinda, m. Homer SHELDON, Oct. 8, 1846, by E.
        Huntington   2   23
    Reuben P*, m. Ann M. COY (colored), b. of New Milford,
        Apr. 9, 1854, by Rev. A. B. Pulling ("P" uncertain)   2   97
WHITTEMORE, Ann, witnessed marriage of David SANDS &
    Paulina LEACH   1   277
WHITTLESEY, Ann, m. William COGSWELL, Nov. 4, 1762, by
    Rev. Noah Wadhams   LR11   16
    George, m. Cornelia KEELER, Feb. 28, 1822, by Rev.
        Andrew Eliot   1   39
    Harvey, of Farmington, m. Dolly M. SPERRY, of New
        Milford, Aug. 31, 1842, by N. Porter   1   377
    Laura, of Washington, m. Enos CAMP, Jr., of New Milford,
        Apr. 17, 1804   1   172
WILCOX, Edwin, of Chester, Mass., m. Fanny EGGLESTON, of
    New Milford, June 14, 1840, by Rev. E. Huntington   2   38
WILDER, Abigail, m. Stanley CARPENTER, b. of New Milford,
    (colored), Nov. 25, 1830, by Rev. Heman Rood   1   425
WILDMAN, Abigail, d. Josiah & Abigail, b. July 20, 1783   LR12   5
    Eden, s. Josiah & Abigail, b. Mar. 5, 1778   LR12   5
    Eliza, m. Gerardus FARVOUR, June 26, 1832, by Nathan
        Gaylord, J. P.   1   252
    Ezra, of Brookfield, m. Harriet N. BARLOW, of Bridgewater,
        Feb. 23, 1841, by Albert B. Camp   1   352

	Vol.	Page
WILDMAN, (cont.)		
George G., of Danbury, m. Eliza HULL, of New Milford, May 16, 1837, by Rev. Francis Donnelly	1	305
James, m. Hannah MESSER, Apr. 4, 1833, by Rev. Luther Mead	1	260
Mary, d. Josiah & Abigail, b. June 10, 1775	LR12	5
Mary Jane, of New Milford, m. Sidney S. PECK, of Bethel, Nov. 27, 1850, by Rev. D. Williams	2	69
Mindwell, of Danbury, m. William BRADSHAW, of New Milford, June 14, 1769	LR10	16
Mindwell, d. Josiah & Abigail, b. Mar. 16, 1773	LR12	5
Polly, of Brookfield, m. Jerome WAY, of New Milford, Feb. 4, 1829, by Rev. John Lovejoy	1	228
Sally, m. Lysander COLE, Jan. 8, 1839, by E. Huntington	1	334
Samuel, of Danbury, m. wid. Paulina BLACKNEY, of New Milford, Apr. 6, 1830, by E. Huntington	1	133
Samuel C., m. Laura A. BOSTWICK, Sept. 1, 1835, by Edward C. Bull	1	314
WILKINSON, WILCURSON, WILKERSON, WILCORSON, WILKYERSON, WILKISON, Abell, s. John & Jerusha, b. Mar. 5, 1752	LR5	11
Abel, m. Hannah SUMMERS, b. of New Milford, Dec. 23, 1773, by Samuell Bostwick, J. P.	LR12	4
Abigal, d. David & Darcos, b. July 28, 1776	LR7	4
Abigail, m. Josiah LOCKWOOD, Apr. 21, 1808, by Elisha Bostwick, J. P.	1	78
Amos, m. Annis THAYER, June 30, 1806, by Elisha Bostwick, J. P.	1	125
Ann, d. John & Jerusha, b. Aug. 4, 1749	LR5	11
Anne, m. John SMITH, Mar. 3, 1768	LR11	5
Asahel, s. John & Jerusha, b. May 9, 1762	LR6	2
Augustine, s. David & Darcos, b. Mar. 25, 1768	LR7	1
Daniel, s. John, Jr. & Lydia, b. Aug. 19, 1782	1	4
David, s. John, Jr. & Jerusha, b. Nov. 7, 1745	LR5	12
David, m. Darcos BROWNSON, Feb. 18, 1764	LR7	1
David, d. Feb. 27, 1791, in the 46th y. of his age	LR7	4
Dorcas, m. Amasa SMITH, b. of New Milford, Jan. 15, 1808, by Elisha Bostwick, J. P.	1	155
Dorcas, wid. David, d. Jan. 6, 1824, ae 68 y. wanting 1 m. & 19 d.	LR7	4
Elizabeth, d. David & Darkos, b. May 31, 1774	LR7	1
Eunice, d. David & Darcos, b. Mar. 27, 1766	LR7	1
Eunice, m. Jesse COLE, Feb. 8, 1783	1	4
Gideon, s. David & Darcos, b. Oct. 28, 1771	LR7	1
Ichabod, s. John & Jerusha, b. Dec. 4, 1753	LR5	12
Ichabod, m. Anna TAYLOR, Apr. 13, 1775	LR13	6
Isaac, s. John & Jerusha, b. May 6, 1773	LR6	2
Isaac, m. Tamar SMITH, Dec. 18, 1791	1	32

WILKINSON, WILCURSON, WILKERSON, WILCORSON, WILKYERSON, WILKISON, (cont.)

	Vol.	Page
Jerusha, wid. John, d. May 12, 1796, at Scipio, N. Y.	LR6	2
Jessee, s. Lewis, Jr. & Mary, b. Oct. 1, 1749	LR6	2
Joel Taylor, s. Ichabod & Anna, b. Dec. 14, 1776	LR13	6
John*, m. Jerusha BROWNSON, b. of New Milford, Jan. 14, 1744/5, by Roger Brownson, J. P. *("Jr." crossed out)	LR5	12
John, s. John & Jerusha, b. June 1, 1747	LR5	12
John, s. David & Darcos, b. Oct. 21, 1779	LR7	4
John, Jr., m. Lydia PIERCE, Feb. 22, 1780	1	4
John, d. Oct. 5, 1791	LR6	2
John, m. Anna FORD, b. of New Milford, Nov. 1, 1807, by Elisha Bostwick, J. P.	1	152
Jonathan, s. John & Jerusha, b. Sept. 7, 1758	LR5	12
Levi, s. Lewis & Mary, b. Aug. 14, 1756	LR6	2
Lewiss, s. Lewis, 3rd* & Mary, b. Nov. 1, 1745 *("Jr." crossed out)	LR5	12
Lois, m. Elijah PERRY, b. of New Milford, Feb. 14, [ ]	1	69
Mabel, d. John & Jerusha, b. June 30, 1760	LR6	2
Mary, [d. Lewis & Mary], b. Dec. 17, 1758	LR6	2
Mary, d. Lewis & Mary, d. [ ], 1758	LR6	2
Nathanael, s. Ichabod & Anna, b. Dec. 31, 1780	LR13	6
Orang[e], s. Abel & Hannah, b. Sept. 10, 1774	LR12	4
Peter, s. David & Darcos, b. May 19, 1764	LR7	1
R[e]uben, s. Lewis, Jr. & Mary, b. May 4, 1754	LR6	2
Ruth, d. David & Darcos, b. July 11, 1770	LR7	1
Samuel, s. Lewiss & Mary, b. Dec. 27, 174[ ]	LR5	12
Sarah, m. Samuel SMITH, July 30, 1744, by Samuel Canfield, J. P.	LR5	7
Sarah, d. John & Jerusha, b. Mar. 23, 1757	LR5	12
Susanah, d. Lewis & Mary, d. Nov. 27, 1752* *(Figure "5" uncertain)	LR6	2
WILLIAMS, Betsey, m. Nathaniel BRONSON, Apr. 10, 1836, by E. Huntington	1	297
Charlotte, m. Daniel MARSH, June 11, 1833, by E. Huntington	1	263
David, m. Betsey HIGGINS, b. of New Milford, Dec. 17, 1826, by Grove S. Brownell	1	210
Emily, d. [John A. & Susan], b. Aug. 29, 1840	1	113
Henry, of Sharon, m. Sarah DARLING, of Redding, Dec. 9, 1839, by E. Huntington	1	338
Jehiel, m. Sally THOMSON, Apr. 20, 1825, by Rev. Andrew Eliot	1	193
John A., of Greenfield, m. Susan PEET, of New Milford, Mar. 8, 1831, by H. Rood	1	113
Mariett, m. Taylor SUMMERS, Jan. 10, 1833, by Rev. Luther Mead	1	256
Mary, m. Henry GARLICK, Jan. 18, 1741	LR5	3

	Vol.	Page
WILLIAMS, (cont.)		
Mary, of New Milford, m. Frederick A. **BOARDMAN,** of Boardman, Ohio, Mar. 20, 1848, by Rev. E. Huntington	2	41
Susan E., d. John A. & Susan, b. May 17, 1732	1	113
William, m. Abigail **LOCKWOOD,** b. of New Milford, Apr. 8, 1838, by N. Porter	1	316
WILMOT, Chancy, m. Mary Ann **HUMESON,** Sept. 17, 1828, by Stephen Crane, J. P.	1	222
Mary Jane, m. Bruce **WELLER,** Aug. 3, 1847, by Julius B. Harrison, J. P.	2	30
WILSON, Antoinett, d. Javan & Dora, colored, b. Nov. 13, 1806	1	420
Catharine, d. Javan & Dora (colored), b. Sept. 19, 1802; d. Apr. 1, [ ]	1	420
Catharine, d. Javan & Dora, colored, b. Apr. 5, 1821	1	420
Daniel B., m. Mary G. **MERWIN,** b. of New Milford, Jan. 21, 1845, by John Greenwood	1	397
Frederick, s. Orman & C[h]loe, b. May 7, 1829	1	420
George, s. Javan & Dora, colored, b. Mar. 10, 1804	1	420
Ira, s. Javan & Dora, colored, b. Apr. 4, 1820	1	420
Javan, m. Dora, d. Patience (an emancipated servant), b. of New Milford, Jan. 20, 1802	1	420
Javan & Dora (colored), had Catharine, b. Sept. 19, 1802; d. Apr. 1, [ ]; George, b. Mar. 10, 1804; Antoniett, b. Nov. 13, 1806; Shubael, b. July 2, 1808; Rachel, b. Apr. 1, 1810; Julius Javan, b. Mar. 6, 1814; Ziba, b. Jan. 30, 1817; Ira, b. Apr. 4, 1820; Catharine, b. Apr. 5, 1821.		
Javan d. Feb. 22, 1827, ae 70, Revolutionary Pensioner	1	420
Javan, colored, d. Feb. 22, 1827, ae 70. Revolutionary Pensioner	1	420
Julius Javan, s. Javan & Dora, (colored), b. Mar. 6, 1814	1	420
Miletus, of Sharon, m. Harriet W. **SQUIRES,** of New Milford, Oct. 9, 1823, by Rev. Benjamin Benham	1	31
Orman, m. Cloe **JACKLIN,** May 18, 1828, by Stephen Crane, J. P.	1	420
Shubael, s. Javan & Dora, colored, b. July 2, 1808	1	420
Ziba, d. Javan & Dora, colored, b. Jan. 30, 1817	1	420
WILTON, George & Elizabeth, had s. [ ], b. June 6, 1792; d. June 7, 1792	1	81
Thirza, d. George & Elizabeth, b. Oct. 6, 1790	1	81
WINANS, John M., of Pine Plains, Dutchess Co., N. Y., m. Eunice **DOWNS,** of New Milford, Jan. 31, 1813	1	107
WING, Bennett, witnessed marriage of Jehu **HOAG** & Phebe **WANZER**	1	250
WINTERS, Harriet C., d. Curtis, m. Charles W. **GORDON,** July 29, 1849, by Rev. James L. Scott, of New Preston. Int. Pub.	2	56
Phebe, m. Ashbel **PEET,** Mar. 9, 1823, at the house of Edmond Clark, by Rev. Eleazar Beecher	1	99

	Vol.	Page
WOOD, Abigail, m. John **COLE**, Oct. 20, 1785	1	35
Polly, m. William C. **POWERS**, b. of Middletown, Nov. 21, 1803	1	168
Sarah, m. Asa **BROWNSON**, Sept. 9, 1777	LR13	10
WOODIN, WOODEN, Almeda, m. Anson **BROWN**, b. of New Milford, Nov. 30, 1826, by Rev. C. A. Boardman	1	207
Maron, m. Julia Samantha **HUNT**, b. of New Milford, Nov. 1, [1831], at the house of Edward Hunt, by Henry S. Atwater	1	245
Mary, witnessed marriage of Enoch **CARPENTER** & Sophia **LANE**	1	184
Mary, witnessed marriage of Jacob **WANZER** & Phebe **LEACH**	1	208
Mary, witnessed marriage of David **SANDS** & Paulina **LEACH**	1	277
Philo L., witnessed marriage of Enoch **CARPENTER** & Sophia **LANE**	1	184
Philo P., witnessed marriage of Jacob **WANZER** & Phebe **LEACH**	1	208
Philo S., witnessed marriage of David **SANDS** & Paulina **LEACH**	1	277
Shelden G., m. Lucy **BOSTWICK**, b. of New Milford, Feb. 24, 1833, by Rev. Henry S. Atwater	1	258
Sibel, m. Timothy **RUGGLES**, Apr. 30, 176[ ]	1	3
WOODLEY, John H., witnessed marriage of Jehu **HOAG** & Phebe **WANZER**	1	250
WOODRUFF, Ann, of the parish of Kensington, Farmington, m. John **MALERY**, of New Milford, May 7, 1740, by Rev. William Burnam, of Kensington	LR4	3
Laura, m. David D. **NORTHROP**, b. of New Milford, Apr. 25, 1841, by Rev. Elijah Baldwin	1	354
WOOSTER, Anna, m. Jesse **MOGER**, Feb. 25, 1773, by Bushnel Boswick, J. P.	LR11	13
David C., m. Emily C. **SHERMAN**, b. of Bridgewater, Oct. 27, 1846, by Rev. William Atwill, of Bridgewater	2	27
Deborah, of Derby, m. David **FABRAGUE**, of New Milford, May 13, 1766	LR8	3
Lois, m. Solomon **HOTCHKISS**, b. of New Milford, July 21, 1762	LR7	3
Mary E., m. Harmon **TREAT**, b. of Bridgewater, May 26, 1852, by D. Williams	2	77
Peter, m. Caroline **MORRIS**, b. of New Milford, Oct. 14, 1845, by Rev. William Atwill, of Bridgewater	2	6
Ruth, m. Asa **KNOWLTON**, [ ]	1	54
Susan, m. Lorenzo D. **SANFORD**, b. of Bridgwater, Nov. 8, 1848, by J. Kilbourn	2	45
Susanna, m. Daniel **BRISTOLL**, July 18, 1775	1	60
WORDEN, Eli E., m. Lucy E. **SHERMAN**, b. of New Milford,		

NEW MILFORD VITAL RECORDS 233

	Vol.	Page
WORDEN, (cont.)		
Mar. 11, 1840, by Noah Porter	1	343
WRIGHT, Caroline, m. Neri **HORFORD**, Jan. 19, 1823, by Elder Eleazar Beacher	1	80
James, m. Hannah **COLE**, Dec. 17, 1801, by Elisha Bostwick, J. P.	1	54
Martin, m. Fanny **HALLOCK**, Mar. 14, 1824, by Daniel Gaylord	1	162
WYANT, Charles M., m. Cordelia **RANDALL**, b. of New Milford, Dec. 18, 1853, by Rev. A. B. Pulling	2	91
Irene, m. William **GREGORY**, Feb. 21, 1841, by Rev. Maltby Gelston	1	364
Irene, m. William **GREGORY**, Feb. 21, 1842, by Maltby Gleston	1	376
Laura A., m. William A. **CHAMBERLAIN**, Mar. 28, 1843, by N. M. Urmston	1	385
WYGANT, Eveline, m. Theodore **BLACKMAN**, b. of New Milford, Nov. 12, 1851, by Rev. David P. Sanford	2	74
YALE, James F., of Lebanon, Penn., m. Mary A. **BENNITT**, of New Milford, Dec. 6, 1848, by John Greenwood	2	46
YEATS, Polly, m. David **BOSTWICK**, Jr., Oct. 24, 1780	LR13	17
YORK, Kezia, m. Job **TERRILL**, Dec. 9, 1781, by Rev. Levi Hart	LR13	8
YOUNG, David, of Roxbury, m. Harriet **WELTON**, of Bridgewater, Sept. 15, 1841, by Rev. Albert B. Camp, of Bridgewater	1	360
Elanson D., m. Mrs. Laura A. **FRENCH**, Feb. 14, 1836, by Albert B. Camp	1	292
Harriet, m. Samuel W. **SMITH**, Dec. 20, 1836, by E. Huntington	1	312
Hester, m. John B. **PECK**, b. of New Milford, Feb. 12, 1854, by Rev. David Murdock, Jr.	2	101
Mary E., m. Cornelius W. **PECK**, b. of New Milford, Oct. 4, 1853, by Rev. Rufus King	2	95
Orrin, of Roxbury, m. Orissa **LOVERIDG[E]**, of New Milford, Jan. 15, 1829, by Rev. Andrew Eliot	1	227
Truman, m. Amy **KAHAM**, Feb. 4, 1824, by Rev. Andrew Eliott	1	65
ZEIDLER, Anna Maria Theresa, wid., m. Charles **HEINZE**, journeyman turner, s. Joseph, decd., master turner, Oct. 17, 1758 (Evangelical Pastorate)	2	118
NO SURNAME, Bette, m. Joseph **BOSTWICK**, Jr., Feb. 7, 1750/1, by Rev. Jeadiah Mills, of Ripton	LR7	1
Dinah, m. Nehemiah **LOCKWOOD**, free negro, Oct. 20, 1783	1	422
Jehannah, m. Elnathan **NOBLE**, Feb. 10, 1774	1	2
Jerusha, m. Lewis **BOOTH**, Aug. 30, 1784	1	407
Mary, m. Henry C. **McMAHON**, b. of New Milford, Aug. 29, 1831, by H. Rood	1	244
Nathan, a witness at wedding of Elnathan **BOTSFORD** &		

	Vol.	Page

NO SURNAME, (cont.)
    Dorothy **PRINDLE**, Quakers — LR4 — 14
    Rachel, m. Benjamin **BOSTWICK**, Jan. 11, 1742/3, by Rev.
        Jonathan Ingerson — LR5 — 1
    Rhiley, s. Susanna, before her marriage to Prince **DRAKE**,
        b. Oct. 9, 1804, in Brookfield — 1 — 422
    Sarah, m. Jehiel **HAULEY**, Mar. 30, 1731 — LR5 — 15
    Sarah, m. Thadeus **BALDWIN**, July 15,*, 1762   *("July" &
        "15th" written after erasure) — LR13 — 3
    William, negro, s. Tamer, b. Apr. 2, 1803, in New Fairfield — 1 — 423

NORFOLK VITAL RECORDS
1758 - 1850

	Vol.	Page
ABERNATHY, ABERNETHY, Jrene*, d. Jared & Loes, b. Apr. 30, 1772 *(Irene)	TM	22
Jared, s. Jared & Loes, b. Sept. 12, 1774	TM	24
Loes, d. Jared & Loes, b. Apr. 4, 1769	TM	22
ADAMS, Henry, m. Polly **BABBET**, Nov. 27, 1834, by Rev. Joseph Eldredge	2	17
Zebediah, m. Angeline M. **BABBET**, Dec. 11, 1842, by Rev. J. Eldredge	2	22
AKINS, AKIN, Asher, of Norfolk, m. Rosilla **WILLCOCKS**, of Simsbury, Oct. 1, 1789, by Dudley Humphry, J. P	1	12
Elizabeth B., m. Frederick E. **PORTER**, May 21, 1845, by Rev. Joseph Eldredge	2	26
Hulday, m. Solom **CURTIS**, Aug. 13, 1783	1	7
Rebecca, m. Elizur **DOWD**, [Mar.] 31, [1834], by Rev. Joseph Eldredge	2	15
Sarah E., m. Philo M. **TROWBRIDGE**, of Bethleham, Sept. 18, 1837, by Rev. Joseph Eldredge	2	18
ALFORD, Arba, of Barhamstead, m. Mary **CASE**, [Nov.] 21, [1836], by Rev. Joseph Eldredge	2	18
ALLEN, ALLIN, ALLING, Elihu, s. Noah & Sarah, b. June 6, 1762	TM	11
Elizabeth, ae 25, m. Eleough **STOW**, ae 32, Nov. 30, 1848, by C. W. Watrous	2	32
Elizabeth M., of Norfolk, m. Elihu **STONE**, ae 31, of East Granville, Mass., Nov. 30, 1848, by Rev. C. W. Watrous	2	30
Erastus, 2nd s. Noah & Sarah, b. Sept. 30, 1760	TM	11
Ezra, s. Noah & Sarah, b. Nov. 5, 1758	TM	6
Noah, m. Sarah **KNAP[P]**, Sept. 29, 1758	TM	7
Noah, s. Noah & Sarah, b. June 25, 1764	TM	12
Noah, s. Noah & Sarah, d. Dec. 13, 1765	TM	20
Noah, s. Noah & Sarah, b. Feb. 23, 1775	TM	24
Sarah, d. Noah & Sarah, b. Nov. 30, 1766	TM	15
Theron, m. Emeline **GLEASON**, Oct. [ ], 1823, by Bushnell Knapp, J. P.	2	4
William A., m. Elizabeth **STEVENS**, Mar. 22, 1842, by Rev. J. Eldredge	2	22
ALLIN, [see under **ALLEN**]		
ALLING, [see under **ALLEN**]		
ALVORD, Jesse, m. Sophia **EDGECOMB**, Oct. 26, 1842, by Rev. J. Eldredge	2	22
ANDRUS, Alson Henry H., of Colebrook, m. Experience J.		

	Vol.	Page
ANDRUS, (cont.)		
CALHOUN, of Norfolk, June 6, 1830, by Azariah Clark	2	10
Eliza, m. Mark **HEDDY**, Mar. 22, 1843, by Rev. J. Eldredge	2	22
Ruth, m. William **NETTLETON**, Oct. 18, 1797, by Asahel Humphry, J. P.	1	15
Sarah Ann, m. Asahel **BRONSON**, Jr., Sept. 28, 1840, by Rev. A. Bushnell, Jr.	2	20
Sarah Lavina, d. Abram H., ae 40 & Experience J., ae 40, b. Oct. 21, 1847	2	44
Uriel, m. Sarah **PARRET**, Oct. 25, 1841, by Rev. J. Eldredge	2	22
Uriel, had d. [ ], b. [ ]	2	51
ARMSTRONG, Robert, m. Huldah **GRANT**, Nov. 11, [1829], by Rev. R. Emerson	2	8
ASHLEY, Edmund H., m. Mary M. **JUDD**, Nov. 20, [1836], by Rev. Joseph Eldredge	2	18
Susan, m. James **BIRDSELL**, Nov. 9, [1835], by Rev. Joseph Eldredge	2	17
ASPINWELL, Sarah, m. Amiriah **PLUMB**, Mar. 10, 1757	TM	7
ATWOOD, Nathan W., m. Sarah A. **GILLET**, Mar. 14, 1822, by R. Emerson	2	2
AUSTIN, AUSTEN, Easther, of Sheffield, m. Daniel **SPALDING**, of Norfolk, Aug. 30, 1781, by Rev. John Keep	1	10
Nancy, m. Lorrain **WHITING**, b. of New Marlboro, Mass., Mar. 11, 1834, by Rev. Theron Ellis, of Bap. Ch.	2	15
William H., of New Hartford, m. Elizabeth **CANFIELD**, Jan. 7, 1845, by Rev. Joseph Eldredge	2	26
BABBIT, BABBET, Angeline M., m. Zebediah **ADAMS**, Dec. 11, 1842, by Rev. J. Eldredge	2	22
Eliza, m. James **HUMPHREY**, Nov. 12, [1834], by Rev. Joseph Eldredge	2	16
Jennet J., m. William E. **PHELPS**, Sept. 1, 1841, by Rev. J. Eldredge	2	22
Polly, m. Henry **ADAMS**, Nov. 27, 1834, by Rev. Joseph Eldredge	2	17
Rebecca, m. Jared **POTTER**, Feb. 9, 1841, by Rev. J. Eldredge	2	21
Ruby, m. Truman **SEYMOUR**, Mar. 25, [1835], by Rev. Joseph Eldredge	2	17
BAILEY, -----, of Goshen, m. M. **PENDLETON**, Sept. 27, 1837, by Rev. Joseph Eldredge	2	18
BAKER, Osmyn, m. Cornelia **ROCKWELL**, Oct. 9, [1838], by Rev. Joseph Eldredge	2	19
Stephen, m. Dorothy **PARDE**, Sept. 9, 1760	TM	7
BALCOM, BALCAM, BOLCAM, Daniel Alson, s. Jsaac & Anna, b. Feb. 12, 1794	1	21
Luther, s. Abraham & Abigail, b. Aug. 1, 1794	1	20
Silva, d. Jsaac & Anna, b. May 10, 1792	1	21
BALDWIN, Andrew, m. Louisa **PHELPS**, Sept. 13, [1837], by		

	Vol.	Page
BALDWIN, (cont.)		
Rev. Joseph Eldredge	2	18
Eliza, m. Heman **COITT**, of Goshen, Feb. 25, [1828], by Rev. R. Emerson	2	8
Francis, s. Peter, ae 25 & Rose, ae 26, b. Aug. 27, 1847	2	45
Francis, d. Mar. 25, 1849, ae 6 m.	2	57
George W., of New Marlboro, m. Mary Ann **BROMLEY**, Oct. 30, 1849, by Rev. Joseph Eldredge	2	36
Julia, m. James M. **COWLES**, Mar. 10, 1830, by Rev. George Carrington, of Goshen	2	9
W[illia]m D., of New Marlboro, m. Atta **BARBER**, of Norfolk, Apr. 9, 1834, by Rev. Theron Ellis, of Bap. Ch.	2	15
BALE, Frederick, 1st s. Hendrick & Sarah, b. Dec. 12, 1785	1	11
Hendrick*, m. Sarah **HOTCHKISS**, Dec. 9, 1784, by Giles Pettibone *(Perhaps "Hendrick **BALL**")	1	10
Salmon, 2nd s. [Hendrick & Sarah], b. Dec. 22, 1786	1	11
BALL, Hendrick, see Hendrick **BALE**	1	10
BANDELL, Juliann, m. William W. **DOWD**, Mar. 7, 1830, by Bushnell Knapp, J. P.	2	9
BARBER, Abigail, d. Luther & Hannah, b. Apr. 7, 1767	TM	15
Amos, s. Samuel & Eunis, b. Apr. 17, 1771	TM	19
Atta, of Norfolk, m. W[illia]m D. **BALDWIN**, of New Marlboro, Apr. 9, 1834, by Rev. Theron Ellis, of Bap. Ch.	2	15
Eunis, d. Samuel & Eunic, b. Apr. 19, 1763	TM	14
Eunis, d. Luther & Hannah, b. Mar. 6, 1765	TM	12
Freelove, d. Luther & Hannah, b. Mar. 30, 1776	1	1
Hannah, m. Theodore **DOUD**, b. of Norfolk, Mar. 26, 1793, by Ammi R. Robbins	1	12a
Heman, s. Samuel & [E]unis, b. May 1, 1769	TM	17
John Calven, s. Luther & Hannah, b. Dec. 17, 1773	TM	23
Katurah, d. Samuel & Eunis, b. June 27, 1775	1	1
Luther, m. Hannah **BURR**, Nov. 15, 1761	TM	7
Luther, d. July 24, 1777	1	5
Marten, s. Samuel & Eunis, b. July 11, 1777	1	1
Martine Luther, s. Luther & Hannah, b. Oct. 23, 1771	TM	19
Roda, d. Luther & Hannah, b. June 6, 1769	TM	17
Ruth, d. Samuel & Eunic, b. Mar. 8, 1767	TM	14
Samuel, m. Eunis **COWLS**, Mar. 24, 1762	TM	7
Samuel, s. Samuel & Eunic, b. Dec. 23, 1764	TM	14
Seth, m. Mehetable **CRESSY**, May 24, [1820], by R. Emerson	2	2
Seth, of Conder, N. Y., m. Olive **CRISSEY**, of Norfolk, Jan. 30, 1831, by Rev. Henry Robinson	2	11
Timothy, s. Samuel & Eunis, b. Aug. 16, 1773	TM	22
William, d. Sept. 14, 1783	1	5
BARDEN, BARDIN, BORDEN, BORDON, Abigail, 2nd d. Eber & Mary, b. Jan. 12, 1795	1	36
Abraham Timothy, s. Ebenezer & Mary, b. Apr. 6, 1805	1	46

238 BARBOUR COLLECTION

	Vol.	Page
BARDEN, BARDIN, BORDEN, BORDON, (cont.)		
Ahira, 2nd s. Seth, Jr. & Sarah, b. Oct. 28, 1800	1	36
Almira, 3rd d. Ebenezer & Mary, b. Oct. 29, 1797	1	36
Asenath, d. Seth, b. June 5, 1771	TM	18
Asenath, d. Ebenezer & Mary, b. Jan. 31, 1789	1	12
Cate, d. Seth, b. Feb. 3, 1771	TM	19
Caty, d. John & Alcha, b. Dec. 14, 1788	1	35
Clarissa, 1st d. Seth, Jr. & Sarah, b. Sept. 4, 1792	1	12
Clarrisa M., m. Asa D. **NORTH**, Jan. 29, 1820, by R. Emerson	2	2
Cynthia, d. Ebenezer & Mary, b. May 13, 1807	1	46
Dorcas, d. Samuel & Mary, b. Oct. 11, 1783	1	39
Ebenezer, s. Seth, b. Feb. 7, 1766	TM	19
Ebenezer, 3rd s. Ebenezer & Mary, b. Apr. 3, 1800	1	36
Elijah, s. Seth & Ruth, b. Apr. 13, 1779	1	7
Elijah, s. Ebenezer & Mary, b. Dec. 16, 1792	1	12
Eliphalet, m. Eliza **HYDE**, June 5, 1825, by Bushnell Knapp	2	5
Easther, d. Seth, b. June 18, 1767	TM	18
Esther, m. Ephah **MERRIELS**, Dec. 7, 1781, by Rev. A. M. Robins	1	11
John, s. Seth & Ruth, b. Apr. 21, 1777	1	7
Joseph, s. Ebenezer & Mary, b. Mar. 18, 1787	1	12
Loritte, d. Samuel & Mary, b. Oct. 21, 1786	1	39
Lusinda, 2nd d. Seth, Jr. & Sarah, b. Mar. 17, 1794	1	12
Mahala, m. John H. **BULLARD**, Feb. [ ], 1826, by Bushnell Knapp	2	5
Mary, d. Seth & Ruth, b. July 11, 1783	1	9
Mary, d. 7th child Ebenezer & Mary, b. Aug. 4, 1802	1	41
Ruth, d. Seth, b. Jan. 11, 1769	TM	19
Ruth, m. [ ] **EVANS**, of Canaan, [Mar.] 31, [1833], by Rev. Joseph Eldredge	2	14
Sarah, d. Seth & Ruth, b. June 26, 1775	1	7
Sarah, 3rd d. Seth, Jr. & Sarah, b. July 18, 1798	1	36
Seth, 3rd, 1st s. Seth, Jr. & Sarah, b. Nov. 17, 1795	1	36
Seth, d. Oct. 29, 1808	1	14
Susanna, d. Seth & Ruth, b. Sept. 11, 1773	1	7
Thomas P., s. Samuel & Mary, b. May 15, 1780	1	39
BARLOW, Andrew, m. Sally **BLAKESLEY**, of Canaan, Jan. 10, 1821, by R. Emerson	2	2
Levi, of Plymouth, m. Eliza **WAITE**, Aug. 28, [1836], by Rev. Joseph Eldredge	2	18
BARNES, Chester, m. Amey **ROBBERTS**, Mar. 19, 1844, by Rev. Joseph Eldredge	2	24
Cynthia, of Canaan, m. Hezekiah **WARNER**, of Derby, Nov. 28, [1827], by Rev. R. Emerson	2	8
------, ae 21, m. Patrick **RYAN**, ae 24, Oct. 28, 1848, by Rev. Mr. Riley	2	31
BARRY, Edmund, s. John, b. July 29, 1850	2	53

	Vol.	Page
BARRY, (cont.)		
Martin, s. John, b. Nov. 23, 1848	2	49
BARSLEY, Mehala, Mrs. of Goshen, m. Prentice **BRUMBLEY,** of Cornwall, Oct. 4, 1830, by Rev. Bradley Selleck	2	10
BARSS, Loes, m. Thomas **KNAP[P]**, Feb. 7, 1758	TM	7
BARTLETT, Ellen, ae 24, m. Azuriah **ELDREDGE,** ae 29, June 20, 1849, by Rev. Joseph Eldredge	2	31
Ellen, m. Azariah **ELDREDGE,** of New Bedford, [June] 20, [1849], by Rev. Joseph Eldredge	2	33
BATTELL, BATTALL, Irene, m. W[illia]m A. **LARNED,** June 1, 1843, by Rev. Joseph Eldredge	2	24
Joseph, m. Sarah **ROBBINS,** July 24, 1805, by Rev. A. R. Robbins	1	44
Joseph, s. Joseph & Sarah, b. Apr. 17, 1806	1	48
Phillip, s. Joseph & Sarah, b. Nov. 28, 1807	1	48
Sarah, of Norfolk, m. Rev. Joseph **ELDREDGE,** of Norfolk, [Oct.] 12, [1836], by Frances L. Robbins	2	17
Urania, of Norfolk, m. James **HUMPHREY,** of Amhurst, Mass., [Oct.] 11, [1836], by Frances L. Robbins	2	17
BEACH, BEECH, Albert, of Goshen, m. Adaline **PINNEY,** of Norfolk, Sept. 11, 1831, by Rev. Luther Mead	2	12
Amanda, d. Caleb & Loes, b. Sept. 11, 1768	TM	16
Archelus, s. Caleb & Loes, b. Mar. 24, 1766	TM	13
Asenath, d. Linus & Elesabath, b. Sept. 6, 1787	1	11
Chester Riley, [s. Joshua], b. Sept. 2, 1799	2	37
Clarissa, of Goshen, m. Ezra **FOOT,** June 3, [1829], by Rev. R. Emerson	2	8
Easther, d. John & Hannah, b. Sept. 27, 1763	TM	13
George W., m. Louisa **DORMAN,** Oct. 5, 1823, by Rev. R. Emerson	2	6
George Willis, [s. Joshua], b. Oct. 26, 1804	2	37
Harriet Loisa, [d. Joshua], b. Mar. 29, 1801	2	37
Hilard*, 3rd s. Linus & Elizabeth, b. Feb. 21, 1785 *("Hyland"?)	1	19
Jerry Johnson, s. Joshua, b. Apr. 12, 1798	2	37
Joel, m. Lucy **BURNHAM,** Feb. 13, 1825, by Rev. R. Emerson	2	6
John, m. Sarah **BURR,** June 4, 1782, by Rev. Mr. Robbins	1	10
John, Jr., 2nd s. John & Sarah, b. Nov. 24, 1786	1	10a
Joshua Harlo, [s. Joshua], b. Dec. 30, 1812	2	37
Joshua Nelson, [s. Joshua], b. Nov. 30, 1807	2	37
Joshua Nelson, s. Joshua, d. Dec. 14, 1808	2	55
Lumen, s. Abner & Mary, b. Mar. 18, 1778	1	2
Luman Loomis, [s. Joshua], b. Apr. 9, 1809	2	37
Marian Wait, [d. Joshua], b. Jan. 10, 1803	2	37
Miranda Barnwell, [d. Joshua], b. Jan. 4, 1811	2	37
Moses Tiler, 2nd s. Caleb, b. Aug. 11, 1762	TM	10
Phebe Rosetta, d. Joel, farmer, ae 47 & Lucy, ae 40, b.		

240 BARBOUR COLLECTION

	Vol.	Page
BEACH, BEECH, (cont.)		
Jan. 8, 1848	2	43
Reuben, s. Linus & Eleazabath, b. Nov. 29, 1782	1	7
Salla, d. John & Sarah, b. Aug. 18, 1789	1	21
Salmon, 1st s. John & Sarah, b. Oct. 8, 1782	1	10a
Samuel, s. John & Hannah, b. Oct. 18, 1749	TM	13
Silvia, d. Luman & Ann, b. Sept. 21, 1764	TM	13
Thomas, s. John & Hannah, b. May 4, 1762	TM	13
BECKLEY, Elisha M., m. Lucy Ann **SMITH**, Aug. 23, 1848, by Rev. Joseph Eldredge	2	28
Jane, m. Newman B. **GILLETT**, of Winchester, Oct. 26, 1845, by Rev. Joseph Eldredge	2	26
BECKWITH, James Everit, s. Luke, b. May 29, 1850	2	52
Luke, m. Mary E. **SWIFT**, Dec. 31, 1844, by Rev. Joseph Eldredge	2	26
BEEBE, Mary A., m. [ ] **THOMPSON**, Jan. 5, 1835, by Rev. Joseph Eldredge	2	17
Robert M., m. Huldah **CASE**, [Aug.] 22, [1837], by Rev. Joseph Eldredge	2	18
BELCHER, Clarissa, m. Humphrey **SMITH**, b. of Norfolk, Mar. 22, 1845, by Rev. A. B. Hubbard	2	25
BELDEN, Austin, m. Charlotte T. **HAWLEY**, May 26, 1830, by Thomas Lascombe	2	10
Austin, m. Mary L. **NETTLETON**, Dec. 20, 1841, by Rev. J. Eldredge	2	22
Ensign, m. Caroline C. **JUDD**, May 19, [1841], by Rev. J. Eldredge	2	21
BELL*, Marther, m. Miles **RIGGS**, Feb. 28, 1775 *(Note says "BULL")	1	10
BELOEW, BELWAR, Peter, m. Rose **MENDES**, Apr. 19, [1846], by Rev. Joseph Eldredge	2	27
Peter M., s. Peter, b. Apr. 20, 1849	2	48
BENEDICT, Abigal, m. Miles **RIG[G]S**, Jr., Oct. 19, 1797, by Asahel Humphry, J. P.	1	15
Almeda, m. Washington J. **SMITH**, Apr. 25, 1821, by Elder Rufus Babcock	2	1
Daniel, s. Francis & Mary, b. Sept. 26, 1772	1	43
Francis, s. Francis & Mary, b. Feb. 13, 1770	1	43
Lois, d. Francis & Mary, b. Dec. 17, 1763	1	43
Olive, d. Francis & Mary, b. June 9, 1766	1	43
BENNETT, BENNET, George, ae 36 m. Eliza B. **PHELPS**, ae 30, Sept. [ ], 1848, by Joseph Eldredge	2	31
George, of Montreal, N. Y., m. Eliza R. **PHELPS**, Sept. [ ], 1848, by Rev. Joseph Eldredge	2	33
BENSON, Dillason, s. Orrin, b. Apr. 6, 1850	2	52
Hannah L., m. Joseph **SIGLOMIRE**, [Oct.] 15, [1849], by Rev. Mr. Robinson	2	33
Joseph, s. Orren, ae 38 & Lucy, ae 32, b. Feb. 27, 1848	2	43

	Vol.	Page
BENSON, (cont.)		
Joseph, d. Mar. 6, 1850, ae 2 y.	2	59
BETH *, Olive, m. Nathan R. **GREEN**, b. of Norfolk, Feb. 24, 1822, by Bushnell Knapp, J. P. *("**BETTS**"?)	2	1
BETTIS, Eliza Ann, m. John **PHELPS**, Dec. 5, [1821], by R. Emerson	2	2
BETTS (?)*, Olive, m. Nathan R. **GREEN**, b. of Norfolk, Feb. 24, 1822, by Bushnell Knapp, J. P. *(Mss. Copy had "Beth")	2	1
[BIGELOW], BIGALOW, Electa, 1st d. Benj[amin] & Eunice, b. Sept. 14, 1793; d. Aug. 29, 1794	1	37
Lemuel Akins, 1st s. Benj[amin] & Eunice, b. Nov. 4, 1795	1	37
Mark, 3rd s. Benjamin & Eunice, b. Aug. 22, 1799	1	37
Robert, 2nd s. Benjamin & Eunice, b. Oct. 17, 1797	1	37
BILLINGS, Sarah, d. Oct. [ ], 1849, ae 4 y.	2	60
William Otis, s. William, laborer, ae 50 & Mernerva, ae 28, b. Feb. 21, 1848	2	43
BILLS, Julia, m. Alfred **COOPER**, Mar. 2, 1836, by Rev. Joseph Eldredge	2	17
BINGHAM, Augustus, s. Ozias & Sarah, b. Apr. 4, 1772	TM	22
Sarah, m. Philo **GUITEAU**, Jan. 26, 1795	1	48
BIRD, David, Jr., of Winchester, m. Eunice A. **PHELPS**, of Norfolk, Oct. 20, 1830, by Frederick Marsh	2	11
BIRDSELL, James, m. Susan **ASHLEY**, Nov. 9, [1835], by Rev. Joseph Eldredge	2	17
BISHOP, Bile, m. Mamre **GILLET**, Oct. 15, 1761	TM	7
BLAKESLEE, BLAKSLEE, BLAKESLEY, BLAKESLY, BLACKLEY, BLAKLEY, Amasiah, s. Bayley & Eunis, b. Nov. 22, 1772	TM	23
Amos, 2nd s. Mathew & Ruth, b. July 2, 1793	1	34
Anson, 1st s. Mathew & Ruth, b. Sept. 6, 1791	1	34
Anson, s. Matthew & Ruth, b. [ ]	1	21
Betsey, d. Mathew & Ruth, b. July 13, 1789	1	11
Levi, 3rd s. Mathew & Ruth, b. May 31, 1795	1	34
Lydia, 3rd d. Mathew & Ruth, b. Apr. 11, 1801	1	36
Polly Barber, 2nd d. Mathew & Ruth, b. Aug. 8, 1797	1	35
Sally, of Canaan, m. Andrew **BARLOW**, Jan. 10, 1821, by R. Emerson	2	2
BLISS, Ralph, of Springfield, m. Mary **THOMPSON**, Aug. 10, [1828], by Rev. R. Emerson	2	8
Ralph, of Springfield, Mass., m. Louisa P. **THOMPSON**, Oct. 13, [1834], by Rev. Joseph Eldredge	2	16
BOLCAM, [see under **BALCOM**]		
BOLLES, Anna, m. Zalmon **PARRET**, May 17, 1821, by Rev. Rufus Babcock, of Colebrook	2	1
BORDEN, [see under **BARDEN**]		
BORDMAN, Rebecka, m. Adna **COWLS**, Oct. 19, 1773	TM	9
BOYD, John, m. Jerusha **HINSDALE**, Dec. 7, [1843], by Rev.		

	Vol.	Page
BOYD, (cont.)		
Joseph Eldredge	2	24
BOYLARD, [see also **BOYLIN**], Sarah J., d. Michael, b. Jan. 14, 1849	2	51
BOYLIN, [see also **BOYLARD**], James, s. Michael, b. May 26, 1850	2	52
Patrick, d. June 16, 1850, ae 53 y.	2	59
BOYNTON, Hiram H., of New Haven, m. Mary E. **MALTBIE**, Nov. 5, 1845, by Rev. Joseph Eldredge	2	26
BRADLEY, Laura, m. W[illia]m **GRANGER**, [, 1821], by R. Emerson	2	2
Sally Maria, m. Solomon **CURTIS**, Oct. 18, [1827], by Rev. R. Emerson	2	8
Tryphena, of Norfolk, m. Augustus **JAMES**, of New Marlborough, Jan. 15, 1832, by Rev. Harmon Ellis, of 1st Bap. Ch.	2	13
BRAMBLE, Mary E., of Norfolk, m. Rev. David **LYMAN**, of Salisbury, July 21, 1846, by Rev. George C. Bancroft	2	25
BRIGGS, A. B., d. Mar. [ ], 1849, ae 15 m.	2	59
A. F., child of W[illia]m, b. Mar. [ ], 1849	2	49
Bert, s. Ander & Judith C., b. Nov. 19, 1847	2	47
BROMLEY, Mary Ann, m. George W. **BALDWIN**, of New Marlboro, Oct. 30, 1849, by Rev. Joseph Eldredge	2	36
Prentice, had d. [ ], b. Aug. 27, 1849	2	49
BRONSON, Asahel F., m. Sarah Ann **ANDRUS**, Sept. 28, 1840, by Rev. A. Bushnell, Jr.	2	20
Frederick, m. Mary **RIGGS**, Apr. 21, 1840, by Rev. J. Eldredge	2	21
John, s. William & Betsy, b. Apr. 5, 1795	1	12a
BROWN, BROW, Aaron, m. Lucy **STURDEVANT**, Nov. 3, 1784	1	12
Aaron, s. Aaron & Lucy, b. Apr. 30, 1789	1	41
Abigals, d. Cornelious, b. July 12, 1750	TM	11
Abigail M., m. Silvanus M. **MO[O]RE**, of New Hartford, Aug. 13, [1837], by Rev. Joseph Eldredge	2	18
Abraham, s. Jonathan & Anne, b. Mar. 30, 1771; d. July 12, 1772	TM	19
Anna, m. David **SAXTON**, Feb. 18, 1802, by Rev. A. R. Robbins	1	44
Anna Maria, d. Jonathan, Jr. & Rosanna, b. Oct. 12, 1792	1	20
Betsey, m. Joseph **HALL**, Jr., [ ], by R. Emerson	2	2
Betty, m. Daniel **BURR**, Oct. 7, 1773	TM	9
Caroline, m. Thomas **MOSES**, Nov. 11, 1839, by Rev. J. Eldredge	2	21
Clarinda, d. Jonathan, Jr. & Rosannah, b. Apr. 2, 1796	1	46
Cornelious, s. Cornelious, b. Jan. 5, 1740	TM	11
Cornelius, d. July 5, 1769	TM	20
Edmond, m. Anna **BURR**, May 9, 1764	TM	7
Edward Quincy, s. Warren L., blacksmith, ae 31 & Sarah		

	Vol.	Page
BROWN, BROW, (cont.)		
Ann, ae 29, b. Nov. 9, 1847	2	43
Eunice C., of Norfolk, m. Samuel **PALMER**, of Goshen, May 9, [1839], by Rev. Grant Powers	2	20
Ezra, s. Aaron & Lucy, b. Nov. 24, 1795	1	41
George, m. Eunice **MOSES**, b. of Norfolk, Mar. 24, 1831, by Rev. Diodate Brockway, of Ellington	2	12
Harriet, d. Jacob & Anna, b. Feb. 1, 1800	1	36
Horrace Stevens, s. Jonathan, Jr. & Rosannah, b. Aug. 6, 1803	1	46
Horace Mathews, s. Jonathan, Jr. & Rosannah, b. July 30, 1806	1	46
Horatio W., d. July 5, 1850, ae 8 y.	2	59
James*, s. Aaron & Lucy, b. Jan. 26, 1801 *("James Sturdivant **BROWN**" in Church Rec.)	1	41
John, m. Eliza **SMITH**, Jan. 18, 1832, by Michael F. Mills, J. P.	2	13
Jonathan, s. Jonathan & Anna, b. Sept. 10, 1765	TM	17
Jonathan, m. Rosanna **STEPHENS**, Mar. 15, 1791	1	13a
Lovina, d. Jonathan, Jr. & Rosannah, b. May 11, 1798	1	45
Lovisa, m. Milo **DYKE**, Jan. 4, 1832, by George Carrington, of Goshen	2	13
Lucy Ann, m. James **GRISWOLD**, July 22, [1841], by Rev. J. Eldredge	2	32
Mary Ann, m. John C. **SAGE**, b. of Norfolk, Sept. 6, 1845, by Rev. Lewis Gunn	2	25
Nathan, s. Jonathan & Anna, b. Nov. 10, 1763	TM	17
Philinda, d. Jonathan & Rosanna, b. Apr. 13, 1794	1	20
Ruben, s. Stephen & Hepsibah, b. May 12, 1768	TM	16
Rhoda, d. Aaraon & Lucy, b. Oct. 12, 1785; d. [ ], 1797	1	41
Rosannah, d. Jonathan, Jr. & Rosannah, b. Oct. 12, 1800	1	46
Samuel, s. Stephen, 2nd, b. Mar. 2, 1773	TM	24
Sarah, d. Cornelious, b. Mar. 15, 1743	TM	11
Seth G., had d. [ ], b. Oct. 5, 1748	2	48
Stephen, s. Cornelious, b. May 12, 1745	TM	11
Stephen, m. Hepsibah **DOWD**, June 12, 1767	TM	7
Stephen, s. Stephen & Hesibah, b. May*, 10, 1770 *(First written "June")	TM	19
Sibel, d. Cornelious, b. Mar. 16, 1748	TM	11
Thomas, d. July 4, 1850, ae 17 y.	2	59
Titus, s. Aaron & Lucy, b. June 2, 1792	1	41
William, d. May 13, 1849, ae 26	2	57
BRUMBLEY, Prentice, of Cornwall, m. Mrs. Mehala **BARSLEY**, of Goshen, Oct. 4, 1830, by Rev. Bradley Selleck	2	10
BULL, Marther*, m. Miles **RIGGS**, Feb. 28, 1775 *(Mss. Copy has "Marther **BELL**")	1	10
Ruth, d. Oct. 1, 1848, ae 101 y.	2	57
BULLARD, John H., m. Mahala **BORDEN**, Feb. [ ], 1826, by Bushell Knapp	2	5
BUNNELL, BUNNEL, Clarissa E., of Norfolk, m. John C.		

	Vol.	Page
BUNNELL, BUNNEL, (cont.)		
MAHON, of Winsted, Nov. 19, 1843, by Rev. Lewis Gunn	2	23
Fra[ ] (?), m. Mary **WHITE**, Dec. 4, 1844, by Rev. Joseph Eldredge	2	24
BURNHAM, Lucy, m. Joel **BEACH**, Feb. 13, 1825, by Rev. R. Emerson	2	6
BURNS, Thomas, d. Sept. 22, 1848, ae 65 y.	2	58
BURR, Aaron, m. Martha **TOBEY**, b. of Norfolk, Dec. 17, 1778, by Rev. A. R. Robbins	1	10
Aaron, s. Aaron & Martha, b. Sept. 19, 1779	1	11a
Aaron, m. Lois **CAMP**, Oct. 23, 1810, by Benjamin Welch	1	44
Anna, m. Edmond **BROWN**, May 9, 1764	TM	7
Asa, s. Oliver & Sarah, b. Dec. 10, 1766	TM	14
Beulah, s. Oliver & Sarah, b. July 31, 1772	TM	22
Caroline, m. Daniel **GRANT**, May 10, 1843, by Rev. Joseph Eldredge	2	24
Charlotte, m. Philip **ROBINSON**, June 17, [1841], by Rev. J. Eldredge	2	21
Daniel, m. Betty **BROWN**, Oct. 7, 1773	TM	9
Daniel, s. Daniel & Betty, b. Mar. 16, 1781	1	11a
Ebenezer, m. Sarah **PHELPS**, Nov. 27, 1760	TM	7
Ebenezer, s. Daniel & Betty, b. Nov. 30, 1791	1	11
Ebenezer, m. Sarah **EVERSON**, July 15, 1800, by Adonijah Strong, J. P.	1	15
Ebenezer, m. Sarah **EVERSON**, July 15, 1800, by Adonijah Strong	1	36
Elisha, 3rd s. Aaron & Martha, b. Feb. 14, 1786	1	39
Elisebeth, d. Daniel & Betty, b. June 16, 1776	1	1
Elizabeth, m. William **OAKLEY**, of Canaan, [Oct.] 24, [1832], by Rev. Joseph Eldredge	2	14
El[l]en T., m. Albert **HORTON**, [Jan.] 9, [1838], by Rev. Joseph Eldredge	2	19
Erastus, m. Nancy **POTTER**, of Canaan, Mar. 24, 1847, by Rev. Joseph Eldredge	2	27
Eunice, d. Daniel & Betty, b. Jan. 14, 1797	1	11a
Eunice, m. Benjamin W. **CRESSEY**, Mar. 4, [1828], by Rev. R. Emerson	2	8
Hannah, m. Luther **BARBER**, Nov. 15, 1761	TM	7
Harriot, 5th d. Aaron & Martha, b. July 7, 1794	1	39
Hepsibah, d. Ebenezer & Sarah, b. Jan. 31, 1767; d. same day	TM	16
Hepsibah, d. Oliver & Sarah, b. Oct. 26, 1768	TM	16
Jerusha, 3rd d. Aaron & Martha, b. June 23, 1790	1	39
Loes, d. Ebenezer & Sarah, b. Apr. 5, 1765	TM	12
Loes, d. Ebenezer, d. Apr. 17, 1766	TM	20
Loes, d. Ebenezer & Sarah, b. [ ]* *(Entry crossed out)	TM	16
Lucy, d. Daniel & Betty, b. July 5, 1774	TM	24

	Vol.	Page
BURR, (cont.)		
Lucy Abilene, d. Ebenezer & Sarah, b. Mar. 30, 1768	TM	16
Lucy Abilene, d. Ebenezer, [ ]* *(Entry crossed out)	TM	16
Martha, 2nd d. Aaron & Martha, b. Apr. 14, 1788	1	39
Martha, d. Silas, farmer, ae 53 & Sarah, ae 42, b. Feb. 16, 1848	2	43
Mary, 4th d. Daniel & Bettey, b. Sept. 28, 1783	1	11a
Mary, m. William HILL, of New Jersey, Mar. 6, [1849], by Rev. Joseph Eldredge	2	33
Mary, ae 31, m. William HILL, ae 32, Mar. [ ], 1849, by Joseph Eldredge	2	32
Mary E., d. Erastus, ae 25 & Nancy, ae 20, b. Feb. 9, 1848	2	46
Nancy, 4th d. Aaron & Martha, b. May 20, 1792	1	39
Oliuer, m. Sarah CAMFIELD, July 9, 1766	TM	7
Oliver, d. Sept. 23, 1848, ae 67 y.	2	58
Rachael, d. Daniel & Betty, b. Aug. 31, 1778	1	11a
Reliance, 1st d. Aaron & Martha, b. Dec. 22, 1783	1	9a
Ruby, d. Daniel & Betty, b. May 2, 1789	1	11
Sarah, d. Ebenezer, Jr. & Sarah, b. May 2, 1762	TM	10
Sarah, m. John BEACH, June 4, 1782, by Rev. Mr. Robbins	1	10
Silus, s. Daniel & Bettey, b. Sept. 19, 1794	1	12
Silas, m. Sarah CALHOUN, Mar. 11, [1835], by Rev. Joseph Eldredge	2	17
Susanah, 4th d. Daniel & Betty, b. July 30, 1785	1	9a
BUTLER, Amanda, d. Jsaac & Hannah, b. July 13, 1779	1	11a
Charles, s. Uri, b. Mar. 12, 1850	2	53
Edwin, m. Eliza GAYLORD, Jan. 15, 1840, by Rev. J. Eldredge	2	21
Egbert T., m. Jennett PORTER, May 1, [1839], by [Rev. Joseph Eldredge]	2	20
Elizabeth, d. Levi, ae 28 & Clarinda E., ae 22, b. June 27, 1848	2	46
Elizur, [s. Hezekiah G.], b. June 11, 1794	2	38
Hannah, d. Jsaac & Hannah, b. Feb. 8, 1776	1	11a
Hezekiah G., [s. Hezekiah G.], b. June 7, 1798	2	38
J. Sullivan, m. Celestia M. GAYLORD, Mar. 8, [1849], by Rev. Joseph Eldredge	2	33
Josiah, m. Livia DEAN, June 16, [1835], by Rev. Joseph Eldredge	2	17
Laura, of Norfolk, m. Starr* CARRINGTON, of Middletown, Aug. 16, 1841, by Michael F. Mills, J. P. *(Note says "Nathan Starr CARRINGTON")	2	21
Mary, m. David STANTON, Dec. 16, 1812	2	1
Mary Merana, [d. Hezekiah G.], b. May 5, 1802	2	38
Merian, m. Amos PEIRCE, May 13, [1841], by Rev. J. Eldredge	2	21
Oliver B., [s. Hezekiah G.], b. Sept. 26, 1791	2	38
Rosanna W., m. H. Edward HUBBARD, Jan. 11, 1843, by		

	Vol.	Page
BUTLER, (cont.)		
Rev. J. Eldredge	2	22
Sarah C., [d. Hezekiah G.], b. June 18, 1789	2	38
Sarah J., d. Edwin, ae 39 & Eliza, ae 31, b. Oct. 9, 1847	2	46
Sullivan, ae 27, m. Celestia M. **GAYLORD,** ae 25, Jan. [,], by Rev. Joseph Eldredge	2	31
William, m. Harriet **MUNSON,** May 29, 1842, by Rev. J. Eldredge	2	22
William, d. Feb. 11, 1849, ae 2 y.	2	58
William G., s. Edwin, b. Nov. 16, 1849	2	51
-----, m. [ ] **COY,** Apr. 10, [1849], by Rev. Joseph Eldredge	2	33
BUTTON, Albert M., s. Joseph M., ae 24 & Frances E., ae 19, b. Feb. 6, 1848	2	46
Joseph, of Tolland, Mass., m. Elvira **PARRET,** of Norfolk, Apr. 24, 1845, by Rev. A. B. Hubbard	2	25
BYRNES, Ann, d. July 16, 1850, ae 53 y.	2	59
CADY, CADEY, Amos, s. Abel & Elisebath, b. Sept. 26, 1772	TM	22
Eunice, 3rd d. Lemuel & Eunice, b. Sept. 12, 1783	1	19
Jacob, 1st s. Lemuel & Eunice, b. July 6, 1781	1	19
Lemuel, m. Eunis **DOUDE,** July 1, 1773	TM	9
Loamni, 1st d. Lemuel & Eunice, b. Aug. 1, 1776	1	19
Lucina, m. George Wilson **FOSTER,** July 11, [1825], by Rev. R. Emerson	2	6
Reuhamah, 2nd d. Lemuel & Eunice, b. Mar. 11, 1779* *(First written "1781")	1	19
CALDER, Caroline, m. Charles **FERGUSON,** Oct. 13, [1832], by Rev. Joseph Eldredge	2	14
CALHOUN, Eliza A., m. Daniel B. **HURLBUT,** Apr. 17, [1837], by Rev. Joseph Eldredge	2	18
Experience J., of Norfolk, m. Alson Henry H. **ANDRUS,** of Colebrook, June 6, 1830, by Azariah Clark	2	10
Sarah, m. Silas **BURR,** Mar. 11, [1835], by Rev. Joseph Eldredge	2	17
CAMP, Abel, m. Caroline **HUMPHREY,** Mar. 1, 1841, by Rev. J. Eldredge	2	21
Ann, m. Charles **HART,** Nov. 22, 1841, by Rev. J. Eldredge	2	22
Charles Wellford, s. Samuel S., ae 47 & Betsey, ae 44, b. July 31, 1848	2	45
Darius, m. Ruth **PARROT,** Nov. 30, [1837], by Rev. Joseph Eldredge	2	19
Frank, s. John E., b. Feb. 16, 1849	2	50
George, m. Julia Ann **SHEFFIELD,** Jan. 21, [1828], by Rev. R. Emerson	2	8
John P., m. Charity A. **HASKINS,** Feb. 25, 1824, by Rev. R. Emerson	2	6
Joseph, m. Mary **MAN,** ae 20, Aug. 22, [1849], by [ ]	2	34
Lois, m. Aaron **BURR,** Oct. 23, 1810, by Benjamin Welch	1	44

NORFOLK VITAL RECORDS 247

	Vol.	Page
CAMP, (cont.)		
Maria S., m. Chancey **FORD**, Mar. 22, 1848, by Rev. Joseph Eldredge	2	28
Maria S., ae 21, of Norfolk, m. Chancy **FORD**, mason, ae 30, of Cornwall, Mar. 22, 1848, by Rev. Joseph Eldredge	2	29
Mary S., m. Julius **RICHARDS**, Apr. 27, 1831, by Frederick Marsh	2	12
Sarah M., m. Philip G. **CURTISS**, Mar. 21, 1850, by Rev. Joseph Eldredge	2	36
Sarah S., ae 19, m. Philip E. **CURTIS**, ae 25, Mar. 21, 1850, by Rev. Joseph Eldredge	2	34
Susan, of Norfolk, m. A. **NICKERSON**, of New Britain, Sept. 29, [1835], by Rev. Joseph Eldredge	2	17
CAMPBELL, Amasa, m. Lucy **WHITE**, Dec. 7, 1834, by Rufus Babcock, of Colebrook	2	16
CANADA, Thomas, m. Mary **WEASNER**, Dec. 1, 1822, by Bushnell Knapp, J. P.	2	3
CANFIELD, CANFELD, CAMFIELD, Elizabeth, m. William H. **AUSTIN**, of New Hartford, Jan. 7, 1845, by Rev. Joseph Eldredge	2	26
Elmore, m. Anna **SAXTON**, Apr. 25, [1838], by Rev. Joseph Eldredge	2	19
Harriet C., m. Hiram **HOTCHKISS**, Dec. 24, 1845, by Rev. Joseph Eldredge	2	26
Lucy R., d. Edward B., b. Nov. 23, 1848	2	50
Lucy R., d. Oct. 14, 1849, ae 10 m.	2	59
Mary M., m. W[illia]m **ELLIS**, [Oct.] 17, [1847], by Rev. Joseph Eldredge	2	28
Naomi, m. Calvin R. **WARD**, b. of Marlboro, Mass., June 14, [1849], by Rev. Joseph Eldredge	2	33
Naoma, ae 32, m. Calvin **WARD**, ae 33, June 20, 1849, by Joseph Eldredge	2	32
Rama, 4th, s. Daniel & Ruth, b. Mar. 27, 1789	1	37
Rufus, 5th s. Daniel & Ruth, b. May 19, 1791	1	37
Samuel, Jr., m. Rebecca **SAXTON**, Apr. 1, 1839, by [Rev. Joseph Eldredge]	2	20
Sarah, m. Oliver **BURR**, July 9, 1766	TM	7
William P., of New Marlboro, m. Nancy **SHEFFIELD**, of Norfolk, Nov. 24, 1845, by Michael F. Mills, J. P.	2	25
CAREY, Ellen, ae 22, m. [ ], June 3, 1850, by Mr. Tucker	2	34
Ellen, d. Jeremiah & Mary, m. Garrett **PEIRCE**, s. Patrick & Mary Ann, June 4, 1850, by Rev. H. Tucker. Witnesses: Richard Peirce & Catharine Carey	2	34
CARRINGTON, Nathan Starr, see Starr **CARRINGTON**	2	21
Starr*, of Middletown, m. Laura **BUTLER**, of Norfolk, Aug. 16, 1841, by Michael F. Mills, J. P. *(Note says "Nathan Starr **CARRINGTON**")	2	21
CASE, Aaron Titus, s. Aaron, b. Dec. 19, 1821	2	38

248 BARBOUR COLLECTION

	Vol.	Page
CASE, (cont.)		
Abijah, m. Thankfull COWLES, Jan. 12, 1784, by Hosea Willcocks, J. P.	1	19
Ann Everit, d. Asahel E. & Huldah A., b. June 25, 1814	2	40
Asahel, s. Asahel & Dorothy, b. Nov.* 8, 1756 *(First written "Sept.")	TM	6
Asahel Everet, s. Asahel & Eunice, b. Mar. 2, 1789; m. Huldah Akin CURTIS, July 7, 1813	2	40
Asenath, d. Asahel & Dorothy, b. Dec. 1, 1760	TM	6
Charlottee, d. Aaron & Lodama, b. Oct. 6, 1808	1	46
Dorathy, d. Asahel & Dorathy, b. Jan. 17, 1755	TM	6
Dorothy P., m. Philo SMITH, Mar. 14, [1820], by R. Emerson	2	2
Fanny, d. Aaron, b. Nov. 27, 1818	2	38
Fanny, m. Asahel G. PHELPS, Nov. 9, [1841], by Rev. J. Eldredge	2	22
Flora, 1st d. Aaron & Lodama, b. Mar. 12, 1796	1	37
Hezekiah, s. Ezra & Mehetable, b. Dec. 9, 1775	1	1
Hiram, 2nd s. Aaron & Lodema, b. June 1, 1812	2	37
Hiram, had s. [ ], b. Apr. [ ], 1849	2	49
Huldah, 2nd d. Asahel E. & Huldah A., b. Feb. 24, 1817	2	40
Huldah, m. Robert M. BEEBE, Aug. 22, 1837, by Rev. Joseph Eldredge	2	18
Joseph, s. Asahel & Dorathy, b. July 22, 1753	TM	6
Lucy Lucretia, d. Aaron, ae 26 & Harriet M., ae 25, b. Oct. 26, 1847	2	44
Lucy Maria, 3rd d. Asahel E. & Huldah A., b. Feb. 6, 1827	2	40
Luy (?), d. Abijah & Thankfull, b. Feb. 11, 1785	1	19
Marcus, s. Aaron & Lodama, b. Oct. 19, 1804	1	41
Mary, d. Aaron, b. June 2, 1815	2	38
Mary, m. Arba ALFORD, of Barkhamstead, [Nov.] 21, [1836], by Rev. Joseph Eldredge	2	18
Rachel, 2nd d. Aaron & Lodama, b. Dec. 25, 1799	1	37
Sarah, d. Asahel & Dorothy, b. Sept. 9, 1758	TM	6
Susan, d. Hiram, ae 36 & Salome, ae 33, b. Apr. 16, 1848	2	45
Sylvia, 3rd, d. Aaron & Lodama, b. Aug. 28, 1801	1	37
Sylvia, m. Robbins STILLMAN, of Colebrook, Mar. 1, 1826, by Rev. R. Emerson	2	6
CASSON, Sam[ue]l S., of Bethleham, m. Almira GAYLORD, Dec. 9, 1824, by Rev. R. Emerson	2	6
CATEBY, Mary Ann, m. Orrange GILBERT, b. of Goshen, Aug. 26, 1834, by Rev. Thomas Sparkes	2	16
CATLIN, CATLEN, Elizabeth, m. John ROGERS, May 4, 1826, by Rufus Babcock, of Colebrook	2	5
Henry, m. Theodosia HAWLEY, Nov. 29, 1827, by Rufus Babcock, of Colebrook	2	7
Lewis, ae 33, m. Sarah M. HOTCHKISS, ae 27, Nov. 30, 1848, by Rev. Joseph Eldredge	2	31
Lewis, of Canaan, m. Sarah M. HOTCHHKISS, [ ] 31,		

	Vol.	Page
CATLIN, CATLEN, (cont.)		
[1848], by Rev. Joseph Eldredge	2	33
Ruth, m. Butler **MINER**, Dec. 25, 1823, by Rufus Babcock	2	4
Sarah Lydia, d. Lewis, b. Feb. 6, 1850	2	53
[CAULKINS], CAUKINS, John, m. [ ] **LOCKWOOD**, Nov. 17, [1833], by Rev. Joseph Eldredge	2	14
CAY, Lucy*, m. Samuell **MILLS**, Jr., b. of Norfolk, Feb. 29, 1776, by Giles Pettibone *(Perhaps "Lucy **COY**")	1	11
CHAPIN, Prudence, of New Marlboro, m. William W. **DOWD**, of Norfolk, May 1, 1843, by Rev. A. B. Hubbard	2	23
Samuel D., of Somers, m. Sally W. **PHELPS**, [May] 28, [1829], by Rev. R. Emerson	2	8
CHASE, Philena, m. W[illia]m H. **WALTER**, b. of Norfolk, Jan. 19, 1843, by Rev. A. B. Hubbard	2	21
CHITTENDEN, Josiah, m. Charity **HOLCOM**, Jan. 26, 1775	TM	9
CLAPP, Lyman, of Bu[r]lington, m. Lucia **COWLES**, Jan. 31, 1826, by Rev. R. Emerson	2	6
-----, Mrs., m. Jeremiah **WEED**, of Sharon, Aug. 13, 1834, by Rev. Joseph Eldredge	2	16
CLARK, CLERK, Ebi, Rev. of Winchester, m. Sarah **LAWRENCE**,	2	14
Sept. 19, 1832, by Rev. Joseph Eldredge		
Job Rathbone, made affidavit Apr. 18, 1772, that Samuel **KNAP** & s. Elaxander were members of Bap. Ch., in Canaan & New Marlborough that they are bap. persons by immersion and have attended worship for about 2 y.	TM	8
Jonathan, of Guilford, Chanango Cty, N. Y.,,, m. Sarah **MOORE**, of Norfolk, Oct. [ ], 1824, by Bushnell Knapp, J. P.	2	5
Marietta, ae 26, m. Edward **KIMBERLEY**, ae 23, Oct. 1, 1850, by Rev. Joseph Eldredge	2	35
Mary J., m. Edward **KIMBERLY**, of Goshen, [ ], 1849, by Rev. Joseph Eldredge	2	33
CLEMMONS, CLEMEN, CLEMENS, Jane, ae 21, m. Thomas **McDERMOTT**, ae 25, Mar. [ ], 1850, by Harlow Ray	2	35
Philo, of Granby, m. Annice **WILCOX**, Jan. 6, 1828, by Rev. R. Emerson	2	8
Rhoda L., of Hartland, m. Sylvester **TERRALL**, of Norfolk, Dec. 29, 1831, by Azariah Clark	2	13
COBB, Lydia, ae 22, m. A. Wheeler **HARLEY**, ae 23, Mar. 6, 1849, by Amos D. Waters	2	32
	1	10
COE, Martha, m. John **WHEELER**, Mar. 12, 1770		
COITT, Heman, of Goshen, m. Eliza **BALDWIN**, Feb. 25, [1828], by Rev. R. Emerson	2	8
COLDEN, [see also **GOLDEN**], Charlotte, m. W[illia]m **HYDURIN**, Apr. 25, [1835], by Rev. Joseph Eldredge	2	17
COLLAR, Almiria L., of New Marlboro, Mass., m. Romulus **HAWLEY**, of Winsted, Mar. 16, 1845, by Rev. A. B.	2	25

	Vol.	Page
COLLAR, (cont.)		
Mary M., m. Franklin B. **MILLARD**, b. of New Marlboro, Mass., Jan. 12, 1845, by Rev. A. B. Hubbard	2	24
COLLINS, Squire, of Torrington, m. Fanny **KNAPP**, Sept. 28, [1832], by Rev. Joseph Eldredge	2	14
COMSTOCK, Martha, m. Abram **KNAP[P]**, Jan. 27, 1756	TM	7
Pattee, d. Serajah & Anna, b. Aug. 5, 1763	1	43
Peter, s. Peter & Sarah, b. Nov. 19, 1777	1	2
CONE, Elizabeth, m. Payne K. **KILBOURNE**, Aug. 3, 1842, by Rev. J. Eldredge	2	22
John, m. Harriet **WATSON**, Oct. 13, [1841], by Rev. J. Eldredge	2	22
COOE, Jerusha, m. John **LUKUS**, Dec. 5, 1765	TM	7
COOK, Caroline H., m. Warren **JOHNSON**, Sept. 9, 1841, by Rev. J. Eldredge	2	22
John R., of Winsted, m. Marietta A. **PHELPS**, Oct. 15, 1845, by Rev. Joseph Eldredge	2	26
Silvia, m. Matiah **STANNARD**, Apr. 20, 1840, by Rev. J. Eldredge	2	21
COOPER, Alfred, m. Julia **BILLS**, Mar. 2, 1836, by Rev. Joseph Eldredge	2	17
COTTON, Micheil, m. Mindwill **THRALL**, Oct. 29, 1783, by Hos. Willcocks, J. P.	1	3a
Michael, Jr., s. Michael & Mindwill, b. Sept. 17, 1784	1	3a
COUCH, Eliza P., m. Lorenzo **WHITING**, Jan. 15, 1844, by Rev. Joseph Eldredge	2	24
Rachel, 3rd d. Thomas & Rachel, b. Feb. 18, 1795	1	36
COWLES, COWLS, COULS, Abigail F., m. Joel **GRANT**, Oct. 12, 1845, by Rev. Joseph Eldredge	2	26
Adna, m. Submit **GRAVES**, Mar. 7, 1768	TM	7
Adna, m. Rebecka **BORDMAN**, Oct. 19, 1773	TM	9
Amasa, s. Amasa & Lucey, b. Apr. 22, 1771	TM	18
Asahel, s. Amasa & Lucy, b. Jan. 20, 1777	1	1
Clarissa, d. Noah & Olbe (?)*, b. Dec. 8, 1781 *(Note says "Olle")	1	3
Ebenezer, s. Daniel & Huldah, b. Mar. 7, 1767	1	2
Ebenezer, s. Ebenezer & Mercy, b. Aug. 13, 1768	TM	19
Edward, m. Harriet M. **GAYLORD**, May 9, 1844, by Rev. Joseph Eldredge	2	24
Enos, s. Samuel, Jr. & Sibel, b. Jan. 26, 1778	1	2
Eunis, m. Samuel **BARBER**, Mar. 24, 1762	TM	7
Fanna, m. William **PHELPS**, b. of Norfolk, Apr. 10, 1832, by Rev. Frederick Marsh, of Winchester	2	13
Henry, Rev. of Colebrook, m. Alice **WELCH**, of Norfolk, July 27, 1830, by Azariah Clark	2	10
Henry, d. Feb. 6, 1850	2	59
Jra, 1st s. Amasa & Lucy, b. June 18, 1768	TM	15
Jsrael, s. Ebenezer & Mercy, b. Jan. 4, 1771	TM	19

	Vol.	Page
COWLES, COWLS, COULS, (cont.)		
James M., m. Julia **BALDWIN**, Mar. 10, 1830, by Rev. George Carrington, of Goshen	2	9
Jemima, had s. Zebediah, b. Jan. 14, 1784; f. Zebediah **JONSON**	1	3a
Joseph, m. Sarah **MILLS**, June 18, 1771	TM	7
Joseph Brooks, s. Joseph & Sarah, b. June 27, 1774	TM	24
Josiah, s. Samuel, Jr. & Sibbel, b. May 20, 1774	TM	23
Levy, d. Aug. 29, 1774	TM	21
Lucia, m. Lyman **CLAPP**, of Bu[r]lington, Jan. 31, 1826, by Rev. R. Emerson	2	6
Noah, m. Olbe* **MILLS**, b. of Norfolk, Dec. 14, 1780, by Rev. Mr. A. M. Robbins *(Written over "Olle")	1	10
Olive, d. Amasa & Luse, b. Feb. 5, 1774	TM	24
Rachel*, 2nd d. Adna & Rebeckah, b. Apr. 16, 1778 *(Written "Rachel **COLE**")	1	1
Rebackah, d. Adna & Rebackah, b. Sept. 18, 1784	1	7
Riley, of Norfolk, m. Elizabeth J. **HAMILTON**, of Toland, Mass., Dec. 15, 1844, by Rev. A. B. Hubbard	2	24
Samuel, d. Feb. 22, 1762	TM	14
Samuel, s. Samuel & Sibbel, b. Mar. 11, 1769	TM	16
Samuel, s. Samuel, Jr., d. Jan. 1, 1770	TM	20
Samuel, s. Samuel, Jr. & Sible, b. Mar. 12, 1771	TM	18
Samuel, s. Joseph & Sarah, b. June 8, 1776	TM	24
Sarah, d. Joseph & Sarah, b. Apr. 10, 1772	TM	22
Sophronia, m. Alva **SEYMOUR**, of Colebrook, Mar. 16, 1825, by Rev. R. Emerson	2	6
Submit, d. Adna & Rebecka, b. May 16, 1776	TM	24
Thankfull, d. Samuel & Sibbel, b. June 26, 1767	TM	14
Thankfull, m. Abijah **CASE**, Jan. 12, 1784, by Hosea Willcocks, J. P.	1	19
Thomas J.*, m. Louisa **ROCKWELL**, Aug. 31, [1828], by Rev. R. Emerson *(Written over "Trumbull")	2	8
Zilpah, m. Joel **GRANT**, Jan. 3, 1782	1	19
COY, Anna, m. Raswell **GRANT**, Mar. 24, 1784, by Rev. Am R. Robbins	1	10
Lucy, see Lucy **CAY**	1	11
-----, m. [ ] **BUTLER**, Apr. 10, [1849], by Rev. Joseph Eldredge	2	33
COYNE, James, m. Sarah **O'BRIEN**, Jan. 4, 1850, by Harlow Roy	2	34
CRISSEY, CRESSEY, CRESSY, Benjamin W., m. Eunice **BURR**, Mar. 4, [1828], by Rev. R. Emerson	2	8
Mehetable, m. Seth **BARBER**, May 24, [1820], by R. Emerson	2	2
Olive, of Norfolk, m. Seth **BARBER**, of Conder, N. Y., Jan. 30, 1831, by Rev. Henry Robinson	2	11
CROFUT, Comfort, ae 65, of Canaan, m. Mrs. Prudence C. **DOWD**, ae 37, of New Marlboro, Mass., Dec. 31, 1848, by Rev. C. W. Watrous	2	30

BARBOUR COLLECTION

	Vol.	Page
CURTIS, CURTISS, Anna, 1st d. Solomon & Huldah, b. Feb. 23, 1784	1	9a
Charlotte, d. Gideon & Pol[l]y, b. May 21, 1799	1	41
Cyrus, s. Thomas, b. Mar. 21, 1767	TM	15
Cyrus, m. Editha **MILLS**, b. of Norfolk, Apr. 19, 1789, by Dudley Humphry, J. P.	1	12
Gideon, m. Polly **RICE**, Sept. 14, 1797, by Rev. R. Robbins	1	13a
Henry, d. Feb. 23, 1849, ae 61 y.	2	58
Henry Akins, 2nd, s. Solomon & Huldah, b. Dec. 19, 1787	1	6
Henry Thomas, s. Thomas, b. June 17, 1850	2	51
Huldah, d. Solomon & Huldah, b. Sept. 1, 1790	1	11
Huldah Akin, m. Asahel Everet **CASE**, s. Asahel & Eunice, July 7, 1813	2	40
Isaac Sweet, s. Gideon & Polly, b. Mar. 23, 1801	1	41
Marther, wid., m. Richard **LIWIS**, Nov. 3, 1778	1	7
Mary, d. Thomas & Mather, b. Dec. 16, 1774	1	11
Mary, d. Gideon & Polly, b. Nov. 12, 1803	1	41
Peter, s. Thomas, b. Feb. 18, 1815	2	38
Philip E., ae 25, m. Sarah S. **CAMP**, ae 19, Mar. 21, 1850, by Rev. Joseph Eldredge	2	34
Philip G., m. Sarah M. **CAMP**, Mar. 21, 1850, by Rev. Joseph Eldredge	2	36
Sarah, [d. Thomas], b. Feb. 1, 1818	2	38
Solom[on], m. Hulday **AKINS**, Aug. 13, 1783	1	7
Solomon, s. Solomon, decd, & Huldah, b. Aug. 20, 1796	1	34
Solomon, m. Sally Marie **BRADLEY**, Oct. 18, [1827], by Rev. R. Emerson	2	8
Thomas, d. Aug. 18, 1776	1	5
Thomas, 1st s. Solomon & Huldah, b. Dec. 6, 1785	1	9a
Thomas S., ae 27, m. Mary White **DOWD**, ae 25, Mar. 20, 1849, by Rev. Mr. Curtiss	2	31
DABOT, Mary, ae 22, m. Henry **HOLT**, ae 23, Sept. 28, 1847, by Rev. Mr. Goodwin	2	30
DANFORTH, Julian, m. Maria **PLUMB**, (colored), Oct. 2, 1837, by Rev. Joseph Eldredge	2	19
DANWELL, Emeline, of Colebrook, m. W[illia]m H. **SEYMOUR**, Nov. 28, [1833], by Rev. Joseph Eldredge	2	15
DARBE, Eben[eze]r, 2nd s. Moses & Dorothy, b. July 17, 1786	1	11
Samuell, s. Moses & Dorothy, b. July 21, 1784	1	3a
Sarah, 1st d. Moses & Dorothy, b. Nov. 15, 1782	1	3a
DEAN, DEANE, Abigal, 3rd, d. Joseph & Sarah, b. Aug. 28, 1764	TM	12
Anna, d. Joseph & Sarah, b. Feb. 23, 1760	TM	6
Azubah, d. Jonathan & Patience, b. Aug. 20, 1760	TM	10
Fanny, of Norfolk, m. Sidney **MANSFIELD**, of Canaan, Apr. 24, 1845, by Harley Goodwin	2	25
Joseph, s. Joseph & Sarah, b. Aug. 14, 1762	TM	11
Lydia, m. Osee **ROYS**, Sept. 8, 1785, by Rev. Jonathan Lee	1	10
Livia, m. Josiah **BUTLER**, June 16, [1835], by Rev. Joseph		

	Vol.	Page
DEAN, DEANE, (cont.)		
Eldredge	2	17
Olive, m. J. W. **PHELPS**, Jr., Nov. 21, [1821], by R. Emerson	2	2
Samuel, s. Joseph & Sarah, b. July 12, 1772	TM	22
Sarah, d. Joseph & Sarah, b. Dec. 10, 1769	TM	17
DECKER, Albert, s. Albert, manufacturer, ae 31 & Malinda, ae 34, b. July 26, 1847	2	42
James, m. Mabel **ORVIS**, Aug. 27, 1829, by Rev. Rufus Babcock, of Colebrook	2	7
DENNIS, Alfred L., m. Eliza A. **SHEPARD**, Sept. 14, 1841, by Rev. J. Eldredge	2	22
DEWITT, John, m. Mary **HUMPHREY**, Jan. 1, 1826, by Rev. R. Emerson	2	6
DIBBLE, Thankful, m. Seth **DONOLDS**, b. of Canaan, Dec. 10, 1839, by Michael F. Mills, J. P.	2	20
DICKINSON, DICKENSON, Charles Fredrick, 1st s. Charles F. & Abigail, b. Feb. 7, 1803	1	37
Lemira, 2nd d. Charles F. & Abigail, b. Sept. 14, 1800	1	37
Loes, d. Thomas & Mary, b. Apr. 20, 1762	TM	11
Lois, d. Samuel **DICKINSON** & Polly **LEE**, b. June 5, 1799	1	37
Thomas, m. Mary **STEPHENS**, June 25, 1760	TM	7
Thomas, s. Thomas & Marey, b. Feb. 15, 1764	TM	11
William Samuel, s. Thomas & Mary, b. May 4, 1766	TM	13
DIXON, John, of Sheffield, m. Huldah **JOHNSON**, Mar. 4, [1847], by Rev. Joseph Eldredge	2	27
DOCHESTER, Daniel, m. Live (?) **HAWLEY**, Oct. 31, [ ], by Asahel Humphry, J. P.	1	15
DONOLD, DONOLDS, J. H., ae 21, m. [ ], Nov. 7, 1848, by Rev. Joseph Eldredge	2	31
Seth, m. Thankful **DIBBLE**, b. of Canaan, Dec. 10, 1839, by Michael F. Mills, J. P.	2	20
DOOLITTLE, Sallah, m. Abiel **WEDBSTER**, Sept. 28, 1820, by Elder Rufus Babcock. Witness: David Doolittle	2	1
----, m. Mary **HOLT**, June [ ], 1831, by Amos Pettibone, J. P.	2	12
DORMAN, Louisa, m. George W. **BEACH**, Oct. 5, 1823, by Rev. R. Emerson	2	6
DOWD, DOUD, DOUDE, Betsey, of Norfolk, m. Jonathan **GILLETT**, of Kingsville, Ashtubula Co., O., Oct. 23, 1851, by Rev. Elisha Whittlesey	2	35
Content, m. Ebenezer **NORTON**, Dec. 24, 1769	TM	7
Currants, w. John, d. Apr. 3, 1807	1	14
Eli, 3rd s. Theodore & Hannah, b. Mar. 24, 1798	1	35
Elizur, m. Rebecca **AKINS**, [Mar.] 31, [1834], by Rev. Joseph Eldredge	2	15
Eunis, m. Lemuel **CADY**, July 1, 1773	TM	9
Hepsibah, m. Stephen **BROWN**, June 12, 1767	TM	7
Hiram, 2nd s. Theodore & Hannah, b. Feb. 10, 1796	1	35
Lent, s. Theodore & Hanna, b. May 19, 1794	1	21

	Vol.	Page
DOWD, DOUD, DOUDE, (cont.)		
Mabel, m. Isaac **HOLT**, May 8, 1764	TM	7
Mary White, ae 25, m. Thomas S. **CURTISS**, ae 27, Mar. 20, 1849, by Rev. Mr. Curtiss	2	31
Noah, s. Cornelis & Thankful, b. Feb. 4, 1763	TM	11
Prudence C., Mrs. ae 37 of New Marlboro, Mass., m. Comfort **CROFUT**, ae 65, of Canaan, Dec. 31, 1848, by Rev. C. W. Watrous	2	30
Thankfull, d. Limwel & Eunis, b. May 9, 1774	TM	24
Theodore, m. Hannah **BARBER**, b. of Norfolk, Mar. 26, 1793, by Ammi R. Robbins	1	12a
William W., m. Juliann **BANDELL**, Mar. 7, 1830, by Bushnell Knapp, J. P.	2	9
William W., of Norfolk, m. Prudence **CHAPIN**, of New Marlboro, May 1, 1843, by Rev. A. B. Hubbard	2	23
DRAKELY, Robert, m. Louisa **VANHOESER**, Jan. 28, 1841, by Rev. J. Eldredge	2	21
DUDLEY, Sibbil, m. Nathan **LEE**, Aug. 19, 1773	1	37
DUETT, Humphrey, m. Cynthia **HITCHCOCK**, of Colebrook, Nov. 7, [1848], by Rev. Joseph Eldredge	2	33
DUNBAR, Emeline, ae 20, m. Warren P. **HURLBUT**, ae 23, Apr. 16, 1850, by Joseph Eldredge	2	35
Emeline M., of Torringford, m. Warren P. **HURLBUT**, of Winsted, Apr. 16, 1850, by Rev. Joseph Eldredge	2	36
DUNHAM, Charlotte, of Canaan, m. Henry **JOHNSON**, Nov. 4, 1849, by Rev. Joseph Eldredge	2	36
Esther, d. Feb. 12, 1850, ae 81 y.	2	60
DUTTON, Jane, m. Rodney **PEARSE**, Aug. 30, 1841, by Rev. J. Eldredge	2	22
Sarah, wid., d. Jan. 30, 1818	2	55
Thankfull, m. Erastus **HALL**, b. of Norfolk, Oct. 6, 1830, by Azariah Clark	2	10
DYKE, Milo, m. Lovisa **BROWN**, Jan. 4, 1832, by George Carrington, of Goshen	2	13
Milo, m. Martha **GRISWOLD**, [Mar.] 15, [1846], by Rev. Joseph Eldredge	2	26
EDGECOMB, Sophia, m. Jesse **ALVORD**, Oct. 26, 1842, by Rev. J. Eldredge	2	22
[EGGLESTON], EGGSLESTON, EGSLESTON, Guestus, m. Clarriss **STURTEVANT**, Mar. 25, 1824, by Rev. R. Emerson	2	6
Rufus, of Torrington, m. Sally **STAFFORD**, [Jan.] 23, [1828], by Rev. R. Emerson	2	8
ELDREDGE, Azariah, ae 29, m. Ellen **BARTLETT**, ae 24, June 20, 1849, by Rev. Joseph Eldredge	2	31
Azariah, of New Bedford, m. Ellen **BARTLETT**, [June] 20, [1849], by Rev. Joseph Eldredge	2	33
Irene, [d. Rev. Joseph & Sarah], b. July 27, 1840	2	41

NORFOLK VITAL RECORDS 255

	Vol.	Page
ELDREDGE, (cont.)		
Isabella P., d. Joseph, clergyman, ae 43 & Sarah, ae 37, b. Apr. 10, 1848	2	42
Isabella Purple, d. Joseph & Sarah, b. Apr. 10, 1848	2	41
Joseph, Rev., of Norfolk, m. Sarah **BATTELL**, of Norfolk, [Oct.] 12, [1836], by Frances L. Robbins	2	17
Joseph Battall, s. Joseph & Sarah, b. Mar. 6, 1845	2	41
Mary, [d. Rev. Joseph & Sarah], b. May 14, 1842	2	41
Sarah, d. Rev. Joseph & Sarah, b. Nov. 11, 1837	2	41
ELLIOTT, W.*, m. Clarissa E. **ROYS**, June 26, 1848, by Rev. Joseph Eldredge *(Perhaps "Elliot **WOODWARD**")	2	28
ELLIS, W[illia]m, m. Mary M. **CANFIELD**, [Oct.] 17, [1847], by Rev. Joseph Eldredge	2	28
EMMONS, Horace, m. Lucy **ROY**, [Mar.] 12, [1828], by Rev. R. Emerson	2	8
ENSIGN, Edward, m. Maria **WOOLCOT**, Oct. 1, [1849], by Rev. Joseph Eldredge	2	33
EVANS, Ruth, had illeg. s. [ ], b. Sept. 5, 1848	2	50
Ruth, ae 38, m. Ichabod **PARSONS**, ae 54, Oct. 1, 1848, by Rev. Joseph Eldredge	2	31
Ruth, m. Ichabod **PARSONS**, [ ], 1848, by Rev. Joseph Eldredge	2	33
----, of Canaan, m. Ruth **BORDEN**, [Mar.] 31, [1833], by Rev. Joseph Eldredge	2	14
EVERRIT, Mary, of Woodbury, m. David **FRISBIE**, of Norfolk, Dec. 5, 1776, by Rev. Joseph Bellamy	1	10
EVERSON, Sarah, m. Ebenezer **BURR**, July 15, 1800, by Adonijah Strong, J. P.	1	15
Sarah, m. Ebenszer **BURR**, July 15, 1800, by Adonijah Strong	1	36
FARLEY, Julia, d. Matthew, ae 34 & Julia, ae 24, b. May [ ] 1848	2	47
FELLOWS, Lucy, m. Thomas J. **SACKET**, June 26, [1821], by R. Emerson	2	2
FERGUSON, Charles, m. Caroline **CALDER**, Oct. 13, [1832], by Rev. Joseph Eldredge	2	14
FERRY, Joseph, Jr., m. Lois **WILLCOCK**, Apr. 5, 1803, by Rev. R. Robbins	1	13a
Truman, s. Joseph & Lois, b. Feb. 25, 1804	1	41
FINCH, Ezra, s. Elias S., ae 41 & Harriet, ae 37, b. July [ ], 1848	2	46
FINKLE, Egbert Erwin, s. Egbert, colier, ae 33 & Katharine, ae 31, b. Mar. 15, 1848	2	44
John A., s. Egbert, b. Mar. 10, 1850	2	52
FITCH, Ezekiel, of New Marlboro, Mass., m. Betsey **PRATT**, of Canaan, Jan. 1, 1834, by Rev. Theron Ellis, of Bap. Ch.	2	15
FOOT[E], Almira Mills, d. Asa & Sarah, b. June 25, 1788	1	39
Amasa, s. Asa & Sarah, b. June 27, 1786	1	39
Dorinda, d. Apr. 29, 1850, ae 58 y.	2	60
Ezra, m. Clarissa **BEACH**, of Goshen, June 3, [1829], by Rev. R. Emerson	2	8

256 BARBOUR COLLECTION

	Vol.	Page
FOOT[E], (cont.)		
Lauren B., m. Abigail **MOSES**, Apr. 7, [1829], by Rev. R. Emerson	2	8
Luman, of Canaan, m. Maria **RIGGS**, of Norfolk, Sept. 25, 1844, by Alfred E. Ives	2	23
Miles, m. Sarah **SMITH**, May 16, [1837], by Rev. Joseph Eldredge	2	18
Plinney, ae 61, m. Ann **MOSES**, ae 35, Aug. 19, 1850, by Joseph Eldredge	2	35
Pliney, m. Ann **MOSES**, of Canaan, Aug. 19, 1850, by Rev. Joseph Eldredge	2	36
FORD, Chancey, m. Maria S. **CAMP**, Mar. 22, 1848, by Rev. Joseph Eldredge	2	28
Chancy, mason, ae 30, of Cornwall, m. Maria S. **CAMP**, ae 21, of Norfolk, Mar. 22, 1848, by Rev. Joseph Eldredge	2	29
FOSTER, George Wilson, m. Lucina **CADY**, July 11, [1825], by Rev. R. Emerson	2	6
Paulina, m. Chancey **GAYLORD**, Nov. 14, [1827], by Rev. R. Emerson	2	8
FOX, David, m. Rhoda **NORTHWAY**, July 4, 1822, by Bushnell Knapp, J. P.	2	3
John, m. Eliza **YOUNG**, Apr. 11, 1830, by Rufus Babcock, of Colebrook	2	9
FRAZIER, Morris, had twin, s. [ ], b. June 24, 1849	2	49
FREEBOURN, Amanda U., m. Andrew **VANNESS**, May 19, [1838], by Rev. Joseph Eldredge	2	19
FREEDOM, Barnard, s. Victor, b. Feb. 26, 1798	2	38
FREEMAN, Anthony, s. Anthony, laborer, colored, ae 32 & Lucy ae 33, b. July 12, 1848	2	43
FRENCH, Lepha, m. Spencer **PEACE**, Jan. 11, 1841, by Rev. J. Eldredge	2	21
Polly Maria, m. William **PEASSE**, Oct. 28, 1841, by Rev. J. Eldredge	2	22
Ryley, m. Diantha **KNAPP**, May 5, 1822, by Bushnell Knapp, J. P.	2	3
FRISBIE, FRISBEE, Caroline C., ae 30, m. Jeremiah **JOHNSON**, ae 36, Oct. 30, [1849], by John F. Norton	2	32
David, of Norfolk, m. Mary **EVERRIT**, of Woodbury, Dec. 5, 1776, by Rev. Joseph Bellamy	1	10
David, 2nd s. David & Mary, b. Jan. 10, 1785	1	6
Jrene, 2nd d. David & Mary, b. Mar. 5, 1780	1	6
John Colven, 1st s. David & Mary, b. Feb. 13, 1783	1	6
Martain Luther, 3rd, s. David & Mary, b. May 24, 1787	1	6
Olive Steal, 1st d. David & Mary, b. Aug. 29, 1778	1	6
Polly, m. Hervey **LEWIS**, July 24, [1827], by Rev. R. Emerson	2	8
GAINS, James, s. Levi & Mary, b. [ ], 1848	2	47
GAYLORD, GAYAYLORD, Abiram, m. Jerusha **LEWIS**, Nov.		

NORFOLK VITAL RECORDS 257

	Vol.	Page
GAYLORD, GAYAYLORD, (cont.)		
14, 1822, by Rev. R. Emerson	2	6
Almira, m. Sam[ue]l S. **CASSON**, of Bethleham, Dec. 9, 1824, by Rev. R. Emerson	2	6
Amasa, s. Roys & Sarah, b. Aug. 27, 1769	TM	17
Amasa, s. Amasa & Mindwell, b. July 23, 1794	1	46
Amon, s. Edward & Welthena, b. Aug. 28, 1766	TM	24
Andrew J., s. Anson, ae 48 & Jenette J., ae 39, b. July 17, 1848	2	47
Celestia M., ae 25, m. Sullivan **BUTLER**, ae 27, Jan. [ ], by Rev. Joseph Eldredge	2	31
Celestia M., m. J. Sullivan **BUTLER**, Mar. 8, [1849], by Rev. Joseph Eldredge	2	33
Chancey, m. Paulina **FOSTER**, Nov. 14, [1827], by Rev. R. Emerson	2	8
Dame, d. Justus & Elesebeth, b. Nov. 4, 1766	TM	14
Edward, m. Welthana **HOPKINS**, Oct. 31, 1765	TM	9
Elezer, s. Justus & Elesebeth, b. Sept. 26, 1768	TM	15
Eliza, m. Edwin **BUTLER**, Jan. 15, 1840, by Rev. J. Eldredge	2	21
Ezekiel, s. Edward & Welthena, b. Aug. 28, 1768	TM	24
Giles, s. Amasa & Mindwell, b. Jan. 9, 1796; d. Feb. 9, 1797	1	46
Giles, s. Amasa & Mindwell, b. Jan. 17, 1800	1	46
Harriet M., m. Edward **COWLES**, May 9, 1844, by Rev. Joseph Eldredge	2	24
Hariel Ursula, d. Amasa & Mindwell, b. Apr. 16, 1802	1	46
Jsaac, s. Edward & Welthena, b. Mar. 29, 1771	TM	24
Jemimah, 3rd, d. Justus, b. Apr. 16, 1760	TM	10
Jerusha, m. Miron **LORING**, of New Marlboro, Jan. 1, 1833, by Rev. Joseph Eldredge	2	14
Joseph, m. Rachel **TIBBALS**, Apr. 27, 1766	TM	7
Laura, m. Charles **STONE**, Oct. 25, [1843], by Rev. Joseph Eldredge	2	24
Lodame, d. Justus & Elisibeth, b. Aug. 5, 1764	TM	12
Loes, d. Timothy & Lydia, b. Apr. 30, 1764	TM	12
Louisa, m. Hiram **MILLS**, Apr. 3, 1823, by Rev. R. Emerson	2	6
Lucenda, d. Edward & Welthena, b. Sept. 18, 1773	TM	24
Lud, 3rd s. Justus & Elisabeth, b. Mar. 26, 1762	TM	10
Lydia, d. Timothy & Lydia, b. Mar. 17, 1762	TM	12
Lydia, m. Hiram **MILLS**, [Apr.] 26, [1829], by Rev. R. Emerson	2	8
Maria, m. Albert **HART**, May 19, 1842, by Rev. J. Eldredge	2	22
Miron, s. Amasa & Mindwell, b. Feb. 27, 1793	1	46
Munson, s. Timothy, 2nd & Rosannah, b. Oct. 21, 1772	TM	19
Salley, m. Alvin **WATSON**, Oct. 25, 1797, by Asahel Humphry, J. P.	1	15
Samuel Norton, s. Roys & Sarah, b. Mar. 1, 1773	TM	22
Sarah Melissa, d. Amasa & Mindwell, b. Feb. 19, 1798	1	46
Timothy, s. Roys & Sarah, b. Feb. 28, 1775	TM	24

	Vol.	Page
GAYLORD, GAYAYLORD, (cont.)		
Timothy, 3rd, m. Sally **WHITE**, Apr. 17, 1822, by R. Emerson	2	2
Timothy, d. May 7, 1848, ae 73	2	56
Wait, s. Ross & Sarah, b. Apr. 19, 1768	TM	15
GEER, Robert A., ae 40, of Ledgward, m. 2nd w. Gennett **MURRY,** ae 30, of Winchester, Dec. 2, 1847, by Frederick Marsh	2	29
Robert A., had s. [ ], b. June 15, 1849	2	48
GILBERT, Aaron, m. Maria M. **ROBBINS,** b. of Norfolk, Aug. 8, 1831, by Pitkin Cowles	2	12
James, farmer, ae 23, m. Lucy M. **ROYS,** ae 24, Oct. 17, 1847, by Mr. Zell	2	29
Mariann M., d. James, b. Nov. 19, 1849	2	52
Mary E., d. Aaron, b. Feb. 14, 1850	2	51
Orrange, m. Mary Ann **CATEBY,** b. of Goshen, Aug. 26, 1834, by Rev. Thomas Sparkes	2	16
GILLETT, GILLET, Jonathan, of Kingsville, Ashtubula Co., O., m. Betsey **DOWD,** of Norfolk, Oct. 23, 1851, by Rev. Elisha Whittlesey	2	35
Mamre, m. Bile **BISHOP,** Oct. 15, 1761	TM	7
Newman B., of Winchester, m. Jane **BECKLEY,** Oct. 26, 1845, by Rev. Joseph Eldredge	2	26
Samuel, m. Lidian L. **STANNARD,** Sept. 2, 1840, by Rev. J. Eldredge	2	21
Sarah A., m. Nathan W. **ATWOOD,** Mar. 14, 1822, by R. Emerson	2	2
GINGILL, GINGELL, Robert P., s. Richard, b. Jan. 1, 1849	2	47
William, ae 21, of Norfolk, m. Mary Ann **WILLIAMS,** ae 16, of New Marlboro, Mass., Sept. 24, 1848, by Rev. C. W. Watrous	2	28
William, ae 21, m. Mary **WILLIAMS,** ae 17, Sept. 29, 1848, by C. W. Watrous	2	32
GLEASON, Edwin, of New Marlborough, m. Lucretia **SACKET,** May 1, [1828], by Rev. R. Emerson	2	8
Emeline, m. Theron **ALLEN,** Oct. [ ], 1823, by Bushnell Knapp, J. P.	2	4
GOLDEN, [see also **COLDEN**], Mary Ann, d. Patrick, b. June 13, 1850	2	53
[GOODWIN], GOODWINE, Mary, d. Thomas & Silance, b. May 18, 1760	TM	10
Thomas, m. Silance [ ], Oct. 26, 1759	TM	7
GORHAM, Abigail Foot, m. Noah **MINER,** [Nov.] 13, [1828], by Rev. R. Emerson	2	8
GRANGER, W[illia]m, m. Laura **BRADLEY,** [, 1821], by R. Emerson	2	2
GRANT, Daniel, m. Caroline **BURR,** May 10, 1843, by Rev. Joseph Eldredge	2	24

	Vol.	Page
GRANT, (cont.)		
Elijah, 1st s. Joel & Zilpah, b. Oct. 28, 1782	1	19
Garry C., s. Ryley A., b. Oct. 20, 1849	2	53
Harry M.,had s. [ ], b. Oct. 30, 1848	2	49
Huldah, m. Robert **ARMSTRONG**, Nov. 11, [1829], by Rev. R. Emerson	2	8
James, s. Joel & Zilpha, b. Jan. 29, 1790	1	12a
Jerusha, 1st d. Joel & Zilpah, b. Apr. 3, 1785	1	19
Joel, m. Zilpah **COWLES**, Jan. 3, 1782	1	19
Joel, m. Abigail F. **COWLES**, Oct. 12, 1845, by Rev. Joseph Eldredge	2	26
Keziah, of Norfolk, m. Cecero **PHELPS**, of Groton, N. Y., about Sept. 14, 1825, by Rev. Mr. Marsh, of Winchester	2	5
Levi, s. Elijah & Mary, b. May 12, 1771	TM	18
Lewis, m. Emma **WALDORPH**, Feb. 12, 1840, by Rev. J. Eldredge	2	21
Lois Lusena, d. Moses & Sarah, b. Sept. 2, 1795	1	12a
Mahala, 1st d. Roswell & Anna, b. July 31, 1785	1	9
Mary Ann, ae 40, m. Hiram **MILLS**, ae 50, [ ], 1849, by Rev. Ira Pettibone	2	31
Moses, 3rd s. Elijah & Marey, b. Aug. 15, 1765	TM	12
Nancy*, d. Joel & Zilpha, b. Apr. 25, 1788 *(Written Nancy **GRAND**")	1	12a
Raswell, m. Anna **COY**, Mar. 24, 1784, by Rev. Am R. Robbins	1	10
Roxe Matilda, d. Moses & Sarah, b. Nov. 12, 1793	1	12a
Salley Mallana, d. Moses & Sarah, b. Mar. 27, 1797	1	12a
Zilpha, d. Joel & Zilpha, b. May 30, 1794	1	12a
GRAVES, Submit, m. Adna **COWLS**, Mar. 7, 1768	TM	7
GRAY, Franklin D., m. Ann O. **PHELPS**, July 4, 1843, by Rev. Joseph Eldredge	2	24
GREEN, Nathan R., m. Olive **BETH***, b. of Norfolk, Feb. 24, 1822, by Bushnell Knapp, J. P. *("**BETTS**"?)	2	1
GRIFFIN, Emeline, m. Augustus **TYLER**, b. of New Haven, last evening, [Apr. 22, 1833], by Frances L. Robbins. Int. Pub. at New Haven	2	14
GRISWOLD, GRISWOULD, Annette, d. James, b. June 23, 1849	2	51
James, m. Lucy Ann **BROWN**, July 22, [1841], by Rev. J. Eldredge	2	22
Kezia, m. Dudley **HUMPHREY**, Oct. 14, 1761	TM	7
Martha, m. Milo **DYKE**, [Mar.] 15, [1846], by Rev. Joseph Eldredge	2	26
Martha Ann, d. James, b. June 23, 1849	2	50
GUITEAU, Asa, s. Ephraim & Phebe, b. Jan. 17, 1764	TM	11
Columbus, s. Philo & Sarah, b. Nov. 4, 1805	1	48
Coredon, s. Philo & Sarah, b. Jan. 19, 1803	1	48
Delia, d. Philo & Sarah, b. Mar. 6, 1797	1	48
Ephraim, m. Phebe **HUMPHREY**, Oct. 21, 1762	TM	7

	Vol.	Page
GUITEAU, (cont.)		
Louisa, d. Ephraim & Phebe, b. June 26, 1769	TM	17
Miras, d. Philo & Sarah, b. Dec. 24, 1798	1	48
Phebe Sophia, d. Ephraim & Phebe, b. Dec. 23, 1767	TM	15
Philo, 2nd s. Ephraim & Phebe, b. Apr. 8, 1766	TM	13
Philo, m. Sarah **BINGHAM**, Jan. 26, 1795	1	48
Philo, d. Nov. 25, 1809	1	14
Sheridan, s. Philo & Sarah, b. Apr. 17, 1801	1	48
HADSDEL, Grastus, of Burlington, m. Jemima **ROOT**, Nov. 3, [1828], by Rev. R. Emerson	2	8
HALL, Caroline, d. Josiah & Clarinda, b. July 4, 1848	2	47
Catharine, d. Jonah B., b. Aug. [ ], 1848	2	49
Catharine A., d. Mar. [ ], 1849	2	58
Erastus, m. Thankfull **DUTTON**, b. of Norfolk, Oct. 6, 1830, by Azariah Clark	2	10
Hannah, d. Highland & Hannah, b. Sept. 26, 1780	1	11a
Harrison, m. Caroline **ROYS**, [Mar.] 4, [1846], by Rev. Joseph Eldredge	2	26
Hiland, of Norfolk, m. Hannah **PARKER**, of Norfolk, Dec. 28, 1779, by Giles Pettibone, J. P.	1	10
Jane, m. Samuel **SMITH** (colored), Oct. 6, 1847, by Rev. Joseph Eldredge	2	28
Jerusha, m. Jonathan **WEBSTER**, Oct. 17, [1820], by R. Emerson	2	2
Joel, m. Laura G. **WALTER**, June 26, 1822, by Rev. R. Emerson	2	6
Joseph, Jr., m. Betsey **BROWN**, [ ], by R. Emerson	2	2
Sally, m. Daniel **LOVELAND**, Jr., Apr. 20, 1820, by R. Emerson	2	2
	2	58
Stephen, d. Mar. [ ], 1849, ae 3 y.	2	
HAMBLIN, [see also **HAMILTON**], Joel, m. Hanah **NORTON**, Apr. 27, 1774	1	10 2
Zerah, 1st s. Joel & Hanah, b. Jan. 3, 1775	1	
HAMILTON, [see also **HAMBLIN**], Elizabeth J., of Toland, Mass., m. Riley **COWLES**, of Norfolk, Dec. 15, 1844, by Rev. A. B. Hubbard	2	24
HANCHET, Ezekiel, of New Haven, m. Laura **MALTBIE**, June 7, [1836], by Rev. Joseph Eldredge	2	18
HANNEGAN, Peter, s. John, ae 24 & Margaret, ae 24, b. May 2, 1848	2	46
HARD, Hervey, m. Polly C. **STURTEVANT**, Oct. 24, [1820], by R. Emerson	2	2
HARLEY, A. Wheeler, ae 23, m. Lyddia **COBB**, ae 22, Mar. 6, 1849. by Amos D. Waters	2	32
HART, Albert, m. Maria **GAYLORD**, May 19, 1842, by Rev. J. Eldredge	2	22 51
Albert S., had s. [ ], b. Mar. 30, 1849	2	22
Charles, m. Ann **CAMP**, Nov. 22, 1841, by Rev. J. Eldredge	2	

	Vol.	Page
HART, (cont.)		
Charles, of Litchfield, m. Elizabeth M. **KILBORN**, Mar. 4, 1846, by Rev. Joseph Eldredge	2	26
Edward, d. Apr. 5, 1849, ae 6 d.	2	58
Eliz[abeth] L., m. A. **WILSON**, of Harwinton, [Nov.] 23, [1836], by Rev. Joseph Eldredge	2	18
Fanny Maria, d. Aug. 17, 1850, ae 31 y.	2	59
Fanny Maria **GAYLORD**, d. Albert S., b. June 22, 1850	2	52
Louisa S., m. Austin A. **SPAULDING**, Mar. 24, [1841], by Rev. J. Eldredge	2	21
HASKINS, Charity A., m. John P. **CAMP**, Feb. 25, 1824, by Rev. R. Emerson	2	6
HASTINGS, Joseph, Elder, certified, June 12, 1776, to the following statement of Jabez **RIMINGTON**, of Norfolk, "I, Jabez **RIMING**, of Norfolk am of the Anne baptis perswasion and do indeavor at all times to attend that worship beleaveing in my concience that it is true worship of God".	TM	8
HATCH, Anna, 4th d. [Eliphalet], b. Mar. 5, 1782	1	10a
Eliphelet, 2nd s. [Eliphelet], b. July 30, 1775; d. Oct. 13, 1777	1	10a
Eliphelet, 3rd s. [Eliphelet], b. Sept. 27, 1779	1	10a
Joseph, s. David & Submit, b. Feb. 18, 1776	1	7
Lucratia, 1st d. Eliphelet & Rebeca. b. Mar. 10, 1770	1	10a
Mabil, d. David & Submit, b. [ ] 9, 1773	1	7
Moses, 1st s. Eliphelut & Rebecca, b. Jan. 1, 1768	1	10a
Myrandah, 2nd d. Eliphelet, b. Sept. 24, 1772	1	10a
Rebeca, 3rd d. [Eliphelet], b. Oct. 16, 1777	1	10a
Roswell, s. David & Submit, b. Aug. 6, 1780	1	7
Salmon, 4th s. [Eliphelet], b. Oct. 23, 1784; d. July 28 [?], 1787	1	10a
HAWKS, E., of Canaan, m. Orrin **WILCOX**, of New Marlboro, Mass., Mar. 23, 1845, by Rev. A. B. Hubbard	2	25
HAWLEY, HAWLLEY, Charlotte T., m. Austin **BELDEN**, May 26, 1830, by Thomas Lascombe	2	10
Live (?), m. Daniel **DOCHESTER**, Oct. 31, [ ], by Asahel Humphry, J. P.	1	15
M. Lamartine, child of Austin, ae 26 & Mary G., ae 25, b. Nov. 1, 1847	2	46
Mathew and John **McEUERT** made affidavit Oct. 29, 1760, "that Thomas **KNAP** of Norfolk was a member of Bap. Ch. in Phillips Patten and a sober christian desenter and faithfull subject to xxx King George".	TM	8
Romulus, of Winsted, m. Almiris L. **COLLAR**, of New Marlboro, Mass., Mar. 16, 1845, by Rev. A. B. Hubbard	2	25
Theodosia, m. Henry **CATLIN**, Nov. 29, 1827, by Rufus Babcock, of Colebrook	2	7
HEADY, Clark, had child b. Oct. 3, 1848	2	47
Clark, d. Oct. 6, 1849, ae 3 d.	2	58

	Vol.	Page
HEADY, (cont.)		
Lucy Ann, of Norfolk, m. W[illia]m **SCOVELL**, of Sheffield, Mar. 19, 1943, by Rev. A. B. Hubbard	2	23
Mark, m. Eliza **ANDRUS**, Mar. 22, 1843, by Rev. J. Eldredge	2	22
Polly, d. Nov. [ ], 1848, ae 88 y.	2	57
HEDGER, Robert L., of New Marlborough, m. Livia A. **NORTHWAY**, of Norfolk, Oct. 19, 1831, by Rev. William Mitchell	2	12
[HEWITT], HEWET, HEWIT, Abijah, s. William & Sarah, b. Jan. 4, 1782	1	3
Abram C., m. Charlotte **McKEEN**, [Oct.] 17, [1823], by Rev. R. Emerson	2	6
Amus, s. William & Sarah, b. Oct. 2, 1774	1	3
Oliver, s. William & Sarah, b. Jan. 10, 1779	1	3
Sarah, Jr., d. William & Sarah, b. Mar. 4, 1777	1	3
Sarah, Jr., d. William & Sarah, d. June 24, 1778	1	3
William, Jr., s. William & Sarah, b. Dec. 2, 1772	1	3
HILL, William, of New Jersey, m. Mary **BURR**, Mar. 6, [1849], by Rev. Joseph Eldredge	2	33
William, ae 32, m. Mary **BURR**, ae 31, Mar.[ ], 1849, by Joseph Eldredge	2	32
HINE, HINES, Bennett H., m. Lucy **WILLY**, Apr. 9, 1843, by Rev. J. Eldredge	2	22
Harriet R., m. George E. **HOSFORD**, Feb. 6, 1842, by Rev. J. Eldredge	2	22
Lucinda, m. Stephen B. **TREAT**, b. of Norfolk, Nov. 11, 1838, by Michael F. Mills, J. P.	2	20
HINMAN, Abner, ae 30, m. Caroline R. **ROY**, ae 28, Feb. 22, [1849], by Joseph Eldredge	2	32
Abner, of New York, s. Caroline B. **HOLT**, Feb. 22, 1849, by Rev. Joseph Eldredge	2	33
HINSDALE, Jerusha, m. John **BOYD**, Dec. 7, [1843], by Rev. Joseph Eldredge	2	24
HITCHCOCK, Cynthia, of Colebrook, m. Humphrey **DUETT**, Nov. 7, [1848], by Rev. Joseph Eldredge	2	33
HODGES, Eunice W., of Torrington, m. John M. **WADBOUN**, of Goshen, Oct. 30, 1837, by Rev. Joseph Eldredge	2	19
HODLEY, Sarah, m. Moses **WALTER**, Feb. 12, 1792, by Dudley Humphry, J. P.	1	12a
HOLCOMB, HOLCOM, Charity, m. Josiah **CHITTENDEN**, Jan. 26, 1775	TM	9
Eunis, d. Amasa & Loes, b. Feb. 4, 1773	TM	24
Margrat, m. Giles **PETTIBONE**, June 20, 1776	TM	9
Timothy, s. Amasa & Loes, b. Nov. 24, 1775	1	1
HOLDEN, Susannah, m. Jesse **ORVIS**, Feb. 23, 1792, by Giles Pettibone	1	15
HOLT, Caroline B., m. Abner **HINMAN**, of New York, Feb. 22, 1849, by Rev. Joseph Eldredge	2	33

	Vol.	Page
HOLT, (cont.)		
Eleazer, m. Elisebeth **STONE**, May 1, 1775	TM	9
Elizabeth, d. [ ], 1848, ae 88 y.	2	58
Elizur P., s. Roger & Mariaetta, b. Mar. 13, 1848	2	47
Harrison, d. Dec. 9, 1847, ae 27	2	56
Henry, ae 23, m. Mary **DABOT**, ae 22, Sept. 28, 1847, by Rev. Mr. Goodwin	2	30
Isaac, m. Mabel **DOWD**, May 8, 1764	TM	7
Jacob, d. Aug. 29, 1774	TM	21
Lucy, m. Elisha Hiram **RICHARDS**, Apr. 19, 1827, by Rev. R. Emerson	2	8
Mary, m. [ ] **DOOLITTLE**, June [ ], 1831, by Amos Pettibone, J. P.	2	12
HOPKINS, Welthana, m. Edward **GAYLORD**, Oct. 31, 1765	TM	9
HORTON, Albert, m. Elen T. **BURR**, [Jan.] 9, [1838], by Rev. Joseph Eldredge	2	19
HOSFORD, George E., m. Harriet R. **HINE**, Feb. 6, 1842, by Rev. J. Eldredge	2	22
HOSMER, Sophia, m. Isaiah **PALMER**, Feb. 6, 1834, by Rev. Joseph Eldredge	2	15
HOTCHKISS, HOTCHKIN, Abigail, m. Amos Roberts **TREAT**, [Nov.] 3, [1828], by Rev. R. Emerson	2	8
Abraham, twin with Hannah, s. Samuel & Jarusha, b. July 16, 1778	1	11a
Amarilla, m. Franklin **SCHOVIL**, b. of Norfolk, Oct. 6, 1830, by Rev. George Carrington, of Goshen	2	11
Betsa, 2nd d. Samuell & Elizabeth, b. Sept. 2, 1780	1	4
Charlotte, m. Daniel **WHITE**, [Mar.] 25, 1823, by Rev. R. Emerson	2	6
Chloe, d. Samuell & Elizabeth, b. Nov. 10, 1777	1	4
Dammeros, 3rd d. Samuell & Elizabeth, b. Mar. 2, 1783	1	4
Elisebeth, d. Emos & Elesebeth, b. Nov. 28, 1758	TM	11
Elisabeth, d. Enos, b. Nov. 28, 1758	TM	18
Elen M., d. William L. ae 26 & Margaret, ae 20, b. Jan. 24, 1848	2	46
Hannah, twin with Abraham, d. Samuel & Jarusha, b. July 16, 1778	1	11a
Hiram, m. Harriet C. **CANFIELD**, Dec. 24, 1845, by Rev. Joseph Eldredge	2	26
Hiram D., s. Hiram, b. Apr. 22, 1850	2	53
Hulda, d. Enos, b. Apr. 5, 1765	TM	18
James, m. Mary **MINOR**, Nov. 25, 1823, by Rufus Babcock	2	4
John, s. Enos, b. Jan. 21, 1764	TM	1/8
Merret E., s. Martin S., b. Sept. 1, 1848	2	48
Ruth, d. Enos & Elesabeth, b. Sept. 1, 1760	TM	11
Ruth, d. Enos, b. Sept. 1, 1760	TM	18
Samuel, s. Samuel & Jerusha, b. Nov. 5, 1774	1	11a
Samuell, Jr., 1st s. Samuell & Elizabeth, b. Mar. 31, 1785	1	4

	Vol.	Page
HOTCHKISS, HOTCHKIN, (cont.)		
Sarah, m. Hendrick **BALE***, Dec. 9, 1784, by Giles Pettibone *(Perhaps "BALL"?)	1	10
Sarah, d. June 18, 1850, ae 53 y.	2	60
Sarah M., ae 27, m. Lewis **CATLIN**, ae 33, Nov. 30, 1848, by Rev. Joseph Eldredge	2	31
Sarah M., m. Lewis **CATLIN**, of Canaan, [ ] 31, [1848], by Rev. Joseph Eldredge	2	33
HOWE, HOW, Elisebeth, d. Joshua, d. May 7, 1763	TM	20
Emily E., m. Miles W. **SMITH**, Dec. 1, 1844, by Rev. Joseph Eldredge	2	24
Eunis, d. Joshua & Meriam, b. Apr. 26, 1769	TM	17
Joseph, s. Joshua & Meriam, b. Dec. 22, 1776	1	1
Joshua, s. Joshua & Miram, b. July* 20, 1772 *(First written "Aug.")	TM	22
Josiah, of Canaan, m. Aba **LAKE**, of [ ] late of Norfolk, Sept. 3, 1789, by D. Humphry, J. P.	1	12
Ruth, d. Joshua & Memiram, b. May 3, 1774	TM	23
Sarah, m. Samuell **TURNER**, Dec. 26, 1754	1	9
HUBBARD, H. Edward, m. Rosanna W. **BUTLER**, Jan. 11, 1843, by Rev. J. Eldredge	2	22
-----, m. Philura **ROBBINS**, Jan. 25, 1842, by Rev. J. Eldredge	2	22
HULL, Anson, s. Jehiel & Ruth, b. Nov. 18, 1771	TM	20
Jahiel, s. Jahiel & Ruth, b. May 27, 1762	TM	20
Samuel Phelps, [s. Jahiel & Ruth], b. June 17, 1766	TM	20
HUMPHREY, HUMPHRY, Almira, 1st d. Dr. Hosea & Persis, b. Dec. 18, 1782	1	9
Asahel, m. Prudence **MERRELS**, Aug. 26, 1773	TM	7
Asahel, m. Prudence **MERRILS**, Aug. 26, 1775	TM	9
Asahel, Jr., s. Asahel & Prudence, b. Apr. 24, 1779	1	11a
Asahel, Dr. of Norfolk, m. Clarissa **STEEL**, of Cornwall, May 5, 1807	1	44
Caroline, m. Abel **CAMP**, Mar. 1, 1841, by Rev. J. Eldredge	2	21
Clarrissa, w. Dr. Asahel, d. Mar. 12, 1809	1	14
Daniel, 1st s. Daniel & Rachel, b. June [ ], 1761; d. June [ ]	TM	14
Daniel Granvelle, 2nd s. Daniel & Rachel, b. June 14, 1766	TM	14
Dudley, m. Kezia **GRISWOLD**, Oct. 14, 1761	TM	7
Dudley, s. Asahel & Prudance, b. June 5, 1775	TM	24
Dudley, d. Mar. 25, 1794, ae 54	1	20
Dudley, m. Polly **PHELPS**, Oct. 16, 1798, by Rev. Publius Virgilius Boge	1	35
Edward Steel, [twin with Edwin **STEEL**], s. Asahel & Clarrissa, b. Nov. 28, 1808	1	46
James, m. Eliza **BABBET**, Nov. 12, [1834], by Rev. Joseph Eldredge	2	16
James, of Amhurst, Mass., m. Urania **BATTALL**, of Norfolk, [Oct.] 11, [1836], by Frances L. Robbins	2	17
James, s. James & Uerania, b. Dec. 3, 1837	2	41

	Vol.	Page
HUMPHREY, HUMPHRY, (cont.)		
James Merrils, 3rd s. Asahel & Prudence, b. Oct. 16, 1786	1	21
John Phelps, 1st s. Dudley & Polly, b. June 18, 1801	1	37
Kezia, 2nd d. Asahel & Prudence, b. July 14, 1781	1	11
Lucy, 5th d. Asahel & Prudence, b. Sept. 12, 1793	1	21
Marcy, 3rd d. Asahel & Prudence, b. May 4, 1783	1	11
Martha, 4th d. Michael, d. Jan. 17, 1763	TM	14
Martha, 1st d. Asahel & Prudence, b. Mar. 25, 1778	1	2
Martha, m. Jsaac **TURNER,** Nov. 19, 1794, by Ammi R. Robbins	1	12a
Mary, m. John **DEWITT,** Jan. 1, 1826, by Rev. R. Emerson	2	6
Mercy, wid., d. May 14, 1793, in the 76th y. of her age	1	20
Michael, made affidavit Apr. 18, 1772, that Samuel **KNAP** & s. Alexander were members of Bap. Ch., in Canaan & New Marlborough that they are bap. persons by immersion and have attended worship for about 2 y.	TM	8
Michael, d. Jan. 26, 1778	1	5
Michael, d. Jan. 26, 1778	1	10
Phebe, m. Ephraim **GUITEAU,** Oct. 21, 1762	TM	7
Polley, 2nd d. Daniel & Rachel, b. Mar. 18, 1764	TM	14
Prudence Harriot, 4th d. Asahel & Prudence, b. May 24, 1788	1	21
Sarah, 1st d. Daniel & Rachel, b. Apr. 7, 1762	TM	14
Steven P., of Goshen, m. P. S. **ROBBINS,** [Mar.] 21, [1833], by Rev. Joseph Eldredge	2	14
HUNT, Ezra, m. Maria Eliza **PETTIBONE,** b. of St. Charles, Mo., Mar. 17, 1830, by Pitkin Cowles	2	9
HURLBUT, HURLBERT, Alice P., d. William, b. July 22, 1850	2	51
Daniel B., m. Eliza A. **CALHOUN,** Apr. 17, [1837], by Rev. Joseph Eldredge	2	18
Ellen G., d. W[illia]m, d. May 19, 1848, ae 3	2	56
Frances Louisa, d. W[illia]m, mechanic, ae 25 & Sarah Ann, ae 24, b. July 16, 1847	2	42
Halsey, of Enfield, m. Betsey **MOSES,** of Norfolk, Mar. 24, 1831, by Rev. Diodate Brockway, of Ellington	2	12
Joseph B., s. Joseph W., b. June 18, 1850	2	51
Warren P., ae 23, m. Emeline **DUNBAR,** ae 20, Apr. 16, 1850, by Joseph Eldredge	2	35
Warren P., of Winsted, m. Emeline M. **DUNBAR,** of Torringford, Apr. 16, 1850, by Rev. Joseph Eldredge	2	36
HYDE, Eliza, m. Eliphalet **BORDEN,** June 5, 1825, by Bushnell Knapp	2	5
James, m. Susan **ROBERTS,** Dec. 26, 1842, by Rev. J. Eldredge	2	22
HYDURIN, W[illia]m, m. Charlotte **COLDEN,** Apr. 25, [1835], by Rev. Joseph Eldredge	2	17
IVES, JIVES, JVES, JUES, Charles, s. George A. & Rebecca, b. Oct. 23, 1795	1	43
Erastus, s. Titus & Dorothy, b. June 9, 1775	TM	24

	Vol.	Page
IVES, JIVES, JVES, JUES, (cont.)		
Eunis, d. Titus & Dorothy, b. Mar. 24, 1772	TM	19
George Anson, s. Titus & Dorothy, b. Apr. 4, 1768	TM	15
Hannah, m. [Sa]muel **TIBBALS**, May 25, 1775	1	10
John, s. Titus & Dorothy, b. Feb. 18, 1770	TM	17
Mary, m. Earl P. **PEASE**, Apr. 8, 1802, by Rev. Mr. Morgan	1	44
Miron, s. George A. & Rebecca, b. Feb. 6, 1799	1	43
Sally, d. George A. & Rebecca, b. Mar. 17, 1797	1	43
Sarah, d. Titus & Dorotha, b. Apr. 13, 1764	TM	13
Titus Ho[w]el[l], s. Titus & Dorotha, b. Feb. 28, 1766	TM	13
JACKSON, George W., m. Mary A. **THOMPSON**, Apr. 26, [1838], by Rev. Joseph Eldredge	2	19
Sarah, m. Alexander **KNAPP**, of Canaan, May 29, 1825, by Rev. R. Emerson	2	6
JAMES, Augustus, of New Marlborough, m. Tryphena **BRADLEY**, of Norfolk, Jan. 15, 1832, by Rev. Harmon Ellis, of 1st Bap. Ch.	2	13
JAQUA, Henry, had d. [ ], b. July 15, 1849	2	50
JENKS, Hannah, d. Ebenezer & Elizabeth, b. May 9, 1778, in North Providence, R. I.	1	11
Nathan, s. Ebenezer & Elizabeth, b. June 29, 1776, in North Providence, R. I.	1	11
Sarah, d. Ebenezer & Elizabeth, b. May 31, 1773, in North Providence, R. I.	1	11
Sarah, m. Solomon **TURNER**, b. of Norfolk, May 1, 1791, by D. Humphry, J. P.	1	12a
Uriah, s. Ebenezer & Elizabeth, b. Jan. 31, 1791	1	11
JOHNSON, JONSON, David, s. Daved & Jerusha, b. Feb. 3, 1762	TM	15
Diana, d. David & Jerusha, b. Sept. 24, 1758	TM	15
Eliza, m. Uriel **NORTON**, Sept. 30, [1835], by Rev. Joseph Eldredge	2	17
Henry, m. Charlotte **DUNHAM**, of Canaan, Nov. 4, 1849, by Rev. Joseph Eldredge	2	36
Huldah, m. John **DIXON**, of Sheffield, Mar. 4, [1847], by Rev. Joseph Eldredge	2	27
Jeremiah, m. Clarissa **NORTON**, [Mar.] 20, [1839], by [Rev. Joseph Eldredge	2	20
Jeremiah, ae 36, m. Caroline C. **FRISBIE**, ae 30, Oct. 30, [1849], by John F. Norton	2	32
Jerusha, d. Daved & Jerusha, b. Sept. 21, 1756	TM	15
Levine, d. Daved & Jerusha, b. June 8, 1767	TM	15
Louisa, m. Joel **SCHOVILLE**, Aug. 25, 1844, by Rev. Joseph Eldredge	2	24
Mary A., m. Philemon **JOHNSON**, May 7, 1845, by Rev. Joseph Eldredge	2	26
Miron, had d. [ ], b. June 29, 1849	2	48
Norton, d. Aug. [ ], 1850	2	60
Philemon, m. Mary A. **JOHNSON**, May 7, 1845, by Rev.		

	Vol.	Page
JOHNSON, JONSON, (cont.)		
Joseph Eldredge	2	26
Phelmon, had s. [ ], b. Mar. 2, 1849	2	49
Philemon, his child, b. May 17, 1850	2	53
Rebecca, d. Daved & Jerusha, b. June 7, 1753	TM	15
Ruth, d. Daved & Jerusha, b. Mar. 10, 1765	TM	15
Thomas, s. Daved & Jarusha, b. Dec. 13, 1751	TM	15
Timothy, s. David & Jerusha, b. Nov. 12, 1754	TM	15
Warren, m. Caroline H. **COOK**, Sept. 9, 1841, by Rev. J. Eldredge	2	22
Zebediah, reputed s. Zebediah **JONSON** & Jemima **COWLS**, b. Jan. 14, 1784	1	3a
JOLIET, Frances B., d. July 20, 1849, ae 2 y.	2	57
JONES, Clarissa, d. Joseph & Abigail, b. Oct. 28, 1783	1	7
Harlow, 4th, s. Joseph & Abigail, b. Feb. 4, 1786	1	21
Joseph, m. Abigal **SEWARD**, Sept. 3, 1772	TM	9
Joseph, 1st s. Joseph & Abigail, b. Oct. 3, 1776	1	1
Joseph, Jr., d. Sept. 13, 1777	1	5
Joseph, s. Joseph & Abigail, b. Aug. 24, 1778	1	10
Kezia, d. Joseph & Abigail, b. Feb. 22, 1792	1	21
Laura, d. Joseph & Abigail, b. Aug. 19, 1790; [d.?] Jan. 18, 1793	1	21
Lewis, s. Joseph & Abigail, b. Apr. 8, 1781	1	10
Prudence, d. Joseph & Abigal, b. June 8, 1773	TM	23
JUDD, Caroline C., m. Ensign **BELDEN**, May 19, [1841], by Rev. J. Eldredge	2	21
Mary M., m. Edmund H. **ASHLEY**, Nov. 20, 1836, by Rev. Joseph Eldredge	2	18
Mindwell, 3rd d. Timothy & Mindwell, b. Oct. 22, 1778	1	1
Timothy, 2nd s. Timothy & Mindwell, b. Nov. 30, 1775	1	1
KENDRICK, James, s. Alvan, b. May 30, 1849	2	49
KILBANE, [see also **KILBOURN**], Mary A., m. Hiram H. **RIGGS**, Mar. 9, [1836], by Rev. Joseph Eldredge	2	17
[KIMBOURN], KILBORN, KILBOURNE, Elizabeth M., m. Charles **HART**, of Litchfield, Mar. 4, 1846, by Rev. Joseph Eldredge	2	26
Marilla, m. H. H. **RIGGS**, Dec. 11, 1843, by Rev. Joseph Eldredge	2	24
Payne K., m. Elizabeth **CONE**, Aug. 3, 1842, by Rev. J. Eldredge	2	22
KILBERLY, KIMBERLEY, Edward, of Goshen, m. Mary J. **CLERK**, [ ], 1849, by Rev. Joseph Eldredge	2	33
Edward, ae 23, m. Marietta **CLARK**, ae 26, Oct. 1, 1850, by Rev. Joseph Eldredge	2	35
KING, Ariel, of New Marlborough, m. Roxay **MOSES**, of Norfolk, Dec. [ ], 1826, by Bushnell Knapp	2	6
KINNEY, Michael, s. John, b. Aug. 6, 1849	2	52
KNAPP, KNAP, Abigail, of Goshen, m. W[illia]m **KNAPP**, of		

KNAPP, KNAP, (cont.)

	Vol.	Page
Canaan, Feb. 1, 1822, by Bushnell Knapp, J. P.	2	1
Abram, m. Martha **COMSTOCK**, Jan. 27, 1756	TM	7
Abram, s. Abram & Martha, b. Sept. 25, 1759	TM	16
Alexander, of Canaan, m. Sarah **JACKSON**, May 29, 1825, by Rev. R. Emerson	2	6
Alexander, see Samuel **KNAP**		
Ann Eliza, d. Oct. 10, 1848, ae 26 y.	2	57
Abuzah*, d. Abram & Martha, b. Apr. 9 [?], 1767 *("Azubah?]	TM	16
Bouton D., s. Lockard, ae 40 & Charlotte, ae 35, b. Jan. 1, 1848	2	47
Cyrus, s. Abram & Martha, b. Mar. 26, 1761	TM	16
David B., m. Olive **MOREY**, Nov. 24, 1822, by Bushnell Knapp, J. P.	2	3
Diantha, m. Ryley **FRENCH**, May 5, 1822, by Bushnell Knapp, J. P.	2	3
Dorothy, d. Abram & Martha, b. Jan. 26, 1772	TM	22
Elaxander, see Samuel **KNAP**	TM	8
Elizabeth, m. Aaron **ROY**, Aug. 20, 1793, by Rev. Ammi R. Robbins	2	1
Emeline, m. Jedediah **KNAPP**, of Canaan, Nov. 15, [1825], by Rev. R. Emerson	2	6
Fanny, m. Squire **COLLINS**, of Torrington, Sept. 28, [1832], by Rev. Joseph Eldredge	2	14
Henry W., ae 27 y., m. Lois A. **ROOD**, ae 20 y., b. of Norfolk, Nov. 7, 1847, by Rev. C. W. Watrous	2	27
Henry W., ae 27, m. Lois Ann **ROOD**, ae 20, Nov. 7, 1847, by Charles Watrous	2	30
Jedediah, of Canaan, m. Emeline **KNAPP**, Nov. 15, [1825], by Rev. R. Emerson	2	6
Lockwood, m. Sharlott **WALKER**, b. of Norfolk, Nov. 21, 1834, by Gladden Bishop, Elder	2	16
Marcy, m. Jsaac **SPALDING**, b. of Norfolk, July 9, 1778	1	10
Martha, d. Abram & Martha, b. Mar. 21, 1763	TM	16
Mary C., m. Emerson **WILLIAMS**, Sept. 29, 1850, by Rev. Joseph Eldredge	2	36
Olive, wid. of Norfolk, m. W[illia]m B. **SLADE**, of New Haven, June 2, 1844, by Rev. A. B. Hubbard	2	23
Rosanna, d. Abram & Martha, b. Jan. 21, 1765	TM	16
Samantha, m. Samuel A. **PETTIBONE**, [Apr.] 24, [1822], by R. Emerson	2	2
Samuel and s. Elaxander "members of Bap. Ch., in Canaan & New Marlborough and that they are bap. persons by immersion and have attended worship for about 2 years. "Affidavit made Apr. 18, 1772, Canaan, by Jedediah Stevens, Job Rathbone Clark, Michael Humphry & Joshua Steven	TM	8

	Vol.	Page

KNAPP, KNAP, (cont.)

	Vol.	Page
Sam[ue]ll, 2nd, "has attended Cong. Meeting and paid to the support thereof to me Joseph Marshal. "Dated Feb. 13, 1786	1	13a
Samuel Comstock, s. Abram & Martha, b. Dec. 12, 1770; d. Dec. 30, 1770	TM	18
Sarah, d. Abram & Martha, b. Oct. 25, 1757	TM	16
Sarah, m. Noah **ALLING**, Sept. 29, 1758	TM	7
Thomas, m. Loes **BARSS**, Feb. 7, 1758	TM	7
Thomas, of Norfolk, "member of Bap. Ch., in Phillips Patten, is a sober christian desenter and a faithfull subject to xxx King George". Affidavit made by John McEuert & Mathew Hawlley, Oct. 29, 1760	TM	8
William, s. Elijah & Rachel, b. Oct. 10, 1771	1	9
W[illia]m, 2nd, 1st s. William & Anna, b. Oct. 8, 1797	1	36
W[illia]m, of Canaan, m. Abigail KNAPP, of Goshen, Feb. 1, 1822, by Bushnell Knapp, J. P.	2	1
Zuruiah, d. Thomas & Loes, b. Nov. 17, 1759	TM	6

KNIGHT, Henry M., m. Mary Fitch **PHELPS**, Oct. 2, 1850, by Rev. Joseph Eldredge | 2 | 36

LaBOUTE, Rume, m. Eunice **PROUT**, May 23, [1847], by Rev. Joseph Eldredge | 2 | 28

LAKE, Aba, of [ ], late of Norfolk, m. Josiah **HOW**, of Canaan, Sept. 3, 1789, by D. Humphry, J. P. | 1 | 12

Caleb M., of Sharon, m. Laura C. **TUTTLE**, Oct. 28, 1845, by Rev. Joseph Eldredge | 2 | 26

LARNED, W[illia]m A., m. Irene **BATTELL**, June 1, 1843, by Rev. Joseph Eldredge | 2 | 24

LAWRENCE, LAWRANCE, Analetta, d. Frederick, d. Apr. 25, 1848 | 2 | 57

	Vol.	Page
Annatta, d. Frederick & Hellen, b. Apr. 9, 1848	2	47
Azariah, s. John & Elesibath, b. May 18, 1771	TM	18
Bette, d. Nehemiah & Elesebeth, b. Aug. 17, 1762	TM	11
Betty, of Canaan, m. Phineas **PEAS**, of Norfolk, Nov. 25, 1779, by Dudley Humphrey, J. P.	1	10
E. G., m. Jerusha **STEVENS**, b. of Norfolk, Aug. 27, 1827, by Rev. James Beach, of Winsted	2	7
Elisebeth, 1st d. Stephen & Mary, b. Apr. 27, 1764	TM	12
Elezabeth, m. Jonathan **MUNGER**, Oct. 9, 1782, by Giles Pettibone	1	10
Ezekiel, [twin with Susanna], s. Arial & Lucey, b. Apr. 22, 1778	1	2
Frederick, of Canaan, m. Elizabeth A. **PEARS**, of Norfolk, Jan. 1, 1838, by Rev. Joseph Eldredge	2	19
Frederick, m. Hellen E. **PEARSE**, Jan. 11, 1844, by Rev. Joseph Eldredge	2	24
Jeremiah, s. Nehemiah & Elesebeth, b. June 15. 1760	TM	6
John Marten, s. John & Elesebeth, b. July 21. 1772	TM	19

270   BARBOUR COLLECTION

	Vol.	Page
LAWRENCE, LAWRANCE, (cont.)		
Lucy, d. Aeiel & Lucy, b. Apr. 16, 1774	TM	23
Samuel, s. John, 2nd & Elesebeth, b. Feb. 1, 1769	TM	18
Sarah, m. Rev. Ebi **CLARK**, of Winchester, Sept. 19, 1832, by Rev. Joseph Eldredge	2	14
Susanna, [twin with Ezekiel], s. Arial & Lucey, b. Apr. 22, 1778	1	2
William, s. Grove & Elizabeth, b. June 28, 1801, in Paris, N. Y.	1	48
LeBARON, Elisebeth, Mrs. of Pleinoth*, m. Ammi R. **ROBBINS**, May 13, 1762 *("Plymouth")	TM	7
LEE, Clarrissa, 6th d. [Nathan & Sibbil], b. May 4, 1794	1	36
Irenae, 4th d. [Nathan & Sibbil], b. Nov. 3, 1784	1	36
Nathan, m. Sibbil **DUDLEY**, Aug. 19, 1773	1	37
Nathan, 1st s. [Nathan & Sibbil], b. June 4, 1787	1	36
Polly, 1st d. Nathan & Sibbil, b. Jan. 12, 1775	1	36
Polly, had d. Lois, b. June 5, 1799; f. Samuel **DICKINSON**	1	37
Ruth, m. Nath[anie]ll **MUNGER**, Feb. 8, 1769	1	11
Ruth, 3rd d. [Nathan & Sibbil], b. June 24, 1782	1	36
Sally, 5th d. [Nathan & Sibbil], b. Apr. 8, 1792	1	36
Stephen, 2nd s. [Nathan & Sibbil], b. Apr. 27, 1790	1	36
Silvie, 2nd d. [Nathan & Sibbil], b. Sept. 10, 1778 *("Sylvia")	1	36
LEWIS, LIWIS, Clarandah, 3rd d. Edward & Jane, b. July 19, 1778	1	3
Hervey, m. Polly **FRISBIE**, July 24, [1827], by Rev. R. Emerson	2	8
James S., of Goshen, m. Harriet **PECK**, Mar. 31, 1836, by Rev. Joseph Eldredge	2	18
Jerusha, m. Abiram **GAYLORD**, Nov. 14, 1822, by Rev. R. Emerson	2	6
Marcus, m. Philander **THOMPSON**, of Goshen, [Sept.] 24, [1833], by Rev. Joseph Eldredge	2	15
Richard, m. wid. Marther **CURTIS**, Nov. 3, 1778	1	7
LOCKWOOD, ----, m. John **CAUKINS**, Mar. 17, [1833], by Rev. Joseph Eldredge	2	14
LOOMIS, Sabra, m. Charles F. **THOMPSON**, Apr. 24, 1842, by Rev. J. Eldredge	2	22
LORAIN, [see under **LORRAIN**]		
LORING, Miron, of New Marlboro, m. Jerusha **GAYLORD**, Jan. 1, 1833, by Rev. Joseph Eldredge	2	14
Virginia, d. John B., ae 30 & Emily, ae 28, b. Oct. 26, 1847	2	46
LORRAIN, LORAIN, Barbara, twin with Isabella, d. John, b. Apr. 18, 1849	2	48
Isabella, twin with Barbara, d. John, b. Apr. 18, 1849	2	48
John, m. Mary Joseph **MAUNDRANCE**, Feb. 27, 1847, by Rev. Joseph Eldredge	2	27
LOVELAND, Daniel, Jr., m. Sally **HALL**, Apr. 20, 1820, by R.		

	Vol.	Page
LOVELAND, (cont.)		
Emerson	2	2
[LOVERIDGE], LOVERIGE, Sarah, d. James & Mahitable, b. Dec. 31, 1782	1	3
LUCAS, LUKUS, Easther, d. John & Jerusha, b. July 2, 1768	TM	16
John, m. Jerusha COOE, Dec. 5, 1765	TM	7
Nancy, of Norfolk, m. Samuel E. WILCOX, of Goshen, Feb. 16, 1831, by Rev. George Carrington, of Goshen	2	11
Rosanna, d. John & Jerusha, b. Sept. 12, 1766	TM	13
LYMAN, David, Rev. of Salisbury, m. Mary E. BRAMBLE, of Norfolk, July 21, 1846, by Rev. George C. Bancroft	2	26
Sally Marina, d. Daniel & Sally, b. Feb. 21, 1794	1	46
McCORMICK, Sarah J., d. William, b. July 26, 1849	2	51
McDERMOTT, Joseph, s. Thomas, b. June 19, 1850	2	52
Thomas, ae 25, m. Jane CLEMEN, ae 21, Mar. [ ], 1850, by Harlow Ray	2	35
McEUERT, John, and Matthew HAWLLEY, made affidavit Oct. 29, 1760 "that Thomas KNAP, of Norfolk was member of Bapt. Ch. in Phillips Patten and a sober christian desenter and faithfull subject to xxx King George".	TM	8
MACK, Daniel, has w. [ ], d. Mar. 10, 1772	TM	21
Elisebath, d. Daniel, d. Nov. 16, 1776	1	5
Orlander, s. Damer & Elisebeth, b. Oct.* 28, 1769 *(First written "Nov.")	TM	17
McKEAN, McKEEN, Charlotte, d. Linus & Polly, b. Dec. 14, 1800	1	48
Charlotte, m. Abram C. HEWET, [Oct.] 17, [1823], by Rev. R. Emerson	2	6
Linus, b. Guilford, Aug. 25, 1778; m. Polly STEEL, of Bethlem, Nov. 14, 1799	1	48
Lucy Ann, d. Linus & Polly, b. Mar. 1, 1808	1	48
William, s. Linus & Polly, b. May 30, 1806	1	48
McMANUS, Elizabeth, d. John, b. Apr. 28, 1850	2	52
MAHON, John C., of Winsted, m. Clarissa E. BUNNELL, of Norfolk, Nov. 19, 1843, by Rev. Lewis Gunn	2	23
MALLORY, MALERY, Eliza, d. James, b. Oct. [ ], 1848	2	49
Freeman, s. W[illia]m, farmer, ae 40 & Susan, ae 44, b. May 2, 1848	2	44
Truman, d. May 2, 1849, ae 10 m.	2	57
MALTBIE, Allen, s. Jehiel & Phebe, b. Mar. 28, 1789	1	20
Almira, [d. Jacob], b. Aug. 25, 1808	2	37
Charles Benjamin, [s. Elan], b. May 20, 1821	2	40
Daniel Munson, s. Daniel & Margret, b. Aug. 28, 1770	TM	23
Elizur, [s. Elan], b. Apr. 24, 1808	2	40
Eliza, [d. Jacob], b. May 25, 1811	2	37
Jesse Alonzo, [s. Elan], b. Apr. 27, 1814	2	40
Laura, [d. Elan], b. May 7, 1812	2	40
Laura, m. Ezekiel HANCHET, of New Haven, June 7, [1836], by Rev. Joseph Eldredge	2	18

272 BARBOUR COLLECTION

	Vol.	Page
MALTBIE, (cont.)		
Mary E., m. Hiram H. **BOYNTON**, of New Haven, Nov. 5, 1845, by Rev. Joseph Eldredge	2	26
Mary Elizabeth, [d. Elan], b. Mar. 29, 1827	2	40
Milo Harrison, [s. Elan], b. June 26, 1810	2	40
Rhoda Julia, [d. Elan], b. Sept. 3, 1824	2	40
Saley, d. Daniel & Margret, b. July 14, 1772	TM	23
Seth, s. Jehiel & Phebe, b. Nov. 12, 1793	1	20
Warren, [s. Jacob], b. May 13, 1806	2	37
William, s. Jacob, b. Jan. 8, 1804	2	37
William Henry, [s. Elan], b. June 2, 1816	2	40
Zaceus, s. Daniel & Margret, b. Aug. 19, 1772	TM	23
MAN, Mary, ae 20, m. Joseph **CAMP**, Aug. 22, [1849], by [ ]	2	34
MANSFIELD, Sidney, of Canaan, m. Fanny **DEAN**, of Norfolk, Apr. 24, 1845, by Harley Goodwin	2	25
MARANDREAR, [see also **MAUNDRANCE**], Mary H. m. Henry **MELLER**, Apr. 20, 1847, by Rev. Joseph Eldredge	2	28
MARKHAM, Rachel Case, d. Abraham, b. May 4, 1819	2	38
MARS, Jupeter, d. June 23, 1818, ae 67	2	55
MARSH, Eunice, w. Nath[anie]ll, d. Dec. 17, 1785	1	20
MARSHALL, Helen, of Colebrook, m. Timothy **ROCKWELL**, Sept. 24, [1828], by Rev. R. Emerson	2	8
MASON, MASONS, Elijah, m. Susannah **MILLS**, May 12, 1768	TM	7
Elijah, s. Elijah & Susanna, b. Nov. 27, 1775	1	1
Elijah, s. Elijah & Susanna, d. Sept. 8, 1778	1	11a
Elijah, s. Elijah & Susanna, d. Sept. 8, 1778, ae 2 y. 9 m. 12 d.	1	11a
Elijah, s. Elijah & Susanna, b. May 1, 1783	1	7
Eliphalet, s. Elijah & Susanna, b. Feb. 2, 1769	TM	18
Mahitable, d. Elijah & Susannah, b. Sept. 13, 1773	TM	22
Phebe, d. Elijah & Susanna, b. Aug. 4, 1778	1	11a
Susanna, d. Elijah & Susannah, b. Oct. 7, 1770	TM	18
Susanna, d. Elijah & Susanna, d. Aug. 30, 1778, ae 7 y. 10 m, 13 d.	1	11a
Susanna, d. Elijah & Susanna, b. Nov. 18, 1780	1	11a
Sibel, d. Elijah & Susanna, b. Oct. 30, 1789	1	21
Uri, s. Elijah & Susanna, b. May 5, 1787	1	3
MAUNDRANCE, [see also **MARANDREAR**], Mary Joseph, m. John **LORRAIN**, Feb. 27, 1847, by Rev. Joseph Eldredge	2	27
MAURISY, William, s. Martin, b. July 8, 1849	2	50
MEACHAM, Horace, of Summers, m. Electa H. **PHELPS**, Jan. 24, 1827, by Rev. R. Emerson	2	6
MEEKER, Phinehas, Jr., s. Phinehas & Mary, b. Aug. 2, 1771	1	7
Sarah, w. Phineas, d. July 29, 1769	TM	20
MELLER, [see also **MILLER**], Henry, m. Mary H. **MARANDREAR**, Apr. 20, 1847, by Rev. Joseph Eldredge	2	28

NORFOLK VITAL RECORDS 273

	Vol.	Page
MENDES, Nancy, m. Levi N. **PARSONS**, Nov. 2, [1846], by Rev. Joseph Eldredge	2	27
Rose, m. Peter **BELOEW**, Apr. 19, [1846], by Rev. Joseph Eldredge	2	27
MERRILL, MERREL, MERRILS, MERRILLS, MERRIELS, MERRELS, Aaron, s. Epha & Easter, b. Apr. 22, 1786	1	3
Alvin, 6th s. Ephah & Esther, b. Dec. 5, 1799	1	35
Asahel, s. Ephah & Esther, b. Dec. 16, 1792	1	12
Carrodon R., m. Coven H. **WILMOT**, b. of New Hartford, Mar. 6, 1848, by Rev. Joseph Eldredge	2	28
Ephah, m. Esther **BORDEN**, Dec. 7, 1781, by Mr. A. M. Robins	1	11
Ephraim, s. Ephah & Esther, b. Oct. 16, 1790	1	12
Esthor, d. Ephah & Esther, b. June 9, 1784	1	6
Hiram A., of Norfolk, m. Nancy A. **WARNER**, of Canaan, May 3, 1843, at Canaan, by Rev. A. B. Hubbard	2	23
Jack, had s. [ ], b. Feb. 23, 1849	2	49
John Warner, 5th s. Ephah & Esther, b. Aug. 16, 1797	1	35
Lucy, d. Ephah & Esther, b. Oct. 10, 1782	1	11
Moses Knap[p], 7th s. Ephah & Esther, b. Nov. 13, 1801	1	39
Philander, 4th s. Ephah & Esther, b. May 16, 1795	1	35
Prudence, m. Asahel **HUMPHRY**, Aug. 26, 1773	TM	7
Prudence, m. Asahel **HUMPHRY**, Aug. 26, 1775	TM	9
Ruth, 3rd d. Ephah & Esther, b. June 27, 1788	1	21
Truman, of New Hartford, m. Polly Mariah **WHITE**, of Norfolk, Sept. 3, 1822, by Elder Rufus Babcock	2	3
MERWIN, Samuel H., of Goshen, m. Sarah Ann M. **MINOR**, Sept. 18, 1837, by Rev. Joseph Eldredge	2	18
MILLARD, Franklin B., m. Mary M. **COLLAR**, b. of New Marlboro, Mass., Jan. 12, 1845, by Rev. A. B. Hubbard	2	24
MILLER, [see also **MELLER**], Louisa, d. Henry, ae 26 & Mary, [b.] Jan. 18, 1848	2	45
MILLS, MILL, Abigail, [d. Samuel & Abigail], b. Mar. 14, 1758	TM	6
Abigal, m. Hosea **WILLCOCKS**, Jr., b. of Norfolk, Nov. 2, 1774, by Rev. A. R. Robbins	1	10
Abigal, wid., m. Miles **RIGGS**, Apr. 20, 1779	1	10
Abram, 1st s. Samuell, Jr. & Lucy, b. June 2, 1778	1	11
Alfred, 2nd, s. Constantine & Philecta, b. Aug. 10, 1794	1	35
Almiry, d. Simeon & Abigal, b. June 16, 1771	1	11
Alvin, s. Simeon & Abigail, b. July 30, 1769	1	11
Asa, s. Samuel & Abigail, b. Aug. 20, 1766	TM	14
Benjamin, s. Benjamin & Hannah, b. Feb. 1, 1758; d. Apr. 1, 1758	TM	6
Benjamin, s. Benjamin & Hannah, b. May 11, 1759	TM	6
Benoney, s. Joseph & Susanna, b. Aug. 8, 1767	TM	15
Charry, 1st d. Constantine & Philecta, b. Jan. 19, 1788	1	35
Constantine, s. Joseph & Susanna, b. Sept. 6, 1761	TM	10
Constantine, m. Philecta **WAY**, Apr. 29, 1784	1	35

MILLS, MILL, (cont.)

	Vol.	Page
Syntha*, d. Simeon & Abigal, b. Sept. 22, 1774 *("Cynthia")	1	11
Daniel, 2nd s. Samuell, Jr. & Lucy, b. Dec. 3, 1779	1	11
Daniel J., m. Polly SMITH, b. of Norfolk, Feb. 17, 1830, by Pitkin Cowles	2	9
Dorinda*, 2nd d. Constantine & Philecta, b. Sept. 23, 1791 *("Pandora" in baptism)	1	35
Eben Augustus, 3rd s. Constantine & Philecta,b. Aug. 13, 1796	1	35
Eden, m. Rossanna WILLCOCKS, Apr. 16, 1786, by Dudley Humphry, J. P.	1	12
Editha, m. Cyrus CURTIS, b. of Norfolk, Apr. 19, 1789, by Dudley Humphry, J. P.	1	12
Ezekiel Willcocks, 1st s. Eden & Rosanna, b. Nov. 10, 1786	1	3a
Francies, s. Asa & Arthusa, b. Feb. 25, 1792	1	12
George S., m. Mary Ann WOODRUFF, May 11, 1846, by Rev. Joseph Eldredge	2	27
George Silvester, s. Eden & Rosanna, b. Dec. 16, 1795	1	34
Hannah, 1st d. Samuell, Jr. & Lucy, b. Oct. 23, 1781	1	11
Hannah, m. Seth THOMSON, Apr. 29, 1802	1	15
Hewit, 3rd s. Samuell, Jr. & Lucy, b. Dec. 8, 1783	1	7
Hiram, m. Louisa GAYLORD, Apr. 3, 1823, by Rev. R. Emerson	2	6
Hiram, m. Lydia GAYLORD, [Apr.] 26, [1829], by Rev. R. Emerson	2	8
Hiram, m. Charlotte PETTIBONE, Oct. 19, [1834], by Rev. Joseph Eldredge	2	16
Hiram, ae 50, m. Mary Ann GRANT, ae 40, [ ], 1849, by Rev. Ira Pettibone	2	31
Jrad, s. Eden & Rosanna, b. Jan. 13, 1793	1	34
Jsrael, s. Samuel & Abigale, b. Oct. 31, 1760	TM	6
John Milton, 2nd s. Eden & Rosanna, b. Oct. 30, 1788	1	34
Joseph Lewis, s. Dr. Joseph & Sarah, b. Nov. 3, 1781	1	12
Lawrence, d. Sept. 6, 1849, ae 83 y.	2	59
Lusina, d. Joseph & Hannah, b. May 28, 1772; d. July 23, 1772	TM	23
Lusine, d. Joseph & Hannah, b. Dec. 26, 1774	TM	23
Lydia, d. Samuel & Abigail, b. Dec. 16, 1755	TM	6
Margaret J., m. John A. SHEPARD, Oct. 8, 1826, by Rev. R. Emerson	2	6
Martin, 1st s. Constantine & Philecta, b. Feb. 14, 1785	1	35
Martin, m. Clarissa TUTTLE, Nov. 20, 1805, by William Battell	1	44
Michael F., m. Sally PETTIBONE, Oct. 16, 1803, by Giles Pettibone	1	15
Olle, d. Samuel & Abigail, b. Sept. 15, 1762	TM	14
Olle, m. Noah COWLES, b. of Norfolk, Dec. 14, 1780, by Rev. Mr. A. M. Robbins	1	10
Pandora, see under Dorinda		

MILLS, MILL, (cont.)

	Vol.	Page
Roger, s. Joseph & Hannah, b. Sept. 6, 1773	TM	23
Rosanna Selina, d. Eden & Rosanna, b. May 17, 1791	1	34
Roxy M., m. George **NETTLETON**, Mar. 16, 1823, by Rev. R. Emerson	2	6
Samuel, s. Samuel & Abigail, b. July 10, 1754	TM	6
Samuel, Jr., m. Lucy **CAY**, b. of Norfolk, Feb. 29, 1776, by Giles Pettibone *(Perhaps "Lucy **COY**")	1	11
Sarah, m. Joseph **COWLS**, June 18, 1771	TM	7
Sarah P., m. Jedediah **SAGE**, Sept. 26, 1826, by Asahel Gaylord	2	5
Starling, s. Joseph & Lusina, b. Apr. 8, 1769	TM	23
Susanna, w. Joseph, d. Aug. 8, 1767	TM	20
Susannah, m. Elijah **MASON**, May 12, 1768	TM	7
Timothy, s. Samuel[l] & Abigale, b. Oct. 26, 1764	TM	14

MINOR, MINER, Butler, m. Ruth **CATLEN**, Dec. 25, 1823, by Rufus Babcock

	Vol.	Page
	2	4
Mary, m. James **HOTCHKISS**, Nov. 25, 1823, by Rufus Babcock	2	4
Noah, m. Abigail Foot **GORHAM**, [Nov.] 13, [1828], by Rev. R. Emerson	2	8
Olive E., m. Appleton R. **STANNARD**, [Mar.] 11, [1845], by Rev. Joseph Eldredge	2	26
Sarah, m. Oliver **PHELPS**, Feb. 5, 1783, by Rev. Ami R. Robins	1	10
Sarah Ann M., m. Samuel H. **MERWIN**, of Goshen, Sept. 18, 1837, by Rev. Joseph Eldredge	2	18

MONTGOMERY, Elizabeth, ae 22, m. Michael **WALSH**, ae 27, Oct. 22, 1849, by Mr. Tucker

	Vol.	Page
	2	34

[MOORE], MOOR, MORE, Andrew, m. Thanks **PHELPS**, Aug. 5, 1762

	Vol.	Page
	TM	7
Andrew, s. Andrew & Thanks, b. May 27, 1769	TM	23
Andrew, Lieut., d. June 9, 1776	TM	21
Chancey, s. Andrew & Thanks, b. June 29, 1771	TM	23
Darius, s. Andrew & Thanks, b. Oct. 24, 1764; d. Dec. 4, 1767	TM	23
Job, s. Job & Mahitable, b. Dec. 6, 1764	TM	12
John, s. Andrew & Thanks, b. Oct. 21, 1775	TM	24
Rhoda, d. Andrew & Thanks, b. July 28, 1767; d. Oct. 3, 1772	TM	23
Rhoda, d. Andrew & Thanks, b. Oct. 29, 1773	TM	23
Roselenda, d. Job & Mahitable, b. Sept. 17, 1763	TM	12
Sarah, of Norfolk, m. Jonathan **CLARK**, of Guilford, Chenengo Cty., N. Y., Oct. [ ], 1824, by Bushnell Knapp, J. P.	2	5
Silvanus M., of New Hartford, m. Abigail M. **BROWN**, Aug. 13, [1827], by Rev. Joseph Eldredge	2	18
Thanks, 1st d. Andrew & Thanks, b. Jan. 7, 1763	TM	23

MOREY, Olive, m. David B. **KNAPP**, Nov. 24, 1822, by Bushnell Knapp, J. P.

	Vol.	Page
	2	3

	Vol.	Page
MORLEY, Clarissa, m. Benjamin MOSES, b. of Norfolk, Dec. 6, 1831, by Rev. Asahel Gaylord	2	13
MORMAS, Catharine, d. John, manufacturer, ae 31 & Ann M., ae 28, b. Apr. 26, 1848	2	42
MORRIS, Augustus C., of Goshen, m. Cordelia E. ROYS, [May] 25, [1849], by Rev. Joseph Eldredge	2	33
Charles, ae 30, m. Cordelia E. ROY, ae 29, May 24, [1849], by Joseph Eldredge	2	32
Edward, m. Minerva SHEFFIELD, Mar. 12, [1821], by R. Emerson	2	2
MOSES, Abigail, m. Lauren B. FOOT, Apr. 7, [1829], by Rev. R. Emerson	2	8
Ann, ae 35, m. Plinney FOOT, ae 61, Aug. 19, 1850, by Joseph Eldredge	2	35
Ann, of Canaan, m. Pliney FOOT, Aug. 19, 1850, by Rev. Joseph Eldredge	2	36
Benjamin, m. Clarissa MORLEY, b. of Norfolk, Dec. 6, 1831, by Rev. Asahel Gaylord	2	13
Betsey, of Norfolk, m. Halsey HURLBUT, of Enfield, Mar. 24, 1831, by Rev. Diodate Brockway, of Ellington	2	12
Eunice, m. George BROWN, b. of Norfolk, Mar. 24, 1831, by Rev. Diodate Brockway, of Ellington	2	12
Jacob, m. Elizabeth A. ROOT, Mar. 4, 1821, by R. Emerson	2	2
Jonah, s. Joshua & Abigail, b. Oct. 25, 1777	1	40
Julia, m. Nathaniel OVIATT, of Richfield, O., [June] 9, [1836], by Rev. Joseph Eldredge	2	18
Laura, ae 22, m. William W. WAUGH, ae 32, [ ], by Joseph Eldredge	2	35
Louisa, m. William W. WAUGH, of Winchester, June [ ], 1850, by Rev. Joseph Eldredge	2	36
Roxay, of Norfolk, m. Ariel KING, of New Marlborough, Dec. [ ], 1826, by Bushnell Knapp	2	6
Ruth, m. Harlow ROYS, Mar. 29, [1838], by Rev. Joseph Eldredge	2	19
Thomas, m. Caroline BROWN, Nov. 11, 1839, by Rev. J. Eldredge	2	21
MOSS, Elminah Georgeannah, d. [James], b. May 25, 1831	2	39
George Leveret, s. James, b. Dec. 13, 1829	2	39
MUNDAY, Louisa, d. John, b. Feb. 17, 1849	2	48
MUNGER, Antha, 2nd, d. [Jonathan & Elezabath], b. May 25, 1785	1	9a
Charlotte, 1st d. Jonathan & Elezabath, b. Oct. 3, 1783	1	9a
Jonathan, m. Elezabath LAWRANCE, Oct. 9, 1782, by Giles Pettibone	1	10
Nath[anie]ll, m. Ruth LEE, Feb. 8, 1769	1	11
Rachel, d. Nath[anie]ll & Ruth, b. Jan. 4, 1770	1	11
Sam[ue]ll, s. Nath[anie]ll & Ruth, b. July 16, 1772	1	11
MUNSON, Augustus, of Canaan, m. Harriet W. ROYS, [Nov.] 4, [1846], by Rev. Joseph Eldredge	2	27

	Vol.	Page
MUNSON, (cont.)		
Harriet, m. William **BUTLER**, May 39, 1842, by Rev. J. Eldredge	2	22
MURPHY, Margaret, m. George L. **WHITE**, b. of Norfolk, Jan. 23, 1848, by Rev. C. W. Watrous	2	28
Margaret, ae 18, m. George **WHITE**, ae 24, Jan. 23, 1848, by C. W. Watrous	2	29
MURRY, Gennett, ae 30, of Winchester, m. Robert A. **GEER**, ae 40, of Ledgward, Dec. 2, 1847, by Frederick Marsh	2	29
Mary Ellen, d. Frances, b. Apr. 11, 1850	2	52
MYRON (?), Margaret, ae 21, m. Jarer **ROBERTS**, ae 21, Jan. 26, [ ], by H. S. Gross	2	32
NETTLETON, George, m. Roxy M. **MILLS**, Mar. 16, 1823, by Rev. R. Emerson	2	6
John, m. Elizabeth **PHELPS**, Oct. 18, 1837, by Rev. Joseph Eldredge	2	19
Mary L., m. Austin **BELDEN**, Dec. 20, 1841, by Rev. J. Eldredge	2	22
Titus, m. Polley **WELCH**, May 9, 1793, by D. Humphry, J. P.	1	12a
William, m. Ruth **ANDRUS**, Oct. 18, 1797, by Asahel Humphry, J. P.	1	15
NICKERSON, A., of New Britain, m. Susan **CAMP**, of Norfolk, Sept. 29, [1835], by Rev. Joseph Eldredge	2	17
NORTH, Asa D., m. Clarrisa M. **BARDEN**, Jan. 29, 1820, by R. Emerson	2	2
Joel, m. Harriet **TAYLOR**, of Colebrook, July 30, 1823, by Rev. R. Emerson	2	6
John, m. Amey **RUSSEL**, Nov. 17, 1763	TM	7
Mary, d. John & Amey, b. Feb. 2, 1767	TM	13
Oliuer, 1st s. John & Amey, b. Aug. 27, 1764	TM	12
Russel, s. John & Aney, b. Jan. 14, 1769	TM	16
Sarah, d. John & Amey, b. Feb. 14, 1771	TM	18
NORTHWAY, Livia A., of Norfolk, m. Robert L. **HEDGER**, of New Marlborough, Oct. 19, 1831, by Rev. William Mitchell	2	12
Rhoda, m. David **FOX**, July 4, 1822, by Bushnell Knapp, J. P.	2	3
Samuel D., m. Sarah S. **POTTER**, of Canaan, Feb. 19, 1845, by Rev. Joseph Eldredge	2	26
NORTON, Alven, 2nd s. Salvanus & Thanks, b. Sept. 22, 1782	1	10a
Birdsey, m. Clarissa **THOMPSON**, Mar. 24, 1834, by Rev. Joseph Eldredge	2	15
Chandler, s. Ebenezer & Content, b. Dec. 22, 1779	1	40
Clarissa, m. Jeremiah **JOHNSON**, [Mar.] 20, [1839], by [Rev. Joseph Eldredge]	2	20
Desiah, m. Marcus **OVIATT**, of Goshen, Feb. 12, 1829, by Rev. R. Emerson	2	8
Dudley, 3rd s. Salvanus & Thanks, b. Feb. 26, [28?], 1786	1	10a
Dudley, m. Mrs. **SPAULDING**, Mar. 23, 1837, by Rev. Joseph		

NORTON, (cont.)

	Vol.	Page
Eldredge	2	18
Ebenezer, m. Content DOWD, Dec. 24, 1769	TM	7
Elisha, s. Ebenezer & Content, b. Oct. 14, 1770	TM	19
Eunice, 1st d. Salvanus & Thanks, b. Sept. 23, 1779	1	10a
Hanah, m. Joel HAMBLIN, Apr. 27, 1774	1	10
Hannah, wid. Stephen, d. May 20, 1848, ae 75	2	56
Hannah M., m. Henry TERRELL, Mar. 17, 1850, by Rev. Joseph Eldredge	2	36
Horace W., of New Marlboro, Mass., m. Martha J. PETTIBONE, of St. Lawrence Co., N. Y., Nov. 9, 1847, by Rev. Ira Pettibone, of Winsted	2	27
Jsaac, s. Ebenezer & Content, b. Feb. 18, 1775	TM	24
Isaac S., of Norfolk, m. Betsey ROOD, of Canaan, Dec. 12, 1830, by Rufus Babcock	2	11
James, s. Silvanus & Eunis, b. Nov. 7, 1773	TM	23
Marina, ae 48, m. Henry TYREL, ae 22, Mar. 17, 1850, by Rev. Joseph Eldredge	2	35
Rebeckah, d. Ebenezer & Content, b. July 23, 1777	1	2
Silvenus, s. Silvanus & Eunes, b. Feb. 8, 1772	TM	23
Silvanus, his w. [ ], d. Jan. 26, 1775	TM	21
Thank, m. Allen WEBSTER, of Sandisfield, Apr. 28, [1828], by Rev. R. Emerson	2	8
Theodoror, 1st s. Salvanus & Thanks, b. Jan. 27, 1778	1	10a
Uriel, m. Eliza JOHNSON, Sept. 30, [1835], by Rev. Joseph Eldredge	2	17
William J., m. Rebecca PHELPS, Mar. 13, 1839, by [Rev. Joseph Eldredge]	2	20
OAKLEY, William, of Canaan, m. Elizabeth BURR, [Oct.] 24, [1832], by Rev. Joseph Eldredge	2	14
O'BRIEN, Sarah, m. James COYNE, Jan. 4, 1850, by Harlow Roy	2	34
ODELL, William C., ae 26, m. Catharine ROYS, ae 21, Sept. 17, 1849, by Rev. Robert Codling	2	34
ODINE, Emma, illeg. d. Daniel ODINE, laborer, ae 25 & Mary SULLIVAN, ae 22, b. Feb. 7, 1848	2	43
ORVIS, Almira, d. Roger & Ruth, b. Aug. 4, 1780	1	40
Alva, s. Jesse & Susannah, b. Apr. 3, 1792; d. Sept. 17, 1794	1	40
Diantha, d. Roger & Ruth, b. June 18, 1785	1	40
Eleazar, s. Roger & Ruth, b. Sept. 16, 1782; d. Mar. 26, 1783	1	40
Eunice, d. Eleazar & Hannah, b. Oct. 13, 1769	1	40
Jesse, s. Eleazar & Hannah, b. June 11, 1772	1	40
Jesse,m. Susannah HOLDEN,Feb. 23, 1792,by Giles Pettibone		
Jesse, s. Jesse & Susannah, b. Aug. 15, 1803	1	15
Lovina, d. Jesse & Susannah, b. Dec. 1, 1799	1	40
Mabel, m. James DECKER, Aug. 27, 1829, by Rev. Rufus Babcock, of Colebrook	1	40
Philander, s. Roger & Ruth, b. Oct. 11, 1772	2	7
Polly, m. Augustus ROOD, June 1, 1823, by Bushnell	1	40

NORFOLK VITAL RECORDS 279

	Vol.	Page
ORVIS, (cont.)		
Knapp, J. P.	2	3
Prudence, d. Jesse & Susannah, b. June 19, 1796	1	40
Rachel, d. Roger & Ruth, b. Jan. 11, 1775	1	40
Salome, d. Roger & Ruth, b. July 24, 1789	1	40
Samuel, s. Roger & Ruth, b. Jan. 26, 1778	1	40
Susannah, d. Roger & Ruth, b. Feb. 4, 1784	1	40
Urania, d. Roger & Ruth, b. May 4, 1787	1	40
OSBORN, Noah Humphrey, s. John & Sarah, b. Aug. 25, 1802	1	43
Ruth Clark, d. John & Sarah, b. July 8, 1806	1	43
Sarah Marshsal, d. John & Sarah, b. June 1, 1804	1	43
OVIATT, Marcus, of Goshen, m. Desiah **NORTON**, Feb. 12, 1829, by Rev. R. Emerson	2	8
Nathaniel, of Richfield, O., m. Julia **MOSES**, [June] 9, [1836], by Rev. Joseph Eldredge	2	18
PALMER, Elias, s. Capt. George & Hannah, b. Sept. 29, 1751	TM	10
Hannah, d. Capt. George & Hannah, b. Sept. 13, 1760	TM	10
Isaiah, m. Sophia **HOSMER**, Feb. 6, 1834, by Rev. Joseph Eldredge	2	15
Samuel, of Goshen, m. Eunice C. **BROWN**, of Norfolk, May 9, 1839, by Rev. Grant Powers	2	20
[PARDEE], PARDE, Dorothy, m. Stephen **BAKER**, Sept. 9, 1760	TM	7
PARKER, Elue (?), m. Thomas **TIBBALS**, Jr., Aug. 22, 1780	1	15
Hannah, m. Hiland **HALL**, b. of Norfolk, Dec. 28, 1779, by Giles Pettibone, J. P.	1	10
PARROT, PARRET, Albert, m. Nancy **WHITE**, Nov. 18, 1824, by Rufus Babcock	2	4
Christe, child, of Lewis, b. Nov. 24, 1849	2	52
Elvira, of Norfolk, m. Joseph **BUTTON**, of Tolland, Mass., Apr. 24, 1845, by Rev. A. B. Hubbard	2	25
Ruth, m. Darius **CAMP**, Nov. 30, [1837], by Rev. Joseph Eldredge	2	19
Sarah, m. Uriel **ANDRUS**, Oct. 25, 1841, by Rev. J. Eldredge	2	22
Sarah J., d. Burr G., b. Mar. 9, 1849	2	50
Zalmon, m. Anna **BOLLES**, May 17, 1821, by Rev. Rufus Babcock, of Colebrook	2	1
PARSONS, Betsey L., d. Mary, b. Dec. 16, 1848	2	50
Emily, d. Levi, ae 26 & Nancy, ae 20, b. [ ]	2	45
Ichabod, ae 54, m. Ruth **EVANS**, ae 38, Oct. 1, 1848, by Rev. Joseph Eldredge	2	31
Ichabod, m. Ruth **EVANS**, [ ], 1848, by Rev. Joseph Eldredge	2	33
Levi N., m. Nancy **MENDES**, Nov. 2, [1846], by Rev. Joseph Eldredge	2	27
Lewis J., b. Oct. 29, 1829	2	39
Mary, had illeg. d. Betsey L., b. Dec. 16. 1848	2	50
Mary S., d. Ichabod, b. Sept. 16. 1824	2	39
William Lawrence, s. Alexander, b. Sept. 5, 1821	2	39

280   BARBOUR COLLECTION

	Vol.	Page
PEARS, [see also PEASE & PIERCE], Elizabeth A., of Norfolk, m. Frederick LAWRENCE, of Canaan, Jan. 1, 1838, by Rev. Joseph Eldredge	2	19
PEARSE, [see under PIERCE]		
PEASE, PEAS, PEACE, PEASSE, [see also PEARS], Augustus P., d. July 17, 1848, ae 56	2	56
Earl P., m. Mary IVES, Apr. 8, 1802, by Rev. Mr. Morgan	1	44
Eliza, d. Earl P. & Mary, b. Mar. 19, 1803	1	48
Emily A., of Norfolk, m. Martial R. WEED, of South Farms, Apr. 2, [1834], by Rev. Joseph Eldredge	2	15
Joseph Ives, s. Earl P. & Mary, b. Aug. 9, 1809	1	48
Pearcey, m. [ ] RICHARDS, b. of Norfolk, Nov. [ ], 1830, by Amos Pettibone, J. P.	2	12
Phineas, of Norfolk, m. Betty LAWRENCE, of Canaan, Nov. 25, 1779, by Dudley Humphrey, J. P.	1	10
Spencer, m. Lepha FRENCH, Jan. 11, 1841, by Rev. J. Eldredge	2	21
William, m. Polly Maria FRENCH, Oct. 28, 1841, by Rev. J. Eldredge	2	22
PECK, Arabela, d. Harlow & Lucy Ann, b. Mar. 5, 1848	2	47
Charles W., s. W[illia]m K., b. Oct. 6, 1850	2	53
Eliza, m. Nath[anie]l WHITE, b. of Norfolk, Oct. 23, 1823, by Rufus Babcock	2	4
Harriet, m. James S. LEWIS, of Goshen, Mar. 31, 1836, by Rev. Joseph Eldredge	2	18
PENDLETON, Clarrissa, d. Mar. 30, 1850, ae 4 y.	2	59
Frederick, m. Flora PINNEY, b. of Norfolk, Mar. 18, 1828, by Rev. E. Washburn	2	7
Grove, d. Apr. 5, 1850, ae 6 y.	2	59
Henry, farmer, ae 34 & Martha Adaline, ae 26, had child b. July 17, 1848	2	44
Joseph, s. James, b. Apr. 1, 1850	2	52
Lucinda, d. Apr. 6, 1850, ae 1 y. 9 m.	2	60
M., m. [ ] BAILEY, of Goshen, Sept. 27, 1837, by Rev. Joseph Eldredge	2	18
Sally, m. Damon PINNEY b. of Norfolk, Jan. 12, 1830, by Rev. Bradley Selleck	2	9
PERCY, Mary Ann, m. Lewis O. ROGERS, Mar. 22, 1842, by Rev. J. Eldredge	2	22
PERKINS, Cyrus, s. Gilbert, b. Nov. 6, 1848	2	49
PETERS, Thomas, m. Dinah VALONE, June 24, 1803, by Giles Pettibone	1	15
Thomas Benjamin, s. Thomas & Dinah, b. May 19, 1804	1	41
PETTIBONE, Amos, s. Samuel & Martha, b. Sept. 4, 1770	TM	19
Amos, m. Julia PETTIBONE, [Apr.] 22, [1834], by Rev. Joseph Eldredge	2	15
Andrew, 3rd s. Elijah & Mabel, b. June 4, 1781	1	19
Asher, 4th s. Elijah & Mabel, b. Nov. 12, 1782	1	19

	Vol.	Page
PETTIBONE, (cont.)		
Augustus, 3rd s. Giles & Desiah, b. Feb. 19, 1766	TM	13
Augustus, 3rd s. [Giles & Desier], b. Feb. 19 (?), 1769	1	6
Cephas, 2nd s. [Giles & Desier], b. Sept. 16, 1763	1	6
Cephas, s. Giles & Deziah, b. Sept. 16, 1763	TM	11
Charlotte, d. Giles, Jr. & Louisa, b. Sept. 19, 1797	1	43
Charlotte, m. Hiram **MILLS**, Oct. 19, [1834], by Rev. Joseph Eldredge	2	16
Cloe, 1st d. Elijah & Mabel, b. Apr. 24, 1785	1	19
Deziah, d. [Giles & Desier], b. Feb. 2, 1769	1	6
Daziah, d. Giles & Daziah, b. Feb. 2, 1769	TM	17
Desiah, w. Giles, d. June 24, 1774	TM	21
Deziah H., m. Halsey **STEVENS**, Oct. 5, [1829], by Rev. R. Emerson	2	8
Desire Humphry, d. Giles, Jr. & Louisa, b. Oct. 3, 1803	1	43
Eben[eze]r, s. Elijah & Mabel, b. Apr. 26, 1778	1	19
Elijah, Jr., 2nd s. Elijah & Mabel, b. Oct. 10, 1779	1	19
Eunice, d. Giles, Jr. & Louisa, b. Jan. 26, 1790	1	41
Giles, s. Giles & Dezeiah, b. May 15, 1760	TM	10
Giles, Jr., 1st s. Giles & Desier, b. May 15, 1769 (?) *("1760" in Humphrey Genealogy)	1	6
Giles, m. Margrat **HOLCOMB**, June 20, 1776	TM	9
Jsaac, d. July 31, 1771	TM	20
Jacob, s. Eli & Phebe, b. Jan. 8, 1760	TM	6
Jno, of Ogdensburg, N. Y., m. Louisa P. **WELD**, of Norfolk, Oct. 4, 1830, by Frederick Marsh	2	10
Jonathan, 4th s. Giles & Margrit, b. Jan. 15, 1777	1	6
Jonathan Humphry, s. Giles, Jr. & Louisa, b. Jan. 15, 1793	1	41
Josiah, 7th s. [Giles & Margrit], b. Jan. 16, 1782	1	6
Judith, m. Joel **WALTER**, May 13, 1762	TM	7
Julia, d. Giles, Jr & Louisa, b. May 1, 1787	1	41
Julia, m. Amos **PETTIBONE**, [Apr.] 22, [1834], by Rev. Joseph Eldredge	2	15
Levi, 6th s. [Giles & Margrit], b. Dec. 17, 1780	1	6
Louisa, d. Giles, Jr. & Louisa, b. Jan. 16, 1785	1	41
Louisa, d. Giles, Jr. & Louisa, d. Jan. 1, 1806	1	14
Luman, s. Samuel & Martha, b. July 10, 1766	TM	19
Maria Eliza, m. Ezra **HUNT**, b. of St. Charles, Mo., May 17, 1830, by Pitkin Cowles	2	9
Martha, d. Samuel & Martha, b. Sept. 21, 1776	1	1
Martha J., of St. Lawrence Co., N. Y., m. Horace W. **NORTON**, of New Marlboro, Mass., Nov. 9, 1847, by Rev. Ira Pettibone, of Winsted	2	27
Mary, d. Isaac & Hepzibah, b. May 26, 1758	TM	6
Mary, d. Eli & Phebe, b. Dec. 7, 1757; d. Apr. 13, 1760	TM	6
Mary, 6th d. Isaac & Hepzibah, b. Aug. 12, 1765	TM	12
Philo, s. Samuel & Martha, b. Aug. 21, 1773	TM	19
Polly, d. Giles, Jr. & Louisa, b. July 26, 1782	1	41

282 BARBOUR COLLECTION

	Vol.	Page
PETTIBONE, (cont.)		
Polly, m. Giles **THOMSON,** Apr. 14, 1803, by Giles Pettibone, J. P.	1	15
Roswill, s. Isaac & Hepziba, b. Aug. 14, 1760	TM	6
Rufus, 8th s. [Giles & Margrit], b. May 26, 1784	1	6
Sally, m. Michael F. **MILLS,** Oct. 16, 1803, by Giles Pettibone	1	15
Samuel, s. Samuel, d. Feb. 17, 1763	TM	20
Samuel, m. Martha **PHELPS,** Sept. 22, 1763	TM	7
Samuel, s. Samuel & Martha, b. Sept. 14, 1768	TM	19
Samuel A., m. Samantha **KNAPP,** [Apr.] 24, [1822], by R. Emerson	2	2
Sarah, d. [Giles & Desier], b. May 12, 1771; d. May 13, 1771	1	6
Sarah, d. Giles & Desiah, b. May 12, 1771; d. May 12, 1771	TM	18
Sarah, d. Giles, Jr. & Louisa, b. June 29, 1780	1	41
Sarah, m. Eb[eneze]r B. **WETMORE,** May 16, [1823], by Rev. R. Emerson	2	6
Sereno, 5th s. [Giles & Margrit], b. Nov. 9, 1778	1	6
Susannah, d. Giles, Jr. & Louisa, b. Oct. 23, 1795	1	41
PHELPS, PHELP, Abel, 2nd, s. Joseph & Huldah, b. Apr. 29, 1785	1	9
Abigail, 2nd d. Oliver & Sarah, b. Aug. 1, 1786	1	10a
Ann O., m. Franklin D. **GRAY,** July 4, 1843, by Rev. Joseph Eldredge	2	24
Anna, 2nd d. Dauid & Triphene, b. Dec. 8, 1758	TM	10
Asahel G., m. Fanny **CASE,** Nov. 9, [1841], by Rev. J. Eldredge	2	22
Asenath, 4th d. Dauid [& Triphene], b. Sept. 24, 1761; d. Nov. 28, 1761	TM	10
Charlotte, m. Sam[ue]l **SEYMOUR,** of Colebrook, Apr. 24, 1823, by Rev. R. Emerson	2	6
Cecero, of Groton, N. Y., m. Keziah **GRANT,** of Norfolk, about Sept. 14, 1825, by Rev. Mr. Marsh, of Winchester (Cicero)	2	5
Daved, s. Daved & Tripheney, b. Aug. 4, 1764	TM	17
Electa H., m. Horace **MEACHAM,** of Summers, Jan. 24, 1827, by Rev. R Emerson	2	6
Eliza B., ae 30, m. George **BENNETT,** ae 36, Sept. [ ], 1848, by Joseph Eldredge	2	31
Eliza B., m. George **BENNET,** of Montreal, N. Y., Sept. [ ], 1848, by Rev. Joseph Eldredge	2	33
Elizabeth, m. John **NETTLETON,** Oct. 18, 1837, by Rev. Joseph Eldredge	2	19
Elkanah, 8th s. Joel & Jerusha, b. Jan. 11, 1775	1	2
Elkanah, s. Elkanah & Abigal, b. Jan. 8, 1776	1	2
Elkanah, d. Oct. 10, 1777	1	5
Ellen E., d. Asahel G., b. Nov. 15, 1848	2	48
Eunice A., of Norfolk, m. David **BIRD,** Jr., of Winchester,,		

	Vol.	Page
PHELPS, PHELP, (cont.)		
Oct. 20, 1830, by Frederick Marsh	2	11
Ezekiel Willcocks, 9th s. Joel & Jerusha, b. May 13, 1777; d. [ ]* *(Entry crossed out)	1	2
Ezekiel Willcocks, d. Oct. 18, 1777	1	5
Fredrick, 6th s. John & Thanks, b. June 27, 1765	TM	13
Fredrick, m. Anna **THOMSON**, Dec. 20, 1807, by Rev. Ammi R. Robbins	1	44
Helen, d. Joseph & Huldah*, b. Sept. 6, 1781 *(First written "Helen")	1	11a
J. W., Jr., m. Olive **DEAN**, Nov. 21, [1821], by R. Emerson	2	2
Jerusha, d. Daved & Tryphena, b. Feb. 6, 1771	TM	19
Jerusha, 7th d. David & Triphena, b. Feb. 6, 1771	1	5
Joel, 4th, s. Joel & Jerusha, b. Sept. 21, 1765	TM	12
John, m. Eliza Ann **BETTIS**, Dec. 5, [1821], by R. Emerson	2	2
John G., d. Dec. 24, 1848, ae 7 y.	2	58
Joseph, s. Joseph & Huldah, b. Apr. 9, 1778	1	11a
Louisa, m. Andrew **BALDWIN**, Sept. 13, [1837], by Rev. Joseph Eldredge	2	18
Lovina, w. Bethuel, b. Norfolk, d. Sept. 29, 1847, in Ohio, ae 57	2	56
Luman, s. Daved & Tryphena, b. Mar. 10, 1768	TM	17
Luman, s. Matthew & Jerusha, b. Jan. 25, 1772	TM	22
Luman, s. Daved, d. Jan. 31, 1772	TM	20
Lumen, twin with Truman, s. David & Triphena, b. May 5, 1775	1	5
Margaret, m. C. C. **ROCKWELL**, June 15, 1848, by Rev. Joseph Eldredge	2	28
Margaret, ae 25, of Norfolk, m. C. Columbus **ROCKWELL**, attorney, ae 24, b. Norfolk, res. Lexington, Ia., June 15, 1848, by Joseph Eldredge	2	29
Marietta A., m. John R. **COOK**, of Winsted, Oct. 15, 1845, by Rev. Joseph Eldredge	2	26
Martha, m. Samuel **PETTIBONE**, Sept. 22, 1763	TM	7
Martain, 7th s. Joel & Jerusha, b. Sept. 10, 1772	1	2
Mary, of Norfolk, m. Sylvester **PLATT**, of Winchester, Sept. 4, 1833, by Rev. Joseph Eldredge	2	15
Mary Fitch, m. Henry M. **KNIGHT**, Oct. 2, 1850, by Rev. Joseph Eldredge	2	36
Mercy, m. David W. **RICE**, Sept. 8, 1803, by Eleazur Holt	1	10
Olive, d. Daved & Trypena, b. Apr. 4, 1766	TM	17
Olive, m. John Treat **WARNER**, May 10, [1829], by Rev. R. Emerson	2	8
Oliver, m. Sarah **MINER**, Feb. 5, 1783, by Rev. Ami R. Robbins	1	10
Oral, 8th d. David & Triphena, b. Nov. 4, 1777	1	5
Philo, 6th s. Joel & Jerusha, b. May 18, 1770	1	2
Philura, 2nd d. Joseph & Hulday, b. Feb. 4, 1788	1	11

PHELPS, PHELP, (cont.)

	Vol.	Page
Phenias, 5th s. Joel & Jerusha, b. Feb. 14, 1778	1	2
Polly, m. Dudley HUMPHRY, Oct. 16, 1798, by Rev. Publius Virgilius Boge	1	35
Rebecca, m. William J. NORTON, Mar. 13, 1839, by [Rev. Joseph Eldredge]	2	20
Robert, s. Darius, d. June 16, 1848, ae 10	2	56
Ruth*, d. Matthew & Jerusha, b. Dec. 26, 1766 *(First written "Vashti")	TM	14
Sally W., m. Samuel D. CHAPIN, of Somers, [May] 28, [1829], by Rev. R. Emerson	2	8
Salmon, 1st w. Elijah & Pheby, b. Jan. 21, 1772	1	11
Samuel Nash, 3rd s. Joel & Jerusha, b. Mar. 24, 1763	TM	11
Sarah, m. Ebenezer BURR, Nov. 27, 1760	TM	7
Sarah, d. Capt. Elijah & Phebey*, b. Mar. 11, 1782 *(First written "Tripheny")	1	7
Sarah, d. Elijah, b. Mar. 11, 1782 *(Entry crossed out)	1	11
Solomon, s. Daved & Tryphena, b. Feb. 11, 1770	TM	17
Susannah, 1st d. Dauid & Triphenah, b. Sept. 3, 1751	TM	10
Salvester, 2nd s. Elijah & Pheby, b. Apr. 11, 1775	1	11
Thanks, m. Anderw MOOR, Aug. 5, 1762	TM	7
Triphena, 3rd d. Dauid & Triphene, b. Apr. 1, 1760	TM	10
Truman, twin with Lumen, s. David & Triphena, b. May 5, 1775	1	5
William, m. Fanna COWLES, b. of Norfolk, Apr. 10, 1832, by Rev. Frederick Marsh, of Winchester	2	13
William C., ae 41 & Parny, ae 41, had child, b. Feb. 19, 1848	2	45
William E., m. Jennet J. BABBIT, Sept. 1, 1841, by Rev. J. Eldredge	2	22
Zerah, s. Elkanah & Abigal, b. Dec. 21, 1766	1	2

[PIERCE], PEIRCE, PEARSE, [see also PEARS], Amos, m.

Merian BUTLER, May 13, [1841], by Rev. J. Eldredge	2	21
Garrett, s. Patrick & Mary Ann, m. Ellen CAREY, d. Jeremiah & Mary, June 4, 1850, by Rev. H. Tucker. Witnesses: Richard Pierce & Catharine Carey	2	34
Hellen E., m. Frederick LAWRENCE, Jan. 11, 1844, by Rev. Joseph Eldredge	2	24
Rodney, m. Jane DUTTON, Aug. 30, 1841, by Rev. J. Eldredge	2	22

PINNEY, Adaline, of Norfolk, m. Albert BEACH, of Goshen,

Sept. 11, 1831, by Rev. Luther Mead	2	12
Damon, m. Sally PENDLETON, b. of Norfolk, Jan. 12, 1830, by Rev. Bradley Selleck	2	9
Flora, m. Frederick PENDLETON, b. of Norfolk, Mar. 18, 1828, by Rev. E. Washburn	2	7
Henry, of Colebrook, m. Delana RIGG, of Norfolk, Jan. 12, 1825, by Rev. F. Marsh, of Winchester	2	4

PLATT, Abi, ae 56, m. Hiram ROY, ae 55, Jan. 7, 1850, by Rev.

	Vol.	Page
PLATT, (cont.)		
Frederick Marsh	2	34
Sylvester, of Winchester, m. Mary **PHELPS**, of Norfolk, Sept. 4, 1833, by Rev. Joseph Eldredge	2	15
PLUMB, PLUME, Amiriah, m. Sarah **ASPINWELL,** Mar. 10, 1757	TM	7
Amiriah, s. Amiriah & Sarah, b. Apr. 23, 1760	TM	10
Joseph, s. Amiriah & Sarah, b. Jan. 11, 1757	TM	10
Mabel, d. Amariah & Sarah, b. Mar. 10, 1762	TM	10
Maria, m. Julian **DANFORTH** (colored), Oct. 2, 1837, by Rev. Joseph Eldredge	2	19
PORTER, Frederick E., m. Elizabeth B. **AKINS,** May 21, 1845, by Rev. Joseph Eldredge	2	26
Jennett, m. Egbert T. **BUTLER,** May 1, [1839], by Rev. Joseph Eldredge	2	20
Luther, of Colebrook, m. Naomi H. **ROGERS,** of Norfolk, May 8, 1822, by Michael F. Mills, J. P.	2	2
POTTER, Easther, of Canaan, m. Miles **RIGGS,** Apr. 16, [1845], by Rev. Joseph Eldredge	2	26
Jared, m. Rebecca **BABBET,** Feb. 9, 1841, by Rev. J. Eldredge	2	21
Nancy, of Canaan, m. Erastus **BURR,** Mar. 24, 1847, by Rev. Joseph Eldredge	2	27
Sarah S., of Canaan, m. Samuel D. **NORTHWAY,** Feb. 19, 1845, by Rev. Joseph Eldredge	2	26
PRATT, Betsey, of Canaan, m. Ezekiel **FITCH,** of New Marlboro, Mass., Jan. 1, 1834, by Rev. Theron Ellis, of Bap. Ch.	2	15
PRESTON, Sibel Maria, d. Seth, b. May 31, 1812	2	38
PROPER, Nelson, of New York, m. Elizabeth **VAN OSTRUM,** of Norfolk, July 22, 1849, by Harlow Goodwin, of Canaan	2	30
PROUT, Eunice, m. Rume **LaBOUTE,** May 23, [1847], by Rev. Joseph Eldredge	2	28
RANDELL, [see under **BANDELL**]		
RANSOM, Esther, 3rd d. Samuel & Esther, b. Mar. 12, 1766	TM	13
George Palmer, s. Samuel & Easter, b. Jan. 3, 1762	TM	22
Lovisa Lawrance, d. Samuel & Easter, b. May 28, 1768	TM	22
Mary, d. Samuel & Easter, b. May 20, 1772	TM	22
Sibbel, d. Samuel & Easter, b. Feb. 1, 1764	TM	22
William, s. Samuel & Easter, b. May 26, 1770	TM	22
RAY, [see under **ROYS**]		
[**REMINGTON**], **RIMINGTON,** Jabez, of Norfolk, affidavit "am of the Anne baptis perswasion and do indeavor at all times to attend that worship beleaveing in my concience that it is true worship of God". Witness: Elder Joseph Hastings, June 12, 1776	TM	8
RICE, [see also **ROYS**], Amy, m. Bazil **TREAT,** Mar. 10, 1801, by Rev. A. R. Robins	1	44
David W., 6th s. Nathaniel & Elenor, b. Aug. 30, 1775	1	10

RICE, (cont.)

	Vol.	Page
David W., m. Mercy **PHELPS**, Sept. 8, 1803, by Eleazur Holt	1	10
Elizabeth, m. Nathaniel **STEVENS**, Nov. 19, 1789	1	44
Polly, m. Gideon **CURTIS**, Sept. 14, 1797, by Rev. R. Robbins	1	13a
RICHARDS, Elisha Hiram, m. Lucy **HOLT**, Apr. 19, 1827, by Rev. R. Emerson	2	8
Julius, m. Mary S. **CAMP**, Apr. 27, 1831, by Frederick Marsh	2	12
----, m. Pearcey **PEASE**, b. of Norfolk, Nov. [ ], 1830, by Amos Pettibone, J. P.	2	12
RIGGS, RIGG, RIGS, Delana, of Norfolk, m. Henry **PINNEY**, of Colebrook, Jan. 12, 1825, by Rev. F. Marsh, of Winchester	2	4
Eden, 2nd s. Miles & Abigal, b. June 30, 1785	1	11
H. H., m. Marilla **KILBOURNE**, Dec. 11, 1843, by Rev. Joseph Eldredge	2	24
Hiram H., m. Mary A. **KILBANE**, Mar. 9, [1836], by Rev. Joseph Eldredge	2	17
Joseph, 1st s. Miles & Abigal, b. Feb. 2, 1780	1	11
Maria, of Norfolk, m. Luman **FOOT**, of Canaan, Sept. 25, 1844, by Alfred E. Ives	2	23
Marther, w. Miles, d. Sept. 9, 1778	1	14
Mary, m. Frederick **BRONSON**, Apr. 21, 1840, by Rev. J. Eldredge	2	21
Mary E., d. Miles, b. June 3, 1849	2	48
Miles, m. Marther **BELL***, Feb. 28, 1775 *(Note says "BULL")	1	10
Miles, Jr., 1st s. Miles, b. Dec. 20, 1777	1	11
Miles, m. wid. Abigal **MILLS**, Apr. 20, 1779	1	10
Miles, Jr., m. Abigal **BENEDICT**, Oct. 19, 1797, by Asahel Humphry, J. P.	1	15
Miles, m. Easther **POTTER**, of Canaan, Apr. 16, [1845], by Rev. Joseph Eldredge	2	26
Norman, had s. [ ], b. July 24, 1848	2	49
[**RILEY**], **RYLEY**, Mary Ellen, d. John, b. Feb. 10, 1849	2	50
ROBBINS, Ammi R., m. Mrs. Elisebeth **LeBARON**, of Pleinoth*, May 13, 1762 *("Plymouth")	TM	7
Ammi Ruhamah, s. Ammi R. & Elizabeth, b. Jan. 3, 1768	TM	16
Elisebeth, 1st d. Ammi R. & Elisebeth, b. Jan. 5, 1766; d. Jan. 9, 1766	TM	13
Elisebeth, d. Ami R. & Elisebeth, b. Jan. 8, 1770	TM	19
Francis LeBaron, s. Ammi R. & Elizabeth, b. Mar. 9, 1775	1	1
Francis LeBaron, s. Ammi R. & Elizabeth, d. Sept. 3, 1777	1	5
Hannah, w. Nathaniel, d. Nov. 17, 1811	2	55
James, s. Ammi R. & Elizabeth, b. Apr. 19, 1782	1	5
Louisa, m. Joel **SACKET**, [Apr.] 20, [1829], by Rev. R. Emerson	2	8
Mara, d. Ammi R. & Elizabeth, b. Jan. 8, 1767; d. Jan. 9, 1767	TM	16

	Vol.	Page
ROBBINS, (cont.)		
Maria M., m. Aaron **GILBERT**, b. of Norfolk, Aug. 8, 1831, by Pitkin Cowles	2	12
Nathaniel, s. Ami R. & Elisebeth, b. June 18, 1772	TM	19
P. S., m. Steven P. **HUMPHREY**, of Goshen, [Mar.] 21, [1833], by Rev. Joseph Eldredge	2	14
Philemon, 1st s. Ammi R., b. Mar. 13, 1763; d. Mar. 20, 1763	TM	11
Philemon, 2nd s. Ammi Ruhamah & Elisebeth, b. Feb. 28, 1764	TM	12
Philemon, 2nd s. Ammi R., d. Sept. 26, 1766	TM	14
Philura, m. [ ] **HUBBARD**, Jan. 25, 1842, by Rev. J. Eldredge	2	22
Sarah, d. Ammi R. & Elizabeth, b. Aug. 22, 1779	1	5
Sarah, m. Joseph **BATTELL**, July 24, 1805, by Rev. A. R. Robbins	1	44
Thomas, s. Ammi R. & Elizabeth, b. Aug. 11, 1777	1	1
ROBERTS, ROBBERTS, Amey, m. Chester **BARNES**, Mar. 19, 1844, by Rev. Joseph Eldredge	2	24
Jarer, ae 21, m. Margaret **MYRON** (?), ae 21, Jan. 26, [ ], by H. S. Gross	2	32
Levi, d. May 12, 1848, ae 25	2	56
Susan, m. James **HYDE**, Dec. 26, 1842, by Rev. J. Eldredge	2	22
ROBINSON, Martha, d. Philip, farmer, ae 37 & Elizabeth, ae 30, b. Nov. 18, 1847	2	42
Mathew, d. Oct. 30, 1848, ae 11 y.	2	58
Philip, m. Charlotte **BURR**, June 17, [1841], by Rev. J. Eldredge	2	21
ROCKWELL, C. C., m. Margaret **PHELPS**, June 15, 1848, by Rev. Joseph Eldredge	2	28
C. Columbus, attorney, ae 24, b. Norfolk, res. Lexington, Ia., m. Margaret **PHELPS**, ae 25, of Norfolk, June 15, 1848, by Joseph Eldredge	2	29
Cornelia, m. Osmyn **BAKER**, Oct. 9, [1838], by Rev. Joseph Eldredge	2	19
Joseph, made affidavit Nov. 20, 1809, "that he was of the Baptist Perswation"	1	44
Louisa, m. Thomas J.* **COWLES**, Aug. 31, [1828], by Rev. R. Emerson *(Written over "**TRUMBULL**")	2	8
Timothy, m. Helen **MARSHALL**, of Colebrook, Sept. 24, [1828], by Rev. R. Emerson	2	8
ROGERS, Asa, 1st s. Abiathar & Naomi, b. Aug. 9, 1782	1	39
Betsey, 1st d. Abiathar & Naomi, b. Apr. 17, 1784; d. Aug. 4, 1786	1	39
Darius, s. Abiathar & Naomi, b. Mar. 9, 1807	1	43
David, s. Abiathar & Naomi, b. Aug. 22, 1797	1	39
Eunice, d. Abiathar & Naomi, b. Mar. 12, 1787	1	39
Isaac Lewis, s. Lewis, colored & Mary Ann, ae 25, b. July 5, 1848	2	44

	Vol.	Page
ROGERS, (cont.)		
John, s. Abiathar & Naomi, b. July 29, 1802	1	39
John, m. Elizabeth **CATLEN**, May 4, 1826, by Rufus Babcock, of Colebrook	2	5
Lewis O., m. Mary Ann **PERCY**, Mar. 22, 1842, by Rev. J. Eldredge	2	22
Naomi, d. Abiathar & Naomi, b. Mar. 4, 1791; d. Feb. 19, 1792	1	39
Naomi, d. Abiather & Naomi, b. Jan. 7, 1793; d. Mar. 7, 1794	1	39
Naomi H., of Norfolk, m. Luther **PORTER**, of Colebrook, May 8, 1822, by Michael F. Mills, J. P.	2	2
Naomi Harrinton, d. Abiathar & Naomi, b. Sept. 19, 1795	1	39
Rene, d. Abiathar & Naomi, b. Feb. 24, 1789	1	39
Samuel Rose, s. Abiathar & Naomi, b. Mar. 3, 1800	1	39
ROOD, Augustus, m. Polly **ORVIS**, June 1, 1823, by Bushnell Knapp, J. P.	2	3
Betsey, of Canaan, m. Isaac S. **NORTON**, of Norfolk, Dec. 12, 1830, by Rufus Babcock	2	11
Elizabeth P., m. Miles B. **TOBEY**, Oct. 1, 1844, by Rev. Joseph Eldredge	2	24
Lois A., ae 20 y., m. Henry W. **KNAPP**, ae 27 y., b. of Norfolk, Nov. 7, 1847, by Rev. C. W. Watrous	2	27
Lois Ann, ae 20, m. Henry W. **KNAPP**, ae 27, Nov. 7, 1847, by Charles Watrous	2	30
ROOT, Elizabeth A., m. Jacob **MOSES**, Mar. 4, 1821, by R. Emerson	2	2
Jemima, m. Grastus **HADSDEL**, of Burlington, Nov. 3, [1828], by Rev. R. Emerson	2	8
Sarah Ann, had illeg. s. [ ], b. [ ], 1849	2	48
Sidney G., m. Delia S. **SEYMOUR**, [Jan.] 8, [1838], by Rev. Joseph Eldredge	2	19
William, m. Abigail **STONE**, Oct. 26, 1797, by Asahel Humphry, J. P.	1	15
ROSS, Stephen, ae 30, m. Urania **SCHUDER**, ae 14, Jan. 1, 1850, by Harlow Ray	2	35
ROYS, ROY, [see also RICE], Aaron, m. Elizabeth **KNAPP**, Aug. 20, 1793, by Rev. Ammi R. Robbins	2	1
Caroline, m. Harrison **HALL**, [Mar.] 4, [1846], by Rev. Joseph Eldredge	2	26
Caroline R., ae 28, m. Abner **HINMAN**, ae 30, Feb. 22, [1849], by Joseph Eldredge	2	32
Catharine, ae 21, m. William C. **ODELL**, ae 26, Sept. 17, 1849, by Rev. Robert Codling	2	34
Clarissa E., m. W. **ELLIOTT**, June 26, 1848, by Rev. Joseph Eldredge	2	28
Clarissa E., ae 20, of Norfolk, m. Eliot **WOODWARD**, druggist, ae 22, of Waltham, June 26, 1848, by Joseph Eldredge	2	29

	Vol.	Page
ROYS, ROY, (cont.)		
Cordelia E., ae 29, m. Charles **MORRISS**, ae 30, May 24, [1849], by Joseph Eldredge	2	32
Cordelia E., m. Augustus C. **MORRIS**, of Goshen, [May] 25, [1849], by Rev. Joseph Eldredge	2	33
Daniel, d. July 8, 1850, ae 67 y.	2	59
Ella Frances, d. Lorenzo, b. Nov. 1, 1848	2	48
Harlow, m. Ruth **MOSES**, Mar. 29, [1838], by Rev. Joseph Eldredge	2	19
Harriet W., m. Augustus **MUNSON**, of Canaan, [Nov.] 4, [1846], by Rev. Joseph Eldredge	2	27
Hiram, ae 55, m. Abi **PLATT**, ae 56, Jan. 7, 1850, by Rev. Frederick Marsh	2	34
Lorenzo, m. Helen **WATROUS**, [Oct.] 27, [1847], by Rev. Joseph Eldredge	2	28
Lorenzo, ae 24, m. Hellen **WATROUS**, ae 23, Oct. 18, 1847, by Joseph Eldredge	2	30
Louisa H., m. Luther **SALMON**, of Richmond, Mass., Nov. 14, [1838], by Rev. Joseph Eldredge	2	19
Louisa Hanah, d. Aaron & Elizabeth, b. Mar. 29, 1802	2	37
Lucy, m. Horace **EMMONS**, [Mar.] 12, [1828], by Rev. R. Emerson	2	8
Lucy M., ae 24, m. James **GILBERT**, farmer, ae 23, Oct. 17, 1847, by Me. Zell	2	29
Lucy P., d. Aug. 13, 1848, ae 44	2	57
Mercy, Mrs., m. Seth **WILSON**, Nov. 17, [1834], by Rev. Joseph Eldredge	2	16
Osee, m. Lydia **DEAN**, Sept. 8, 1785, by Rev. Jonathan Lee	1	10
Reuben Dean, 1st s. Osee & Lydia, b. Oct. 16, 1786	1	9a
Susanah, 6th d. John & Mary, b. Apr. 27, 1782	1	3
RUSSEL[L], Alice, d. Harris, b. Mar. 8, 1850	2	53
Amey, m. John **NORTH**, Nov. 17, 1763	TM	7
RYAN, Charles John, d. Jan. 25, 1849, ae 1 y. 7 m.	2	58
Edmund, [s. Charles & Mary], b. Aug. 18, 1844	2	41
Elizabeth, d. Charles & Mary, b. Nov. 9, 1840	2	41
El[l]en, [d. Charles & Mary], b. Nov. 9, 1842	2	41
El[l]en F., d. Michael, b. Jan. 26, 1849	2	50
Harriet, d. Charles, b. May 18, 1849	2	53
Harriet F., d. Charles, b. May 18, 1849	2	50
Henry C., s. Charles. b. Nov. 11, 1851	2	53
James, s. John, b. July 18, 1849	2	51
Joseph, s. Charles & Mary, b. Apr. 7, 1839	2	41
Patrick, ae 24, m. [ ] **BARNES**, ae 21, Oct. 28, 1848, by Rev. Mr. Riley	2	31
Thomas Michael, d. Jan. 27, 1849, ae 3 y.	2	58
W[illia]m M., s. Matthew, manufacturer, ae 48 & Ann A., ae 36, b. June 2, 1847	2	42
SACKETT, SACKET, Edwin Nagrave, s. Joseph, ae 32 & Phelena,		

	Vol.	Page
SACKETT, SACKET, (cont.)		
ae 36, b. Sept. 10, 1847	2	45
Joel, m. Louisa **ROBBINS**, [Apr.] 20, [1829], by Rev. R. Emerson	2	8
Lucretia, m. Edwin **GLEASON**, of New Marlborough, May 1, [1828], by Rev. R. Emerson	2	8
Rhoda, m. Daniel R. **SPAULDING**, May 16, [1838], by Rev. Joseph Eldredge	2	19
Thomas J., m. Lucy **FELLOWS**, June 26, [1821], by R. Emerson	2	2
SAGE, Burret, m. Francis **THOMPSON**, Feb. 27, 1837, by Rev. Joseph Eldredge	2	18
Jedediah, m. Sarah P. **MILLS**, Sept. 26, 1826, by Asahel Gaylord	2	5
John, had d. [ ], b. Aug. 6, 1848	2	48
John C., m. Mary Ann **BROWN**, b. of Norfolk, Sept. 6, 1845, by Rev. Lewis Gunn	2	25
Marian, d. Nov. 22, 1849, ae 28 y.	2	60
William B., s. Henry W., b. Mar. 29, 1849	2	49
SALMON, Luther, of Richmond, Mass., m. Louisa H. **ROYS**, Nov. 14, [1838], by Rev. Joseph Eldredge	2	19
SAXTON, SEXTON, Anna, m. Elmore **CANFIELD**, Apr. 25, [1838], by Rev. Joseph Eldredge	2	19
David, m. Anna **BROWN**, Feb. 18, 1802, by Rev. A. R. Robbins	1	44
David Jason, s. David & Anna, b. Oct. 21, 1808	1	46
Delia, d. David & Anna, b. Jan. 25, 1804	1	41
Delia, d. Feb. 26, 1807	1	14
Jerusha, 1st d. Jonathan & Prudence, b. Apr. 18, 1800	1	41
Norman, s. Jonathan, b. Feb. 7, 1807	2	38
Rebecca, m. Samuel **CANFIELD**, Jr., Apr. 1, 1839, by [Rev. Joseph Eldredge]	2	20
SCHUDDER, SCHUDER, John B., d. July 22, 1849, ae 40 y.	2	57
Urania, ae 14, m. Stephen **ROSS**, ae 30, Jan. 1, 1850, by Harlow Ray	2	35
[**SCOTT**], **SCOOT**, Nathaniell, s. Ethel & Eunice, b. May 31, 1786	1	0a
[**SCOVILLE**], **SCOVELL, SCHOVEL, SCHOVIL, SCHOVILLE, SCOVIL**, Franklin, m. Amarilla **HOTCHKISS**, b. of Norfolk, Oct. 6, 1830, by Rev. George Carrington, of Goshen	2	11
Joel, m. Louisa **JOHNSON**, Aug. 25, 1844, by Rev. Joseph Eldredge	2	24
Reuben, of Colebrook, m. Elen A. **SMITH**, [Nov.] 19, [1848], by Rev. Joseph Eldredge	2	33
Sarah, d. William, ae 27 & Lucy Ann, ae 21, b. Apr. 3, 1848	2	46
W[illia]m, of Sheffield, m. Lucy Ann **HEADY**, of Norfolk, Mar. 19, 1843, by Rev. A. B. Hubbard	2	23
W[illia]m, his infant child d. [, 1849], ae 6 m.	2	58

	Vol.	Page
SEWARD, SEAWARD, Abigail, m. Joseph JONES, Sept. 3, 1772	TM	9
Caroline, d. Joseph & Elesebeth, b. Aug. 26, 1766	TM	13
Charles, s. Joseph & Elisebath, b. Mar. 20, 1762	TM	11
Maryanne Doctia, d. Capt. Joseph & Elisebeth, b. Oct. 24, 1769	1	1
Mindwel, 1st d. Joseph, d. Sept. 18, 1766	TM	14
Rosamond, d. Brotherton & Abigail, d. Jan. 14, 1805	1	14
Rozine, d. Joseph & Elisebeth, b. Sept. 15, 1764	TM	12
SEXTON, [see under SAXTON]		
SEYMOUR, Alva, of Colebrook, m. Sophronia COWLES, Mar. 16, 1825, by Rev. R. Emerson	2	6
Delia S., m. Sidney G. ROOT, [Jan.] 8, [1838], by Rev. Joseph Eldredge	2	19
Isabella, d. Truman, b. May [ ], 1849	2	50
Sam[ue]l, of Colebrook, m. Charlotte PHELPS, Apr. 24, 1823, by Rev. R. Emerson	2	6
Truman, m. Ruby BABBET, Mar. 25, [1835], by Rev. Joseph Eldredge	2	17
W[illia]m H., m. Emeline DANWELL, of Colebrook, Nov. 28, [1833], by Rev. Joseph Eldredge	2	15
SHEFFIELD, Julia Ann, m. George CAMP, Jan. 21, [1828], by Rev. R. Emerson	2	8
Minerva, m. Edward MORRIS, Mar. 12, [1821], by R. Emerson	2	2
Nancy, of Norfolk, m. William P. CANFIELD, of New Marlboro, Nov. 24, 1845, by Michael F. Mills, J. P.	2	25
SHEPARD, SHEEPORD, SHEPORD, SHEAPARD, Claranda, d. Zebelon & Hannah, b. July 29, 1778	1	3a
Eliza A., m. Alfred L. DENNIS, Sept. 14, 1841, by Rev. J. Eldredge	2	22
Giles, s. Zebulon & Hannah, b. Oct. 18, 1792	1	12a
Hannah, d. Zebelon & Hannah, b. Dec. 13, 1782	1	3a
Jerusha, d. Zebelon & Hannah, b. May 10, 1776	1	3a
Jerusha, d. May 4, 1782	1	5
John A., m. Margaret J. MILLS, Oct. 8, 1826, by Rev. R. Emerson	2	6
Pellitiah, s. Zebelon & Hannah, b. Apr. 10, 1781	1	3a
Rizpah, 3rd d. Zeblon & Hannah, b. Jan. 28, 1788	1	6
Ruth, d. Zebelon & Ruth, b. May 20, 1774	1	3a
Zebelon, m. Hannah THRALL, Apr. 11, 1775, by Giles Pettibone	1	3a
Zebulon, Jr., s. Zebulon & Hannah, b. July 14, 1784	1	7
SHOOK, John Bennet, s. John, d. Mar. 20, 1848, ae 5 w.	2	56
John Burnett, s. John, colier, ae 22 & Maria A. Elizabeth, ae 20, b. Feb. 14, 1848	2	44
SIGLOMIRE, Joseph, m. Hannah L. BENSON, [Oct.] 15, [1849], by Rev. Mr. Robinson	2	33
SIMONS, Julia R., ae 19, of Canaan, m. Eugene WEBSTER, of		

292   BARBOUR COLLECTION

	Vol.	Page
SIMONS, (cont.)		
New Marlboro, Mass., Nov. 26, 1848, by Rev. C. W. Watrous	2	30
Royal, m. Lucy **SPAULDING**, Mar. 3, 1825, by Rev. R. Emerson	2	6
SLADE, W[illia]m B., of New Haven, m. wid. Olive **KNAPP**, of Norfolk, June 2, 1844, by Rev. A. B. Hubbard	2	23
SMITH, Asahel C., d. Sept. 27, 1847, ae 21	2	56
Eliza, m. John **BROWN**, Jan. 18, 1832, by Michael F. Mills, J. P.	2	13
Elen A., m. Reuben **SCOVIL**, of Colebrook, [Nov.] 19, [1848], by Rev. Joseph Eldredge	2	33
Humphrey, m. Clarissa **BELCHER**, b. of Norfolk, Mar. 22, 1845, by Rev. A. B. Hubbard	2	25
Lucy Ann, m. Elisha M. **BECKLEY**, Aug. 23, 1848, by Rev. Joseph Eldredge	2	28
Miles W., m. Emily E. **HOWE**, Dec. 1, 1844, by Rev. Joseph Eldredge	2	24
Philo, m. Dorothy P. **CASE**, Mar. 14, [1820], by R. Emerson	2	2
Polly, m. Daniel J. **MILLS**, b. of Norfolk, Feb. 17, 1830, by Pitkin Cowles	2	9
Samuel, m. Jane **HALL** (colored), Oct. 6, 1847, by Rev. Joseph Eldredge	2	28
Sarah, m. Miles **FOOT**, May 16, [1837], by Rev. Joseph Eldredge	2	18
Selena E., m. Joel **TAYLER**, of Salisbury, May 20, [1849], by Rev. Joseph Eldredge	2	33
Washington J., m. Almeda **BENEDICT**, Apr. 25, 1821, by Elder Rufus Babcock	2	1
William H., m. Lucy **WILLIAMS**, b. of Norfolk, Oct. 5, 1828, by Daniel Coe	2	7
SPAULDING, SPALDING, Austin A., m. Louisa S. **HART**, Mar. 24, [1841], by Rev. J. Eldredge	2	21
Daniel, s. Jacob & Rachel, b. July 25, 1758	TM	6
Daniel, m. Easther **AUSTIN**, Aug. 30, 1781* *(Entry crossed out)	1	10
Daniel, of Norfolk, m. Easter **AUSTEN**, of Sheffield, Aug. 30, 1781, by Rev. John Keep	1	10
Daniel R., m. Rhoda **SACKET**, May 16, [1838], by Rev. Joseph Eldredge	2	19
Jsaac, s. Jacob & Rachel, b. May 30, 1757	TM	6
Jsaac, m. Marcy **KNAPP**, b. of Norfolk, July 9, 1778	1	10
Jsaac, Jr., 3rd s. Jsaac & Marcy, b. Mar. 13, 1782	1	10
Jacob, 2nd, s. Jsaac & Marcy, b. June 1, 1780	1	10
Jeremiah, 1st s. Jsaac & Marcy, b. Dec. 14, 1778	1	10
Lockwood, of Northampton, N. Y., m. Mary A. **SPALDING**, of Norfolk, Sept. 14, [1834], by Rev. Joseph Eldredge	2	16
Lucy, m. Royal **SIMONS**, Mar. 3, 1825, by Rev. R. Emerson	2	6

	Vol.	Page
SPAULDING, SPALDING, (cont.)		
Mary A., of Norfolk, m. Lockwood **SPAULDING**, of Northampton, N. Y., Sept. 14, [1834], by Rev. Joseph Eldredge	2	16
Mary Alice, d. Frederick A., ae 38 & Mary, b. Feb. 10, 1848	2	47
Sarah, d. Daniel & Easther, b. Jan. 26, 1783	1	10
Sarah J., m. Julian J. **WHITING**, Oct. 10, 1842, by Rev. J. Eldredge	2	22
----, Mrs., m. Dudley **NORTON**, Mar. 23, 1837, by Rev. Joseph Eldredge	2	18
SPELMAN, Elizur, had s. [ ], b. July 16, 1849	2	48
Lee Morris, s. Elizer, farmer, ae 38 & Samantha, ae 25, b. Oct. 8, 1847	2	44
STAFFORD, Sally, of Stafford, m. Rufus **EGSLESTON**, of Torrington, [Jan.] 23, [1828, by Rev. R. Emerson	2	8
STANNARD, Appleton R., m. Olive E. **MINOR**, [Mar.] 11, [1846], by Rev. Joseph Eldredge	2	26
Lidian L., m. Samuel **GILLETT**, Sept. 2, 1840, by Rev. J. Eldredge	2	21
Matiah, m. Silvia **COOK**, Apr. 20, 1840, by Rev. J. Eldredge	2	21
Obed Humphrey, s. Apleton R., b. Jan. 30, 1849	2	49
STANTON, David, m. Mary **BUTLER**, Dec. 16, 1812	2	1
STEEL, Clarissa, of Cornwall, m. Asahel **HUMPHRY**, M. D., of Norfolk, May 5, 1807	1	44
Polly, of Bethlem, b. Sept. 17, 1780; m. Linus **McKEAN**, Nov. 14, 1799	1	48
STEVENS, STEVEN, STEPHENS, Benjamin Roys, s. Nethaniel, Jr. & Elezebath, b. Aug. 31, 1790	1	21
Elizabeth, d. Nathaniell, Jr. & Elizabeth, b. July 24, 1795	1	46
Elizabeth, m. William A. **ALLEN**, Mar. 22, 1842, by Rev. J. Eldredge	2	22
Halsey, s. Nathaniell, Jr. & Elizabeth, b. Mar. 27, 1803	1	46
Halsey, m. Deziah H. **PETTIBONE**, Oct. 5, [1829], by Rev. R. Emerson	2	8
Jedediah, made affidavit Apr. 18, 1772, that Samuel **KNAP** & s. Elaxander, were members of Bap. Ch. in Canaan & New Marlborough, that they are bap. persons by immersion and have attended worship for about 2 y.	TM	8
Jerusha, d. Nathaniell, Jr. & Elizabeth, b. Sept. 3, 1806	1	46
Jerusha, m. E. G. **LAWRENCE**, b. of Norfolk, Aug. 27, 1827, by Rev. James Beach, of Winsted	2	7
Joshua, made affidavit Apr. 18, 1772, that Samuel **KNAP** & s. Elaxander were members of Bap. Ch., in Canaan & New Marlborough, that they are bap. persons by immersion and have attended worship for about 2 y.	TM	8
Mary, m. Thomas **DICKENSON**, June 25, 1760	TM	7
Nathaniel, s. Nathaniel & Lois, b. Feb. 20, 1768	TM	15
Nathaniel, m. Elizabeth **RICE**, Nov. 19, 1789	1	44

STEVENS, STEVEN, STEPHENS, (cont.)

	Vol.	Page
Nathaniel, s. Nathaniell, Jr. & Elizabeth, b. Mar. 30, 1798	1	46
Phebe, d. Nethaniel & Elezebeth, b. Sept. 2, 1792	1	21
Rosanna, m. Jonathan BROWN, Mar. 15, 1791	1	13a
Samuel, s. Nathaniel & Loes, b. Mar. 6, 1766	TM	13
Samuel, s. Nathaniell, Jr. & Elizabeth, b. July 28, 1800	1	46
William Pitt, s. Nathaniel & Loes, b. Nov. 30, 1770	TM	24
STILLMAN, Robbins, of Colebrook, m. Sylvia CASE, Mar. 1, 1826, by Rev. R. Emerson	2	6
Sally, m. Stephen TIBBALS, Aug. 13, 1805, by Rev. R. Robbins	1	13a
STIMPSON, Lavet, m. E. A. VAN OSTRUM, ae 15, July [ ], 1849, by Rev. Joseph Eldredge	2	31
STONE, [see also STOW], Abigail, m. William ROOT, Oct. 26, 1797, by Asahel Humphry, J. P.	1	15
Charles, m. Laura GAYLORD, Oct. 25, [1843], by Rev. Joseph Eldredge	2	24
Elihu*, ae 31, of East Granville, Mass., m. Elizabeth M. ALLEN, of Norfolk, Nov. 30, 1848, by Rev. C. W. Watrous *("Stow"?)	2	30
Elisebeth, m. Eleazer HOLT, May 1, 1775	TM	9
STOW, [see also STONE], Eleough*, ae 32, m. Elizabeth ALLING, ae 25, Nov. 30, 1848, by C. W. Watrous *("Eleough STONE"?)	2	32
STRONG, STRONGE, Aaron, s. Oliver & Loes, b. Mar. 21, 1773	TM	22
Anna, d. Oliver & Loes, b. Sept. 18, 1780	1	11a
Daniel, s. Oliver & Loes, b. Apr. 21, 1771	TM	18
John, s. Oliver & Loes, b. Apr. 11, 1777	1	1
Loes, d. Oliver & Loes, b. July 12, 1767	TM	15
Oliver, s. Oliver & Loes, b. May 20, 1769	TM	17
Sarah, d. Oliver & Loes, b. June 18, 1775	TM	24
[STURDIVANT], STURDEVANT, STURTEVANT, Clarriss[a], m. Guestus EGGSLESTON, Mar. 25, 1824, by Rev. R. Emerson	2	6
Lucy, m. Aaron BROWN, Nov. 3, 1784	1	12
Polly C., m. Hervey HARD, Oct. 24, [1820], by R. Emerson	2	2
SULLIVAN, Mary, ae 22, had illeg. child Emma, b. Feb. 7, 1848; f. Daniel ODINE, laborer. ae 25	2	13
SWIFT, Mary E., m. Luke BECKWITH, Dec. 31, 1844, by Rev. Joseph Eldredge	2	16
TAYLOR, TAYLER, Harriet, of Colebrook, m. Joel NORTH, July 30, 1823, by Rev. R. Emerson	2	6
Joel, of Salisbury, m. Selena E. SMITH, May 20, [1849], by Rev. Joseph Eldredge	2	13
TERRELL, TERRALL, TYREL, Henry, ae 22, m. Marina NORTON, ae 48, Mar. 17, 1850, by Rev. Joseph Eldredge	2	15
Henry, m. Hannah M. NORTON, Mar. 17, 1850, by Rev.		

TERRELL, TERRALL, TYREL, (cont.)

	Vol.	Page
Joseph Eldredge	2	36
Sylvester, of Norfolk, m. Rhoda L. **CLEMMONS**, of Hartland, Dec. 29, 1831, by Azariah Clark	2	13
THOMPSON, THOMSON, Anna, m. Frederick **PHELPS**, Dec. 20, 1807, by Rev. Ammi R. Robbins	1	44
Charles, 2nd s. Seth & Hannah, b. Apr. 7, 1804	1	41
Charles F., m. Sabra **LOOMIS**, Apr. 24, 1842, by Rev. J. Eldredge	2	22
Clarissa, m. Birdsey **NORTON**, Mar. 24, 1834, by Rev. Joseph Eldredge	2	15
Ella P., d. Giles, mechanic, ae 39 & Nancy, ae 38, b. Sept. 11, 1847	2	42
Francis, m. Burret **SAGE**, Feb. 27, 1837, by Rev. Joseph Eldredge	2	18
Frances Louisa, d. Giles, mechanic, ae 67 & Mary, ae 45, b. July 30, 1847	2	43
Giles, m. Polly **PETTIBONE**, Apr. 14, 1803, by Giles Pettibone, J. P.	1	15
James Jackson, s. Giles, b. Feb. 5, 1813	2	37
Levi, s. Seth & Hannah, b. Sept. 8, 1802	1	39
Louisa P., m. Ralph **BLISS**, of Springfield, Mass., Oct. 13, [1834], by Rev. Joseph Eldredge	2	16
Mary, 1st d. Giles & Polly, b. Mar. 18, 1804	1	41
Mary, m. Ralph **BLISS**, of Springfield, Aug. 10, [1828], by Rev. R. Emerson	2	8
Mary A., m. George W. **JACKSON**, Apr. 26, [1838], by Rev. Joseph Eldredge	2	19
Philander, of Goshen, m. Marcus **LEWIS**, [Sept.] 24, [1833], by Rev. Joseph Eldredge	2	15
Seth, 2nd s. Levi & Mary, b. May 2, 1783	1	9a
Seth, m. Hannah **MILLS**, Apr. 29, 1802, by [ ]	1	15
Seth, d. Sept. 1, 1848, ae 65 y.	2	59
----, m. Mary A. **BEEBE**, Jan. 5, 1835, by Rev. Joseph Eldredge	2	17
THRALL, Hannah, m. Zebelon **SHEEPORD**, Apr. 11, 1775, by Giles Pettibone	1	3a
Lewis, s. Lorrain, b. Feb. 23, 1813	2	38
Mindwill, m. Micheil **COTTON**, Oct. 29, 1783, by Hos. Willcocks, J. P.	1	3a
TIBBALLS, TIBBALS, Amos, s. Thomas & Rachel, b. Aug. 2, 1771	1	1
Auren, s. Thomas, Jr. & Elue, b. Apr. 10, 1790	1	40
Charlotte, d. Thomas & Elue, b. Aug. 21, 1800	1	40
Charlotte, d. [Thomas Jr. & Elue], d. May 1, 1802	1	14
Elbert Plumb, s. Sheldon & Jeannette, b. Feb. 24, 1842	2	41
Elue, d. Thomas, Jr. & Elue, b. July 5, 1787	1	40
Eunice, d. Samuell & Hannah, b. Sept. 8, 1778	1	10

TIBBALLS, TIBBALS, (cont.)

	Vol.	Page
Halsey, s. Samuel & Hannah, b. Mar. 15, 1776	1	1
Hannah, d. Samuell & Hannah, b. May 27, 1781	1	10
Julina Sally, d. Stephen & Sally, b. May 29, 1807	1	43
Noah, s. Thomas & Rachel, b. May 19, 1760	1	1
Olive, d. Thomas, Jr. & Elue, b. Feb. 22, 1794	1	40
Olive, d. May 15, 1833, ae 39	2	55
Rachel, m. Joseph GAYLORD, Apr. 27, 1766	TM	7
Rachel, d. Thomas & Rachel, b. Oct. 6, 1767	1	1
Rachel, d. Thomas, Jr. & Elue, b. June 9, 1784	1	40
Rachael, d. Thomas, Jr. & Elue, d. Mar. 10, 1792	1	14
[Sa]muel, m. Hannah JVES, May 25, 1775	1	10
Samuell, Jr., 4th s. Lieut. Samuell & Hannah, b. Mar. 23, 1784	1	4
Sam[ue]ll, Jr., 2nd s. Ens. Samuell & Hannah, b. Mar. 23, 1784	1	19
Sarah, 3rd d. Lieut. Samuell & Hannah, b. Jan. 4, 1787	1	4
Shelden, s. Thomas & Elue, b. Feb. 22, 1797	1	40
Sheldon, d. Mar. 25, 1850, ae 54 y.	2	60
Stephen, s. Thomas, Jr. & Elue, b. Sept. 18, 1781	1	40
Stephen, m. Sally STILLMAN, Aug. 13, 1805, by Rev. R. Robbins	1	13a
Thomas, Jr., m. Elue PARKER, Aug. 22, 1780	1	15
Thomas, d. Feb. 22, 1826, ae 72	2	55
TOBEY, Martha, m. Aaron BURR, b. of Norfolk, Dec. 17, 1778, by Rev. A. R. Robbins	1	10
Miles B., m. Elizabeth P. ROOD, Oct. 1, 1844, by Rev. Joseph Eldredge	2	24
TOMPKINS, Julia E., d. Enos., b. Mar. 13, 1849	2	48
TREAT, Abijah, s. Bazil & Amy, b. Feb. 16, 1802	1	43
Abijah, s. Bazil & Amy, d. Mar. 4, 1803	1	14
Amos Roberts, m. Abigail HOTCHKISS, [Nov.] 3, [1828], by Rev. R. Emerson	2	8
Bazil, m. Amy RICE, Mar. 10, 1801, by Rev. A. R. Robins	1	44
Jason Abijah, 2nd s. Bazil & Amy, b. Dec. 1, 1803	1	43
Jason Abijah, d. June 2, 1827, ae 23 1/2 y.	2	55
Lucius, 3rd s. Bazil & Amy, b. Sept. 10, 1805	1	43
Stephen B., m. Lucinda HINE, b. of Norfolk, Nov. 11, 1838, by Michael F. Mills, J. P.	2	20
TROWBRIDGE, Philo M., of Bethleham, m. Sarah E. AKIN, Sept. 18, 1837, by Rev. Joseph Eldredge	2	18
TUBBS, Thankfull, d. Nathan & Elisebeth, b. Oct. 1, 1765	TM	12
TURNER, Abigail, d. John & Mary, b. Oct. 28, 1763	TM	20
Baits, 2nd s. Sam[ue]ll & Sarah, b. Oct. 30, 1760	1	9
Daniel, s. Samuell & Sarah, b. Mar. 21, 1756* *(First written "1786")	1	9
Elizabeth, d. Sam[ue]ll & Sarah, b. Dec. 3, 1757	1	9
Hannah, 2nd d. Sam[ue]ll & Sarah, b. June 23, 1759	1	9
Hezekiah, s. John & Mary, b. Oct. 20, 1768	TM	20

	Vol.	Page
TURNER, (cont.)		
Jsaac, 6th s. Samuell & Sarah, b. Oct. 16, 1769	1	9
Jsaac, m. Martha **HUMPHRY**, Nov. 19, 1794, by Ammi R. Robbins	1	12a
John, s. John & Mary, b. Jan. 16, 1757	TM	20
Josiah, 8th s. Samuell & Sarah, b. Oct. 18, 1775	1	9
Mabel, d. John & Mary, b. May 7, 1765	TM	20
Martha, d. John & Mary, b. Dec. 14, 1755	TM	20
Mary, d. John & Mary, b. Sept. 22, 1754	TM	20
Moses, s. John & Mary, b. Jan. 9, 1759	TM	20
Nath[anie]ll, 7th s. Sam[ue]ll & Sarah, b. Mar. 11, 1772	1	9
Samuell, m. Sarah **HOW**, Dec. 26, 1754	1	9
Sam[ue]ll, Jr., 4th s. Samuell & Sarah, b. Feb. 8, 1766	1	9
Sarah, d. John & Mary, b. Feb. 14, 1770	TM	20
Solomon, 5th s. Samuell & Sarah, b. Oct. 20, 1767	1	9
Solomon, m. Sarah **JENKS**, b. of Norfolk, May 1, 1791, by D. Humphry, J. P.	1	12a
Susannah, d. John & Mary, b. Nov. 11, 1761	TM	20
Uriah, 3rd s. Sam[ue]ll & Sarah, b. Dec. 4, 1762	1	9
William, s. John & Mary, b. June 18, 1760	TM	20
TUTTLE, Clarrisa, m. Martin **MILLS**, Nov. 20, 1805, by William Battell	1	44
Laura C., m. Caleb M. **LAKE**, of Sharon, Oct. 28, 1845, by Rev. Joseph Eldredge	2	26
TYLER, Augustus, m. Emeline **GRIFFIN**, b. of New Haven, last evening, [Apr. 22, 1833], by Frances L. Robbins. Int. Pub. at New Haven	2	14
TYREL, [see under **TERRELL**]		
VAIL, Samuel S., m. Mary S. **WATTELL**, Oct. 14, [1838], by Rev. Joseph Eldredge	2	19
VALONE, Dinah, m. Thomas **PETERS**, June 24, 1803, by Giles Pettibone	1	15
VANHOESER, Louisa, m. Robert **DRAKELY**, Jan. 28, 1841, by Rev. J. Eldredge	2	21
VANNESS, Andrew, m. Amanda U. **FREEBOURN**, May 19, [1838], by Rev. Joseph Eldredge	2	19
VAN OSTRUM, E. A., ae 15, m. Lavet **STIMPSON**, July [ ], 1849, by Rev. Joseph Eldredge	2	31
Elizabeth, of Norfolk, m. Nelson **PROPER**, of New York, July 22, 1849, by Harlow Goodwin, of Canaan	2	30
VICTOR, Samuel, m. Ruth A. **WARD**, Jan. 13, 1850, by Rev. Mr. Robinson	2	33
VICTORY, Harriet, d. Mar. 24, [ ], ae 40 y.	2	57
WADBOUN, John M., of Goshen, m. Eunice W. **HODGES**, of Torrington, Oct. 30, 1837, by Rev. Joseph Eldredge	2	19
WAITE, Eliza, m. Levi **BARLOW**, of Plymouth, Aug. 28, [1836], by Rev. Joseph Eldredge	2	18
WALDORPH, Emma, m. Lewis **GRANT**, Feb. 12, 1840, by Rev.		

WOLDORPH, (cont.)

	Vol.	Page
J. Eldredge	2	21
WALKER, Sharlott, m. Lockwood KNAPP, b. of Norfolk, Nov. 21, 1834, by Gladden Bishop, Elder	2	16
WALSH, Michael, ae 27, m. Elizabeth MONTGOMERY, ae 22, Oct. 22, 1849, by Mr. Tucker	2	34
WALTER, Abigail, of Colebrook, m. Joseph W. WENTWORTH, of Winchester, May 31, 1849, by Rev. J. H. Robinson	2	30
Asahel, 8th s. Lieut. W[illia]m & Buley, b. Dec. 21, 1781	1	9a
Betty, d. Charles & Eleazabath, b. Oct. 8, 1784	1	19
Charles, Jr., s. Charles & Elizabeth, b. Dec. 11, 1781	1	19
Elihu, 5th s. Stephen & Mercy, b. Oct. 30, 1791	1	34
Elijah, s. William & Patience. b. July 26, 1758	TM	10
George, 7th s. Stephen & Mercy, b. Sept. 28, 1796	1	34
Hannah, d. William & Patience, b. Feb. 8, 1756	TM	10
Joel, m. Judith PETTIBONE, May 13, 1762	TM	7
Joel, s. Joel & Judeth, b. Mar. 1, 1764	TM	17
Judith, d. Joel & Judith, b. Oct. 10, 1768	TM	17
Laura G., m. Joel HALL, June 26, 1822, by Rev. R. Emerson	2	6
Lorane, d. Joel & Judeth, b. Jan. 9, 1763	TM	11
Marcy, Jr., [twin with Michaeil], 2nd d. Stephen & Marcy, Mar. 28, 1785	1	9a
Michaeil, [twin with Marcy], 3rd s. Stephen & Marcy, b. Mar. 28, 1785	1	9a
Moses, m. Sarah HODLEY, Feb. 12, 1792, by Dudley Humphry, J. P.	1	12a
Nancy, 1st d. Stephen & Marcy, b. May 10, 1783	1	9a
Sam[ue]ll, 9th s. Lieut. W[illia]m & Buley, b. Nov. 26, 1783	1	9a
Sarah, d. William & Patience, b. Nov. 8, 1753	TM	10
Sarah Samantha, 3rd d. Stephen & Mercy, b. July 12, 1789	1	34
Seth, s. William, Jr. & Rowlandy, b. Jan. 31, 1765	TM	12
Stephen, Jr., 2nd s. Stephen & Marcy, b. Mar. 24, 1781	1	9a
Timothy, s. William & Patience, b. Feb. 13. 1761	TM	10
Tru Mills, 4th s. Stephen & Mercy, b. Mar. 21, 1787	1	34
William, Jr., d. Sept. 7, 1793	1	20
William, 6th s. Stephen & Mersey, b. Mar. 6, 1794	1	34
W[illia]m H., m. Philena CHASE, b. of Norfolk, Jan. 19, 1843, by Rev. A. B. Hubbard	2	21
Zeluk, 1st s. Stephen & Marcy, b. Apr. 2, 1779	1	9a
WARD, Calvin, ae 33, m. Naoma CANFIELD, ae 32, June 20, 1849, by Joseph Eldredge	2	32
Calvin R., m. Naomi CANFIELD, b. of Marlboro, Mass., June 14, [1849], by Rev. Joseph Eldredge	2	33
Ruth A., m. Samuel VICTOR, Jan. 13, 1850, by Rev. Mr. Robinson	2	33
WARNER. Hezekiah, of Derby, m. Cynthia BARNES, of Canaan, Nov. 28. [1827], by Rev. R. Emerson	2	8
John Treat. m. Olive PHELPS, May 10, [1829], by Rev. R.		

	Vol.	Page
WARNER, (cont.)		
Emerson	2	8
Nancy A., of Canaan, m. Hiram A. **MERRELS**, of Norfolk, May 3, 1843, at Canaan, by Rev. A. B. Hubbard	2	23
WATROUS, Hellen, ae 23, m. Lorenzo **ROYS**, ae 24, Oct. 18, 1847, by Joseph Eldredge	2	30
Helen, m. Lorenzo **ROYS**, [Oct.] 27, [1847], by Rev. Joseph Eldredge	2	28
WATSON, Alvin, m. Salley **GAYLORD**, Oct. 25, 1797, by Asahel Humphry, J. P.	1	15
Harriet, m. John **CONE**, Oct. 13, [1841], by Rev. J. Eldredge	2	22
WATTELL, Mary S., m. Samuel S. **VAIL**, Oct. 14, [1838], by Rev. Joseph Eldredge	2	19
WAUGH, William W., of Winchester, m. Louisa **MOSES**, June [ ], 1850, by Rev. Joseph Eldredge	2	36
William W., ae 32, m. Laura **MOSES**, ae 22, [ ], by Joseph Eldredge	2	35
WAY, Philecta, m. Constantine **MILLS**, Apr. 29, 1784	1	35
WEASNER, Mary, m. Thomas **CANADA**, Dec. 1, 1822, by Bushnell Knapp, J. P.	2	3
WEBSTER, WEDBSTER, Abiel, m. Sallah **DOOLITTLE**, Sept. 28, 1820, by Elder Rufus Babcock	2	1
Allen, of Sandisfield, m. Thank **NORTON**, Apr. 28, [1828], by Rev. R. Emerson	2	8
Eugene, of New Marlboro, Mass., m. Julia R. **SIMONS**, ae 19, of Canaan, Nov. 26, 1848, by Rev. C. W. Watrous	2	30
Jonathan, m. Jerusha **HALL**, Oct. 17, [1820], by R. Emerson	2	2
WEED, Jeremiah, of Sharon, m. Mrs. [ ] **CLAPP**, Aug. 13, 1834, by Rev. Joseph Eldredge	2	16
Martial H., of South Farms, m. Emily A. **PEASE**, of Norfolk, Apr. 2, [1834], by Rev. Joseph Eldredge	2	15
WEEKS, Catharine, had d. Philantha, b. Feb. 23, 1795	1	35
Philantha, d. Catharine, b. Feb. 23, 1795	1	35
WELCH, Abigael, 4th d. [Hopestill], b. May 20, 1774	1	4
Alice, of Norfolk, m. Rev. Henry **COWLES**, of Colebrook, July 27, 1830, by Azariah Clark	2	10
Benjamin, 2nd s. Hopestill & [ ], b. Feb. 3, 1768	1	4
Benjamin, Dr., d. Dec. 17, 1849, ae 82 y.	2	59
Charlotte, 7th d. [Hopestill], b. Sept. 1, 1780	1	4
Eleazabath, 8th d. [Hopestill], b. June 9, 1782	1	4
Eunis, 3rd d. [Hopestill], b. Mar. 20, 1772	1	4
Hopestill, Jr., 3rd s. [Hopestill], b. Mar. 16, 1785	1	4
Lucy, 6th d. [Hopestill], b. Aug. 20, 1778	1	4
Phebe S., of Norfolk, m. Daniel M. **WELTON**, of Goshen, July 7, 1833, by Henry Cowles	2	14
Polley, m. Titus **NETTLETON**, May 9, 1793, by D. Humphry, J. P.	1	12a
Sarah, 2nd d. [Hopestill], b. Dec. 8, 1769	1	4

BARBOUR COLLECTION

	Vol.	Page
WELCH, (cont.)		
Susana*, 5th d. [Hopestill], b. May 20, 1776 *(First written "Lucy")	1	4
William, s. William W., b. Apr. 8, 1850	2	51
WELD, Louisa P., of Norfolk, m. Jno **PETTIBONE**, of Ogdensburg, N. Y., Oct. 4, 1830, by Frederick Marsh	2	10
WELTON, Daniel M., of Goshen, m. Phebe S. **WELCH**, of Norfolk, July 7, 1833, by Henry Cowles	2	14
WENTWORTH, Joseph W., of Winchester, m. Abigail **WALTER**, of Colebrook, May 31, 1849, by Rev. J. N. Robinson	2	30
WETMORE, Eb[eneze]r B., m. Sarah **PETTIBONE**, May 16, [1823], by Rev. R. Emerson	2	6
WHEELER, Elisebeth, 1st d. John & Martha, b. Feb. 8, 1771	1	2
John, m. Martha **COE**, Mar. 12, 1770	1	10
Joseph, 2nd s. John & Martha, b. Dec. 15, 1774	1	2
Martha, d. John & Martha, b. May 6, 1779	1	11a
Mary M., d. Hiram, b. May 18, 1849	2	50
Phenihas Elmar, 1st s. John & Martha, b. Jan. 25, 1773	1	2
Prudence, 2nd d. John & Martha, b. Feb. 2, 1777	1	2
Sarah Jane, d. June 23, 1850, ae 38 y.	2	60
WHITE, Caroline, d. Turner, b. Sept. 21, 1829	2	39
Daniel, m. Charlotte **HOTCHKISS**, [Mar.] 25, 1823, by Rev. R. Emerson	2	6
Emily Maria, d. James, b. Jan. 18, 1823	2	39
Esther, d. Nov. 16, 1847, ae 86	2	57
George, ae 24, m. Margaret **MURPHY**, ae 18, Jan. 23, 1848, by C. W. Watrous	2	29
George L., m. Margaret **MURPHY**, b. of Norfolk, Jan. 23, 1848, by Rev. C. W. Watrous	2	28
Hannah, m. Reuben **WHITE**, Mar. 18, 1827, by Rufus Babcock	2	6
Lucy, m. Amasa **CAMPBELL**, Dec. 7, 1834, by Rufus Babcock, of Colebrook	2	16
Mary, m. Fra[ ] (?) **BUNNEL**, Dec. 4, 1344, by Rev. Joseph Eldredge	2	24
Mary Charlotte, d. Daniel, b. June 19, 1824	2	39
Nancy, m. Albert **PARRET**, Nov. 18, 1824, by Rufus Babcock	2	4
Nath[anie]l, m. Eliza **PECK**, b. of Norfolk, Oct. 23, 1823, by Rufus Babcock	2	4
Polly Mariah, of Norfolk, m. Truman **MERREL**, of New Hartford, Sept. 3, 1822, by Elder Rufus Babcock	2	3
Rebecca D., of Norfolk, m. Daniel C. **WHITMAN**, of New Marlborough, Mass., Aug. 30, 1847, by Rev. Amos R. Hubbard	2	27
Reuben, m. Hannah **WHITE**, Mar. 18, 1827, by Rufus Babcock	2	6
Sally, m. Timothy **GAYLORD**, 3rd, Apr. 17, 1822, by R. Emerson	2	2

	Vol.	Page
WHITEHEAD, Rufus, his child, b. July 16, 1850	2	53
WHITING, Julian J., m. Sarah J. SPAULDING, Oct. 10, 1842, by Rev. J. Eldredge	2	22
Lorenzo, m. Eliza P. COUCH, Jan. 15, 1844, by Rev. Joseph Eldredge	2	24
Lorrain, m. Nancy AUSTIN, b. of New Marlboro, Mass., Mar. 11, 1834, by Rev. Theron Ellis, of Bap. Ch.	2	15
WHITMAN, Daniel C., of New Marlborough, Mass., m. Rebecca D. WHITE, of Norfolk, Aug. 30, 1847, by Rev. Amos R. Hubbard	2	27
WHITNEY, Dauid, s. Joshua & Ami, b. Mar. 25, 1757	TM	6
Elisebeth Sarah, d. Joshua & Ami, b. Dec. 18, 1759; d. Feb. 3, 1760	TM	6
WILCOX, WILLCOCK, WILLCOCKS, Annice, m. Philo CLEMENS, of Granby, Jan. 6, 1828, by Rev. R. Emerson	2	8
Charlotte, d. Ezekiel & Rosanna, b. Apr. 4, 1766	TM	18
Dyantha, 2nd d. Hosea, Jr. & Abigal, b. Feb. 18, 1784	1	7
Hosea, Jr., m. Abigal MILLS, b. of Norfolk, Nov. 2, 1774, by Rev. A. R. Robbins	1	10
Joseph, s. Hosea & Sarah, b. July 1, 1780	1	3
Lois, m. Joseph FERRY, Jr., Apr. 5, 1803, by Rev. R. Robbins	1	13a
Moses Case, s. Hosea, Jr. & Abigal, b. Aug. 9, 1781	1	3
Orrin, of New Marlboro, Mass., m. E. HAWKS, of Canaan, Mar. 23, 1845, by Rev. A. B. Hubbard	2	25
Philura, d. Hosea & Sarah, d. Dec. 27, 1786, in the 19th y. of her age	1	14
Rhoda, d. Hosea, Jr. & Abigal, b. Dec. 20, 1777	1	3
Rosanna, d. Ezekiel & Rosanna, b. Mar. 1, 1769	TM	18
Rossanna, m. Eden MILLS, Apr. 16, 1786, by Dudley Humphry, J. P.	1	12
Rosilla, of Simsbury, m. Asher AKINS, of Norfolk, Oct. 1, 1789, by Dudley Humphry, J. P.	1	12
Samuel E., of Goshen, m. Nancy LUCAS, of Norfolk, Feb. 16, 1831, by Rev. George Carrington, of Goshen	2	11
Sylvester, 3rd s. Hosea, Jr. & Abigail, b. Sept. 20, 1786	1	10a
WILLIAMS, Emerson, m. Mary C. KNAPP, Sept. 29, 1850, by Rev. Joseph Eldredge	2	36
Lucy, m. William H. SMITH, b. of Norfolk, Oct. 5, 1828, by Daniel Coe	2	7
Mary, ae 17, m. William GINGILL, ae 21, Sept. 29, 1848, by C. W. Watrous	2	32
Mary Ann, ae 16, of New Marlboro, Mass., m. William GINGILL, ae 21, of Norfolk, Sept. 24, 1848, by Rev. C. W. Watrous	2	28
WILLY, Lucy, m. Bennett H. HINES, Apr. 9, 1843, by Rev. J. Eldredge	2	22

	Vol.	Page
WILMOT, Coven H., m. Carrodon R. **MERREL**, b. of New Hartford, Mar. 6, 1848, by Rev. Joseph Eldredge	2	28
WILSON, A., of Harwinton, m. Eliz[abeth] L. **HART**, [Nov.] 23, [1836], by Rev. Joseph Eldredge	2	18
Miram, b. July 26, 1824	2	39
Seth, m. Mrs. Mercy **ROYS**, Nov. 17, [1834], by Rev. Joseph Eldredge	2	16
[WOLCOTT], WOOLCOT, Maria, m. Edward **ENSIGN**, Oct. 1, [1849], by Rev. Joseph Eldredge	2	33
WOODRUFF, Mary Ann, m. George S. **MILLS**, May 11, 1846, by Rev. Joseph Eldredge	2	27
WOODWARD, Eliot*, druggist, ae 22, of Waltham, m. Clarissa E. **ROY**, ae 20, of Norfolk, June 26, 1848, by Joseph Eldredge *(Perhaps "Woodward **ELIOT**")	2	29
WOOSTER, Autin F., s. Austin, b. May 6, 1849	2	50
WRIGHT, Levi & Emily, had child, b. Apr. 24, 1848	2	45
YOUNG, Eliza, m. John **FOX**, Apr. 11, 1830, by Rufus Babock, of Colebrook	2	9
NO SURNAME, Constantine*, [ ] *(Crossed out)	TM	15
Silance, m. Thomas **GOODWINE**, Oct. 26, 1759	TM	7

NORTH STONINGTON VITAL RECORDS
1807 - 1852

	Page
ADAMS, John Q., of Lebanon, m. Lucy A. **BAILEY**, of N. Stonington, Sept. 12, 1844, by Philo Judson	210
Mary, of Norwich, m. Aaron B. **RIX**, of N. Stonington, Feb. 16, 1846, by Rev. John Sheffield	221
AKINS, William H., of Stonington, m. Mary E. **CHAPMAN**, of N. Stonington, Oct. 17, 1847, by Rev. John Sheffield	230
ALEXANDER, Mary Ann, of N. Stonington, m. Nathan L. **PENDLETON**, of Stonington, Oct. 27, 1839, by Charles Bennet, J. P.	180
ALLEN, Amos H., m. Dolly **BROWN**, b. of N. Stonington, Nov. 14, 1821, by William Randall, Jr., J. P.	70
Dolly, m. Joshua **BLIVIN**, b. of N. Stonington, Mar. 22, 1835, by Ezra Hewitt, J. P.	153
Elnathan, s. Ichabod & Nabby, b. July 16, 1798	53
Ethan, m. Wealthy **PARTLO[W]**, b. of N. Stonington, Aug. 23, 1820, by John Langworthy, J. P.	66
Hannah, m. Samuel H. **SMITH**, Jan. 1, 1843	211
Ichabod, m. Nabby **BUTTON**, July 6, 1782	53
John, s. Ichabod & Nabby, b. Aug. 16, 1793	53
Latham H., s. Ethan & Wealthy, b. May 6, 1822	131
Lucy, d. Ichabod & Nabby, b. Feb. 26, 1787	53
Lucy B., m. Palmer **CRUMB**, July 26, 1840, by Cyrus W. Brown, Jr. J. P.	184
Lydia, d. Ichabod & Nabby, b. June 21, 1785	53
Nabby, d. Ichabod & Nabby, b. Apr. 17, 1796	53
Nancy, of N. Stonington, m. Asa **WILLCOX**, of Lynn, Dec. 1, 1845, by Matthew Brown, J. P.	219
Prudence, d. Ichabod & Nabby, b. Apr. 27, 1789	53
Sally, d. Ichabod & Nabby, b. Mar. 6, 1800	53
Sally, m. David **CRUMB**, b. of N. Stonington, Feb. 3, 1833, by Asher Miner, Elder	143
Wealthy R., d. Ethan & Wealthy, b. July 20, 1827	131
William, s. Ichabod & Nabby, b. July 27, 1806	53
William J. S., of Stonington, m. Mary E. **WENTWORTH**, of Westerly, R. I., Oct. 17, 1852, by Rev. O. T. Walker	261
AMES, Rufus, of Preston, m. Eunice **BURDICT**, of N. Stonington, Jan. 2, 1825, by Stephen Avery, J. P.	91
AMSBURY, Julia, d. Levi & Orrilla, b. Jan. 12, 1807	51
L. Allen, s. Levi & Orrilla, b. May 27, 1811	51
Levi, b. Sept. 28, 1785; m. Orrilla	51
Levi, s. Levi & Orrilla, b. Apr. 12, 1806	51
Maria, d. Levi & Orrilla, b. Dec. 4, 1808	51
Nelson, s. Levi & Orilla, b. July 25, 1814	51

	Page
AMSBURY, (cont.)	
Orrilla, w. Levi, b. May 14, 1788	51
ANDERSON, Catharine, m. Silas **ORCHARD**, b. colored & of N. Stonington, Nov. 24, 1837, by P. H. Shaw	163
Emeline, m. Thomas **WARD**, persons of color, Feb. 7, 1839, by P. H. Shaw	173
ANGTERS, Isabel, had d. Sophronia **SMITH**, b. Mar. 23, 1796	40
ASHLEY, Sally L., of Groton, m. William H. **COGSHALL**, of N. Stonington, May 24, 1818, by Elder Roswell Burrows	69
AUSTIN, Dorcas, of Westerly, m. Benjamin **WORDEN**, of Hopkinton, Oct. 10, 1824, by Asher Miner, Elder	69
Jedediah, Jr., m. Lydia **BRUMLEY**, July 27, 1813, by Peleg Randall, Elder	18
Jedediah, of Hopkinton, & Betsey **COOK**, Aug. 16, 1823, by Ichabod Brown, J. P.	82
Russ, m. Hannah **HYDE**, July 4, 1813, by Peleg Randall, Elder	18
William, of New London, m. Maria **ELLINGTON**, of N. Stonington, Dec. 24, 1826, by Elias Hewit, J. P.	99
AVERY, Albert, of Groton, m. Phebe E. **WHEELER**, of N. Stonington, Mar. 15, 1837, by Rev. Joseph Ayer, Jr.	160
Albert L., of Groton, m. Joanna P. **WHEELER**, of N. Stonington, Jan. 1, 1839, by P. H. Shaw	171
Alexander Har[r]ington, s. Stephen & Betsey, b. June 28, 1814	1
Alfred, of Windham, m. Fanny F. **WHEELER**, of N. Stonington, Mar. 1, 1827, by Rev. Joseph Ayer, Jr.	99
Almira W., of N. Stonington, m. George **AYER**, of Groton, May 16, 1831, by Rev. J[oseph] Ayer, Jr.	129
Anna, w. Stephen, d. Aug. 11, 1801, in her 38th year	1
Benjamin F., of Preston, m. Dimus **BAILEY**, of N. Stonington, Feb. 25, 1829, by Rev. Augustus B. Collins	112
Betsey, d. Jonathan & Anna, b. Oct. 21, 1800	64
Calvin Goddard, s. Stephen & Betsey, b. Feb. 9, 1812	1
Charles G., m. Ede D. **WHEELER**, b. of N. Stonington, Nov. 4, 1823, by William Randall, Jr., J. P.	86
Charles Grandison, s. Stephen & Anna, b. Apr. 9, 1796	1
Christopher, Elder, m. Mary **ELDREDGE**, a single woman. Marriage agreement signed Nov. 7, 1803, in presence of Latham & Desire Hull, and recorded at the request of the widow, Sept. 20, 1823. Interest indorsed to July 5, 1822	83
Cornelia Culver, d. Roswell R. & Mary, b. May 18, 1823	74
Cyrus Wheeler, s. Stephen & Anna, b. Oct. 10, 1798	1
Eliza Adaline, d. Stephen & Betsey, b. Sept. 29, 1807	1
Eliza Adeline, m. Elisha **PARKE**, b. of N. Stonington, Mar. 20, 1823, by Asher Miner, Elder	80
Elizabeth W., m. Gurdon S. **CRANDALL**, Dec. 2, 1828, by Rev. Joseph Ayer, Jr.	109
Emma Wheeler, d. Roswell R. & Mary, b. June 27, 1828; d. Sept. 8, 1829	74

	Page
AVERY, (cont.)	
Erastus Randall, s. Stephen & Betsey, b. Aug. 8, 1818	1
Esther, m. Nathan **SWAN**, Mar. 10, 1776	8
Frances M., of N. Stonington, m. Capt. Richard A. **WHEELER**, of Stonington, Jan. 12, 1843, by Rev. Philo Judson	196
Frances Mary, d. Stephen & Betsey, b. Sept. 23, 1821	1
Frederick, s. Fred[eric]k & Betsey, b. Apr. 28, 1819	70
Hannah, wid. Elder Nathan, d. Oct. 10, 1810, in her 85th year	1
Hannah Mary, d. Stephen & Anna, b. July 18, 1789	1
Harriet W., d. Cha[rle]s G. & Ede D., b. May 27, 1825	86
Jonathan, m. Anna **HEWIT[T]**, Feb. 2, 1800	64
Lucy, w. Oliver, d. Nov. 3, 1836	46
Margarit, w. Oliver, d. May 22, 1805	46
Martha W., m. Silas M. **CRANDALL**, of New York, Aug. 7, 1837, by P. H. Shaw	162
Mary Ann, d. Jona[tha]n & Anna, b. Feb. 20, 1817	64
Mary Ann, d. Roswell R. & Mary, b. Dec. 31, 1820	74
Nancy, d. Stephen & Anna, b. Dec. 29, 1783	1
Nancy W., m. Frances H. **WHEELER**, b. of N. Stonington, June 3, 1846, by Rev. Myron N. Morris	222
Oliver, m. Lucy **BUDDINGTON**, Apr. 18, 1806, by Christopher Avery, Elder	46
Ralph Hurlburt, s. Stephen & Betsey, b. Apr. 22, 1816	1
Rebecca Wheeler, d. Roswell R. & Mary, b. Mar. 25, 1826	74
Roger Griswold, s. Stephen & Betsey, b. Sept. 4, 1809	1
Roswell R., m. Mary **WHEELER**, b. of N. Stonington, Apr. 9, 1818, by Asher Miner, Elder	74
Roswell Randall, s. Stephen & Anna, b. Nov. 5, 1791	1
Stephen, m. Anna **WHEELER**, b. of Stonington, Dec. 9, 1781, by Rev. Nath[anie]l Eells	1
Stephen, 2d, of Stonington, m. Betsey **MORGAN**, of Groton, Aug. 18, 1804, by Jer[emia]h Halsey, J. P.	1
Stephen Lyman, s. Stephen & Anna, b. May 12, 1786	1
Zilpha, d. July 11, 1823, "a person of color"	1
AYER, Albert G., of Preston, m. Jane **PENDLETON**, of N. Stonington, Sept. 23, 1845, by Rev. James R. Stone	217
Ann W., m. John **GRANT**, b. of N. Stonington, Sept. 26, 1826, by Rev. Joseph Ayer, Jr.	96
Bridget, m. Ephraim **WHEELER**, b. of N. Stonington, Oct. 8, 1829, by Rev. Joseph Ayer, Jr.	116
Charles Lathrop, s. Joseph & Frances, b. June 25, 1826	96
George, of Groton, m. Almira W. **AVERY**, of N. Stonington, May 16, 1831, by Rev. J[oseph] Ayer, Jr.	129
Harriet, m. Thomas **PRENTICE**, Jr., b. of N. Stonington, Apr. 26, 1831, by Rev. Joseph Ayer, Jr.	128
Joseph Curtis, s. Latham H. & Susan A., b. Apr. 3, 1832	136
Lucy, m. Eph[rai]m **SMITH**, b. of N. Stonington, Feb. 9, 1826, by Rev. Joseph Ayer, Jr.	95

	Page
BABCOCK, Augustus L., of Hopkinton, R. I., m. Hannah **PECKHAM**, of N. Stonington, Nov. 10, 1811, by Stephen Avery, J. P.	34
Benj[ami]n F., m. Harriet N. **WALKER**, Feb. 25, 1838, by Amos C. Main, J. P.	165
Bethiah, of N. Stonington, m. Marvin **HERREN**, of Groton, Mar. 18, 1810, by Elias Hewit, J. P.	8
Betsey, m. Cyrus **BROWN**, Jr., b. of N. Stonington, Dec. 21, 1826, by Asher Miner, Elder	98
Betsey, of N. Stonington, m. Benjamin **PALMER**, of Voluntown, Jan. 1, 1838, by Rev. Benj[ami]n N. Harris	164
Charles D., s. Stephen, b. Dec. 24, 1810	231
Charles D., m. Betsey **CHADSEY**, b. of N. Stonington, Mar. 15, 1855, by Rev. Tho[ma]s W. Clark	265
Cha[rle]s Henry, s. Henry & Dolly, b. Apr. 28, 1813	60
Elizabeth, m. Libeus **COON**, Sept. 14, 1786	44
Emma, d. Lodo[wic]k & Mary, b. Aug. 22, 1815	42
Esther J., of N. Stonington, m. Daniel **YORK**, Jan. 28, 1838, by Rev. Alfred Gates	164
Eunice, d. Lodo[wic]k & Mary, b. Apr. 15, 1811	42
Henry, m. Dolly **STANTON**, Nov. 10, 1811, by Peleg Randall, Elder	60
Hoxie, m. Elizabeth **WHITE**, Nov. [ ], 1837, by Leland D. Miner, J. P.	163
Huldah, m. Christopher **DEWEY**, Jr., Nov. 13, 1809, by Asher Miner, Elder	23
Lodowick, m. Mary **DAVIS**, Dec. 13, 1801	42
Lodowick, s. Lodo]wic]k & Mary, b. June 23, 1809	42
Mark D., of Hopkinton, R. I., m. Rachel **SHESUCKS**, of N. Stonington, Nov. 24, 1839, by Charles Bennett, J. P.	180
Mary, d. Lo[dowi]ck & Mary, b. Oct. 30, 1803	42
Melissa, d. Lodo[wic]k & Mary, b. Nov. 23, 1807	42
Nancy A., of N. Stonington, m. Bailey P. **PARK**, of New Jersey, Jan. 3, 1854, by Rev. J. G. Post	263
Orin A., s. Augustus L. & Hannah, b. May 22, 1814	34
Samuel, m. Caroline **STANTON**, b. of N. Stonington, Feb. 28, 1832, by Rev. Asher Miner	136
Sam[ue]l, m. Mary **CASWELL**, Mar. 28, 1838, by Leland D. Miner, J. P.	166
Sarah L., of N. Stonington, m. Hiram **CLARK**, of Leyden, Mass., Aug. 9, 1829, by David Coats, J. P.	114
Silas, of N. Stonington, m. Mary **COOK**, of Preston, Oct. 1, 1820, by Rev. John Hyde	67
Stanton, s. Lod[owic]k & Mary, b. Mar. 20, 1813	42
Thankful, d. Lodo[wic]k & Mary, b. July 15, 1805	42
W[illia]m A., Dr., m. Harriet B. **COATS**, b. of N. Stonington, Apr. 14, 1845, by Rev. James R. Stone	216
William Avery, s. Henry & Dolly, b. Sept. 4, 1817	60
BAILEY, Caroline, of N. Stonington, m. Denison **SWAN**, Jan. 4, 1832, by Rev. Augustus B. Collins	133

	Page
BAILEY. (cont.)	
Charlotte, of Stonington, m. Bradford **PHILLIPS**, of N. Stonington, Nov. 28, 1850, by Rev. O. T. Walker	249
Dimus, of N. Stonington, m. Benjamin F. **AVERY**, of Preston, Feb. 25, 1829, by Rev. Augusuts B. Collins	112
Frances E., of N. Stonington, m. Aaron **PIERCE**, of Westerly, R. I., Apr. 16, 1855, by Rev. Stephen Hubbell	266
Lucy A., of N. Stonington, m. John Q. **ADAMS**, of Lebanon, Sept. 12, 1844, by Philo Judson	210
William W., m. Philena **MAIN**, b. of N. Stonington, Jan. 5, 1848, by Rev. Thomas Barber	233
BAKER, David, m. Emeline **COATS**, Oct. 3, 1831, by Rev. S. Heath	153
BALDWIN, Abby, d. John & Nabby, b. Mar. 21, 1797	45
Abigail, m. Henry **BALDWIN**, Sept. 17, 1818, by Asher Miner, Elder	45
Almira, d. Tho[ma]s & Nancy, b. May 24, 1807	28
Amos, of N. Stonington, m. Sally **WHITE**, of Hartford, May 2, 1807	28
Amos Brown, s. Amos & Sally, b. Aug. 13, 1816	28
Andrew, m. Polly **BOARDMAN**, Nov. 22, 1801	27
Andrew, twin with Damson, s. Andrew & Polly, b. Sept. 16, 1802; d. Apr. 26, 1803	27
Avery Swan, s. Andrew & Polly, b. July 21, 1815	27
Benjamin Franklin, s. David & Susan, b. Sept. 20, 1807; d. Jan. 6, 1808	39
Benjamin Franklin, s. John & Nabby, b. Jan. 15, 1809; d. Mar. 7, 1809	45
Betsey M., m. William S. **GRANT**, b. of N. Stonington, May 16, 1827, by Asher Miner, Elder	100
Betsey Mason, d. John & Nabby, b. Apr. 18, 1801	45
Charles Washington, s. G[eorge] W. & M[ary] C., b. June 19, 1813	26
Damson, twin with Andrew, s. Andrew & Polly, b. Sept. 16, 1802	27
Daniel, m. Eunice **FRINK**, b. of Stonington, Apr. 22, 1804, by Stephen Avery, J. P.	26
Daniel, of Stonington, m. Lucy **BOARDMAN**, of Preston, Feb. 22, 1807, by Rev. Levi Hart	46
Daniel, Capt., of N. Stonington, m. Hannah **STANTON**, of Preston, Apr. 21, 1808, by Alexander Stewart, J. P.	46
Daniel, s. Andrew & Polly, b. Oct. 22, 1808	27
Daniel Avery, s. Daniel & Hannah, b. July 2, 1811	46
David, m. Susan **SWEET**, May 29, 1793	39
David, Capt., d. Oct. 7, 1807	39
David, s. David & Susan, b. May 5, 1798	39
Elizabeth, m. Thomas **HOLMES**, 2nd, Nov. 19, 1789	26
Emily A., m. John S. **HEWIT**, Jr., b. of N. Stonington, Nov. 16, 1826, by Elias Hewit, J. P.	97
Emily Angeline, d. John & Nabby, b. Apr. 26, 1810	45
Emma Hannah, d. Amos & Sally, b. Mar. 8, 1812	28
Eunice, w. Daniel, d. May 7, 1805	46
Eunice Williams, d. John & Nabby, b. Sept. 27, 1806	45
George W., m. Mary C. **PHINNEY**, at Preston, Nov. 16, 1809, by Eben[eze]r Stewart, J. P.	26

	Page
BALDWIN, (cont.)	
Giles Washington, s. Amos & Sally, b. Aug. 9, 1814	28
Henry, m. Abigail **BALDWIN**, Sept. 17, 1818, by Asher Miner, Elder	45
Joanna Salvia, d. G[eorge] W. & M[ary] C., b. Oct. 1, 1811	26
John, Jr., m. Nabby **BOARDMAN**, Jan. 31, 1796	45
John, Jr., of Windham, m. Ann L. **FRINK**, of Stonington, Feb. 24, 1839, by P. H. Shaw	176
John Addams, s. John & Nabby, b. May 26, 1799; d. June 8, 1805	45
John Denison, s. Daniel & Hannah, b. Sept. 29, 1809	46
John Nicholas, s. Amos & Sally, b. Feb. 9, 1808	28
Loiza, d. Andrew & Polly, b. Apr. 12, 1811; d. Oct. 15, 1814	27
Lucy, w. Daniel, d. Aug. 27, 1807	46
Lucy, m. Isaac A. **SWAN**, b. of N. Stonington, Aug. 31, 1823, by Levi Walker	84
Lucy Ann, d. Tho[ma]s & Nancy, b. Jan. 6, 1815	28
Lucy Prentice, d. John & Nabby, b. Nov. 13, 1803	45
Mary, m. Stephen **FRENCH**, b. of Stonington, Mar. 22, 1807, by Rev. Christopher Avery	3
Mary Ann, d. Andrew & Polly, b. Aug. 1, 1804	27
Mary Anna, d. G[eorge] W. & M[ary] C., b. July 29, 1815	26
Nabby, w. John, d. July 30, 1814	45
Nancy, d. Tho[ma]s & Nancy, b. Jan. 30, 1803	28
Nancy, of N. Stonington, m. Amos **SHEFFIELD**, of Exeter, R. I., Feb. 23, 1823, by Asher Miner, Elder	79
Nancy Adeline, d. Daniel & Hannah, b. Apr. 27, 1815	46
Polly, m. Tho[ma]s **HOLMES**, Jan. 1, 1815, by Asher Miner, Elder	29
Rebecca had illeg. s. William **DENISON**, b. of May 23, 1798, in Stonington	36
Rhoda, m. Benjamin **FRINK**, Jan. 14, 1821, b. of N. Stonington, by Asher Miner, Elder	68
Sally, m. Isaac R. **TAYLOR**, b. of N. Stonington, Sept. 24, 1834, by Rev. Joseph Ayer, Jr.	152
Sally Adelaide, d. Daniel & Hannah, b. July 17, 1813; d. Apr. 11, 1814	46
Sally Almyra, d. Andrew & Polly, b. June 4, 1813	27
Sally Ann, d. John & Nabby, b. June 1, 1814	45
Sally Eliza, d. Amos & Sally, b. Jan. 29, 1810	28
Sarah A., of N. Stonington, m. George N. **GRIFFIN**, of Wallingford, Sept. 1, 1839, by Rev. Augustus B. Collins, of Preston	179
Stewert, s. David & Susan, b. Mar. 6, 1796	39
Susan, d. David & Susan, b. Mar. 2, 1794	39
Susan, m. Samuel H. **PRENTICE**, Nov. 27, 1814	39
Thomas, m. Nancy **SPAULDING**, b. of Stonington, Apr. 16, 1801, by Simeon Brown, Elder	28
Thomas H., of Gilbertsville, Otsego Co., N. Y., m. Hannah E. **FRINK**, of N. Stonington, May 23, 1847, by Rev. Thomas Barber	232
Thomas Harvie, s. Tho[ma]s & Nancy, b. Apr. 1, 1812	28
Tho[ma]s Jefferson, s. Tho[ma]s & Nancy, b. Feb. 5, 1805;	

	Page
BALDWIN, (cont.)	
d. Apr. 3, 1811	28
William, alias **DENISON**, s. Rebecca **BALDWIN**, b. May 23, 1798, in Stonington	36
William, s. Andrew & Polly, b. Nov. 15, 1806; d. Dec. 27, 1807	27
W[illia]m Henry, s. Henry & Abigail, b. May 28, 1816	45
Wolcott, s. David & Susan, b. Oct. 20, 1801	39
BALL, Thomas D., of Stonington, m. Emma **BROWN**, of N. Stonington, Mar. 1, 1847, by Rev. Thomas Barber	232
BARBER, Esther, of N. Stonington, m. William **DOUGLAS**, of Voluntown, June 14, 1846, by Rev. Levi Walker	239
Paul M., of Westerly, m. Almanda **DEWEY**, of N. Stonington, Dec. 30, 1827, by Asher Miner, Elder	103
Susan E., of Granville, Mass., m. Thomas W. **PECKHAM**, of Stonington, May 3, 1847, by Rev. Thomas Barber	226
BAKER, Jared, of Westerly, m. Eliza **STANTON**, of N. Stonington, Feb. 12, 1825, by Asher Miner, Elder	91
BARNES, Eunice, m. Charles **SWAN**, Mar. 21, 1779	37
BATES, Hannah, m. Isaac **SIMS**, b. of N. Stonington, Sept. 26, 1841, by Rev. Philo Judson	188
BATTLES, Samuel, Jr., m. Polly **LAMPHEAR**, b. of Hopkinton, R. I., but now residing in N. L. County, Jan. 26, 1823, by Nathan Pendleton, J. P.	79
BENJAMIN, Stephen P., of Colchester, m. Sally P. **PHILLIPS**, of N. Stonington, Nov. 15, 1824, by Levi Meech, Elder	90
BENNETT, BENNET, Aaron, Jr., m. Lucy **WILLIAM**, Apr. 10, 1796	81
Aaron, s. Aaron & Lucy, b. Dec. 1, 1800	81
E. William, s. Aaron & Lucy, b. June 7, 1799	81
Elisha W., m. Huldah **LEWIS**, June 18, 1820, by Paris Hewit, J. P.	65
Esther Jane, d. Aaron & Lucy, b. Mar. 29, 1810	81
Jesse, s. Aaron & Lucy, b. Oct. 3, 1807	81
John, s. Aaron & Lucy, b. May 15, 1813; d. Oct. 19, 1819	81
Lucy Ann, d. Aaron & Lucy, b. Apr. 21, 1805	81
Lucy Jane, m. Lyman **CHAMPLAIN**, b. of N. Stonington, Sept. 29, 1855, by Rev. S. H. Peckham	267
Mary Ann, of Stonington, m. Joshua **PRENTICE**, of N. Stonington, Jan. 13, 1820, by Paris Hewit, J. P.	65
Nathan Denison, s. Aaron & Lucy, b. Dec. 20, 1802	81
Salah, s. Aaron & Lucy, b. May 25, 1797	81
BENT, Martha, of Hopkinton, R. I., m. Henry **GARDINER**, of N. Stonington, Jan. 6, 1847, by Rev. Levi Walker	237
BENTLEY, Adam Clark, s. Henry F. & Mary H., b. May 13, 1842	162
Anna C., d. George W. & Anna, b. Sept. 23, 1827	53
Cha[rle]s W., s. George W. & Anna, b. July 2, 1815	53
Cynthia, see Sinthey	
David N., s. Ezekiel, b. July 24, 1785	5
Edwin, s. George W. & Anna, b. July 3, 1824	53
Frances Mary, d. George W. & Anna, b. Oct. 14, 1830	53

	Page
BENTLEY, (cont.)	
Franklin Tyler, s. David, b. June 4, 1842	244
George, d. Oct. 28, 1814, aged 83 years	5
George R., s. George W. & Anna, b. June 10, 1810	53
George W., s. Ezekiel, b. May 21, 1783	5
George W., m. Anna **WILLIAMS**, b. of N. Stonington, June 18, 1809	53
Henry, s. Ezekiel, b. Aug. 23, 1789; d.	5
Henry, s. George W. & Anna, b. Jan. 21, 1813	53
Henry F., m. Mary H. **WHEELER**, b. of N. Stonington, Oct. 24, 1837, by Dea. C. D. Fillmore	162
Henry F., Jr., s. Henry F. & Mary H., b. Oct. 12, 1838	162
James Knox Polk, s. David, b. Mar. 12, 1846	244
John, s. Ezekiel, b. Mar. 2, 1796	5
John, m. Phebe S. **WILLIAMS**, b. of N. Stonington, Nov. 24, 1823, by Paris Hewit, J. P.	86
John Denison, s. Henry F. & Mary H., b. Nov. 4, 1845	162
John S., m. Mary E. **DAVIS**, b. of N. Stonington, Aug. 13, 1854, by Rev. John Sheffield	264
John Sands, s. David, b. Jan. 25, 1844	244
John Stanton, s. John & Phebe, b. Mar. 27, 1828	86
Jonathan, s. Ezekiel, b. Aug. 17, 1787; d.	5
Lucy, d. Ezekiel, b. Sept. 16, 1793	5
Martha E., m. John H. **CRARY**, b. of N. Stonington, Nov. 12, 1845, by Rev. James R. Stone	218
Mary, d. Ezekiel, b. May 2, 1778	5
Mary Wheeler, d. Henry F. & Mary H., b. Aug. 28, 1840	162
Nancy, d. Ezekiel, b. Apr. 19, 1798	5
Phebe Ann, d. John & Phebe, b. Oct. 17, 1824	86
Polly Williams, d. John & Phebe, b. Dec. 23, 1825	86
Roxane, of N. Stonington, m. W[illia]m G. **JOHNSON**, of Charleston, R. I., Nov. 22, 1829, by Rev. Seth Higby	119
Russell, m. Susanna **STANTON**, b. of N. Stonington, Dec. 18, 1821, by Asher Miner, Elder	73
Sinthey, d. Ezekiel, b. Aug. 7, 1791; d.	5
William, s. Ezekiel, b. May 28, 1780	5
BERRY, B. Gage, of Norwich, N. Y., m. Adaline M. **WHEELER**, of N. Stonington, June 29, 1854, by Stephen Hubbell	264
BILLINGS, Benjamin F., s. Gilbert & Lucy, b. Jan. 15, 1811	21
Ebenezer, s. Elisha & Lucretia, b. Feb. 13, 1788	20
Elisha, m. Lucretia **STANTON**, b. of Stonington, Oct. 4, 1778	20
Elisha, s. Elisha & Lucretia, b. Sept. 13, 1781	20
Elisha P., s. Nathan & Patty, b. Feb. 5, 1809	51
Eunice, d. Nathan & Patty, b. June 14, 1807	51
George W., s. Gilbert & Lucy, b. Dec. 9, 1803	21
Gilbert, m. Lucy **SWAN**, b. of Stonington, Apr. 19, 1792	21
Gilbert, m. Mary A. **HEWITT**, b. of N. Stonington, Sept. 3, 1852, by Rev. Nehemiah B. Cook, of Stonington	259
Horatio N., s. Gilbert & Lucy, b. Nov. 26, 1805	21

NORTH STONINGTON VITAL RECORDS 311

	Page
BILLINGS, (cont.)	
James. s. Gilbert & Lucy, b. Jan. 2, 1802	21
John, s. Gilbert & Lucy, b. Mar. 4, 1809; d. Aug. 28, 1812	21
Joseph, s. Josephus & Phebe, b. Jan. 14, 1810	51
Josephus, m. Phebe **BROWN**, July 2, 1809	51
Joshua, s. Elisha & Lucretia, b. Jan. 5, 1784	20
Lucy, d. Gilbert & Lucy, b. June 30, 1794; d. Dec. 9, 1794	21
Lucy, d. Gilbert & Lucy, b. Oct. 9, 1794 [sic]	21
Mary, d. Elisha & Lucretia, b. July 5, 1778	20
Mary, d. Gilbert & Lucy, b. June 24, 1813	21
Nathan, m. Patty **BROWN**, Aug. 11, 1803, by Stephen Avery, J. P.	51
Priscilla, d. Nathan & Patty, b. Sept. 14, 1804	51
Rebeckah, d. Elisha & Lucretia, b. Aug. 7, 1791	20
Robert, s. Gilbert & Lucy, b. May 2, 1800	21
Sanford, s. Gilbert & Lucy, b. June 21, 1792	21
Susan A., m. Gershom A. **MAIN**, Dec. 7, 1840, by Rev. Charles S. Weaver, of Voluntown	185
-----, 6th s. Gilbert & Lucy, b. Sept. 19, 1807; d. Nov. 19, 1807	21
BIRCH, [see also **BURCH**], Frederick, of Stonington, m. Mary Ann **THOMPSON**, of N. Stonington, May 21, 1845, by Rev. James R. Stone	216
BLANCHARD, Benjamin, m. Waty **MARTIN**, b. of N. Stonington, Sept. 20, 1823, by Levi Walker	84
BLIVIN, Barker N., m. Mary **HANDCOCK**, Mar. 26, 1820, by Stephen Avery, J. P.	67
Henry, of Westerly, R. I., m. Lucy Ann **SISSON**, of N. Stonington, Nov. 28, 1822, by Elias Hewit, J. P.	76
Joshua, m. Dolly **ALLEN**, b. of N. Stonington, Mar. 22, 1835, by Ezra Hewitt, J. P.	153
Rebeckah Ann, m. Josiah **BROWN**, Jr., Mar. 6, 1823, b. of N. Stonington, by Asher Miner, Elder	80
Robert A., of Westerly, R. I., m. Emily **SISSON**, of N. Stonington, by Rev. Joseph Ayer, Jr. Recorded Aug. 20, 1836	158
Russell, m. Lucy **CRUMB**, Nov. 20, 1825, by William Randall, Jr. J. P.	96
Susan, of N. Stonington, m. Dudley **BROWN**, of Leicester, N. Y., Nov. 6, 1834, by Rev. Asher Miner	152
BOARDMAN, Lucy, of Preston, m. Daniel **BALDWIN**, of Stonington, Feb. 22, 1807, by Rev. Levi Hart	46
Nabby, m. John **BALDWIN**, Jr., Jan. 31, 1796	45
Polly, m. Andrew **BALDWIN**, Nov. 22, 1801	27
BOGGS, George A., of Charleston, R. I., m. Ann **CONNER**, of New York City, Mar. 7, 1858, by Rev. Joseph Burnett	274
BOTSFORD, Tarsus, of Sharon, m. Abigail C. **SWAN**, of N. Stonington, Sept. 9, 1822, by Rev. John Hyde	76
BOWER, Phenety, of N. Stonington, m. James **MEEDS**, of Hartford, Oct. 21, 1823, by Paris Hewit, J. P.	85
BRADLEY, Sally M., of New London, m. Sherman **WILLIAMS**, of	

	Page
BRADLEY, (cont.)	
Russia. N. Y., Oct. 18, 1831, by Rev. Joseph Ayer, Jr.	131
BRAND, Patty, m. Nathan **YORK**, Nov. 25, 1810, by Jedediah Randall, Elder	11
BREED, Abel, s. Jabish & Sally, b. Oct. 13, 1806	35
Abel, of Oxford, N. Y., m. Rebecca **PEABODY**, of N. Stonington, Nov. 8, 1829, by Asher Miner, Elder	35
Allen, s. Jabish & Sally, b. May 10, 1793	35
Andrew, s. Jabish & Sally, b. Jan. 26, 1790	35
Anna, d. Jabish & Sally, b. Jan. 26, 1801	35
Betsey, d. Jabish & Sally, b. Nov. 24, 1808	35
Esther Randall, d. Jabish & Sally, b. Apr. 26, 1803	35
Gershom, s. Jabish & Sally, b. Feb. 10, 1795	35
Hannah, d. Jabish & Sally, b. Dec. 18, 1784	35
Hannah W., m. Joseph **YORK**, Aug. 22, 1825, by W[illia]m Randall, Jr., J. P.	93
Isaac S., of Stonington, m. Phebe P. **HEWIT**, of N. Stonington, Nov. 25, 1827, by Asher Miner, Elder	101
Lucy, d. Jabish & Sally, b. Mar. 21, 1797	35
Patty, d. Jabish & Sally, b. Aug. 19, 1791	35
Polly, d. Jabish & Sally, b. Apr. 17, 1788	35
Polly, m. Elias **CHAPMAN**, b. of N. Stonington, June 28, 1818, by Jonathan Miner, Elder	106
Sally, d. Jabish & Sally, b. Mar. 22, 1783	35
William, s. Jabish & Sally, b. Jan. 20, 1799	35
William, m. Silva **PALMER**, b. of N. Stonington, Oct. 1, 1820, by David Coats, J. P.	66
BREWSTER, Cynthia, m. Charles **SWAN**, Jr., Dec. 25, 1803	33
Sally, of Preston, m. Chester **SMITH**, of Stonington, Dec. 7, 1788, by Sam[ue]l Mott, J. P.	57
BRIG[G]S, Sarah R., of Greenwich, R. I., m. John B. **WHEELER**, of N. Stonington, Jan. 1, 1834, by Jonathan Miner, Elder	149
BROMLEY, BROMBLEY, BRUMBLEY, BRUMLEY, Alice, m. Tho[ma]s **BURDICK**, b. of N. Stonington, Oct. 22, 1826, by Asher Miner, Elder	97
Betsey, of N. Stonington, m. William **BURDICK**, of Stonington, Mar. 6, 1823, by Asher Miner, Elder	80
Fanny E., m. Daniel **WRIGHT**, b. of N. Stonington, Jan. 17, 1842, by Peleg Clarke, J. P.	189
Hannah, m. Gilbert **BROWN**, June 11, 1837, by Matthew Brown, J. P.	161
Laura, of N. Stonington, m. Levi S. **CLARK**, of Lyme, May 24, 1835, by Rev. Asher Miner	154
Lydia, m. Jedediah **AUSTIN**, Jr., July 27, 1813, by Peleg Randall, Elder	18
Sabra A., m. Albert T. **CRUMB**, Oct. 20, 1855, by Charles P. White, J. P.	269
William G., m. Betsey **DAVIS**, b. of N. Stonington, Oct. 11, 1844, by Charles S. Brown, J. P.	211

NORTH STONINGTON VITAL RECORDS 313

	Page
BROOKS, John H., of Lisbon, m. Frances E. PECKHAM, of N. Stonington, Jan. 22, 1838, by Rev. Joseph Ayer, of Lisbon	175
BROWN, Abby C., of Westerly, m. Jesse CHAPMAN, of N. Stonington, Sept. 13, 1820, by Jonathan Miner, Elder	54
Abby Mary, d. Sandford & Clarissa, b. Dec. 19, 1818	64
Alanson, of Stonington, m. Eliza A. DAVIS, of N. Stonington, Jan. 12, 1840, by Rev. Philo Judson	182
Almira M., m. Henry D. LANPHEAR, Sept. 2, 1834, by Stephen Main, J. P.	151
Betsey, m. Ransford COATES, b. of N. Stonington, Nov. 29, 1807, by Joshua Babcock, J. P.	15
Charles, s. Eph[rai]m & Deborah, b. July 3, 1804	21
Charles, m. Rhod[a] Ann BROWN, Oct. 19, 1820, by Asher Miner, Elder	67
Charles F., m. Nancy BROWN, b. of N. Stonington, Dec. 25, 1832, by Thomas H. Hewitt, J. P.	141
Charles F., m. Lucy BROWN, of N. Stonington, Dec. 25, 1832, by Thomas H. Hewitt, J. P.	275
Charles L., m. Mary RILEY, b. of N. Stonington, Apr. 7, 1851, by Rev. M. N. Morris	250
Charles Prentice, s. Sanford & Polly, b. Apr. 10, 1815	43
Charlotte, d. Jonas & Mary, b. Oct. 22, 1775	6
Charlotte Ann, d. Christ[ophe]r & Charlotte, b. Aug. 7, 1807; d. July 16, 1808	37
Christopher, Jr., m. Charlotte PENDLETON, b. of Stonington, Nov. 27, 1806, by Stephen Avery, J. P.	37
Christopher Franklin, s. Christ[ophe]r & Charlotte, b. Jan. 12, 1809	37
Clarissa, d. Sandford & Clarissa, b. Sept. 15, 1811	64
Clark L., m. Content WILCOX, b. of N. Stonington, Feb. 10, 1833, by Jonathan Miner, Elder	143
Cyrus, Jr., m. Betsey BABCOCK, b. of N. Stonington, Dec. 21, 1826, by Asher Miner, Elder	98
Daniel P., m. Jerusha Ann BROWN, b. of N. Stonington, Apr. 17, 1843, by Erastus Denison	200
Darius, m. Prudence BROWN, b. of N. Stonington, Jan. 29, 1826, by Asher Miner, Elder	94
Deborah, d. Josiah & Deborah, b. Oct. 9, 1786; d. June 29, 1792	3
Deborah, 2d d. Josiah & Deborah, b. Sept. 12, 1802	3
Deborah, d. Eph[rai]m & Deborah, b. Aug. 27, 1796	21
Deborah Ann, d. Hampton, of Westerly, m. William, s. Charles SWAN, of N. Stonington, Apr. 20, 1825, by Benajah Gavitt, J. P.	92
Denison W., m. Juliett BROWN, b. of N. Stonington, Feb. 10, 1833, by Rev. Joseph Ayer, Jr.	142
Dolly, m. Amos H. ALLEN, b. of N. Stonington, Nov. 14, 1821, by William Randall, Jr., J. P.	70
Dudley, s. Temperance, b. July 19, 1802	56
Dudley, of Leicester, N. Y., m. Susan BLIVIN, of N. Stonington, Nov. 6, 1834, by Rev. Asher Miner	152

	Page
BROWN, (cont.)	
Eliza, d. Eph[rai]m & Deborah, b. Oct. 10, 1800	21
Eliza Ann, of N. Stonington, m. Daniel **RODMAN**, of S. Kingston, R. I., Nov. 26, 1835, by Rev. Asher Miner	156
Eliza Ann, of N. Stonington, m. William M. **DEEWEY**, of Stonington, Feb. 16, 1843, by John Sheffield, J. P.	201
Ellen Rebecca, d. Henry C. & Rebecca, b. Aug. 2, 1831	140
Emma, of N. Stonington, m. Thomas D. **BALL**, of Stonington, Mar. 1, 1847, by Rev. Thomas Barber	232
Ephraim, s. Jed[idia]h & Anna, b. Aug. 28, 1768	21
Ephraim, s. Ephraim & Deborah, b. Feb. 21, 1794	21
Ephraim, m. Hannah H. **HOLMES**, Sept. 5, 1807, by Asher Miner, Elder	21
Erastus A., m. Sarah M. **CHAMPLAIN**, b. of N. Stonington, Nov. 26, 1855, by Stephen Hubbell, Pastor	268
Erastus N., m. Celia **EDWARDS**, b. of N. Stonington, Aug. 12, 1832, by Rev. Asher Miner	136
Esther, m. Thatcher **BROWN**, b. of Stonington, Aug. 3, 1800, by Jer[emia]h Haley, J. P.	23
Esther Randall, d. Jabish & Sally, b. Apr. 26, 1803 (* **BREED** is handwritten in margin)	35
Eunice, d. Jonas & Mary, b. Feb. 10, 1778 *(**BROWN** handwritten in margin)	6
Eunice, d. Eph[rai]m & Hannah H., b. June 22, 1808	21
Frances Maria, m. Isaac H. **PECKHAM**, b. of Groton, Oct. 30, 1837, by Rev. Joseph Ayer, Jr.	162
George E., m. Jane E. **MANNING**, of Norwich, Apr. 28, 1844, by Rev. Philo Judson	206
Gilbert, m. Hannah **BROMLEY**, June 11, 1837, by Matthew Brown, J. P.	161
Hannah, d. Jonas & Mary, b. Apr. 27, 1769	6
Harriet, m. Nathan **YORK**, Jr., b. of N. Stonington, Mar. 24, 1842, by Rev. Philo Judson	193
Henry, s. Jonas & Mary, b. Aug. 31, 1790	6
Henry D., of N. Stonington, m. Hellen M. **POTTER**, of Voluntown, Nov. 29, 1855, by Stephen Hubbell	268
James, m. Temperance **BROWN**, b. of N. Stonington, Dec. 2, 1824, by Stephen Avery, J. P.	90
Jedediah, s. Thatcher & Esther, b. June 23, 1805	23
Jepthah, m. Lydia **BROWN**, of N. Stonington, Nov. 15, 1823, by Stephen Avery, J. P.	85
Jerusha Ann, m. Daniel P. **BROWN**, b. of N. Stonington, Apr. 17, 1843, by Rev. Erastus Denison	200
John Franklin, of Rochester, N. Y., m. Lucy Ellen **DENISON**, of N. Stonington, Mar. 15, 1858, by Rev. Stephen Hubbell	275
Jonas, s. Jonas & Mary, b. May 10, 1773	6
Josiah, s. Josiah & Deborah, b. Apr. 15, 1793; d. Dec. 18, 1793	3
Josiah, 2d s. Josiah & Deborah, b. Sept. 11, 1799	3

BROWN, (cont.)

Josiah, Jr., m. Rebeckah Ann **BLIVIN**, b. of N. Stonington, Mar. 6, 1823, by Asher Miner, Elder	80
Juliett, m. Denison W. **BROWN**, b. of N. Stonington, Feb. 10, 1833, by Rev. Joseph Ayer, Jr.	142
Kathiah Williams, d. Thatcher & Esther, b. Oct. 13, 1807	23
Keturah R., of N. Stonington, m. Charles S. **PENDLETON**, of Stonington, Dec. 30, 1828, by Rev. Ira Hart	112
Latham, s. Jere[mia]h, b. June 15, 1785	40
Leonard, m. Lydia Ann **POTTER**, b. of N. Stonington, Nov. 25, 1846, by Charles Bennet, J. P.	224
Lizzie, of N. Stonington, m. Orrin **FLINT**, of Windham, Jan. 14, 1821, by Asher Miner, Elder	68
Louisa A., of N. Stonington, m. Edwin R. **LEWIS**, of Hopkinton, R. I., Dec. 17, 1850, by Rev. O. T. Walker	249
Lucretia, m. Azariah **HILLIARD**, b. of N. Stonington, Mar. 5, 1834, by Rev. Asher Miner	150
Lucy, m. Prentice **GRANT**, Dec. 28, 1808	33
Lucy, of N. Stonington, m. Charles F. **BROWN**, Dec. 25, 1832, by Thomas H. Hewitt, J. P.	275
Lucy A., m. Benj[ami]n N. **HARRIS**, Jr., b. of N. Stonington, Apr. 3, 1838, by Rev. Benj[ami]n N. Harris	178
Lucy Ann, m. Stanton **LOOMIS**, Jan. 20, 1822, by W[illia]m Randall, Jr., J. P.	76
Lucy E., m. Reuben W. **YORK**, b. of N. Stonington, Oct. 8, 1840, by Levi Meech, Elder	183
Lydia, d. Jer[emia]h, b. Oct. 7, 1773	40
Lydia had s. Dudley **DENISON**, b. Aug. 19, 1794	40
Lydia, d. Eph[rai]m & Deborah, b. Oct. 17, 1798	21
Lydia, of N. Stonington, m. Jepthah **BROWN**, Nov. 15, 1823, by Stephen Avery, J. P.	85
Lydia, of N. Stonington, m. Stephen **BROWN**, of Stonington, Mar. 30, 1824, by Stephen Avery, J. P.	87
Lydia E., of N. Stonington, m. Simeon **HALEY**, Jr., of Mystic, May 12, 1839, by Rev. Fernando Bester	177
Lydia M., m. Jonathan A. **WRIGHT**, b. of N. Stonington, Jan. 2, 1840, by Matthew Brown, J. P.	181
Mabel, see Mayba	
Martha Esther, m. Rowland **COON**, Jan. 9, 1839, by W[illia]m Randall, Jr., J. P.	174
Mary Reed, d. Christ[ophe]r & Charlotte, b. Oct. 15, 1812	37
Mayba, d. Jonas & Mary, b. Nov. 27, 1783	6
Molly, m. David **COATS**, b. of Stonington, June 29, 1788, by Eleazer Brown, Elder	49
Molly, b. Aug. 29, 1766	49
Nancy, d. Josiah & Deborah, b. Dec. 18, 1789	3
Nancy, m. John **MINER**, Apr. 5, 1812, by Jed[idia]h Randall, Elder	52
Nancy, m. Chandler **MAIN**, b. of N. Stonington, Feb. 22, 1821,	

316 BARBOUR COLLECTION

	Page
BROWN, (cont.)	
by Asher Miner, Elder	69
Nancy, m. Charles F. **BROWN**, b. of N. Stonington, Dec. 25, 1832, by Thomas H. Hewitt, J. P.	141
Oliver, m. Sarah E. **GRANT**, b. of N. Stonington, Aug. 29, 1855, by Rev. Stephen Hubbell	266
Patty, m. Nathan **BILLINGS**, Aug. 11, 1803, by Stephen Avery, J. P.	51
Patty Smith, d. Eph[rai]m & Hannah H., b. Dec. 13, 1811	21
Phebe, m. Josephus **BILLINGS**, July 2, 1809	51
Phebe, of Preston, m. Asher **HOLMES**, of Stonington, Jan. 1, 1823, by Levi Meech, Elder	78
Phebe E., of N. Stonington, m. Maxon **KENYON**, of Richmond, R. I., May 11, 1851, by Rev. O. T. Walker	253
Phebe S., m. Amos **COLLINS**, b. of N. Stonington, July 1, 1838, in Hopkinton, by Rev. Amos R. Wells. Witnesses: Sarah Wells, Phebe Reynolds	167
Polly, d. Jonas & Mary, b. Apr. 18, 1771	6
Polly, w. Sanford, b. Sept. 30, 1792	43
Polly, m. Henry **PALMER**, Apr. 6, 1808, by Jer[emia]h Haley, Esq.	61
Polly P., of Westerly, m. Asa S. **MINER**, of N. Stonington, Jan. 29, 1852, by Rev. O. T. Walker	258
Prudence, m. Darius **BROWN**, b. of N. Stonington, Jan. 29, 1826, by Asher Miner, Elder	94
Ralph Isham, s. Christ[ope]r & Charlotte, b. Nov. 20, 1810	37
Ralph R., m. Mary Ann **WHEELER**, b. of N. Stonington, Oct. 12, 1842, by John Sheffield, J. P.	196
Rhoda Ann, d. Thatcher & Esther, b. Jan. 15, 1803	23
Rhoda [A]nn, m. Charles **BROWN**, Oct. 19, 1820, by Asher Miner, Elder	67
Sanford, s. Jonas & Mary, b. Jan. 27, 1787	6
Sanford, s. Jere[mia]h, b. May 5, 1789	43
Sanford, m. Polly	43
Sandford, m. Clarissa **PALMER**, Nov. 4, 1810, by Stephen Meech, J.P.	64
Sanford, m. Polly **DYE**, May 15, 1814, by Asher Miner, Elder	22
Sandford, of Preston, m. Frances **WALKER**, of N. Stonington, Oct. 10, 1824, by Levi Meech, Elder	89
Sandford P., s. Sandford & Clarissa, b. June 8, 1814	64
Sandford P., m. Lucinda G. **WHEELER**, July 4, 1838, by P. H. Shaw	168
Sarah B., of N. Stonington, m. Joseph N. **DEWEY**, of Stonington, Mar. 26, 1843, by John Sheffield, J. P.	201
Sarah E., m. George H. **CHAMPLAIN**, b. of N. Stonington, Dec. 31, 1855, by William B. Hull, J. P.	269
Sarah M., of N. Stonington, m. George A. **STANTON**, of Charleston, R. I., June 5, 1848, by Rev. Isaac Fargo, of Hamburgh, N. Y.	233
Simeon, s. Josiah & Deborah, b. May 8, 1795	3
Smith, m. Rebecca B. **MAIN**, b. of N. Stonington, Feb. 16, 1834, by Rev. Asher Miner	149
Stephen, of Stonington, m. Lydia **BROWN**, of N. Stonington, Mar. 30,	

	Page
BROWN. (cont.)	
1824, by Stephen Avery, J. P.	87
Taphena, m. Amos **STANTON**, Jr., b. of N. Stonington, Sept. 24, 1826, by Asher Miner, Elder	97
Temperance, d. Jer[emia]h & Nabby, b. Feb. 22, 1771	56
Temperance had s. Dudley, b. July 19, 1802	56
Temperance, m. James **BROWN**, b. of N. Stonington, Dec. 2, 1824, by Stephen Avery, J. P.	90
Thatcher, m. Esther **BROWN**, b. of Stonington, Aug. 3, 1800, by Jer[emia]h Haley, J. P.	23
Thatcher, s. Thatcher & Esther, b. Aug. 31, 1800	23
Thatcher, m. Eunice **SPAULDING**, Oct. 3, 1821, b. of N. Stonington, by Asher Miner, Elder	72
Thomas J., of N. Stonington, m. Mary **SHEFFIELD**, of Charlestown, R. I., Dec. 20, 1846, by Rev. Thomas Barber	231
BROWNING, Adaline, twin with Catherine, d. Tho[ma]s & Amy, b. July 21, 1821	214
Adaline, of N. Stonington, m. William C. **OSGOOD**, of Norwich, Sept. 15, 1844, by Rev. Augustus B. Collins, of Preston	202
Amos Wheeler, s. L[atham] H. & E[meline], b. July 3, 1835	124
Ann, m. Asa **PRENTICE**, Jr., Feb. 15, 1818, b. of Stonington, by Rev. Gustavus Davis	60
Anna, twin with Sarah, d. William T. & Cata, b. Aug. 9, 1794	55
Benjamin F., s. W[illia]m T. & Cata, b. Feb. 18, 1808	55
Catharine, d. William T. & Cata, b. Jan. 28, 1786	55
Catharine, m. Rufus **WILLIAMS**, Nov. 11, 1810, b. of N. Stonington, by Elias Hewit, J. P.	10
Catherine, twin with Adaline, d. Tho[ma]s & Amy, b. July 21, 1821	214
Charles Downer, s. Sam[ue]l & Sophia, b. Nov. 3, 1812	38
Charles Phelps, s. John & Lucy, b. Mar. 22, 1802	32
Cyrus S., of Brooklyn, N. Y., m. Fanny A. **WHEELER**, of N. Stonington, July 14, 1831, by Rev. Joseph Ayer, Jr.	130
Cyrus Swan, s. John & Lucy, b. June 7, 1807	32
Elizabeth B., of N. Stonington, m. Latham **HULL**, Aug. 15, 1811, by Rev. Christopher Avery	24
Elizabeth Backus, d. William T. & Cata, b. July 1, 1792	55
Elizabeth H., d. Tho[ma]s & Amy, b. Feb. 11, 1824	214
Frances A., d. Tho[ma]s & Amy, b. Dec. 28, 1825	214
George S., of Griswold, m. Frances E. **HEWITT**, of N. Stonington, Feb. 24, 1836, by Rev. Joseph Ayer, Jr.	158
Harriet A., d. Tho[ma]s & Amy, b. Feb. 14, 1828	214
Henry Latham, s. L[atham] H. & Emeline, b. Jan. 28, 1832	124
James, s. L[atham] H. & E[meline], b. Jan. 6, 1840	124
John, m. Lucy **SWAN**, Mar. 10, 1799	32
John H., s. W[illia]m [T.] & Cata, b. July 28, 1801	55
Joseph, s. W[illia]m [T.] & Cata, b. June 21, 1798	55
Joshua P., s. Tho[ma]s & Amy, b. June 2, 1819; d. July 29, 1819	214
Latham H., s. W[illia]m [T.] & Cata, b. Apr. 13, 1804	55

318   BARBOUR COLLECTION

Page

BROWNING, (cont.)
Latham H., Capt., m. Emeline **WHEELER**, of N. Stonington, Nov. 18,
    1830, by Rev. Augustus B. Collings   124
Lucy, d. John & Lucy, b. Dec. 16, 1799   32
Lucy S., m. Cyrus **WHEELER**, b. of N. Stonington, Mar. 24, 1822, by
    Rev. Syrel Lee Hart, of Stonington   74
Lucy Wheeler, d. L[atham] H. & E[meline], b. Dec. 22, 1837   124
Mary, d. William T. & Cata, b. Feb. 4, 1788   55
Mary P., d. Tho[ma]s & Amy, b. Dec. 28, 1814   214
Mary P., m. Denison **HEWITT**, Apr. 3, 1839, by Rev. Augustus B.
    Collins, of Preston   176
Mason B., s. Tho[ma]s & Amy, b. Mar. 26, 1816   214
Oren T., s. W[illia]m [T.] & Cata, b. Mar. 31, 1806   55
Robert, m. Hannah **DEWEY**, Dec. 12, 1810, by Jedediah Randall,
    Elder   10
Sally Maria, d. John & Lucy, b. Mar. 8, 1805   32
Sally Maria, m. Dudley R. **WHEELER**, Mar. 4, 1828   75
Sally Mariah, m. Dudley R. **WHEELER**, b. of N. Stonington, Mar. 4,
    1828, by Rev. Joseph Ayer, Jr.   104
Samuel, m. Sophia **PRENTICE**, Nov. 28, 1811   38
Sarah, twin with Anna, d. of William T. & Cata, b. Aug. 9, 1794   55
Sarah A., b. Oct. 10, 1817   164
Sarah A., m. Oliver **HEWITT**, b. of N. Stonington, Dec. 28, 1842, by
    Rev. Benj[ami]n C. Phelps, of Mystic   164
Sarah A., d. Tho[ma]s & Amy, b. Oct. 10, 1817   214
Sophia P., of N. Stonington, m. Samuel **PRENTICE**, of Norwich,
    [Dec.] 31, 1849, by Rev. N. S. Hunt, of Preston   244
Susan A., d. W[illia]m [T.] & Cata, b. Nov. 8, 1810   55
Thomas, s. William T. & Cata, b. Nov. 21, 1790   55
Thomas Lathrop, s. L[atham] H. & E[meline], b. Feb. 28, 1842   124
Welcome A., of Griswold, m. Catherine M. **WILLIAMS**, of N.
    Stonington, Sept. 2, 1846, by Rev. James R. Stone   223
William, s. W[illia]m [T.] & Cata, b. Aug. 25, 1796   55
William Gardner, s. Sam[ue]l & Sophia, b. Aug. 6, 1815   38
W[illia]m T., s. Tho[ma]s & Amy, b. Feb. 2, 1814   214
BRUMBLEY, BRUMLEY, [see under **BROMLEY**]
BUDDINGTON, Lucy, m. Oliver **AVERY**, Apr. 18, 1806, by Christopher
    Avery, Elder   46
BULLOCK, Mary Catharine, of N. Kingston, R. I., m. Henry S. **MOWRY**,
    July 2, 1844, by Rev. James R. Stone   208
BURCH, [see also **BIRCH**], Paul B., of Stonington, m. Abby M.
    THOMPSON, of N. Stonington, May 14, 1851, by Rev. O. T.
    Walker   251
BURDICK, BURDICT, Betsey, m. Albert **WHITE**, Sept. 4, 1826, by
    William Randall, Jr., J. P.   96
Caleb, of Penn, m. Harriet **EDWARDS**, of Hopkinton, R. I.,
    Nov. 29, 1844, by Dewitt C. Pendleton, J. P.   246
Charles H., m. Angeline **ECCLESTON**, b. of N. Stonington,

	Page
BURDICK, BURDICT, (cont.)	
Apr. 1, 1856, by Cha[rle]s C. Lewis	271
Content, of Stonington, m. Daniel **GREEN**, of Springfield, N. Y., at Hopkinton, Feb. 15, 1795, by Abram Coon, J. P.	43
Dorcas, b. Nov. 29, 1760; m. Stephen **PALMER**, Dec. 12, 1784, by Eleazer Brown, Elder	41
Emma, of Griswold, m. Thomas **EDGECOMB**, of N. Stonington, Apr. 7, 1852, by Rev. O. T. Walker	258
Ethan L., of Charleston, R. I., m. Mary **BURDICK**, of Hopkinton, R. I., Feb. 28, 1846, by Rev. Levi Walker	238
Eunice, of N. Stonington, m. Rufus **AMES**, of Preston, Jan. 2, 1825, by Stephen Avery, J. P.	91
Eunice E., formerly of N. Stonington, m. Ezekiel C. **TURNER**, of N. Stonington, July 20, 1851, by Rev. O. T. Walker	253
Harriet E., m. Latham H. **ECCLESTON**, Oct. 19, 1856, by Rev. Charles C. Lewis	272
Jenet L., m. Andrew N. **MASON**, b. of N. Stonington, Feb. 6, 1831, by Rev. Joseph Ayer, Jr.	126
Lucinda, m. Gershom **HOLMES**, Mar. 12, 1815	49
Maryett, m. William H. **HILLIARD**, b. of N. Stonington, Dec. 30, 1851, by Rev. O. T. Walker	257
Mary, of N. Stonington, m. Billings **MERRET**, of Stonington, Aug. 1, 1830, by Rev. Gershom Holmes	123
Mary, of Hopkinton, R. I., m. Ethan L. **BURDICK**, of Charleston, R. I., Feb. 28, 1846, by Rev. Levi Walker	238
Mary E., m. John E. **CLARK**, b. of N. Stonington, July 28, 1833, by Jonathan Miner, Elder	146
Mary R., m. Henry A. **ECCLESTON**, b. of N. Stonington, Jan. 7, 1855, by Rev. Thomas W. Clark	265
Oliver S., m. Eunice M. **ECCLESTON**, Oct. 19, 1856, by Rev. Charles C. Lewis	272
Sarah S., m. Edwin **SPAULDING**, Nov. 26, 1857, by Rev. Joseph Burnett	274
Susanna, m. Joshua **CLARK**, Mar. 1, 1810	42
Tho[ma]s, m. Alice **BRUMBLEY**, b. of N. Stonington, Oct. 22, 1826, by Asher Miner, Elder	97
Thomas E., m. Fanny E. **MINER**, Mar. 6, [1857], by Rev. Charles C. Lewis	273
William, of Stonington, m. Betsey **BRUMBLEY**, of N. Stonington, Mar. 6, 1823, by Asher Miner, Elder	80
BURTON, Caroline, of Hopkinton, R. I., m. Nathan W. **PERKINS**, of Groton, Mar. 16, 1845, by Rev. James R. Stone	215
BUTTLES, Mary, m. Dan **DEWEY**, Feb. 23, 1812, by Jedediah Randall, Elder	14
BUTTON, Lucy, of Hopkinton, m. Varnum **LAMPHEAR**, Jan. 1, 1824, by Nathan Pendleton, J. P.	87
Nabby, m. Ichabod **ALLEN**, July 6, 1782	53
CARD, Henry C., of Westerly, R. I., m. Lois Ann **PHILIPS**, of N.	

	Page
CARD, (cont.)	
Stonington, Nov. 14, 1842, by Rev. Erastus Denison	199
CARDNER, Charles L., of Westerly, R. I., m. Elizabeth A. **ECCLESTON**, of Hopkinton, R. I., Sept. 1, 1847, by Rev. Thomas Barber	228
CARPENTER, Delacy A., of Stonington, m. Samuel **DENNIS**, of Newport, R. I., May 10, 1852, by M. N. Morris	258
Mary, m. Richard **WANSLEY**, b. of N. Stonington, Aug. 4, 1850, by Mathew Brown, J. P.	247
CARR, Daniel, m. Susan **COLE**, Nov. 16, 1815, by Asher Miner, Elder	27
CASE, Ann Elizabeth, m. Nathan H. **LANGWORTHY**, b. of N. Stonington, Feb. 20, 1837, by Rev. Amos R. Wells	159
William H., m. Eliza H. **MUMFORD**, b. of Kingston, Aug. 10, 1829, by Rev. Joseph Ayer, Jr.	115
CASSON, Salvina, m. John **WILKSINSON**, b. of N. Stonington, Mar. 10, 1814, by Elias Hewit, J. P.	20
CASWELL, Daniel N., of N. Stoningtn, m. Janettie **McCRACKEN**, of Colchester, Nov. 13, 1853, by W[illia]m B. Hull, J. P.	263
Mary, m. Sam[ue]l **BABCOCK**, Mar. 28, 1838, by Leland, D. Miner, J. P.	166
Sally, m. Joseph **WOODMANCEE**, b. of N. Stonington, Oct. 3, 1842, by Enoch B. Pendleton, J. P.	197
CHADSEY, Betsey, m. Charles D. **BABCOCK**, b. of N. Stonington, Mar. 15, 1855, by Rev. Tho]ma]s W. Clark	265
Hannah, of Groton, m. Jared **HOLMES**, of N. Stonington, Mar. 11, 1811, by Stephen Avery, J. P.	25
CHAMPLAIN, Eunice, of R. I., m. Elias A. **MINER**, of Stoughton, Nov. 29, 1847, by Oliver Hewitt, J. P.	230
George H., m. Sarah E. **BROWN**, b. of N. Stonington, Dec. 31, 1855, by William B. Hull, J. P.	269
Isaac F., m. Susan A. **CRUMB**, b. of N. Stonington, Apr. 12, 1846, by Rev. Thomas Barber	225
Jeffrey, of Griswold, m. Mrs. Abigail **McDONALD**, of Westerly, R. I., Jan. 11, 1846, by Rev. Levi Walker	220
Lyman, m. Lucy Jane **BENNET**, b. of N. Stonington, Sept. 29, 1855, by Rev. S. H. Peckham	267
Sarah A., of Griswold, m. John C. **NORTHROP**, of N. Kingston, R. I., Feb. 3, 1856, by S. W. Peckham	270
Sarah M., m. Erastus A. **BROWN**, b. of N. Stonington, Nov. 26, 1855, by Stephen Hubbell, Pastor	268
CHAPMAN, Abby C., w. Jesse, d. May 17, 1832	151
Abby Elizabeth, d. Smith & Eunice C., b. Dec. 12, 1824	94
Albert Taylor, [s. Prentice & Martha], b. July 21, 1839	277
Alexander, s. Ezra & Charlotte, b. Aug. 6, 1815; d. July 29, 1826	53
Alexander Hamilton, s. Ezra & Charlotte, b. June 11, 1826	53
Betsey, d. Nahum & Mercy, d. Jan. 4, 1822	59
Betsey, [d. Prentice & Martha], b. Dec. 19, 1843	277
Catharine H., [d. Prentice & Martha], b. Aug. 7, 1841	277
Charles, m. Elizabeth **BROWN**, b. of N. Stonington, Sept. 20, 1810,	

CHAPMAN, (cont.)

	Page
by Elias Hewit, J. P.	50
Charles Faxon, s. Ezra & Charlotte, b. Aug. 26, 1823	53
Clarissa Avaline, d. Amos & Polly, b. Mar. 11, 1814	27
Dorcas, m. Silas CHAPMAN, b. of N. Stonington, Sept. 7, 1821, by Asher Miner, Elder	71
Edgar H., of N. Stonington, m. Mary H. SMITH, of Stonington, Nov. 2, 1849, by Rev. O. T. Walker	244
Edwin Prentice, [s. Prentice & Martha], b. Sept. 26, 1834	277
Elias, m. Polly BREED, b. of N. Stonington, June 28, 1818, by Jonathan Miner, Elder	106
Elias, m. Eunice MINER, b. of N. Stonington, Jan. 3, 1833, by Jonathan Miner, Elder	143
Elias, m. Lydia MINER, June 21, 1835, by Rev. Asher Miner	155
Elisha, m. Abigail PEABODY, b. of N. Stonington, Oct. 13, 1822, by David Coats, J. P.	77
Elisha, d. Oct. 2, 1823	77
Eliza Ann, of N. Stonington, m. Lyman JOHNSON, of Union, Apr. 22, 1838, by Rev. Benj[ami]n N. Harris	178
Eliza Peabody, d. Nathan & Hannah, b. July 12, 1810	25
Eunice, m. John HOLMES, Jr., b. of N. Stonington, Mar. 15, 1835, by Stephen Main, J. P.	153
Ezra, m. Charlotte HULL, b. of N. Stonington, Nov. 13, 1814, by Jonathan Miner, Elder	53
Fidela, [d. Prentice & Martha], b. June 11, 1830	277
Franklin S., s. Jesse & Lois, d. Sept. 23, 1835	157
Franklin Story, s. Jesse & Louisa, b. May 27, 1816	54
George, of Griswold, m. Mrs. Martha CRUMB, of N. Stonington, Nov. 26, 1846, by Rev. Levi Walker	237
George C., m. Celia WHEELER, b. of Stonington, Aug. 31, 1851, by Rev. O. T. Walker	254
Gideon, m. Hannah WHEELER, b. of N. Stonington, Sept. 4, 1808, by Stephen Avery, J. P.	9
Gideon, s. Gideon & Hannah, b. May 8, 1809	9
Gurdon P., of Norwich, m. Frances Ann COTRELL, of Westerly, R. I., Feb. 14, 1836, by Rev. Amos R. Wells	157
Hannah Maria, d. Palmer & Maria, b. May 15, 1826	106
Harriet O., of N. Kingston, m. Dewitt R. PARK, of New York City, Sept. 22, 1847, by Rev. James M. Phillips	229
Henry S., m. Lydia E. WHEELER, b. of N. Stonington, Aug. 12, 1849, by Rev. John Sheffield	242
Henry T., m. Nancy E. SMITH, b. of N. Stonington, Feb. 3, 1846, by Rev. Thomas Barber	220
Israel Clark, s. Jesse & Louisa, b. Feb. 10, 1821	54
James Davis, s. Sam[ue]l & Lucy, b. July 22, 1816	19
James Maddison, s. Nathan & Hannah, b. May 29, 1815	25
Jason Lee, s. Amos & Polly, b. Mar. 11, 1816	27
Jesse, m. Louisa PARKE, b. of N. Stonington, Oct. 31, 1813, by	

CHAPMAN, (cont.)

	Page
Nathan Pendleton, J. P.	54
Jesse, of N. Stonington, m. Abby C. **BROWN**, of Westerly, Sept. 13, 1820, by Jonathan Miner, Elder	54
Jesse, m. Ursula **PARK**, b. of N. Stonington, Dec. 9, 1832, by Jonathan Miner, Elder	54
Jesse, of N. Stonington, m. Keturah **MAIN**, of Stonington, May 24, 1835, by Rev. Asher Miner	157
Joseph, Lieut., d. Jan. 17, 1810, in his 60th year	7
Joseph, of Preston, m. Betsey **JOHNSON**, of N. Stonington, Nov. 27, 1814, by Jonathan Miner, Elder	57
Julyet, [d. Prentice & Martha], b. Feb. 12, 1832	277
Lois Ann, of N. Stonington, m. William D. **CHAPMAN**, of Griswold, Feb. 20, 1850, by Rev. T. O. Walker	245
Louis Ann, d. Jesse & Ursula, b. Sept. 6, 1833	151
Louisa, w. Jesse, d. July 23, 1821	54
Lucinda, of N. Stonington, m. Daniel **GRIFFIN**, of Rhode Island, Jan. 3, 1841, by Rev. Levi Walker	195
Lucy, d. Sam[ue]l & Lucy, b. June 8, 1818	19
Manssel Harris, s. Jesse & Louisa, b. Sept. 26, 1818	54
Marcy, w. Nahum, d. May 10, 1815	29
Martha Ann, [d. Prentice & Martha], b. July 18, 1828	277
Mary, w. Lieut. Joseph, d. Aug. 29, 1793, in her 28th year	7
Mary, m. Martin **YORK**, b. of N. Stonington, Mar. 13, 1824, by Asher Miner, Elder	87
Mary E., m. Enoch B. **PENDLETON**, b. of N. Stonington, Oct. 30, 1843, by Rev. Charles Randall	210
Mary E., of N. Stonington, m. William H. **AKINS**, of Stonington, Oct. 17, 1847, by Rev. John Sheffield	230
Mary Meigs, d. Sam[ue]l & Lucy, b. Nov. 13, 1820	19
Melissa, [d. Prentice & Martha], b. Aug. 6, 1836	277
Nahum, m. Hannah **PEABODY**, b. of N. Stonington, May 4, 1822, by Jonathan Miner, Elder	59
Nathan, Dea., d. Feb. 14, 1824	94
Nathan, Jr., of N. Stonington, m. Hannah **RANDALL**, of Voluntown, May 29, 1808, by Peleg Randall, Elder, in Voluntown	25
Nathan Randall, s. Nathan & Hannah, b. Apr. 25, 1809	25
Noyes Lee, s. Elias & Polly, b. Feb. 24, 1821	106
Noyes Palmer, s. Stephen & Keturah, b. Jan. 14, 1811	7
Phebe Esther, d. Ezra & Charlotte, b. June 25, 1817	53
Polly, w. Elias, d. June 15, 1822	106
Rufus Edwin, s. Rufus M. & Mary Esther, b. Mar. 24, 1846, as per affidavits of Rufus M. **CHAPMAN** & Mrs. Fanny M. **MILLER**, sister of Mary Esther **CHAPMAN**	221
Rufus M., of Griswold, m. Mary E. **ECCLESTON**, of N. Stonington, Nov. 28, 1844, by Rev. John Sheffield	212
Russell H., m. Maria B. **INGRAHAM**, b. of N. Stonington, Aug. 6, 1844, by Rev. James R. Stone	209

	Page
CHAPMAN, (cont.)	
Samuel, m. Lucy W. **RANDALL**, Jan. 1, 1812, by Asher Miner, Elder	19
Samuel Edwin, s. Sam[ue]l & Lucy, b. June 27, 1814	19
Sanford, s. Cha[rle]s & Elizabeth, b. Apr. 3, 1816	50
Sandford, s. Nahum, d. June 20, 1816	29
Silas, m. Dorcas **CHAPMAN**, b. of N. Stonington, Sept. 7, 1821, by Asher Miner, Elder	71
Stephen, m. Keturah **PALMER**, b. of N. Stonington, Sept. 27, 1807	7
Stephen, s. Stephen & Keturah, b. Oct. 2, 1808	7
Susan K., of N. Stonington, m. Stephen **MAIN**, of N. Y., Apr. 21, 1833, by Jonathan Miner, Elder	145
Ursula, w. Jesse, d. May 12, 1835	157
Ursula, m. Lewis L. **MAIN**, b. of N. Stonington, Oct. 20, 1850, by Rev. O. T. Walker	248
Ursula M., d. Jesse & Ursula, b. May 5, 1835	157
Washington, s. Ezra & Charlotte, b. Dec. 17, 1819	53
William Burrows, s. Elias & Polly, b. Dec. 7, 1818	106
William D., of Griswold, m. Lois Ann **CHAPMAN**, of N. Stonington, Feb. 20, 1850, by Rev. O. T. Walker	245
William Randall, s. Samuel & Lucy, b. June 12, 1829	19
CHEESEBROUGH, Bridget, m. Jabish **EDGECOMB**, Apr. 13, 1815, by Asher Miner, Elder	24
Charles Wheeler, s. Silas & Phebe E[sther], b. May 29, 1822	84
Esther, w. Dea. William & d. William **WILLIAMS**, deceased, d. June 8, 1814, in her 72nd year	22
Eunice, d. Silas & Phebe E[sther], b. Mar. 22, 1824	84
Ezra Denison, s. Henry & Sally, b. Apr. 16, 1814	57
Henry, of N. Stonington, m. Martha **WILLIAMS**, of Stonington, Jan. 27, 1812	57
Henry, of N. Stonington, m. Sally P. **WILLIAMS**, of Stonington, July 18, 1813	57
Henry, s. Silas & Phebe E[sther], b. July 22, 1827	84
Martha, w. Henry, d. Mar. 19, 1812	57
Martha Williams, d. Henry & Sally, b. Nov. 11, 1815	57
Rebecca Wheeler, d. Silas & Phebe E[sther], b. Feb. 19, 1829	84
Rhoda, of Stonington, m. Cyrus **GRANT**, of N. Stonington, Nov. 19, 1820	100
Silas, of N. Stonington, m. Phebe Esther **WILLIAMS**, of Stonington, Jan. 29, 1819	84
Silas James, s. Silas & Phebe E[sther], b. Apr. 6, 1820	84
CHESTER, Elderkin A., of East Haddam, m. Lucy **MORGAN**, of N. Stonington, Oct. 17, 1822, by Levi Meech, Elder	77
CHURCH, Lodowick, m. Betsey **COOK**, Dec. 13, 1829, by Sands Cole, J. P.	120
CLAPSON, Frances A., m. Chandler D. **MAIN**, b. of N. Stonington, Jan. 25, 1853, by Rev. Philo J. Williams	262
CLARK, Eliza, d. John T. & Ruama, b. June 3, 1813	49
Ephraim, m. Polly **COON**, May 14, 1818, by Sands Cole, J. P.	74

CLARK, (cont.)

	Page
Hannah K., of Charleston, R. I., m. James C. **TUCKER**, of Richmond, R. I., Nov. 26, 1838, by Rev. Pierpoint Brocket	171
Hiram, of Leyden, Mass., m. Sarah L. **BABCOCK**, of N. Stonington, Aug. 9, 1829, by David Coats, J. P.	114
John B., m. Eliza J. **DAVIS**, b. of N. Stonington, Aug. 8, 1853, by Rev. Philo J. Williams	262
John E., s. Joshua & Susanna, b. Mar. 31, 1814	42
John E., m. Mary E. **BURDICK**, b. of N. Stonington, July 28, 1833, by Jonathan Miner, Elder	146
John Franklin, s. John T. & Ruama, b. Apr. 20, 1816	49
John T., m. Ruama **SPENCER**, b. of N. Stonington, Oct. 25, 1810, by Elias Hewett, J. P.	49
Joshua, m. Susanna **BURDICK**, Mar. 1, 1810	42
Levi S., of Lyme, m. Laura **BROMBLEY**, of N. Stonington, May 24, 1835, by Rev. Asher Miner	154
Lucinda, of N. Stonington, m. Sumner **HISCOX**, of Preston, Aug. 19, 1832, by Rev. Asher Miner	137
Lucinda B., d. Joshua & Susanna, b. Jan. 24, 1811	42
Lucy S., of N. Stonington, m. John B. **PENDLETON**, of Stonington, Mar. 20, 1845, by Nehemiah B. Cook	212
Ruth Caroline, d. John T. & Ruama, b. Apr. 12, 1811	49
Susan, m. William W. **COLLINS**, b. of N. Stonington, Feb. 18, 1833, by David Coats, J. P.	144
Thomas, m. Sarah E. **WHEELER**, b. of N. Stonington, June 20, 1855, by Rev. Henry Clark	266
W[illia]m H., of N. Stonington, m. Sarah C. **PARK**, of Ledyard, Sept. 5, 1858	264
COATES, COATS, Alfred W., s. Amos & Anna, b. Jan. 8, 1813	63
Alfred W., Dr., m. Martha E. **WHEELER**, b. of N. Stonington, Sept. 18, 1843, by Rev. Tubal Wakefield	204
Amos, s. John & Anna, b. Oct. 17, 1761	63
Amos, m. Anna **PEABODY**, Nov. 6, 1783	63
Amos, s. Amos & Anna, b. June 21, 1784	63
Anne, d. Amos & Anna, b. Sept. 16, 1788	63
Anner, w. Lieut. John, d. Jan. 10, 1806	49
Ansel, s. David & Molly, b. Mar. 14, 1794	49
Ansel, s. David & Mary, b. Mar. 14, 1794	105
Ansel, m. Eunice **RANDALL**, Jan. 18, 1826, by Rev. Gideon Perry	105
Ansel, s. Ansel & Eunice, b. Mar. 6, 1827	105
Asher, s. David & Molly, b. Oct. 28, 1790	49
Betsey, d. Amos & Anna, b. Aug. 6, 1795	63
Catharine, d. Edw[ar]d, b. June 12, 1794	48
Celesta, d. Amos & Anna, b. Nov. 16, 1805	63
Clarissa, d. David & Molly, b. June 16, 1801	49
Cynthia Williams, d. Edward & Cynthia, b. Jan. 8, 1816	48
David, m. Molly **BROWN**, b. of Stonington, June 29, 1788, by Eleazer Brown, Elder	49

	Page
COATES, COATS, (cont.)	
David. b. Dec. 17, 1766	49
David, s. David & Molly, b. Jan. 4, 1789	49
David, Jr., m. Susannah **MAIN**, b. of N. Stonington, Oct. 14, 1824, by Asher Miner, Elder	89
Edward, s. Edw[ar]d, b. Dec. 12, 1786	48
Edward, Jr., m. Cynthia **SWAN**, Oct. 15, 1809, by Stephen Avery, J. P.	48
Elias, twin with Silas, s. Amos & Anna, b. Apr. 2, 1793	63
Eliza Mary, d. Ransford & Betsey, b. Feb. 21, 1811	15
Elizabeth, m. Ephraim **WHEELER**, b. of N. Stonington, Dec. 29, 1852, by Rev. Franklin A. Slater, of Groton	261
Emeline, m. David **BAKER**, Oct. 3, 1831, by Rev. S. Heath	153
Erastus, s. Amos & Betsey, b. Oct. 11, 1800	63
Eunice Wheeler, d. Edward & Cynthia, b. Sept. 4, 1831	48
Frederick Brown, s. Ransford & Betsey, b. Dec. 25, 1809	15
Harriet B., m. Dr. W[illia]m A. **BABCOCK**, b. of N. Stonington, Apr. 14, 1845, by Rev. James R. Stone	216
John, Lieut., d. May 22, 1811	49
John Calvin, s. David & Molly, b. Nov. 1, 1811	49
John Noyes, s. Amos & Anna, b. Aug. 11, 1809	63
Lucretia, d. Amos & Betsey, b. Aug. 11, 1798	63
Lucy, d. Edw[ar]d, b. June 20, 1784	48
Lucy A., of N. Stonington, m. Hurlbutt W. **GEER**, of Preston, Nov. 18, 1833, by David Coats, J. P.	148
Lucy Ann, m. Charles T. **RICHARDS**, of Groton, Sept. 15, 1847, by Rev. H. R. Knapp, of Groton	228
Lucy Avery, d. Edward & Cynthia, b. Oct. 14, 1810	48
Lucy P., m. Austin **WHEELER**, Feb. 9, 1843, by Rev. B. C. Grafton	213
Lucy Palmer, d. David & Molly, b. July 22, 1806	49
Mary Ann, d. David Jr. & Susan[nah], b. Mar. 24, 1826	89
Nancy, of Voluntown, m. Thomas **HOLMES**, of N. Stonington, Nov. 11, 1810, by Peleg Randall, Elder	26
Polly, d. David & Molly, b. Feb. 28, 1799	49
Polly, m. Cyrus **SWAN**, b. of N. Stonington, Apr. 24, 1817, by Elias Hewit, J. P.	59
Ralph, s. David, Jr. & Susan[nah], b. Apr. 30, 1828; d. Dec. 18, 1834	89
Ransford, s. Amos & Anna, b. July 7, 1786	63
Ransford, m. Betsey **BROWN**, b. of N. Stonington, Nov. 29, 1807, by Joshua Babcock, J. P.	15
Rebeckah, d. Amos & Anna, b. Feb. 16, 1791	63
Russell B., m. Abby Lucinda **HEWITT**, b. of N. Stonington, Sept. 27, 1838, by Rev. Timothy Tuttle, of Ledyard	170
Sally Palmer, twin with Sophia Breed, d. Amos & Anna, b. June 19, 1803	63
Silas, twin with Elias, s. Amos & Anna, b. Apr. 2, 1793	63
Sophia Breed, twin with Sally Palmer, d. Amos & Anna, b. June 19, 1803	63
COGSHALL, Sally Latham, d. W[illia]m H. & Sally L., b. Sept. 16, 1820	69

	Page
COGSHALL, (cont.)	
William Ashby, s. W[illia]m H. & Sally L., b. Dec. 22, 1824	69
William H., of N. Stonington, m. Sally L. **ASHLEY**, of Groton, May 24, 1818, by Elder Roswell Burrows	69
COLE, Susan, m. Daniel **CARR**, Nov. 16, 1815, by Asher Miner, Elder	27
COLEMAN, Edwin, of Coventry, m. Ellen **MAGLOIN**, of New York, Nov. 30, 1843, by Rev. Philo Judson	203
COLLINGS, Sarah, m. Harris **GEER**, Apr.16, 1815, by Jonathan Miner, Elder	46
COLLINS, Amos, m. Phebe S. **BROWN**, b. of N. Stonington, July 1, 1838, in Hopkinton, by Rev. Amos R. Wells. Witnesses: Sarah Wells, Phebe Reynolds	167
Harriet, of N. Stonington, m. William **WALKER**, of Lenox, Mass., July 8, 1833, by Rev. Joseph Ayer, Jr.	146
Thomas M., m. Charlotte **PALMER**, b. of N. Stonington, May 11, 1823, by Nathan Pendleton, J. P	81
William W., m. Susan **CLARK**, b. of N. Stonington, Feb. 18, 1833, by David Coats, J. P.	144
CONGDON, Isaiah, m. Louis **MURPHY**, Oct. 22, 1840, by Cyrus W. Brown, Jr., J. P.	184
James M., of New London, m. Sarah **LINCOLN**, of N. Stonington, Feb. 14, 1842, by Rev. Philo Judson	190
Sarah, of Voluntown, m. Levi W. **PARK**, of N. Stonington, Apr. 11, 1852, by Rev. O. T. Walker	260
CONNER, Ann, of New York City, m. George A. **BOGGS**, of Charleston, R. I., Mar. 7, 1858, by Rev. Joseph Burnett	274
CONWAY, Nancy H., m. James H. **KENYON**, b. of Stonington, Nov. 30, 1848, by Rev. D. H. Miller	236
COOK, Albert, m. Eliza **CRUMB**, b. of N. Stonington, Mar. 30, 1834, by Rev. Asher Miner	150
Benedict Franklin, s. John & Thankfull, b. May 12, 1812, in Stonington	48
Betsey, m. Jedediah **AUSTIN**, of Hopkinton, Aug. 16, 1823, by Ichabod Brown, J. P.	82
Betsey, m. Lodowick **CHURCH**, Dec. 13, 1829, by Sands Cole, J. P.	120
Henry S., m. Mary D. **MINOR**, b. of Norwich, Nov. 2, 1844, by Levi Meech, Elder	211
James, of Norwich, m. Nancy **PEABODY**, of N. Stonington, May 27, 1851, by Rev. O. T. Walker	252
John, of Preston, m. Thankfull **ECCLESTON**, of Stonington, Apr. 20, 1803	48
Mary, of Preston, m. Silas **BABCOCK**, of N. Stonington, Oct. 1, 1820, by Rev. John Hyde	67
COON, Asa Spaulding, s. Libeus & Elizabeth, b. Apr. 6, 1800	44
Betsey, d. Libeus & Elizabeth, b. Jan. 16, 1791	44
Clark Burdick, s. Libeus & Elizabeth, b. Sept. 20, 1802	44
Desire, d. Libeus & Elizabeth, b. June 8, 1805	44
Elisha Crandall, s. Libeus & Elizabeth, b. Jan. 27, 1793	44

COON, (cont.)

	Page
Libeus, m. Elizabeth **BABCOCK**, Sept. 14, 1786	44
Libeus, s. Libeus & Elizabeth, b. May 28, 1789	44
Libeus, m. Lydia **RANDALL**, Feb. 22, 1842, by Enoch B. Pendleton, J. P.	190
Phebe A., m. Samuel **MINER**, b. of N. Stonington, July 3, 1842, by Rev. Philo Judson	194
Polly, d. Libeus & Elizabeth, b. Apr. 2, 1795	44
Polly, m. Ephraim **CLARK**, May 14, 1818, by Sands Cole, J. P.	74
Rowland, m. Martha Esther **BROWN**, Jan. 9, 1839, by W[illia]m Randall, Jr., J. P.	174
Sally, d. Libeus & Elizabeth, b. May 3, 1797	44

COOPER, Otis, Dr., of Warwick, R. I., m. Emeline Matilda **REYNOLDS**, of N. Kingston, R. I., Feb. 18, 1845, by Rev. James R. Stone — 215

COT[T]RELL, Frances Ann, of Westerly, R. I., m. Gurdon P. **CHAPMAN**, of Norwich, Feb. 14, 1836, by Rev. Amos R. Wells — 157

CRANDALL, Anna, of Westerly, R. I., m. Humphrey **ELDREDGE**, of Hopkinton, R. I., July 4, 1846, by Rev. Levi Walker — 238

Betsey, of N. Stonington, m. Jonathan **WHITE**, of Hopkinton, R. I., Dec. 20, 1829, by Asher Miner, Elder — 118

Charles H., of Stonington, m. Lucy M. **HILLIARD**, of N. Stonington, Oct. 13, 1852, by Rev. O. T. Walker — 260

Charlotte, of N. Stonington, m. Lewis **CRANDALL**, of New London, Sept. 20, 1835, by Rev. Joseph Ayer, Jr. — 155

Eliza, of N. Stonington, m. Jacob **WALTERS**, of Philadelphia, Dec. 14, 1826, by Asher Miner, Elder — 98

George Fenton, s. W[illia]m H. & Harriet Crandall, b. June 13, 1826 — 67

Gurdon S., m. Elizabeth W. **AVERY**, Dec. 2, 1828, by Rev. Joseph Ayer, Jr. — 109

Harriet, w. W[illia]m H., d. May 2, 1831 — 67

Harriet Francis, d. W[illia]m H. & Harriet, b. Sept. 24, 1828 — 67

Henry, m. Sally M. **TRUMAN**, b. of N. Stonington, Nov. 29, 1827, by Asher Miner, Elder — 101

Henry, m. Nancy **MAIN**, b. of N. Stonington, Feb. 3, 1839, by Rev. Pierpoint Brockett — 173

Horace Irvin, s. W[illia]m H. & Harriet, b. Feb. 27, 1824 — 67

James, of N. Stonington, m. Sally **GAVIT**, of Westerly, R. I., Dec. 28, 1829, by Asher Miner, Elder — 119

Lewis, of New London, m. Charlotte **CRANDALL**, of N. Stonington, by Rev. Joseph Ayer, Jr., Sept. 20, 1835 — 155

Lucy, of Stonington, m. Richard **SLOCUM**, of Hopkinton, Aug. 6, 1797, by Sam[ue]l Northup, Elder — 31

Oliver, m. Phebe E. **HOLMES**, b. of N. Stonington, Jan. 12, 1840, by Levi Meech, Elder — 182

Oliver, m. Louisa T. **PALMER**, b. of N. Stonington, Feb. 16, 1851, by Rev. W[illia]m C. Walker — 250

Russell, of Brookfield, N. Y., m. Lucy **WITTER**, of Hopkinton. R. I., June 5, 1825, by Stephen Avery, J. P. — 92

BARBOUR COLLECTION

Page

CRANDALL, (cont.)
Russell, of Richmond, R. I., m. Patience **WRIGHT**, of N. Stonington, Nov. 30, 1828, by Asher Miner, Elder ... 110
Ruth, of Warwick, R. I., m. Asa **LANGWORTHY**, of Stonington, July 14, 1813, by Rev. David Curtis. Recorded Mar. 25, 1831 ... 128
Sarah, m. John B. **MINER,** b. of N. Stonington, Apr. 29, 1841, by Philo Judson ... 187
Silas M., of New York, m. Martha W. **AVERY**, Aug. 7, 1837, by P. H. Shaw ... 162
Silas Maxon, s. Josel & Kitte, b. Apr. 17, 1815 ... 74
Tho[ma]s Franklin, s. Joel & Kitte, b. Mar. 9, 1818 ... 74
Thomas Wells, s. W[illia]m H. & Harriet, b. Mar. 30, 1831; d. Feb. 25, 1833 ... 67
William Edwin, s. W[illia]m H. & Harriet, b. Feb. 2, 1822 ... 67
W[illia]m H., m. Harriet **LEWIS**, Sept. 28, 1820, by Asher Miner, Elder ... 67
CRANE, Origen, of Mansfield, m. Bridget S. **GREEN**, of N. Stonington, Nov. 22, 1829, by Rev. Joseph Ayer, Jr. ... 117
CRARY, Cyrus W., m. Mary **PEABODY**, b. of N. Stonington, Mar. 12, 1838 ... 164
Cyrus W., m. Mary **PEABODY**, b. of N. Stonington, Nov. 21, 1846, by Rev. Thomas Barber ... 225
John H., m. Martha E. **BENTLEY**, b. of N. Stonington, Nov. 12, 1845, by Rev. James R. Stone ... 218
Nathan B., m. Mrs. Mary **WOODMANCEY**, b. of N. Stonington, Apr. 26, 1849, by Oliver Hewitt, T. C. ... 238
Nathaniel M., m. Rebeckah **STEWART**, b. of N. Stonington, m. July 18, 1824, by Rev. Gideon Perry ... 88
Polly, of N. Stonington, m. Hezekiah **PRENTICE**, of Griswold, Nov. 9, 1834, by Rev. Asher Miner ... 153
Sally, of N. Stonington, m. John **RIPLEY**, of Groton, Oct. 30, 1832, by Asher Miner. Elder ... 141
Sarah H., of Voluntown, m. Charles E. **MAIN**, of N. Stonington, Oct. 6, 1850, by Rev. O. T. Walker ... 247
CRUMB, Albert T., m. Sabra A. **BROMLEY**, Oct. 20, 1855, by Charles P. White, J. P. ... 269
Augusta J., m. James A. **PEABODY**, Nov. 10, 1856, by Rev. W[illia]m **STOW**, at Stonington ... 273
David, m. Sally **ALLEN**, b. of N. Stonington, Feb. 3, 1833, by Asher Miner, Elder ... 143
Eliza, m. Albert **COOK**, b. of N. Stonington, Mar. 30, 1834, by Rev. Asher Miner ... 150
Lucy, m. Russell **BLIVIN**, Nov. 20, 1825, by William Randall, Jr., J. P. ... 96
Martha, of N. Stonington, m. George **CHAPMAN**, of Griswold, Nov. 26, 1846, by Rev. Levi Walker ... 237
Nathan, m. Phebe **RICHARDSON**, b. of N. Stonington, Sept. 5, 1833, by Jonathan Miner, Elder ... 147

	Page
CRUMB, (cont.)	
Palmer, m. Lucy B. **ALLEN**, July 26, 1840, by Cyrus W. Brown, J. P.	184
Susan A., m. Isaac F. **CHAMPLAIN**, b. of N. Stonington, Apr. 12, 1846, by Rev. Thomas Barber	225
Susanna, m. Sands **PALMER**, Jan. 29, 1823, by Sands Cole, J. P.	79
CURTIS, Thomas, m. Phebe J. **WHEELER**, b. of Norwich, May 30, 1849, by M. N. Morris	236
DARROW, Moses, of New London, m. Jane M. **MINER**, of N. Stonington, Aug. 15, 1853, by Rev. O. T. Walker	263
DART, Giles, of Waterford, m. Nancy **GRANT**, of N. Stonington, Dec. 27, 1826, by Asher Miner, Elder	98
DAVIS, Betsey, m. Elias **THOMPSON**, Mar. 19, 1795	33
Betsey, m. William G. **BROMLEY**, b. of N. Stonington, Oct. 11, 1844, by Charles S. Brown, J. P.	211
Eliza A., of N. Stonington, m. Alanson **BROWN**, of Stonington, Jan. 12, 1840, by Rev. Philo Judson	182
Eliza J., m. John B. **CLARK**, b. of N. Stonington, Aug. 8, 1853, by Rev. Philo J. Williams	262
Gustavus Fellows, s. Gustavus F. & Abigail, b. Jan. 4, 1818	62
James A., of Stonington, m. Nancy A. **MAIN**, of N. Stonington, Apr. 3, 1851, by Rev. O. T. Walker	253
Marvin, b. Jan. 17, 1760; m. William **PALMER**, Dec. 11, 1783	17
Mary, m. Lodowick **BABCOCK**, Dec. 13, 1801	42
Mary E., m. John S. **BENTLEY**, b. of N. Stonington, Aug. 13, 1854, by Rev. John Sheffield	264
Phineas M., m. Phebe **HULL**, b. of N. Stonington, Nov. 6, 1842, by Rev. Philo Judson	196
DEAN, Thomas Andrew, of N. Y. C., m. Keturah **SISSON**, of N. Stonington, Aug. 19, 1832, by Rev. Joseph Ayer, Jr.	138
DENISON, Clarissa, m. Osamus **SMITH**, Aug. 24, 1823, by Paris Hewit, J. P.	85
Dudley, s. Lydia **BROWN**, b. Aug. 19, 1794	40
Dudley, m. Sophia **SMITH**, b. of N. Stonington, Oct. 20, 1814, by Stephen Avery, J. P.	40
Lucy Ellen, of N. Stonington, m. John Franklin **BROWN**, of Rochester, N. Y., Mar. 15, 1858, by Rev. Stephen Hubbell	275
Lydia, d. Dudley & Sophronia, b. Sept. 7, 1815	40
William, alias **BALDWIN**, s. Rebecca **BALDWIN**, b. May 23, 1798, in Stonington	36
William B., m. Lucy A. **MINER**, b. of N. Stonington, Jan. 18, 1830, by Rev. Joseph Ayer, Jr.	121
DENNIS, Samuel, of Newport, R. I., m. Delacy A. **CARPENTER**, of Stonington, May 10, 1852, by M. N. Morris	258
DEVERLL, Thomas J., s. Tho[ma]s J. & Elizabeth, b. Sept. 3, 1821	74
DEWEY, Abby, d. Christ[ophe]r & Huldah, b. Mar. 4, 1810	23
Almanda, of N. Stonington, m. Paul M. **BARBER**, of Westerly, Dec. 30, 1827, by Asher Miner, Elder	103
Amelia S., of N. Stonington, m. Dea. Samuel S. **PECKHAM**, of	

330 BARBOUR COLLECTION

	Page
DEWEY, (cont.)	
Portsmouth, R. I., Mar. 6, 1853, by Rev. O. T. Walker	262
Charles H., s. Christ[ophe]r & Huldah, b. May 17, 1811	23
Christopher, Jr., m. Huldah **BABCOCK**, Nov. 13, 1809, by Asher Miner, Elder	23
Dan, m. Mary **BUTTLES**, Feb. 23, 1812, by Jedediah Randall, Elder	14
Daniel, s. Dan & Mary, b. Mar. 11, 1815	14
Erastus, s. Christ[ophe]r & Huldah, b. Oct. 17, 1812	23
Esther, m. Thomas **PEABODY**, b. of N. Stonington, Sept. 4, 1832, by Rev. Asher Miner	139
Hannah, m. Robert **BROWNING**, Dec. 12, 1810, by Jedediah Randall, Elder	10
Joseph N., of Stonington, m. Sarah B. **BROWN**, of N. Stonington, Mar. 26, 1843, by John Sheffield, J. P.	201
Marilla, m. William M. **HILLIARD**, b. of N. Stonington, May 18, 1830, by Asher Miner, Elder	92
Sophia, m. Joseph **GEER**, Apr. 10, 1834, by Saxyon Miner, J. P.	159
Sophia, m. Joseph **GEER**, b. of N. Stonington, Apr. [ ], 1836, by Saxton Miner, J. P.	178
Thomas Harris, s. Christ[ophe]r & Huldah, b. Dec. 31, 1814	23
William Earl, s. Dan & Mary, b. Feb. 18, 1813	14
William M., of Stonington, m. Eliza Ann **BROWN**, of N. Stonington, Feb. 16, 1843, by John Sheffield, J. P.	201
DIVEREAU, Amanda, m. W[illia]m **STEWART**, b. of N. Stonington, Oct. 31, 1802, by Stephen Avery, J. P.	94
DOUGLASS, Charles L., of N. Stonington, formerly of Voluntown, m. Marinda **NED**, of N. Stonington, Oct. 1, 1843, by Latham Hull, J. P.	202
Joseph A., of Hopkinton, R. I., m. Lucy E. **THOMPSON**, of N. Stonington, July 3, 1844, in N. Stonington, by Rev. Leander Wakefield of Hopkinton, R. I.	208
William, of Voluntown, m. Esther **BARBER**, of N. Stonington, June 14, 1846, by Rev. Levi Walker	239
DOWNER, Anna, m. Thomas **PRENTICE**, Apr. 17, 1787	38
DUNHAM, John, m. Eliza **WILCOX**, of N. Stonington, Jan. 14, 1856, at Mystic, by Nehemiah B. Cook	270
DYE, Deborah, b. Feb. 1766	43
Polly, m. Sanford **BROWN**, May 15, 1814, by Asher Miner, Elder	22
DYER, Samule F., m. Mrs. Sally R. **ELDRED**, b. of N. Kingston, R. I., Oct. 6, 1845, by Rev. R. Stone	217
***EATON**, Rachel, m. Elisha **FRINK**, Dec. 25, 1807 * Handwritten in original manuscript.	
EBBINS, Betsey, of N. Stonington, m. Coddington **PETERS**, of Stonington, Mar. 29, 1821, by Asher Miner, Elder	70
ECCLESTON, ECLESTON, [EGGLESTON], Abigail, m. Jared **MAIN**, b. of N. Stonington, Sept. 10, 1801, by Joshua Babcock, Esq.	40
Almira, d. W[illia]m & Lucy, b. July 1, 1811	50
Almira, of N. Stonington, m. Charles **MAIN**, of Voluntown, Dec. 18,	

	Page
ECCLESTON, ECLESTON, [EGGLESTON], (cont.)	
1833, by Thomas H. Hewitt, J. P.	148
Angeline, m. Charles H. BURDICK, b. of N. Stonington, Apr. 1, 1856, by Cha[rle]s C. Lewis	271
Anna, d. Gershom & Avis, b. June 13, 1788	32
Avery N., s. W[illia]m & Lucy, b. Aug. 13, 1808	50
Clarissa, d. W[illia]m & Lucy, b. Aug. 31, 1802	50
Content, d. Gershom & Avis, b. Feb. 5, 1786; d. July 22, 1786	32
Deborah, d. Gershom & Avis, b. Aug. 23, 1784	32
Desire, of N. Stonington, m. Sam[ue]l REED, of Canterbury, Sept. 15, 1833, by David Coats, J. P.	147
Elias, s. W[illia]m & Lucy, b. Oct. 4, 1804	50
Elizabeth A., of Hopkinton, R. I., m. Charles L. CARDNER, of Westerly, R. I., Sept. 1, 1847, by Rev. Thomas Barber	228
Ellenner, d. Gershom & Avis, b. Feb. 9, 1791	32
Emeline, s. W[illia]m & Lucy, b. Nov. 5, 1810	50
Emily, of N. Stonington, m. Asa RIX, of Griswold, Nov. 27, 1845, by Rev. John Sheffield	221
Enoch B., m. Ruth MAIN, b. of N. Stonington, Oct. [ ], 1849, by Dewitt C. Pendleton, J. P.	246
Eunice M., m. Oliver S. BURDICK, Oct. 19, 1856, by Rev. Charles C. Lewis	272
Gershom, of Stonington, m. Avis LAMPHEIR, of Hopkinton, Apr. 4, 1784, by William Tanner, J. P., of Hopkinton	32
Gershom, s. Gershom & Avis, b. Oct. 14, 1801	32
Gershom, Jr., m. Fanny ROGGERS, b. of N. Stonington, Dec. 9, 1824, by Jonathan Miner, Elder	107
Henry A., m. Mary R. BURDICK, b. of N. Stonington, Jan. 7, 1855, by Rev. Thomas W. Clark	265
Latham H., m. Harriet E. BURDICK, Oct. 19, 1856, by Rev. Charles C. Lewis	272
Lucy, d. William & Lucy, b. Feb. 19, 1794	50
Mary E., of N. Stonington, m. Rufus M. CHAPMAN, of Griswold, Nov. 28, 1844, by Rev. John Sheffield	212
Oliver, s. W[illia]m & Lucy, b. Mar. 28, 1813	50
Priscilla, d. W[illia]m & Lucy, b. Aug. 15, 1800	50
Rowland, s. Gershom & Avis, b. Aug. 19, 1796	32
Sarah Almira, of N. Stonington, m. Oliver S. MILLER, of Clinton, Sept. 23, 1849, by Rev. John Sheffield	242
Stephen, s. W[illia]m & Lucy, b. Jan. 29, 1798	50
Thankfull, of Stonington, m. John COOK, of Preston, Apr. 20, 1803	48
Thankful, m. John LAW, Jr., b. of N. Stonington, Dec. 29, 1808, by Joshua Babcock, J. P.	25
Thankfull, m. Lester MAIN, b. of N. Stonington, Mar. 13, 1856, by Rev. J. G. Park, at Griswold	271
William, s. W[illia]m & Lucy, b. Nov. 2, 1795	50
W[illia]m N., Jr., m. Mrs. Fanny M. MILLER, b. of N. Stonington, Jan. 26, 1840, by Rev. Levi Walker	195

332 BARBOUR COLLECTION

	Page
EDGECOMB, EDGCOME, Jabish, m. Bridget **CHEESEBROUGH**, Apr. 13, 1815, by Asher Miner, Elder	24
Julia, m. Cyrus H. **MAIN**, Oct. 27, 1847, by Rev. D. H. Miller	236
Mary Jane, m. Willard N. **HILL**, Oct. 12, 1856, by Henry W. Webber	272
Thomas, of N. Stonington, m. Emma* **BURDICK**, of Griswold, Apr. 7, 1852, by Rev. O. T. Walker *(Abbie corrected in handwriting)	258
EDWARDS, Celia, m. Erastus N. **BROWN**, b. of N. Stonington, Aug. 12, 1832, by Rev. Asher Miner	136
Freelove, m. Jabish **MAIN**, Mar. 15, 1795	7
George W., m. Lucinda **WILLCOX**, Jan. 7, 1838, by Leland D. Miner, J. P.	166
Harriet, of Hopkinton, R. I., m. Caleb **BURDICK**, of Penn., Nov. 29, 1844, by Dewitt C. Pendleton, J. P.	246
Isaac C., of Hopkinton, R. I., m. Lucy Ann **MAIN**, of N. Stonington, Sept. 27, 1835, by Rev. Asher Miner	192
EGGLESTON, [see under **ECCLESTON**]	
ELDREDGE, ELDRED, Humphrey, of Hopkinton, R. I., m. Anna **CRANDALL**, of Westerly, R. I., July 4, 1846, by Rev. Levi Walker	238
Joshua, Jr., of Groton, m. Elizabeth **KENYON**, of N. Stonington, Feb. 20, 1825, by William Williams, J. P.	92
Mary, singlewoman, m. Elder Christopher **AVERY**, of Stonington. Marriage agreement signed Nov. 7, 1803, in presence of Latham & Desire **HULL**, to return her property to her brothers and sisters, she to have no right of dower.	83
Sally R., m. Samuel F. **DYER**, b. of N. Kingston, R. I., Oct. 6, 1845, by Rev. James R. Stone	217
ELLINGTON, Maria, of N. Stonington, m. William **AUSTIN**, of New London, Dec. 24, 1826, by Elias Hewit, J. P.	99
ELLIS, Betsey Ann, m. Benjamin R. **HOXSIE**, b. of W. Greenwich, R. I., Apr. 28, 1835, by Rev. Asher Miner	154
***EATON**, Rachel, m. Elisha **FRINK**, Dec. 25, 1807 *(corrected in handwriting from **ESTES**)	48
FAGANS, FAGINS, FAGGAN, FAGGINS, PHAGINS, Abby, m. John **RANDALL**, colored people, b. of N. Stonington, Nov. 27, 1851, by M. N. Morris	256
Eunice, of N. Stonington, m. William **WILLIAMS**, of Groton, colored people, June 22, 1823, by Asher Miner, Elder	82
Gilbert W., m. Eliza Ann **WILSON**, b. of N. Stonington, Nov. 25, 1846, by Charales Bennet, J. P.	224
Harriet, m. Alexander **WATSON**, b. of color, Feb. 8, 1821, by William Randall, J. P.	69
Henry, m. Freelove **SHELLEY**, b. of N. Stonington, June 25, 1838, by Rev. Pierpoint Brocket	167
Laura, of N. Stonington, m. Albert **WATSON**, of Charlestown, R. I., Nov. 30, 1843, by Rev. Erastus Denison, of Groton	203
Sulliven, of Preston, m. Mrs. Hannah M. **RANDALL**, of N. Stonington, b. colored person, July 1, 1847, by Rev. Myron N. Morris	226

NORTH STONINGTON VITAL RECORDS 333

Page

FARNHAM, Sally, of N. Stonington, m. Dudley RANDALL, Mar. 28,
    1830, by Rev. Jabez S. Swan   122
FELLOWS, Prudence, of N. Stonington, m. Nathan MINER, of Norwich,
    Mar. 14, 1821, by Stephen Avery, J. P.   70
FISH, Charles, m. Lucy HEWITT, b. of N. Stonington, Mar. 23, 1843, by
    Asher Prentice, Jr., J. P.   199
Sarah J., m. George F. WILKINSON, b. of N. Stonington, Feb. 27,
    1848, by Rev. James M. Phillips   233
Susan, of N. Stonington, m. W[illia]m R. SWEET, of Voluntown,
    May 15, 1842, by Asher Prentice, Jr., J. P.   193
FISK, Eunice, of Voluntown, m. Spicer STANTON, of N. Stonington,
    Mar. 9, 1823, by Asher Miner, Elder   79
FLINT, Orrin, of Windham, m. Lizzie BROWN, of N. Stonington, Jan.
    14, 1821, by Asher Miner, Elder   68
FRANKLIN, Edward W., of Norwich, m. Charlotte HULL, of N.
    Stonington, June 29, 1823, by Elias Hewit, J. P.   82
Elcy M., of W. Greenwich, m. Samuel WOODMANSIE, Jr., of Exeter,
    b. of R. I., Mar. 11, 1832, by Rev. John G. Wightman   135
FRENCH, Latham Hull, s. Stephen & Mary, b. Mar. 17, 1810   3
Stephen, m. Mary BALWIN, b. of Stonington, Mar. 22, 1807, by Rev.
    Christopher Avery   3
Stephen, s. Stephen & Mary, b. Oct. 11, 1807   3
FRINK, Alexander G., of Stonington, m. Mary MINER, of N. Stonington,
    Dec. 10, 1828, by Rev. Joseph Ayer, Jr.   110
Ann L., of Stonington, m. John BALDWIN, Jr., of Windham, Feb. 24,
    1839, by P. H. Shaw   176
Benadam, s. Benj[ami]n & Eunice, b. Dec. 16, 1794   4
Benjamin, m. Eunice MAIN, b. of Stonington, Oct. 2, 1792, by Joshua
    Babcock, J. P.   4
Benjamin, m. Rhoda BALDWIN, Jan. 14, 1821, b. of N. Stonington,
    by Asher Miner, Elder   68
Colins, m. Adaline WOODMANCEY, b. of N. Stonington, Aug. 26,
    1851, by Rev. John Sheffield   256
Elisha, m. Rachel *EATON, Dec. 25, 1807 *(corrected from ESTES,
    in handwriting in margin of original)   48
Elvira, see Ulvira
Eunice, m. Daniel BALDWIN, b. of Stonington, Apr. 22, 1804, by
    Stephen Avery, J. P.   46
Gustavus, d. Elisha & Rachel, b. Jan. 22, 1811   48
Hannah E., of N. Stonington, m. Thomas H. BALDWIN, of
    Gilbertsville, Otsego Co., N. Y., May 23, 1847, by Rev. Thomas
    Barber   232
Jefferson, m. Martha HARVEY, of N. Stonington, Sept. 30, 1855, by
    Rev. William Clift   267
John H., m. Lucy A. MAIN, b. of N. Stonington, Oct. 10, 1855, by
    Rev. John Sheffield   267
Mary, m. Nathaniel M. MAIN, b. of N. Stonington, Mar. 21, 1847, by
    Rev. Levi Walker   240

	Page
FRINK, (cont.)	
Randall, s. Benj[ami]n & Eunice, b. Dec. 20, 1800	4
Randall, m. Eliza **MORGAN**, b. of N. Stonington, Nov. 28, 1824, by David Coats, J. P.	90
Robert, s. Benj[amin] & Eunice, b. May 28, 1807	4
Sally A., m. William L. **MAIN**, of Ledyard, Feb. 26, 1837, by Matthew Brown, J. P.	160
Ulrika, d. Elisha & Rachel, b. May 26, 1809	48
Ulvira, d. Elisha & Rachel, b. Aug. 27, 1813	48
GALLUP, Asa L., of Ledyard, m. Eliza **GALLUP**, of N. Stonington, Dec. 9, 1840, by Levi Meech, Elder	185
Benjamin A., m. Harriet A. **GRANT**, of N. Stonington, Oct. 11, 1855, by Rev. O. T. Walker	267
Eliza, of N. Stonington, m. Asa L. **GALLUP**, of Ledyard, Dec. 9, 1840, by Levi Meech, Elder	185
Erastus, of Groton, m. Frances E. **SHEFFIELD**, of N. Stonington, Aug. 27, 1846, by Rev. John Sheffield	223
Hannah, d. Jabez & Eunice, b. Apr. 17, 1834	152
John D., s. Jabez & Eunice, b. Nov. 27, 1832	152
Martha, d. Jabez & Eunice, b. Feb. 16, 1830	152
Martha, m. Dudley R. **HEWITT**, b. of N. Stonington, Oct. 10, 1854, by Rev. Stephen Hubbell	265
Mary J., m. Elisha **WHEELER**, Nov. 2, 1856, by Rev. Charles C. Lewis	272
Peleg H., of Voluntown, m. Clarinda E. **MAIN**, of N. Stonington, Dec. 3, 1845, by Rev. Thomas Barber	219
Sophia, m. Thomas Hazard **PECKHAM**, Jr., Sept. 30, 1813, by Stephen Avery, J. P.	58
GARDINER, Henry, of N. Stonington, m. Martha **BENT**, of Hopkinton, R. I., Jan. 6, 1847, by Rev. Levi Walker	237
GARDNER, [see also **CARDNER**], Albert, m. Mary E. **WHEELER**, b. of N. Stonington, Nov. 3, 1850, by J. B. Maryatt, J. P.	250
John, of Groton, m. Mary **RANDALL**, of Stonington, Mar. 1, 1830, by Rev. Asher Miner	122
GAVITT, **GAVIT**, Hannah, of N. Stonington, m. Paris **SWAN**, of Genesee, N. Y., Sept. 27, 1821, by Elias Hewit, J. P.	72
Sally, of Westerly, R. I., m. James **CRANDALL**, of N. Stonington, Dec. 28, 1829, by Asher Miner, Elder	119
GAY, Betsey, m. Thomas **STANTON**, b. of N. Stonington, Feb. 20, 1828, by Sam[ue]l Chapman, J. P.	103
Thomas W., s. Jed[edia]h & Dolly, b. July 11, 1800	70
GAYANT, Hannah, m. Elisha W. **HULL**, b. of Stonington, July 11, 1844, by Rev. Levi Walker	237
GAYART, Hannah, m. Elisha W. **HULL**, b. of N. Stonington, July 14, 1844, by Rev. Levi Walker	209
GEER, Anna, d. George & Amey, b. Jan. 25, 1796	41
Betsey, d. George & Amey, b. Oct. 2, 1799	41
Ezra, of N. Stonington, m. Esther **THOMPSON**, of Westerly, Mar.	

	Page
GEER, (cont.)	
19, 1827, by Elias Hewit, J. P.	99
Harris, s. George & Amey, b. Apr. 1, 1793	41
Harris, m. Sarah **COLLINGS,** Apr. 16, 1815, by Jonathan Miner, Elder	46
Harris, s. Harris & Sarah, b. Oct. 13, 1815	46
Henry C., m. Emily M. **MAIN,** b. of N. Stonington, Aug. 14, 1848, by Rev. Thomas Barber	234
Hurlbutt W., of Preston, m. Lucy A. **COATS,** of N. Stonington, Nov. 18, 1833, by David Coats, J. P.	148
Jefferson, s. George & Amey, b. Nov. 12, 1803	41
John Baker, s. Joseph & S., b. Dec. 24, 1841	178
Joseph, m. Sophia **DEWEY,** Apr. 10, 1834, by Saxton Miner, J. P.	159
Joseph, m. Sophia **DEWEY,** b. of N. Stonington, Apr. [ ], 1836, by Saxton Miner, J. P.	178
Joseph Abner, s. Joseph & S., b. Sept. 19, 1839	178
Lucy, twin with Lurey, d. George & Amey, b. Jan. 20, 1809	41
Lurey, twin with Lucy, d. George & Amey, b. Jan. 20, 1809	41
Mariah, m. John **MAIN,** b. of N. Stonington, Oct. 5, 1825, by Nathan Pendleton, J. P.	93
GOULD, Julia A., m. Lorenzo D. **KNAPP,** b. of Stonington, Nov. 24, 1850, by Rev. Milo Tracy	249
GRANT, Almira, d. Joshua & Lucy, b. Apr. 6, 1800	16
Almira, of N. Stonington, m. Noyes **WEAVER,** of Farsalia, N. Y., Nov. 11, 1824, by Levi Walker	89
Almira C., d. Cyrus & Rhoda, b. Mar. 26, 1822	100
Ann M., of N. Stonington, m. Orren **SAFFORD,** of Preston, Dec. 29, 1830, by Rev. Asher Miner	125
Anna, of N. Stonington, m. James **TREAT,** of Preston, Sept. 29, 1839, by Rev. Nathan E. Shaler, of Preston	179
Betsey, d. Joshua & Lucy, b. Oct. 2, 1792	16
Bridget, twin with Phebe, d. Daniel & Polly, b. Aug. 24, 1807	3
Bridget, m. George W. **NOYES,** b. of N. Stonington, Mar. 12, 1833, by Rev. Asher Miner	144
Caleb, s. Joshua & Lucy, b. June 19, 1797	16
Charles, s. Joshua & Lucy, b. Jan. 12, 1788	16
Charles Prentice, s. Prentice & Lucy, b. Oct. 12, 1813	33
Cyrus, of N. Stonington, m. Rhoda **CHEESEBROUGH,** of Stonington, Nov. 19, 1820	100
Daniel, m. Polly **SWAN,** b. of Stonington, Apr. 10, 1783	3
Daniel, s. Daniel & Polly, b. Feb. 24, 1805	3
Denison P., s. Cyrus & Rhoda, b. Dec. 29, 1827	100
Erastus, s. Prentice & Lucy, b. Oct. 27, 1811	33
Eunice, m. Allen **YORK,** Oct. 1, 1820, by Asher Miner, Elder	66
Ezra C., s. Cyrus & Rhoda, b. Mar. 19, 1826	100
Francis Nelson, s. Prentice & Lucy, b. Sept. 4, 1815	33
Henry, s. Joshua & Lucy, b. July 25, 1790	16
John, m. Ann W. **AYER,** b. of N. Stonington, Sept. 26, 1826, by Rev. Joseph Ayer, Jr.	96

336   BARBOUR COLLECTION

	Page
GRANT, (cont.)	
Joshua, m. Lucy **GREEN**, Jan. 1, 1778	16
Joshua, s. Joshua & Lucy, b. Nov. 17, 1778	16
Lucinda, m. Stanton **HEWIT**, May 15, 1784	38
Lucy, d. Joshua & Lucy, b. Dec. 24, 1781	16
Lucy, m. Timothy S. **WHEELER**, Dec. 18, 1796, by Christ[ophe]r Avery, Pastor	50
Mary, d. Daniel & Polly, b. Mar. 24, 1819	3
Miner, s. Daniel & Polly, b. Aug. 4, 1815	3
Nancy, of N. Stonington, m. Giles **DART**, of Waterford, Dec. 27, 1826, by Asher Miner, Elder	98
Nathan B., s. Cyrus & Rhoda, b. May 29, 1824	100
Phebe, twin with Bridget, d. Daniel & Polly, b. Aug. 24, 1807	3
Phebe, of N. Stonington, m. Justin **HINCKLEY**, of Lebanon, Mar. 22, 1829, by Rev. Joseph Ayer, Jr.	113
Prentice, s. Joshua & Lucy, b. Nov. 29, 1783	16
Prentice, m. Lucy **BROWN**, Dec. 28, 1808	33
Prentice, s. Prentice & Lucy, b. Jan. 27, 1809; d. Sept. 27, 1811	33
Sally, d. Joshua & Lucy, b. Nov. 11, 1785	16
Sarah E., m. Oliver **BROWN**, b. of N. Stonington, Aug. 29, 1855, by Rev. Stephen Hubbell	266
Wealthy, m. Sandford **PALMER**, b. of Stonington, Feb. 10, 1788	62
Wealthy, d. Daniel & Polly, b. Aug. 17, 1811	3
William F., m. Harriet N. **WILLIAMS**, b. of N. Stonington, Mar. 12, 1856, by Timothy Tuttle, at Ledyard	270
William S., m. Betsey M. **BALDWIN**, b. of N. Stonington, May 16, 1827, by Asher Miner, Elder	100
GRAY, Alva, d. John & Lucy, b. Mar. 12, 1805	11
Alva, m. Priscilla **WHEELER**, b. of N. Stonington, Oct. 30, 1831, by Rev. Asher Miner	132
Eunice Ann, m. Gilbert **SISSON**, b. of N. Stonington, Mar. 7, 1845, by Rev. James R. Stone	215
John, s. John & Nancy, b. May 10, 1795	11
John, m. Lucy **YORK**, July 9, 1804	11
Lucy York, d. John & Nancy, b. Apr. 8, 1803	11
Lyman M., m. Eunice **LAREY**, b. of N. Stonington, Jan. 6, 1822, by Asher Miner, Elder	73
Lyman Main, s. John & Nancy, b. Aug. 20, 1800	11
Mary, m. Charles S. **HEWITT**, b. of N. Stonington, May 8, 1837, by William Williams, J. P.	161
Melissa, d. John & Lucy, b. Sept. 17, 1806	11
Nancy, d. John & Nancy, b. Oct. 17, 1797	11
Nancy M., m. William **WHIPPLE**, Aug. 30, 1829, by Paris Hewit, J. P.	116
William Wilbur, s. John & Lucy, b. Dec. 20, 1809	11
GREEN, Bethany, d. Daniel & Content, b. Oct. 18, 1801	43
Bettey, d. Daniel & Content, b. May 11, 1815	4
Bridget S., of N. Stonington, m. Origen **CRANE**, of Mansfield,	

	Page
GREEN, (cont.)	
Nov. 22, 1829, by Rev. Joseph Ayer, Jr.	117
Calvin, s. Daniel & Content, b. Mar. 9, 1799	43
Content, w. Daniel, b. Apr. 6, 1790	43
Content, d. Daniel & Content, b. Nov. 6, 1811	43
Daniel, b. Nov. 30, 1772	43
Daniel, of Springfield, N. Y., m. Content **BURDICK**, of Stonington, at Hopkinton, Feb. 15, 1795, by Abram Coon, J. P.	43
Daniel, s. Daniel & Content, b. Apr. 5, 1809	43
Dorcas, d. Daniel & Content, b. May 9, 1806	43
Dudley, m. Lydia M. **WRIGHT**, Sept. 2, 1849, by Rev. Milo Tracey	241
John L., of Voluntown, m. Mary E. **YORK**, of N. Stonington, Nov. 29, 1832, by Jonathan Miner, Elder	141
Lucy, m. Joshua **GRANT**, Jan. 1, 1778	16
Martha, d. Daniel & Content, b. Feb. 1, 1796	43
Melissa L., b. Oct. 25, 1855	274
Thomas, s. Daniel & Content, b. Feb. 15, 1804	43
GRIFFIN, Daniel, of Rhode **ISLAND**, m. Lucinda **CHAPMAN**, of N. Stonington, Jan. 3, 1841, by Rev. Levi Walker	195
George N., of Wallingford, m. Sarah A. **BALDWIN**, of N. Stonington, Sept. 1, 1839, by Rev. Augustus B. Collins, of Preston	179
Russell, of Wallingford, m. Emily A. **HEWITT**, of N. Stonington, Sept. 1, 1839, by Rev. Augustus B. Collins, of Preston	179
GRINNELL, Julia A., m. Ephraim **SWAN**, b. of N. Stonington, Nov. 29, 1831, by Rev. Asher Miner	132
HAKES, Bridget, m. Nathan **RATHBOURN**, b. of N. Stonington, Apr. 6, 1828, by Benjamin Pomeroy, J. P.	104
Hannah, m. David **HOLMES**, b. of N. Stonington, Apr. 30, 1826, by Asher Miner, Elder	95
Henry B., of Preston, m. Ann W. **WOODWARD**, of N. Stonington, Jan. 6, 1841, by Rev. Augustus B. Collins, of Preston	186
HALEY, Simeon, Jr., of Mystic, m. Lydia E. **BROWN**, of N. Stonington, May 12, 1839, by Rev. Fernando Bester	177
HALLET, Alfred, m. Laura **WHEELER**, b. of N. Stonington, July 11, 1848, by Rev. Levi Walker	240
HANDCOCK, Mary, m. Barker N. **BLIVEN**, Mar. 26, 1820, by Stephen Avery, J. P.	67
HARRINGTON, Janette, m. Daniel **LANPHEAR**, b. of Preston, July 19, 1847, by Rev. John Sheffield	227
HARRIS, Benj[ami]n N., Jr., m. Lucy A. **BROWN**, b. of N. Stonington, Apr. 3, 1838, by Rev. Benj[ami]n N. Harris	178
HARVEY, Martha, of N. Stonington, m. Jefferson **FRINK**, Sept. 30, 1855, by Rev. William Clift	267
Wa[i]ty, m. Stanton H. **PERRY**, b. of Charlestown, R. I., Mar. 31, 1842, by Elias Hewitt, J. P.	192
HASKELL. [see also **HESKALL**], Moses, m. Hannah **SHELLEY**, b. of N. Stonington, June 23, 1839, by Charles Bennet, J. P.	181
HAWKINS. Hannah, m. Daniel **SWAN**, Apr. 3, 1803	52

338 BARBOUR COLLECTION

	Page
HECKOCK, Lorenzo D., of Wallingford, m. Julia Ann **WILLIAMS**, of N. Stonington, July 20, 1828, by Asher Miner, Elder	107
HERREN, Lydia Ann, d. Marvin & Bethiah, b. Dec. 24, 1810	8
Marvin, of Groton, m. Bethiah **BABCOCK**, of N. Stonington, Mar. 18, 1810, by Elias Hewit, J. P.	8
HESKALL, [see also **HASKELL**], Hezekiah, of Preston, m. Sally A. **HEWIT**, of N. Stonington, Apr. 24, 1825, by Levi Meech, Elder	92
HEWIT, HEWITT, Abby Lucinda, m. Russell B. **COATS**, b. of N. Stonington, Sept. 27, 1838, by Rev. Timothy Tuttle, of Ledyard	170
Abby P., m. Richard H. **MAIN**, b. of N. Stonington, Feb. 11, 1833, by Rev. Joseph Ayer, Jr.	142
Alpheas M., s. Elias & Polly, b. Sept. 16, 1818	134
Anna, m. Jonathan **AVERY**, Feb. 2, 1800	64
Austin D., m. Eunice A. **HEWITT**, b. of N. Stonington, Dec. 9, 1828, by William Williams, J. P.	111
Benadam, s. Eli & Betsey, b. Apr. [ ], 1808	22
Betsey, d. Eli & Betsey, b. Aug. 30, 1799; d. Mar. 7, 1803	22
Charles, s. Stanton & Lucinda, b. July 13, 1786	38
Charles, s. Paris & Nancy, b. Sept. 27, 1813	23
Charles, of Preston, m. Eliza **STANTON**, of N. Stonington, Oct. 22, 1850, by Rev. M. V. Morris	247
Charles Grandison, s. Eli & Betsey, b. Dec. 20, 1801	22
Charles S., m. Cynthia W. **HEWIT**, Sept. 4, 1825, by Paris Hewit, J. P.	93
Charles S., m. Mary **GRAY**, b. of N. Stonington, May 8, 1837, by William Williams, J. P.	161
Cynthia, d. Paris & Nancy, b. June 10, 1804	23
Cynthia, of Groton, m. Coddington **SWAN**, of N. Stonington, Apr. 5, 1818, by Ralph Hurlbutt, J. P.	61
Cynthia W., m. Charles S. **HEWIT**, Sept. 4, 1825, by Paris Hewit, J. P.	93
D. Matilda, of N. Stonington, m. J. S. **SCHOONEVER**, of Groton, May 13, 1851, by Rev. M. N. Morris	251
Denison, s. Stanton & Lucinda, b. Jan. 19, 1811	38
Denison, m. Mary P. **BROWN**, Apr. 3, 1839, by Rev. Augustus B. Collins, of Preston	176
Desire, of N. Stonington, m. Ezra **MINER**, of Stonington, Oct. 9, 1823, by Asher Miner, Elder	85
Desire Matilda, d. Elias & Polly, b. Nov. 24, 1825	134
Dudley R., m. Martha **GALLUP**, b. of N. Stonington, Oct. 10, 1854, by Rev. Stephen Hubbell	265
Eli, m. Betsey **WILLIAMS**, Apr. 24, 1796	22
Eli, d. Feb. 10, 1814	22
Eli, s. Eli & Betsey, b. June 28, 1810	22
Elias, Jr., Lieut., m. Polly W. **MINER**, b. of N. Stonington, Feb. 6, 1817, by Stephen Avery, J. P.	58
Elias, Jr., b. May 5, 1792 (Recorded Feb. 22, 1832)	58
Eliza, d. Stanton & Lucinda, b. Apr. 17, 1803	38
Eliza, m. Henry **PRENTICE**, Nov. 30, 1824, by Rev. John Hyde	90
Eliza Stanton, d. Eli & Betsey, b. Mar. 10, 1806	22

	Page
HEWIT, HEWITT, (cont.)	
Elizabeth A., m. Elias **HILLIARD**, b. of N. Stonington, Oct. 10, 1824, by David Coats, J. P.	89
Elizabeth Ann, d. E[phraim] G. & Eliza, b. Jan. 23, 1825	86
Emily A., of N. Stonington, m. Russell **GRIFFIN**, of Wallinford, Sept. 1, 1839, by Rev. Augustus B. Collins, of Preston	179
Emily Augusta, d. E[phraim] G. & Eliza, b. Apr. 30, 1834	86
Emmarella, of N. Stonington, m. Joseph **ROBINSON**, of Stonington, Dec. 25, 1827, by Asher Miner, Elder	103
Ephraim, s. Stanton & Lucinda, b. Apr. 20, 1801	38
Ephraim G., m. Eliza **PRENTICE**, Dec. 4, 1823, by Rev. John Hyde	86
Ephr[ai]m N., s. Ephr[ai]m G. & Eliza, b. Aug. 3, 1827; d. July 2, 1828	86
Erastus W., s. Elias & Polly, b. Jan. 14, 1821	134
Eunice, d. Paris & Nancy, b. Aug. 5, 1806	23
Eunice A., m. Austin D. **HEWITT**, b. of N. Stonington, Dec. 9, 1828, by William Williams, J. P.	111
Frances A., d. Elias & Polly, b. Aug. 31, 1828	134
Frances E., of N. Stonington, m. George S. **BROWNING**, of Griswold, Feb. 24, 1836, by Rev. Joseph Ayer, Jr.	158
Frances M., of N. Stonington, m. Charles G. **MAIN**, of Brooklyn, Ct., Tuesday, Sept. 11, 1838, by Rev. Peirpoint Brockett	169
George Williams, s. Eli & Betsey, b. June 26, 1797	22
George Williams, s. Paris & Nancy, b. May 26, 1811	23
Hannah, twin with Nancy, d. Paris & Nancy, b. May 30, 1800	23
Hannah C., m. Marland **STANTON**, Oct. 26, 1820, by Elias Hewit, J. P.	68
Hannah Lord, d. Eli & Betsey, b. Feb. 20, 1804	22
Harriet N., d. Ephr[ai]m G. & Eliza, b. Mar. 26, 1829	86
Harriet P., of N. Stonington, m. S. A. **MAIN**, Sept. 24, 1856, by Rev. A. L. Whitman, of Pawcatuck	272
Henry, s. Paris & Nancy, b. Sept. 7, 1802	23
John S., Jr., m. Emily A. **BALDWIN**, b. of N. Stonington, Nov. 16, 1826, by Elias Hewit, J. P.	97
Joseph D., m. Emily L. **STANTON**, b. of N. Stonington, Mar. 14, 1839, by Rev. Peirpoint Brockett	175
Julia, w. O[liver], d. Apr. 25, 1842	164
Lucinda, d. Stanton & Lucinda, b. Apr. 17, 1797	38
Lucy, m. Charles **FISH**, b. of N. Stonington, Mar. 23, 1843, by Asher Prentice, Jr., J. P.	199
Lydia, m. Dudley R. **WHEELER**, Dec. 1, 1818, by Asher Miner, Elder	75
Mary, d. Stanton & Lucinda, b. May 19, 1808	38
Mary, d. Paris & Nancy, b. Oct. 16, 1808	23
Mary, m. Moses **THOMPSON**, Oct. 26, 1817, by Stephen Avery, J. P.	23
Mary, m. Asher **PRENTICE**, Jr., b. of N. Stonington, Dec. 25, 1828, by Rev. Timothy Tuttle, of Groton	111
Mary A., m. Gilbert **BILLINGS**, b. of N. Stonington, Sept. 3, 1852, by Rev. Nehemiah B. Cook, of Stonington	259
Mary E., d. E[phraim] G. & Eliza, b. Jan. 1, 1831	86

340 BARBOUR COLLECTION

Page

HEWIT, HEWITT, (cont.)
Mary L., of N. Stonington, m. W[illia]m W. MAIN, of Brooklyn, Ct.,
   Tuesday, Sept. 11, 1838, by Rev. Pierpoint Brocket   169
Nancy, twin with Hannah, d. Paris & Nancy, b. May 30, 1800   23
Nancy M., m. Charles G. SISSON, b. of N. Stonington, June 21, 1840,
   by Rev. Philo Judson   183
Nancy Mary, d. Elias & Polly, b. Aug. 2, 1823   134
Oliver, s. Stanton & Lucinda, b. Oct. 15, 1795   38
Oliver, b. Oct. 15, 1795   164
Oliver, m. Julia PENDLETON*, at Preston (Poquetannock), Feb. 28,
   1819, by Jonah Witter, Esq. *(PUNDERSON corrected in
   handwriting on original manuscript)   164
Oliver, m. Sarah A. BROWNING, b. of N. Stonington, Dec. 28, 1842,
   by Rev. Benj[ami]n C. Phelps, of Mystic   164
Oliver Pendleton, s. Oliver & Julia, b. June 4, 1826   164
Paris, m. Nancy WILLIAMS, Feb. 12, 1797   23
Paris, s. Charles & Hannah, b. Apr. 29, 1770   23
Paris, s. Paris & Nancy, b. Feb. 24, 1798   23
Patty, of N. Stonington, m. Darius MINER, of Goshen, Dec. 21, 1812,
   by Rev. Christopher Avery   14
Phebe E., of N. Stonington, m. Lathrop W. HULL, of Stonington,
   Sept. 1, 1841, by M. N. Morris   255
Phebe Esther, d. Elias & Polly, b. Mar. 23, 1831   134
Phebe P., of N. Stonington, m. Isaac S. BREED, of Stonington, Nov.
   25, 1827, by Asher Miner, Elder   101
Polly, w. [Lieut.] Elias, [Jr.], b. May 9, 1798 (Recorded Feb. 22, 1832)   58
Sally A., of N. Stonington, m. Hezekiah HESKALL, of Preston,
   Apr. 24, 1825, by Levi Meech, Elder   92
Stanton, m. Lucinda GRANT, May 15, 1784   38
Stanton, s. Stanton & Lucinda, b. July 11, 1788   38
Wealthy A., of N. Stonington, m. William RANDALL, Jr., of
   Stonington, Dec. 23, 1813, by Stephen Avery, J. P.   56
William, s. Stanton & Lucinda, b. Jan. 23, 1792   38
-----, s. E[phraim] G. & Eliza, b. Mar. 2, 1838   86
HILL, [see also HILLS], Gurdon, of Groton, m. Lucy YEARINGTON, of
   N. Stonington, Nov. 1821, by John Spicer, J. P.   73
Ruth C., m. Alfred HURLBURT, b. of N. Stonington, Dec. 10, 1837,
   by Rev. Alfred Gates   163
Willard N., m. Mary Jane EDGCOME, Oct. 12, 1856, by Henry W.
   Webber   272
HILLIARD, Albert W., m. Emily M. RANDALL, b. of N. Stonington, Nov.
   25, 1851, by Rev. O. T. Walker   257
Azariah, m. Lucretia BROWN, b. of N. Stonington, Mar. 5, 1834, by
   Rev. Asher Miner   150
Elias, m. Eliza A. HEWIT, b. of N. Stonington, Oct. 10, 1824, by
   David Coats, J. P.   89
Frances A., m. Benjamin THOMPSON, b. of N. Stonington, Oct. 30,
   1852, by Rev. O. T. Walker   261

HILLIARD, (cont.)

	Page
Lucy M., of N. Stonington, m. Charles H. **CRANDALL**, of Stonington, Oct. 13, 1852, by Rev. O. T. Walker	260
Sophia, of Preston, m. Ephraim **MEECH**, of N. Stonington, Oct. 14, 1813, by Rev. John Hyde	55
William H., m. Maryett **BURDICK**, b. of N. Stonington, Dec. 30, 1851, by Rev. O. T. Walker	257
William M., m. Cynthia S. **WHEELER**, b. of N. Stonington, Aug. 7, 1825, by Elias Hewit, J. P.	102
William M., m. Cynthia S. **WHEELER**, b. of N. Stonington, Aug. 7, 1825, by Elias Hewit, J. P.	92
William M., m. Marilla **DEWEY**, b. of N. Stonington, May 18, 1830, by Asher Miner, Elder	92

HILLS, [see also **HILL**], Clarissa, m. Amos **STEWART**, b. of N. Stonington, Nov. 30, 1826, by David Coats, J. P. — 97

HINCKLEY, Justin, of Lebanon, m. Phebe **GRANT**, of N. Stonington, Mar. 22, 1829, by Rev. Joseph Ayer, Jr. — 113

Phalla, of Stonington, m. Joseph **VINCENT**, of Westerly, Jan. 28, 1802, by Simon Brown, Elder — 9

William H., s. Elijah W. & Rebeckah, b. Feb. 27, 1818 — 60

HISCOX, HISSCOX, Mary E., of R. I., m. Miles **PATTERSON**, of Newport, R. I., Dec. 1, 1847, by Rev. Thomas Barber — 234

Sumner, of Preston, m. Lucinda **CLARK**, of N. Stonington, Aug. 19, 1832, by Rev. Asher Miner — 137

William E., of Charleston, R. I., m. Mary Ann **WORDEN**, of Richmond, R. I., Sept. 1, 1845, by Rev. Thomas Barber — 213

HOLLAND, Hannah, of South Kingstown, m. Rufus **WHEELER**, of N. Stonington, Sept. 23, 1821, by Elias Hewit, J. P. — 72

HOLLEY, Joseph, of N. Stonington, m. Ann **THOMPSON**, of Westerly, Jan. 27, 1822, at Milltown, by Tho[ma]s J. DeVerell — 74

HOLMES, Albert, s. James & Esther, b. Jan. 1, 1782, in Stonington — 13

Albert Smith, s. Tho[ma]s & Elizabeth, b. Sept. 7, 1807 — 26

Almira Angeline, d. Tho[ma]s & Nancy, b. May 16, 1818 — 26

Almira Angeline, d. Tho[ma]s & Nancy, d. Aug. 10, 1826, ae 8 y. 2 m. 25 d. — 105

Andrew Billings, s. Tho[ma]s & Elizabeth, b. Mar. 9, 1795 — 26

Asher, of Stonington, m. Phebe **BROWN**, of Preston, Jan. 1, 1823, by Levi Meech, Elder — 78

Betsey, d. Tho[ma]s & Elizabeth, b. Mar. 1, 1800 — 26

Charles, Jr., of N. Stonington, m. Thankfull **RICHARDSON**, of Stonington, Dec. 11, 1828, by Asher Miner, Elder — 110

Charles, s. Charles, Jr., & Thankfull, b. Sept. 15, 1829 — 110

Charles, m. Watey **MARTIN**, b. of N. Stonington, Mar. 24, 1834, by Jonathan Miner, Elder — 150

Charles Burrows, s. Tho[ma]s & Nancy, b. Apr. 27, 1823 — 105

Daniel, s. Tho[ma]s & Elizabeth, b. June 30, 1797 — 26

David, s. Thomas & Elizabeth, b. Dec. 2, 1792 — 26

David, m. Anna **MINER**, July 24, 1814, by Asher Miner, Elder — 30

342   BARBOUR COLLECTION

Page

HOLMES, (cont.)
David, m. Hannah **HAKES**, b. of N. Stonington, Apr. 30, 1826, by Asher Miner, Elder	95
Elias Atwood, s. John & Nancy, b. Aug. 25, [1834?]	127
Elizabeth, w. Tho[ma]s, d. Mar. 4, 1810, aged 38 y. 10 m. 21 d.	26
Ephraim, s. James & Esther, b. Apr. 18, 1778, in Westerly	13
Esther, twin with Eunice, d. of James & Esther, b. Mar. 5, 1784	13
Esther, d. James & Esther, b. Sept. 12, 1790	13
Eunice, twin with Esther, d. of James & Esther, b. Mar. 5, 1784	13
Eunice, m. Ezra **HUNTLEY**, Dec. 29, 1796, in Stonington	17
Frank, s. John & Nancy, b. Dec. 22, 1807	27
Franklin Haris, twin with Frederick Noyes, s. Tho[ma]s & Nancy, b. May 12, 1816	26
Frederick Noyes, twin with Franklin Haris, s. Tho[ma]s & Nancy, b. May 12, 1816	26
George, s. Charles [Jr.] & Thankfull, b. May 25, 1831	110
Gershom, m. Lucinda **BURDICK**, Mar. 12, 1815	49
Hannah, m. Stephen **WILLCOX**, b. of N. Stonington, Oct. 22, 1809, by Stephen Avery, J. P.	59
Hannah H., m. Ephraim **BROWN**, Sept. 5, 1807, by Asher Miner, Elder	21
Hannah Wheeler, d. W[illia]m & Hannah, b. Feb. 24, 1804	5
Hazard, s. James & Esther, b. Jan. 1, 1788	13
Henry Palmer, s. Jared & Hannah, b. Aug. 6, 1817	25
Henry Tyler, s. Tho[ma]s & Nancy, b. Aug. 8, 1812	26
James, s. James & Esther, b. Mar. 24, 1792	13
Jared, of N. Stonington, m. Hannah **CHADSEY**, of Groton, Mar. 11, 1811, by Stephen Avery, J. P.	25
Jared Ransford, s. Jared & Hannah, b. Mar. 9, 1812	25
John, Jr., of Preston, m. Nancy A. **WILLIAMS**, of N. Stonington, Mar. 10, 1831, by Benj[amin] Pomeroy, J. P.	127
John, Jr., m. Eunice **CHAPMAN**, b. of N. Stonington, Mar. 15, 1835, by Stephen Main, J. P.	153
John Clinton, s. Tho[ma]s & Nancy, b. Mar. 17, 1821, at Griswold	105
Lucinda W., of N. Stonington, m. Robert **WORDEN**, of Albany, N. Y., July 19, 1841, by Rev. Tho[ma]s Dowling	188
Lucy Ann, of N. Stonington, m. David W. **NICHOLS**, of Plainfield, Dec. 24, 1843, by Rev. Tubal Wakefield	231
Lucy Coats, d. John & Ruth, b. Dec. 4, 1822	27
Lura, d. Jared & Martha, b. Apr. 29, 1800	68
Maria S., m. Ransom S. **PERRY**, Nov. 26, 1857, by Rev. John Sheffield	274
Martha, d. John & Nancy, b. July 5, 1804; d. Oct. 3, 1806	27
Martha Ann, d. Gershom & Lucinda, b. Feb. 10, 1816	49
Martha Esther, d. Russell & Patty, b. Nov. 7, 1819	65
Mary, m. Thomas **PARTELOW**, b. of N. Stonington, Oct. 6, 1831. by Thomas P. Wattles. J. P.	131
Mary Esther, d. Tho[ma]s & Nancy, b. June 21. 1825	105

NORTH STONINGTON VITAL RECORDS 343

	Page
HOLMES, (cont.)	
May, of Kingston, R. I., m. Sands **PERKINS**, of Danbury, Mar. 11, 1828, by Rev. Joseph Ayer, Jr.	104
Nancy, d. James & Esther, b. Aug. 20, 1780, in Westerly	13
Nancy, w. John, d. Aug. 8, 1819	27
Nancy Angeline, d. John & Nancy, b. Feb. 1, 1837	127
Nancy Eliza, d. John & Ruth, b. Mar. 1, 1821	27
Nathan W., s. John & Nancy, b. Mar. 28, 1819; d. Oct. 9, 1819	27
Nelson Baldwin, s. Tho[ma]s & Elizabeth, b. Feb. 14, 1805	26
Noyes, s. James & Esther, b. Apr. 18, 1793	13
Patty, m. Russel[l] **HOLMES**, b. of N. Stonington, Jan. 26, 1819, by Stephen Avery, J. P.	65
Phebe E., m. Oliver **CRANDALL**, b. of N. Stonington, Jan. 12, 1840, by Levi Meech, Elder	182
Prudence, d. W[illia]m & Hannah, b. Dec. 16, 1805	5
Russel[l], m. Patty **HOLMES**, b. of N. Stonington, Jan. 26, 1819, by Stephen Avery, J. P.	65
Sabra, d. Tho[ma]s & Elizabeth, b. Nov. 4, 1802	26
Silence Wheeler, d. W[illia]m & Hannah, b. Oct. 23, 1813	5
Thomas, 2nd, m. Elizabeth **BALDWIN**, Nov. 19, 1789	26
Thomas, s. Thomas & Elizabeth, b. Jan. 17, 1791	26
Thomas, of N. Stonington, m. Nancy **COATS**, of Voluntown, Nov. 11, 1810, by Peleg Randall, Elder	26
Tho[ma]s, m. Polly **BALDWIN**, Jan. 1, 1815, by Asher Miner, Elder	29
Thomas, m. Lucy Ann **PARTELO[W]**, Mar. 30, 1836, by Matthew Brown, J. P.	157
William Burrows, s. W[illia]m & Hannah, b. July 27, 1808	5
HOOD, Philena, m. John **MAIN**, Jr., b. of N. Stonington, Mar. 20, 1836, by Thomas Hewitt, J. P.	158
HOWELL, Elisabeth A., of N. Stonington, m. Elisha **RUDE**, of Preston, Dec. 23, 1845, by Rev. Augustus B. Collins, of Preston	219
HOXSIE, Benjamin R., m. Betsey Ann **ELLIS**, b. of W. Greenwich, R. I., Apr. 28, 1835, by Rev. Asher Miner	154
HULL, Amos, m. Esther **WHEELER**, Sept. 12, 1799	52
Amos, m. Serviah **WHEELER**, Jan. 31, 1810	52
Charlotte, m. Ezra **CHAPMAN**, b. of N. Stonington, Nov. 13, 1814, by Jonathan Miner, Elder	53
Charlotte, of N. Stonington, m. Edward W. **FRANKLIN**, of Norwich, June 29, 1823, by Elias Hewit, J. P.	82
Christopher, Jr., of S. Kingston, R. I., m. Bridget **SWAN**, of N. Stonington, Jan. 4, 1829, by Asher Miner, Elder	112
Elisha W., m. Hannah **GAYANT**, b. of Stonington, July 11, 1844, by Rev. Levi Walker	237
Elisha W., m. Hannah **GAYART**, b. of N. Stonington, July 14, 1844, by Rev. Levi Walker	209
Eliza Smith, d. John W. & Elizabeth, b. May 22, 1812	12
Esther, d. Amos & Esther, b. May 22, 1802; d. Apr. 17, 1804	52
Esther, d. Amos & Esther, b. Sept. 13, 1807	52

344 BARBOUR COLLECTION

	Page
HULL, (cont.)	
Esther, w. Amos, d. July 13, 1808	52
Esther W., m. Russell **WHEELER**, Oct. [ ], 1827, by Rev. Joseph Ayer, Jr.	100
Eunice Billings, d. John W. & Elizabeth, b. July 17, 1814	12
John Pomeroy, s. John W. & Elizabeth, b. May 10, 1816	12
John W., s. Latham & Desire, b. Jan. 5, 1789	12
John W., of N. Stonington, m. Elizabeth **SMITH**, of Waterford, May 16, 1811, by Samuel West, Elder	12
Joshua, m. Rachel **THOMPSON**, b. of N. Stonington, Jan. 1, 1815, by Jonathan Miner, Elder	39
Latham, d. Dec. 18, 1807	4
Latham, m. Elizabeth B. **BROWNING**, of N. Stonington, Aug. 15, 1811, by Rev. Christopher Avery	24
Latham, s. Latham & Elizabeth B., b. Oct. 28, 1812	24
Lathrop W., s. Amos & Esther, b. Mar. 11, 1804	52
Lathrop W., of Stonington, m. Phebe E. **HEWITT**, of N. Stonington, Sept. 1, 1851, by M. N. Morris	255
Nathan, s. Nathan & Sally, b. Feb. 22, 1801	4
Patty, d. Amos & Serviah, b. Mar. 23, 1811	52
Phebe, m. Phineas M. **DAVIS**, b. of N. Stonington, Nov. 6, 1842, by Rev. Philo Judson	196
Sally, of N. Stonington, m. Samuel G. **HULL**, of West Greenwich, Oct. 31, 1830, by Rev. Joseph Ayer, Jr.	124
Samuel G., of W. Greenwich, m. Sally **HULL**, of N. Stonington, Oct. 31, 1830, by Rev. Joseph Ayer, Jr.	124
William B., m. Susan M. **WATTLES**, b. of N. Stonington, Aug. 6, 1851, by M. N. Morris	254
William Browning, s. Latham & Elizabeth B., b. Nov. 7, 1815	24
HUNT, W[illia]m, of Bolton, m. Clarinda M. **SPRAGUE**, of Coventry, May 6, 1839, by Rev. Fernando Bester of 2nd Bapt. Ch. N. Stonington	177
HUNTLEY, Ezra, m. Eunice **HOLMES**, Dec. 29, 1796, in Stonington	17
Ezra, s. Ezra & Eunice, b. July 25, 1798	17
Harriet, d. Ezra & Eunice, b. Dec. 12, 1811	17
Henry Holmes, s. Ezra & Eunice, b. July 6, 1808	17
Julia Ann, d. Ezra & Eunice, b. Jan. 10, 1815	17
Lucy Hagley, d. Ezra & Eunice, b. Mar. 23, 1810	17
Oliver Denison, s. Ezra & Eunice, b. July 3, 1802	17
Polly Ann, d. Ezra & Eunice, b. May 14, 1804	17
HURLBURT, Alfred, m. Ruth C. **HILL**, b. of N. Stonington, Dec. 10, 1837, by Rev. Alfred Gates	163
HYDE, Hannah, m. Russ **AUSTIN**, July 4, 1813, by Peleg Randall, Elder	18
INGRAHAM, Maria B., m. Russell H. **CHAPMAN**, b. of N. Stonington, Aug. 6, 1844, by Rev. James R. Stone	209
IRISH, Benjamin, of New London, m. Emily A. **WILLIAMS**, of N. Stonington, Apr. 16, 1851, by Rev. Myron N. Morris	251
Daniel Babcock, s. George & Betsey, b. Feb. 9, 1818	139
Eliza, d. George & Betsey, b. Nov. 24, 1808	139

	Page
IRISH, (cont.)	
Eliza, m. Benjamin **LANGWORTHY**, b. of N. Stonington, Aug. 24, 1835, by Rev. Amos R. Wells	156
Emeline Maria, d. George & Betsey, b. May 23, 1815	139
George, Jr., s. George & Betsey, b. Feb. 7, 1810	139
James Reed, s. George & Betsey, b. Dec. 18, 1811	139
Lucy Ann, d. George & Betsey, b. June 7, 1819	139
Mary, d. George & Betsey, b. Sept. 27, 1821	139
Oliver Babcock, s. George & Betsey, b. Aug. 12, 1826	139
JACKSON, David, of Lisbon, m. Lucinda **WHEELER**, of N. Stonington, persons of color, Aug. 7, 1828, by Sam[ue]l Chapman, J. P.	107
Ezra, m. Hannah **PART[E]LO[W]**, Aug. 18, 1822, by W[illia]m Randall, Jr., J. P.	78
Ezra, of N. Stonington, m. Ann **MURPHY**, of Staten Island, July 21, 1856, by Rev. Stephen Hubbell	271
John, of Lisbon, m. Elizabeth T. **WHEELER**, of N. Stonington, Jan. 24, 1824, by Asher Miner, Elder	86
Lucius, of Lisbon, m. Sarah **STEWART**, of N. Stonington, Dec. 2, 1829, by David Coats, J. P.	118
JAMES, Rebecca W., m. Oliver E. **TABOR**, b. of Providence, R. I., Sept. 13, 1831, by Rev. Joseph Ayer, Jr.	130
JOHNSON, Betsey, of N. Stonington, m. Joseph **CHAPMAN**, of Preston, Nov. 27, 1814, by Jonathan Miner, Elder	57
Lyman, of Union, m. Eliza Ann **CHAPMAN**, of N. Stonington, Apr. 22, 1838, by Rev. Benj[ami]n N. Harris	178
W[illia]m G., of Charleston, R. I., m. Roxane **BENTLEY**, of N. Stonington, Nov. 22, 1829, by Rev. Seth Higby	119
W[illia]m M., of Windham, m. Lydia H. **WHEELER**, of N. Stonington, Jan. 1, 1836, by Rev. Joseph Ayer, Jr.	156
KENYON, KINION, KINYON, Beriah, m. Clarissa **PALMER**, b. of N. Stonington, Jan. 29, 1832, by Rev. Joseph Ayer, Jr.	133
Betsey, w. Rowland, d. May 14, 1829, aged 25 years	137
Clarissa, m. James H. **MUMFORD**, b. of S. Kingstown, Sept. 10, 1829, by Rev. Joseph Ayer, Jr.	115
Elizabeth, of N. Stonington, m. Joshua **ELDREDGE**, Jr., of Groton, Feb. 20, 1825, by William Williams, J. P.	92
Emily A., m. Calvin N. **ROBINSON**, b. of N. Stonington, Mar. 1, 1851, at Richmondtown, R. I., by Rev. Steadman Kenyon. Recorded Aug. 15, 1863	257
Franklin P., m. Abby A. **LEWIS**, b. of N. Stonington, Oct. 28, 1850, by Rev. O. T. Walker	248
James H., m. Nancy H. **CONWAY**, b. of Stonington, Nov. 30, 1848, by Rev. D. H. Miller	236
Lucinda, of South Kingston, R. I., m. Seth J. **PADDOCK**, of Middletown, Dec. 4, 1833, by Rev. Asher Miner	148
Mary Ann, d. Rowland & Ede, b. Sept. 2, 1830	137
Maxon, of Richmond, R. I., m. Phebe E. **BROWN**, of N. Stonington, May 11, 1851, by Rev. O. T. Walker	253

	Page
KENYON, KINION, KINYON, (cont.)	
Rowland, m. Betsey **PALMER**, Jan. 28, 1821	137
Ruth M., of Richmond, R. I., m. Joseph D. **SEGAR**, of Lebanon, Mar. 15, 1846, by Rev. Thomas Barber	221
KINGSLEY, Abby A., of N. Kingston, R. I., m. John W. **SUNDERLAND**, of Exeter, R. I., May 2, 1847, by Rev. Thomas Barber	232
KINION, KINYON, see under **KENYON**	
KINNEY, Lot Wheeler, s. Pierpont & Ann, b. Aug. 31, 1826	95
Pierpont, of Griswold, m. Ann **WHEELER**, of N. Stonington, Feb. 16, 1826, by Elias Hewit, J. P.	95
KNAPP, Lorenzo D., m. Julia A. **GOULD**, b. of Stonington, Nov. 24, 1850, by Rev. Milo Tracy	249
KNIGHT, Eunice, of N. Stonington, m. Charles D. **WILLCOX**, of Westerly, R. I., Oct. 4, 1844, by Dewitt C. Pendleton, J. P.	246
Horace T., m. Mary **WILLIAMS**, b. of N. Stonington, May 16, 1844, by Oliver Hewitt, J. P.	207
Permelia, m. David O. **MAIN**, b. of N. Stonington, Oct. 4, 1844, by Dewitt C. Pendleton, J. P.	245
LAMPHERE, LAMPHEIR, LANPHEAR, LAMPHEAR, Avis, of Hopkinton, m. Gershom **ECLESTON**, of Stonington, Apr. 4, 1784, by William Tanner, J. P., of Hopkinton	32
Carrington, m. Laura **WHEELER**, b. of N. Stonington, May 15, 1843, by Levi Walker	207
Daniel, m. Janette **HARRINGTON**, b. of Preston, July 19, 1847, by Rev. John Sheffield	227
Emma, of Hopkinton, m. Christopher D. **LEWIS**, of N. Stonington, Feb. 18, 1830, by Rev. Asher Miner	121
Henry D., m. Almira M. **BROWN**, Sept. 2, 1834, by Stephen Main, J. P.	151
Polly, m. Samuel **BATTLES**, Jr., b. of Hopkinton, R. I., but now residing in N. L. County, Jan. 26, 1823, by Nathan Pendleton, J. P.	79
Sylvester, of Hopkinton, R. I., m. Emeline **SPAULDING**, of North Stonington, Feb. 17, 1831, by Rev. Asher Miner	127
Varnum, m. Lucy **BUTTON**, of Hopkinton, Jan. 1, 1824, by Nathan Pendleton, J. P.	87
William C., m. Mary S. **SPENCER**, b. of N. Stonington, Nov. 28, 1855, by Charles P. White, J. P.	269
LANGWORTHY, Abby Altana, d. Asa & Ruth, b. Dec. 6, 1825	128
Albana B., d. John & Sarah, b. Apr. 8, 1817	10
Ann Ruth, d. Asa & Ruth, b. Apr. 17, 1817	128
Asa, of Stonington, m. Ruth **CRANDALL**, of Warwick, R. I., July 14, 1813, by Rev. David Curtis. Recorded Mar. 25, 1831	128
Asa Albert, s. John & Sarah, b. Mar. 17, 1808	10
Benjamin, m. Eliza **IRISH**, b. of N. Stonington, Aug. 24, 1835, by Rev. Amos R. Wells	156
Benjamin Franklin, s. John & Sarah, b. May 7, 1810	10
Charles Davis, s. John & Sarah, b. Feb. 25, 1804	10

LANGWORTHY, (cont.)

	Page
Content, d. John, of N. Stonington, m. Dea. Daniel **LEWIS**, of Hopkinton, R. I., June 1, 1823, by Matthew Stillman, Elder	82
Edwin Philip, s. Asa & Ruth, b. Oct. 2, 1821	128
Isaac Pendleton, s. John & Sarah, b. Jan. 19, 1806	10
James B., s. John & Sarah, b. June 23, 1819	10
John, m. Sarah **PENDLETON**, b. of Stonington, Nov. 29, 1798, by Joshua Babcock, J. P.	10
John Avery, s. John & Sarah, b. Dec. 27, 1799	10
Nathan H., m. Ann Elizabeth **CASE**, b. of N. Stonington, Feb. 20, 1837, by Rev. Amos R. Wells	159
Nathan Handy, s. John & Sarah, b. Oct. 17, 1812	10
Oliver Babcock, s. Asa & Ruth, b. Sept. 2, 1823	128
Sarah A., m. Albert G. **PALMER**, b. of N. Stonington, Mar. 27, 1837, by Rev. Amos R. Wells, at house of John Langworthy	160
Sarah Amelia, d. John & Sarah, b. Dec. 1, 1814	10
Thomas Henry, s. Asa & Ruth, b. Aug. 15, 1829	128
Thomas Jefferson, twin with William Pendleton, s. John & Sarah, b. Mar. 20, 1802	10
Thomas Jefferson, d. July 21, 1828	10
William Asa, s. Asa & Ruth, b. June 17, 1819	128
William Pendleton, twin with Thomas Jefferson, s. John & Sarah, b. Mar. 20, 1802	10

LAREY, Eunice, m. Lyman M. **GRAY**, b. of N. Stonington, Jan. 6, 1822, by Asher Miner, Elder — 73

LARKIN, Eliza E., of Richmond, R. I., m. Ralph **THOMPSON**, of N. Stonington, Oct. 11, 1863, by Rev Stanton Austin, at Hopkinton — 275
Patrick, of N. Stonington, m. Sarah **RILEY**, of Stonington, June 15, 1848, by Rev. John Sheffield — 235

LAROACH, Peter, of Stonington, m. Lucy **SISSON**, of N. Stonington, May [ ], 1838, by Oliver Hewitt, J. P. — 165

LATHAM, Prudence, m. John H. **REYNOLDS**, Jr., b. of N. Stonington, Feb. 9, 1833, by Rev. Asher Miner — 144

LAW, Betsey Ann, d. John & Thankful, b. June 10, 1810 — 25
Cynthia, d. John & Thankful, b. Jan. 19, 1817 — 25
John, Jr., m. Thankful **ECLESTON**, b. of N. Stonington, Dec. 29, 1808, by Joshua Babcock, J. P. — 25
Mary Laura, d. John & Thankful, b. May 13, 1812 — 25
Olive Augusta, d. John & Thankful, b. Sept. 2, 1814 — 25
Sophronia, b. Aug. 27, 1812 — 40
Zerviah Mason, d. John & Thankful, b. Mar. 2, 1819 — 25

LEAVENS, Lewis, of Peekskill, N. Y., m. Mary R. **THAYER**, of N. Stonington, Jan. 25, 1856, by Cha[rle]s C. Lewis — 270

LEWIS, Abby A., m. Franklin P. **KENYON**, b. of N. Stonington, Oct. 28, 1850, by Rev. O. T. Walker — 248
Christopher D., of N. Stonington, m. Emma **LANPHEAR**, of Hopkinton, Feb. 18, 1830, by Rev. Asher Miner — 121
Christopher Dewey, s. Bariah & Sarah, b. June 30, 1805 — 74

348   BARBOUR COLLECTION

Page

LEWIS, (cont.)
Cynthia, of Stonington, m. William **PECKHAM**, of N. Stonington,
   Aug. 29, 1811, by Rev. Christopher Avery   56
Daniel, Dea., of Hopkinton, R. I., m. Content, d. John
   LANGWORTHY, of N. Stonington, June 1, 1823, by Matthew
   Stillman, Elder   82
Edwin R., of Hopkinton, R. I., m. Louisa A. **BROWN**, of N.
   Stonington, Dec. 17, 1850, by Rev. O. T. Walker   249
Eleanor, of Hopkinton, R. I., m. John **MAIN**, of N. Stonington, Oct. 29,
   1807, by Stephen Coon, Elder   44
Eliza Diana, d. Clark & Lucy, b. June 20, 1832   140
Emeline, d. Bariah & Sarah, b. Feb. 22, 1822   74
Eunice, of N. Stonington, m. Lucius H. **TRACY**, of Preston, Apr.
   24, 1828, by Rev. Joseph Ayer, Jr.   106
George Henry, s. Bariah & Sarah, b. Apr. 10, 1809   74
Harriet, d. Bariah & Sarah, b. Jan. 17, 1802   74
Harriet, m. W[illia]m H. **CRANDALL**, Sept. 28, 1820, by Asher
   Miner, Elder   67
Huldah, m. Elisha W. **BENNET**, June 18, 1820, by Paris Hewit, J. P.   65
Julia Ann, d. Bariah & Sarah, b. Nov. 23, 1819   74
Lucretia, d. Clark & Lucy, b. Nov. 25, 1830   140
Martha, of Voluntown, m. Alexander **THOMSON**, 2nd, of N.
   Stonington, Mar. 5, 1818, by Alexander Campbell, J. P.   61
Nathan B., of Griswold, m. Lucy A. **PARK**, of N. Stonington, Oct. 6,
   1850, by Rev. O. T. Walker   248
Nathan Saunders, s. Bariah & Sarah, b. June 9, 1812   74
Phebe Mary, d. Bariah & Sarah, b. Feb. 15, 1816   74
Thomas, m. Almira **SLOCUM**, of N. Stonington, Oct. 23, 1831, by
   Jonathan Miner, Elder   135
LINCOLN, Lyman, of Windham, m. Julina **MAIN**, of N. Stonington,
   [1821-2], by Asher Miner, Elder   73
Sarah, of N. Stonington, m. James M. **CONGDON**, of New London,
   Feb. 14, 1842, by Rev. Philo Judson   190
LOOMIS, Stanton, m. Lucy Ann **BROWN**, Jan. 20, 1822, by W[illia]m
   Randall, Jr., J. P.   76
LYSTER, James L., of Griswold, m. Lucy **WHEELER**, of N. Stonington,
   Sept. 5, 1820, by Asher Miner, Elder   66
MAGLOIN, Ellen, of New York, m. Edwin **COLEMAN**, of Coventry, Nov.
   30, 1843, by Rev. Philo Judson   203
MAIN, Abby E., d. Rufus, b. May 15, 1830   30
Adah, d. Nath[anie]l & Abigail, b. Feb. 14, 1787   44
Adah, m. Israel P. **PARKE**, Oct. 28, 1810   54
Adam, s. Simeon & Martha, b. Oct. 29, 1811   19
Adam, m. Lucy M. **MAIN**, Apr. 6, 1843, by Thomas P. Wattles, J. P.   204
Almira, d. Jared & Abigail, b. Mar. 8, 1811   41
Amos, s. Peter & Patience, b. Aug. 16, 1776   13
Amos, 2nd, b. Aug. 16, 1776; m. Abigail **SLOCUM**, Dec. 25, 1797   40
Amos C., m. Susan **WHEELER**, Mar. 29, 1804, by Christopher

NORTH STONINGTON VITAL RECORDS 349

	Page
MAIN, (cont.)	
Avery, Elder	47
Amos S., s. Amos & Abigail, b. Nov. 25, 1798	40
Aner, d. Peter & Patience, b. Aug. 4, 1767	13
Azariah, s. Amos & Abigail, b. Aug. 29, 1802	40
Betsey, d. Nath[anie]l & Abigail, b. Feb. 10, 1785	44
Bridget, d. Amos C. & Susan, b. July 23, 1807	47
Bridget W., m. Leeland D. **MINER**, b. of N. Stonington, Apr. 15, 1829, by Asher Miner, Elder	114
Cary C., s. Amos & Abigail, b. Dec. 6, 1799	40
Chandler, s. David & Esther, b. Jan. 29, 1790	6
Chandler, m. Nancy **BROWN**, b. of N. Stonington, Feb. 22, 1821, by Asher Miner, Elder	69
Chandler D., m. Frances A. **CLAPSON**, b. of N. Stonington, Jan. 25, 1853, by Rev. Philo J. Williams	262
Charles, of Voluntown, m. Almira **ECCLESTON**, of N. Stonington, Dec. 18, 1833, by Thomas H. Hewitt, J. P.	148
Charles B., m. [ ] **STAR**, b. of N. Stonington, Nov. 28, 1847, by Rev. Thomas Barber	234
Charles E., of N. Stonington, m. Sarah H. **CRARY**, of Voluntown, Oct. 6, 1850, by Rev. O. T. Walker	247
Charles G., of Brooklyn, Ct., m. Frances M. **HEWITT**, of N. Stonington, Tuesday, Sept. 11, 1838, by Rev. Peirpoint Brockett	169
Charlotte, d. John & Eleanor, b. Dec. 16, 1810	44
Charlotte, of N. Stonington, m. John **MAIN**, Feb. 19, 1832, by Jonathan Miner, Elder	135
Christopher, s. Jabish & Freelove, b. Nov. 6, 1810	7
Clarinda, d. Jabish & Freelove, b. Mar. 30, 1808	7
Clarinda E., of N. Stonington, m. Peleg H. **GALLUP**, of Voluntown, Dec. 3, 1845, by Rev. Thomas Barber	219
Clarissa, d. Nath[anie]l & Abigail, b. Oct. 3, 1793	44
Clarissa, of N. Stonington, m. Elias **SPRAGUE**, of Coventry, Dec. 20, 1831,by Jonathan Miner, Elder	134
Clark B., of N. Stonington, m. Abby E. **MITCHELL**, of Groton, Apr. 10, 1854, by Rev. P. J. Williams	264
Collings, s. Jabish & Freelove, b. Dec. 16, 1797	7
Cynthia, d. Jabish & Freelove, b. June 23, 1804	7
Cyrus H., m. Julia **EDGECOMB**, Oct. 27, 1847, by Rev. D. H. Miller	236
Daniel, s. Simeon & Martha, b. June 21, 1814	19
Daniel, m. Mary A. **MAIN**, b. of N. Stonington, Apr. 12, 1857, by Rev. S. H. Peckham	274
David, m. Hannah **WORDEN**, b. of Stonington, May 28, 1773	6
David, m. Judah **PALMER**, Apr. 27, 1781	6
David, m. Esther **PALMER**, Jan. 8, 1787	6
David, s. David & Judah, b. July 26, 1781	6
David, s. Peter & Patience, b. Aug. 20, 1784	13
David, 2d, b. Aug. 20, 1785; m. Dorcas **PALMER**, Nov. 21, 1811, by Jed[idia]h Randall, Elder	42

	Page
MAIN, (cont.)	
David, of N. Stonington, m. Phelana **SAWYER**, of Windham, Feb. 7, 1825, by Stephen Avery, J. P.	91
David, m. Mrs. Sally **NEWTON**, b. of N. Stonington, July 16, 1843, by Rev. Charles Randall	210
David C., s. Miall & Eunice, b. Nov. 8, 1810	35
David O., m. Permelia **KNIGHT**, b. of N. Stonington, Oct. 4, 1844, by Dewitt C. Pendleton, J. P.	245
Deborah, d. Peter & Patience, b. May 6, 1782	13
Desire, m. Gilbert **SISSON**, Mar. 22, 1791	47
Dianthia Harriet, d. Jabish & Freelove, b. June 8, 1823	7
Ede, d. Rufus, b. Dec. 18, 1809	30
Edgar Ray, s. Lewis & Hannah, b. Sept. 24, 1808	51
Edwin C., of Wisconsin, m. Ellen **WHEELER**, of N. Stonington, June 13, 1852, by Rev. O. T. Walker	260
Emily M., m. Henry C. **GEER**, b. of N. Stonington, Aug. 14, 1848, by Rev. Thomas Barber	234
Ephraim W., s. Amos C. & Susan, b. Oct. 31, 1812	47
Ephraim W., m. Catharine **THOMPSON**, b. of N. Stonington, Nov. 5, 1845, by Rev. James R. Stone	218
Erastus Franklin, s. Stephen & Lucinda, b. May 28, 1818	45
Eunice, m. Benjamin **FRINK**, b. of Stonington, Oct. 2, 1792, by Joshua Babcock, J. P.	4
Eunice, d. Amos & Abigail, b. Apr. 10, 1807	40
Eunice, m. William **RANDALL**, June 10, 1824, by W[illia]m Randall, Jr., J. P.	88
Eunice Ann, d. Miall & Eunice, b. June 11, 1813	35
Ezra, s. Nath[anie]l & Abigail, b. Oct. 3, 1793	44
Fanny Mary, d. Jabish & Freelove, b. Feb. 23, 1817; d. Mar. 13, 1817	7
Filena, d. Jared & Abigail, b. June 13, 1807 (see Philena)	41
Francis, s. of David & Esther, b. Oct. 29, 1791	6
Franklin B., of Guilderland, N. Y., m. Zerviah **MAIN**, of North Stonington, May 23, 1824, by Nathan Pendleton, J. P.	88
Freelove, d. Jabish & Freelove, b. June 10, 1800	7
Gardner, s. Nath[anie]l & Abigail, b. Nov. 20, 1782	44
George W., s. John & Eleanor, b. Nov. 11, 1814	44
George W., of Ledyard, m. Lucy A. **WHEELER**, of N. Stonington, Mar. 20, 1844, by Rev. Stephen H. Peckham	205
George W., m. Lucy B. **MINER**, b. of N. Stonington, Nov. 29, 1855, by Elder John Green	268
Gershom, s. Jared & Abigail, b. Mar. 11, 1814	41
Gershom A., m. Susan A. **BILLINGS**, Dec. 7, 1840, by Rev. Charles S. Weaver, of Voluntown	185
Hannah, w. David, d. Nov. 27, 1779	6
Hannah, d. Nath[anie]l & Abigail, b. Oct. 31, 1795	44
Hannah, d. Amos & Abigail, b. Oct. 14, 1817	40
Henry, s. Amos & Abigail, b. Sept. 3, 1811	40
Hiram Leonard, s. Jabish & Freelove, b. Sept. 26, 1814; d. July	

	Page
MAIN, (cont.)	
27, 1818	7
Huldah, d. Simeon & Martha, b. Oct. 11, 1806	19
Huldah, m. Zebulon B. MINER, b. of N. Stonington, Apr. 20, 1834, by Rev. Asher Miner	151
Ira, s. Jared & Abigail, b. Mar. 11, 1809	41
Jabish, m. Freelove EDWARDS, Mar. 15, 1795	7
Jabish, s. Jabish & Freelove, b. Apr. 20, 1796	7
Jared, s. Peter & Patience, b. Jan. 22, 1778	13
Jared, m. Abigail ECLESTON, b. of N. Stonington, Sept. 10, 1801, by Joshua Babcock, Esq.	40
Jared, s. Jared & Abigail, b. Mar. 18, 1802	41
Jesse, 2d, m. Hannah PARTELOW, Nov. 27, 1838, by W[illia]m Randall, Jr., J. P.	174
Joanna, d. Simeon & Martha, b. Dec. 29, 1801	19
Job, s. Nath[anie]l & Abigail, b. May 17, 1781	44
John, s. Peter & Patience, b. Apr. 6, 1780	13
John, s. Amos & Abigail, b. June 16, 1805	40
John, of N. Stonington, m. Eleanor LEWIS, of Hopkinton, R. I., Oct. 29, 1807, by Stephen Coon, Elder	44
John, s. John & Eleanor, b. July 23, 1808	44
John, m. Mariah GEER, b. of N. Stonington, Oct. 5, 1825, by Nathan Pendleton, J. P.	93
John, m. Charlotte MAIN, of N. Stonington, Feb. 19, 1832, by Jonathan Miner, Elder	135
John, Jr., m. Philena HOOD, b. of N. Stonington, Mar. 20, 1836, by Thomas H. Hewitt, J. P.	158
John Van Renssalear, s. Jared & Abigail, b. Jan. 12, 1806	41
Jonas C., s. Jabish & Freelove, b. Mar. 7, 1806	7
Joseph, s. Peter & Patience, b. Sept. 21, 1769	13
Judah, w. David, d. Nov. 16, 1783	6
Julina, of N. Stonington, m. Lyman LINCOLN, of Windham, [1821-2], by Asher Miner, Elder	73
Keturah, of Stonington, m. Jesse CHAPMAN, of N. Stonington, May 24, 1835, by Rev. Asher Miner	157
Lester, m. Thankfull ECCLESTON, b. of N. Stonington, Mar. 13, 1856, by Rev. J. G. Park, at Griswold	271
Lewis L., m. Ursula CHAPMAN, b. of N. Stonington, Oct. 20, 1850, by Rev. O. T. Walker	248
Lucinda, d. Stephen & Lucinda, b. Apr. 22, 1811; d. [ ]	45
Lucinda, d. Stephen & Lucinda, b. Apr. 13, 1813	45
Lucy A., m. John H. FRINK, b. of N. Stonington, Oct. 10, 1855, by Rev. John Sheffield	267
Lucy Ann, d. David & Dorcas, b. June 15, 1813	42
Lucy Ann, of N. Stonington, m. Isaac C. EDWARDS, of Hopkinton, R. I., Sept. 27, 1835, by Rev. Asher Miner	192
Lucy B., d. Sanford & Rebecca, b. Aug. 7, 1822	108
Lucy B., of N. Stonington, m. W[illia]m F. SHEFFIELD, of	

352   BARBOUR COLLECTION

	Page
MAIN, (cont.)	
Stonington, Mar. 8, 1854, by Rev. Harris H. Tinker	264
Lucy M. m. Adam MAIN, Apr. 6, 1843, by Thomas P. Wattles, J. P.	204
Lucy Wheeler, d. Stephen & Lucinda, b. May 11, 1823	45
Martha, w. Simeon, b. Dec. 16, 1777	19
Mary, d. Amos & Abigail, b. July 4, 1808	40
Mary, d. John & Eleanor, b. June 16, 1813	44
Mary A., m. Daniel MAIN, b. of N. Stonington, Apr. 12, 1857, by Rev. S. H. Peckham	274
Matilda, d. David & Dorcas, b. Apr. 3, 1812	42
Mial, s. David & Esther, b. May 27, 1788	6
Miall, m. Eunice PALMER, June 15, 1808	35
Nabby, d. Nath[anie]l & Abigail, b. July 11, 1791	44
Nancy, d. Rufus, b. Feb. 9, 1819	30
Nancy, m. Henry CRANDALL, b. of N. Stonington, Feb. 3, 1839, by Rev. Pierpoint Brockett	173
Nancy A., of N. Stonington, m. James A. DAVIS, of Stonington, Apr. 3, 1851, by Rev. O. T. Walker	253
Nancy B., m. Nathan YORK, b. of N. Stonington, Jan. 2, 1834, by Rev. Asher Miner	149
Nancy W., m. Bibby P. PARK, b. of N. Stonington, Jan. 22, 1843, by Rev. William Flint	197
Nathaniel, m. Abigail THURSTON, Aug. 7, 1780	44
Nathaniel M., m. Mary FRINK, b. of N. Stonington, Mar. 21, 1847, by Rev. Levi Walker	240
Noyes M., m. Sarah A. MITCHELL, Dec. 6, 1843, by Thomas P. Wattles, J. P.	205
Patty, d. David & Hannah, b. Feb. 10, 1778	6
Peter, Jr., m. Patience STANTON, b. of Stonington, Mar. 3, 1765, by John Burdict, J. P., at Hopkinton, R. I.	13
Peter, s. Peter & Patience, b. Dec. 4, 1765	1
Peter Nelson, s. Jared & Abigail, b. Mar. 23, 1816	41
Phebe, d. Simeon & Martha, b. July 27, 1803	19
Phebe, d. Rufus, b. Nov. 17, 1813	30
Phebe, of N. Stonington, m. Dudley MICHEL, of Groton, Sept. 15, 1822, by Stephen Avery, J. P.	76
Philena, m. William W. BAILEY, b. of N. Stonington, Jan. 5, 1848, by Rev. Thomas Barber. (see Filena)	233
Polly, d. Peter & Patience, b. May 9, 1774	13
Polly, m. John PARTLO, b. of N. Stonington, June 28, 1821, by William Randall, Jr., J. P.	70
Polly, m. Silas MILLER, May 12, 1822, by W[illia]m Randall, Jr., J. P.	78
Prentice, s. Simeon & Martha, b. Feb. 22, 1797	19
Prudence, d. Peter & Patience, b. May 3, 1789	13
Prudence, d. Amos & Abigail, b. Jan. 28, 1804	40
Prudence M., d. Rufus, b. Sept. 26, 1827	30
Ralph Hewllet, s. Amos C. & Susan, b. Apr. 13, 1816	47

MAIN, (cont.)

	Page
Rebecca B., d. Sanford & Rebecca, b. Jan. 21, 1819	108
Rebecca B., m. Smith **BROWN**, b. of N. Stonington, Feb. 16, 1834, by Rev. Asher Miner	149
Reuben P., s. Rufus, b. Sept. 9, 1824	30
Rhoda, d. David & Esther, b. May 16, 1794	6
Richard H., s. Simeon & Martha, b. Feb. 27, 1809	19
Richard H., m. Abby P. **HEWITT**, b. of N. Stonington, Feb. 11, 1833, by Rev. Joseph Ayer, Jr.	142
Robert, s. David & Judah, b. Jan. 19, 1783	6
Robert P., s. David & Dorcas, b. Aug. 16, 1814	42
Ruby, d. Nath[anie]l & Abigail, b. Dec. 13, 1800	44
Rufus, m. Feb. 3, 1803	30
Rufus W., s. Rufus, b. Nov. 9, 1803	30
Russell, s. Nath[anie]l & Abigail, b. May 31, 1789	44
Ruth, m. Enoch B. **ECCLESTON**, b. of N. Stonington, Oct. [ ], 1849, by Dewitt C. Pendleton, J. P.	246
S. A., m. Harriet P. **HEWITT**, of N. Stonington, Sept. 24, 1856, by Rev. A. L. Whitman, of Pawcatuck	272
Sally, d. Rufus, b. Sept. 15, 1815	30
Samuel, s. Amos & Abigail, b. Apr. 8, 1812	40
Sands B., m. Eliza C. **PERRY**, b. of N. Stonington, Oct. 1, 1847, by Rev. Thomas Barber	229
Sanford A., s. Sanford & Rebecca, b. May 9, 1828	108
Sextus, s. David & Esther, b. Aug. 27, 1796	6
Sidney Cresson, s. Jabish & Freelove, b. May 6, 1818	7
Silence, d. Amos & Abigail, b. Aug. 29, 1814	40
Simeon, b. Nov. 27, 1768	19
Simeon, m. Martha	19
Stephen, s. Rufus, b. June 8, 1805	30
Stephen, m. Lucinda **RAY**, Jan. 14, 1810, by Peleg Randall, Elder	45
Stephen, of N. Y., m. Susan K, **CHAPMAN**, of N. Stonington, Apr. 21, 1833, by Jonathan Miner, Elder	145
Stephen, of New York City, m. Lydia **YORK**, of N. Stonington, Mar. 6, 1842, by Rev. Tho[ma]s Dowling	191
Stephen, of New York, m. Ann E. **STEWART**, of N. Stonington, June 8, 1847, by Rev. James M. Phillips	227
Stephen Nelson, s. Stephen & Lucinda, b. June 5, 1815	45
Susan, d. Amos C. & Susan, b. May 24, 1806	47
Susannah, m. David **COATS**, Jr., b. of N. Stonington, Oct. 14, 1824, by Asher Miner, Elder	89
Thomas Jefferson, s. Rufus, b. Mar. 14, 1807	30
Timothy H., s. Rufus, b. Apr. 26, 1821	30
William, s. Amos & Abigail, b. May 9, 1801	40
William L., of Ledyard, m. Sally A. **FRINK**, of N. Stonington, Feb. 26, 1837, by Matthew Brown, J. P.	160
William S., s. Rufus, b. Feb. 17, 1811	30
W[illia]m W., of Brooklyn, Ct., m. Mary L. **HEWITT**, of N.	

354   BARBOUR COLLECTION

Page

MAIN, (cont.)
   Stonington, Tueday, Sept. 11, 1838, by Rev. Peirpoint Brocket 169
   Zacheus, s. Jabish & Freelove, b. June 22, 1812 7
   Zerviah, d. Jabish & Freelove, b. Dec. 20, 1801 7
   Zerviah, of N. Stonington, m. Franklin B. MAIN, of Guilderland,
     N. Y., May 23, 1824, by Nathan Pendleton, J. P. 88
MANDELL, London, m. Jane MASON, persons of color, Sept. 1, 1822, by
   Paris Hewit, J. P. 77
MANNING, Jane E., of Norwich, m. George E. BROWN, Apr. 28, 1844, by
   Rev. Philo Judson 206
MARTIN, Waty, m. Benjamin BLANCHARD, b. of N. Stonington, Sept.
   20, 1823, by Levi Walker 84
   Watey, m. Charles HOLMES, b. of N. Stonington, Mar. 24, 1834, by
   Jonathan Miner, Elder 150
MASON, Andrew N., m. Jenet L. BURDICK, b. of N. Stonington, Feb. 6,
   1831, by Rev. Joseph Ayer, Jr. 126
   Jane, m. London MANDELL, persons of color, Sept. 1, 1822, by Paris
   Hewit, J. P. 77
MAYNARD, Jeremiah, of Norwich, m. Lucy E. PITCHER, of N.
   Stonington, Oct. 14, 1851, by Rev. O. T. Walker 255
McCRACKEN, Janettie, of Colchester, m. Daniel N. CASWELL, of N.
   Stonington, Nov. 13, 1853, by W[illia]m B. Hull, J. P. 263
McDONALD, Abigail, of Westerly, R. I., m. Jeffrey CHAMPLAIN, of
   Griswold, Jan. 11, 1846, by Rev. Levi Walker 220
McGLADE, Margaret, m. Joseph THOMAS, b. of N. Stonington, Sept. 1,
   1852, at the residence of Mrs. William R. Wheeler, by Rev.
   O. T. Walker 259
MEECH, Amey, m. John PRENTICE, Jan. 31, 1813, by Rev. John Hyde 20
   Daniel Bishop, s. Capt. Daniel, b. Oct. 31, 1803 19
   Ephraim, of N. Stonington, m. Sophia HILLIARD, of Preston, Oct. 14,
   1813, by Rev. John Hyde 55
   Harriet Newell, d. Eph[rai]m & Sophia, b. Feb. 1, 1816, in Preston 55
   Hezekiah, s. Eph[rai]m & Sophia, b. July 11, 1814 55
   Maria, d. Capt. Daniel, b. Nov. 5, 1799 19
   Zerviah, d. Capt. Daniel, b. July 1, 1797 19
MEEDS, James, of Hartford, m. Phenety BOWER, of N. Stonington, Oct.
   21, 1823, by Paris Hewit, J. P. 85
MERRET, MERITT, Billings, of Stonington, m. Mary BURDICK, of N.
   Stonington, Aug. 1, 1830, by Rev. Gershom Holmes 123
   Mary E., m. Perry G. PALMER, Feb. 15, 1857, by Rev. Milo Tracy 273
MILLER, Fanny M., m. W[illia]m N. ECCLESTON, Jr., b. of N.
   Stonington, Jan. 26, 1840, by Rev. Levi Walker 195
   Oliver S., of Clinton, m. Sarah Almira ECCLESTON, of N.
   Stonington, Sept. 23, 1849, by Rev. John Sheffield 242
   Silas, m. Polly MAIN, May 12, 1822, by W[illia]m Randall, Jr., J. P. 78
MINER, MINOR, Alpheas, m. Desire WHEELER, b. of Stonington, Feb.
   5, 1797 18
   Alura Ann, d. Robert & Alura, b. Dec. 25, 1819 108

	Page
MINER, MINOR, (cont.)	
Anna, m. David **HOLMES**, July 24, 1814, by Asher Miner, Elder	30
Asa S., s. Asher & Lucy, b. Mar. 8, 1811	126
Asa S., m. Abba **PALMER**, b. of N. Stonington, Sept. 26, 1832, by Rev. Asher Miner	140
Asa S., of N. Stonington, m. Polly P. **BROWN**, of Westerly, Jan. 29, 1852, by Rev. O. T. Walker	258
Asher, s. Asher & Lucy, b. Sept. 10, 1799	126
Clarissa, of N. Stonington, m. Elias H. **MINER**, of Stonington, Mar. 22, 1853, by Rev. Philo J. Williams	262
Cyrus Lazell, s. Denison & Phebe, b. Mar. 26, 1826	64
Darius, of Goshen, m. Patty **HEWIT**, of N. Stonington, Dec. 21, 1812, by Rev. Christopher Avery	14
Denison W., m. Clarissa M. **PARK**, b. of N. Stonington, [1832], by Jonathan Miner, Elder. Recorded Sept. 5, 1832	138
Elias A., of Stoughton, m. Eunice **CHAMPLAIN**, of R. I., Nov. 29, 1847, by Oliver Hewitt, J. P.	230
Elias H., of Stonington, m. Clarissa **MINER**, of N. Stonington, Mar. 22, 1853, by Rev. Philo J. Williams	262
Elisha Parke, s. Denison & Phebe, b. Mar. 25, 1821	64
Eliza H., m. Elisha **PALMER**, b. of N. Stonington, Mar. 12, 1833, by Jonathan Miner, Elder	145
Eunice, d. John & Nancy, b. Mar. 3, 1813	52
Eunice, m. Elias **CHAPMAN**, b. of N. Stonington, Jan. 3, 1833, by Jonathan Miner, Elder	143
Eunice, B., d. Asher & Lucy, b. Oct. 5, 1815	126
Eunice B., of N. Stonington, m. Benjamin **NOYES**, of S. Kingstown, R. I., Nov. 14, 1836, by Rev. John G. Wightman	159
Ezra, of Stonington, m. Desire **HEWIT**, of N. Stonington, Oct. 9, 1823, by Asher Miner, Elder	85
Fanny E., m. Thomas E. **BURDICK**, Mar. 6, [1857], by Rev. Charles C. Lewis	273
George Lewellyn, s. Robert & Alura, b. Feb. 2, 1827	108
Gilbert Smith, s. Robert & Alura, b. Nov. 8, 1821	108
Hannah H., d. Asher & Lucy, b. July 3, 1813	126
Harriet N., m. Sanford **WHEELER**, b. of N. Stonington, Mar. 31, 1844, by Rev. Philo Judson	206
Harriet Newell, d. Denison & Phebe, b. June 17, 1815	64
James Henry, s. Denison & Phebe, b. Dec. 9, 1818	64
Jane M., of N. Stonington, m. Moses **DARROW**, of New London, Aug. 15, 1853, by Rev. O. T. Walker	263
Jedediah R., s. Asher & Lucy, b. Sept. 23, 1806	126
John, m. Nancy **BROWN**, Apr. 5, 1812, by Jed[idia]h Randall, Elder	52
John B., m. Sarah **CRANDALL**, b. of N. Stonington, Apr. 29, 1841, by Philo Judson	187
John Billings, s. Denison & Phebe, b. July 19, 1813	64
John J., s. Asher & Lucy, b. Nov. 15, 1808	126
Leeland D., m. Bridget W. **MAIN**, b. of N. Stonington, Apr. 15,	

	Page
MINER, MINOR, (cont.)	
1829, by Asher Miner, Elder	114
Lucy A., m. William B. **DENISON**, b. of N. Stonington, Jan. 18, 1830, by Rev. Joseph Ayer, Jr.	121
Lucy Ann, d. Denison & Phebe, b. May 25, 1809	64
Lucy B., m. George W. **MAIN**, b. of N. Stonington, Nov. 29, 1855, by Elder John Green	268
Luther, m. Nancy **MOORE**, b. of N. Stonington, Feb. 7, 1813, by Elias Hewit, J. P.	15
Lydia, m. Elias **CHAPMAN**, June 21, 1835, by Rev. Asher Miner	155
Martha, d. Asher & Lucy, b. Feb. 12, 1795	126
Mary, of N. Stonington, m. Alexander G. **FRINK**, of Stonington, by Rev. Joseph Ayer, Jr., Dec. 10, 1828	110
Mary Ann, m. Edgar R. **PALMER**, b. of N. Stonington, May 27, 1851, by Van R. Gray, J. P.	252
Mary D., m. Henry S. **COOK**, b. of Norwich, Nov. 2, 1844, by Levi Meech, Elder	211
Mary Elizabeth, d. Robert & Alura, b. Aug. 8, 1824	108
Nathan, of Norwich, m. Prudence **FELLOWS**, of N. Stonington, Mar. 14, 1821, by Stephen Avery, J. P.	70
Oliver, of N. Stonington, m. Resilla **SAFFORD**, of Norwich, Sept. 1, 1852, by Rev. O. T. Walker	259
Phebe Esther, d. Denison & Phebe, b. Nov. 5, 1805	64
Polly, d. Alpheas & Desire, b. May 9, 1798	18
Polly W., m. Lieut. Elias **HEWIT**, Jr., b. of N. Stonington, Feb. 6, 1817, by Stephen Avery, J. P.	58
Robert Tyler, s. Robert & Alura, b. Jan. 26, 1818	108
Samuel, m. Phebe A. **COON**, b. of N. Stonington, July 3, 1842, by Rev. Philo Judson	194
Stanton B., s. John & Nancy, b. Dec. 15, 1815	52
William Denison, s. Denison & Phebe, b. May 15, 1807	64
Zebulon B., m. Huldah **MAIN**, b. of N. Stonington, Apr. 20, 1834, by Rev. Asher Miner	151
MITCHELL, MICHEL, Abby E., of Groton, m. Clark B. **MAIN**, of N. Stonington, Apr. 10, 1854, by Rev. P. J. Williams	264
Dudley, of Groton, m. Phebe **MAIN**, of N. Stonington, Sept. 15, 1822, by Stephen Avery, J. P.	76
Sarah A., m. Noyes M. **MAIN**, Dec. 6, 1843, by Thomas P. Wattles, J. P.	205
MOORE, MORE, Anna, d. David & Lydia, b. June 4, 1789	34
Cyrus, s. David & Lydia, b. July 26, 1785; d. July 25, 1787	34
David, m. Lydia **WHEELER**, Mar. 16, 1782	34
David, m. Sally **PRENTICE**, Mar. 29, 1808	34
David Wells, s. George W. & Bridget, b. Dec. 2, 1808	29
Eliza R., d. David & Sally, b. Jan. 18, 1814; d. Mar. 11, 1814	34
George W., m. Bridget **WELLS**, Feb. 22, 1808	29
George Washington, s. David & Lydia, b. Dec. 1, 1787	34
Lydia, w. David, d. June 27, 1806	34

	Page
MOORE, MORE, (cont.)	
Mariah, d. George W. & Bridget, b. May 22, 1816	29
Mary, d. David & Lydia, b. June 4, 1792	34
Mary Ann, d. George W. & Bridget, b. Mar. 26, 1810	29
Matilda, d. George W. & Bridget, b. Apr. 4, 1812	29
Nancy, m. Luther MINER, b. of N. Stonington, Feb. 7, 1813, by Elias Hewit, J. P.	15
Phebe Emeline, d. David & Sally, b. Nov. 17, 1809	34
Sally, d. David & Lydia, b. Jan. 25, 1784	34
William, s. George W. & Bridget, b. July 18, 1814	29
MORGAN, Betsey, of Groton, m. Stephen AVERY, 2nd, of Stonington, Aug. 18, 1804, by Jer[emia]h Halsey, J. P.	1
Eliza, m. Randall FRINK, b. of N. Stonington, Nov. 28, 1824, by David Coats, J. P.	90
Lucy, of N. Stonington, m. Elderkin A. CHESTER, of East Haddam, Oct. 17, 1822, by Levi Meech, Elder	77
Nabby, of Voluntown, m. Uzziel PALMER, of Stonington, Mar. 25, 1790 by Allen Campbell, J. P.	55
MORSE, Esther, of N. Stonington, m. John TYLER, of Griswold, May 29, 1822, by Rev. Horatio Waldo	75
MOWRY, Henry S., m. Mary Catharine BULLOCK, of N. Kingston, R. I., July 2, 1844, by Rev. James R. Stone	208
MUMFORD, Eliza H., m. William H. CASE, b. of Kingston, Aug. 10, 1829, by Rev. Joseph Ayer, Jr.	115
James H., m. Clarissa KENYON, b. of S. Kingstown, Sept. 10, 1829, by Rev. Joseph Ayer, Jr.	115
MURPHY, Ann, of Staten Island, m. Ezra JACKSON, of N. Stonington, July 21, 1856, by Rev. Stephen Hubbell	271
Louis, m. Isaiah CONGDON, Oct. 22, 1840, by Cyrus W. Brown, Jr. J. P.	184
MURRAY, Jacob B., of New York City, m. Martha H. WHEELER, of N. Stonington, June 20, 1855, by Henry W. Beecher, of Brooklyn, N. Y.	266
MYERS, Maggie, m. Oliver H. WRIGHT, May 29, 1864, in Norfolk	276
NED, Marinda, of N. Stonington, m. Charles L. DOUGLASS, of N. Stonington, formerly of Voluntown, Oct. 1, 1843, by Latham Hull, J. P.	202
NEDSON, Hannah M., m. Jedediah RANDALL, Aug. 31, 1846, by Rev. Levi Walker	239
NEWTON, Sally, m. David MAIN, b. of N. Stonington, July 16, 1843, by Rev. Charles Randall	210
Warran, of Norwich, N. Y., m. Lydia A. WHEELER, of N. Stonington, May 28, 1851, by Rev. M. N. Morris	252
NICHOLS, David W., of Plainfield, m. Lucy Ann HOLMES, of N. Stonington, Dec. 24, 1843, by Rev. Tubal Wakefield	231
NILES, Elizabeth, of N. Stonington, m. Horace ROSS, of Stonington, persons of color, Nov. 14, 1838, by P. H. Shaw	170
Simeon, of N. Stonington, m. Mary Ann PALMER, of Stonington,	

	Page
NILES, (cont.)	
Feb. 10, 1834, by Rev. Asher Miner	149
NORTHROP, John C., of N. Kingston, R. I., m. Sarah A. **CHAMPLAIN**, of Griswold, Feb. 3, 1856, by S. W. Peckham	270
NOYES, Benjamin, m. Sally M. **THOMPSON**, b. of N. Stonington, Mar. 20, 1829, by Asher Miner, Elder	81
Benjamin, of S. Kingstown, R. I., m. Eunice B. **MINER**, of North Stonington, Nov. 14, 1836, by Rev. John G. Wightman	159
George W., m. Bridget **GRANT**, b. of N. Stonington, Mar. 12, 1833, by Rev. Asher Miner	144
OLIN, Benjamin, of Preston, m. Susan **PARTLO**, of N. Stonington, Dec. 26, 1824, by Stephen Avery, J. P.	90
ORCHARD, Silas, m. Catharine **ANDERSON**, b. colored & of N. Stonington, Nov. 24, 1837, by P. H. Shaw	163
OSGOOD, William C., of Norwich, m. Adaline **BROWNING**, of N. Stonington, Sept. 15, 1844, by Rev. Augusuts B. Collins, of Preston	202
PADDOCK, Seth J., of Middletown, m. Lucinda **KENYON**, of South Kingston, R. I., Dec. 4, 1833, by Rev. Asher Miner	148
PALMER, Abba, m. Asa S. **MINER**, b. of N. Stonington, Sept. 26, 1832, by Rev. Asher Miner	140
Albert G., m. Sarah A. **LANGWORTHY**, b. of N. Stonington, Mar. 27, 1837, by Rev. Amos R. Wells, at house of John Langworthy	160
Alpheas, s. W[illia]m & Marvin, b. Feb. 6, 1794	17
Amos, s. Israel & Lydia, b. Feb. 20, 1794	18
Amos, s. Stephen & Dorcas, b. Apr. 19, 1796	41
Benadam, s. W[illia]m & Marvin, b. Feb. 5, 1792	17
Benjamin, of Voluntown, m. Betsey **BABCOCK**, of N. Stonington, Jan. 1, 1838, by Rev. Benj[ami]n N. Harris	164
Betsey, d. Cyrus & Betsey, b. May 2, 1804	31
Betsey, m. Rowland **KINION**, Jan. 28, 1821	137
Calvin Goodard, s. Sandford & Wealthy, b. Feb. 11, 1810	62
Celissa, see Selissa	
Charlotte, m. Thomas M. **COLLINS**, b. of N. Stonington, May 11, 1823, by Nathan Pendleton, J. P.	81
Christopher, of Exeter, N. Y., m. Desire **WHEELER**, of N. Stonington, Nov. 1, 1823, by Asher Miner, Elder	84
Clarissa, m. Sandford **BROWN**, Nov. 4, 1810, by Stephen Meech, J. P.	64
Clarissa, m. Beriah **KENYON**, b. of N. Stonington, Jan. 29, 1832, by Rev. Joseph Ayer, Jr.	133
Clarissa Angeline, d. Israel & Lydia, b. Aug. 5, 1809	18
Daniel, s. Stephen & Dorcas, b. Oct. 1, 1793	41
Denison, s. Sandford & Wealthy, b. Dec. 3, 1800	62
Desire, d. W[illia]m & Marvin, b. Mar. 27, 1786	17
Dorcas, d. Stephen & Dorcas, b. Aug. 20, 1785	41
Dorcas, b. Aug. 20, 1785	42
Dorcas, m. David **MAIN**, Nov. 21, 1811, by Jed[idia]h Randall, Elder	42
Edgar R., m. Mary Ann **MINER**, b. of N. Stonington, May 27, 1851,	

	Page
PALMER, (cont.)	
by Van R. Gray, J. P.	252
Elisha, s. Elisha & Eunice, b. Mar. 26, 1811	43
Elisha, m. Eliza H. MINER, b. of N. Stonington, Mar. 12, 1833, by Jonathan Miner, Elder	145
Elisha Randall, s. Uzziel & Nabby, b. Apr. 6, 1811	55
Elmina, of N. Stonington, m. W[illia]m C. WALKER, of Griswold, Nov. 25, 1839, by Rev. Levi Walker	195
Esther, s. David MAIN, Jan. 8, 1787	6
Ethal, s. Cyrus & Betsey, b. Apr. 7, 1807	31
Eunice, d. W[illia]m & Marvin, b. Feb. 16, 1799	17
Eunice, d. Cyrus & Betsey, b. Feb. 14, 1806	31
Eunice, d. Oliver & Nancy, b. Apr. 20, 1808	78
Eunice, m. Miall MAIN, June 15, 1808	35
Eunice, m. David SMITH, b. of N. Stonington, Mar. 20, 1841, by Benj[ami]n Gallup, J. P. in Voluntown	187
Ezra, s. Israel & Lydia, b. Feb. 21, 1800	18
Fanny, d. Uzziel & Nabby, b. May 1, 1800	55
Gideon Avery, s. Uzziel & Nabby, b. Jan. 24, 1803	55
Hannah, twin with Jane, d. Israel & Lydia, b. Feb. 2, 1801	18
Hannah, d. Oliver & Nancy, twin with Phelena, b. July 26, 1806	78
Harvey, s. Cyrus & Betsey, b. Mar. 7, 1803	31
Henry, s. Henry & Polly, b. Jan. 6, 1807	61
Henry, m. Polly BROWN, Apr. 6, 1808, by Jer[emia]h Haley, Esq.	61
Isaac, m. Mary Ann PRINCE, b. of N. Stonington, Nov. 4, 1841, by Rev. Levi Walker	209
Israel, s. Israel & Lydia, b. Nov. 15, 1793	18
Jane, twin with Hannah, d. Israel & Lydia, b. Feb. 2, 1801	18
Joshua, s. Israel & Lydia, b. Aug. 4, 1798	18
Judah, m. David MAIN, Apr. 27, 1781	6
Julius, m. Susannah YORK, b. of N. Stonington, Nov. 19, 1809, by Joshua Babcock, J. P.	31
Julius Lathrop, s. Julius & Susannah, b. Jan. 30, 1811	31
Kathariah, d. Sandford & Wealthy, b. Oct. 1, 1789	62
Keturah, m. Stephen CHAPMAN, b. of N. Stonington, Sept. 27, 1807	7
Louisa T., m. Oliver CRANDALL, b. of N. Stonington, Feb. 16, 1851, by Rev. W[illa]m C. Walker	250
Lucy, d. Israel & Lydia, b. Mar. 7, 1804	18
Lydia, d. Israel & Lydia, b. Dec. 10, 1796	18
Maranda, d. Cyrus & Betsey, b. Nov. 20, 1808	31
Martin, s. Uzziel & Nabby, b. Oct. 23, 1805	55
Mary, d. W[illia]m & Marvin, b. Mar. 28, 1796	17
Mary Ann, of Stonington, m. Simeon NILES, of N. Stonington, Feb. 10, 1834, by Rev. Asher Miner	149
Merie, d. Elisha & Eunice, b. June 20, 1814	43
Miner, m. Esther THOMPSON, b. of N. Stonington, Feb. 4, 1816, by Jonathan Miner, Elder	30
Nabby, d. Uzziel & Nabby, b. June 7, 1791	55

360   BARBOUR COLLECTION

                                                                              Page
PALMER. (cont.)
Nathan, s. Stephen & Dorcas, b. Aug. 30, 1789   41
Nathan D., of Preston, m. Nancy **SWAN**, of N. Stonington, Oct. 7,
    1830, by Rev. Augustus B. Collings   123
Noyes, s. Sandford & Wealthy, b. June 27, 1798   62
Noyes, Deac., of Stonington, m. Harriet **WHEELER**, of N. Stonington,
    Mar. 28, 1844, by Rev. Philo Judson   206
Perry G., m. Mary E. **MERITT**, Feb. 15, 1857, by Rev. Milo Tracy   273
Phebe, d. Sandford & Wealthy, b. Aug. 1, 1803   62
Phelena, d. Oliver & Nancy, b. July 26, 1806, twin with Hannah   78
Randall, s. Sandford & Wealthy, b. Feb. 25, 1807   62
Rhoda, of N. Stonington, m. Stephen B. **WEAVER**, of Farralie, N. Y.,
    July 22, 1821, by David Coats, J. P.   71
Robert, s. Stephen & Dorcas, b. Oct. 24, 1791   41
Samuel, twin with Sanford, s. Uzziel & Nabby, b. Mar. 3, 1798   55
Sands, s. Stephen & Dorcas, b. Sept. 1, 1798   41
Sands, m. Susanna **CRUMB**, Jan. 29, 1823, by Sands Cole, J. P.   79
Sandford, m. Wealthy **GRANT**, b. of Stonington, Feb. 10, 1788   62
Sanford, twin with Samuel, s. Uzziel & Nabby, b. Mar. 3, 1798   55
Sandford Billings, s. Sandford & Wealthy, b. Dec. 13, 1791   62
Selissa, d. Uzziel & Nabby, b. [ ], 31, 1808   55
Silva, m. William **BREED**, b. of N. Stonington, Oct. 1, 1820, by
    David Coats, J. P.   66
Simeon Hewit, s. Oliver & Nancy, b. Feb. 10, 1803   78
Sophia, d. Sandford & Wealthy, b. Dec. 15, 1795   62
Sophia, d. Israel & Lydia, b. Apr. 12, 1811   18
Stephen, b. Aug. 28, 1758   41
Stephen, m. Dorcas **BURDICK**, Dec. 12, 1784, by Eleazer Brown,
    Elder   41
Stephen, s. Stephen & Dorcas, b. July 28, 1787   41
Stephen Wheeler, s. W[illia]m & Marvin, b. Mar. 10, 1790   17
Susan, d. Julius & Susan[nah], b. Dec. 25, 1813   31
Susannah, d. Israel & Lydia, b. Dec. 28, 1803   18
Uzziel, of Stonington, m. Nabby **MORGAN**, of Voluntown, Mar. 25,
    1790, by Allen Campbell, J. P.   55
Uzziel, s. Uzziel & Nabby, b. Feb. 1, 1793   55
William, b. June 27, 1759   17
William, m. Marvin **DAVIS**, Dec. 11, 1783   17
William, s. W[illia]m & Marvin, b. Jan. 22, 1788   17
William B., s. Uzziel & Nabby, b. May 9, 1795   55
PARK, PARKE, Abigail, w. Israel P., d. Apr. 7, 1810   54
Alvin Hart, s. Israel P. & Adah, b. Aug. 12, 1811   54
Anson Earl, s. Israel P. & Abigail, b. Dec. 21, 1809   54
Bailey P., m. Nancy W. **MAIN**, b. of N. Stonington, Jan. 22, 1843, by
    Rev. William Flint   197
Bailey P., of New Jersey, m. Nancy A. **BABCOCK**, of N. Stonington,
    Jan. 3, 1854, by Rev. J. G. Post   263
B[a]illey Partteous, s. Israel P. & Adah, b. May 6, 1813   54

NORTH STONINGTON VITAL RECORDS 361

Page

PARK, PARKE, (cont.)
Charles Clinton, twin with Ursula, s. of Israel P. & Abigail,
    b. Nov. 12, 1807   54
Clarissa M., m. Denison W. **MINER,** b. of N. Stonington, [1832], by
    Jonathan Miner, Elder. Recorded Sept. 5, 1832.   138
Clarissa Maria, d. Israel P. & Adah, b. Dec. 12, 1814   54
Dewitt R., of New York City, m. Harriet O. **CHAPMAN,** of N.
    Kingston, Sept. 22, 1847, by Rev. James J. Phillips   229
Elbert O., m. Fanny E. **PARK,** b. of N. Stonington, Feb. 19, 1843, by
    Rev. William Flint   198
Elisha, m. Eliza Adeline **AVERY,** b. of N. Stonington, Mar. 20, 1823,
    by Asher Miner, Elder   80
Elisha, of N. Stonington, d. Jan. 24, 1828   80
Emala Ann, d. Elisha & E[liza] Adeline, b. July 4, 1824   80
Emily, d. Israel P. & Abigail, b. June 12, 1804   54
Fanny E., m. Elbert D. **PARK,** b. of N. Stonington, Feb. 19, 1843, by
    Rev. William Flint   198
Faxon B., m. Cynthia A. **SMITH,** b. of N. Stonington, Nov. 5, 1851,
    by Rev. O. T. Walker   256
Israel P., m. Abigail **STORY,** Apr. 1, 1794   54
Israel P., m. Adah **MAIN,** Oct. 28, 1810   54
Levi W., of N. Stonington, m. Sarah **CONGDON,** of Voluntown,
    Apr. 11, 1852, by Rev. O. T. Walker   260
Lois, d. Israel P. & Abigail, b. Sept. 12, 1794   54
Louisa, m. Jesse **CHAPMAN,** b. of N. Stonington, Oct. 31, 1813, by
    Nathan Pendleton, J. P.   54
Lucy A., of N. Stonington, m. Nathan B. **LEWIS,** of Griswold,
    Oct. 6, 1850, by Rev. O. T. Walker   248
Lucy C., m. Jesse B. **SLOCUM,** b. of N. Stonington, Jan. 11, 1846,
    by Rev. Thomas Barber   220
Mary, m. Samuel B. **PHILLIPS,** Oct. 11, 1792   39
Sarah C., of Ledyard, m. W[illia]m H. **CLARK,** of N. Stonington,
    Sept. 5, 1858   264
Story, s. Israel P. & Abigail, b. May 12, 1797   54
Ursula, twin with Charles Clinton, d. of Israel P. & Abigail, b.
    Nov. 12, 1807   54
Ursula, m. Jesse **CHAPMAN,** b. of N. Stonington, Dec. 9, 1832, by
    Jonathan Miner, Elder   54
PARKER, Daniel, s. Daniel & Polly, b. Jan. 11, 1810   16
Stephen Avery, s. Daniel & Polly, b. Aug. 13, 1812   16
PARTELOW, PARTELO, PARTLO, Amos, m. Hannah **ROBBINS,** Mar.
    3, 1822, by W[illia]m Randall, Jr., J. P.   76
Hannah, m. Ezra **JACKSON,** Aug. 18, 1822, by W[illia]m Randall, Jr.
    J. P.   78
Hannah, m. Jesse **MAIN,** 2d, Nov. 27, 1838, by W[illia]m Randall, Jr.
    J. P.   174
John, m. Polly **MAIN,** b. of N. Stonington, June 28, 1821, by
    William Randall, Jr., J. P.   70

362 BARBOUR COLLECTION

	Page
PARTELOW, PARTELO, PARTLO, (cont.)	
Jonas, m. Phebe WHEELER, Dec. 26, 1822, by Asher Miner, Elder	78
Lucy Ann, m. Thomas HOLMES, Mar. 30, 1836, by Matthew Brown, J. P.	157
Mary Esther, of N. Stonington, m. Thomas C. PHILIPS, of Hopkinton, R. I., Mar. 26, 1843, by Rev. Erastus Denison, of Groton	200
Phebe, m. Rev. Milo TRACEY, b. of N. Stonington, Nov. 22, 1849, by N. E. Shailer, Missionary	243
Rebecca, m. Joseph WOLIZER, b. of N. Stonington, Nov. 13, 1855, by Rev. John Taylor	268
Susan, of N. Stonington, m. Benjamin OLIN, of Preston, Dec. 26, 1824, by Stephen Avery, J. P.	90
Thomas, m. Mary HOLMES, b. of N. Stonington, Oct. 6, 1831, by Thomas P. Wattles, J. P.	131
Wealthy, m. Ethan ALLEN, b. of N. Stonington, Aug. 23, 1820, by John Langworthy, J. P.	66
PATTERSON, Miles, of Newport, R. I., m. Mary E. HISSCOX, of R. I., Dec. 1, 1847, by Rev. Thomas Barber	234
PEABODY, Abigail, m. Elisha CHAPMAN, b. of N. Stonington, Oct. 13, 1822, by David Coats, J. P.	77
Anna, d. Sam[ue]l & Abigail, b. July 31, 1766	63
Anna, m. Amos COATS, Nov. 6, 1783	63
Benjamin, m. Patty PECKHAM, Mar. 5, 1812, by Stephen Avery, J. P.	24
Fanny A., d. Benj[ami]n & Patty, b. June 29, 1825	24
Fanny A., of N. Stonington, m. Russell WELLES, of Groton, Oct. 1, 1845, by Rev. James R. Stone	217
Francis Starr, s. Benj[ami]n & Patty, b. Nov. 29, 1815	24
Giles Holmes, s. Benj[ami]n & Abigail, b. Sept. 25, 1807	5
Hannah, m. Nahum CHAPMAN, b. of N. Stonington, May 4, 1822, by Jonathan Miner, Elder	59
James A., s. Benj[ami]n & Patty, b. May 30, 1831	24
James A., m. Augusta J. CRUMB, Nov. 10, 1856, by Rev. W[illia]m Stow, at Stonington	273
Martha Esther, d. Benj[ami]n & Patty, b. Apr. 24, 1819	24
Mary, d. Benj[ami]n & Patty, b. May 2, 1822	24
Mary, m. Cyrus W. CRARY, b. of N. Stonington, Mar. 12, 1838	164
Mary, m. Cyrus W. CRARY, b. of N. Stonington, Nov. 21, 1846, by Rev. Thomas Barber	225
Nancy, d. Benj[ami]n & Patty, b. Sept. 5, 1828	24
Nancy, of N. Stonington, m. James COOK, of Norwich, May 27, 1851, by Rev. O. T. Walker	252
Rebecka, d. Benj[ami]n & Abigail, b. Sept. 5, 1809	5
Rebecca, of N. Stonington, m. Abel BREED, of Oxford, N. Y., Nov. 8, 1829, by Asher Miner, Elder	117
Thomas, m. Esther DEWEY, b. of N. Stonington, Sept. 4, 1832, by Rev. Asher Miner	139
Thomas Hazard, s. Benjamin & Patty, b. Mar. 10, 1813	24
PECKHAM, Emily Ann, d. Tho[ma]s H. & Sophia, b. May 30, 1814	58

NORTH STONINGTON VITAL RECORDS 363

	Page
PECKHAM, (cont.)	
Frances E., of N. Stonington, m. John H. **BROOKS**, of Lisbon, Jan. 22, 1838, by Rev. Joseph Ayer, of Lisbon	175
Hannah, of N. Stonington, m. Augustus L. **BABCOCK**, of Hopkinton, R. I., Nov. 10, 1811, by Stephen Avery, J. P.	34
Isaac H., m. Frances Maria **BROWN**, b. of Groton, Oct. 30, 1837, by Rev. Joseph Ayer, Jr.	162
Isaac Miner, s. Tho[ma]s H. & Sophia, b. Aug. 19, 1816	58
Maryette, d. W[illia]m & Cynthia, b. May 29, 1812	56
Martha Ann, d. W[illia]m & Cynthia, b. Sept. 22, 1814	56
Nancy, m. Jesse **WHEELER**, May 30, 1811	32
Patty, m. Benjamin **PEABODY**, Mar. 5, 1812, by Stephen Avery, J. P.	24
Samuel S., Dea., of Portsmouth, R. I., m. Amelia S. **DEWEY**, of N. Stonington, Mar. 6, 1853, by Rev. O. T. Walker	262
Thomas Hazard, Jr., m. Sophia **GALLUP**, Sept. 30, 1813, by Stephen Avery, J. P.	58
Thomas W., of Stonington, m. Susan E. **BARBER**, of Granville, Mass., May 3, 1847, by Rev. Thomas Barber	226
William, of N. Stonington, m. Cynthia **LEWIS**, of Stonington, Aug. 29, 1811, by Rev. Christopher Avery	56
PENDLETON, Azalia, d. Isaac & Bridget, b. Oct. 25, 1809, in Groton	12
Caroline, m. Samuel S. **WOODMANSIE**, b. of N. Stonington, July 3, 1831, by Rev. Joseph Ayer, Jr.	129
Charles Henry, s. Nathan & Phebe, b. Jan. 19, 1807	11
Charles S., of Stonington, m. Keturah R. **BROWN**, of N. Stonington, Dec. 30, 1828, by Rev. Ira Hart	112
Charlotte, m. Christopher **BROWN**, Jr., b. of Stonington, Nov. 27, 1806, by Stephen Avery, J. P.	37
Dewitt Clinton, s. Nathan & Phebe, b. May 27, 1812	11
Emily, m. Paul L. **TEFFT**, Feb. 7, 1836, by Rev. John G. Wightman	159
Enoch B., m. Mary E. **CHAPMAN**, b. of N. Stonington, Oct. 30, 1843, by Rev. Charles Randall	210
Enoch Burrows, s. Nathan & Phebe, b. Sept. 5, 1808	11
Isaac, m. Bridget **STANTON**, Jan. 22, 1809, by Asher Miner, Elder	12
Jane, of N. Stonington, m. Albert G. **AYER**, of Preston, Sept. 23, 1845, by Rev. James R. Stone	217
John B., of Stonington, m. Lucy S. **CLARK**, of N. Stonington, Mar. 20, 1845, by Nehemiah B. Cook	212
*Julia, b. Mar. 4, 1800 *(**PUNDERSON** handwritten in original manuscript)	164
*Julia, m. Oliver **HEWITT**, Feb. 28, 1819, at Preston (Poquetannock), by Jonah Witter, Esq*. *(handwritten in original manuscript)	164
*Julia, d. Apr. 25, 1842, w. Oliver **HEWITT** *(**PUNDERSON** handwritten in original manuscript)	164
Lydia Ann, d. Isaac & Bridget, b. Sept. 28, 1811	12
Nancy Maria, d. Nathan & Phebe, b. Mar. 1, 1820	11
Nathan L., of Stonington, m. Mary Ann **ALEXANDER**, of N. Stonington, Oct. 27, 1839, by Charles Bennet, J. P.	180

PENDLETON, (cont.)

	Page
Nathan Sands, s. Nathan & Phebe, b. Jan. 18, 1805	11
Phebe Esther, d. Nathan & Phebe, b. Nov. 30, 1810	11
Sally Ann, d. Nathan & Phebe, b. May 23, 1816	11
Sarah, m. John LANGWORTHY, b. of Stonington, Nov. 29, 1798, by Joshua Babcock, J. P.	10
Susan Amelia, d. Nathan & Phebe, b. Mar. 18, 1818	11
William Franklin, s. Nathan & Phebe, b. Apr. 5, 1814	11

PERKINS, Nathan W., of Groton, m. Caroline BURTON, of Hopkinton, R. I., Mar. 16, 1845, by Rev. James R. Stone — 215
Sands, of Danbury, m. May HOLMES, of Kingston, R. I., Mar. 11, 1828, by Rev. Joseph Ayer, Jr. — 104

PERRY, Alfred H., m. Hannah E. SHERMAN, Mar. 16, 1857, by Rev. Charles C. Lewis — 273
Eliza C., m. Sands B. MAIN, b. of N. Stonington, Oct. 1, 1847, by Rev. Thomas Barber — 229
Ransom S., m. Maria S. HOLMES, Nov. 26, 1857, by Rev. John Sheffield — 274
Ruth, m. Charles WHITE, Jan. 26, 1812, by Jedediah Randall, Elder — 12
Stanton H., m. Wa[i]ty HARVEY, b. of Charlestown, R. I., Mar. 31, 1842, by Elias Hewitt, J. P. — 192

PETERS, Coddington, of Stonington, m. Betsey EBBINS, of N. Stonington, Mar. 29, 1821, by Asher Miner, Elder — 70

PETERSON, Abraham, of Stonington, m. Sophia WHEELER, of N. Stonington, persons of color, Feb. 10, 1825, by Stephen Avery, J. P. — 91

PHAGINS, see under FAGINS

PHILLIPS, PHILIPS, Bradford, of N. Stonington, m. Charlotte BAILEY, of Stonington, Nov. 28, 1850, by Rev. O. T. Walker — 249
Caty Ann, d. Sam[ue]l B. & Mary, b. Jan. 26, 1806 — 39
Elisha P., m. Margaret WILKINSON, b. of N. Stonington, Mar. 30, 1835, by Stephen Geer, J. P., at house of George Wilkinson — 155
Eliza, d. Sam[ue] B & Mary, b. Aug. 1, 1794 — 39
Emily Augusta, d. Sam[ue]l B. & Mary, b. June 19, 1808 — 39
Gardner B., Dr., of New Shoreham, R. I., m. Dolly B. REYNOLDS, of N. Kingston, R. I., May 5, 1845, by Rev. James R. Stone — 216
Katy, see Caty
Lois Ann, of N. Stonington, m. Henry C. CARD, of Westerly, R. I., Nov. 14, 1842, by Rev. Erastus Denison — 199
Maria, d. Sam[ue]l B. & Mary, b. Feb. 12, 1797 — 39
Sally P., of N. Stonington, m. Stephen P. BENJAMIN, of Colchester, Nov. 15, 1824, by Levi Meech, Elder — 90
Samuel B., m. Mary PARKE, Oct. 11, 1792 — 39
Samuel B., s. Sam[ue]l B. & Mary, b. June 3, 1803 — 39
Sarah P., d. Sam[ue]l B. & Mary, b. Jan. 28, 1801 — 39
Thomas C., of Hopkinton, R. I., m. Mary Esther PARTELO, of N. Stonington, Mar. 26, 1843, by Rev. Erastus Denison, of Groton — 200

PHINNEY, Mary C., m. George W. BALDWIN, at Preston, Nov. 16, 1809,

	Page
PHINNEY, (cont.)	
by Eben[eze]r Stewart, J. P.	26
PIERCE, Aaron, of Westerly, R. I., m. Frances E. **BAILEY**, of N. Stonington, Apr. 16, 1855, by Rev. Stephen Hubbell	266
Nathaniel C. R., m. Eliza **REYNOLDS**, b. of Richmond, R. I., Oct. 24, 1841, by Rev. Tho[ma]s Dowling	189
Truman, m. Betsey, wid. of Lodowick **WHEELER**, Sept. 13, 1835, by Amos C. Main, J. P.	155
PITCHER, Ann Elizabeth, d. Joel & Perlina, b. Dec. 16, 1834	154
Harriet Newell, d. Joel & Perlina, b. May 16, 1832	154
Joel W[illia]m, s. Joel & Perlina, b. Nov. 14, 1828	154
Lucy E., d. Joel & Perlina, b. Oct. 13, 1826	154
Lucy E., of N. Stonington, m. Jeremiah **MAYNARD**, of Norwich, Oct. 14, 1851, by Rev. O. T. Walker	255
POMEROY, Benjamin, of N. Stonington, m. Jerusha **WILLIAMS**, of Stonington, Jan. 1, 1818	62
Benjamin, s. Benj[ami]n & Jerusha, b. Nov. 2, 1818	62
POTTER, Betsey, of Voluntown, m. Charles W. **THOMPSON**, of N. Stonington, Jan. 25, 1821 [1824?], by Amos Frink, J. P.	87
Hellen M., of Voluntown, m. Henry D. **BROWN**, of N. Stonington, Nov. 29, 1855, by Stephen Hubbell	268
Henry, m. Maria **YORK**, b. of N. Stonington, Mar. 16, 1834, by Jonathan Miner, Elder	150
Lydia Ann, m. Leonard **BROWN**, b. of N. Stonington, Nov. 25, 1846, by Charles Bennet, J. P.	224
PRENTICE, Abby, m. Lathrop **WILLIAMS**, b. of N. Stonington, Nov. 8, 1818, by Rev. John Hyde	4
Alex[ande]r S., s. Sam[ue]l H. & Susan, b. Mar. 9, 1824	194
Asa, Jr., m. Ann **BROWNING**, b. of N. Stonington, Feb. 15, 1818, by Rev. Gustavus Davis	60
Asher, Jr., m. Mary **HEWIT**, b. of N. Stonington, Dec. 25, 1828, by Rev. Timothy Tuttle, of Groton	111
Charles, s. Tho[ma]s & Anna, b. Apr. 26, 1797	38
Cha[rle]s F., s. Samuel & Amy, b. Aug. 8, 1820	34
Chester S., s. Samuel & Amy, b. Aug. 16, 1816	34
David N., s. Sam[ue]l H. & Susan, b. Jan. 28, 1817	194
Dewitt C., s. Sam[ue]l H. & Susan, b. July 30, 1830	194
Eliza, m. Ephraim G. **HEWITT**, Dec. 4, 1823, by Rev. John Hyde	86
Eliza Ann, d. Tho[ma]s & Anna, b. Nov. 6, 1804	38
Henry, s. Tho[ma]s & Anna, b. Sept. 7, 1802	38
Henry, m. Eliza **HEWIT**, Nov. 30, 1824, by Rev. John Hyde	90
Hezekiah, of Griswold, m. Polly **CRARY**, of N. Stonington, Nov. 9, 1834, by Rev. Asher Miner	153
John, m. Amey **MEECH**, Jan. 31, 1813, by Rev. John Hyde	20
Joshua, d. Sept. 9, 1794	34
Joshua, s. John & Rebeckah, b. Apr. 29, 1798	15
Joshua, of N. Stonington, m. Mary Ann **BENNET**, of Stonington,	

	Page
PRENTICE, (cont.)	
Jan. 13, 1820, by Paris Hewit, J. P.	65
Joshua Downer, s. Tho[ma]s & Anna, b. June 12, 1795; d. July 17, 1796	38
Lucy, m. John Denison **WHEELER,** Dec. 11, 1814, by Rev. John Hyde	108
Nancy, d. Tho[ma]s & Anna, b. Feb. 8, 1789; d. July 28, 1789	38
Paul P., s. Sam[ue]l H. & Susan, b. Sept. 2, 1821	194
Polly, d. Joshua, d. Apr. 4, 1806	34
Sally, m. David **MORE,** Mar. 29, 1808	34
Samuel, m. Amy **SMITH,** Dec. 23, 1810	34
Samuel, h. Amy, d. May 25, 1837, ae 49 years	34
Samuel, s. Sam[ue]l & Susan, b. Aug. 4, 1819	194
Samuel, of Norwich, m. Sophia P. **BROWNING,** of N. Stonington, [Dec.] 31, 1849, by Rev. N. S. Hunt, of Preston	244
Samuel H., m. Susan **BALDWIN,** Nov. 27, 1814	39
Samuel S., s. Samuel & Amy, b. Oct. 28, 1814; d. July 17, 1815	34
Sary L., of N. Stonington, m. Sandford **WILLIAMS,** of Stonington, Jan. 6, 1825, by Parke Williams, J. P.	91
Sophia, d. Tho[ma]s & Anna, b. May 31, 1791	38
Sophia, m. Samuel **BROWNING,** Nov. 28, 1811	38
Susan R., d. Sam[ue]l H. & Susan, b. Sept. 2, 1834	194
Thomas, m. Anna **DOWNER,** Apr. 17, 1787	38
Thomas, s. Tho[ma]s & Anna, b. July 7, 1793	38
Thomas, Jr., m. Harriet **AYER,** b. of N. Stonington, Apr. 26, 1831, by Rev. Joseph Ayer, Jr.	128
William B., s. Tho[ma]s & Anna, b. May 21, 1807	38
PRINCE, Mary Ann, m. Isaac **PALMER,** b. of N. Stonington, Nov. 4, 1841, by Rev. Levi Walker	209
***PUNDERSON,** Julia, b. Mar. 4, 1800	164
Julia, m. Oliver **HEWITT,** Feb. 28, 1819, at Preston (Poquetannock), by Jonah Witter, Esq.*	164
Julia, d. Apr. 25, 1842, w. Oliver **HEWITT**	164
* Above was handwritten in orginal manuscript)	
RANDALL, Darius Hewit, s. W[illia]m & Wealthy, b. July 28, 1823	56
Desire, of Stonington, m. Dr. Thomas T. **WELLS,** of N. Stonington, Dec. 31, 1812, in Presence of Stephen & Betsey Avery	15
Dudley, m. Sally **FARNHAM,** of N. Stonington, Mar. 28, 1830, by Rev. Jabez S. Swan	122
Elisha D., of Stonington, m. Eunice P. **VINCENT,** of N. Stonington, Feb. 27, 1843, by Rev. Erastus Denison, of Groton	198
Emily M., m. Albert W. **HILLIARD,** b. of N. Stonington, Nov. 25, 1851, by Rev. O. T. Walker	257
Emily Miner, d. W[illia]m & Wealthy, b. Jan. 4, 1829	56
Eunice, d. William & Wealthy, b. Aug. 11, 1804	105
Eunice, m. Ansel **COATS,** Jan. 18, 1826, by Rev. Gideon Perry	105
Hannah, of Voluntown, m. Nathan **CHAPMAN,** Jr., of N. Stonington, May 29, 1808, in Voluntown, by Peleg Randall, Elder	25

	Page
RANDALL, (cont.)	
Hannah M., of N. Stonington, m. Sullivan **FAGAN**, of Preston, b. colored person, July 1, 1847, by Rev. Myron N. Morris	226
Hannah Marcy, d. William & Wealthy, b. Aug. 31, 1816	56
Hannah Mary, of N. Stonington, m. Capt. John **RANDALL**, of Norwich, N. Y., Nov. 3, 1816, by Stephen Avery, J. P.	57
Henry Clay, s. W[illia]m & Wealthy, b. Dec. 7, 1825	56
Jedediah, m. Hannah M. **NEDSON**, Aug. 31, 1846, by Rev. Levi Walker	239
John, Capt., of Norwich, N. Y., m. Hannah Mary **RANDALL**, of N. Stonington, Nov. 3, 1816, by Stephen Avery, J. P.	57
John, m. Abby **PHAGINS**, colored people, b. of N. Stonington, Nov. 27, 1851, by M. N. Morris	256
Lucy W., m. Samuel **CHAPMAN**, Jan. 1, 1812, by Asher Miner, Elder	19
Lydia, m. Libeus **COON**, Feb. 22, 1842, by Enoch B. Pendleton, J. P.	190
Mary, of Stonington, m. John **GARDNER**, of Groton, Mar. 1, 1830, by Rev. Asher Miner	122
Mary H., of N. Stonington, m. Ezra **WHEELER**, of Stonington, Nov. 25, 1840, by Rev. Tho[ma]s Dowling	186
Roswell, Capt., d. May 1, 1815	1
Thankfull S., m. George **WHEELER**, b. of Stonington, Nov. 13, 1817, in Stonington, by Asher Miner, Elder	172
Wealthy Avery, d. W[illia]m & Wealthy, b. Jan. 11, 1821	56
William, Jr., of Stonington, m. Wealthy A. **HEWIT**, of N. Stonington, Dec. 23, 1813, by Stephen Avery, J. P.	56
William, m. Eunice **MAIN**, June 10, 1824, by W[illia]m Randall, Jr., J. P.	88
William Harrison, s. W[illia]m & Wealthy, b. Aug. 11, 1818	56
RATHBOURN, Nathan, m. Bridget **HAKES**, b. of N. Stonington, Apr. 6, 1828, by Benjamin Pomeroy, J. P.	104
RAY, Lucinda, m. Stephen **MAIN**, Jan. 14, 1810, by Peleg Randall, Elder	45
READ, REED, Nab[b]y, of Hopkinton, m. Lodowick **STANTON**, of Stonington, Dec. 6, 1801, by Henry Joslin, Bapt. Elder	14
Sam[ue]l, of Canterbury, m. Desire **EGGLESTON**, of N. Stonington, Sept. 15, 1833, by David Coats, J. P.	147
REYNOLDS, Dolly B., of N. Kingston, R. I., m. Dr. Gardner B. **PHILIPS**, of New Shoreham, R. I., May 5, 1845, by Rev. James R. Stone	216
Eliza, m. Nathaniel C. R. **PIERCE**, b. of Richmond, R. I., Oct. 24, 1841, by Rev. Tho[ma]s Dowling	189
Emeline Matilda, of N. Kingston, R. I., m. Dr. Otis **COOPER**, of Warwick, R. I., Feb. 18, 1845, by Rev. James R. Stone	215
John H., Jr., m. Prudence **LATHAM**, b. of N. Stonington, Feb. 9, 1833, by Asher Miner, Minister	144
Luke C., b. Dec. 30, 1785, in Stonington	276
RICHARDS, Charles T., of Groton, m. Lucy Ann **COATS**, Sept. 15, 1847, by Rev. H. R. Knapp, of Groton	228
RICHARDSON, Phebe, m. Nathan **CRUMB**, b. of N. Stonington, Sept. 5, 1833, by Jonathan Miner, Elder	147

	Page
RICHARDSON, (cont.)	
Thankfull, of Stonington, m. Charles **HOLMES**, Jr., of N. Stonington, Dec. 11, 1828, by Asher Miner, Elder	110
Thankful, m. Benjamin **WILBUR**, Nov. 26, 1829, by Sands Cole, J. P.	120
Thankful, m. Benjamin **WILBUR**, Nov. 26, 1829, by Sands Cole, J. P. Recorded Jan. 27, 1839	172
RILEY, Mary, m. Charles L. **BROWN**, b. of N. Stonington, Apr. 7, 1851, by Rev. M. N. Morris	250
Sarah, of Stonington, m. Patrick **LARKIN**, of N. Stonington, June 15, 1848, by Rev. John Sheffield	235
RIPLEY, John, of Groton, m. Sally **CRARY**, of N. Stonington, Oct. 30, 1832, by Asher Miner, Elder	141
RIX, Aaron B., of N. Stonington, m. Mary **ADAMS**, of Norwich, Feb. 16, 1846, by Rev. John Sheffield	221
Asa, of Griswold, m. Emily **ECCLESTON**, of N. Stonington, Nov. 27, 1845, by Rev. John Sheffield	221
ROBBINS, Hannah, m. Amos **PARTLO**, Mar. 3, 1822, by W[illia]m Randall, Jr. J. P.	76
ROBERTS, Betsey, m. Cyrus **SHELLEY**, Apr. 8, 1822, by Paris Hewit, J. P.	75
ROBINSON, Calvin N., of N. Stonington, m. Emily A. **KENYON**, of N. Stonington, Mar. 1, 1851, at Richmondtown, R. I., by Rev. Steadman Kenyon. Recorded Aug. 15, 1863	257
Joseph, of Stonington, m. Emmarella **HEWIT**, of N. Stonington, Dec. 25, 1827, by Asher Miner, Elder	103
ROCHE, Sarah A., m. John M. **TERWILLIGER**, Jan. 12, 1834, by Elder McJimpsey	154
RODMAN, Daniel, of S. Kingston, R. I., m. Eliza Ann **BROWN**, of N. Stonington, Nov. 26, 1835, by Rev. Asher Miner	156
ROGGERS, Fanny, m. Gershom **ECCLESTON**, Jr., b. of N. Stonington, Dec. 9, 1824, by Jonathan Miner, Elder	107
ROSS, Horace, of Stonington, m. Elizabeth **NILES**, of N. Stonington, persons of color, Nov. 14, 1838, by P. H. Shaw	170
RUDE, Elisha, of Preston, m. Elizabeth A. **HOWELL**, of N. Stonington, Dec. 23, 1845, by Rev. Augustus B. Collins, of Preston	219
SAFFORD, Orren, of Preston, m. Ann M. **GRANT**, of N. Stonington, Dec. 29, 1830, by Rev. Asher Miner	125
Resilla, of Norwich, m. Oliver **MINER**, of N. Stonington, Sept. 1, 1852, by Rev. O. T. Walker	259
SAUNDERS, John, m. Huldah **SLACK**, b. of Griswold, Nov. 29, 1827, by Levi Meech, Elder	102
SAWYER, Phelana, of Windham, m. David **MAIN**, of N. Stonington, Feb. 7, 1825, by Stephen Avery, J. P.	91
SCHOONEVER, J. S., of Groton, m. D. Matilda **HEWITT**, of N. Stonington, May 13, 1851, by Rev. M. N. Morris	251
SEGAR, Joseph D., of Lebanon, m. Ruth M. **KINYON**, of Richmond, R. I., Mar. 15, 1846, by Rev. Thomas Barber	221
SHEFFIELD, Amos, of Exeter, R. I., m. Nancy **BALDWIN**, of N.	

NORTH STONINGTON VITAL RECORDS 369

	Page
SHEFFIELD, (cont.)	
Stonington, Feb. 23, 1823, by Asher Miner, Elder	79
Frances E., of N. Stonington, m. Erastus **GALLUP**, of Groton, Aug. 27, 1846, by Rev. John Sheffield	223
Mary, of Charlestown, R. I., m. Thomas J. **BROWN**, of N. Stonington, Dec. 20, 1846, by Rev. Thomas Barber	231
W[illia]m F., of Stonington, m. Lucy B. **MAIN**, of N. Stonington, Mar. 8, 1854, by Rev. Harris H. Tinker	264
SHELLEY, Cyrus, m. Betsey **ROBERTS**, Apr. 8, 1822, by Paris Hewit, J. P.	75
Freelove, m. Henry **FAGGINS**, b. of N. Stonington, June 25, 1838, by Rev. Pierpoint Brocket	167
Hannah, m. Moses **HASKELL**, b. of N. Stonington, June 23, 1839, by Charles Bennet, J. P.	181
Noyes, s. Samuel & Esther, b. Mar. 20, 1788	22
SHERMAN, Hannah E., m. Alfred H. **PERRY**, Mar. 16, 1857, by Rev. Charles C. Lewis	273
SHESUCKS, Rachel, of N. Stonington, m. Mark D. **BABCOCK**, of Hopkinton, R. I., Nov. 24, 1839, by Charles Bennett, J. P.	180
SHIRLEY, Martha E., m. Lemuel D. **STEVENS**, b. of N. Stonington, Dec. 22, 1855, by Stephen Hubbell	269
SIMMS, SIMS, Isaac, m. Hannah **BATES**, b. of N. Stonington, Sept. 26, 1841, by Rev. Philo Judson	188
M[ar]y Ann, d. Isaac & Hannah, b. Jan. 10, 1843	188
SISSON, Benjamin Franklin, s. Gilbert & Desire, b. Apr. 20, 1811	47
Benjamin Franklin, m. Marilla **YORK**, b. of N. Stonington, Tuesday, Aug. 28, 1838, by Rev. Peirpoint Brockett	168
Betsey, d. Gilbert & Desire, b. Sept. 19, 1796	47
Charles G., m. Martha **WHEELER**, b. of N. Stonington, May 11, 1829, by Rev. Joseph Ayer, Jr.	113
Charles G., m. Nancy M. **HEWITT**, b. of N. Stonington, June 21, 1840, by Rev. Philo Judson	183
Charles Grandison, s. Gilbert & Desire, b. Apr. 15, 1807	47
Cyrus Swan, s. Gilbert & Desire, b. Mar. 5, 1813; d. Mar. 22, 1813	47
Emily, d. Gilbert & Desire, b. June 7, 1809	47
Emily, of N. Stonington, m. Robert A. **BLIVIN**, of Westerly, R. I., by Rev. Joseph Ayer, Jr. Recorded Aug. 20, 1836	158
Esther, d. Gilbert & Desire, b. Dec. 8, 1793	47
Gilbert, m. Desire **MAIN**, Mar. 22, 1791	47
Gilbert, s. Gilbert & Desire, b. Sept. 1, 1800	47
Gilbert, m. Eunice Ann **GRAY**, b. of N. Stonington, Mar. 7, 1845, by Rev. James R. Stone	215
Keturah, of N. Stonington, m. Thomas Andrew **DEAN**, of N. Y. C., Aug. 19, 1832, by Rev. Joseph Ayer, Jr.	138
Lucy, of N. Stonington, m. Peter **LAROACH**, of Stonington, May [ ], 1838, by Oliver Hewitt, J. P.	165
Lucy Ann, d. Gilbert & Desire, b. Dec. 3, 1804	47
Lucy Ann, of N. Stonington, m. Henry **BLIVIN**, of Westerly, R. I.;	

370 BARBOUR COLLECTION

	Page
SISSON, (cont.)	
Nov. 28, 1822, by Elias Hewitt, J. P.	76
Noyes, s. Gilbert & Desire, b. Sep. 21, 1798	47
Polly, d. Gilbert & Desire, b. Nov. 17, 1791; d. Aug. 17, 1794	47
William, s. Gilbert & Desire, b. Sept. 6, 1802	47
SLACK, Huldah, m. John SAUNDERS, b. of Griswold, Nov. 29, 1827, by Levi Meech, Elder	102
Sylvia, of Stonington, m. Ephraim WHEELER, of N. Stonington, Jan. 15, 1815, by Stephen Avery, J. P.	36
SLOCUM, Abigail, b. Sept. 15, 1771	40
Abigail, m. Amos MAIN, 2d, Dec. 25, 1797	40
Almira, d. W[illia]m & Lydia, b. Sept. 22, 1806 [probably 1808]	14
Almira, of N. Stonington, m. Thomas LEWIS, Oct. 23, 1831, by Jonathan Miner, Elder	135
Burrill, s. W[illia]m & Lydia, b. Sept. 10, 1815	14
Charles Crandall, s. Richard & Lucy, b. Jan. 31, 1809	31
Esther Crandall, d. Richard & Lucy, b. Jan. 10, 1803	31
James Thomson, s. Richard & Lucy, b. Jan. 5, 1814	31
Jesse B., m. Lucy C. PARKS, b. of N. Stonington, Jan. 11, 1846, by Rev. Thomas Barber	220
Lucinda, d. Richard & Lucy, b. June 10, 1816	31
Lucy, d. Richard & Lucy, b. Jan. 26, 1800	31
Philura, d. W[illia]m & Lydia, b. Aug. 23, 1806	14
Polly, d. Richard & Lucy, b. Jan. 10, 1812	31
Richard, of Hopkinton, m. Lucy CRANDALL, of Stonington, Aug. 6, 1797, by Sam[ue]l Northup, Elder	31
Richard, s. Richard & Lucy, b. Oct. 21, 1801	31
Sally, d. Richard & Lucy, b. Feb. 18, 1806	31
Samuel, s. W[illia]m & Lydia, b. Nov. 21, 1811; d. Feb. 25, 1815	14
SMITH, Amy, m. Samuel PRENTICE, Dec. 23, 1810	34
Anna, d. Chester & Sally, b. Feb. 1, 1791	57
Anna Reed, d. George W. & Lucretia, b. Feb. 8, 1813	7
Charles, s. Chester & Sally, b. Jan. 2, 1801	57
Chester, of Stonington, m. Sally BRE[W]STER, of Preston, Dec. 7, 1788, by Sam[ue]l Mott, J. P	57
Cynthia A., m. Faxon B. PARK, b. of N. Stonington, Nov. 5, 1851, by Rev. O. T. Walker	256
David, m. Eunice PALMER, b. of N. Stonington, Mar. 20, 1841, by Benj[ami]n Gallup, J. P., in Voluntown	187
Elizabeth, of Waterford, m. John W. HULL, of N. Stonington, May 16, 1811, by Samuel West, Elder	12
Ephraim, s. Chester & Sally, b. Feb. 8, 1797	57
Eph[rai]m, m. Lucy AYER, b. of N. Stonington, Feb. 9, 1826, by Rev. Joseph Ayer, Jr.	95
Ezra Brewster, s. Chester & Sally, b. Mar. 23, 1794	57
George, s. Samuel H. & Hannah, b. Oct. 1, 1844	211
John Leland, s. Sheffield & Polly, b. July 1, 1805	19
Lucy, m. Jedediah SPAULDING, Oct. 29, 1807	54

NORTH STONINGTON VITAL RECORDS 371

Page
SMITH, (cont.)
Mary H., of Stonington, m. Edgar H. **CHAPMAN**, of N. Stonington,
   Nov. 2, 1849, by Rev. O. T. Walker 244
Nancy E., m. Henry T. **CHAPMAN**, b. of N. Stonington, Feb. 3, 1846,
   by Rev. Thomas Barber 220
Osamus, m. Clarissa **DENISON**, Aug. 24, 1823, by Paris Hewit, J. P. 85
Prudence Wheeler, d. George W. & Lucretia, b. May 22, 1805 7
Samuel H., m. Hannah **ALLEN**, Jan. 1, 1843 211
Sophia, m. Dudley **DENISON**, b. of N. Stonington, Oct. 20, 1814, by
   Stephen Avery, J. P. [See **SMITH**, Sophronia] 40
Sophronia, d. Isabel **ANGTERS**, b. Mar. 23, 1796 [see **SMITH**,
   Sophia] 40
Susan, d. Chester & Sally, b. Dec. 31, 1792 57
SPAULDING, Asa, Dr., d. Feb. 21, 1811 54
Edwin, m. Sarah S. **BURDICK**, Nov. 26, 1857, by Rev. Joseph
   Burnett 274
Emeline, of N. Stonington, m. Sylvester **LANPHEAR**, of Hopkinton,
   R. I., Feb. 17, 1831, by Rev. Asher Miner 127
Eunice, m. Thatcher **BROWN**, b. of N. Stonington, Oct. 3, 1821, by
   Asher Miner, Elder 72
Jedediah, m. Lucy **SMITH**, Oct. 29, 1807 54
Lydia, of N. Stonington, m. Adam **STILLMAN**, of Westerly, Mar. 18,
   1824, by Asher Miner, Elder 88
Nancy, m. Thomas **BALDWIN**, b. of Stonington, Apr. 16, 1801, by
   Simeon Brown, Elder 28
SPENCER, Mary S., m. William C. **LANPHEAR**, b. of N. Stonington,
   Nov. 28, 1855, by Charles P. White, J. P. 269
Ruama, m. John T. **CLARK**, b. of N. Stonington, Oct. 25, 1810, by
   Elias Hewett, J. P. 49
SPICER, Eldridge, of Groton, m. Lydia **STANTON**, of N. Stonington, May
   31, 1820, by Asher Miner, Elder 70
SPRAGUE, Clarinda M., of Coventry, m. W[illia]m **HUNT**, of Bolton,
   May 6, 1839, by Rev. Fernando Bester of 2d Bapt. Ch., N.
   Stonington 177
Elias, of Coventry, m. Clarissa **MAIN**, of N. Stonington, Dec.
   20, 1831, by Jonathan Miner, Elder 134
STANTON, Albert, s. Lod[owic]k & Nabby, b. Feb. 26, 1811 14
Amos, Jr., m. Taphena **BROWN**, b. of N. Stonington, Sept. 24, 1826,
   by Asher Miner, Elder 97
Betsey, d. W[illia]m & Hannah, b. Jan. 30, 1782 5
Bridget, m. Isaac **PENDLETON**, Jan. 22, 1809, by Asher Miner, Elder 12
Caroline, m. Samuel **BABCOCK**, b. of N. Stonington, Feb. 28, 1832,
   by Rev. Asher Miner 136
Daniel, s. Lod[owic]k & Nabby, b. May 23, 1805 14
Dolly, m. Henry **BABCOCK**, Nov. 10, 1811, by Peleg Randall, Elder 60
Eliza, of N. Stonington, m. Jared **BARKER**, of Westerly, Feb. 12,
   1825, by Asher Miner, Elder 91
Eliza, of N. Stonington, m. Charles **HEWITT**, of Preston, Oct.

STANTON, (cont.)

	Page
22, 1850, by Rev. M. V. Morris	247
Elizabeth S., m. Zebulon T. **YORK**, b. of N. Stonington, Mar. 6, 1842, by Rev. Tho[ma]s Dowling	191
Emily L., m. Joseph D. **HEWITT**, b. of N. Stonington, Mar. 14, 1839, by Rev. Peirpoint Brockett	175
George A., of Charleston, R. I., m. Sarah M. **BROWN**, of N. Stonington, June 5, 1848, by Rev. Isaac Fargo, of Hamburgh, N. Y.	233
Hannah, d. W[illia]m & Hannah, b. Apr. 5, 1779	5
Hannah, of Preston, m. Capt. Daniel **BALDWIN**, of N. Stonington, Apr. 21, 1808, by Alexander Stewart, J. P.	46
Hosea W., m. Mary E. **THOMPSON**, b. of N. Stonington, Feb. 24, 1848, by Rev. Thomas Barber	235
Ledyard, s. Lod[owic]k & Nabby, b. Mar. 27, 1807	14
Lodowick, s. Joshua & Molly, b. Dec. 12, 1775, in Stonington	14
Lodowick, m. Nab[b]y **READ**, of Hopkinton, Dec. 6, 1801, by Henry Joslin, Bapt. Elder	14
Lodowick, s. Lodowick & Nabby, b. July 30, 1803	14
Lucretia, m. Elisha **BILLINGS**, b. of Stonington, Oct. 4, 1778	20
Lydia, of N. Stonington, m. Eldridge **SPICER**, of Groton, May 31, 1820, by Asher Miner, Elder	70
Marland, m. Hannah C. **HEWIT**, Oct. 26, 1820, by Elias Hewit, J. P.	68
Nancy Maria, d. Lod[owic]k & Nabby, b. Feb. 14, 1809	14
Patience, m. Peter **MAIN**, Jr., b. of Stonington, Mar. 3, 1765, by John Burdict, J. P., at Hopkinton, R. I.	13
Polly, d. W[illia]m & Hannah, b. Mar. 11, 1784	5
Spicer, of N. Stonington, m. Eunice **FISK**, of Voluntown, Mar. 9, 1823, by Asher Miner, Elder	79
Susanna, m. Russell **BENTLEY**, b. of N. Stonington, Dec. 18, 1821, by Asher Miner, Elder	73
Thomas, m. Betsey **GAY**, b. of N. Stonington, Feb. 20, 1828, by Sam[ue]l Chapman, J. P.	103
William, s. W[illia]m & Hannah, b. Mar. 20, 1777	5
STAR[R], -----, m. Charles B. **MAIN**, b. of N. Stonington, Nov. 28, 1847, by Rev. Thomas Barber	234
STEVENS, Lemuel D., m. Martha E. **SHIRLEY**, b. of N. Stonington, Dec. 22, 1855, by Stephen Hubbell	269
Thomas M., of Stonington, m. Frances A. **THOMPSON**, of N. Stonington, July 26, 1851, by Rev. O. T. Walker	254
STEWART, STEWERT, Amos, m. Clarissa **HILLS**, b. of N. Stonington, Nov. 30, 1826, by David Coats, J. P.	97
Ann E., of N. Stonington, m. Stephen **MAIN**, of New York, June 8, 1847, by Rev. James M. Phillips	227
Betsey, m. Frederick **SWAN**, b. of N. Stonington, Jan. 14, 1828, by David Coats, J. P.	103
Emeline, m. William R. **WHEELER**, b. of N. Stonington, Dec. 16, 1830, by Rev. Joseph Ayer, Jr.	125

	Page
STEWART, STEWERT, (cont.)	
Julia A., of N. Stonington, m. Henry A. **THOMLINSON**, of New York City, May 1, 1856, by George W. Wooding	271
Rebeckah, m. Nathaniel M. **CRARY**, b. of N. Stonington, July 18, 1824, by Rev. Gideon Perry	88
Russell D., s. W[illia]m & Amanda, b. Feb. 1, 1805	94
Sarah, of N. Stonington, m. Lucius **JACKSON**, of Lisbon, Dec. 2, 1829, by David Coats, J. P.	118
W[illia]m, m. Amanda **DIVEREAU**, b. of N. Stonington, Oct. 31, 1802, by Stephen Avery, J. P.	94
STILLMAN, Adam, of Westerly, m. Lydia **SPAULDING**, of N. Stonington, Mar. 18, 1824, by Asher Miner, Elder	88
STORY, Abigail, m. Israel P. **PARKE**, Apr. 1, 1794	54
SUNDERLAND, John W., of Exeter, R. I., m. Abby A. **KINGSLEY**, of N. Kingston, R. I., May 2, 1847, by Rev. Thomas Barber	232
SWAN, Abigail C., d. Daniel & Hannah, b. Mar. 19, 1805	52
Abigail C., of N. Stonington, m. Tarsus **BOTSFORD**, of Sharon, Sept. 9, 1822, by Rev. John Hyde	76
Amos, s. Cha[rle]s & Eunice, b. Sept. 12, 1780; d. May 27, 1812	37
Amos, s. Charles & Cynthia, b. Jan. 2, 1813	33
Asa, s. Nathan & Esther, b. Oct. 17, 1780	8
Asa A., m. Fanny **WHEELER**, b. of N. Stonington, Feb. 16, 1809, by Stephen Avery, J. P.	26
Avery, s. Nthan & Esther, b. July 21, 1776	8
Bridget, of N. Stonington, m. Christopher **HULL**, Jr., of S. Kingston, R. I., Jan. 4, 1829, by Asher Miner, Elder	112
Charles, m. Eunice **BARNES**, Mar. 21, 1779	37
Charles, s. Cha[rle]s & Eunice, b. Apr. 3, 1782	37
Charles, Jr., m. Cynthia **BREWSTER**, Dec. 25, 1803	33
Charles, s. Charles & Cynthia, b. Apr. 1, 1810	33
Christopher, s. Charles & Eunice, b. Mar. 30, 1787; d. Apr. 16, 1816	37
Clarissa, d. Asa A. & Fanny, b. Jan. 22, 1812	26
Coddington, s. Cha[rle]s & Eunice, b. Jan. 15, 1794	37
Coddington, of N. Stonington, m. Cynthia **HEWIT**, of Groton, Apr. 5, 1818, by Ralph Hurlburt, J. P.	61
Cynthia, d. Nathan & Esther, b. May 24, 1787	8
Cynthia, d. Charles & Cynthia, b. Feb. 26, 1805	33
Cynthia, m. Edward **COATS**, Jr., Oct. 15, 1809, by Stephen Avery, J. P.	48
Cynthia, of N. Stonington, m. John **WOODMANSEY**, of Preston, Oct. 19,1828, by Rev. Asher Miner	109
Cyrus, s. Nathan & Esther, b. Mar. 25, 1793	8
Cyrus, m. Polly **COATS**, b. of N. Stonington, Apr. 24, 1817, by Elias Hewit, J. P.	59
Damaris, m. Lathrop **WILLIAMS**, b. of N. Stonington, Nov. 26, 1807, by Christopher Avery	4
Daniel, m. Hannah **HAWKINS**, Apr. 3, 1803	52
Dansa, d. Cha[rle]s & Eunice, b. Feb. 6, 1786; d. Mar. 18,1786	37

	Page
SWAN, (cont.)	
Danason, s. Cha[rle]s & Eunice, b. Nov. 6, 1791	37
Denison, m. Caroline **BAILEY**, of N. Stonington, Jan. 4, 1832, by Rev. Augustus B. Collins	133
Dim[m]is, d. Nathan & Esther, b. Apr. 28, 1785	8
Eliza A., of N. Stonington, m. Henry F. **WORTH**, of New Bedford, Mass., Sept. 22, 1851, by Rev. O. T. Walker	255
Ephraim, s. Charles & Eunice, b. Aug. 2, 1802	37
Ephraim, m. Julia A. **GRINNELL**, b. of N. Stonington, Nov. 29, 1831, by Rev. Asher Miner	132
Eunice, m. John **WHEELER**, b. of Stonington, May 9, 1785	47
Eunice, d. Cha[rle]s & Eunice, b. Sept. 13, 1796	37
Eunice, d. Charles & Cynthia, b. Oct. 3, 1808	33
Frederick, s. Cha[rle]s & Eunice, b. July 18, 1784	37
Frederick, m. Bestey **STEWART**, b. of N. Stonington, Jan. 14, 1828, by David Coats, J. P.	103
Harriet, d. Charles & Cynthia, b. Dec. 31, 1815	33
Harriet, m. Phinehas M. **WHEELER**, Aug. 23, 1846, by Rev. N. V. Steadman, of Preston	222
Harriet Y., d. Daniel & Hannah, b. Dec. 20, 1812	52
Henry T., s. Daniel & Hannah, b. July 28, 1806	52
Isaac, s. Nathan & Esther, b. Aug. 25, 1798	8
Isaac A., m. Lucy **BALDWIN**, b. of N. Stonington, Aug. 31, 1823, by Levi Walker	84
Lucy, m. Gilbert **BILLINGS**, b. of Stonington, Apr. 19, 1792	21
Lucy, m. John **BROWNING**, Mar. 10, 1799	32
Lucy, d. Asa A. & Fanny, b. Apr. 9, 1814	26
Lucy A., m. Eldredge A. **WHIPPLE**, Dec. 25, 1856, by Rev. John Sheffield	273
Mary Ann, d. Asa A. & Fanny, b. Dec. 13, 1810	26
Nancy, d. Charles & Cynthia, b. Nov. 10, 1806	33
Nancy, of N. Stonington, m. Nathan D. **PALMER**, of Preston, Oct. 7, 1830, by Rev. Augustus B. Collings	123
Nathan, m. Esther **AVERY**, Mar. 10, 1776	8
Nathan, s. Nathan & Esther, b. Oct. 10, 1790	8
Nelson, s. Charles & Cynthia, b. Nov. 28, 1811	33
Oliver, s. Nathan & Esther, b. Dec. 21, 1782	8
Paris, of Genesee, N. Y., m. Hannah **GAVITT**, of N. Stonington, Sept. 27, 1821, by Elias Hewit, J. P.	72
Polly, m. Daniel **GRANT**, b. of Stonington, Apr. 10, 1783	3
Prentice, s. Nathan & Esther, b. Sept. 5, 1795	8
Robert, s. Nathan & Esther, b. Oct. 22, 1778	8
Sally, d. Cha[rle]s & Eunice, b. July 24, 1789	37
Thomas E., s. Daniel & Hannah, b. Apr. 8, 1809	52
William, s. Charles & Eunice, b. Feb. 24, 1799	37
William, s. Charles, of N. Stonington, m. Deborah Ann, d. of Hampton **BROWN**, of Westerly, Apr. 20, 1825, by Benajah Gavitt, J. P.	92

	Page
SWEET, Susan, m. David **BALDWIN**, May 29, 1793	39
W[illia]m R., of Voluntown, m. Susan **FISH**, of N. Stonington, May 15, 1842, by Asher Prentice, Jr., J. P.	193
TABOR, Oliver E., m. Rebecca W. **JAMES**, b. of Providence, R. I., Sept. 13, 1831, by Rev. Joseph Ayer, Jr.	130
TAYLOR, Isaac R., m. Sally **BALDWIN**, b. of N. Stonington, Sept. 24, 1834, by Rev. Joseph Ayer, Jr.	152
TEFFT, Paul L., m. Emily **PENDLETON**, Feb. 7, 1836, by Rev. John G. Wightman	159
TERWILLIGER, John M., m. Sarah A. **ROCHE**, Jan. 12, 1834, by Elder McJimpsey	154
THAYER, Mary R., of N. Stonington, m. Lewis **LEAVENS**, of Peekskill, N. Y., Jan. 25, 1856, by Cha[rle]s C. Lewis	270
THOMAS, Joseph, m. Margaret **McGLADE**, b. of N. Stonington, Sept. 1, 1852, at the residence of Mrs. William R. Wheeler, by Rev. O. T. Walker	259
THOMLINSON, Henry A., of New York City, m. Julia A. **STEWART**, of N. Stonington, May 1, 1856, by George W. Wooding	271
THOMPSON, THOMSON, Aaron, m. Elmina **YORK**, b. of N. Stonington, May 22, 1825, by Jonathan Miner, Minister	91
Abby M., of N. Stonington, m. Paul B. **BURCH**, of Stonington, May 14, 1851, by Rev. O. T. Walker	251
Alexander, 2d, of N. Stonington, m. Martha **LEWIS**, of Voluntown, Mar. 5, 1818, by Alexander Campbell, J. P.	61
Amos Sheffield, s. Joshua & Rachel, b. Dec. 30, 1805	17
Ann, of Westerly, m. Joseph **HOLLEY**, of N. Stonington, Jan. 27, 1822, at Milltown, by Tho[ma]s J. DeVerell	74
Anna, w. Moses, d. Nov. 16, 1815	23
Benjamin, m. Frances A. **HILLIARD**, b. of N. Stonington, Oct. 30, 1852, by Rev. O. T. Walker	261
Benjamin Franklin, s. Elias & Betsey, b. Mar. 15, 1803; d. Mar. 8, 1810	33
Betsey, d. Elias & Betsey, b. July 5, 1801	33
Catharine, m. Ephraim W. **MAIN**, b. of N. Stonington, Nov. 5, 1845, by Rev. James R. Stone	218
Charles W., of N. Stonington, m. Betsey **POTTER**, of Voluntown, Jan. 25, 1821 [1824?], by Amos Frink, J. P.	87
Clarke Davis, s. Elias & Betsey, b. Oct. 22, 1797	33
Elias, m. Betsey **DAVIS**, Mar. 19, 1795	33
Elias, s. Elias & Betsey, b. Apr. 20, 1796	33
Eliza, d. Joshusa & Rachel, b. Sept. 30, 1803	17
Esther, d. Joshua & Rachel, b. July 7, 1792	17
Esther, m. Miner **PALMER**, b. of N. Stonington, Feb. 4, 1816, by Jonathan Miner, Elder	30
Esther, of Westerly, m. Ezra **GEER**, of N. Stonington, Mar. 19, 1827, by Elias Hewit, J. P.	99
Frances A., of N. Stonington, m. Thomas M. **STEVENS**, of Stonington, July 26, 1851, by Rev. O. T. Walker	254

Page

THOMPSON, THOMSON, (cont.)
Harriet Caroline, d. Elias & Betsey, b. June 4, 1816 — 33
Joshua, m. Rachel **TILEY**, Sept. 9, 1790, by Simeon Brown, Elder — 17
Joshua Hale, s. Joshua & Rachel, b. Oct. 6, 1794 — 17
Lucian, d. Elias & Betsey, b. Aug. 20, 1807 — 33
Lucy E., of N. Stonington, m. Joseph A. **DOUGLASS**, of Hopkinton, R. I., July 3, 1844, in N. Stonington, by Rev. Leander Wakefield, of Hopkinton, R. I. — 208
Martin, s. Joshua & Rachel, b. Sept. 2, 1799 — 17
Mary Ann, d. Joshua & Rachel, b. July 24, 1808 — 17
Mary Ann, of N. Stonington, m. Frederick **BIRCH**, of Stonington, May 21, 1845, by Rev. James R. Stone — 216
Mary E., m. Hosea W. **STANTON**, b. of N. Stonington, Feb. 24, 1848, by Rev. Thomas Barber — 235
Moses, m. Mary **HEWIT**, Oct. 26, 1817, by Stephen Avery, J. P. — 23
Nancy, d. Elias & Betsey, b. Aug. 4, 1811 — 33
Oliver, s. Elias & Betsey, b. Aug. 3, 1799 — 33
Philurah, d. Joshua & Rachel, b. June 21, 1801 — 17
Prudence, d. Joshua & Rachel, b. Nov. 2, 1797 — 17
Rachel, m. Joshua **HULL**, b. of N. Stonington, Jan. 1, 1815, by Jonathan Miner, Elder — 39
Ralph, of N. Stonington, m. Eliza E. **LARKIN**, of Richmond, R. I., Oct. 11, 1863, by Rev. Stanton Austin, at Hopkinton — 275
Rebecca, d. Joshua & Rachel, b. Jan. 13, 1791 — 17
Rufus Cranston, s. Elias & Betsey, b. Sept. 3, 1809 — 33
Sally M., m. Benjmain **NOYES**, b. of N. Stonington, Mar. 20, 1829, by Asher Miner, Elder — 81
Susan, of N. Stonington, m. Jason L. **WEST**, of Stonington, May 14, 1837, by Matthew Brown, J. P. — 161
Tyler Brown, s. Elias & Betsey, b. Jan. 26, 1814 — 33
THURSTON, Abigail, m. Nathaniel **MAIN**, Aug. 7, 1780 — 44
TILEY, Rachel, m. Joshua **THOMPSON**, Sept. 9, 1790, by Simeon Brown, Elder — 17
TOMLINSON, see under **THOMLINSON**
TRACY, TRACEY, Eleanor Jane, m. William **VINCENT**, b. of N. Stonington, Mar. 16, 1858, by Rev. Charles C. Lewis — 275
Lucius H., of Preston, m. Eunice **LEWIS**, of N. Stonington, Apr. 24, 1828, by Joseph Ayer, Jr., Minister — 106
Milo, Rev., m. Mrs. Phebe **PARTELO[W]**, b. of N. Stonington, Nov. 22, 1849, by N. E. Shailer, Missionary — 243
TREAT, James, of Preston, m. Anna **GRANT**, of N. Stonington, Sept. 29, 1839, by Rev. Nathan E. Shaler, of Preston — 179
TRUMAN, Sally M., m. Henry **CRANDALL**, b. of N. Stonington, Nov. 29, 1827, by Asher Miner, Elder — 101
TUCKER, James C., of Richmond, R. I., m. Hannah K. **CLARK**, of Charleston, R. I., Nov. 26, 1838, by Rev. Pierpoint Brocket — 171
TURNER, Ezekiel C., of N. Stonington, m. Eunice E. **BURDICK**, formerly of N. Stonington, July 20, 1851, by Rev. O. T. Walker — 253

	Page
TYLER, John, of Griswold, m. Esther **MORSE**, of N. Stonington, May 29, 1822, by Rev. Horatio Waldo	75
VINCENT, Benjamin, s. Joseph & Phalla, b. Dec. 11, 1804	9
Eunice P., of N. Stonington, m. Elisha D. **RANDALL**, of Stonington, Feb. 27, 1843, by Rev. Erastus Denison, of Groton	198
Joseph, of Westerly, m. Phalla **HINCKLEY**, of Stonington, Jan. 28, 1802, by Simon Brown, Elder	9
Joseph Reed, s. Joseph & Phalla, b. Aug. 12, 1802	9
Phalla, d. Joseph & Phalla, b. Feb. 28, 1806	9
Thomas Hinckley, s. Joseph & Phalla, b. Mar. 14, 1811	9
William, m. Eleanor Jane **TRACY**, b. of N. Stonington, Mar. 16, 1858, by Rev. Charles C. Lewis	275
Zervia, d. Joseph & Phalla, b. Dec. 5, 1808	9
WALKER, Frances, of N. Stonington, m. Sandford **BROWN**, of Preston, Oct. 10, 1824, by Levi Meech, Elder	89
Harriet N., m. Benj[ami]n F. **BABCOCK**, Feb. 25, 1838, by Amos C. Main, J. P.	165
Hettey, of Saybrook, m. Warren **WILKINSON**, of N. Stonington, July 11, 1849, by Rev. Levi Walker	241
William, of Lenox, Mass., m. Harriet **COLLINS**, of N. Stonington, July 8, 1833, by Rev. Joseph Ayer, Jr.	146
W[illia]m C., of Griswold, m. Elmina **PALMER**, of N. Stonington, Nov. 25, 1839, by Rev. Levi Walker	195
WALTERS, Jacob, of Philadelphia, m. Eliza **CRANDALL**, of N. Stonington, Dec. 14, 1826, by Asher Miner, Elder	98
WAMSLEY, Richard, m. Mary **CARPENTER**, b. of N. Stonington, Aug. 4, 1850, by Matthew Brown, J. P.	247
WARD, Thomas, m. Emeline **ANDERSON**, persons of color, Feb. 7, 1839, by P. H. Shaw	173
WATSON, Albert, of Charlestown, R. I., m. Laura **TAGANS**, of N. Stonington, Nov. 30, 1843, by Rev. Erastus Denison, of Groton	203
Alexander, m. Harriet **FAGINS**, b. of color, Feb. 8, 1821, by William Randall, J. P.	69
WATTLES, Susan M., m. William B. **HULL**, b. of N. Stonington, Aug. 6, 1851, by M. N. Morris	254
Susan Miner, d. Tho[ma]s P. & Lucy, b. May 27, 1829	101
Thomas P., Dr., m. Lucy P. **WHEELER**, Nov. 25, 1827, by Rev. Joseph Ayer, Jr.	100
Thomas Wheeler, s. Tho[ma]s P. & Lucy, b. Aug. 24, 1832	101
WEAVER, Lydia N., m. John W. **WILKINSON**, b. of N. Stonington, Aug. 2, 1846, by Rev. Levi Walker	239
Noyes, of Farsalia, N. Y., m. Almira **GRANT**, of N. Stonington, Nov. 11, 1824, by Levi Walker	89
Stephen B., of Farralie, N. Y., m. Rhoda **PALMER**, of N. Stonington, July 22, 1821, by David Coats, J. P.	71
WELLS, WELLES, Albert Gallatin, s. Randall & Patience, b. Apr. 30, 1803	2
Amos Griffing, s. Tho[ma]s J. & Desire, b. Sept. 17, 1815	15
Betsey, d. Randall & Patience, b. Oct. 16, 1812	2

	Page
WELLS, WELLES, (cont.)	
Bridget, m. George W. **MORE**, Feb. 22, 1808	29
James Bidwell, s. Randall & Patience, b. Mar. 26, 1806	2
Loiza, d. Randall & Patience, b. Dec. 28, 1809	2
Randall, made affidavit regarding religious belief Oct. 31, 1807, in presence of Stephen & Hannah **AVERY**. He was evidently not born in Stonington.	2
Russell, of Groton, m. Fanny A. **PEABODY**, of N. Stonington, Oct. 1, 1845, by Rev. James R. Stone	217
Thomas T., Dr., m. Desire **RANDALL**, of Stonington, Dec. 31, 1812, in presence of Stephen & Betsey Avery	15
William Randall, s. Tho[ma]s J. & Desire **WELLS**, b. Sept. 20, 1813	15
William Randall, s. Randall & Patience, b. Jan. 19, 1816	2
WENTWORTH, Mary E., of Westerly, R. I., m. William J. S. **ALLEN**, of Stonington, Oct. 17, 1852, by Rev. O. T. Walker	261
WEST, Edwin, m. Sarah A. **YERRINGTON**, b. of N. Stonington, Mar. 18, 1855, by Rev. H. H. Tinker	265
Jason L., of Stonington, m. Susan **THOMPSON**, of N. Stonington, May 14, 1837, by Matthew Brown, J. P.	161
WHEELER, Adaline, d. Timothy S. & Lucy, b. Oct. 28, 1814	50
Adaline M., of N. Stonington, m. B. Gage **BERRY**, of Norwich, N. Y., June 29, 1854, by Stephen Hubbell	264
Allen, s. Allen & Jemima Ann, b. Aug. 8, 1823	77
Ann, of N. Stonington, m. Pierpont **KINNEY**, of Griswold, Feb. 16, 1826, by Elias Hewit, J. P.	95
Anna, m. Stephen **AVERY**, b. of Stonington, Dec. 9, 1781, by Rev. Nath[anie]l Eells	1
Anna, d. John & Eunice, b. Dec. 13, 1804	47
Anna, d. Allen & Jemima Ann, b. Jan. 24, 1822	77
Austin, s. John D[enison] & Lucy, b. June 15, 1816	108
Austin, m. Lucy P. **COATS**, Feb. 9, 1843, by Rev. B. C. Grafton	213
Betsey, wid. Lodowick, m. Truman **PIERCE**, Sept. 13, 1835, by Amos C. Main, J. P.	155
Celia, m. George C. **CHAPMAN**, b. of Stonington, Aug. 31, 1851, by Rev. O. T. Walker	254
Chauncey Goodrich, s. Dudley R. & Lydia, b. Nov. 30, 1823	75
Cynthia S., m. William M. **HILLIARD**, b. of N. Stonington, Aug. 7, 1825, by Elias Hewit, J. P.	92
Cynthia S., m. William M. **HILLIARD**, b. of N. Stonington, Aug. 7, 1825, by Elias Hewit, J. P.	102
Cyrus, m. Lucy S. **BROWNING**, b. of N. Stonington, Mar. 24, 1822, by Rev. Syrel Lee Hart, of Stonington	74
Desire, m. Alpheas **MINER**, b. of Stonington, Feb. 5, 1797	18
Desire, of N. Stonington, m. Christopher **PALMER**, of Exeter, N. Y., Nov. 1, 1823, by Asher Miner, Elder	84
Dudley, s. Dudley R. & Lydia, b. Nov. 4, 1821; d. Oct. 7, 1822	75
Dudley R., m. Lydia **HEWIT**, Dec. 1, 1818, by Asher Miner, Elder	75
Dudley R., m. Sally Maria **BROWNING**, Mar. 4, 1828	75

WHEELER, (cont.)

	Page
Dudley R., m. Sally Mariah **BROWNING**, b. of N. Stonington, Mar. 4, 1828, by Rev. Joseph Ayer, Jr.	104
Ede D., m. Charles G. **AVERY**, b. of N. Stonington, Nov. 4, 1823, by William Randall, Jr.	86
Elias, s. John & Eunice, b. Mar. 23, 1793	47
Elisha, s. Allen & Jemima Ann, b. Jan. 15, 1827	27
Elisha, d. Feb. 11, 1835	134
Elisha, m. Mary J. **GALLUP**, Nov. 2, 1856, by Rev. Charles C. Lewis	272
Elisha Peckham, s. Jesse & Nancy, b. Dec. 15, 1815	32
Eliza A., m. Amos N. **WILLCOX**, b. of N. Stonington, Feb. [ ], 1844, by Levi Walker	208
Elizabeth T., of N. Stonington, m. John **JACKSON**, of Lisbon, Jan. 24, 1824, by Asher Miner, Elder	86
Ellin, d. Allen & Jemima [Ann], b. Apr. 13, 1833	77
Ellen, of N. Stonington, m. Edwin C. **MAIN**, of Wisconsin, June 13, 1852, by Rev. O. T. Walker	260
Emeline, of N. Stonington, m. Capt. Latham H. **BROWNING**, Nov. 18, 1830, by Rev. Augustus B. Collings	124
Ephraim, of N. Stonington, m. Sylvia **SLACK**, of Stonington, Jan. 15, 1815, by Stephen Avery, J. P.	36
Ephraim, m. Bridget **AYER**, b. of N. Stonington, Oct. 8, 1829, by Rev. Joseph Ayer, Jr.	116
Ephraim, m. Elizabeth **COATS**, b. of N. Stonington, Dec. 29, 1852, by Rev. Franklin A. Slater, of Groton	261
Esther, m. Amos **HULL**, Sept. 12, 1799	52
Esther, d. Timothy S. & Lucy, b. May 15, 1804	50
Eunice, d. Timohty S. & Lucy, b. Aug. 23, 1801	50
Eunice K., d. Geo[rge] & Thankfull, b. June 4, 1825	172
Ezra, of Stonington, m. Mary H. **RANDALL**, of N. Stonington, Nov. 25, 1840, by Rev. Tho[ma]s Dowling	186
Fanny, d. John & Eunice, b. June 29, 1790	47
Fanny, m. Asa A. **SWAN**, b. of N. Stonington, Feb. 16, 1809, by Stephen Avery, J. P.	26
Fanny A., of N. Stonington, m. Cyrus S. **BROWNING**, of Brooklyn, N. Y., July 14, 1831, by Rev. Joseph Ayer, Jr.	130
Fanny F., of N. Stonington, m. Alfred **AVERY**, of Windham, Mar. 1, 1827, by Rev. Joseph Ayer, Jr.	99
Frances H., m. Nancy W. **AVERY**, b. of N. Stonington, June 3, 1846, by Rev. Myron N. Morris	221
Francis Abby, d. Allen & Jemima [Ann], b. Apr. 14, 1839	77
George, m. Thankfull S. **RANDALL**, b. of Stonington, Nov. 13, 1817, in Stonington, by Asher Miner, Elder	172
George T., s. Geo[rge] & Thankful, b. July 8, 1819	172
Hannah, m. Gideon **CHAPMAN**, b. of N. Stonington, Sept. 4, 1808, by Stephen Avery, J. P.	9
Harriet, d. Allen & Jemima [Ann], b. Feb. 1, 1831	77
Harriet, of N. Stonington, m. Deac. Noyes **PALMER**, of Stonington,	

BARBOUR COLLECTION

WHEELER, (cont.)	Page
Mar. 28, 1844, by Rev. Philo Judson	206
Henry Dwight, s. Dudley R. & Sall M[aria], b. June 22, 1829	75
Horace C., s. Geo[rge] & Thankfull, b. Aug. 20, 1821	172
Jerusha, m. James **WOODMANSEE**, b. of N. Stonington, Nov. 2, 1845, by Rev. James R. Stone	218
Jesse, m. Nancy **PECKHAM**, May 30, 1811	32
Joanna P., of N. Stonington, m. Albert L. **AVERY**, of Groton, Jan. 1, 1839, by P. H. Shaw	171
John, m. Eunice **SWAN**, b. of Stonington, May 9, 1785	47
John, s. John & Eunice, b. Sept. 9, 1787; d. Feb. 28, 1813	47
John A., s. Austin & Lucy, b. Apr. 7, 1844	213
John B., of N. Stonington, m. Sarah R. **BRIGS**, of Greenwich, R. I., Jan. 1, 1834, by Jonathan Miner, Elder	149
John Denison, m. Lucy **PRENTICE**, Dec. 11, 1814, by Rev. John Hyde	108
John Owen, s. Jesse & Nancy, b. June 5, 1818	32
Laura, m. Carrington **LANPHEAR**, b. of N. Stonington, May 15, 1843, by Levi Walker	207
Laura, m. Alfred **HALLET**, b. of N. Stonington, July 11, 1848, by Rev. Levi Walker	240
Louis, w. Elisha, d. Feb. 16, 1832, in her 67th year	134
Louisa Desire, d. Dudley R. & Lydia, b. Oct. 10, 1819	75
Lucinda, of N. Stonington, m. David **JACKSON**, of Lisbon, persons of color, Aug. 7, 1828, by Sam[ue]l Chapman, J. P.	107
Lucinda G., m. Sandford P. **BROWN**, July 4, 1838, by P. H. Shaw	168
Lucy, d. John & Eunice, b. Mar. 20, 1785	47
Lucy, d. Timothy S. & Lucy, b. July 29, 1800; d. aged 10 weeks	50
Lucy, of N. Stonington, m. James L. **LYSTER**, of Griswold, Sept. 5, 1820, by Asher Miner, Elder	66
Lucy A., of N. Stonington, m. George W. **MAIN**, of Ledyard, Mar. 20, 1844, by Rev. Stphen H. Peckham	205
Lucy Ann, d. Timothy S. & Lucy, b. Feb. 20, 1811	50
Lucy P., m. Dr. Thomas P. **WATTLES**, Nov. 25, 1827, by Rev. Joseph Ayer, Jr.	101
Luke, s. John & Eunice, b. Oct. 29, 1795	47
Lydia, m. David **MORE**, Mar. 16, 1782	34
Lydia, w. Dudley R., d. Sept. 7, 1826	75
Lydia A., of N. Stonington, m. Warren **NEWTON**, of Norwich, N. Y., May 28,, 1851, by Rev. M. N. Morris	252
Lydia Ann, d. Dudley R. & Lydia, b. July 26, 1825	75
Lydia E., m. Henry S. **CHAPMAN**, b. of N. Stonington, Aug. 12, 1849, by Rev. John Sheffield	242
Lydia H., of N. Stonington, m. W[illia]m M. **JOHNSON**, of Windham, Jan. 1, 1836, by Rev. Joseph Ayer, Jr.	156
Martha, d. Lodowick & Polly, b. Apr. 26, 1797	25
Martha, m. Cyrus **WILLIAMS**, b. of Stonington, Aug. 31, 1806, by Rev. Christopher Avery	24

WHEELER, (cont.)

	Page
Martha, m. Timothy C. **WILKINSON**, Mar. 24, 1814, by Elias Hewit, Esq.	63
Martha, m. Charles G. **SISSON**, b. of N. Stonington, May 11, 1829, by Rev. Joseph Ayer, Jr.	113
Martha E., m. Dr. Alfred W. **COATS**, b. of N. Stonington, Sept. 18, 1843, by Rev. Tubal Wakefield	204
Martha H., of N. Stonington, m. Jacob B. **MURRAY**, of New York City, June 20, 1855, by Henry W. Beecher, of Brooklyn, N. Y.	266
Mary, m. Roswell R. **AVERY**, b. of N. Stonington, Apr. 9, 1818, by Asher Miner, Elder	74
Mary Ann, m. Ralph R. **BROWN**, b. of N. Stonington, Oct. 12, 1842, by John Sheffield, J. P.	196
Mary E., m. Albert **GARDNER**, b. of N. Stonington, Nov. 3, 1850, by J. B., Maryatt, J. P.	250
Mary H. m. Henry F. **BENTLEY**, b. of N. Stonington, Oct. 24, 1837, by Dea. C. D. Fillmore	162
Mary Haskell, d. John D[enison] & Lucy, b. Feb. 20, 1818	108
Phebe, m. Jonas **PARTLO**, Dec. 26, 1822, by Asher Miner, Elder	78
Phebe E., of N. Stonington, m. Albert **AVERY**, of Groton, Mar. 15, 1837, by Rev. Joseph Avery, Jr.	160
Phebe J., m. Thomas **CURTIS**, b. of Norwich, May 30, 1849, by M. N. Morris	236
Phinehas M., m. Harriet **SWAN**, Aug. 23, 1846, by Rev. N. V. Steadman, of Preston	222
Prentice G., m. Sarafiner **WHEELER**, b. of N. Stonington, Nov. 28, 1827, by Elias Hewit, J. P.	101
Priscilla, m. Alva **GRAY**, b. of N. Stonington, Oct. 30, 1831, by Rev. Asher Miner	132
Reuben, d. Aug. 1, 1832, in his 45th year	146
Richard, s. Allen & Jemima Ann, b. Feb. 16, 1829	77
Richard A., Capt., of Stonington, m. Frances M. **AVERY**, of N. Stonington, Jan. 12, 1843, by Rev. Philo Judson	196
Rufus, s. Lodowick & Polly, b. July 27, 1795	25
Rufus, of N. Stonington, m. Hannah **HOLLAND**, of South Kingstown, Sept. 23, 1821, by Elias Hewit, J. P.	72
Russell, m. Esther W. **HULL**, Oct. [ ], 1827, by Rev. Joseph Ayer, Jr.	100
Sally, d. Timothy S. & Lucy, b. June 26, 1797	50
Sanford, m. Harriet N. **MINER**, b. of N. Stonington, Mar. 31, 1844, by Rev. Philo Judson	206
Sarafiner, m. Prentice G. **WHEELER**, b. of N. Stonington, Nov. 28, 1827, by Elias Hewit, J. P.	101
Sarah E., m. Thomas **CLARK**, b. of N. Stonington, June 2, 1855, by Rev. Henry Clark	266
Sarah Emeline, d. William R. & Emeline, b. Aug. 20, 1832	125
Sophia, of N. Stonington, m. Abraham **PETERSON**, of Stonington, persons of color, Feb. 10, 1825, by Stphen Avery, J. P.	91
Stephen Hazard, s. Jesse & Nancy, b. Mar. 6, 1812	32

382   BARBOUR COLLECTION

Page

WHEELER, (cont.)
Susan, m. Amos C. **MAIN,** Mar. 29, 1804, by Christopher Avery,
  Elder   47
Swan, s. Timothy S. & Lucy, b. Sept. 23, 1807   50
Thomas William, s. Jesse & Nancy, b. Oct. 20, 1822   32
Timothy S., m. Lucy **GRANT,** Dec. 18, 1796, by Christ[ope]r Avery,
  Pastor   50
William R., m. Emeline **STEWART,** b. of N. Stonington, Dec. 16,
  1830, by Rev. Joseph Ayer, Jr.   125
S[Z]erviah, m. Amos **HULL,** Jan. 31, 1810   52
WHIPPLE, Eldredge A., m. Lucy A. **SWAN,** Dec. 25, 1856, by Rev. John
  Sheffield   273
William, m. Nancy M. **GRAY,** Aug. 30, 1829, by Paris Hewit, J. P.   116
WHITE, Albert, m. Betsey **BURDICK,** Sept. 4, 1826, by William Randall,
  Jr., J. P.   96
Charles, m. Ruth **PERRY,** Jan. 26, 1812, by Jedediah Randall, Elder   12
Charles Perry, s. Charles & Ruth, b. Nov. 13, 1812   12
Elizabeth, m. Hoxie **BABCOCK,** Nov. [ ], 1837, by Leland D. Miner,
  J. P.   163
Jonathan, of Hopkinton, R. I., m. Betsey **CRANDALL,** of N.
  Stonington, Dec. 20, 1829, by Asher Miner, Elder   118
Sally, of Hartford, m. Amos **BALDWIN,** of N. Stonington, May 2,
  1807   28
WILBUR, Benjamin, m. Thankful **RICHARDSON,** Nov. 26, 1829, by
  Sands Cole, J. P.   120
Benjamin, m. Thankfull **RICHARDSON,** Nov. 26, 1829, by Sands
  Cole, J. P. Recorded Jan. 27, 1839   172
Desire, m. Isaiah **WILBUR,** b. of Westerly, R. I., Aug. 14, 1825, by
  W[illia]m Randall, Jr., J. P.   93
Isaiah, m. Desire **WILBUR,** b. of Westerly, R. I., Aug. 14, 1825, by
  W[illia]m Randall, Jr., J. P.   93
WILCOX, WILLCOX, Amos N., s. Lyman & Eliza, b. Dec. 22, 1810   36
Amos N., m. Eliza A. **WHEELER,** b. of N. Stonington, Feb. [ ],
  1844, by Levi Walker   208
Asa, of Lynn, m. Nancy **ALLEN,** of N. Stonington, Dec. 1, 1845, by
  Matthew Brown, J. P.   219
Charles D., of Westerly, R. I., m. Eunice **KNIGHT,** of N. Stonington,
  Oct. 4, 1844, by Dewitt C. Pendleton, J. P.   246
Content, d. Francis & Martha, b. July 2, 1772   36
Content, d. Lyman & Eliza, b. Feb. 16, 1812   36
Content, m. Clark L. **BROWN,** b. of N. Stonington, Feb. 10, 1833, by
  Jonathan Miner, Elder   143
Eliza, of N. Stonington, m. John **DUNHAM,** Jan. 14, 1856, at Mystic,
  by Nehemiah B. Cook   270
Eliza Ann, d. Lyman & Eliza, b. June 1, 1816   36
Francis, s. Francis & Martha, b. Feb. 17, 1774   36
Henry, twin with Stephen, s. Stephen & Hannah, b. July 6, 1810   59
Joshua, s. Francis & Martha, b. June 28, 1782   36

	Page
WILCOX, WILLCOX, (cont.)	
Lucinda, d. Lyman & Eliza, b. Apr. 15, 1808	36
Lucinda, m. George W. **EDWARDS**, Jan. 7, 1838, by Leland D. Miner, J. P.	166
Lyman, s. Francis & Martha, b. Sept. 25, 1784	36
Robertson, s. Francis & Martha, b. Mar. 23, 1794	36
Stephen, m. Hannah **HOLMES**, b. of N. Stonington, Oct. 22, 1809, by Stephen Avery, J. P.	59
Stephen, twin with Henry, s. of Stephen & Hannah, b. July 6, 1810	59
WILKINSON, Dolly E., d. William **WILKINSON**, b. Mar. 14, 1846	243
Fidelia, see Phedelia	
George F., m. Sarah J. **FISH**, b. of N. Stonington, Feb. 27, 1848, by Rev. James M. Phillips	233
John, m. Salvina **CASSON**, b. of N. Stoningnton, Mar. 10, 1814, by Elias Hewit, J. P.	20
John W., m. Lydia N. **WEAVER**, b. of N. Stonington, Aug. 2, 1846, by Rev. Levi Walker	239
John Washington, s. John & Salvina, b. Aug. 31, 1814	20
Lucy, d. Timothy C. & Martha, b. Oct. 24, 1817	63
Margaret, m. Capt. Elisha P. **PHILLIPS**, b. of N. Stonington, Mar. 30, 1835, by Stephen Geer, J. P., at house of George Wilkinson	155
Mary Ann, d. Timothy C. & Martha, b. May 6, 1815	63
Phebe Ann N., d. John & Salvina, b. Sept. 15, 1825	20
Phedelia, d. John & Salvina, b. July 4, 1821	20
Polly, d. John & Salvina, b. Mar. 17, 1819	20
Timothy C., m. Martha **WHEELER**, Mar. 24, 1814, by Elias Hewit, Esq.	63
Warden, s. John & Salvina, b. Nov. 15, 1816 (Perhaps "Worden")_	20
Warren, of N. Stonington, m. Hettey **WALKER**, of Saybrook, July 11, 1849, by Rev. Levi Walker	241
William Pantiere, s. John & Salvina, b. Mar. 19, 1824; d. Oct. 23, 1824	20
WILLIAMS, Anna, m. George W. **BENTLEY**, b. of N. Stonington, June 18, 1809	53
Asa Preston, s. Rufus & Catherine, b. Jan. 14, 1821	10
Benedam, s. Rufus & Catherine, b. Nov. 6, 1811	10
Betsey, m. Eli **HEWIT**, Apr. 24, 1796	22
Catherine M., of N. Stonington, m. Welcome A. **BROWNING**, of Griswold, Sept. 2, 1846, by Rev. James R. Stone	223
Cyrus, m. Martha **WHEELER**, b. of Stonington, Aug. 31, 1806, by Rev. Christopher Avery	23
Cyrus, at his house, Liph, s. Rose, a woman of color, b. Sept. 20 - 24, 1811	1
Damaris, w. Capt. Lathrop, d. Apr. 2, 1817, aged 32 years.	4
Emily A., of N. Stonington, m. Benjamin **IRISH**, of New London, Apr. 16, 1851, by Rev. Myron N. Morris	251
Esther, d. William, and w. of Dea. William **CHEESBROUGH**, d. June 8, 1814, in her 72nd year.	22

384 BARBOUR COLLECTION

Page

WILLIAMS, (cont.)
George, s. Rufus & Catherine, b. May 19, 1819 — 10
George Lathrop, s. Lathrop & Abby, b. Feb. 16, 1820 — 4
Harriet N., m. William F. **GRANT,** b. of N. Stonington, Mar. 12, 1856, by Timothy Tuttle, at Ledyard — 270
Jerusha, of Stonington, m. Benjaminn **POMEROY,** of N. Stonington, Jan. 1, 1818 — 62
Joanna Wheeler, d. Cyrus & Martha, b. Oct. 24, 1807 — 24
Joseph Browning, s. Rufus & Catherine, b. Feb. 18, 1815 — 10
Julia Ann, of N. Stonington, m. Lorenzo D. **HECKOCK,** of Wallingford, July 20, 1828, by Asher Miner, Elder — 107
Keturah, w. Lieut. John, d. Mar. 2, 1810 — 7
Lathrop, m. Damaris **SWAN,** b. of N. Stonington, Nov. 26, 1807, by Christopher Avery — 4
Lathrop, m. Abby **PRENTICE,** b. of N. Stonington, Nov. 8, 1818, by Rev. John Hyde — 4
Lucy, m. Aaron **BENNET[T],** Jr., Apr. 10, 1796 — 81
Martha, of Stonington, m. Henry **CHEESEBROUGH,** of N. Stonington, Jan. 27, 1812 — 57
Martha Esther, d. Cyrus & Martha, b. Jan. 24, 1816 — 24
Mary, m. Horace T. **KNIGHT,** b. of N. Stonington, May 16, 1844, by Oliver Hewitt, J. P. — 207
Nancy, d. George & Nancy, b. Sept. 13, 1779 — 23
Nancy, m. Paris **HEWIT,** Feb. 12, 1797 — 23
Nancy, w. Capt. Isaac, d. Dec. 7, 1821 — 1
Nancy A., of N. Stonington, m. John **HOLMES,** Jr., of Preston, Mar. 10, 1831, by Benj[amin] Pomeroy, J. P. — 127
Phebe Esther, of Stonington, m. Silas **CHEESEBROUGH,** of N. Stonington, Jan. 29, 1819 — 84
Phebe S., m. John **BENTLEY,** b. of N. Stonington, Nov. 24, 1823, by Paris Hewit, J. P. — 86
Polly, m. Appleton **WOODWARD,** b. of N. Stonington, Dec. 30, 1815 — 58
Rufus, m. Catharine **BROWING,** b. of N. Stonington, Nov. 11, 1810, by Elias Hewit, J. P. — 10
Rufus Lathrop, s. Rufus & Catherine, b. July 21, 1817 — 10
Sally, d. Cyrus & Martha, b. July 31, 1818 — 24
Sally P., of Stonington, m. Henry **CHEESEBROUGH,** of N. Stonington, July 18, 1813 — 57
Sandford, of Stonington, m. Sary L. **PRENTICE,** of N. Stonington, Jan. 6, 1825, by Parke Williams, J. P. — 91
Sherman, of Russia, N. Y., m. Sally M. **BRADLEY,** of New London, Oct. 18, 1831, by Rev. Joseph Ayer, Jr. — 131
Thomas Wheeler, s. Cyrus & Martha, b. Nov. 14, 1809 — 24
Tirsah Moss, d. Cyrus & Martha, b. Sept. 8, 1820 — 24
William, of Groton, m. Eunice **FAGINS,** of N. Stonington, colored people, June 22, 1823, by Asher Miner, Elder — 82
William Browning, s. Rufus & Catherine, b. Aug. 18, 1813 — 10
WILSON, Eliza Ann, m. Gilbert W. **FAGANS,** b. of N. Stonington, Nov.

	Page
WILSON, (cont.)	
25, 1846, by Charles Bennet, J. P.	224
WITTER, Lucy, of Hopkinton, R. I., m. Russell **CRANDALL**, of Brookfield, N. Y., June 5, 1825, by Stephen Avery, J. P.	92
WOLIZER, Joseph, m. Rebecca **PARTELO**, b. of N. Stonington, Nov. 13, 1855, by Rev. John Taylor	268
WOODMANCEY, WOODMANSEE, WOODMANSEY, WOODMANSIE, Adaline, m. Colins **FRINK**, b. of N. Stonington, Aug. 26, 1851, by Rev. John Sheffield	256
James, m. Jerusha **WHEELER**, b. of N. Stonington, Nov. 2, 1845, by Rev. James R. Stone	218
John, of Preston, m. Cynthia **SWAN**, of N. Stonington, Oct. 19, 1828, by Rev. Asher Miner	109
Joseph, m. Sally **CASWELL**, b. of N. Stonington, Oct. 3, 1842, by Enoch B. Pendleton, J. P.	197
Mary, m. Nathan B. **CRARY**, b. of N. Stonington, Apr. 26, 1849, by Oliver Hewitt, T. C.	238
Samuel, Jr., of Exeter, m. Elcy M. **FRANKLIN**, of West Greenwich, b. of R. I., Mar. 11, 1832, by Rev. John G. Wightman	135
Samuel S., m. Caroline **PENDLETON**, b. of N. Stonington, July 3, 1831, by Rev. Joseph Ayer, Jr.	129
WOODWARD, Ann W., of N. Stonington, m. Henry B. **HAKES**, of Preston, Jan. 6, 1841, by Rev. Augustus B. Collins, of Preston	186
Anna, [d. Appleton & Polly], b. Mar. 26, 1820	58
Appleton, m. Polly **WILLIAMS**, b. of N. Stonington, Dec. 30, 1815	58
Appleton A., s. Appleton & Polly, b. May 26, 1815	58
Cynthia R., d. Appleton & Polly, b. Dec. 27, 1824	58
Harriet F., d. Appleton & Polly, b. Jan. 4, 1827	58
Mary Anna S., d. Appleton & Polly, b. July 6, 1816	58
Phebe A., [d. Appleton & Polly], b. June 3, 1822	58
William H., s. Appleton & Polly, b. Apr. 11, 1829	58
WORDEN, Benjamin, of Hopkinton, m. Dorcas **AUSTIN**, of Westerly, Oct. 10, 1824, by Asher Miner, Elder	89
Hannah, m. David **MAIN**, b. of Stonington, May 28, 1773	6
Mary Ann, of Richmond, R. I., m. William E. **HISSCOX**, of Charleston, R. I., Sept. 1, 1845, by Rev. Thomas Barber	213
Robert, of Albany, N. Y., m. Lucinda W. **HOLMES**, of N. Stonington, July 19, 1841, by Rev. Tho[ma]s Dowling	188
WORTH, Henry F., of New Bedford, Mass., m. Eliza A. **SWAN**, of N. Stonington, Sept. 22, 1851, by Rev. O. T. Walker	255
WRIGHT, Allen H., s. Daniel & Fanny E., b. May 1, 1844	189
Daniel, m. Fanny E. **BROMLEY**, b. of N. Stonington, Jan. 17, 1842, by Peleg Clarke, J. P.	189
Jonathan A., m. Lydia M. **BROWN**, b. of N. Stonington, Jan. 2, 1840, by Matthew Brown, J. P.	181
Lydia M., m. Dudley **GREEN**, Sept. 2, 1849, by Rev. Milo Tracey	241
Oliver H., m. Maggie **MYERS**, May 29, 1864, in Norfolk	276
Patience, of N. Stonington, m. Russell **CRANDALL**, of Richmond,	

	Page
WRIGHT, (cont.)	
R. I., Nov. 30, 1828, by Asher Miner, Elder	110
YERRINGTON, Lucy, of N. Stonington, m. Gurdon **HILL**, of Groton, Nov. [ ], 1821, by John Spicer, J. P.	73
Sarah A., m. Edwin **WEST**, b. of N. Stonington, Mar. 18, 1855, by Rev. H. H. Tinker	265
YORK, Allen, m. Eunice **GRANT**, Oct. 1, 1820, by Asher Miner, Elder	66
Almira, d. Zebulon, b. May 9, 1809	16
Bill, m. Deborah **YORK**, Feb. 16, 1809, by Rev. Jedediah Randall	8
Daniel, s. Bill & Deborah, b. Sept. 22, 1812	8
Daniel, m. Esther J. **BABCOCK**, of N. Stonington, Jan. 28, 1838, by Rev. Alfred Gates	164
Deborah, m. Bill **YORK**, Feb. 16, 1809, by Rev. Jedediah Randall	8
Elmina, m. Aaron **THOMPSON**, b. of N. Stonington, May 22, 1825, by Rev. Jonathan Miner	91
Eunice Esther, d. Zebulon, b. May 16, 1815	16
Horace Franklin, s. Nathan & Patty, b. Nov. 14, 1828	11
Isaac, s. Bill & Deborah, b. July 14, 1810	8
Jabish Reed, s. Reuben & Hannah, b. June 25, 1811	6
Jesse, s. W[illia]m & Noamy, b. Apr. 19, 1809	12
John Calvin, s. Zebulon, b. Apr. 3, 1812	16
Joseph, m. Hannah W. **BREED**, Aug. 22, 1825, by W[illia]m Randall Jr., J. P.	93
Lois, d. Reuben & Hannah, b. Oct. 25, 1807	6
Lucy, m. John **GRAY**, July 9, 1804	11
Lydia, of N. Stonington, m. Stephen **MAIN**, of New York City, Mar. 6, 1842, by Rev. Tho[ma]s Dowling	191
Maria, m. Henry **POTTER**, b. of N. Stonington, Mar. 16, 1834, by Jonathan Miner, Elder	150
Maryette, s. W[illia]m & Noamy, b. Apr. 1, 1814	12
Marila, d. Nathan & Patty, b. Sept. 26, 1815	11
Marilla, m. Benjamin Franklin **SISSON**, b. of N. Stonington, Tuesday, Aug. 28, 1838, by Rev. Peirpoint Brockett	168
Martin, m. Mary **CHAPMAN**, b. of N. Stonington, Mar. 13, 1824, by Asher Miner, Elder	87
Mary E., of N. Stonington, m. John L. **GREEN**, of Voluntown, Nov. 29, 1832, by Jonathan Miner, Elder	141
Mary Esther, d. Reuben & Hannah, b. June 27, 1813	6
Nabby, d. Zebulon, b. July 9, 1807	16
Nathan, m. Patty **BRAND**, Nov. 25, 1810, by Jedediah Randall, Elder	11
Nathan, s. Nathan & Patty, b. Sept. 16, 1811	11
Nathan, m. Nancy B. **MAIN**, b. of N. Stonington, Jan. 2, 1834, by Rev. Asher Miner	149
Nathan, Jr., m. Harriet **BROWN**, b. of N. Stonington, Mar. 24, 1842, by Rev. Philo Judson	193
Patty Paulina, d. Nathan & Patty, b. Jan. 7, 1814	11
Reuben W., m. Lucy E. **BROWN**, b. of N. Stonington, Oct. 8, 1840, by Levi Meech, Elder	183

	Page
YORK, (cont.)	
Reuben Wheeler, s. Nathan & Patty, b. Jan. 22, 1819	11
Speda, d. William & Noamy, b. Feb. 4, 1806	12
Stephen, s. W[illia]m & Noamy, b. Aug. 3, 1811	12
Susannah, m. Julius **PALMER**, b. of N. Stonington, Nov. 19, 1809, by Joshua Babcock, J. P.	31
Thomas Jefferson, s. Reuben & Hannah, b. Feb. 5, 1806	6
Zebulon T., m. Elizabeth S. **STANTON**, Mar. 6, 1842, by Rev. Tho[ma]s Dowling	191

www.ingramcontent.com/pod-product-compliance
Lightning Source LLC
Chambersburg PA
CBHW071231290426
44108CB00013B/1368